Healthcare Quality and HIT - International Standards, China Practices

Top international standards shape top hospitals, and top international standards must incorporate best practices elements from China.

Cai Xiujun
President, Sir Run Run Shaw Hospital Affiliated to Zhejiang University School of Medicine

IT development is like growing the nervous system of a hospital, which requires us to adopt international standards and a global vision to lead our journey forward.

Zhao Guoguang
President, Xuanwu Hospital, Capital Medical University

JCI - quality and safety, HIMSS - efficiency and convenience. They are like a pair of wings that lift the hospital upwards.

Jiang Jie
President, The First Affiliated Hospital of Xiamen University

JCI accreditations and HIMSS EMRAM/(O)EMRAM Stage 7s have guided and witnessed our transformation from baby step progresses to giant leap forward.

Xia Huimin
President, Guangzhou Women and Children's Medical Center

HIMSS has witnessed the growth of innovation of China together with the rest of the world.

Guo Qiyong
Former President, Shengjing Hospital of China Medical University

The combination of JCI accreditation, HIMSS methodology and traditional medicine adds to the significant leap forward.

Xiao Zhen
President, Longhua Hospital Shanghai University of Traditional Chinese Medicine

To lead an internationally renowned hospital that always put patients and customers first through our journey towards excellence and quality services.

Wang Jianan
President, The Second Affiliated Hospital of Zhejiang University School of Medicine

Write down what you should do. Do what you have noted down. Document what you have done.

Huang Guoying
President, Children's Hospital of Fudan University

A pioneer in pursuing excellence over one hundred years, improvement and innovation is the core spirit of Huashan Hospital through generations.

Ma Xin
Vice President, Huashan Hospital Affiliated to Fudan University

We learn from the world and open our doors for the world to learn from us. We shall deliver even better performance on the international stage.

Liu Xiaocheng
President, TEDA International Cardiovascular Hospital

To turn standards into daily habits and align habits with standards.

Bai Xizhuang
President and secretary of Party committee, People's Hospital of Liaoning Province

As the first children's hospital in China, our goal is to grow it into a world-class hospital for children.

Yu Guangjun
President, Children's Hospital of Shanghai

IT adoption is an important task to achieve further healthcare reform as well as the strategic support to the hospital development in the new era.

Shi Jun
Former President, The First Affiliated Hospital of Nanchang University

To realize modern hospital management through IT development and to improve patient care quality through smart technology.

Jia Weiping
Former President, People's Shanghai No.6 People's Hospital

JCI and HIMSS EMRAM Stage 6 are our efforts to pursue excellence and innovation at United Family Healthcare.

Pan Zhongying
Vice President, United Family Healthcare

Smart hospital for greater value of healthcare.

Jiang Zhongyi
President, Shanghai Children's Medical Center Affiliated to Shanghai Jiao Tong University School of Medicine

JCI standards and HIMSS validation have fueled our hospital towards world-class practice and our goal to build a beautiful hospital providing heart-warming care.

Wang Weilin
Former President, The First Affiliated Hospital of Zhejiang University

Let us always stay true to our mission and keep our goal in heart. Let us share the standards that lead the development of hospitals and carry out the "Belt and Road" initiative.

Wen Hao
Former President, The First Affiliated Hospital of Xinjiang Medical University

To build the best platform of chain healthcare services together with patients, healthcare organizations and payers through technologies supported by standards.

Fan Shaofei
Chairman of the Board and CEO, Ping An Wanjia Healthcare

Healthcare Quality and HIT - International Standards, China Practices

Edited by Jilan Liu

CRC Press
Taylor & Francis Group
Boca Raton London New York

CRC Press is an imprint of the
Taylor & Francis Group, an **informa** business
A PRODUCTIVITY PRESS BOOK

HIMSS

CRC Press
Taylor & Francis Group
6000 Broken Sound Parkway NW, Suite 300
Boca Raton, FL 33487-2742

Printed on acid-free paper

International Standard Book Number-13: 978-1-138-32251-6 (Hardback)
International Standard Book Number-13: 978-0-429-45153-9 (e-Book)

Library of Congress Cataloging-in-Publication Data

Names: Liu, Jilan, 1964- author.
Title: Healthcare quality and HIT : international standards, China practices / Jilan Liu.
Description: Boca Raton, FL : Taylor & Francis, 2019.
Identifiers: LCCN 2018057575 (print) | LCCN 2018060262 (ebook) |
ISBN 9780429451539 (e-Book) | ISBN 9781138322516 (hardback : alk. paper)
Subjects: | MESH: Healthcare Information and Management Systems Society. |
Joint Commission International. | Quality of Health Care—standards |
Hospitals—standards | Health Information Management | Medical Informatics |
Electronic Health Records—organization & administration | China
Classification: LCC RA971.6 (ebook) | LCC RA971.6 (print) | NLM WX 153 | DDC
362.110285—dc23
LC record available at https://lccn.loc.gov/2018057575

Visit the Taylor & Francis Web site at
http://www.taylorandfrancis.com

and the CRC Press Web site at
http://www.crcpress.com

Contents

Foreword

I am very pleased to see the fruition of the work of 20 amazing Chinese healthcare organizations exhibited in this book: 'International Standards, China Practices.'

We live in an era of amazing opportunities and significant challenges. Technology and informational advancements such as big data analytics, artificial intelligence, cloud computing, mobile technologies, and advanced robotics have begun to reshape our day-to-day work and lives. Meanwhile, the increasingly pervasive use of information technology (IT) is being met with greater security and safety threats.

HIMSS is a not-for-profit, cause-based organization with the mission of transforming healthcare through information and technology. We accomplish this goal by sharing our mission and collaborating with likeminded individuals, organizations, and government agencies on a variety of initiatives globally.

Since my first visit in 1987 and over the past three decades, the world has witnessed China's rapid growth in both economic terms and the transformation of the way in which it cares for its people. As the two largest economies in the world, both China and the US have aspired to improve their respective healthcare systems.

The Central Government of China has set impressive goals in its Healthy China 2030 initiative. By staging these extraordinary changes, China has promoted the exceptional value of adopting IT to support and improve health service delivery and operations.

The Chinese EMRAM offered by Chinese National Hospital Management Institute and the Interoperability certification program offered by the Center for Health Statistics and Information have created an important foundation which should have a long-lasting and successful impact on reshaping China's healthcare IT adoption. I congratulate China for initiating their own programs with such widespread and significant impacts.

By creating a Greater China arm in 2014, HIMSS found a place in China's healthcare IT journey by introducing HIMSS EMRAM and O-EMRAM. These programs are roadmaps that we hope will complement the Chinese programs in assisting Chinese hospitals and outpatient facilities by building and using their IT systems and maximize their value and productivity. In a very short time, by adopting HIMSS EMRAM, China has become the largest EMRAM Stage 7 country outside the US.

More importantly, the momentum is building as more and more Chinese hospitals recognize the phenomenal improvements achieved by engaging in interoperability and in both Chinese and HIMSS EMRAMs. By utilizing these programs, they improve their patient safety, quality of care, and operational efficiency.

China has always been a key player in the global landscape. Under the strong leadership of the Chinese government, we expect an ever more prosperous China. As part of this progress, we foresee a healthcare system that is transformed through IT, just as is depicted in the Healthy China 2030 initiative.

It has been an honor for HIMSS to participate in China's great endeavors in transforming healthcare systems through IT. At the end of the day, the grand vision of Health for All is a goal shared by all of us.

Harold (Hal) Wolf III, President and CEO
Healthcare Information and Management Systems Society

As the CEO of Joint Commission International (JCI), I have had the privilege of working with Dr. Jilan Liu for more than seven years. During that time, Jilan has taught me about health care and hospitals in China and also a great deal of what it takes to be a top-performing healthcare provider. In her book 'International Standards, China Practices', Dr. Liu shares the wealth of experience she has gained from advising and helping hospitals and other healthcare providers in China. She also provides insight into how much an organization can change as a result of preparing for and going through a JCI survey. This book is a vital resource for healthcare professionals interested in improving the quality and safety of the care they deliver in their healthcare organizations.

Paula Wilson, CEO
Joint Commission International

Acknowledgment

This book gathers together the thoughts and experiences of many individuals and organizations regarding their transformation in healthcare delivery. I want to thank all the authors, translators, editorial committee members and staff for their hard work and participation. This project would not have been possible without their contributions!

Jilan Liu

Editorial Board

Editor

Jilan Liu MD, MHA, CEO of HIMSS Greater China

Dr. Liu has extensive knowledge and experience in international healthcare. Not only has she worked and consulted in over 30 countries, she has experience in many diverse healthcare sectors. These include third-party accreditation/consulting agencies, public/private hospitals and academic medical centers, large physician group practices, health insurance companies, health maintenance organizations (HMOs), information technology (IT) companies, health policy research projects, and many others. Dr. Liu has been credited by some as one of the individuals contributing to reshaping healthcare delivery systems around the world.

As CEO of HIMSS Greater China since 2014, Dr. Liu has helped Chinese hospitals embrace international Health Information Technology (HIT) standards and best practices. With Dr. Liu's advice and support, these institutions have forcefully promoted value-driven IT investment and have successfully engineered senior leadership-led evolution of clinical/operation strategies incorporating IT. Through this work, Dr. Liu and her team have made a major contribution to transforming healthcare organizations' adoption of HIT, which in turn has fostered the maturity and growth of HIT industry in China. With her leadership and with the hard work of the institutions that they have worked with, China now has the second highest number of hospitals that have attained HIMSS EMRAN Stage 7 in the world. This has led many healthcare organizations and HIT companies that have worked with Dr. Liu and her team to testify to the transformational experience they have had while incorporating their approach to both information and technologies as together they reshape the entire healthcare industry.

Until 2017, Dr. Liu was the Principal Consultant and the Director for Greater China Practice for Joint Commission International. In this role, Dr. Liu and her colleagues provided consulting services to hundreds of hospitals in about 30 countries. This work focused on helping these hospitals to refocus on patient-centered care and services. The result was a transformation of their clinical and managerial operations toward better patient safety, higher quality, more personalized care and services, greater operational performance, and improved patient satisfaction.

Contributors

Bai Xizhuang
President and Secretary of Party Committee
People's Hospital of Liaoning Province
Shenyang, China

Jeremy T. Bonfini
Former Executive Vice President
HIMSS International
Pittsburgh, Pennsylvania

Cai Bin
Director, Quality Management Office
Sir Run Run Shaw Hospital Affiliated to Zhejiang University School of Medicine
Hangzhou, China

Cai Chengfu
Director of Human Resources and HIMSS Office
The First Affiliated Hospital of Xiamen University
Xiamen, China
and
Vice Dean
School of Medicine of Xiamen University
Xiamen, China

Cai Xiujun
President
Sir Run Run Shaw Hospital of Zhejiang University School of Medicine
Hangzhou, China

Cao Lei
CIO
The First Affiliated Hospital of Nanchang University
Nanchang, China

Cao Xiaojun
Deputy Director, Data Center
Guangzhou Women and Children's Medical Center
Guangzhou, China

Chang Li
Deputy Director, Hospital Standardization Management Office
Affiliated Hospital of Jining Medical University
Jining, China

Chen Dongfeng
Former President
Affiliated Hospital of Jining Medical University
Jining, China

Chen Min
Engineer, IT Department
Children's Hospital of Shanghai
Shanghai, China

Chen Ting
Staff, IT Department
People's Shanghai No. 6 People's Hospital
Shanghai, China

Chen Weiwen
Assistant Director, Pharmacy Department
Children's Hospital of Fudan University
Shanghai, China

Chen Xinlin
Vice President
Longhua Hospital Shanghai University of Traditional Chinese Medicine
Shanghai, China

Cui Mei
Director, Medical Records Management
TEDA International Cardiovascular Hospital
Tianjin, China

Dai Xiaona
Staff
The Second Affiliated Hospital of Zhejiang University School of Medicine
Hangzhou, China

John H. Daniels
Global Vice President
Healthcare Advisory Services Group HIMSS Analytics
Chicago, Illinois

Deng Pei
Engineer, IT Department
The First Affiliated Hospital of Nanchang University
Nanchang, China

Ding Chunguang
Deputy Director, Medical Affairs Department
Guangzhou Women and Children's Medical Center
Guangzhou, China

Dong Jun
Executive Vice President
TEDA International Cardiovascular Hospital
Tianjin, China

Dong Liang
CIO
Longhua Hospital Shanghai University of Traditional Chinese Medicine
Shanghai, China

Fan Shaofei
Chairman of the Board and CEO
Ping An Wanjia Healthcare (a subsidiary of Ping An Group)
Shenzhen, China

Fan Ying
Head Nurse, Nursing Department
The First Affiliated Hospital of Xinjiang Medical University
Ürümqi, China

Fei Xiaolu
Chief Engineer, IT Department
Xuanwu Hospital Affiliated to Capital Medical University
Beijing, China

Feng Shuting
Director, Medical Affairs Department and JCI Accreditation Office
People's Hospital of Liaoning Province
Shenyang, China
and
President
People's Hospital of Liaozhong District
Shenyang, China

Fu Yimin
Staff, IT Department
People's Shanghai No. 6 People's Hospital
Shanghai, China

Gao Chunhui
Vice President
Children's Hospital of Shanghai
Shanghai, China

Gao Xing
Deputy CIO
Shengjing Hospital of China Medical University
Shenyang, China

Gao Xuan
Deputy Director, Pharmacy Department
Children's Hospital of Fudan University
Shanghai, China

Gao Yunfei
Engineer, IT Department
TEDA International Cardiovascular Hospital
Tianjin, China

Ge Xiaoling
Director, Medical Statistics Department
Children's Hospital of Fudan University
Shanghai, China

Gong Jianguo
Engineer, IT Department
The First Affiliated Hospital of Nanchang University
Nanchang, China

Gu Shibo
Auditor, Wanjia Accreditation and Validation Committee
Ping An Wanjia Healthcare
Shenzhen, China

Guo Qiyong
Former President
Shengjing Hospital
China Medical University
Taiwan, China
and
Former Vice President
China Medical University
Taiwan, China

Han Li
Deputy Director, Medical Education Department
TEDA International Cardiovascular Hospital
Tianjin, China

He Jielang
Staff, Quality Management Office
Sir Run Run Shaw Hospital Affiliated to Zhejiang University School of Medicine
Hangzhou, China

He Xinzhu
Auditor, Wanjia Accreditation and Validation Committee
Ping An Wanjia Healthcare
Shenzhen, China

He Yi
Director, IT Department
Shanghai Children's Medical Center
Shanghai, China

John P. Hoyt
Former Global Vice President
Healthcare Advisory Services Group HIMSS Analytics
Chicago, Illinois

Allen Hsiao
CMIO
Yale New Haven Health and Yale School of Medicine
New Haven, Connecticut

Huang Chen
Information Nurse
Sir Run Run Shaw Hospital Affiliated to Zhejiang University School of Medicine
Hangzhou, China

Huang Guoying
President
Children's Hospital of Fudan University
Shanghai, China

Huang Shujuan
Chairman, Wanjia Accreditation and Validation Committee
Ping An Wanjia Healthcare
Shenzhen, China

Huang Xin
Assistant Director
The Second Affiliated Hospital of Zhejiang University School of Medicine
Hangzhou, China

Huang Yan
Auditor, Wanjia Accreditation and Validation Committee
Ping An Wanjia Healthcare
Shenzhen, China

Ji Bingxin
Deputy Director of Medical Affairs Department
Xuanwu Hospital Affiliated to Capital Medical University
Beijing, China

Ji Nan
Assistant Director
The Second Affiliated Hospital of Zhejiang University School of Medicine
Hangzhou, China

Ji Xianfeng
Director, Emergency Department
People's Hospital of Liaoning Province
Shenyang, China

Jia Weiping
Shanghai Clinical Center of Diabetes
People's Shanghai No. 6 People's Hospital
Shanghai, China

Jiang Jie
President
The First Affiliated Hospital of Xiamen University
Xiamen, China
and
Vice Dean
School of Medicine of Xiamen University
Xiamen, China

Jiang Zhixin
Assistant Director
The Second Affiliated Hospital of Zhejiang University School of Medicine
Hangzhou, China

Jiang Zhongyi
President
Shanghai Children's Medical Center
Shanghai, China

Jiang Zhou
Director, Neonatology Department
Sir Run Run Shaw Hospital Affiliated to Zhejiang University School of Medicine
Hangzhou, China

Jin Jianmin
Coordinator, Quality Control Department
The First Affiliated Hospital of Zhejiang University
Hangzhou, China

Jin Jingfen
Director, Nursing Department
The Second Affiliated Hospital of Zhejiang University School of Medicine
Hangzhou, China

Lan Chunyu
Engineer, IT Department
The First Affiliated Hospital of Nanchang University
Nanchang, China

Li Jia
Vice Secretary of the CPC (Communist Party of China) Committee and Secretary of Discipline Inspection Commission
Xuanwu Hospital Affiliated to Capital Medical University
Beijing, China

Li Lijuan
Director, Medical Records Management Department
Guangzhou Women and Children's Medical Center
Guangzhou, China

Li Min
Videographer, Cultural Propoganda Center
People's Hospital of Liaoning Province
Shenyang, China

Li Minqing
Director, Prevention Healthcare Department
Guangzhou Women and Children's Medical Center
Guangzhou, China

Li Tao
Responsible Staff, IT Department
Shengjing Hospital of China Medical University
Shenyang, China

Li Xiaoyu
Deputy Director of Outpatient Department
Xuanwu Hospital Affiliated to Capital Medical University
Beijing, China

Li Yandong
Director, Hospital Standardization Management Office
Affiliated Hospital of Jining Medical University
Jining, China

Li Yun
Director, Medical Records Department
Huashan Hospital Affiliated to Fudan University
Shanghai, China

Li Zhiping
Director, Pharmacy Department
Children's Hospital of Fudan University
Shanghai, China

Liang Zhigang
CIO
Xuanwu Hospital Affiliated to Capital Medical University
Beijing, China

Ling Qiming
Deputy CIO
Children's Hospital of Shanghai
Shanghai, China

Liu Dongyang
Director, IT Department
TEDA International Cardiovascular Hospital
Tianjin, China

Liu Fei
Deputy Director, IT Department
TEDA International Cardiovascular Hospital
Tianjin, China

Liu Gongbao
Director, Medical Affairs Department
Children's Hospital of Fudan University
Shanghai, China

Liu Haifeng
Vice President
Children's Hospital of Shanghai
Shanghai, China

Liu Hong
Director, Quality Control Center
TEDA International Cardiovascular Hospital
Tianjin, China

Liu Hongyang
Director, President's Executive Office and Medical Reform Office
People's Hospital of Liaoning Province
Shenyang, China

Liu Jianjun
Assistant President and Director of Medical Education Department
TEDA International Cardiovascular Hospital
Tianjin, China

Liu Qiang
Engineer, IT Department
The First Affiliated Hospital of Nanchang University
Nanchang, China

Liu Xiaocheng
President
TEDA International Cardiovascular Hospital
Tianjin, China

Liu Yang
Deputy Director, Outpatient Department
Huashan Hospital Affiliated to Fudan University
Shanghai, China

Liu Yongbin
Director of Medical Affairs Department
Children's Hospital of Shanghai
Shanghai, China

Liu Zhen
Staff, Pharmacy Department
Affiliated Hospital of Jining Medical University
Jining, China

Christopher A. Longhurst
Chief Information Officer
UC San Diego Health
San Diego, California

Lu Xiaoyang
Director, Pharmaceutical Department
The First Affiliated Hospital of Zhejiang University
Hangzhou, China

Lu Yan
Director, Human Resource Department
The Second Affiliated Hospital of Zhejiang University School of Medicine
Hangzhou, China

Lu Zhaohui
Director of the President's Office and the IT Center
Shanghai Children's Medical Center
Shanghai, China

Luo Xi
Auditor, Wanjia Accreditation and Validation Committee
Ping An Wanjia Healthcare
Shenzhen, China

Lv Na
Staff
The Second Affiliated Hospital of Zhejiang University School of Medicine
Hangzhou, China

Ma Lei
Quality Management Officer, Nursing Department
The First Affiliated Hospital of Xiamen University
Xiamen, China
and
Vice Dean
School of Medicine of Xiamen University
Xiamen, China

Ma Wenhui
Staff, Hospital Infection Management Department
Xuanwu Hospital Affiliated to Capital Medical University
Beijing, China

Ma Xin
Vice President
Huashan Hospital Affiliated to Fudan University
Shanghai, China

Ma Xuexian
Director, Standardization Management Department
The First Affiliated Hospital of Xinjiang Medical University
Ürümqi, China

Meng Fanfeng
Auditor, Wanjia Accreditation and Validation Committee
Ping An Wanjia Healthcare
Shenzhen, China

Mu Rongrong
Staff, IT Department
Shengjing Hospital of China Medical University
Shenyang, China

Pan Hongming
Vice President
Sir Run Run Shaw Hospital Affiliated to Zhejiang University School of Medicine
Hangzhou, China

Pan Hongying
Deputy Director, Nursing Department
Sir Run Run Shaw Hospital Affiliated to Zhejiang University School of Medicine
Hangzhou, China

Pan Zhongying
Vice President
United Family Healthcare
Beijing, China

Michael A. Pfeffer
CIO
UCLA Health Sciences
Los Angeles, California

Qian Yin
Head Nurse
Sir Run Run Shaw Hospital Affiliated to Zhejiang University School of Medicine
Hangzhou, China

Qiao Di
Staff, Pharmaceutical Department
The First Affiliated Hospital of Zhejiang University
Hangzhou, China

Qiao Kai
Vice Secretary of the CPC (Communist Party of China) Committee and Director of IT Department
Sir Run Run Shaw Hospital Affiliated to Zhejiang University School of Medicine
Hangzhou, China

Qiao Man
Staff, Hospital Standardization Management Office
Affiliated Hospital of Jining Medical University
Jining, China

Qiu Zhiyuan
Deputy Director, Medical Affairs Department
Huashan Hospital Affiliated to Fudan University
Shanghai, China

Qu Xiaowen
Vice President
Children's Hospital of Fudan University
Shanghai, China

Quan Yu
CIO
Shengjing Hospital of China Medical University
Shenyang, China

Rao Chunmei
Information Nurse, Nursing Department
The First Affiliated Hospital of Xiamen University
Xiamen, China
and
Vice Dean
School of Medicine of Xiamen University
Xiamen, China

Ren Anjie
Assistant Vice President
HIMSS Greater China

Shao Zhiyu
Director, Drug Manufacturing Room
The First Affiliated Hospital of Xiamen University
Xiamen, China
and
Vice Dean
School of Medicine of Xiamen University
Xiamen, China

Shen Nanping
Deputy Director, Nursing Department
Shanghai Children's Medical Center
Shanghai, China

Shi Jingyi
Director of President's Office
Longhua Hospital Shanghai University of Traditional Chinese Medicine
Shanghai, China

Shi Jun
Former President
First Affiliated Hospital of Nanchang University
Nanchang, China

Shi Min
United Family Healthcare
Beijing, China

Shi Minhua
Engineer, IT Department
Children's Hospital of Shanghai
Shanghai, China

Sun Benzheng
Staff, Security Guard Department
Affiliated Hospital of Jining Medical University
Jining, China

Sun Di
Assistant to the General Manager
United Family Healthcare
Beijing, China

Sun Huajun
Director of Pharmacy Department
Children's Hospital of Shanghai
Shanghai, China

Sun Xin
Director, Medical Affairs Department
Guangzhou Women and Children's Medical Center
Guangzhou, China

Sun Xuemei
Team Leader of Software, IT department
Xuanwu Hospital Affiliated to Capital Medical University
Beijing, China

Sun Yu
Staff, IT Department
People's Shanghai No. 6 People's Hospital
Shanghai, China

Tang Guobao
Director, Community Office
The First Affiliated Hospital of Xiamen University
Xiamen, China
and
Vice Dean
School of Medicine of Xiamen University
Xiamen, China

Tang Mingkun
Secretary, Administrative Personnel Department
The First Affiliated Hospital of Xiamen University
Xiamen, China
and
Vice Dean
School of Medicine of Xiamen University
Xiamen, China

Tang Yijun
Officer of JCI Office
Longhua Hospital Shanghai University of Traditional Chinese Medicine
Shanghai, China

Tian Mu
Former Manager, Quality Control Department
United Family Healthcare
Beijing, China

Tong Suijun
Vice Secretary of the CPC (Communist Party of China) Committee
The First Affiliated Hospital of Xiamen University
Xiamen, China
and
Vice Dean
School of Medicine of Xiamen University
Xiamen, China

Wang Bo
Staff, Hospital Standardization Management Office
Affiliated Hospital of Jining Medical University
Jining, China

Wang Chuanqing
Director, Hospital Infection Control and Prevention Office
Children's Hospital of Fudan University
Shanghai, China

Wang Guoqian
Staff, Hospital Standardization Management Office
Affiliated Hospital of Jining Medical University
Jining, China

Wang Huafen
Director, Quality Department
The Second Affiliated Hospital of Zhejiang University School of Medicine
Hangzhou, China

Wang Huiying
Director, Medical Affairs Department
Huashan Hospital Affiliated to Fudan University
Shanghai, China

Wang Jialing
Director, Party Office
Sir Run Run Shaw Hospital Affiliated to Zhejiang University School of Medicine
Hangzhou, China

Wang Jianan
President
The Second Affiliated Hospital of Zhejiang University School of Medicine
Hangzhou, China

Wang Lihong
Director of Hospital Infection Management Department
Xuanwu Hospital Affiliated to Capital Medical University
Beijing, China

Wang Weilin
President
The First Affiliated Hospital of Zhejiang University
Hangzhou, China

Wang Xin
Director, Pharmacy Department
TEDA International Cardiovascular Hospital
Tianjin, China
and
Assistant Director
The Second Affiliated Hospital of Zhejiang University School of Medicine
Hangzhou, China

Wang Yanxia
Director, Performance Evaluation
TEDA International Cardiovascular Hospital
Tianjin, China

Wang Yongxin
Deputy Director, Trauma Center
The First Affiliated Hospital of Xinjiang Medical University
Ürümqi, China

Wei Lan
Team Leader of Data, IT department
Xuanwu Hospital Affiliated to Capital Medical University
Beijing, China

Wei Li
Head Nurse
Sir Run Run Shaw Hospital Affiliated to Zhejiang University School of Medicine
Hangzhou, China

Wei Mingyue
Deputy CIO
Children's Hospital of Shanghai
Shanghai, China

Wei Xingling
Staff
The Second Affiliated Hospital of Zhejiang University School of Medicine
Hangzhou, China

Wen Hao
Former President
The First Affiliated Hospital of Xinjiang Medical University
Ürümqi, China

Weng Zihan
Staff, IT Department
Shanghai Children's Medical Center
Shanghai, China

Wu Dingying
Assistant Director, Quality Management Office
Sir Run Run Shaw Hospital Affiliated to Zhejiang University School of Medicine
Hangzhou, China

Wu Jing
Director, Healthcare Performance Department
Ping An HealthKonnect
Shenzhen, China

Wu Weizhe
Pharmacist
Guangzhou Women and Children's Medical Center
Guangzhou, China

Wu Xiaohu
Director, Human Resource Department
Children's Hospital of Fudan University
Shanghai, China

Wu Yunqi
Deputy Director, Medical Education Department
TEDA International Cardiovascular Hospital
Tianjin, China

Xi Yan
Deputy Director of Pharmacy Department and Director of Traditional Chinese Medicine Department
Longhua Hospital Shanghai University of Traditional Chinese Medicine
Shanghai Shi, China

Xia Chengfeng
Inspector, Medical Quality Department
TEDA International Cardiovascular Hospital
Tianjin, China

Xia Huimin
President
Guangzhou Women and Children's Medical Center
Guangzhou, China

Xiang Ying
Staff, IT Department
Shanghai Children's Medical Center
Shanghai, China

Xiao Zhen
President
Longhua Hospital Shanghai University of Traditional Chinese Medicine
Shanghai, China

Xie Linling
Auditor, Wanjia Accreditation and Validation Committee
Ping An Wanjia Healthcare
Shenzhen, China

Xu Hong
Vice Secretary of the CPC (Communist Party of China) Committee
Children's Hospital of Fudan University
Shanghai, China

Xu Jiahua
Director, Quality Control Office
Children's Hospital of Fudan University
Shanghai, China

Xu Liwen
Director of Pharmacy Department
Longhua Hospital Shanghai University of Traditional Chinese Medicine
Shanghai, China

Xu Meifang
Executive Vice-President
Shulan Health
Hangzhou, China

Xu Ran
Staff, Hospital Standardization Management Office
Affiliated Hospital of Jining Medical University
Jining, China

Xue Qiang
Deputy CIO
Affiliated Hospital of Jining Medical University
Jining, China

Yang Chenjing
Deputy Director, Propoganda Department
TEDA International Cardiovascular Hospital
Tianjin, China

Yang Minjie
Doctor in Charge, Emergency Room
Huashan Hospital Affiliated to Fudan University
Shanghai, China

Yang Yi
Director, Nursing Department
The First Affiliated Hospital of Xinjiang Medical University
Ürümqi, China

Yang Yinling
Head Nurse
The First Affiliated Hospital of Xiamen University
Xiamen, China
and
Vice Dean
School of Medicine of Xiamen University
Xiamen, China

Yang Yuanyuan
Director, Medical Administration Department
The First Affiliated Hospital of Xinjiang Medical University
Ürümqi, China

Ye Chengjie
CIO
Children's Hospital of Fudan University
Shanghai, China

Ye Feng
Director, Medical Oncology Department
The First Affiliated Hospital of Xiamen University
Xiamen, China
and
Vice Dean
School of Medicine of Xiamen University
Xiamen, China

Ye Jinming
Deputy CIO
Sir Run Run Shaw Hospital Affiliated to Zhejiang University School of Medicine
Hangzhou, China

Ye Xiaoyun
Director, Customer Service Department
The Second Affiliated Hospital of Zhejiang University School of Medicine
Hangzhou, China

Yin Shankai
Vice President
People's Shanghai No. 6 People's Hospital
Shanghai, China

Ying Bo
Deputy Director of Nursing Department
Xuanwu Hospital Affiliated to Capital Medical University
Beijing, China

Yu Guangjun
President
Children's Hospital of Shanghai
Shanghai, China

Zhang Faming
Engineer, IT Department
The First Affiliated Hospital of Nanchang University
Nanchang, China

Zhang Lili
Staff
The Second Affiliated Hospital of Zhejiang University School of Medicine
Hangzhou, China

Zhang Min
Director, Quality Control Department
Shanghai Children's Medical Center
Shanghai, China

Zhang Wei
Staff, IT Department
Shengjing Hospital of China Medical University
Shenyang, China

Zhang Ye
Pharmacist
TEDA International Cardiovascular Hospital
Tianjin, China

Zhang Ying
Engineer, IT Department
TEDA International Cardiovascular Hospital
Tianjin, China

Zhang Yishun
Managing Staff, Human Resource Department
Children's Hospital of Fudan University
Shanghai, China

Zhang Zan
Engineer, IT Department
TEDA International Cardiovascular Hospital
Tianjin, China

Zhao Cailian
Director, Quality Control Department
The First Affiliated Hospital of Zhejiang University
Hangzhou, China

Zhao Guoguang
President
Xuanwu Hospital Affiliated to Capital Medical University
Beijing, China

Zhao Min
CIO
The First Affiliated Hospital of Xiamen University
Xiamen, China
and
Vice Dean
School of Medicine of Xiamen University
Xiamen, China

Zhao Qi
Staff, IT Department
Shengjing Hospital of China Medical University
Shenyang, China

Zhao Xiaoying
Former Vice President
The Second Affiliated Hospital of Zhejiang University School of Medicine
Hangzhou, China

Zhao Yong
Assistant Director, Logistics Department
Huashan Hospital Affiliated to Fudan University
Shanghai, China

Zheng Feng
Director, PIVAS
Children's Hospital of Fudan University
Shanghai, China

Zheng Zhi
Staff, IT Department
Shengjing Hospital of China Medical University
Shenyang, China

Zhou Kang
Associate Partner
Ernst & Young (China) Advisory Limited
Tianjin, China

Zhou Yachun
Director, Quality Control Department
TEDA International Cardiovascular Hospital
Tianjin, China

Zhu Haihua
Director, Nursing Department
The First Affiliated Hospital of Xiamen University
Xiamen, China
and
Vice Dean
School of Medicine of Xiamen University
Xiamen, China

Zhu Jianqing
Staff, Medical Affairs Department
Huashan Hospital Affiliated to Fudan University
Shanghai, China

Zhu Yu
United Family Healthcare
Beijing, China

Zhu Yu
Coordinator, Quality Control Department
The First Affiliated Hospital of Zhejiang University
Hangzhou, China

Zhuang Yiyu
Vice President
Sir Run Run Shaw Hospital Affiliated to Zhejiang University School of Medicine
Hangzhou, China

Chapter 1

Preface

Contents

Born and raised in an exciting era, my generation is blessed to have been part of the most extraordinary transformation and profound changes of China. I am personally grateful to witness the realization of the Chinese dream of national rejuvenation.

Healthcare is the foundation of any society, and it directly touches all people's interests and wellbeing; therefore, healthcare-related policies and developments have always been important dimensions for policy makers, healthcare executives, clinicians, healthcare technology industries, and the general public. As Mr. Xi Jinping, stated on the 19th National Congress of the CPC, China will support her traditional industries in upgrading themselves and accelerate development of modern service industries to elevate themselves to international standards. Meanwhile, China's Healthy China Campaign has become the overarching strategy for the entire healthcare industry which accelerates the expansion and growth of healthcare delivery sector into comprehensive improvement of the people's health status and wellbeing. It is not until now has China realized a new era of healthcare industry has truly come. Healthcare needs not only technological innovation and breakthroughs, but also the restructuring of healthcare financing and delivery systems, standardization of clinical processes and more profound understanding of healthcare governance and leadership.

> Reflection in a mirror helps us dress properly; reflection into history helps us understand trends and patterns; and reflection from people helps us govern with clear mission.
>
> *Emperor Taizong of Tang Dynasty*

China has had a tradition of improving and reforming itself by adopting higher standards. In recent years, a series of Chinese health standards in line with international standards have blossomed which had laid a vital foundation for the rapid development of Chinese healthcare industry such as the China's National EMRAM standards, China's National HIT Interoperability Maturity standards, etc. One of the most authoritative standards in Chinese healthcare is the Chinese Hospital Classification system launched by the National Health Commission of People's republic of China.

In the meantime, pioneers of Chinese hospitals have also sought references and validations from the most representative international standards with global influence. The most influential among them are from Joint Commission International (JCI) and from Healthcare Information and Management Systems Society (HIMSS).

As the oldest accrediting body in healthcare globally, The Joint Commission (TJC) and its affiliate, JCI, have a long history in standards research and development and have devoted significant resources globally. Moreover, JCI has partnered with national and regional governments and global organizations, such as World Health Organization, to help establish patient-centered, quality improvement and patient-safety-oriented health systems and to implement the modern hospital governance and administration mechanism. Its impact is much more significant than that the number of JCI accredited hospitals shows. In the United States, the vast majority of U.S. hospitals are accredited by TJC, and outside the United States, around 1,000 hospitals from close to 70 countries are accredited by JCI, of which around 100 come from hospitals that have received the JCI accreditation.

JCI standards provide a basic framework for patient-centered hospital management and operation focusing on safety and continuous quality improvement which also focus on implementation. JCI standards hold state of art concepts with practical and locally implementable approaches to the most fundamental routine requirements for all hospitals. JCI not only encourages hospitals to enhance clinical knowledge and capabilities but also elevate their all-around and foundational performance in general. These often seemingly routine fundamentals, however, are not as easy to realize and maintain and often require strong systems and processes to support: From early stage of designing and planning of the infrastructure; formulation of corresponding operational rules and regulations, standardized workflow process design; habits of compliance in behavior; to monitoring, evaluating, receiving feedback and taking actions to improve on an ongoing basis, these are all essential pieces of a puzzle. Any missing pieces could make the entire system dysfunctional.

HIMSS, Healthcare Information and Management Systems Society, was founded as a grass-root organization by a group of process engineers. It later embraced Information & Technology as their driving force to transform hospital and healthcare operations. The society's mission is to transform healthcare through information and technology. Held by HIMSS annually, the HIMSS global conference and exhibition is the largest health information technology exchange platform. On the other hand, HIMSS Analytics, a wholly owned subsidiary of HIMSS, is the healthcare research and advisory arm for all kinds of healthcare organizations. Its signatures, EMRAM (Electronic Medical Record Adoption Model) and O-EMRAM (Outpatient Electronic Medical Record Adoption Model), are the most commonly used tools for validating hospital and ambulatory care organizations' IT adoption and support of clinical processes, which have seen markedly increasing influence in China. Since the functions and organizational structures of inpatient and outpatient maybe separate/independent, the two models are applied separately. They share the similar technical infrastructure in general while separately having a distinct emphasis on their respective capabilities.

EMRAM is an eight stage (0–7) model. Stage 0 indicates that a hospital has little clinical information system and operates mostly on a manual basis. Stage 1 indicates that three basic ancillaries—laboratory, pharmacy and radiology have installed clinical information systems. In the following stages, each level up requires adoption of different clinical information systems and functions such as nursing documentation, physician documentation and Computerized Physician Order Entry (CPOE) and a series of safety/security measures. Stage 6 requires a hospital to implement all essential clinical systems/functionalities and integrate all the modules with full interoperability within the hospital to support closed-loop process management, clinical decision support for orders, especially medication orders and a start of a document driven clinical decision support capabilities.

Stage 7 is the highest level in EMRAM which combines the features of digital hospital and smart hospital. Digital hospital is signaled by paperless operation and device interface (direct data extraction/incorporation into Electronic Medical Record (EMR) from medical equipment such as monitors in ICU) in all of its clinical processes. Smart hospital is signaled by the extensive incorporation of clinical decision support (incorporation of AI capabilities) to the point of care for all clinicians and the demonstration of advanced analytics (BI) to support managerial decision making and clinical/financial improvements. All clinicians in the hospital should be able to have single sign-on to access and enter all clinical information for the patients he/she provide care/service to. Clinical decision making reflected in the ordering and documentation process should be supported by the evidenced based clinical rules whenever and wherever those decisions are made. Stage 7 hospital also exhibit a high level of interoperability through its own data exchange platform and the HIE capability with external organizations. Extensive closed-loop management, at least on medications, blood and breast milk, should be achieved across departments through process redesign and re-engineering.

IT capability in Stage 7 hospitals or ambulatory centers not only helps the healthcare organizations enhance the standardization and reliability of clinical care to ensure patient safety and quality, but also significantly reduces manual process and unnecessary repetition to improve efficiency and effectiveness. It's a win-win situation for both healthcare providers and patients. The application of advanced Clinical Decision Support System (CDSS) could strengthen the ability of personalized diagnosis and treatment and precision medicine and improve clinical research capabilities. The journey to become a HIMSS EMRAM Stage 7 organization is a process of confidence and capacity building in the organization, as well as a vibrant process of improving technology and using technology to improve satisfaction for patients and providers.

The ideal development path depicted by HIMSS EMRAM of having Clinical Data Repository (CDR) in the early stage (Stage II) is challenging in China and in most of the countries of the world due to the lack of systematic design in the early IT development phase. Most of the information systems modules in many hospitals are purchased from different vendors or self-developed one at a time in the past. It has led to barriers in data exchange among all those silos. But to share data among multidisciplinary providers in multiple departments and locations and to realize various workflows within a same organization would require the interoperability among all functional clinical modules. If the modules are not fully integrated, departments cannot share data and the hospital cannot achieve closed-loop process management. Only when the modules truly achieve a high, standard integration and share data can cross-department processes be implemented for closed loops. CDSS and evidence-based management require a high level of data extraction, cross-referencing, aggregation, a strong evidence-based knowledge base, rules engine and data analysis tools, including machine learning capabilities. From our working experience with many hospitals in China, the real difficulty lies in the building and adoption of appropriate rules and the redesign of hospital processes rather than availability of technology. These cannot be achieved by vendors or IT department alone but with the engagement of the clinical and management departments who know the rules and procedures.

My personal overlap of roles, between 2014 and the end of 2017, as JCI Principal & Consulting Director for Greater China and as Vice President and CEO of HIMSS Greater China might have given rise to the misperception in China that the two organizations are somewhat intertwined, which is untrue. In reality, TJC/JCI and HIMSS are two independent and completely separate organizations. The only reason that I was able to carry both roles at the same time for each of the organizations in China, between 2014 and 2017, is because they share the common goals of improving healthcare in terms of patient safety and quality of care, and operational efficiency in the case of HIMSS. Both organizations allowed me to work with them on a part-time basis. In fact, this unique opportunity enabled me with unique insights into the integration of driving forces, ideals and tools of healthcare at a much greater scale, as would not have been possible otherwise.

JCI standards provide a comprehensive framework of clinical care process and hospital management and show hospitals the essential fundamentals needed as healthcare organizations, basically what the right things are. HIMSS, in addition to safety and quality, further highlights efficiency and effectiveness in hospital and healthcare operations and management, in other words, how to do the right things well. It puts emphasis on planning, implementing, operating and maintaining the technical roadmap to ensure safety, quality and efficiency. One of its core values is to help hospitals use technology and information to standardize the workflows and create a reliable, efficient and durable work environment for clinicians, patients/family and hospitals as a whole. In other words, HIMSS EMRAM criteria provide hospitals with roadmap for outstanding medical care and excellence in management through the effective use of modern information technology. This would provide a sense of self-worthiness and progress in patients and staff. As modern technologies constantly reshape every dimension of life, it seems unthinkable to profoundly transform health without technology.

The reasons for hospitals to participate in international accreditation and validation may vary. One of them for hospitals that already had their domestic recognition is their wish to obtain benchmark for their performance internationally to identify their own advantages, weaknesses and seek opportunities for improvements. Another important impetus to participate in JCI accreditation or HIMSS EMRAM certification is to pursue outstanding management and service and to be recognized internationally. On the journey toward outstanding management, leading managerial philosophies and concepts have always been sought after. Even if people know what to do and how to do it, without a "leverage" (inspiring goals and benchmarks) to motivate people and drive changes, the implementation of large-scale changes to the entire organization is frequently less than desirable. That's where JCI and HIMSS come in, as credible third parties that are internationally recognized to provide external inspiration, motivation and guidance for hospitals and to direct their efforts with the established frameworks to achieve excellence.

To fully understand JCI and HIMSS, we must look back to their origins and histories to learn about the stories behind and how they have found their ways into China.

Many Chinese hospitals have published books after they attain JCI accreditation or HIMSS EMRAM validation. My team and I have provided consulting/validation to most of them in China. Many of my friends and colleagues suggest that I write a book of my JCI and HIMSS consulting experience with Chinese hospitals. Thus, I decided to invite some of the Chinese hospitals who have stories and experiences to share from their JCI and HIMSS journeys. I would like to make this book a stage for the Chinese hospitals to tell their JCI and HIMSS stories, how they have grown and thrived by integrating "international standards" into their "China practices."

Jilan Liu
November 2017

My Journey from JCI to HIMSS

Jilan Liu

HIMSS Greater China

How unique is China and can international standards be applicable to improve China's medical practices? This is the question that has been asked repeatedly. From the initial skepticism to a certain level of acceptance and eventually evident achievements of JCI and HIMSS in China, it has not only represented the success of China's sharing and openness to the world but also the profound transformation in Chinese healthcare. As a participant and a witness of this journey, my story might also reflect our era driven by my generation of Chinese, with open minds to pursue excellence and mission to transform healthcare systems for better care and services for the Chinese people.

My JCI Journey

The adaptation of The Joint Commission Hospital Accreditation Standards to international community began in 1990s. At that time, hospitals from several countries were interested in participating in the then JCAHO (Joint Commission on Accreditation of Healthcare Organizations) accreditation, but many of the standards weren't quite easily adaptable to the countries outside of United States due to difference in laws and regulations. Taking that opportunity, JCAHO established an international arm of the organization to focus on the modification of standards and on using those standards for the consulting and accreditation of healthcare organizations outside of the United States.

Around 2001, JCI had its first opportunity of working in China. Mr. Clifford Peng, Chairman of Hong Kong Clifford Group, decided to build and operate a hospital with international standards, Clifford Hospital, in Panyu District, Guangdong province of China. Starting from the early stage of design and construction, Mr. Peng invited consultants from JCI to give guidance on the hospital design. After the completion of construction, JCI consultants continued their consultation support, and Clifford Hospital was successfully accredited by JCI in 2003. It may have been the first JCI accredited hospital in Asia. I was not among the first consulting team working with the Clifford Hospital, but it somehow brought me to JCI.

From 1992 to 1994, I did my Master of Healthcare Administration at the University of Washington. After my graduation, I worked at analyst, consultant, and manager positions with hospitals, medical insurance companies, health maintenance organizations (HMOs), and physician group organizations. The organization I worked for the longest period in the United States, as the Manager of Practice Performance & Improvement, Group Health Cooperative of Puget Sound, one of the oldest HMOs in the United States, which later merged with and became part of Kaiser Permanente. The latter, as the most well-known of HMOs, operates a diverse integrated portfolio of services, covering medical insurance, physician practice groups, hospitals, and other services to provide healthcare and services to its enrolled members. It is no doubt in my mind one of the most integrated value-driven healthcare organizations. This model of healthcare financing and delivery has had its broad-based influence in the United States and has recently attracted the attention of Chinese healthcare organizations.

I left the then Group Health Cooperative of Puget Sound and was in search of an opportunity to return to China at the end of 1999. At that time, Chinese healthcare sector began to reach out globally. Many of my Chinese friends in the United States were looking for opportunities to go back to China. I was among the first Chinese physicians with healthcare management degrees (MHA) in the United States, and I was at the time, hoping to bring my experience of physician group and hospital management, especially the integrated financing and delivery model back to China. However, most of the open opportunities to returning overseas healthcare professionals were in pharmaceuticals, medical equipment, and academic research. Those skills/experience, most believe, were directly transferable across borders, regardless of social, cultural, and structural differences. There were very few opportunities for healthcare delivery and financing services due to system differences. Though there were many visits and exchanges about the delivery of healthcare and services between China and the United States, gaps and differences were evident in terms of cultures, priorities, and how healthcare systems were organized. This may be why, unlike pharmaceutical and medical equipment/device companies, there were few multinationals existing in healthcare delivery systems, as most people believe, healthcare delivery is very locally driven business.

Unlike most of my friends that went back to China through pharmaceutical or equipment-related multinationals, I felt a bit lost as I was not able to find any healthcare delivery company that can take me back to China. So, I started a consulting company together with some of my friends to provide consulting services to local healthcare organizations in Seattle area and to multinationals that were interested in learning about Chinese healthcare sectors (I grew up in and still had many friends in Chinese healthcare). One of my business partners mentioned that he was providing consultation services to Clifford Hospital on behalf of JCI. Upon hearing that, I suddenly realized: after so many years working with the healthcare delivery and in HMO in the U.S., why shouldn't I go back to China to share my experience in healthcare delivery as a consultant? It was my belief that having in-depth understanding and management experience with healthcare delivery both in the United States and in China would enable me to share the merits of both countries like nobody else could! And I also realized that JCI accreditation may be the most effective in helping me get to Chinese healthcare organizations. That sowed the seeds toward the beginning of my journey with JCI.

At a social gathering in Seattle, I met Mr. Craig Allen, the then Principle of the US Department of Commerce in China. After knowing about my experiences, he asked, "Since you are from China and are so familiar with healthcare management of the United States, why don't you join JCI's efforts in China?" Craig told me that many healthcare organizations in China were very interested in JCI accreditation, and he was requested by the Chinese government at that time to help linking Chinese healthcare organizations with JCI. With his help, Mr. Zhu Qingsheng, the then Vice Minister of China's Ministry of Health, led a delegation including Chinese government officials and hospital executives to JCI headquarter for an official visit. At the same time, Craig was planning to learn more about the value of JCI accreditation toward Chinese hospitals after returning to Beijing. It was his ideas and initiatives that had further aroused my interest.

Later, I had opportunities to participate in some activities when Craig went back to China. On one of the forums where he had dialog with healthcare leaders on JCI, he introduced me to the audience and I briefly introduced my own experience in the United States. That forum allowed me to directly learn about the interest of Chinese hospitals in JCI and seriously evaluated the potential influence of JCI in Chinese healthcare industry.

Around that time (2002), I returned to China as a consultant for the first time to participate in organizing a Hospital Management Training Program for Hospital CEOs and other executives held by Project HOPE in Shanghai. Many of the professors and trainees for that course are still very active leaders in China's healthcare community today. The training program was one of the first hospital management training programs in China supported by an oversea foundation and was very meaningful to me personally. That was the first time I went back to China as a consultant for healthcare delivery management training. It was somewhat embarrassing when I found out that I had lost some of my fluency in Chinese language after having used English as my working language for more than 10 years. I had the pleasure of admiring the fluent, vivid expression and precise, in-depth analysis of problems of Professor Shen Xiaoming, a well-known pediatrician and CEO of the Xinhua Hospital at the time (now the Governor of Hainan Province), when he and I were co-teaching a case study for the class.

After that, introduced by my friend who is JCI consultant for Clifford Hospital, I got in touch with the then JCI Vice President in charge of consultation services, Ms. Ann Rooney. In our first phone call, she asked why I was interested in JCI. I simply said that my background should be beneficial to Chinese healthcare delivery and I wished to do so through JCI. At that time, though the Clifford Hospital had already been connected with JCI, it was still a single unique case in China. The reality was that many Chinese healthcare organizations that had interest in JCI did not believe they should participate in the actual accreditation process as JCI was still considered as quite remote and foreign to Chinese healthcare. JCI, at that time, also did not know whether Chinese hospitals were ready to meet JCI standard requirements. The mainstream of Chinese healthcare in 2003 was very far from modern operations. I remember saying it at the phone interview that the concept of "driving improvement through evaluation" was rooted in Chinese culture and that if JCI's mission was to improve patient safety and quality of healthcare throughout the world, it should not write off the vast number of China's healthcare organizations. Later, I was told that the leadership of the JCI had agreed on that.

Thus, right at the beginning the outbreak of SARS in early 2003, with the support of Mr. Zhou Zhijun of Beijing University I arranged and accompanied the then President/CEO Karen Timmons and Vice President for Consulting Services Ann Rooney to visit China. That was JCI's first ever official visit to China. We met the leaders of China's Ministry of Health and Chinese Hospital Association, as well as with Hospital Management Research Center of Peking University. They showed strong interests in JCI. At that time, China's Ministry of Health had just concluded their visit to the JCI headquarters, and everyone showed great enthusiasm and interests for JCI's visit. During the visit, Karen Timmons, then President of JCI, signed a Memorandum of Understanding with Mr. Cao Ronggui, President of Chinese Hospital Association. After that visit, the Chinese Hospital Association began the translation of JCI hospital standards manual into Chinese language. I also joined JCI and became a JCI consultant. I felt humbled when I went to the first consultant gatherings as I was the youngest JCI consultant ever hired at the time (Figure 1.1).

However, in the first few years of my part-time employment with JCI as its consultant, in the years of after mass of SARS, there were few activities in China. As a matter of fact, the Clifford Hospital was the only one JCI accredited hospital in China at that time. Therefore, for many years after joining JCI, I had been working with hospitals in other countries. My initial training and preceptorship were in India, Singapore, and in the United States. After that, the first hospital I officially consulted was in Jordan, the second was in Korea, and the third to the tenth were in Israel and in Denmark. Later on, I jointed more and more JCI consultation activities in hospitals in the Mideast, in Europe, in Central America, in Africa, and in many other Asian countries. The most activities were concentrated in the Middle East for a period of time. So far, I've been to hundreds of hospitals in nearly 30 countries. Building up my in-depth understanding of healthcare in China and in the United States, such consulting experience to so many other countries and continents on healthcare delivery has given me a unique opportunity to expand my horizons, allowing me to look deeply into healthcare delivery from a truly global perspective. It gave rise to the realization of the absolute needs for incorporating/integrating modern management standards and best

Figure 1.1 Signing ceremony of MoU between Ms. Karen Timmons, then President of JCI and Mr. Cao Ronggui, then President of Chinese Hospital Association in 2003.

practices into local political, economic, and cultural environment to drive changes. When driving the common value into the change equation, I was also enlightened with the need for sensitivity in recognizing the unique culture in every organization and to allow flexibility in making adjustments in approaches to get the buy-in from the leadership and staff.

Back at that time, there were very few Chinese consultants doing hospital management consulting in international community, especially in developed countries. The welcome and respect I had received in all those countries gave me a lot of confidence. For example, it was initially difficult to convince Israeli doctors of the need to conduct physician credentialing, privileging, and performance evaluation as doctors had enjoyed very high autonomy in hospitals in Israel. But they welcomed the straightforward discussions with me as I was among the first physician consultants working with them on their initial JCI accreditation preparation. Now, almost all major hospitals in Israel have had their JCI accreditation, and all of them had implemented their physician credentialing, privileging, and performance evaluation programs, among many other changes brought by JCI accreditation and by our consultation. Some Israeli hospitals I provided consultation with later told me that they regarded me as one of their own. I suppose that came from their respect for my straightforwardness. In the meantime, I also developed/maintained very friendly and professional relationships with hospitals in many countries in the Mideast as well. In Ireland, one of many hospitals that I had provided consultations with had received four rounds of JCI accreditation. I was invited back to their hospital every time for their reaccreditation preparation, and they even awarded me with their staff pin as an honorary employee. In Kazakhstan, I was touched when a doctor told me that he envied me as a healthcare "expert" representing both United States and China, two biggest and strongest countries in the world. Unlike him, he said, when he studied abroad and told people where he came from, people often responded by asking "where is that"?

Within the first few years after I joined JCI, I was busy doing JCI consultation in other countries with limited interactions with the Chinese healthcare community. At the time, United Family Healthcare was very interested in JCI accreditation. After my meeting with Ms. Roberta Lipson, founder of the United Family Hospital Group, I teamed up with another JCI consultant for a visit to the hospital and discussed the details of preparation for JCI accreditation in 2003.

United Family Healthcare decided to officially launch their JCI journey. The Beijing United Family Hospital became the second hospital in China accredited by JCI (Figures 1.2–1.6).

During the same time, Sir Run Run Shaw Hospital in Hangzhou got in touch with us. In the autumn of 2003, Professor He Chao, then CEO of Sir Run Run Shaw Hospital, invited me

Figure 1.2 Sep. 2007, JCI consultants in front of Rigshospitalet Hospital in Copenhagen.

Figure 1.3 Dec. 2008, JCI team in King Abudulaziz medical city in Saudi Arabia.

Figure 1.4 Jun. 2013, a JCI consulting engagement at a Children's hospital in Kenia.

Figure 1.5 2014, taking participants to a hospital in Seoul to demonstrate tracer methodology.

Figure 1.6 2015, hangout with other JCI faculty in Tokyo during a JCI Tokyo training program.

and Scott Altman to introduce the JCI hospital accreditation to the hospital. Sir Run Run Shaw Hospital soon embarked on their own JCI accreditation journey and spent much time in the preparation. The JCI consultation team conducted a mock survey. The hospital was then successfully accredited after their initial survey in 2006.

An important turning point occurred in 2010 when Huashan Hospital of Fudan University passed the JCI accreditation. Huashan Hospital first started its JCI journey around 2007 for several reasons: First, Professor Xu Jianguang, then CEO of Huashan Hospital, and Professor Ding Qiang, the successor CEO of the hospital, held strong insight in the value of international standards and practices. They wanted to lead Huashan Hospital to participate in accreditation by international standards in the hope of better meeting the needs generated by increasing patient volume and higher-quality expectations as well as seeking new breakthroughs after its one hundredth anniversary. Second, about 50% of the foreign residents in Shanghai would go to Huashan Hospital for their clinical care. Some foreign insurance companies expected that the hospital be JCI accredited when discussing insurance contracts. The external impetus from the insurance companies, the internal demand for higher service capacity without jeopardizing safety and quality, and the limited space for physical expansion motivated Huashan Hospital toward using JCI accreditation to push for system building, clinical process redesign, and quality improvement.

Our first consultation visit to Huashan Hospital was an 8-day baseline survey in 2007. We were impressed by the earnestness of the hospital after the first day's patient tracer in the hospital. We also found many issues for the hospital that was shocking to them, as many of the issues we identified for them were never brought up to the leadership before (Figure 1.7).

During the baseline, Professor Xu Jianguang, then CEO, was already appointed as the Director-General of the Health Bureau of Shanghai Municipality. He received us both as the CEO of Huashan Hospital and as Director-General of the healthcare authority of Shanghai Municipality and heard our debriefing to learn our perspective on the issues of the hospital. Shortly after the baseline consultation, Professor Ding Qiang became the CEO of Huashan Hospital. The preparation for JCI accreditation was then proceeded under the leadership of Professor. Ding Qiang, the new CEO and Professor Ma Xin, then Director of the Medical Affairs and Director of JCI office

Figure 1.7 Baseline survey at Huashan Hospital in November 2007.

(who later became the Vice President of Medical services for the Hospital). As for me, my job was to provide consultation and guidance to support their improvement efforts throughout.

In fact, it was a long and challenging journey for the hospital, from the baseline consultation, technical support, mock survey to the initial survey. JCI also made some efforts to adjust standard interpretation to the Chinese practice reality. The consulting team and the hospital spent a lot of time discussing potential mechanisms to bridge many of the gaps to the standards and some that appeared to be impossible requirements at the time. For example, the management of outpatient medical records was one of the typical differences between China and the international community. JCI standard requires that a medical record must be established and maintained for each patient. It was interpreted as that hospital should keep all patient records, inpatient and outpatients. That is the standard practice in most of the countries. However, according to the common practice of Chinese hospitals, at the time they only kept the medical records for inpatients, and the outpatient medical records were given to the patients after each encounter. Huashan was not exceptional. Therefore, no outpatient medical record was kept in the hospital. (This is before the era of electronic medical records for China. It is less of the issue now as many hospitals have since embarked on EMR journey for both inpatient and outpatient settings.)

That was one of the issues that we struggled for a long time to resolve. It appeared to be one simple problem of keeping outpatient medical records. But the fundamental issue was that it had significant impact on the continuity of care. It also involved how best to evaluate the compliance of outpatient assessment and care process documentation against relevant JCI standards. During the preparation, I had a lot of communication with JCI central office from the perspective of the Chinese government policy and common practice in Chinese hospitals. At that time, there was no primary care system requirement and Chinese authorities have not encouraged patients to choose their own primary care doctors (they do that now). The Chinese government sponsored insurance was promoting the freedom of choice for care providers as the measure to respect patient choices. They required portability of outpatient medical records (on paper) by patients owning those records directly. We argued that allowing outpatient owning and maintaining their own records (instead of owning and maintaining those outpatient records by hospitals) was the best solution of Chinese hospitals to ensure the continuity of care among different hospitals/clinics. This becomes a major issue as major hospitals like Huashan have millions of outpatient visits per year. Changing the outpatient record ownership from patients to the hospital was not possible to accomplish in a paper record environment, nor did the hospital see the value of doing so.

After our repeated back and force discussion both verbally and in writing with the JCI central office, eventually, following a standard committee discussion and decision, the Vice President responsible for JCI Accreditation at the time issued a clarification, stating how JCI would address the absence of outpatient records maintained by Chinese hospitals. With that clarification, JCI decided that without owning and maintaining outpatient medical records, Chinese hospitals may be scored under the standards related to continuity of care, but it should not be a show stopper. This move by JCI removed a major road block and played an important role in encouraging a large number of Chinese hospitals to follow the path laid by Huashan Hospital for JCI accreditation. It also proved the openness and flexibility of the JCI standards.

The exciting news of Huashan Hospital passing JCI accreditation was thrilling! At the celebration party, an overwhelming number of congratulations were sent to the hospital, including those from the National Health and Family Planning Commission (now called National Health Commission), the People's Government of Shanghai Municipality, and many leaders from peer hospitals. Based on their hard-earned achievement and experience, Huashan Hospital organized many seminars on JCI accreditation and attracted many leaders from hospitals in Shanghai and all over China.

In my opinion, the adoption of JCI standards by Huashan Hospital paved ways for JCI with large government-owned hospitals in China. Other three JCI hospitals before that, namely Clifford Hospital, Sir Run Run Shaw Hospital and Beijing United Family Hospital, all have had strong ties with overseas investment and operations. Both Clifford Hospital and Beijing United Family Hospital were owned and operated by overseas investments/individuals. Though Sir Run Run Shaw Hospital has been owned by the Chinese Government, the founding donor was from Hong Kong, and the hospital was first operated by the Medical Center of Loma Linda University. Therefore, there was a misunderstanding at the time that only English-speaking hospitals could earn the JCI gold seal. But Huashan Hospital, a traditional Chinese hospital owned and operated entirely by Chinese can achieve JCI accreditation, served as an excellent example for and injected a lot of confidence to other Chinese hospitals with high patient volume, limited space and some old buildings. Huashan's pursuit of excellence and success told the local hospitals that JCI, and the international standard in general, was possible to reach! It has also proved to the Chinese healthcare community that the pursuit of quality improvement is an endless journey.

Since then, more Chinese hospitals started to show their interest in JCI accreditation. My team and I also joined their journeys and provided consultation and guidance to most of Chinese hospitals preparing for their JCI accreditation, the list is long, including but not limited to the following:

Shanghai Children's Medical Center of Shanghai Jiaotong University
Children's Hospital of Fudan University
Luoyang Orthopedic Hospital
Zhengzhou No. 5 People's Hospital
Zhenjiang First People's Hospital
Guangzhou Women and Children's Medical Center
Kunming Children's Hospital

The First Affiliated Hospital of Zhejiang University
The Second Affiliated Hospital of Zhejiang University
The First Affiliated Hospital of Xinjiang Medical University
Sir Run Run Shaw Hospital
Clifford Hospital
The First Affiliated Hospital of Xiamen University
Shenzhen Shekou People's Hospital
Shanghai Pudong Hospital
Affiliated Hospital of Jining Medical College
Wuxi Second People's Hospital
Liaoning Provincial People's Hospital
Ningbo No. 2 Hospital
Shanghai Changning Women & Children's Hospital
Shulan (Hangzhou) Hospital
Shanghai Proton and Heavy Ion Center
Kunmin 1st People's Hospital

My JCI colleagues for all these years, both the consultants/surveyors and the leadership/staff, at the corporate/regional level have played a pivotal role in getting JCI brand recognized as a true reflection of the gold seal. The consultants from outside of China that I worked with most closely and those that have become well-known names to Chinese hospitals have brought and shared their experiences, expertise, most of all, their unwavering mission to improve patient safety/quality to all that they touched. Some of them have been the mentor to me when I started my JCI career and have continued supporting me through my own journey with JCI. They are the real embodiment of quality itself. This includes but not limited to the following individuals:

Helen Hoesing, RN, Ph.D
Linda Faber, RN, Ph.D
Derick Pasternak, MD, MBA
Terence Shea, RN, MPA
Richard Wright, MD, MS
Thomas Kozlowski, Ph.D
Francine Westergaard, RN, MBA
Judy Moomjian, RN, MPA
Yvonne Burdick, MHA
Nellie Yeo, RN, MBA
Karen Reno, RN, Ph.D
Jeannell Mansur, D.Ph, MS
Rosanne Pesseri Farrell, RN, MS
Heidi Do, RN, Ph.D
Chinhak Chun, MD

For all those hospitals that invited me and my team to provide consultation services to steer them through their JCI journey, we helped them assess their gaps, train them on the intent of the standards, show them the best practices, and help them identify solutions that would work for them. So far, we have been conducting baseline surveys, technical support, and mock surveys for almost 100 hospitals in China (Figures 1.8–1.11).

Figure 1.8 Sep. 2009, demonstrating medication system tracking in Huashan Hospital.

Figure 1.9 Feb. 2015, demonstrating patient tracking in No. 2 Affiliated Hospital of Zhejiang University College of Medicine.

Every Chinese hospital on the JCI journey with us has proven the value of a patient-centered and employee-oriented approach encouraged by JCI standards. With JCI's evidence-based standards and methodology as well as the support from a stable, professional, and neutral team of consultants and surveyors, the hospitals have gained extensive and profound changes during its JCI accreditation process. Most importantly, the focus on quality and safety and the emphasis on evidence-based methodologies and continuous improvement have inspired the synergy of the hospital staff through team building, capacity, and confidence building.

Meanwhile, the Chinese hospital accreditation program conducted by the National Health Commission has shifted its focus from scale/capacity to safety and quality. I had the privilege to learn from the national team of reviewers led by General Chen Xiaohong, some of the provincial

Figure 1.10 Jan. 2017, site tour in ED of No. 1 Affiliated Hospital of Zhejiang University College of Medicine.

Figure 1.11 Jun. 2017, site tour in tumor ward of Liaoning People's Hospital.

and municipal team of reviewers, and the quality control departments in China and to discuss with them standards and survey methodologies. I am very impressed by the experience and achievements of China during these years of vigorous reforms and improvements. Compared with the past, the safety and quality of Chinese hospitals have been greatly improved. The credit goes to the effective push at a national level.

The later story became quite familiar to many people in the Chinese healthcare community. After a bumpy journey toward mutual understanding and collaboration, JCI has firmly landed in China, and our promotion on the system capacity building and development of Chinese hospitals have served to help improving the quality of patient safety and healthcare services in China.

HIMSS' Adventure in China

It was somewhat a surprise but not totally out of blue for me to join HIMSS' cause of transforming healthcare through IT by serving as HIMSS Vice President and Chief Executive for the Greater China operation. My first interests in health information technology and HIMSS could be dated back to more than a decade ago.

It was around 2004 when I began working with JCI as a part-time consultant. I also had a Seattle-based consulting practice, part of that was to help multinationals identify China-related healthcare opportunities and to develop strategies. At such a capacity, I was involved in help organizing Pacific Health Summit as a consultant, which included helping invite senior healthcare leaders from China to join in the summit. The conference might have been among the first global policy summit centered around individualized care and precision medicine. The summit's seed funding came from Bill & Melinda Gates Foundation and Russell Family Foundation, and co-organized by the Fred Hutchinson Cancer Research Center and the National Bureau of Asian Research. GE, Intel, Microsoft, and many other world-famous technology companies were among the major sponsors. At that time, the human genome project and information technology had just made enough progress to show the glimpse of potential of transforming healthcare into prewarning, precision, preventive, and personalized care. Policymakers, technology pioneers, leading academics, and medical executives gathered together to discuss how we can seize the moment and realize the potential. I was later invited to provide consultation to Intel on healthcare policies and their implications. I was also invited to consult with Perot Healthcare in EMR consulting which engaged me to help explore opportunities in China, before it was sold to Dell.

Later on, while working as a JCI consultant, I continued my role in organizing the Pacific Health Summit and inviting Chinese healthcare leaders to the summit. Though JCI's progress in China was slow in those years, I had the opportunity to work with many movers and shakers of Chinese healthcare through the summit. As a healthcare management consultant and a JCI consultant on a global level, I was invited by HIMSS headquarters and Asia Pacific to speak at HIMSS Global Conference and Asia-Pacific events many times. Through those activities, I learned more about HIMSS.

From 2004 to 2014, I became increasingly occupied with JCI consulting assignments. And I started to recommend more and more IT-based solutions for process reengineering and quality improvements to meet JCI standards both in China and in many other countries. I had a strong conviction that the bigger volume pressure there is for a hospital, the stronger the demand it is for solid IT support. This is especially true for large public hospitals in China.

Chinese people are known for their diligence and practicality. However, the very large-sized, complex modern hospitals could not be operated on a manual process. Compared with hospitals around the world, the staffing ratio of Chinese hospitals is relatively low. Under such circumstances, it was obviously not possible to build hospitals of "excellence" completely "by hand".

Healthcare delivery is both high-tech and high-touch industry. Facing the challenges of staffing shortage, demanding tasks/responsibilities with large patient volumes, and the new payment mechanism and regulations for Chinese hospitals, the answer lies in a high level of incorporation of information technology with healthcare practices. It is precisely the opportunity and the calling of our times. The speed of maturity and potential of information technology is unprecedented in human history. The Chinese government policy has promoted advanced information and technology in healthcare to increase access, operational efficiency, enhance clinical capacity, and improve skills of the professionals. The ultimate goal is to improve healthcare quality, safety, and efficiency. The question is no longer whether to build but how to build an excellent modern hospital? and

- "What must be done manually and what can be done automatically?"
- "What processes can be achieved most effectively through human-machine interactions?"
- "What are the appropriate technologies?"
- "What are the best technology development strategies?" and
- "What is the leverage that can be used to drive changes?"

Even for achieving JCI accreditation, I was strongly aware that without robust information technology support, a significant portion of the processes redesign would not last. A fundamental change should be built on top of the systems, and it is essential for the use of information technology if a hospital wants to make their changes brought by JCI to demonstrate continuous improvement.

My thought coincided with HIMSS' consideration of launching a Greater China operation. In about 2014, I began to realize that the promotion of JCI already had a positive impact on China's healthcare industry, but to sustain and to demonstrate value to clinicians and staff required further support of information technology in such a modern era. However, the HIT industry in China was at an anxious yet puzzled state at the time. The initial surge of claim-driven systems has tapered off, pieces of EMRs from a large number of vendors were laid on top of one another, silos everywhere, the new era for an integrated electronic medical record to support clinical operations had been considered too remote to achieve. Therefore, when I was with hospitals for consultation, I started to provide recommendations on process redesign via adopting information technology, some of which even became selling features for some vendors' products. A few HIT vendors had approached me hoping that I could help them develop IT solutions that help meet JCI standards. Having consulted with hundreds of hospitals on systems/process improvement around the world, it would be meaningful and fulfilling for me personally to see my own ideas become concrete products that could help hospitals to ensure safety, improve quality, and increase efficiency on an even larger scale. When I was approached by HIMSS to lead its Greater China operation, I immediately saw that the offer was exactly what I needed in China which gave me an opinion leadership position to influence hospitals and HIT industry together at a broader level! I was enthusiastic to take on this responsibility. An agreement was soon reached, and HIMSS Greater China operation was rolled out right away.

The first call from HIMSS came to me in February 2014, and I started to work for them in March. I had such a sense of urgency to start working right away as there was such a need to get something done. Though HIMSS had been exploring China opportunities for many years, they did not find an effective and meaningful connection to the Chinese healthcare community before 2014. I am a believer of HIMSS' mission to transform healthcare through information and technology. I was convinced that it was exactly the right moment, at the right time, to ignite that mission with the healthcare community, and I also believed that I was the right person to ignite that mission, as it was exactly the right extension to the work I have built through JCI and Pacific Health Summit over the years with the Chinese hospitals and the entire healthcare community.

As far as I knew, China's HIT industry had heard about HIMSS for many years. From 2006 to 2012, the National Institute of Hospital Administration (affiliated to MOH) and/or the Chinese Healthcare Information Management Association (CHIMA) had organized delegations from government, healthcare industry, and hospitals to attend the HIMSS global conferences in the United States almost every year. In 2010, CHIMA and HIMSS also jointly held a CHIMA/HIMSS annual conference in Beijing. Over the years, both the Statistics and Information Center of the

National Health and Family Planning Commission (now named as National Health Commission), National Institute of Hospital Administration, and CHIMA have stayed in touch with HIMSS.

The HIMSS EMRAM criteria were first released in the United States in 2005 and gradually matured after 2006. CHIMA discussed with HIMSS about the possibility of introducing HIMSS EMRAM model into China, though it was obvious to both sides that "China, as a big and strong country, must have its own standards". I personally agree with that. Soon the National Institute of Hospital Administration took the lead to establish China's own EMRAM standards which had been widely applied to thousands of Chinese hospitals before I joined HIMSS. Though MOH agencies and CHIMA did not participate directly in the introduction of HIMSS EMRAM validation in China, it played a very important role in increasing the HIT community's awareness and in the promotion of HIMSS in China in the early days.

Before I joined HIMSS, there were already four HIMSS EMRAM Stage 6 hospitals in China, namely Peking University People's Hospital, Shengjing Hospital of China Medical University, Chang An Hospital, and Yantai Yuhuangding Hospital. After I started HIMSS Greater China operation, the first news was that Peking University People's Hospital was preparing for HIMSS EMRAM Stage 7 because they strongly agreed with the idea of closed-loop process and interoperability. I decided to cease the moment to support the hospital's journey toward HIMSS EMRAM Stage 7. Thus, it became the first project for me and that was why I immediately started my work with HIMSS—to arrange and organize HIMSS EMRAM Stage 7 consultation and validation for the People's Hospital of Peking University.

In March 2014, a colleague from HIMSS Asia PAC and I went to Beijing to discuss the detailed plan with People's Hospital for their Stage 7 preparation and validation. After the discussion, I coordinated the follow-up consultation and validation arrangements with the HIMSS headquarters. Shortly after, Shengjing Hospital of China Medical University came to me and expressed their interests in HIMSS EMRAM Stage 7. A mock survey was arranged for Shengjing Hospital to assist their HIMSS EMRAM journey as well.

In May 2014, the HIMSS validation team arrived in Beijing for the on-site Stage 7 validation in People's Hospital of Peking University. The team includes John Daniels, Global Vice President of HIMSS Analytics, Dr. Melisa Rizer, CMIO of Ohio State University Health System, and I. After the validation with People's Hospital, we went on to Shenyang for the mock survey with Shengjing Hospital.

The reason that the People's Hospital of Peking University decided to be validated at that time was because they wished to receive the validation award from HIMSS at the CHIMA Annual conference to be held at end of May 2014. The impact and reputation of HIMSS EMRAM in the Chinese hospital community and HIT industry can be partially attributed to the success of People's Hospital of Peking University's achieving HIMSS EMRAM Stage 7. The hospital helped demonstrating our value to the healthcare community in China. It was like a breath of fresh air, we made a big impact to the hospitals and HIT industry in China at the time, and subsequently, this was regarded as a milestone event to connect HIMSS to Chinese healthcare (Figure 1.12).

If the success with People's Hospital of Peking University had earned the initial reputation for HIMSS in China, the Stage 7 validation of Shengjing Hospital had a more profound impact on my own HIMSS career because I participated in the consultation component rather than the validation. The consultation experience helped me better understand the leadership strength of Shenjing hospital and left me with a deeper appreciation on the value of HIMSS EMRAM on hospitals. Through HIMSS consultation and validation of People's Hospital and Shenjing Hospital, both among the top of Chinese Hospitals and in their HIT, I have gained insights with the essence of HIMSS EMRAM maturity model and its profound influence on the transformation of hospital safety, quality, efficiency,

Figure 1.12 Peking University People's Hospital passed HIMSS EMRAM Stage 7 validation in May 2014.

staff growth and patients' satisfaction, as well as its potential to support clinical excellence. I was further convinced that its mission and its knowledge have a unique value to healthcare globally and in China, and I was glad that I have made a right choice to work with HIMSS.

The two HIMSS EMRAM Stage 7 hospitals in China were followed by Zhongshan Hospital of Fudan University, Zhongshan Hospital of Dalian University, and Tianjin Ninghe People's Hospital that were validation for HIMSS EMRAM Stage 6. Learning from our initial success with People's Hospital of Peking University, we issued press releases on social media Wechat for every hospital that achieved HIMSS EMRAM Stages 7 and 6. The year of 2014 became a big year for HIMSS and its EMRAM maturity model. It found its way to China and became widely recognized by China's healthcare community.

Prior to the two Chinese hospitals achieved their EMRAM Stage 7, in 2014 HIMSS EMRAM Stage 7 was unfamiliar to Chinese hospitals and was considered almost an unachievable undertaking. Although there was still insufficient understanding of the criteria and the mechanisms used to build required capabilities, the success of two Stage 7 hospitals and the emergence of several Stage 6 hospitals became a booster to China's healthcare industry. The success of the two Stage 7 hospitals was achieved through the strong leaderships from their then CEOs, Dr. Wang Shan, then CEO, People's Hospital of Peking University, and Dr. Guo Qiyong, then CEO, Shengjing Hospital of China Medical University. The strong support from the hospital leaderships proved to be the core strengths to the hospitals. And it was through the role model of these CEOs, HIMSS Greater China established a strong practice of engaging hospital CEOs and other top leaders for the transformational experience of large scaled organizational change to embrace/effective use of IT technology.

In 2015, Dr. Dong Jun, Executive Vice President of TEDA Cardiovascular Hospital, went to Seoul for JCI practicum training, of which I was among the faculty teaching the program. One significant part of the program was to demonstrate tracer methodology. I took Dr. Dong and other trainees to the two Korean hospitals I had consulted before. She was very impressed with the level of information technology adoption in one of them—Severance Hospital. After that, Dr. Dong and Dr. Liu Xiaocheng, CEO of TEDA Cardiovascular Hospital, invited me to their hospital for a visit. With our help, TEDA Hospital was successively validated by Stage 6 and then Stage 7 in the same year. This was rather rapid progress for any hospital. This was possible because of their strong foundation and with the good guidance from the HIMSS team. The staff of this hospital could not believe that they had achieved so much progress in such a short period of time. We witnessed the growth of more HIMSS EMRAM Stage 6 hospitals in China within that year, for example, the First Affiliated Hospital of Xinjiang Medical University, Xuanwu Hospital of Capital Medical University, Sir Run Run Shaw Hospital of Zhejiang University, Luoyang Orthopedic-Traumatology Hospital and Guangzhou Women and Children's Medical Center (Figures 1.13–1.17).

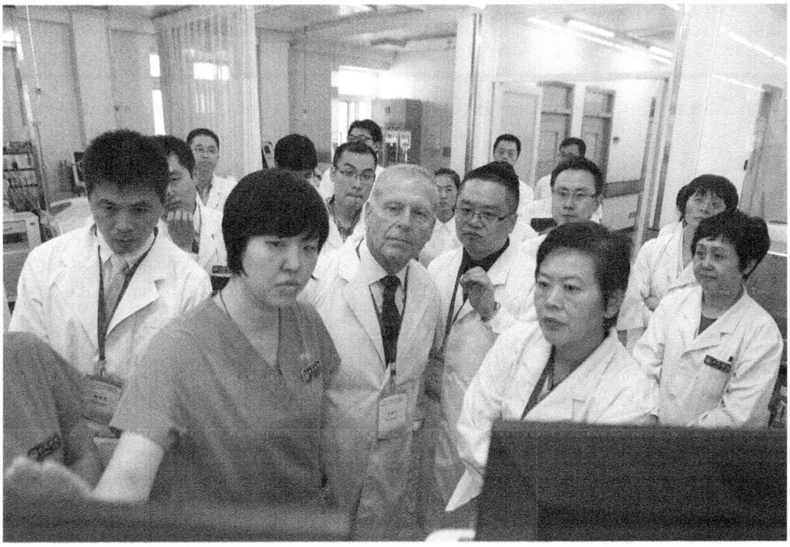

Figure 1.13 HIMSS validation at Xuanwu Hospital.

Figure 1.14 HIMSS validation at Guangzhou Women and Children's Medical Center.

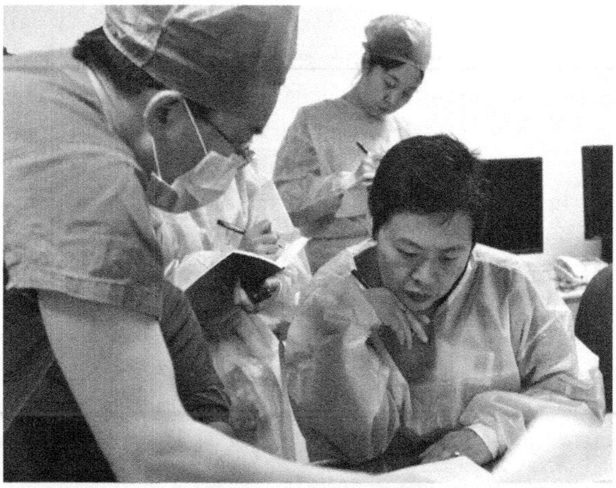

Figure 1.15 HIMSS consulting at The First Affiliated Hospital of Xiamen University.

Figure 1.16 HIMSS Stage 6 validation at Longhua Hospital Affiliated to Shanghai University of Traditional Chinese Medicine.

In 2016, the national government of China started to vigorously promote IT adoption in healthcare organizations, and the trend of "Internet+Hospital" began to take momentum. The strategy of "Health for All" drove up hospitals' interest in HIMSS EMRAM validation, especially among children's hospitals. Guangzhou Women and Children's Medical Center was the only Stage 7 children's hospital at the time, but the number of Stage 6 children's hospitals increased rapidly, including three children's hospitals in Shanghai (Shanghai Children's Hospital, Children's Hospital of Fudan University, Shanghai Children's Medical Center) and Northwest Women & Children's Hospital. Other hospitals obtained their HIMSS EMRAM Stage 6 status in 2016 include The First Affiliated Hospital of Xiamen University, The Affiliated Hospital of Jining Medical University, Linkou Changgung Memorial Hospital in Taiwan, The First Affiliated Hospital of Nanchang University, and Huangshi Central Hospital. Among them, Ningbo Yinzhou

Figure 1.17 HIMSS validation at Sir Run Run Hospital.

No. 2 Hospital stood out for being the first district-level hospital to achieve HIMSS EMRAM Stage 6 as the rest of them were all major teaching medical centers.

Guangzhou Women and Children's Medical Center galvanized enthusiasm and creativity of their physicians and other clinical staff. They had many innovations and realized technical and managerial improvement throughout their Stage 7 efforts; for example, they were the first to deploy hybrid cloud services for their data center provided by their mobile carrier, they were the first in deploying advanced service without prior payment or deposit (Chinese healthcare were primarily built on advanced payment model at the time), and they were also the pioneers in special population registration and disease management through patient portal (APP). They did all of these through a large-scaled system conversion (include the entire CPOE and physician and nursing documentation) in a very short period of time. I felt very gratified to be able to witness the systematic change and clinical transformation in these hospitals!

Since 2017, the number of participating hospitals continued to increase. Not only teaching hospitals, but also municipal hospitals from cities, counties, and provincial levels saw the value in using HIMSS EMRAM to guide and drive the technology adoption. Meanwhile, a larger base of hospitals previously validated at Stage 6 continued their efforts toward Stage 7 in this year. The First Affiliated Hospital of Xiamen University and Sir Run Run Shaw Hospital of Zhejiang University were validated as HIMSS EMRAM Stage 7 hospitals on the same day. Subsequently, Xuanwu Hospital of Capital Medical University and Ningbo Yinzhou No. 2 Hospital also gained their Stage 7 validation. Their experiences were also shared in this book.

Information technology has been evolving rapidly with new tools, methodologies, and solutions emerging in the market. With the advancement of emerging technology, the bar of HIMSS EMRAM criteria have also been rising. In order to show their continued efforts in meeting the requirements and performing up to the best of their abilities, Shengjing Hospital of China Medical University received their triennial revalidation in 2017. It demonstrated the ongoing value of the partnerships between HIMSS and hospitals in China.

As stated by many hospital executives who have worked with HIMSS Greater China team, HIMSS maturity models help them define a vision for digital and smart hospital, provide them with an effective and feasible path to follow, and a validation to recognize their effort. The combination of domestic and overseas expertise in healthcare leadership and in HIT, the face-to-face discussion with the frontline staff, and the individualized services provided to each hospital have helped build the confidence of hospitals in investing in health IT technology and encouraged the engagement of staff in finding proper IT solutions for their own hospitals. In 2017, the following hospitals joined the Stage 6 club:

China Medical University Hospital (Taiwan)
Shanghai Sixth People's Hospital
Kunming Children's Hospital
Wuxi No. 2 People's Hospital
The Fifth Hospital of Xiamen
Ningbo Yinzhou No. 2 Hospital
Henan Children's Hospital
The First Affiliated Hospital of Xiamen University
Huai'an First People's Hospital
The First People's Hospital of Jiande
The First People's Hospital of Tianmen in Hubei Province
Shanghai Tongren Hospital
Hebei Provincial People's Hospital
Binzhou Medical University Hospital
The Second Hospital of Zhejiang University
Beijing United Family Hospital
Shanghai Seventh People's Hospital
Baotou Central Hospital
Yueyang Hospital of Shanghai University of Traditional Chinese Medicine
Taizhou Hospital of Enze Medical Center
The First Hospital of Zhejiang University
Henan Provincial People's Hospital

In addition to the HIMSS EMRAM maturity model focusing on inpatient and emergency services, hospitals have also shown increasing interest in the O-EMRAM criteria for outpatient services. A HIMSS O-EMRAM Stage 7 hospital should be able to interact with patients through Patient portal (APP) to improve patient engagement, chronic disease management, and population health improvement, in addition to required capabilities in outpatient medical care, nursing, ancillary service, and medication management, similar to that of inpatient model. It aims at improved experience of patients with their clinical visits as well as hospital's efforts in health education, patient follow-up, management of chronic disease and to lay a foundation for the IT capability for population management and health improvement.

It was frequently asked: What is the difference between HIMSS EMRAM and Chinese EMRAM, and the Interoperability Maturity Model operated by the Chinese authority? Which one should the hospital use to improve their IT developments? I think all of these criteria are complementary. To a large extent, the Interoperability Maturity Model conducted by the Statistics and Information Center of National Health Commission and the Chinese EMRAM operated by the Institution of Hospital Administration of National Health Commission are tailor-made for Chinese hospitals, which may be more in line with China's healthcare environment. HIMSS, however, assesses the HIT capability of a hospital from a global perspective. For Chinese hospitals, HIMSS EMRAM should be considered only if HIMSS EMRAM model could contribute to the goal of "excellence" of a hospital, to the decision-making process related to IT investment and help build confidence, help building the collaboration, and support from all staff, to help realize the benefit of IT technology in assisting the clinical flow for frontline staff. HIMSS EMRAM and other maturity models, not only helps guide hospitals with their digital transformation, as a global benchmark, also provides Chinese hospitals with the opportunity to showcase their competence globally.

Since the establishment of HIMSS Greater China, China has made considerable achievements in HIMSS EMRAM validation. In the United States, there are currently around 300 Stage 7 hospitals, accounting for about 5% of the total number of hospitals in the country. There are less than 20 Stage 7 hospitals in other countries outside the United States. In the Asia-Pacific region, there are in total ten Stage 7 hospitals. Except for the one in Singapore and another one in South Korea, the remaining eight Stage 7 hospitals are all from China by the end of 2017. China became the country with the second largest number of stage 7 hospitals, next only to the United States. We can tell that Chinese hospitals and HIT companies are fast in their catching up efforts and achievements. We should be more supportive and have more confidence in them.

INTERNATIONAL STANDARDS

I

Chapter 2

JCI: Quality Improvement and Safety

Jilan Liu
HIMSS Greater China

Xu Meifang
Shulan Health

Ren Anjie
HIMSS Greater China

Contents

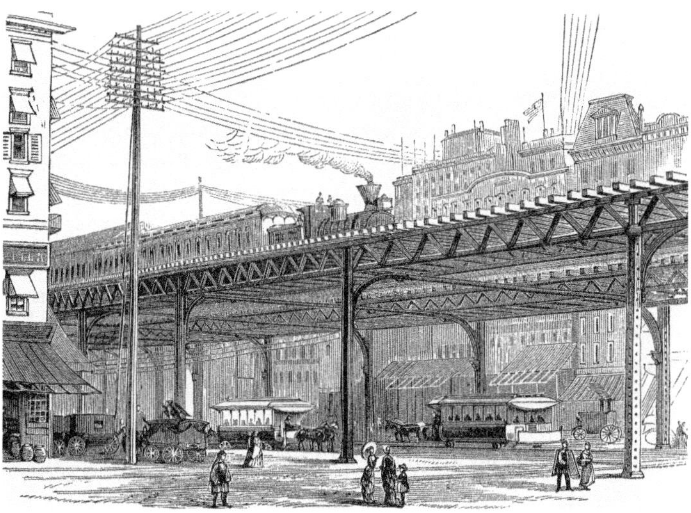

We are lucky to live in this era of openness and sharing that enables us to listen to the voice from all countries and regions. The story of JCI may remind ourselves why we started the journey in the first place.

JCI's Journey

Human history entered a new era in 1776 when James Watt invented the steam engine.[1] The First Industrial Revolution significantly improved the productivity of the human society and changed the ways of production. But without productivity innovation and advancement driven by systematic and proven practices, the "science" at that time was still far away from what could be called matured methodology.[2]

Soon the world was engulfed with the Second Industrial Revolution in the later 19th century when three things happened and totally changed the world: first, the establishment of modern scientific methodology implemented in actual production technology development; second, standardization driven by large-scale industrialization; and third, redesign of the production process and its organization based on the scientific methodology, technical equipment, and standardization.[3] The most widely known example was the Ford Production Line, which marked the emergence of mass industrial production. Such revolution of productive forces and their economic relationship relations soon grew beyond factories and found its way into other industries, including hospitals.

> The story of JCI starts with Dr. Ernest Codman's mission to establish "a system that enable a hospital to track every patient it treated long enough to determine whether or not the treatment was effective. If the treatment was not effective, the hospital would then try to find out how to prevent similar failures in the future".

Dr. Codman developed "End Result Idea" which included the documentation of end medical outcomes and the *explanation on the imperfect end results*.[4] In this system, every patient had his/her "documentation of end medical outcomes" that describes the symptoms and conditions of the patient, the causes indicated by the physician, the diagnostic conclusion and the evidence of treatment, the care plan, the diagnosis upon discharge, and the annual checkup results of the patient. In addition to the "documentation of end medical outcomes," Dr. Codman also analyzed and categorized each "imperfectness," based on which he would review and improve the current care and treatment.

To interpret this process with modern terminology, it is a process consisting of comprehensive analysis of medical record and follow-up records, the standardized coding and final statistics and evidence-based improvement. This happened 100 years ago. But it fully reflected the modern scientific methodology and standardization. Back at that time, this system had already gone far beyond the application level of scientific methodology. Even today, the "End Result Idea" remains as the core component of modern healthcare management principles.

American College of Surgeons (ACS) was the starting point for this idea under the support of Dr. Martin, one of the key founding members of ACS.

ACS focused mainly on how to survive and achieve professional success in the first 3 years after its establishment in 2012. Surprisingly, the topic of "hospital standardization" came first onto the stage. ACS rejected 60% of its membership application. The reason was that "the required fifty medical records could not sufficiently prove the professionalism of the applicant."[5] That means that the submitted 50 medical records as required were too messy to show the competence of the applicant surgeons at the first. It might be hard to imagine today that the physicians at that time could write whatever they wanted in the patient's chart or even chose to leave no trace of the care due to lack of standardized requirement. "Shortly thereafter, John Bowman, PhD, the director of the College, used his influence with the Carnegie Foundation, New York, to obtain a gift of $30,000 to launch a hospital standardization program."[6] This program later evolved into the TJC (The Joint Commission) and much later JCI (Joint Commission International).

There are four important elements that can be found in all successful standards and evaluation organizations throughout the history: (1) a noble mission serving as the guidance and cornerstone of its ideal, (2) an influential organization with a broad and strong reputation among the constituents, (3) scientific standard formulation and evaluation methodologies as its technical core and well trained and competent surveyors to carry out the evaluation, and (4) sustainable operational strategy to obtain and efficiently utilize resources to achieve the goals.

By this, ACS had already formulated half of its concept and technical core (the "End Result System Methodology" proposed by Dr. Codman), the organization (ACS and its "Hospital Standardization Program"), and the start-up capital (the 30,000 dollars from the Carnegie Foundation). There were still one and half ingredients missing from the formula of accreditation success!

"From Oct 19 to 20, 1917, 300 fellows from the Committees on Standards from every state in the union and every province in Canada, as well as 60 leading hospital superintendents, met in Chicago to discuss hospital standardization." On Dec 20, 1917, the American College of Surgeons formally established the Hospital Standardization Program, and in March 1918, the College published a *Standard on Efficiency* in the *Bulletin-the Minimum Standard*. The results of the field trials were announced by Bowman at a conference on hospital standardization in New York on Oct. 24, 1919. Bowman told the audience that 692 hospitals of 100 beds or more had been surveyed and that only 89 hospitals had met the standards.[6]

Although the College made the numbers public, it burned the list of hospitals at midnight in the furnace of the Waldorf Astoria Hotel, New York, to keep it from the press. Some of the most prestigious hospitals in the country had failed to meet the most basic standards. However, 109 hospitals corrected deficiencies after their initial surveys and were subsequently approved. Although the first trial of the evaluation results were disappointing, they dramatically demonstrated the need for a national hospital accreditation program, and they solidified national support for the program.[6]

With the adoption of the *Minimum Standard*, the accreditation process that continues today was set in motion. As news of the program's success spread, more and more hospitals sought approval. The number of approved hospitals rose from 89 in 1919 to 3,290 in 1950, over half of the hospitals in the U.S. (Figure 2.1).[6]

The ACS accreditation was entirely on a voluntary basis without any administrative or financial restriction or compulsion on any organization. In other word, hospitals could ignore the standards if they did not agree with the values advocated by ACS. Thus, the increase in applicants and accredited hospitals was the best testimony of the acceptance and recognition of the value of hospital standardization.

"By 1950, the size and scope of the program had increased significantly, and the College, which had already invested $2 million in the Hospital Standardization Program, was having difficulty in supporting the effort alone."[6] Two million was no doubt an enormous investment for a professional society back at that time. It finally became a burden on the shoulder of ACS.

Meanwhile, other professional associations also followed suit and launched their own evaluation activities with different focuses and values.

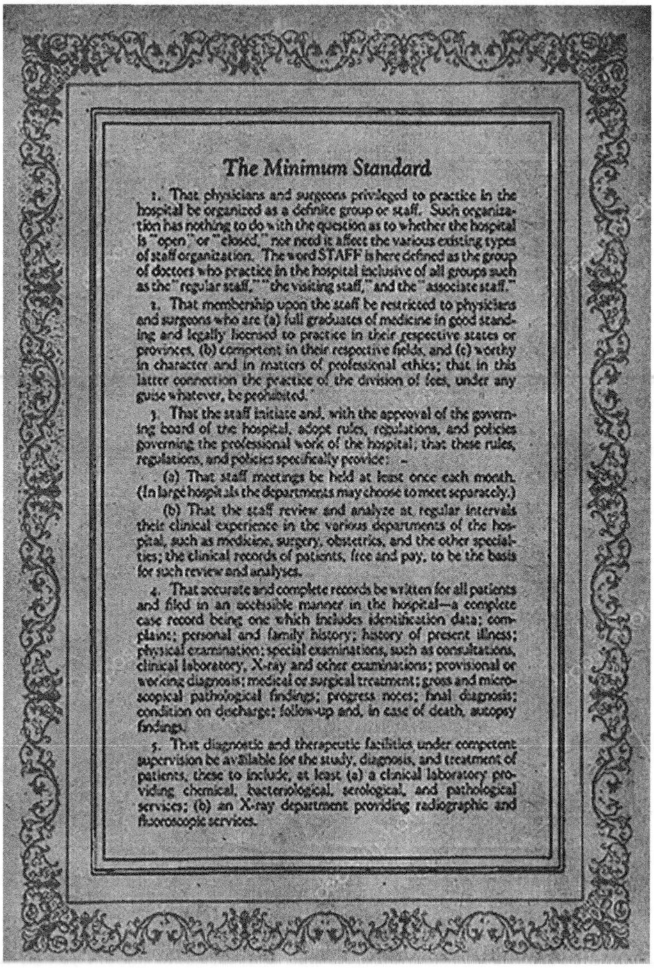

The Minimum Standard

1. That physicians and surgeons privileged to practice in the hospital be organized as a definite group or staff. Such organization has nothing to do with the question as to whether the hospital is "open" or "closed," nor need it affect the various existing types of staff organization. The word STAFF is here defined as the group of doctors who practice in the hospital inclusive of all groups such as the "regular staff," "the visiting staff," and the "associate staff."

2. That membership upon the staff be restricted to physicians and surgeons who are (a) full graduates of medicine in good standing and legally licensed to practice in their respective states or provinces, (b) competent in their respective fields, and (c) worthy in character and in matters of professional ethics; that in this latter connection the practice of the division of fees, under any guise whatever, be prohibited.

3. That the staff initiate and, with the approval of the governing board of the hospital, adopt rules, regulations, and policies governing the professional work of the hospital; that these rules, regulations, and policies specifically provide: –

(a) That staff meetings be held at least once each month. (In large hospitals the departments may choose to meet separately.)

(b) That the staff review and analyze at regular intervals their clinical experience in the various departments of the hospital, such as medicine, surgery, obstetrics, and the other specialties; the clinical records of patients, free and pay, to be the basis for such review and analyses.

4. That accurate and complete records be written for all patients and filed in an accessible manner in the hospital—a complete case record being one which includes identification data; complaint; personal and family history; history of present illness; physical examination; special examinations, such as consultations, clinical laboratory, X-ray and other examinations; provisional or working diagnosis; medical or surgical treatment; gross and microscopical pathological findings; progress notes; final diagnosis; condition on discharge; follow-up and, in case of death, autopsy findings.

5. That diagnostic and therapeutic facilities under competent supervision be available for the study, diagnosis, and treatment of patients, these to include, at least (a) a clinical laboratory providing chemical, bacteriological, serological, and pathological services; (b) an X-ray department providing radiographic and fluoroscopic services.

Figure 2.1 The original document of the *Minimum Standard*.

After considerable deliberation, the American College of Physicians (ACP), the American Hospital Association (AHA), the American Medical Association (AMA) and the Canadian Medical Association (CMA) joined the American College of Surgeons on Dec 15, 1951, to form the Joint Commission on Accreditation of Hospitals (JCAH) as an independent, nonprofit organization. The Canadian Medical Association withdrew in 1959, to participate in the development of its own program, the Canadian Council on Hospital Accreditation. The College officially conveyed its program to the Joint Commission on Dec 6, 1952, and the Joint Commission began to offer accreditation to hospitals in January 1953.

In reviewing this history one element or group emerged that is often not recognized. It became very clear to us that the existence of TJC and JCI was directly the result of physicians wanting to improve patient care. Often TJC and JCI are thought to be an administrative or managerial group. And it is often a surprise to learn that it originated, developed, managed, and continues to be the focus of physicians with the support of many other individuals.

JCAH inherited several important traditions from the ACS program: (1) voluntary participation by hospitals, (2) "professional consensus" as the basis of the standards updated according to the agreement on the most influential elements regarding care quality, (3) education and consultation service in addition to survey and accreditation to maximally benefit the hospital through the process, and (4) regular review and modification of the standards to reflect the latest development of hospitals and healthcare industry. Besides, the results should be publicized after the survey process and the findings were confined to the JCAH and the reviewed hospital. These principles can still be found in today's TJC and JCI activities.

> In August 1966, the Joint Commission board made a major decision to undertake a complete revision of the standards to reflect an optimal achievable rather than a minimal essential level of care. The publication of the optimal achievable standards in the *1970 Accreditation Manual for Hospitals* was a landmark. In little more than 50 years, the one-page set of standards that specified a minimal essential level of performance had developed into a 152-page manual of state-of-the-art standards. The publication of these standards was a clear indication of the tremendous progress hospitals had made since the beginning of this century and of the impact of voluntary accreditation on the quality of hospital care.[6]

Such expansion also went along with the evolution, segmentation and further development of the healthcare industry to meet the needs of service quality improvement evaluation of the newly emerging organizations. The expansion lasted for more than 10 years with new programs added to the list of JCAH activities.

There was another important change to JCAH in the same era—JCAH started to charge for accreditation in 1964. It was safe to say that ACS and JCAH had not been equipped with the four key elements: the mission; the organization; the scientific standards, methodology and human resources; and the sustainable operation strategy. The most important question was the last one: how to ensure the sustainability of the organization and the programs from the operation perspective. In brief, no program could survive without sustainable financial income to support its development and maintenance. This was the driving force behind the restructuring of the Hospital Standardization Program of ACS and the founding of the JCAH. Finally, after over 50 years of development, JCAH found a way to operate the hospital accreditation program for both public benefit and financial sustainability.

> The Joint Commission has important relationship with government. These relationships began in 1965, when Congress passed Public Law 89–97, the Medicare Act. Written into this law was a provision that hospitals accredited by the Joint Commission were deemed to be in compliance with most of the *Medicare Conditions of Participation for Hospitals* and thus, deemed to meet eligibility requirements for participation in the Medicare program.[6]

The U.S. Congress again amended the Social Security Act in 1971, which requested the U.S. Department of Health and Human Services to validate the findings of the JCAH accreditation to ensure that JCAH delivered fair, objective, and accurate conclusions.

In response to that, JCAH established several specialized Accreditation Councils responsible for different specific standards and accreditation programs. In 1979, JCAH disbanded all different committees of accreditation and replaced them with the Professional and Technical Advisory Committee for each program. The American Dental Association (ADA) joined the JCAH in the next year.

Then a subsidiary of JCAH, Quality Healthcare Resources, Inc. (QHR), was founded and was restructured into today's Joint Commission Resources, Inc. (JCR).

Following that, JCAH officially changed its name in 1987 from JCAH to Joint Commission on Accreditation of Healthcare Organizations (JCAHO). It was because that the accreditation programs were expanded to cover various types of healthcare organizations in the U.S. rather than only hospitals since the beginning. It continued to expand accreditation programs under its new name. For example, it launched the home-care organization accreditation program in 1989.

After the World War II, the global pattern had been relatively stabilized with continuous growth of economy in various countries. More countries and regions had overcome the struggle against mere survival. Then a higher-quality healthcare service becomes a pressing topic. With JCAHO's reputation, history, technology, and authority in the U.S., many hospitals outside the country realized that the most systematic way to improve their operation was to apply for the accreditation instead of learning pieces from individual US hospitals. Thus, applications for accreditation started to get into JCAHO from those international hospitals.

Finally, in 1998, JCI was established under QHR as the international arm of accreditation and consultation. With the establishment of JCI, the standards used to evaluate hospitals overseas were also developed accordingly. Many of the JCAHO standards had a strong touch of the American flavor. Some of the requirements based on the American laws and regulations could not be applied directly in other countries and regions governed by totally different legal frameworks and culture.

The JCI standards were initially modified based on the original JCAHO standards. The core concept and basic framework were kept in the international version of the standards, while some detailed requirements only applicable in the U.S. were removed. After that, there were many rounds of revisions/updates. JCI not only established its own accreditation committee but also standard development subcommittee with representation from all over the world. It also sought input from international accredited organizations and many other international sources; it becomes more and more international overtime.

The first JCI Accreditation Standards for Hospitals was published and used in official international survey activities in 2000. By that year, QHR had already been renamed as JCR in 1998.

Then in 2007, JCAHO was formally renamed as TJC.

This was the last move to complete the structure of TJC.

JCI Standards and Accreditation

According to the sixth edition of the Joint Commission International Standards for Hospitals, including Standards for Academic Medical Center Hospitals, there are mainly four pats. The first part includes the qualifications for initial accreditation application as well as the requirements for remaining accredited. The second through fourth parts of the standards book consist of the basic framework of the JCI standards, namely, Patient-Centered Standards, Health Care Organization Management Standards, and Academic Medical Center Standards.

The Patient-Centered Standards, including the following eight chapters:

- International Patient Safety Goals (IPSG)
- Access to Care and Continuity of Care (ACC)
- Patient and Family Rights (PFR)
- Assessment of Patients (AOP)
- Care of Patients (COP)

- Anesthesia and Surgical Care (ASC)
- Medication Management and Use (MMU)
- Patient and Family Education (PFE)

The Health Care Organization Management Standards, including the following six chapters:

- Quality Improvement and Patient Safety (QPS)
- Prevention and Control of Infections (PCI)
- Governance, Leadership and Direction (GLD)
- Facility Management and Safety (FMS)
- Staff Qualifications and Education (SQE)
- Management of Information (MOI)

The Academic Medical Center Standards, including the following two chapters:

- Medical Professional Education (MPE)
- Human Subjects Research Programs (HRP)

To serve as a set of intentionally applicable standards, JCI standards need to respect the laws, regulations, and cultures of different countries and regions. With a focus on the following questions instead of specific hospital technology or service level, it becomes more flexible:

1. whether patient safety is basically ensured
2. whether relevant policies, procedures, and culture are in place
3. whether the hospital is equipped with the evidence-based methodology for continuous improvement and holds the desire in pursuing ongoing improvement

JCI does not focus only on the present situation of a hospital, but more so on the aspiration, capability, system, and culture that could drive the hospital move forward. It does not require a hospital to submit a 100% satisfaction rate survey on patient satisfaction or 100% hand hygiene compliance report, but on what the hospital have done based on its current situation and its policy, procedure, and culture to ensure better performance in the future.

Risk mitigation is the fundamental concept embedded in the JCI standards. Today we enjoy more advanced technologies in various aspects compared with any other era in human history. Such advancement never exists alone. It is always accompanied with risks. This is more predominant in the healthcare industry. The healthcare technology has achieved tremendous progress and saved many lives. But technology is a double-edged sword. If the technology is not used in a proper way, it might harm patients. JCI gives special attention to the overall risk control and mitigation, including the potential risks existing in healthcare activities, facilities, processes, human behavior, strategies, finance, reputation, and even the hospital culture. JCI accreditation process pay attention to the risks that might compromise the best performance of operations, business, and patient care/services in a hospital. Over 1,000 measurable elements in the JCI standards can be regarded as the guide to help hospital control potential risks through the identification, assessment, and mitigation of risks. It not only involves physical facilities, human resources, organization, policies, and procedure, but it also covers various systems, behaviors, communication, competency, intentions, and other aspects.

Thus, "Culture of Safety" is of utmost importance for a hospital to have. "Culture" is a complicated concept that contains profound implication. It could be the belief, values, and habits shared by a group of people. It could also be interpreted as the interaction, relations, and atmosphere in which we influence one another. Culture is like air and water. If a person lives in a polluted environment, he/she may not be able to tell whether the air or the water is fresh or clean. Only those who have experienced fresh air and clean water would know the differences between the two and aspire a better environment. The Culture of Safety in the hospital setting contains two layers of meaning. One is the value centering on safety as the bottom line. The other is the psychological security of the healthcare staff with which they would feel safe to identify, report, and rectify issues and to voice different opinions to their colleagues and superiors.

Adverse event reporting is one of the indicators that could directly reflect the culture of safety. All staff need to contribute to a positive, cooperative and open environment in which they would pursue continuous improvement based on identifying issues, and see hospital as their own home and patients as the ones they care for and care about. With this in place, what they aspire to would go beyond the basis requirement of laws, regulations, and rules. If hospital staff believes that they should simply comply with the basic requirement without thinking, making judgment and decisions, or taking actions centering on patients, the culture of the hospital would never be strong enough to support best practices. That is the reason why JCI standards also stress on the development, promotion and maintenance of a culture of safety in the hospital on top of the requirements on risk management and mitigation.

In terms of evaluation, JCI adopts the "tracer methodology." "Tracer Methodology" was originated from TOYOTA and was applied in the healthcare survey activities for the first time by TJC. As a patient-oriented methodology, the tracer follows the flow of patient care and service to fully evaluate how the clinical and managerial processes ensure patient safety and quality. Currently, this method has been adopted by various hospital evaluation organizations and systems across the world.

There are mainly three types of tracer activities: patient tracer, system tracer, and accreditation program specific tracer. The patient tracer and system tracer are the two types of activities that are commonly seen during a JCI survey in hospital, while accreditation program specific tracer is more often seen in JCI Clinical Care Program Certification accreditation survey process.

Patient tracer is "designed to 'trace' the care experiences that a patient had while at an organization. It is a way to analyze the organization's system of providing care, treatment or services using actual patients as the framework for assessing standards compliance. Patients selected for these tracers will likely be those in high volume, high-risk or problem prone areas or whose diagnosis, age or type of services received may enable the best in-depth evaluation of the organization's processes and practices."

System tracer "includes an interactive session with a surveyor and relevant staff members in tracing one specific 'system' or process within the organization. While individual tracers follow a patient through his or her course of care, the system tracer evaluates the system or process, including the integration of related processes, and the coordination and communication among disciplines and departments in those processes."[7]

The tracer methodology derives from the value and position of "stepping in other people's shoes." Healthcare staff and managers always want to perform well, to treat the ill and save the dying. But when it becomes a daily pattern, they might forget to view the medical activities from a patient's perspective but get influenced by their own emotions and perception. The core of tracer methodology is to view the behavior of staff and the operation of hospital from the patient perspective, to share their feeling so as to see if their needs could be fully met. As a Chinese poet once wrote: "Standing from the front, I see a whole range; standing from the side, I see a single peak; Standing from afar, near, high, low, no two parts looks alike. Why can't I tell the true shape of Mount Lushan? Because I myself am in the middle of the mountain" (Chinese poem by Su Shi,

English translation by Burton Watson). Tracer methodology allows you to stand away from the mountain and to have a bird view of it as a whole.

It usually takes a hospital 18–24 months to prepare for the JCI accreditation survey, especially for public general hospitals in China. Some hospitals would like to get accredited as soon as they start the JCI journey. Some even want to race with other hospitals for the shortest preparation record. We definitely do not encourage this. Hospitals would have their own schedule of the preparation and actual survey. But such decisions should be made based on where they started with, resources available and the dedication of the hospital leadership and staff instead of the unrealistic wish of being quick. The journey is like gestation. You need time to nurture a healthy and mature life in you. To intentionally move the delivery ahead of an appropriate schedule might lead to the risk of giving birth to a premature baby but also potential future troubles.

Many JCI hospitals have experienced the unprecedented unity thanks to the shared goal and pursuit of excellence in a systematic fashion, which is much more sensational than many other improvement projects. As Dr. Wen Hao, the former CEO of The First Affiliated Hospital of Xinjiang Medical University, said, "During the preparation for the JCI survey, all the staff in the hospital showed their dedication and efficiency. They did not complain but tried their best to contribute to the process. They are confident and hard working. They fight as an invincible team. They love the hospital as their own home. This never happened in the past!" It is true. We helped hundreds of hospitals in dozens of countries and regions through the same process. They all experienced the same feeling. Each one of the hospitals has proved their competency in improvement and have harvested a stronger team capable in business and management on the journey.

The highways and railways built in the New York City in the 19th century marked the beginning of a new era of industrialization that has brought mankind closer to science and civilization (Figure 2.2).

Figure 2.2 Jilan Liu and Paula Wilson, CEO of JCI, visited Huashan Hospital in December, 2015.

References

1. Hills R.L., *James Watt, His Time in Scotland, 1736–1774*, Vol 1; *The Years of Toil, 1775–1785*, Vol 2; *Triumph Through Adversity 1785–1819*, Vol 3. Landmark Publishing Ltd: Ashbourne, ISBN 1-84306-045-0, 2002.
2. Perez C. Technological revolutions and techno-economic paradigms. In Working Papers in Technology Governance and Economic Dynamics, Working Paper No. 20, Norway and Tallinn University of Technology: Tallinn, 2009.
3. Williams L.P. *The Rise of Modern Science; History of Science.* Encyclopedia Britannica: Chicago, IL, 2017.
4. Dervishaj O., Wright K.E., Saber A.A., Pappas P.J. Ernest Amory Codman and the end-result system. *The American Surgeon*, 2015, 81(1): 12–5.
5. Schlicke C.P. American surgery's noblest experiment. *The Archives of Surgery*, 1973, 108: 379–385.
6. Roberts J.S. A history of the Joint Commission on Accreditation of Hospitals. *JAMA*, 1987, 258(7): 936–940.
7. The Joint Commission: Facts about the Tracer Methodology, Feb 10, 2017. www.jointcommission.org/facts_about_the_tracer_methodology/.

Chapter 3

HIMSS: Transforming Health through Information and Technology

John H. Daniels, CNM, FACHE, FHIMSS, CPHIMS
Healthcare Advisory Services Group HIMSS Analytics

John H. Daniels *is Global Vice President of the Healthcare Advisory Services Group for HIMSS Analytics at HIMSS, a global, cause-based, not-for-profit organization focused on better health through information technology (IT). For over 30 years, Mr. Daniels, career has spanned behavioral healthcare, healthcare information technology, and hospital administration. As an expert in health IT issues and trends, Daniels is an invited speaker to many conferences in Asia, Europe, Middle East, South America, and the United States. Before joining HIMSS Analytics, Daniels served as Vice President of Strategic Relations for HIMSS North America, and previously served as Senior Vice President and Chief Information Officer for Evolvent Technologies, Inc. Daniels was elected to the HIMSS Board of Directors where he served as both the Vice Chair and Financial Director of the Board. Additionally, Daniels served as Chief Information Officer at the U.S. Air Force Academy Hospital, Vice President of IT Operations for Harris County Hospital District which was the fourth largest public metropolitan health system in the United States, and in several other executive healthcare positions throughout his career.*

Contents

Beginning and History

The Healthcare Information and Management Systems Society (HIMSS) was organized in 1961 as the Hospital Management Systems Society (HMSS), an independent, unincorporated, nonprofit, voluntary association of individuals. The entire detailed history of the organization is captured in its self-published document titled, “History of the Healthcare Information and Management Systems Society (Formerly Hospital Management Systems Society).” This document can be accessed at www.himss.org. This chapter will summarize the history of HIMSS to give readers a glimpse into how HIMSS was formed and how it came to be known as potentially the world’s largest not-for-profit healthcare information technology professional society.

HIMSS was founded on the thesis that an organized exchange of experience among members and other interested parties could promote a better understanding of the principles underlying hospital management systems and could develop new principles for improving the skills of the person who directs hospital programs and the practitioner who analyzes, designs, or improves hospital systems. The purpose of the Society as stated in the original constitution was “to promote the continual improvement of hospital management systems through organized programs of research, education, and professional practice.”

In the 1950s, increasing amounts of management engineering activity in healthcare involved led to various meetings among hospital leaders resulting in a decade of isolated attempts to improve hospital methods and procedures. These activities eventually were converted into an organized methods-improvement movement. In 1952, three major events occurred: The American Hospital Association (AHA) established a Committee on Methods Improvement; a 2-week workshop on hospital work simplification was held at the University of Connecticut; and Earl J. Frederick became the first full-time hospital management engineer as a joint employee of the Cleveland Clinic and St. Luke’s Hospital in Cleveland, Ohio. The shared goal for these three events was to improve the healthcare services to patients and to reduce costs. These events also served as the foundation for HMSS (Figure 3.1).

During the period of 1956–1960, hospital management engineering practitioners were seeking an avenue to allow easy exchange of ideas, particularly to encourage discussions of project studies and approaches among them, while the AHA focused on marketing the profession to hospital administrators. This difference in approaching the profession stimulated sowing the seed for HMSS.

Figure 3.1 Edward Gerner Jr., founder and first CEO of HIMSS.

In collaboration with information and management colleagues at Georgia Tech and the University of Connecticut, a questionnaire was designed to test the extent of interest in forming a new society. In May 1961, this questionnaire was sent to 50 persons known to be involved in hospital management engineering. Favorable responses from 37 practitioners and educators led to the decision to proceed with preliminary plans for a new society. Using the information from the questionnaire responses and from other contacts and sources, ad hoc committees were formed to draft provisions of a constitution for the new society.

During October 1961, a constitution was drafted and circulated for review and comment. The Constitution of the Hospital Management Systems Society was certified at Society headquarters on the campus of the Georgia Institute of Technology on November 1, 1961, with a proviso that persons admitted to membership within 2 months of that date would be considered to be Charter Members. Membership applications were sent from the Atlanta headquarters to all persons believed to be interested in this new society. The first application was received on November 6, 1961. In total, 47 people were admitted as Charter Members of the new society. The first newsletter of the Society was published in March 1962 and HIMSS has continued to publish official newsletter on a quarterly or more frequent basis since then. At that time, plans were already underway to hold the Society's first national convention (Figure 3.2).

The first National Convention was held on April 1, 1962, at the Emerson Hotel in Baltimore in conjunction with the AHA Advanced Institute on Methods Improvement. The Society's first board of directors were elected during the convention and served from the National Convention at which they were elected until the following National Convention. The primary topic of importance at this meeting was the adoption of the "Baltimore Resolution" which established a special committee to negotiate with the AHA concerning affiliation. This committee was to request that AHA establish a personal membership department for "management systems" and to allow the Society to maintain maximum autonomy of membership requirements and admissions.

In 1964, The AHA rejected the Society's request for affiliation citing the lack of a budget and resources to support the addition of new affiliations into the AHA. This decision was

Figure 3.2 Initial founder members and also the first three CEOs of HIMSS.

despite the Society's decision that year to move its headquarters from Atlanta to Chicago in the same building as the AHA headquarters. After more negotiations and increased pressure from the Society and other groups, the AHA agreed to an affiliation with the Society in December 1966. During the ensuing years, the membership criteria of the Society expanded to create membership opportunities for various disciplines associated with hospital management. This membership expansion led to discussions in the 1972 annual convention on whether the AHA should actively pursue the development of a Society for Computer Information Systems. A subcommittee was appointed to look into hospital productivity. The committee later reported that a separate society was not needed and that these individuals could be attracted to the existing society.

In 1980, the Society began to discuss long-term plans related to reaching the professionals interested in management information systems. This resulted in formal recognition at the 1981 annual conference the emergence of information systems in hospitals. A creative campaign was introduced called "Where's Moses?" to appeal to the Society membership the need for leaders to bring the small, scattered pockets of hospital information systems professionals to the "Promised Land," or HMSS. The Board of Directors recognized the growing importance of management information systems and the relation of persons responsible for their installation and operation to the Society. This same year, a management systems engineer serving as the Chief Information Officer (CIO) for the UMASS Medical Center was elected to the Board and may have represented the first CIO to serve on a HMSS board.

Also, during the 1981 conference, a Task Force on Information Systems reported that information systems professionals have different needs from practicing management engineers, and the board of directors reaffirmed the multidisciplinary nature of the Society. The board noted the Society's and its members' continued involvement in both the use of computers and in development of information systems. The task force provided the subsequent conference program director a track on information systems for the 10th Annual Systems Conference held in conjunction with the 21st Annual Convention and meeting in San Diego, Calif. in February 1982.

In 1986, the Long Range Planning Committee developed plans for 1987 and beyond because it became apparent that there was no professional Society within healthcare for information systems professionals. The growth of the position of CIO would create a need for a Society that could embrace all of the professionals who should report to such a position. As the Society had been presenting educational tracks and programs directed at information systems professionals for about 5 years, it seemed logical that the HMSS could fill that role. After a number of meetings of task forces and advisory committees, it was recommended to the board that the name of the Society be changed to the HIMSS and that the Society move to encompass information systems professionals. In a subsequent vote of the membership on the name change, more than 80% of the 1,000 members who voted were in favor of the change. It was now official; the Society's new name became the HIMSS.

With the change in name, a second organization was established within the AHA to assist in the expansion of the Society. This organization, the Center for Healthcare Information Management (CHIM), was established to utilize funds donated by vendors and consultants who supported the expansion of the Society. As the efforts of the Society were approved by the AHA, it became apparent that the telecommunications professionals also belonged within this organization. At the end of the year, discussions about a merger were undertaken with the telecommunications group of the American Society for Hospital Engineers (ASHE), of which it was a part. This was precipitated by the fact that prior to the advance of IT, hospital telecommunications typically were focused on switchboard operations, which generally reported to the engineering department. Directors of plant engineering were represented by the ASHE, another AHA personal membership group.

The year 1987 was a year of change and growth for the newly named organization, HIMSS. HIMSS reached out to new constituencies in addition to its traditional core group of management engineers. With the creation of CHIM, HIMSS reached out to information systems professionals, and through its agreement with the ASHE, HIMSS also reached out to telecommunications professionals. Because of these and other efforts, the Society grew by 50%. Ultimately, CHIM split from HIMSS and became an independent organization 2 years later in 1989.

HIMSS continued to enjoy membership growth and increasing conference attendance in the years 1990–1993. However, in 1991, the Society experienced for the first a financial deficit despite the healthy growth of the organization. This resulted in leadership reappointments, a couple of revisions to the Society's bylaws, and some restructuring within the AHA. The new leadership of the Society worked to revise the bylaws to reflect HIMSS' growth, the diversification of its members' interests, and the intent to foster an organization that supports meeting the needs of its members through the integration of common interests while still recognizing individual interests.

In 1993, HIMSS and AHA began to examine the possibility of an independent HIMSS. During 1992 and into 1993, AHA began a process of restructuring that would eventually see a reduction in the 1,000-person AHA workforce of about 30% and planning for relocation from its historic Chicago Streeterville district headquarters to another, smaller office space. As part of that restructuring, AHA began probing options for its personal membership groups, of which HIMSS was among the most likely to be able to survive as an independent entity. Seizing the moment, HIMSS and AHA agreed in the spring 1993 to examine the possibility of HIMSS becoming independent. In the aftermath of the 1993 conference's success, as well as the Society's continuing membership growth, AHA and HIMSS agreed to dissolve the 27-year affiliation between the two organizations. The separation occurred on September 10, 1993, when HIMSS became an independent, not-for-profit 501(c) (6) corporation. HIMSS then moved into new headquarters 1 month later at 230 E. Ohio St. in Chicago's Streeterville neighborhood, a location within walking distance of both the Blue Cross/Blue Shield Association and the American Medical Association. Timing could not have been better for HIMSS to become an independent organization.

Parallel to HIMSS' steady growth and evolution were several developments that placed information and management systems at the forefront of the healthcare reform dialog in the United States. President Clinton's Health Security Act, unveiled in September 1993, featured a section on the role of information systems. Legislation was introduced that same month that proposed the development of wide-area healthcare information networks with which to streamline administration of healthcare financial and clinical operations. During 1993–1994, other legislation was introduced calling for funding of test bed healthcare information networks and telemedicine pilot projects. In addition to legislation, The Joint Commission on Accreditation of Healthcare Organizations added standards regarding hospitals' information management functions to its 1994 accreditation manual. A number of HIMSS members were reviewers of early drafts of the standard. The Workgroup on Electronic Data Interchange published a revised (upwardly) estimated savings from healthcare electronic data interchange in its October 1993 report (a follow-up to its July 1992 report) on the use of information technology in healthcare. In this setting, HIMSS once again seemed to be heading for a major success with its annual conference—a critical milestone for the now-independent Society. By mid-December 1993, exhibition space for the 1994 conference in Phoenix was already nearly sold out.

HIMSS blossomed as the years ensued seeing many new education programs, publications, research, membership changes, and other initiatives take shape. The annual conference and exhibition seemed to set new all-time high records in terms of attendance and exhibitors, and membership growth expanded significantly. The organization also experienced mergers with other societies and participated in the launch new to institutes to help further the mission of HIMSS. Recognizing a need in the industry for quality and expanded market research services, the Society formed HIMSS Analytics in February 2004, as a wholly owned, for-profit subsidiary, supporting the HIMSS' mission of advancing the delivery of healthcare through the best use of information technology (Figure 3.3).

The Society considered several options in developing the subsidiary, including exploring relationships with existing market research organizations and building a new enterprise. With approval from the HIMSS board of directors, HIMSS Analytics acquired the DORENFEST IHDS+DATABASE™ and related business assets from Sheldon I. Dorenfest & Associates, Ltd., a Chicago-based provider of health information technology consulting and market data. The acquisition was final in July 2004. The subsidiary was headquartered in Chicago, brought together a strategic and experienced senior leadership team with expertise in health IT, market research and consulting. Products and services offered by HIMSS Analytics supported improved decision-making for healthcare organizations, health IT companies, and consulting firms by delivering high-quality data, information, and analytical expertise. The company collected and analyzed healthcare organization data relating to IT processes and environments, products, IS department composition and costs, IS department management metrics, healthcare delivery trends, and purchasing-related decisions. HIMSS Analytics also provided custom market

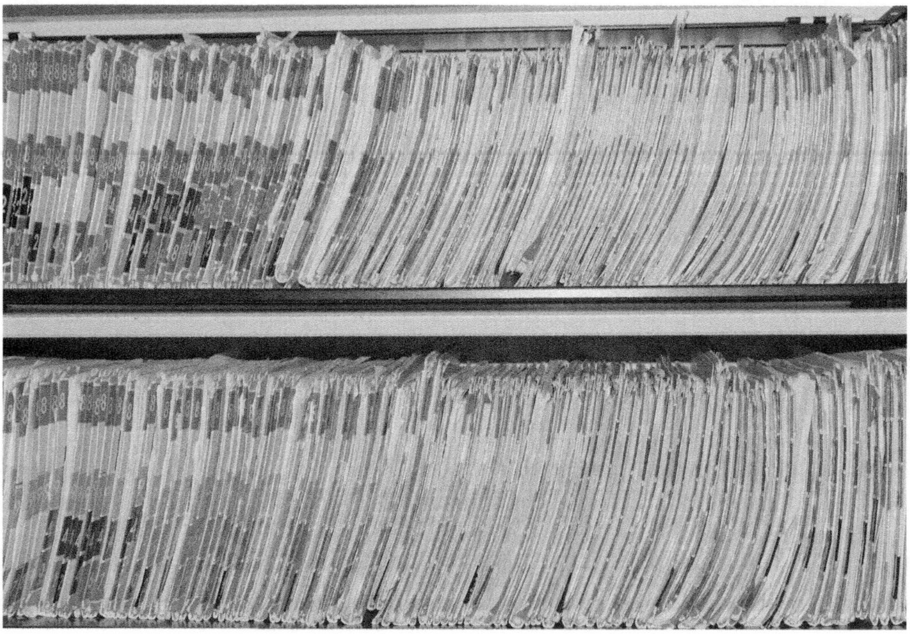

Figure 3.3 A photo of paper health records. HIMSS' mission is transforming healthcare through information and technology. Health IT is the key to solve the current problem of healthcare industry.

research services to support strategic decision-making in areas such as product planning, business and marketing strategy.

In 2005, HIMSS Analytics launched the Electronic Medical Record Adoption Model, or EMRAM. The EMR Adoption Model ("EMRAM") is a progressively sophisticated and aspirational healthcare information technology maturity model widely used and referenced by research institutions and academia across the globe. Facilities scored on the EMRAM go through a comprehensive survey with skilled research professionals to understand the current technology environment of their organization. More about the EMRAM later, but at this time in 2005, the majority of HIMSS and HIMSS Analytics activities were focused in North America.

In 2006, HIMSS began to welcome and cater to the needs of international delegations and attendees from around the world. The Global Business Trade Pavilion featured at the 2006 HIMSS Conference and Exhibition welcomed trade ministries from the United Kingdom, China, Australia and Singapore. To connect international trade representatives with major U.S. healthcare IT vendors and providers, the Global Business Trade Pavilion featured country-specific trade and investment information. HIMSS offered discounts for groups of 30 or more international delegates that were planning to attend the annual conference. Participation in 2006 included more than ten groups from Germany, Japan, Sweden, France, China, Singapore, Australia, and The Netherlands. Included in the group package were special networking events, private U.S. hospital tours specializing in state-of-the-art health IT, a private tour of the Interoperability showcase during non-exhibit hours, opportunities to meet and greet with senior-level executives of U.S. marketed companies, and a special discount on registration.

In HIMSS' fiscal year 2007, the organization officially expanded globally with its membership expansion, outreach, and educational programming to Europe with the introduction of the first annual World of Health IT Conference & Exhibition held in Geneva, Switzerland in collaboration with the European Commission (EC) and the World Health Organization (WHO). Close to 2,000 people attended the conference drawing speakers, attendees and exhibitors from across Europe, the Middle East and Africa, including places as diverse as Andorra and Azerbaijan, Iceland and Israel and Saudi Arabia, and Serbia-Montenegro.

The first HIMSS Asia-Pacific conference was held in 2007 in Singapore attended by 1,139 individuals gaining insights from 47 different education sessions and three different symposia. There were also 51 vendors exhibiting at this event. In 2009, HIMSS held its first HIMSS Middle East conference in Manama, Bahrain, a leadership summit in Muscat, Oman. That same year, HIMSS Analytics recognized the world's first EMRAM Stage 7 hospital in the U.S. In 2010, HIMSS held its first ever conference in China in the form of the HIMSS Asia-Pacific Exposition held in Beijing.

In 2011, HIMSS Analytics services were introduced to the Asia-Pacific and Middle East markets. Hospitals in these regions began leveraging the HIMSS Analytics EMRAM to better understand their current EMR adoption maturity levels. HIMSS Analytics recognized the first EMRAM Stage 7 hospital outside of North America, which was Seoul National University Bundang Hospital in Seoul, South Korea. Moreover, in 2012, HIMSS held events in Australia, Singapore, Malaysia, Denmark, and in the United Arab Emirates, followed by its first event in Latin America in 2013 (Figure 3.4).

HIMSS continued to expand and grow at a phenomenal rate as it pursued its vision of better health through information technology. The organization grew from having only about 54 attendees at its first conference in 1961 to over 42,000 attendees at its annual U.S. conference held in 2017, and the number of attendees continues to grow each year.

Figure 3.4 The first SINO-U.S. summit on transforming healthcare through information and technology and 2014 HIMSS greater China annual conference in Beijing.

HIMSS Standards and Validation

HIMSS Analytics also continued to influence the adoption of information technology as it works with healthcare organizations around the world. As of the writing of this chapter, HIMSS Analytics coverage includes EMR details of about 9,000 hospitals in 46 countries. It has also validated 289 of those hospitals in 11 countries at Stage 7 of the EMRAM, and validated over 2,600 hospitals in 25 countries at Stage 6 of the EMRAM. The bed count in these hospitals ranges from less than 25 beds to over 5,000 beds indicating that the EMRAM roadmap is relevant for any sized hospital.

The EMRAM represents eight distinct stages measuring the adoption and utilization of the core EMR functions required to achieve a near paperless environment that harnesses technology to optimize operations and patient care. HIMSS Analytics continues to survey acute care hospitals and clinics on an ongoing basis in the U.S. and by invitation only everywhere else. This enables each organization and the industry as a whole to understand trends and the rise of technology adoption in healthcare. It provides these organizations with an unbiased, independent analysis of the technology environment of their organization to help identify gaps, demonstrate progress, conduct benchmark comparisons with other like facilities, and overall to support the measurement of value achievement from their IT investments.

In addition to providing EMR adoption scoring and benchmarking, HIMSS Analytics also provides gap analysis assessments that help healthcare providers understand the specific functionalities and technologies needed to achieve advanced EMR capabilities represented in Stage 7 of the EMRAM. Stage 7 organizations have reported reductions in medical errors, improved readmission rates, higher operating margins, lower staffing costs, and reductions in duplicate orders, to name just a few benefits. The EMRAM provides organizations with a roadmap for achieving these benefits. Using this model helps identify gaps in an organization's technology portfolio and uncover opportunities for improved utilization.

The mission of HIMSS is to transform healthcare through the best use of information technology. Healthcare information technology is a key factor in addressing the problems facing the healthcare. The Health and Medicine Division of the National Academies of Sciences, Engineering, and Medicine (formerly known as the Institute of Medicine (IOM)) reported in the year 2000 that over 98,000 people die each year in the U.S. as a result of medical errors.[1] In 2016, Johns Hopkins University reported that medical errors are the third leading cause of death in the United States.[2] Healthcare information technology is often times compared to the banking industry when people talk about interoperability in healthcare. In healthcare, information technology solutions can be the difference in ensuring healthier outcomes. Regardless of the number of deaths reported by the IOM, one patient death due to a medical error is one too many. There are a number of reasons medical errors occur, but they can mostly be summed up in one common theme: The most relevant information needed is not available at the point of care when a care decision is being made.

The IOM published another report in 2001 that suggested the best way to make healthcare delivery safe, timely, effective, efficient, equitable, and patient centered, it would require a significant investment in information technology.[3] High-reliability organization theory also suggests that health information technology is needed to monitor precisely a healthcare organization's system of care, how medications are dispensed to patients, and how much waste is in the system. However, simply automating an already flawed system can contribute to even less efficiency. Therefore, it is critically important to consider both the process of care and how technology can enable improvements in those care processes.[4] This is precisely how the HIMSS Analytics EMRAM can help an organization in understanding how its EMR strategy focuses on the outcomes and process improvements directly impacted by the use of information technology.

For example, medication management processes can be greatly enhanced through the careful integration of information technology into the process. Using auto identification capabilities such as barcoding on both unit-dose medications and on the wristbands of patients in the hospital has proven to significantly reduce medication errors. The closed-loop medication administration process evaluated during an EMRAM assessment ensures the hospital has the ability to improve patient safety at the bedside by enabling the nurse to scan medications and patients allowing the EMR to verify the right patient is receiving the right medications at the right dose, time, and route.

The EMRAM criteria also go beyond just requiring online physician and nursing documentation in an electronic medical record system. The EMRAM requires an organization to demonstrate advanced clinical decision support capabilities to support caregivers at the time they need to make a decision about the care they are providing. In words, the system needs to be sophisticated enough to provide alerts when patient data indicate that intervention is recommended. For example, if a physician adds a new problem to the patient's problem list, the EMR must be able to provide immediate feedback to the physician in the form of recommended protocols specific to the new problem. It is also expected that the system is smart enough to allow organization leadership at all levels to track protocol adherence, a capability that fully supports the ideas of high-reliability organizations in terms of being able to plan and implement specific improvement initiatives.

The EMRAM Stage 7 validation criteria include an assessment of an organization's clinical and business analytics capabilities. To receive a Stage 7 validation, the EMRAM requires an organization to describe and demonstrate how operational, clinical, and business areas and leaders at different levels use clinical and business information collected in various information technology systems to monitor and improve operations on a regular basis. More specifically, the organization

Figure 3.5 A photo of John H. Daniels in HIMSS EMRAM Stage 6 on-site validation of Shanghai Children's Medical Center.

must demonstrate through case studies that analytics is used to identify issues that need to be improved, and that analytics is used to monitor and track improvements over time. Summarily, the organization must demonstrate that it uses its analytics capabilities to influence clinical and business decision-making toward issue identification, resolution, and improvement.

Stage 7 organizations consistently share the same attributes. They use data to drive improved outcomes related to clinical processes, financial operations, and clinical quality and safety outcomes. They are paperless, or near paperless and virtually create no paper during the course of care. All clinically relevant data are in the EMR and at the disposal of the caregiver when needed. They are fully committed to continuous process improvement through collaboration and have strong IT leadership, active non-IT executive champions, and clinicians (physicians, nurses, ancillary professionals) and end-user champions engaged throughout the entire implementation and process-improvement cycle (Figure 3.5).

All of the current EMRAM Stage 7 organizations have successfully demonstrated the benefits they have realized from their information technology investments. Some actual examples of benefits demonstrated by Stage 7 organizations during their on-site validations include the following:

- Medication error rates per 1,000 case mix index (CMI)-adjusted patient days were reduced by 62% once the hospital implemented and achieved a 95% compliance rate with the closed-loop medication administration process (e.g., scanning medications and scanning patients at the bedside).
- Catheter-associated urinary tract infection (CAUTI) rate per 1,000 catheter-days was eliminated after implementing an advanced clinical decision support rule that supported both nurses and physicians.
- Serious Harm Event rate was reduced from two events per 1,000 patient days to 0.2% after implementing an advanced clinical decision support rule that supported both nurses and physicians.
- A children's hospital was able to reduce its non-ICU resuscitation events (code blue) from 1.07 events per 1,000 patient days to 0.12 events after implementing two different interventions including modifying rapid response team processes and then implementing an automated clinical decision support rule that predicted potential resuscitation events allowing the care team to intervene before an event occurred.

- Central line-associated bloodstream infections (CLABSIs) were significantly reduced from over 40 infections per year to less than five infections per year by implementing an advanced clinical decision support rule that supported both nurses and physicians in their monitoring of patients with central lines.
- Reduced chemotherapy order entry time for physicians from 90 min to only 15 min per patient after implementing carefully constructed chemotherapy order sets.
- One hospital eliminated wrong milk administration errors and significantly reduced the number of label errors and storage errors in human (breast) milk administration after including patients and human milk in the closed-loop medication administration process (e.g., human milk received a barcode label and was scanned along with the patient at the bedside). The hospital also demonstrated a time savings of 1 h per nurse per day by implementing the barcoding process for human milk.

Other improvements achieved from Stage 7 organizations include improved venous thromboembolism (VTE) prophylaxis compliance rates among physicians (from 80% to 92% compliance), eliminating patient falls in the hospital, eliminating ventilator acquired pneumonia (VAP), and achieving full compliance with administering antibiotics within an hour from a rate of 70%.

One particular example of benefits realized by an organization that achieved Stage 7 on both the EMRAM and outpatient EMRAM involves the organization's discovery of its unusually high emergency department (ED) utilization rate. Using its advanced clinical and business analytics capabilities, the organization identified a subgroup of its patient population that represented the highest users of the ED. Drilling into that particular group, the organization learned that this group of patients were economically depressed and as a result, would wait until they were seriously ill before seeking medical attention. They were not seeking help from a primary care clinic; the medical attention they sought was primarily in the ED. Armed with this new-found information, the organization began working on a process-improvement initiative that involved clinicians (physicians and nurses) from both the hospital and outpatient care settings, and other analysts from various departments. The resulting solution involved a proactive outreach program targeting this group of patients with the goal of getting them engaged in a primary care (outpatient) clinic on a regular basis. After implementing this program and monitoring its progress over a 1-year period, the organization was able to demonstrate a 50% reduction in that group's utilization of the ED also resulting in a 50% reduction in the costs of the ED.

Stage 7 organizations employ a deliberate and multidisciplinary approach to their information technology projects. Any acute care hospital can use the EMRAM to help measure its EMR implementation progress over time. The EMRAM equips hospitals with an industry-proven, internationally applicable, vendor neutral, and technology agnostic maturity model intended as a roadmap that guides organizations toward a truly advanced, virtually paperless healthcare delivery model.

Using the EMRAM will help the organization understand its current level of EMR adoption progress and understand where gaps may exist in its information technology strategy. Understanding where gaps exist is a powerful tool that informs the strategic planning process allowing decision makers the ability to focus resources toward the right areas. This ability to focus resources helps to ensure successful EMR optimization and cost effectiveness. Fully leveraging the EMRAM will help an organization continue to improve its patient safety, quality, organizational efficiency, and perhaps even its patient and staff satisfaction goals and objectives.

References

1. Kohn, L.T. *To Err Is Human: Building a Safer Health System.* Washington, DC: National Academy Press, 2000.
2. Makary, M.A., and Daniel, M. Medical error—the third leading cause of death in the US. *Bmj*, 2016, 353: i2139. doi:10.1136/bmj.i2139
3. Institute of Medicine (US) Committee on Quality of Health Care in America. *Crossing the Quality Chasm: A New Health System for the 21st Century.* Washington, DC: National Academy Press, 2001.
4. Hines, S., Luna, K., Lofthus, J., et al. Becoming a high reliability organization: Operational advice for hospital leaders. (Prepared by the Lewin Group under Contract No. 290-04-0011.) AHRQ Publication No. 08-0022. Rockville, MD: Agency for Healthcare Research and Quality, April 2008.

Chapter 4

"China and Me": Stories of International Accreditation Professionals

Contents

The Movement for Integrated Care

Jeremy T. Bonfini

HIMSS International

Jeremy T. Bonfini is the CEO of Allegheny County Medical Society and the Allegheny County Medical Society Foundation. Before that, Jeremy served as Executive Vice President for HIMSS International, a non-profit, mission-driven association. Jeremy was responsible for the development of programs in Europe, the Middle East and Asia Pacific. Prior to joining HIMSS, Jeremy served as Intel Corporation's Worldwide Digital Health Policy Manager; an education policy analyst in the House of Commons in London, England; and was employed in the U.S Congress and worked to provide constituent services to the people of Ohio's 18th Congressional District and advocated for legislation favoring economic development.

The last 100 years of modern medicine has been focused on the interaction of patient and clinician at a physical point of care. As the complexity of these interactions has increased, we now have reached the inevitable conclusion that healthcare information technology (IT) is essential to delivering the right care at the right time. HIMSS proudly tracks the adoption of healthcare IT in over 8,500 hospitals worldwide. While hospitals around the world are making steady progress, over 70% of the hospitals have not yet achieved the highest levels of electronic medical record (EMR) adoption. Nevertheless, the adoption of IT in acute care facilities is a mega-trend that is notable and undeniable (Figure 4.1).

Figure 4.1 Portrait of Jeremy Bonfini.

As hospitals modernize and maximize efficiency, they will eventually an absolute ceiling on how much care can be delivered cost effectively. Acute care settings are a critical core of our care delivery system and will be for the foreseeable future. However, the next 10 years of healthcare will be focused on managing chronic disease which acute care settings are poorly equipped to do.

The Next 10 Years of Health and Care

The chronic disease and aging wave will test health and care delivery systems like never before. The real question is whether governments are answering the right question of "How will we enable citizens to live healthy and productive lives outside of healthcare settings." As chronic disease quickly replaces accident and emergency care, hospitals and governments better have the right answers. The movement toward integrated care will define the next 10 years of health and care; however, the blueprint and infrastructure for true integrated care is still in its very early stages.

Core Components for Integrated Care

Integrated care is by its very nature, connected. However, the exchange of health information to support the patient journey is much easier said than done. HIMSS and the Radiological Society of North America founded the **Integrating the Healthcare Enterprise (IHE)** initiative to tackle the very difficult challenge of clinical health information exchange. Elements of IHE have been adopted globally to solve big challenges. The Austrian eHealth Exchange (ELGA) and the Statewide Health Information Network of *New York* (SHIN-*NY*) have been two major adopters. New York, as the second largest state in the US, was especially notable as it had extensive legacy health information exchanges that required tightly constrained interoperability to transport patient health information across the State. The incredible success in New York resulted in the creation of a testing and certification platform now available to the World via the ConCert by HIMSS program.

- The ConCert by HIMSS program streamlines the certification of interoperability in health IT and helps evaluate HIT products and simplifies the task of selecting the right information systems for your organization.
- The ConCert by HIMSS mark means a product is proven to be interoperable with other products.
- ConCert by HIMSS allows vendors to achieve cost-effective, interoperability certification for solutions that facilitate efficient, seamless data exchange.

Continua

As regional health information networks mature, the Body Area Network is evolving in parallel. Throughout our daily lives, the human body creates rich data that can provide early warning indicators of impending illness or provide patients feedback on how to manage known chronic illness. The incredible lost opportunity is that much of these rich data go uncollected. Even worse, the data that are collected are not integrated into a record centered on the patient. Uncollected and disconnected personal health information creates lost care and wellness opportunities that cost societies huge sums in unnecessary healthcare expenditures and lost productivity. The Continua Design Guidelines seek to enable connectivity and aggregation of personal health data. The Design

Guidelines are based on common international standards defined by recognized standards development organizations, and are built on four key principles:

1. Authentic interoperability—connectivity requiring minimal effort on the part of the user
2. Open source development model—the Continua Design Guidelines are universally accessible, nonproprietary, and not for profit
3. Flexibility—designed to provide maximum choice for developers and end users (healthcare buyers, individual clinicians, and consumers)
4. Wisdom of the market—the market in aggregate has more wisdom than any individual stakeholder; thus, the Continua Design Guidelines are developed through a consensus process

Valuable tools and resources support product certification via the Continua Design Guidelines, including: The Continua Enabling Software Library (CESL) and test tool development, representing over $2 million worth of software development created by Continua to enable complete end-to-end functionality. The Continua Council is the Continua Design Guidelines governing body, boasting today's most dynamic, forward-thinking and successful organizations: Fujitsu, Intel, Orange, Philips, Roche Diagnostics, Sharp, and UnitedHealth Group.

Benchmarking the Success of Integrated Care: The Continuity of Care Maturity of Model

Integrated care is the cornerstone for the sustainability of healthcare systems. The core components of integrated care include (1) efficient and effective acute care settings, (2) health information exchange that supports that patient journey, and (3) personal health information capture and exchange that empowers health and wellness.

To support the journey undertaken by nations in Europe to integrate healthcare systems, HIMSS has developed the Continuity of Care Maturity Model (CCMM). The CCMM was created to help optimize outcomes for health systems and patients alike, the CCMM™ goes beyond Stage 7 of the Electronic Medical Record Adoption Model (EMRAM). This global maturity model addresses the convergence of interoperability, information exchange, care coordination, patient engagement, and analytics with the ultimate goal of holistic individual and population health management.

The Next 10 Years Summary

The challenges of integrated care are incredible and come at a crucial time for healthcare systems straining to deal with existing demands of their citizens. However, the old models cannot scale to meet these challenges. Attempts to scale old care delivery models will only lead to systemic collapse as healthcare spend consumes gross national product. A new embrace of health information exchange and personal health data capture and exchange is essential to bringing the right information to the right people to make healthier, less costly, and more empowering decisions about health and wellness. HIMSS, ConCert, and the Personal Connected Health Alliance enthusiastically seek to embrace partners to join us on our mission of healthcare transformation.

HIMSS Stage 7 Experience in China

Michael A. Pfeffer, MD, FACP

UCLA Health Sciences

Michael A. Pfeffer, MD, FACP serves as the Chief Information Officer (CIO) for the UCLA Health Sciences, which is comprised of the UCLA Hospital System, the UCLA Faculty Practice Group, and the David Geffen School of Medicine. Michael is an Associate Professor of Clinical Medicine with a focus Hospital Medicine, supervising residents and medical students in the acute care of patients. He also serves as an Associate Program Director for the new Clinical Informatics Fellowship at UCLA and as a mentor in the Resident Informaticist program. Michael has lectured around the world on clinical informatics with a focus on electronic health records and their impact on organizations and patients.

Leadership—the unifying thread that ties together all of the most successful hospitals I had the opportunity to evaluate in China. To accomplish HIMSS Stage 7 requires a thoughtful, humble leader capable of driving their complex organization toward a unified goal of advanced, patient-focused technology delivery. This person is typically the Chief Executive Officer (CEO) of the hospital, but may also be an executive that reports directly to the CEO with their full support. In either case, this leader is paramount in achieving the change management necessary for HIMSS Stage 7. From my visits, I postulate three key roles of the leader are needed for success: ensure this is not an IT project, convey the "why," and be present (Figure 4.2).

While the presence and functionality of an electronic health record is necessary for HIMSS Stage 7, it is certainly not sufficient. The leader must unify their organization around the idea that this is not an IT project. What does that mean? IT analysts, IT project managers, and even the Chief Information Officer (CIO) cannot be the driving force behind implementing and optimizing the EHR. Rather, the business owners must be responsible for the success and implementation of their respective EHR modules. For example, the pharmacy director must be intimately familiar with the pharmacy module and be an advocate for the EHR. Partnering closely with the pharmacy IT team and ensuring that the tool is built to center around the patient while providing needed efficiencies for their staff is critical. Where I have seen organizations struggle is when the IT team

Figure 4.2 Portrait of Michael A. Pfeffer.

is "pushing" the business to adopt the technology. It is almost a guarantee that the tool will not be built properly, will be frustrating to end users, and will have a higher chance of failing. In addition, organizations that have realized a physician champion dedicated to the project, often called a physician Informaticist or Chief Medical Informatics Officer (CMIO), is a highly successful way of bridging the gap between the business and the IT organization. Such an individual must be highly skilled in change management and adoption techniques, and must have a strong relationship with both the CEO (or executive leader) and the CIO.

HIMSS Stage 7 should never be the primary reason for advancing health IT at an organization—a successful CEO understands this. In order to energize the organization around such a goal, it must be clear to the organization that the purpose of advancing health IT is for improving the health of the patient and populations served. HIMSS Stage 7 criteria serve as a guide to get there, and achieving its recognition is only the start of the possibilities of health IT at the organization, not the end. I refer to this idea as "the why?" Why are we doing this? Why is it good for patients? Why is it good for the organization? Luckily, the answers to these questions can be found from partner health organizations that have achieved HIMSS Stage 7. I'll answer these from my viewpoint as an HIMSS Stage 7 organization, but a savvy CEO will seek out many answers to these questions prior to beginning the change management around advancing health IT.

"Why Are We Doing This?"

A unified, patient-centered electronic health record is fundamentally needed, both now and in the future, to provide ever-increasing complex medical care. The future of medicine—which I believe is precision medicine—requires large amounts of readily available multi-axis datasets to provide clinicians real-time precision clinical decision support. This will pull from genomic data and environmental data, in addition to the phenotypic data currently available in the EHR. A fragmented patient record, a business-centered patient record, or an incomplete/multisystem patient record will not accomplish this goal. In addition, achieving HIMSS Stage 7 ensures numerous critical medical delivery processes are in place, such as closed-loop medication administration, that has clear evidence behind it in reducing adverse medication events.

"Why Is It Good for Patients?"

Patients are the primary focus of our business of promoting and ensuring health. Not fixing illness. Health IT transcends the acute care needs of our patients and allows organizations to promote health of patients and populations. Patient portals, educational apps, and home medical device integrations all allow the organization to envelop the patient in their health without even having to have the patient step foot into the clinic or hospital. That is why new terminology for the patient—member, customer, stakeholder, client—has caught on in the health sphere. One only becomes our patient when they are sick, but is a member of our health community, routinely absorbing health information and education from our organizations through health IT. The obvious—better access to their health information on portals, a legible medical record accessible by all care providers, interoperability, etc.—are worth noting as well.

"Why Is It Good for the Organization?"

Chief Financial Officers (CFO), Chief Operating Officers (COO), board members, etc. are going to want to know how this large investment in capital and resources is going to be good for the

Figure 4.3 A photo of Michael A. Pfeffer in HIMSS EMRAM Stage 7 validation of TEDA Hospital.

organization. As mentioned above, patients are customers. They seek out the best healthcare—and it clear that the best healthcare is delivered by HIMSS Stage 7 organizations. Not just because of their EHR, but because of their leadership and forward-thinking as I mentioned above. HIMSS Stage 7 organizations are acutely aware of the future of healthcare, model their business around the patient, and tend to be highly successful on the revenue front. Coding and billing are more accurate and timely, less duplication in testing and procedures occurs due to accessibility of information from throughout the organization and externally, and key performance indicators based on real-time analytics are readily available to the business to maneuver quickly as needed. Such ideas are just a subset of the critical advantages of an HIMSS Stage 7 site (Figure 4.3).

Finally, the most successful hospital organizations in China have leaders that are present. It is not enough to say this is important—one has to commit their own time to it to show that it is important. The consistent message that, I, the CEO, dedicate my valuable time to the project centered on achieving HIMSS Stage 7 is critical for the organization to see and feel. It provides the fuel for numerous late nights redesigning workflows or testing various interfaces. It reinvigorates the team when a failure occurs (and they will). It provides compromise in situations seemingly without a path forward. It rewards and recognizes successes, even the little ones, in the vast array of tasks and milestones along the path toward the pinnacle of health IT.

In sitting through numerous presentations, touring many hospital floors, speaking with countless business owners in laboratory medicine, pharmacy, medical records, etc., I have seen first hard organizations that have the leader described above and those that do not. An HIMSS Stage 7 organization—a top health IT organization—in China always has a strong leader. That common thread is a must, or the hard work of many in the organization can unravel before one knows it.

My HIMSS Visit to China

Allen Hsiao

Yale New Haven Health and Yale School of Medicine

Allen Hsiao, MD, is Vice President and Chief Medical Information Officer (CMIO), Yale New Haven Health and Yale School of Medicine. Allen also oversees the DBAs, data architects, and the Joint Data Analytics Team, a team of over 45 analysts that provide the reporting and analytics for the System and the School, supporting operational, clinical, and research reporting and data needs. In addition to these operational responsibilities, he serves as Informatics co-director for Yale's Clinical Translational Science Award (CTSA) from the National Institutes of Health. Complementing his CMIO responsibilities, Allen Hsiao is also Associate Professor of Pediatrics and of Emergency Medicine at the Yale School of Medicine, regularly teaching students, residents and fellows and sees patients in the Pediatric Emergency Department at Yale-New Haven Children's Hospital.

Health Information Technology holds great promise and in dramatically improving how healthcare is delivered and how new medical knowledge is discovered. Nowhere is this more true than in China. The large populations of patients that need care, with a wide range of ailments, are both a challenge and a strength. It is a challenge because of the relatively smaller number of available physicians and specialists that work tirelessly to care for the large number of patients who seek care. From my observations, advanced hospitals in the large cities need to support not only their own local population, but large numbers from the surrounding rural areas, many traveling long distances to seek care from the urban physician experts. However, the hospitals and specialists are passionate about doing their best to meet these demands, and many have been leveraging IT to do so (Figure 4.4).

Because of the large number of patients, much larger than I suspect in most countries, and certainly the US where I have the most experience, the use of technology such as close loop medication administration is even more critical. While in a busy emergency department shift the nurse and I may see and treat 30 or 40 patients; in China, they may see and treat four or five times that many. Because time is so short, computerized decision support has even more potential to improve safety in China by electronically verifying medications, dosages, allergies, and drug-drug interactions. However, to be effective, workflows also need to be adopted to make sure the critical information is captured about a patient's past history, current medications, allergies, and similar history.

Figure 4.4 Portrait of Allen Hsiao.

On the other hand, an advantage Chinese EMR designers and users have is they can design and use their systems solely for the purpose of improving clinical care and recording information for future clinical and research use. In the US, a large portion of system design, and unfortunately, system usage and documentation are aimed toward billing: lots of low utility information that is recorded to justify reimbursement of the care to the insurance companies and regulators. Besides the extra time and effort needed to enter this information into the EMR, it makes it more difficult for other clinicians, and ultimately researchers, to extract the information they need because there is so much to scan and read through, much of is extra documentation of exhaustive "review of systems" and negative physical exam findings, social, and family history, etc., to meet billing compliance rules and support billing for higher levels of care. To be clear, such information is often clinically important, but not routinely documented the level they are currently, too often solely to support billing. This has led to a very common complaint of "note bloat" in the US, and some hospitals have resorted to even reorganizing how their electronic notes are structured, from "SOAP" (subjective, objective, assessment, and plan) to "APSO" so physicians can ignore the subjective and objective portions and quickly read the assessment and plan.

Another strength, yet a challenge, I have seen firsthand at multiple hospitals in China is how embedded and close their relationships are with their EMR vendor. It is certainly a strength that they work so closely with the designers and programmers of their systems; the nimbleness of which changes are made in the system is unparalleled. Comments that we have made as part of HIMSS reviews are have at times been addressed and live by the next morning! This is very impressive from a dedication and systems coding/engineering standpoint. On the other hand, however, it is concerning from a change control and clinician testing, usability, and education standpoint. It is possible to be too nimble; if changes are made without really testing how well they work, with the actual physicians and nurses who must use the systems testing and participating in the changes, that is a problem as often there may be unexpected ramifications of the changes that can negatively impact patient care, creating dangerous situations. For clinicians who already see many more times the volume of patients in many other countries, any unexpected changes to the system can be quite detrimental.

Along those lines, what also seems to commonly be missing from the EMR vendor teams are experienced clinicians who participate at the ground level in system and solutions design. While there is certainly no shortage of smart engineers and computer scientists on the EMR teams I have met, none have had a nurse or physician on them. It is critical that experienced clinicians with firsthand, front-line, experience on how patient care is delivered, and how nurses and doctors think, help shape, and design the way the EMR works. The placement of information, the natural workflow and questions asked, the number of clicks, and the way decision support is displayed are just a few ways nurses and physicians can profoundly help EMR design be optimized. Again, because clinicians in China see such large volume of patients, every click saved, every bit of information that is more optimally displayed, is magnified many folds and invaluable.

Speaking of workflow, and challenges to them, is something that appears to be fairly common in China: the "information systems" are very separate. It took me a while to fully appreciate how there was such a separate nursing information system from the physician one (typically called HIS), separate still from the lab information system and such. The work of nurses and physicians are so closely tied, having separate NIS from the HIS is at best extremely cumbersome to nurses and physicians, and at worst dangerous. Much progress has been made at the leading hospitals, typically with a web-based overview that pulls from these various information systems to give the clinician a more comprehensive view. However, it is still view-only, and changes in one system do not often quickly make it into the other system. For instance, at some hospitals, physicians changing a medication order does not populate the nursing task list until the next day, so a physician has to find the nurse and verbally tell them; if they are too busy or forget, the incorrect medication or dose can readily be given, passing all of the closed-loop barcode administration logic that was painstakingly programmed for patient safety. EMR vendors in China need to not think of the nursing and physician systems are being separate; this is an artificial construct that needs to be remedied. True, physicians and nurses have different roles and tasks to do, but they are an intricately tied team taking care of the same patient. That patient's data should, must, be all in the same single database for patient safety and to decrease duplicative work recording and accessing information by the nurses, physicians, and other clinicians. Universally, but in China more than everywhere else, they do not have the time to not be efficient and be performing duplicative or unsynchronized work.

Given the closeness of the EMR companies with the hospitalist they support, it could easily be that local nurses and physicians are identified and tasked to work with them toward better, integrated system designs. In fact, it could be that already many do behind the scenes and I was not made aware of it. If not, however, it should be done more uniformly, and ideally more than one nurse and one physician, so that a range of opinions and ideas can be solicited; also, medicine is so complex with so many specialties, and many clinicians from different areas should participate and have a voice. Their time should also be protected to do so, with clinical load lightened so they can appropriately dedicate time and attention to these important responsibilities. In my limited experience in China, I have met physician CIOs who work tirelessly to guide EMR design in addition to their many other tasks. Having physician CIOs is an excellent model in my humble opinion, but they need help from the US equivalent of CMIOs and CNIOs, and they in turn, from local physician and nursing champions in different medical specialties. In the US, EMR vendors universally hire physicians and nurses full-time to provide them insight as they design their systems, and then they get another round of more specific and broader feedback/advice from the local doctors and nurses using their system in real life.

Another challenge that comes to mind is that the tremendous amount of work being done to create, support, troubleshoot, and optimize EMRs by the various different companies is a lot of duplicative effort and work that ultimately is a lot of "reinventing the wheel." Each hospital and their partner vendor are spending an inordinate amount of time and resources tacking problems and coming up with solutions. In many ways, this is a good thing, as I have seen firsthand in terms of the nimbleness of problem solving, but it is also concerning in the long run. I say this because on one hand because of the huge amount of effort involved at so many busy hospitals around China; great work and a brilliant innovative solution will not be readily shared and utilized by all of the hospitals that may also benefit from it. Another issue is that with all of these custom, relatively locally designed EMR systems, standards are not readily apparent. This makes it challenging, if not impossible, to share data between hospitals. It may be that patients do not travel between hospitals as often as they do in the US, but some portion certainly must as they seek sub-specialists, etc., and for research or population surveillance and population health, have data standards is critical.

In the US, in the late 1980s and in the 1990s, most of our leading academic medical centers did exactly this; spending an inordinate amount of resources to create their own local, home-grown, EMR systems from scratch. Many of them, such as at Harvard (Partners), Vanderbilt, and Intermountain, were extremely sophisticated and capable systems. However, all of those institutions, and in fact, almost all large hospitals in the US, have converted to one of the two leading US EMR companies. This is because the teams (sometimes over 1,000 people) and financial support they needed to maintain those systems was unsustainable given the growing complexity of medicine. While the demands of a EMR system were initially fairly basic (problem, medication, and allergy lists, basic documentation), modern medicine requirements now include sophisticated, structured recording of all of those fields as well as complex decision support, integration of countless devices and all of their interfaces, accounting for their information, exchange of data between hospitals, mobile health technologies, genomic information, machine learning, "big data," and complex predictive and prescriptive algorithms. To expect each hospital, or even fairly large academic medical center and their partner EMR vendor to be able to keep up with so much complexity is not realistic, and why things have dramatically shifted in the US from countless different EMR vendors and a "best of breed" nightmare, to now just a handful. Those leading vendors have also dramatically changed, growing to now having 10,000 employees or larger, and partnering more closely than ever with knowledge experts at the leading hospitals their systems are in.

There are two particular strengths I noticed in China that I would be remiss not to mention. The first is how universal it seems that medical information is very patient centered and readily available to patients. While in the US there is still much debate over how long we should delay results being released to patients, where many doctors think it should be over a week, or even never. In China, every hospital I visited had patient kiosks where as soon as the lab and radiology results were available, the patient would have access and could print it out. Likely, most patients are aware of the results before their doctors do, something nearly unheard of in the US. This patient-centric attitude is tremendous, and can be built upon with online patient portals for results and education, mobile health technologies to monitor patients at home, and technologies like telemedicine.

The second particular strength I noticed is how central a role the government plays in healthcare. Very high-level government officials have participated in the HIMSS visits I have been on, which speaks volumes to the hospital administration and EMR companies about the importance of their work. The realization that the healthcare data they collect can be used to help government officials plan the best use of resources and population health was eye opening to them and made them even more passionate in their work. Also, my understanding is that the government is pushing for great regional sharing of data among hospitals. This will help push for adoption of more data standards between different EMR platforms and enable collection of cleaner data for disease surveillance, public health planning, research, and the like. With the digitization of medicine, China with its extremely large population and great governmental push for data sharing and aggregation is arguably uniquely poised for healthcare knowledge discovery.

EMRAM and China

John P. Hoyt

Healthcare Advisory Services Group HIMSS Analytics

John P. Hoyt, FACHE, FHIMSS Title: Consultant to HIMSS Analytics

Former Executive Vice President, HIMSS Analytics

John P. Hoyt is former Executive Vice President Emeritus, HIMSS Analytics. Before joining HIMSS, Hoyt served as a hospital Chief Operating Officer and twice as a Chief Information Officer with various healthcare organizations accumulating in over 22 years of hospital executive committee leadership experience. Mr. Hoyt served in consultancy practices, including: IBM Healthlink Services and First Data Health Systems Group.

Figure 4.5 Portrait of John P. Hoyt.

Chinese Interest and Drive

There is clearly a strong interest in China to improve quality, safety, and efficiency through the use of e-health investments, notable the EMR. Every hospital that HIMSS Analytics staff has visited for consulting or validation on Stage 6 or Stage 7 of the EMRAM model has shown keen interest in improving their use of EMR tools to improve care quality. There is a desire among many of the Chinese hospitals that HIMSS Analytics staff has seen to emulate the top American hospitals in their use of health IT investments (Figure 4.5).

Capacity Along with Interest and Drive

Combining the interest and drive with the tremendous human resource capacity of China means there is all the potential in the world for China to become a world leader in the effective use of IT in healthcare. China has made great progress in just the few years that HIMSS Analytics has been consulting and validating hospitals in Greater China. Yes, there are a tremendous number of hospitals in China, but given the tremendous human resource capacity, China can quickly become a world leader in the use of EMR.

Still to Achieve

The capacity of skilled Chinese labor can be extended to the broad use of e-health tools. This is extending from using technology to improve the patient scheduling and registration experience to engaging patients in maintaining and improving their own health. China seems to be at the beginning of the movement to engage patients in their own health. The HIMSS Analytics teams are just beginning to see this emerge in the leading Chinese e-health institutions. There is great belief that engaging patients in taking more responsibility in maintaining their own health can improve the overall health of the population. The main emphasis is on the chronic diseases that require diligent maintenance to prevent significant deterioration and early death. The use of e-health tools is believed to energize patients in engaging in their own health. This appears to be just emerging in China where other nations have been working on patient engagement through the use of e-health tools for several years now.

Very Technology Focused

It is clear that China is still very "technology focused" in its software development. This is reminiscent of the US in the late 1980s and early 1990s. Clearly, China needs to move on from a technology model where there are an inordinate number of vendors involved in a health system's EMR to a consolidated vendor who supplies the overwhelming majority of clinical computing software without interfaces. Built with a common clinical architecture with a single data model in a single clinical data repository will not require any interfaces, thus reducing the probability of error and improving the end user experience. All Stage 7 hospitals outside of China (over 300) are built on this architectural concept. China still has a significant way to go to adopt a common clinical data architecture without interfaces for the core clinical processes.

Governance of the system requires the "ownership," and strategic plan of the system to be in the hands of the hands of the end users with the IT Department being a "sub-contractor" to the end users. This, of course, requires an educated end user environment. The end users need to know what is possible and what leading hospitals in the world are doing with advanced e-health investments. China, with its technology focus in the IT department or via an outsourced vendor, has a journey ahead to have true clinical ownership of the system. This goes hand in hand with moving away from a technology focused delivery environment.

HIMSS 7 Site Visit to Guangzhou Women and Children's Medical Center

Christopher A. Longhurst

UC San Diego Health

Christopher A. Longhurst, MD, MS

Chief Information Officer, UC San Diego Health

Clinical Professor of Biomedical Informatics and Pediatrics, UC San Diego School of Medicine

As Chief Information Officer, Dr. Longhurst is responsible for all operations and strategic planning for information and communications technology across the multiple hospitals, clinics and professional schools which encompass UC San Diego Health. Dr. Longhurst is also a Clinical Professor of Biomedical Informatics and Pediatrics at UC San Diego School of Medicine, and continues to see patients. He previously served as Chief Medical Information Officer for Stanford Children's Health and Clinical Professor at the Stanford University School of Medicine. Described as a pragmatic academician, Dr. Longhurst, serves as an Advisor to several companies and speaks internationally on a wide gamut of healthcare IT topics.

My first trip to China was memorable, to say the least. I was scheduled to arrive in Guangzhou on 22 October, but weather delays forced an unexpected layover in Beijing, and I arrived during a half day late on Sunday afternoon. Despite missing the opening presentation, I was quickly impressed with the landmarks achieved by this large medical center in the third largest city in China. Our hosts were proud of their accomplishments and open about their opportunities. Along with Dr. Paul Testa, CMIO from NYU Langone Medical Center, John Daniels, and Yu Quan, we found the case studies impressive and awarded the HIMSS 7 designation without resignation (Figures 4.6 and 4.7).

Three memories really stick out. The first was visiting their women's health clinic, where intake vitals were highly automated and self-service. In fact, Guangzhou Women and Children's Medical

Figure 4.6 Portrait of Christopher Longhurst.

Figure 4.7 A photo of Christopher Longhurst in HIMSS EMRAM Stage 7 validation of Guangzhou Women and Children's Medical Center on Oct. 25, 2016.

Center reported that over 80% of their 4 million annual outpatient visits are self-scheduled from mobile devices! I have shared these stories at UC San Diego Health to encourage our own ambulatory service transformation.

The second was visiting the neonatal intensive care unit, where the physicians all attested that the system made them *more efficient*—a milestone we have not yet achieved in America. It was clear that the medical staff felt very positive toward the benefits of the electronic health record. Although the doctors are clearly not subject to the same regulatory and compliance burden we have created for ourselves in the US, the focus on usability was laudable.

Finally, dinner with Dr. Xia, the pediatric surgeon CEO, was an indulgent and unforgettable experience. Our hosts' generosity was unparalleled, and I hope to return someday to continue to share our innovations on both sides.

CHINA PRACTICES II

Chapter 5

Huashan Hospital Affiliated to Fudan University

Ma Xin, Liu Yang, Li Yun, Qiu Zhiyuan, Zhu Jianqing, Yang Minjie, Zhao Yong, and Wang Huiying
Huashan Hospital Affiliated to Fudan University

Ma Xin *is a Vice President, Professor of Orthopedics and Supervisor of doctoral candidates of Huashan Hospital of Fudan University.*

He is General Secretary and Director of Education of Foot and Ankle Chapter of the Chinese Orthopaedic Association, Vice Chairman of Foot and Ankle Chapter of Chinese Association of Orthopaedic Surgeons and a member of American Orthopaedic Foot & Ankle Society, among others.

Hospital Introduction: Huashan Hospital Affiliated to Fudan University (hereinafter referred as "Huashan Hospital") was established in 1907. It is under direct governance of the National Health Commission and Fudan University. As one of the first hospitals in China accredited as the Level A Tertiary Hospital in 1992, Huashan Hospital also enjoys high reputation as a comprehensive academic medical center with diverse international exchanges. It is also the first public hospital in China accredited by JCI as an Academic Medical Center.

Huashan Hospital focuses on quality improvement and people-centered care following the Red Cross spirit of "humanity, philanthropism and dedication." Under the leadership of the hospital, Huashan people are committed themselves to the new round of healthcare reform in line with the spirit of "being pioneering and dedicated." Our goal is to build the hospital into an international high-quality hospital through discipline development and branding strategies.

International Accreditation: 2010, 2013, and 2016, JCI accreditation and reaccreditation;

CAP certification for Laboratory, six times in a row;

Contents

Preface

Ten Years to Make a Sword; A 100 Years to Build Huashan

In early February 2016, Huashan Hospital received the final report from the headquarters of JCI and learned that we were accredited again, making Huashan the first teaching public hospital that had passed three rounds of JCI surveys. When looking back to the journey we have made, we are proud and pleased. It was the choice made by the inevitable history and the people of Huashan. A choice to start over from zero.

In the past 10 years, China has gone through unprecedented changes. As the reform and opening-up campaign continues to move forward and the rapid development in the healthcare techniques and technologies, the level of healthcare in China has gradually caught up with the advanced international practices. Huashan enjoys profound history and ranks high among all hospitals in Shanghai regarding service volume and clinical strength. However, while embracing the new era, Huashan was confined by its space and facilities in the central downtown Shanghai. It became a challenge to all hospital managers at that time to ensure quality and safety while meeting the increasing healthcare demands. The leadership was aware that the adoption of international quality management system was the ticket to extended international cooperation and competition on the global arena.

JCI, an internationally recognized organization, advocates for the "patient-centered" concept in hospital management for improved care and safe practice. It echoes the goal of Huashan during the period of rapid development. A decision was then made to introduce the JCI standards into the hospital.

For Huashan, it was a journey full of hardships. The decision was challenged by many people: Would the international standards of quality find its way into a traditional Chinese hospital facing so many obstacles waiting to be overcome? Again, Huashan took the lead to reform. Through rounds of painful changes, we completed the trilogy of improvement, transformation, and development.

Change of Concept, Breakthrough of Traditions

There were different opinions in the hospital when we first encountered JCI. The endless pursuit of patient safety and process details advocated by JCI were confronted by the tradition way of service provision and hospital quality management concept in China. For example, JCI requires pain and nutrition assessment upon admission onto the floors or encounter in outpatient clinic, surgery verification including surgical site mark and the pre-op/post-op verification, and adoption of clinical protocols such as clinical guidelines and SOPs, etc. Many staff including the senior experts could not fully understand the standards: after decades of experience as a physician, we had never made such mistakes, and the traditional way of practicing had never posed any threat to patient safety. Why would we need to be judged by the international standards?

In the face of all these questions, the hospital leaders were determined. In July 2007, in order to better understand the role of international standards in improving healthcare quality and the setbacks of the management expertise of the hospital, the hospital sent the key management staff to Boston and Chicago for 1-month JCI training, and invited JCI experts to give lectures to interpret the international hospital management standards.

Gaps Identified via Baseline

Soon, Huashan set up the first JCI Office to specifically facilitate the accreditation preparation. On 28 November 2007, three consultants were sent by JCI headquarters to carry out the 8-day baseline, marking the official start of our JCI journey. Though with thorough preparation and rectification before the baseline, there were still many findings during the first 5 days: from small things as the formulation of policy, environmental cleanness, storage of boxes, patient medication list, expiration date of medication in use, various labeling, informed consent, staff training, to more complicated problems such as privileging, hospital priorities, multidisciplinary plan of care, pathology investigation process, ER process, contingency plans, patient identification, hospital-acquired infection control, physical facilities, patient safety, and privacy. We had never identified or paid attention to these things.

For the first time, many staff had the opportunity to visit each corner of the hospital and learned about the system tracer methodology in that 5 days. We felt exactly our gap from the leading international practice. Though it would be an arduous journey, we were convinced that it would enhance the hospital managerial expertise. We became more determined in continuous improvement to achieve the JCI gold seal.

First JCI Survey

In the 2 years between the baseline and the initial survey, Huashan Hospital implemented comprehensive improvement actions: 4,000 staff files, 259 hospital policies, clinical protocols in all units, 140 informed consent forms, quality indicators in over 20 areas, 80 department-level service plan, and job responsibilities for all staff in the hospital. All these had been put in place. However, that was not sufficient. The surveyors still identified opportunities for improvement during the initial survey, including patient assessment, individualized service targeted at children and the elderly, nursing human resources, observation in ER, continuity of medical records, and the hospital-wide code services. These were, then, added to the list of key improvement projects in the hospital.

Through JCI accreditation, Huashan Hospital successfully provided world-class medical service to the 2010 World Expo in Shanghai. It is our "Golden Key" to the international medical tourism and conference medical service in the future. As a large general hospital with a history over 100 years, Huashan Hospital's JCI experience is the highlight of China's healthcare reform and offers a new example of the reform of the public hospitals in China.

First JCI Triennial Survey

From 2010 to 2012, Huashan Hospital followed the requirements in the fourth edition of the JCI hospital accreditation standards and improved the findings from the initial survey, such as the ER observation service, uniform care in ER, patient care continuity, integrated nursing human resources, standard inpatient assessment and reassessment policy, and the focus on children and young teenagers to further standardize the care processes in the hospital.

Meanwhile, we started to adopt information technology to further optimize the processes, including electronic ledger, ICD, patient handover system, hospital-acquired infection monitoring system, outpatient EMR, adverse event reporting system, etc. A healthcare quality database was established based on all the systems in place to realize delicacy management. To meet the standards regarding medical education and human subject research defined in the fourth edition, we also set higher bars on the oversight on research and education.

During 7–12 January 2013, five surveyors spent 6 days in Huashan Hospital for our triennial survey. The implementation of daily processes by the hospital policies was the guarantee of sufficient preparation for the second survey. We were successfully accredited again as an academic teaching hospital.

As Dr. Ma Xin, then VP of the hospital in charge of medical affairs, said that JCI standards had gained more support from our staff to drive the processes toward the requirements, and more staff had learned the methodology of modern quality management.

However, there were three major findings identified by the surveyors that required SIPs.

1. Only 53% of the open records contained measurable goals for nursing care.
2. During the tracer in the Orthopedics Department, one bag of Type A blood was delivered to the unit at 14:00 and put on the desk in the medication room. But it was not until 14:45

that the transfusion started. According to the hospital policy, the blood/blood product could not be kept at room temperature longer than 30 min.

3. Through the clinical tracer and education interview, it was evidenced that the trainees were not included in the hospital quality improvement program.

We know that there is no perfect system or process in the hospital. Thus, PDCA is necessary for continuous improvement.

Second JCI Triennial Survey

The second triennial survey was scheduled in January 2016. The hospital leadership gradually learned how to utilize JCI survey as a tool to promote quality and safety in the hospital. From the initial survey to the second triennial survey, we also completed our transformation from "wasting away in sorrow and pain" to "taking the survey with zero preparation," and from "listening to the surveyors" to "sharing our experience and ideas with them." Survey is like a bridge of exchanges. Huashan Hospital also revealed our strengths to the surveyors from abroad. Quality is no longer a word with empty shell but a term of the essence. Though the fifth edition made many changes to the previous edition and set even higher bars on the requirements, Huashan Hospital was successfully reaccredited and became the first JCI public hospital that was accredited for the third time. We were not as thrilled as we were 6 years ago during the initial survey. But it left more for us to think about regarding the future path.

Safety and Quality, Always on the Road

Dr. Ding Qiang, CEO of Huashan, commented on the exit meeting,

> Huashan is the first general public hospital in China's mainland to take the JCI challenge and succeeded. Under the leadership of the hospital, the number of hospitals embarking on the JCI journey has increased. The concept of healthcare quality, safety and continuous improvement has gradually embedded in people's mind. In the past decade, we have become more open-minded to the survey. We started to know how to seek our journey ahead through all these imperfections. We gradually learned how to use data to guide the quality improvement and began to think about the balance between quality and efficiency. It is JCI that helps us come back to the very essence of healthcare and lead us into the future.

China is also establishing and optimizing its own hospital management accreditation system, and is exploring the long-effective mechanism of hospital management suitable for the situation in our country. Huashan's experience in the past 10 years would definitely exert profound influence in this regard.

Case 1: Upgrade of PIVAS in ER

Located in the very center of Shanghai, Huashan Hospital does not have much space. The Emergency Room only occupies a small portion of the facility. Before 2009, there was no IV admixture service designated for ER, and all IV fluid was mixed by the ER nurses in the medication room.

PIVAS in ER

After an IV medication was prescribed by a physician, the patient needed to pay for the medication first, went to the Pharmacy to pick up the medication, gave it to the nurse in the Infusion Room, and waited for the mixing before he/she could get the IV treatment. During the process, repetitive queuing and waiting was common. If any problem was identified by a pharmacist during appropriateness review or a nurse during mixing, the patient had to find the prescribing physician for confirmation or adjustment. Such back-and-forth hurt the patient's satisfaction rate heavily. In addition, the process to allow patients to deliver the medications might cause damage to the medication and impose further risks during the care (see Figure 5.1).

In September 2009, a Pareto chart analysis was conducted to find out the causes of patient complaints against the IV infusion service in ER. The top three causes, i.e., long waiting time, wrong prescription, and back-and-forth communication, made up 80% of the complaints (see Figure 5.2).

According to the "80-20 rule," the hospital decided to solve the three top issues. After the discussion on the Quality and Safety Committee, Huashan Hospital launched the process redesign for the IV infusion in ER in 2010: (1) An independent PIVAS was established. (2) Medication delivery chain from the Pharmacy to PIVAS was designed to save the patients from picking up medication by themselves. (3) Electronic physician ordering system was adopted in the ER to facilitate appropriateness review by the pharmacists and the verification by the nurses before mixing the medication. If a problem was identified by the pharmacist or the nurse, he/she could notify the physician for confirmation and invite the patient to settle the payment again. (4) Number calling system was established. Patients are issued with a queuing number for receiving infusion and would be asked to wait for the call.

After we finished the PIVAS transformation in April 2010, the complaints against the IV Infusion Room dropped rapidly (Figures 5.2–5.5).

Second Round of IV Upgrade

In 2016, according to the latest requirements in the fifth edition of the JCI Accreditation Standards for Hospitals, we further optimized the process in the Infusion Room in ER through information technology. The original infusion flow was as follows: patient registration → waiting for number calling → consultation and IV prescription by physician → payment settlement and retrieval of medication at Pharmacy by patient → delivery of medication to the Infusion Room for mixing by patient → waiting for mixing at any seat available → mixing by nurse → calling patient name or

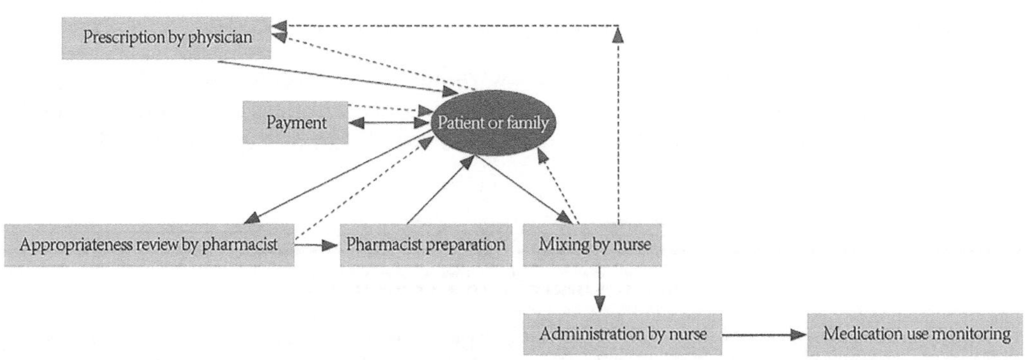

Figure 5.1 ER infusion process before ER PIVAS.

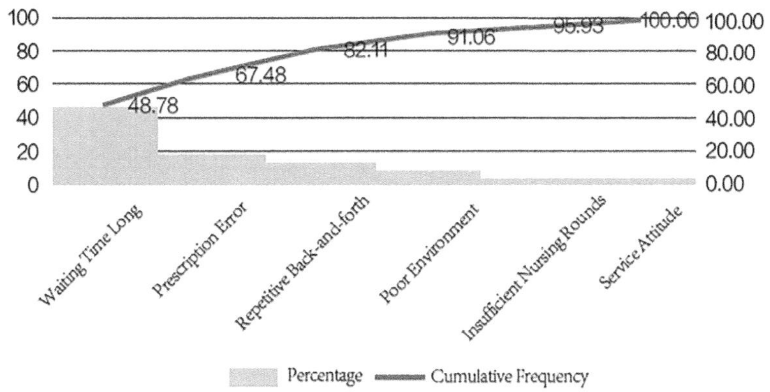

Figure 5.2 Pareto chart of patient complaints before ER PIVAS.

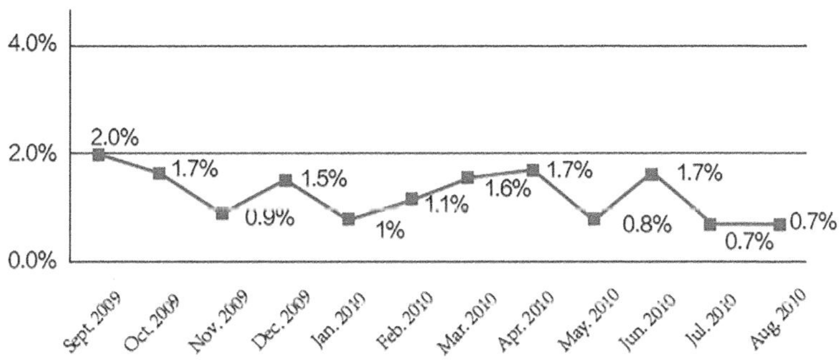

Figure 5.3 Trend of complaints against ER infusion service (September 2009–August 2010).

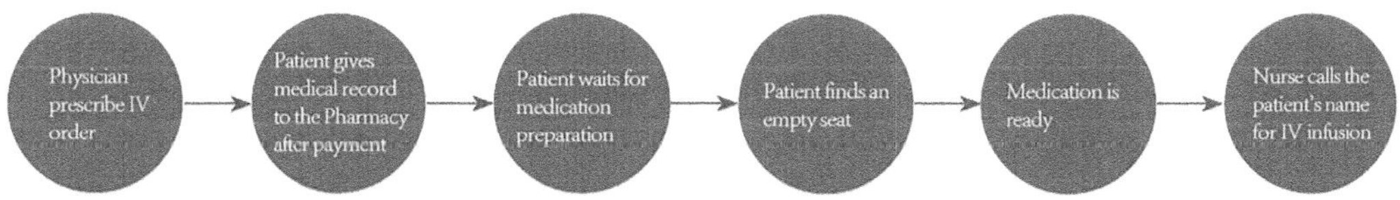

Figure 5.4 Original ER infusion flow.

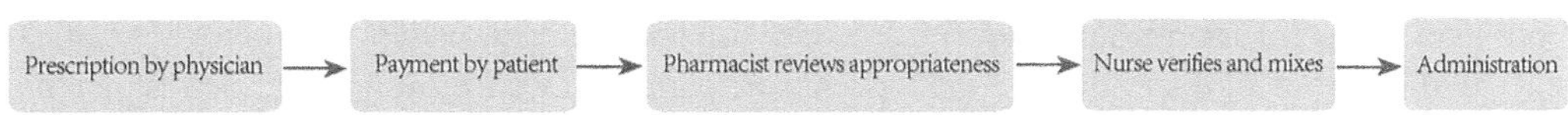

Figure 5.5 ER infusion flow after improvement.

finding patient in the infusion area → administration (if necessary, the accompanying staff seeks follow-up by physician) → completion of infusion and departure of patient from ER.

There were several risks in that process:

1. Patient had to deliver common high-risk medication (e.g., potassium chloride injection) from the Pharmacy to the Infusion Room for mixing.

2. Disputes might occur due to other patient's jumping into the queue while finding seats, which interrupted the nurses' work.
3. Medication error could occur if patients shared the same name or names with similar pronunciation.
4. Physicians often could not find the patients because of seat switches or because patients would leave their seats.
5. Patient's identity and the clinic they had seen could not be identified immediately if a patient complained discomfort due to ineffective communication between the nurses and the physicians.
6. Too many accompanying people influenced the services, making the seat utilization rather low for the patients.
7. Crowded Infusion Room caused interruption of nurses' work as many patients came up for directions and all kinds of questions.

Targeting the above-mentioned problems, the ER redesigned the process in the following five aspects.

1. From screening to triage Patients are classified and scheduled according to the criticality of their conditions based on their major complaints, vital signs, glucose, blood oxygen saturation, consciousness assessment, and pain assessment. Critical patients (Levels I and II) are sent to the ER for resuscitation via the fast track immediately without entering the regular Infusion Room flow. Other patients (Levels III–V) are asked to wait until they are called according to their queue number (priority is given to Level III patients). Data such as vital signs are made available in the HIS for physicians' access.
2. Better clinic consultation flow: The patients see the physician according to the queue number. After thorough and comprehensive assessment by the physician, patients with unstable conditions would enter the fast track, while for other patients, the physician would decide whether IV treatment is necessary based on their history, physical check-up, lab tests and examinations. If IV is required, the physician prescribes medication (including the dosage, frequency, speed, etc.), assesses the needs of enhanced observation and decides on the observation frequency in the system.
3. Number ticket for IV mixing to ensure safety: Patient goes to pay for the service after he/she finishes the consultation with the physician and hands over their medical record and patient card to the Pharmacy at which point, a barcode for IV infusion would be issued to the patient. The barcode is generated by the pharmacist by wiping the patient card, one copy for patient and the other one for the internal medication management flow. The patient then goes to the Infusion Room with the barcode which is then scanned by the nurse at the check-in desk for seat arrangement. At this point, the patient's IV infusion information is matched with the seat number. The other barcode is then dispensed by the pharmacist to the nurse together with the medications to be mixed. The nurse verifies the medication against the physician's order. For each set of medication, there would be a barcode label to be attached to the IV bag indicating the ingredients and dosage. The mixed medication is then delivered by the nurse in the mixing area to the nurse desk of the infusion area. Since the seat is already linked to the patient information in the system, the screen in the infusion area and the physician's workstation would indicate the patient's status as "Waiting for IV" if the medication is under preparation. In the new process, the medication would never be touched by the patient before administration, which further ensures the safety of medication use to the maximum.

4. IV change and real-time verification: When the nurse at the infusion area receives the mixed medication, he/she verifies the order again to make sure that the medication matches the patient's prescription. Then, the nurse uses PDA to scan the barcode to access the seat information. He/she then goes to the patient to verify the patient information and gives the IV. The nurse scans the barcode on the first set of the medication to confirm that the patient's status is "Infusion Going On." When new fluid is started, the nurse scans the barcode on the next set of medication until the entire process finishes. On the screen in the Infusion Room and the physician's workstation, patient's information is updated in real time, including the clinical units (different colors), prescribing physician, total number of IV sets, the sequence number of the current set, and the level of observation.
5. Observation for closed-loop management: For patients without special needs of observation, the nurse only needs to ask the patient's feeling at each change of IV and requires the patient back to the consultation room for follow-up after the IV finishes. For patients with special observation needs, the nurse has to conduct observation according to the physician's order to monitor on blood pressure, glucose, consciousness, etc. The physician in the Infusion Room then documents the information until the IV finishes, or the physician could add more medication or arrange observation in the hospital based on the change of conditions. When patient complains discomfort, the physician or nurse in the Infusion Room immediately contacts the prescribing physician indicated on the screen for response. Patient goes back to the consultation room for reassessment by the physician after the IV finishes. See Figure 5.6 for detailed process.

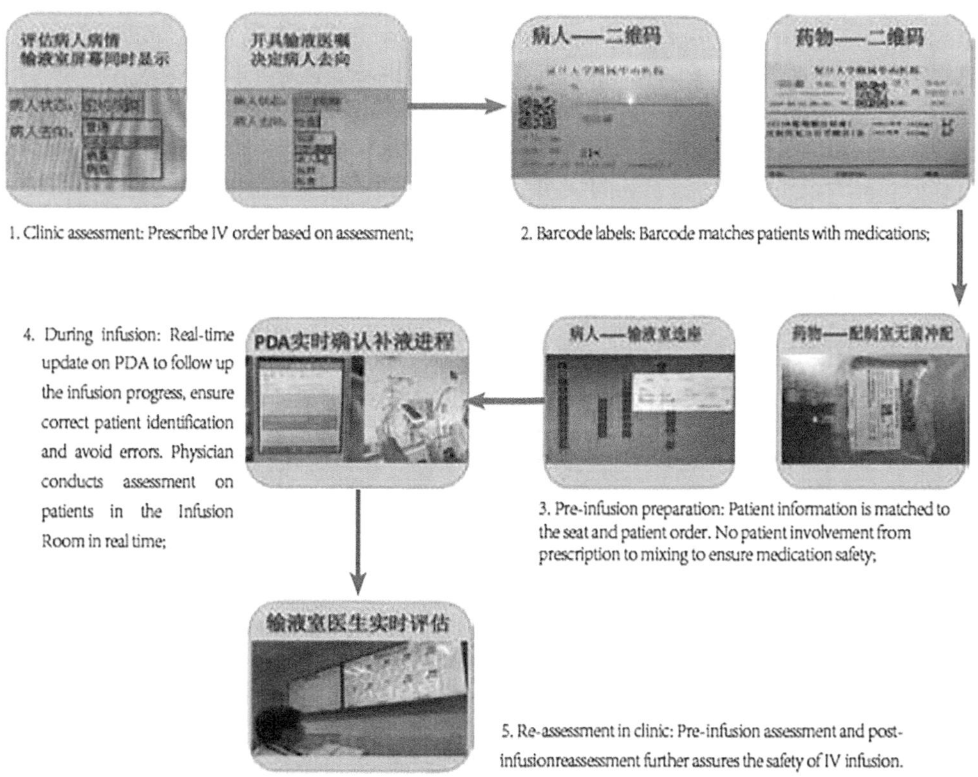

Figure 5.6 Improved ER infusion flow.

The optimized IV process in the ER supported by information technology ensures quick access of staff to the information regarding patient's consultation, condition and location, helping the healthcare staff to identify the patient correctly and better manage the medication in a safe way. During the infusion, healthcare staff could better monitor and follow up the patient's condition in real time to save more human resources. A closed loop has then completed from the triage to the final follow-up at the clinic after infusion to ensure safety and efficiency as well as to minimize potential errors.

Case 2: Make DNT Shorter

Evidence has proved that thrombolysis with intravenous rtPA is the most effective treatment for acute ischemic stroke (AIS). But less than 2% of the patients with AIS have received intravenous thrombolysis treatment. We have to increase the number of AIS patients to receive thrombolysis with intravenous rtPA within the treatment window. Due to the time sensitivity of intravenous rtPA treatment, the 2013 *AHA/ASA Guideline for Early Management of Patients with Acute Ischemic Stroke* clearly defined that the door-to-needle time (DNT) be controlled within 60 min.

Based on the improved ER processes in Huashan Hospital, what we should do was to further reduce the delay in the internal process, shorten the DNT, and comprehensively improve the intravenous thrombolysis treatment effectiveness. In addition, mechanical thrombectomy after intravenous thrombolysis for AIS patients with large vessel occlusion would significantly improve the prognosis of the patients. Therefore, to establish an effective intravascular treatment process was a pressing task of the hospital. Our goal was to transport the patients with suspected stroke to the hospital within the treatment window (4.5 h), improve the intravenous thrombolysis rate within the window (80% patients with DNT less than 60 min), and establish the clinical process for intravascular treatment so as to bring the maximum benefit to specific patients.

Targeted Solutions

From 26 June 2012, we started to provide thrombolysis with intravenous rtPA directly to patients who have no special clinical or medication history without waiting for the platelet count and coagulation results. POCT glucometers have been allocated in the ER for finger-tip test before thrombolysis. As soon as the patient is confirmed with no hyperglycemia, the thrombolysis process could be initiated. The bedside EKG on the inpatient units could save the time waiting for results before the treatment. The thrombolysis team brings the sphygmomanometer to ensure continuous blood pressure monitoring during the transportation of patients. All these actions have been taken to further reduce the delay in the internal process.

The clinical background data were collected between January and December 2014 from the cases receiving thrombolysis with intravenous rtPA for cerebral infarction in the Neurology Department. A thrombolysis team was established to provide 24/7 services. Upon the call from the ER, the thrombolysis team has to arrive at the ER within 15 min for assessment and intervention on patients with suspected stroke.

According to the Procedure for *Suspected Stroke Patient and Clinical Pathway on Emergency Intravenous Thrombolysis*, the hospital further enhanced the monthly training on the neurologists, and emphasized on the importance to call the thrombolysis team within the treatment window without waiting for the CT scan. We then began to give feedback to all physicians the data of each key step on every thrombolysis case on a quarterly basis.

Trainings have been organized for ER nurses on how to triage such patients and call the thrombolysis team. Many specific educations on triage nurses for identifying the symptoms of stroke have been delivered. If the triage nurse identifies suspected patients still within the treatment window, he/she is authorized to call the thrombolysis team immediately.

Continuous Improvement through Data Tracking

Though the mean of DNT had been controlled under 60 min since 2015 and the number under 60 min had been increased from 32% to 69%, there was still gap from the 80% target defined by AHA/ASA. To ensure the 60 min DNT for most thrombolysis patients, the following measures have also been put in place:

- The ER triage nurse assesses the patient and calls the thrombolysis team immediately when a suspected patient is identified to initiate the process.
- All cases responded by the thrombolysis team are continuously documented for monthly discussion and analysis to find out the causes of delayed treatment and to improve the thrombolysis rate.
- The intravascular treatment process has been further standardized to emphasize the time from arrival to femoral artery puncture and the time from arrival to revascularization.

Case 3: Stories Behind Two Anonymous Surveys

In the fifth edition of JCI standards, the hospital's culture of safety was included as one of the key measurable elements, requiring the hospital leadership evaluate the culture of safety regularly. Thus, we did the first questionnaire survey on the culture of safety in October 2014. Improvement actions were taken based on the results, and the effectiveness was assessed in the following year.

Two Anonymous Surveys

The questionnaire was released through the intranet of the hospital. We did two surveys to learn about our staff's opinions toward the culture of safety. The questionnaire was designed with reference to the American organization patient safety environment scale. Based on the JCI standards (fifth edition) and the hospital's reality, we included 35 items in 10 dimensions with a 3-point scoring system (1 means "disagree"; 2 means "neither disagree or agree"; 3 means sssss"agree"). The Cronbach's α coefficient for the two surveys was 0.903 and 0.892, respectively, showing good IC.

In October 2014, the first survey was completed with 938 validated responses. The second survey was done in October 2015 with 1,349 validated questionnaires collected. The two surveys covered physicians, technicians, nurses, and administrators, counting for over 50% of the hospital employees, which showed good objective representation (see Table 5.1).

The top three dimensions that received high recognition among the staff in the first survey in 2014 were continuous education and improvement, cooperation with other clinical units, and feedback summarized after adverse events (all with a score over 0.8). However, the nonpunitive reporting of adverse events, work load, and effective internal communication performed poorly, the highest one only had a score of 0.52. The hospital then took actions to facilitate effective communication and motivate staff in reporting adverse events as the two priorities of improvement (see Table 5.2).

When we further drilled down into the results in "effective internal communication," we found that 41.4% of our staff believed that "Shift change exerts problems to patient care," and 17.2% of the staff believed that there was missing patient information during the shift handover. Those were the evidence of insufficient communication during shift handovers in the hospital. On the

Table 5.1 Results of Culture of Safety Survey

	2014		*2015*	
Staff	*Number of Staff*	*Percentage*	*Number of Staff*	*Percentage*
Physicians	343	36.60	350	25.90
Technicians	88	9.40	90	6.70
Nurses	379	40.40	788	58.40
Administrators	128	13.60	121	9.00
Total	938	100.00	1,349	100.00

Table 5.2 Results of 2014 Culture of Safety Survey

Item	*Average*	*SD*
Leadership factor	0.69	0.135
Organizational learning and continuous improvement	0.89	0.133
Team work	0.87	0.116
Open communication environment	0.71	0.131
Lesson and feedback summarized after adverse events	0.81	0.152
Nonpunitive reporting of adverse events	0.36	0.143
Work load	0.46	0.135
Hospital's support in patient safety	0.73	0.157
Cooperation among different units	0.68	0.150
Effective internal communication	0.52	0.151

other hand, over 25% of the staff identified the phenomenon of "not my business" during patient transfer, which indicated that the roles of different units were poorly defined (see Table 5.3).

Result Analysis and Implementation of Policies

The fifth edition of JCI standards requires that the hospital develops and implements patient handover procedure. In Huashan, quality improvement projects were implemented for shift handover and inter-unit patient transfer, including formulating new policies, designing new work flows, adopting standard tools and templates, and monitoring the implementation.

Specific measures regarding shift handover included (1) update of the Policy on Duty and Shift Handover, (2) standardization of shift handover procedure, (3) identification of roles involved in handover, and (4) standardization of the information exchanged during shift handover. Specific measures to improve patient transportation included formulation of the *Policy on Inter-Unit Patient Transfer*, adoption of patient transfer form for critical patients (see Table 5.4), identification

Table 5.3 Survey Results on Effective Internal Communication

Item	*Percentage of "Agree"*
When a patient is transferred from one unit to another, the problem of "nobody's business" would occur.	25.8
Important patient information is often missing during shift handover.	17.2
Unsatisfactory information exchanges among different departments.	6.6
Shift change exerts problems to patient care.	41.4

of responsibilities of staff involved in the transfer on the transfer template, and automatic reminder in the EMR system.

In the second survey in October 2015 after the new procedures had been put in place, staff's perception on "effective internal communication" was improved (see Table 5.5).

However, soon, staff found out that communication efficiency became the new bottleneck. Thus, efforts were focused on sharing handover information among different processes to reduce repetitive communication and to improve the efficiency within and among units. The regular survey on culture of safety is the guidance and effectiveness evaluation on the quality projects. It is also an important tool for us to enhance the staff's awareness on patient safety through adopting effective measures to further assure an environment of safety.

Table 5.4 Handover List

Scenario	*Accompanying Staff*	*Responsible Staff*	*Handover Sheet*
Critical patients	Responsible physician	Responsible physician–responsible physician	New SBAR sheet
ER to ward	Physician, nurse, and worker	Responsible physician–responsible physician	Special handover sheet
ER to OR	Responsible physician	Responsible physician–anesthesiologist	Special handover sheet
Ward to ICU	Responsible physician	Responsible physician–ICU physician	SBAR sheet+unit transfer document
ICU to ward	ICU nurse	ICU nurse–ward nurse	Special handover sheet
Ward to OR	Ward nurse	Ward nurse–OR nurse	Special handover sheet
OR to ward	Responsible physician	Responsible physician–ward nurse	Special handover sheet
OR to PACU	Anesthesiologist	Anesthesiologist PACU nurse	Special handover sheet (anesthesia)
PACU to ward	Anesthesiologist	Anesthesiologist ward nurse	Special handover sheet

Table 5.5 Results of 2015 Culture of Safety Survey

Item	*Average*	*Variation*	*SD*
Leadership factor	0.69	0.00	0.134
Organizational learning and continuous improvement	0.89	0.00	0.133
Team work	0.87	0.00	0.118
Open communication environment	0.71	0.00	0.128
Lesson and feedback summarized after adverse events	0.81	0.00	0.151
Nonpunitive report of adverse events	0.41	0.06	0.154
Work load	0.46	0.00	0.132
Hospital's support in patient safety	0.72	−0.01	0.155
Cooperation among different units	0.69	0.02	0.137
Effective communication	0.59	0.06	0.133

Case 4: Evolution of Labeling of Medical Waste

JCI requires hospitals properly dispose the medical waste to reduce infection risks. During the process, the hospital needs to develop and implement proper labels to identify hazardous materials and waste. The *Regulation on Medical Waste Management of Shanghai Municipality* also defines in Article 17 and Article 20, respectively, that "medical waste is packed and sealed with specially designed bags, identified with Chinese labels indicating the department/unit, date, category and other information." "The staff responsible for transporting the medical waste checks each one of the medical waste bags and sharp containers for the availability of the Chinese labels and the compliance of the information on the label with applicable regulations." During the survey in 2013, the hospital did not perform well with regard to this standard.

Thus, in the following 2 years, we started from the policy review and the formulation of new plans through our own analysis on the hospital process to further standardize the labeling of the medical waste to ensure that all information regarding the category, department/unit, weight, and time could be tracked and to reduce the infection risks through proper storage.

A Two-Pronged Approach

First, special trainings were organized to enhance the staff's awareness on proper labeling of the waste, in particular the attention from the responsible departments.

After the JCI survey, we started to enhance the training on the waste collection staff as well as the staff in all units and laboratories.

In the past, the waste from all units and wards was sent to the sewage station. However, the staff at the sewage station never checked the labeling and did not pay much attention to the quantity and registration. Thus, the administrative departments also set higher requirements on the responsible departments to conduct random check on the labeling of the medical waste. Furthermore, they are now also responsible for identifying insufficient or substandard labeling and making rectification during the collection, sealing, and weighing process.

Data Analysis for Timely Improvement

In 2014, the random check on waste labeling at the sewage station was extended to the wards. One hundred bags of medical waste were randomly checked every month to find the reasons of substandard practice of waste handling including sealing and weighing. Improvement actions would then be implemented accordingly.

The labeling was improved, but not constantly. The overall performance did not meet the expectation. After the analysis, the following measures were taken: enhanced staff training; and random check on labeling to analyze the causes of substandard handling (see Table 5.6). We also changed the indicator from proper labeling of the waste to proper information on the labels. After rounds of improvement efforts, we had achieved significant progress in 2016. The standard labeling rate had been increasing for consecutive 4 years from 81% in 2013 to 98% in 2016 (Table 5.7).

It seems an easy job to label the medical waste, but it is an indispensable part of staff's daily work flow. Routine checks are performed to sample the practices and collect data for analysis.

Table 5.6 Causes of Substandard Labeling

	2013	*2014*	*2015*	*2016*
No seal or insufficient seal		19	17	6
No label	112	6	5	2
Insufficient information on labels		87	57	11
Total	112	115	79	19

Table 5.7 Standard Labeling Rate

	2013 (%)	*2014 (%)*	*2015 (%)*	*2016 (%)*
January	–	93	94	98
February	–	85	87	98
March	–	88	93	98
April	–	92	94	99
May	–	91	94	98
June	–	91	93	98
July	60	92	94	98
August	71	92	96	98
September	90	94	95	98
October	78	87	90	98
November	91	89	95	99
December	98	91	96	99
Annul average	81	90	93	98

Staff training has also been proven to be an effective way to standardize the labeling on medical waste, which could be further enhanced through routine check and performance evaluation on the staff involved, such as the transport worker and the managers. To standardize the sample statistics and the documentation of the raw data could also facilitate the quality improvement tracking and monitoring.

Chapter 6

People's Hospital of Liaoning Province

Bai Xizhuang, Feng Shuting, Liu Hongyang,
Ji Xianfeng, and Li Min
People's Hospital of Liaoning Province

Bai Xizhuang *is President and Secretary of Party Committee of the People's Hospital of Liaoning Province, Expert who enjoys State Council Special Allowance, National Second-Level Professor, Chief Physician, Adviser to PhD candidates, Hospital Management Expert, and graduated from China Medical University. He was awarded the titles of "Famous Doctors of Liaoning Province," "National Advanced Worker of National Healthy System," "Young-Middle Aged Expert who made outstanding contribution in National Healthy and Family Planning," "Outstanding Technical Worker of Liaoning Province." He is also deputy president of Liaoning Medical Association, committee chairman of Liaoning Medical Association's Sports Medical Branch, Director-designate of Liaoning Hospital Association's Quality Management Branch. He was also awarded the first prize, the second prize, and the third prize of Science and Technology Progress Award, two national invention patents. He also undertook three National Nature Science Foundation Projects and five provincial research projects.*

Feng Shuting *is the Director of Medical Affairs Department and JCI Accreditation Office of the People's Hospital of Liaoning Province, and President of the People's Hospital of Liaozhong District. She studied in Vivantes Klinikum Neukölln in Germany as a visiting doctor in 2017. She won the first Liaoning provincial Chinese Youth Medal and gain title of Liaoning provincial Woman Pacesetter.*

Liu Hongyang *is the Director of President's Executive Office and Medical Reform Office of the People's Hospital of Liaoning Province. She graduated from Liaoning University with a bachelor's degree in biology and graduated from Northeast University with a master's degree in public administration. She is a chief technologist and has been successively engaged in human resource management, hospital administration management, JCI accreditation, and medical reform.*

Hospital Introduction: The People's Hospital of Liaoning Province (northeast China, hereinafter referred to as PHLP), also known as the Red Cross Hospital of Liaoning Province, is a comprehensive tertiary hospital under the direct supervision of Liaoning Provincial Health and Family Planning Commission that provides clinical care, research, education, emergency care, rehabilitation, and wellness care for this province. Located in Shenyang, the capital and geographic center of Liaoning Province, the hospital is a regional medical center.

Established in February 1949, it was named as "Worker's Hospital for Northeast China," the first of its kind in the country. It was moved to Tieling city, about 47 miles from Shenyang, under the national program of "moving healthcare resources to underdeveloped areas" and renamed as "People's Hospital of Tieling Special Area" in 1969. In 1978, it was relocated to Shenyang and has stayed on that location since then.

International Accreditation: JCI accreditation in June 2017.

Contents

Preface

The Rise of PHLP

Overview

When we have a goal for our future,
For which we will even have to pay,
We will always feel cheerful and gay
Just as moths, while flying to the light of fire,
Would rather be the prisoners of raging flames.
With the beautiful tassels whirling in the air,
We are marching forward with non-stop paces.
During the journey of seeking our goal,
Whether it is bitter or sweet,
We will constantly strive to achieve it
Without any regret in the least.
If we could not win, we would rather lose to seeking;
When we get married, we would rather "marry" happiness.

(A verse titled *"Marrying" Happiness* translated by Jiang Longguo and published in the poet anthology *Top Modern Chinese Poems—Wang Guozhen's 80 Poems in English Verse*. Wang Guozhen is a late Chinese poet born in the 20th century.)

This verse is a favorite of Mr. Bai Xizhuang, CEO of the hospital. It has been used to encourage the entire staff throughout the preparation for JCI accreditation in PHLP. On June 30, 2017, happiness was seen on everyone's face as Ken, a JCI surveyor, announced that PHLP has been recommended as a JCI-accredited hospital, which marks the first JCI hospital in northeast China.

JCI accreditation was listed at the top of the strategic goals of PHLP during the Thirteenth Five-Year Period (2016–2020). The preparation for JCI accreditation started on December 8, 2015 and lasted till June 26, 2017 when the survey kicked off. The enthusiasm and motivation of 3,000 some staff members throughout the organization had been sustained by the "goal" and the "seeking." The 500 days and nights were filled with touching montages of us going all out for our goal and memorable moments of us striving for the seeking. That is how our unique story of JCI accreditation came into being.

A Historic Decision

Let's turn the clock back to 2015 in late spring and early summer.

The year of 2015 was destined to be a turning point in the course of PHLP's development. It witnessed a new building rising straight from the ground, upgrading of equipment as well as facilities and the successful handover of administrative power from the outgoing to the upcoming leadership. More importantly, nevertheless, it was in this year that PHLP started a new journey toward novelty and transformation by making the decision to go for JCI accreditation.

In June 2015, Mr. Bai Xizhuang, having worked in the First Hospital of China Medical University, took over the Secretary of Party Committee of PHLP, and then CEO later in August. Bai Xizhuang, a pioneer in sports medicine and joint surgery and a renowned surgeon-turned

CEO, said that he is confident and determined to turn our hospital into a top one in Liaoning Province, northeast China and even the entire country, working with all the colleagues of PHLP. His motto has been that "No roads are longer than the feet; no mountains are higher than human beings" (from Wang Guozhen's verse of *High Mountains and Long Road*, translated by Jiang Longguo and published in the poet anthology *Top Modern Chinese Poems—Wang Guozhen's 80 Poems in English Verse*).

Unlike some new officials who startle the world by applying strict measures, Mr. Bai started with establishing the culture of the hospital, something that moistens everything, silent, and soft. He knows it well that the culture of a hospital has a profound influence on the value as well as the awareness and action of serving people among all the staff, and the business strategies of the hospital. What do we care about? What behavior do we encourage? What are our values? He had many rounds of discussion with administrators and staff members, and we concluded that our mission is "to serve people's health whole-heartedly," our organizational spirit is "benevolence, dedication, professionalism and shouldering responsibilities," and our vision is "to become the hospital of choice among patients where staff enjoy their career."

Compared with university hospitals, PHLP is neither a competitive player nor leader in the healthcare sector. Professional education and development of academic strength are the key to the sustainable growth of a hospital as well as a long-term and arduous task for us though. Mr. Bai Xizhuang has been mulling over questions like how to seize opportunities to draw and train professionals as well as creating good environment for academic research, how to maximize the value of healthcare professionals, and how to achieve phenomenal progress on all aspects from physical environment to inner strength. It has been clear in his mind that the time when healthcare organizations are eager to expand volume and become "massive and all-inclusive hospital like an aircraft carrier" has gone. Rather, the strategic goals for hospital become high quality, cost-efficient, and driven by delicacy management.

With the mission and purpose of our hospital, which is to serve people's health whole-heartedly, we found an echo in JCI standards, an internationally recognized gold standard for hospital management that regards continuous improvement and patient safety as its core purpose.

Back in 2015, there was no JCI-accredited hospital in northeast China. If we could grasp this new opportunity and become the first JCI-accredited organization in northeast China, we will stand shoulder to shoulder with other major hospitals in Liaoning Province with our adoption of international standards and first-rate management. We will become one of the top hospitals with higher reliability of quality and safety which patients have more belief in.

Therefore, Mr. Bai Xizhuang and other leadership members described our target as: to become a first-rate hospital in China managed with modern philosophy by adopting the best technical standards and providing the best quality and safety. It was later expanded to the Five-Strategy Planning of the thirteenth Five-Year Period: (1) to become a hospital managed with modern philosophy by going for JCI accreditation, (2) to achieve the upgrade of IT adoption in the nearest possible future, (3) to establish a "five-in-one" structure for emergency care and response, (4) to implement the "ten-a hundred-a thousand" expert recruitment program, and (5) to develop subjects relevant to the "four beams and eight pillars" structure of healthcare reform.*

By then, JCI accreditation had been listed as the first of the five strategic plans of PHLP. According to the schedule we developed, the survey might be expected in June 2017.

---

* The four beams are public health service system, medical care system, health insurance and essential drugs, and the eight pillars are management, operation, investment, pricing, regulation, personnel, IT adoption, and legal system.

A Morning Spent with a Cup of Coffee

On December 8, 2015, the JCI Accreditation Office of PHLP was established, marking the initiation of preparation for JCI accreditation.

The entire staff started to wonder how to interpret standards and how to get things done. In many training sessions, whether taking place outside or inside our hospital (when we invited external experts to speak), we got to know a name—Jilan Liu, Principal & JCI Consulting Director, Greater China. On December 12, 2015, Ms. Liu moderated the HIMSS Greater China annual conference in Tianjin as HIMSS Vice President & Chief Executive, Greater China at HIMSS. Mr. Bai Xizhuang was also invited to the event.

Recalling the moment when he got to meet Ms. Liu, Mr. Bai said:

> The first time that I met Ms. Liu was in a morning during that conference. I stayed in the cafeteria for breakfast from 8 o'clock to over 11 o'clock with just a cup of coffee. It was the longest breakfast that I had ever had in my life. I kept listening to Ms. Liu the whole morning, trying to understand JCI from her. She explained JCI's core purpose, intent, standards and methodologies in great detail. We were like old friends from the start.

On December 16, 2015, Ms. Jilan Liu came to PHLP for assessment and consultation at the invitation of Mr. Bai Xizhuang to get a general picture of the hospital and see what efforts we need to spend in preparing for JCI accreditation. Ms. Liu provided training to the intermediate leaders by laying out the line of JCI philosophies. From that training, we got a picture of how a first-rate hospital in China managed with modern philosophy would be like. It reaffirmed our resolution to seek further growth of the hospital by dashing toward JCI accreditation. Deeply touched by our enthusiasm and passion, Ms. Liu said:

> If we hold the same aspiration and undertaking and stay together on the journey of JCI standards, that means we cherish the same ideals and follow the same path. I have a yearning desire to exchange thoughts and communicate with people and push forward JCI accreditation as a great cause. It would be a meaningful experience for me to help you on your journey towards JCI accreditation.

That day, Ms. Liu joined PHLP staff in singing *The Red Army Is Not Afraid of the Expedition's Difficulties*, a famous song that lifted the army's morale during the national war in the 1930s.

Propagate the Doctrine, Impart Professional Knowledge, and Resolve Doubts

Everyone in PHLP regards Ms. Liu as our teacher, because she not only masters the precise connotation of JCI standards but also, and more importantly, has spread the JCI philosophies and methods to prepare for accreditation throughout the organization. She led her team and came to provide consultation of JCI standards for four times, when they propagated the philosophies, impart techniques, and resolve our confusion. These consultants walked to every part of the hospital and got the true picture of our hospital through activities like leadership interview, document review, on-site evaluation, patient tracing, facility tours, and sit-down sessions. They went through all the elements in the JCI standards and developed an action plan for the pending tasks with us at the end. Although they just stayed here for a few days, their witty remarks are still resounding. For example, "You will see the problem if you are wearing the JCI glasses." "Everyone of us has two jobs. One is our own job, and the other is to improve the first job." "To identify problems and solve them, you do not need a new department, but you need to get everyone involved in a department."

Prior to the actual survey, she had cared so much about us that she came to PHLP again. That time, she highlighted the solutions to the unresolved issues from the mock survey, took questions from us about the standards by chapter, action plan for the next step and heads-ups for the final survey process. This era is defined by the aspiration to success. We have been longing for success as much as we do for breathing. So how could we succeed? In addition to a proper aim, decision making, and actions, it takes an ideal partner and platform. That is the correct approach to any undertaking.

Develop Ourselves in PHLP

If an egg is broken by outside force, feeding begins. If broken by inside force, life begins. It is true for a hospital as well. If broken by outside force, pressure prevails; if broken by inside force, growth begins. If one waits to be broken by outside force, it is doomed to become food; if one breaks its shell from the inside, that type of growth is regeneration.

In PHLP, we abound with the courage to transform and the determination to regenerate.

The JCI standards center on quality, safety, and the awareness of serving people. Their intention lies in regarding patients as the center of whatever is done and continuous quality improvement. The approach they take toward quality features "whole-process, all-dimensional, full-crew involvement and sustainability." Specifically, they cover not only medical care, nursing, and infection control, but also how patient safety is related to facilities, equipment, general support, fire safety, and supply management. The proper mechanism to improve work for JCI standard compliance is looking into problems specifically, highlighting cause analysis and finding systemic errors. In terms of culture of safety, JCI encourages a non-punitive environment. These new philosophies have stimulated endogenous vigor for improving our culture.

After having worked toward the goal for a year and a half, we perceived changes in PHLP: staff care more about patients, become more aware of serving people and pay more attention to safety and quality; and the hospital becomes more reputable among patients and becomes the cleanest hospital in northeast China. These changes were sort of unbelievable to us because they happened so fast.

Kent Seltman, an expert of management in Mayo Clinic of the U.S., visited our hospital and complimented while giving us a thumb up: "If I were to receive surgery, I would come here."

"This is the cleanest hospital that I have ever been working in. I love to work here" said a maternity matron in the obstetrics ward.

"I take a walk in the square and enjoy piano music in the outpatient hall every day. I become attached to this organization," said an inpatient.

Through striving for JCI accreditation, the overall strength of the hospital has been improved remarkably. First of all, it has become increasingly competitive with strong commitment to quality and patient safety, higher academic capability in clinical disciplines, better compliance to practice standards, rigorous approach to care, and greater reputation among patients. Second, staff become more cohesive as they get to see the potential, goal and future prospects of the hospital, and become better able to perform their function according to the better-defined job expectation and mutual support and collaboration. Third, as our reputation grows, the hospital receives more and more interests on and recognition of its development and transformation.

In truth, it is not that easy to change a large comprehensive hospital. What are the drivers for the rapid changes happening in PHLP? First and foremost, the leadership has carried forward the approach of "being problem-based, target-oriented and outcome-directed." A problem-based perspective allows us to identify gaps, a target-oriented outlook enables us to solve problem, and outcome-directed attitude brings our attention to change. This approach has helped us transform management style from being rough and general to being detail-oriented.

Case 1: Take Picture Whenever You See a Problem

Introduction

The "Take picture whenever you see a problem" initiative is short for "You find it, I corrected it. To show your love of PHLP, take a picture whenever you see a problem," a campaign initiated by Mr. Bai on the tenth day of his office, i.e., August 13, 2015, and conducted by the Executive Office.

It was a time when China was seeing the exponential growth of Internet application and welcoming the era of "Internet+." Many hospital administrators could not help thinking how to improve management with IT adoption. That year, PHLP provided a smart phone for every staff, and Wechat, a most popular Chinese mobile APP of multipurpose social media, became a favorite channel for communication among the staff. Amid the social trend of "no one is living without Wechat," PHLP turned to Wechat and initiated an official account named "Take picture whenever you see a problem" with two intentions: first, to encourage communication by providing an effective channel, and second, to identify gaps to improve. That was how "You find it, I corrected it" originated. During her initial visit to PHLP, Ms. Liu thought highly of the approach of "Take picture whenever you see a problem" initiative and regarded it as the foundation for PHLP to identify, acknowledge and correct problems as well as create a culture of safety and a broader perspective for quality; an excellent example of seeking truth from facts and always counting on the input from frontline staff; and as a means that reflects the major government and Party policies as well as the essence of JCI philosophies. Since then, the growth and application of "Take picture whenever you see a problem" has been pushed to a new height as we proceeded in the preparation for JCI accreditation.

You Find It, I Correct It

Established with the principle of "sharing for patients, colleagues and the hospital" and the intent of "engaging every one," the official Wechat account of "Take picture whenever you see a problem" became an instant eye-catcher among the entire staff since the beginning, in particular since the initiation of JCI preparation. This new and easy form of operation has stimulated the passion and zeal of staff to contribute since all that they need to do to send and see pictures is to follow the official account on the Wechat, which takes only a few taps on the smart phone. It serves as a channel for staff to provide insight.

Again, "Take picture whenever you see a problem" is a problem-based tool, where the more followers, the more problems we can see as administrators, and the more problems that we could work on. The better it operates, the safer and more orderly function we will have in the organization. By doing so, hospital administration, in particular healthcare safety, is no longer the exclusive duty of the leadership and administrative departments. It has become a task that everyone from any level or aspect of the pyramid structure of management can contribute.

The process of "Take picture whenever you see a problem," from "You find it" to "I correct it," is mapped out in Figure 6.1:

Step 1: report a problem. At seeing something unsafe, incorrect or inappropriate, staff takes a picture and sends it to the official account on Wechat and leaves a comment.

Step 2: collect problems. A manager for the official account from the Hospital Affairs Office gathers the pictures received every day and develops a presentation to show in the morning huddle the next day, when the leadership and intermediate leaders of administrative departments discuss and analyze the problems, and propose comments and measures to take.

Step 3: assign problems. The leadership designates a department, or several of them together, to handle a particular problem.

Step 4: solve problems. The departments assigned with the task of taking action to solve it, take pictures of the final result, send them to the official account on Wechat and report that resolution during the morning huddle.

Step 5: provide update. The manager of the official account updates the staff who reported that problem with the resolution. If the problem is not promptly corrected or forgotten, the Hospital Affairs Office sends out a reminder to the responsible department or replays the picture during morning huddle to remind relevant departments to take proper actions.

In essence, the "Take picture whenever you see a problem" means it is a self-repeating PDCA cycle (see Figure 6.1), through which problems are resolved one by one. It has helped with the continuous improvement of the organization as a whole and pushed the hospital forward along a path of spiral development.

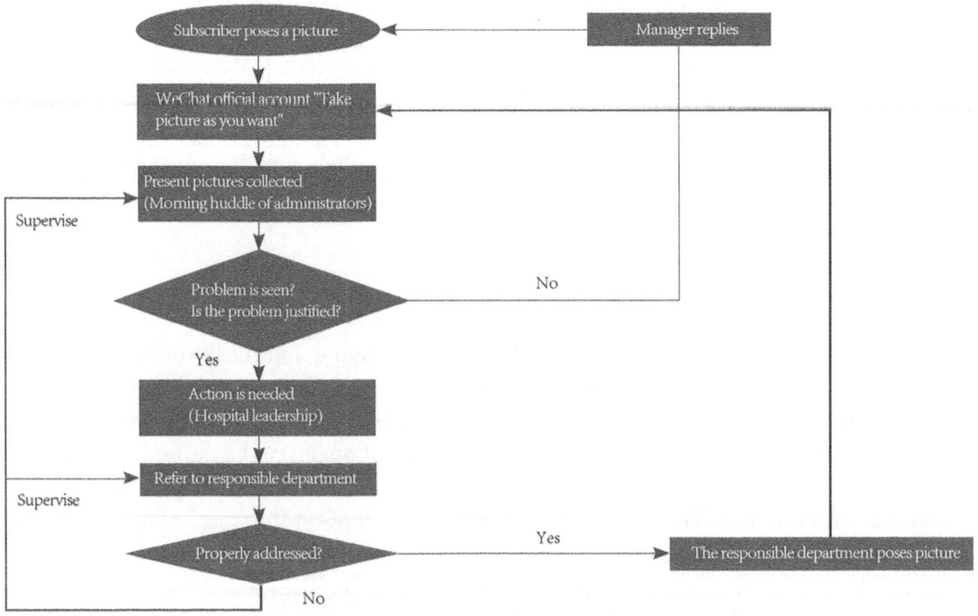

Figure 6.1 The process of "Take picture whenever you see a problem" initiative.

Qualitative Transformation Driven by Every Small Bit of Problem

On August 14, 2015, the official account received its first picture since operation. It was from Mr. Bai, CEO, who commented that the door was not properly closed on the equipment room of the mezzanine of the building. Shortly later, the Infrastructure Office worked together with General Support Center to lock all the doors to equipment rooms.

On October 25, 2015, a picture from an intermediate-level manager indicated that a part of the corridor handrail in the ward came off because of insufficient fixation (two fixation points only) and it had caused patient injury from fall. Later on, another two fixation points were added. This picture and the story were well-received when Mr. Bai presented it in the conference hosted by Mayo Clinic.

On December 15, 2015, a picture from staff showed that the doorsill between the corridor and ward was so high that it was a fall risk. Later on, plastic padding was placed on all the doorsills throughout the hospital that reduced fall risk and allowed easy access of stretcher and wheelchair.

On March 22, 2016, a picture from staff showed that the patient census sheet was just sitting on the nurse station in a ward, creating risk to patient privacy. Later on, we made an organizational change of putting it in a binder instead. When one needs it, he or she opens the binder and closes it when done to protect patient privacy.

From March 31 to November 17, 2016, staff sent in four pictures about problems with wristbands. It was changed five times, from being hand written to printout, from a hard one to a soft one. A special version for surgical patient was tried at one time. And it was finalized as the durable version that we are currently using.

September 29, 2016, a staff from a ward sent in a picture that showed short circuit occurred to the electricity panel in the ward. With this, all the electric circuits were checked, sorted out, and labeled throughout the organization to ensure safety.

On November 30 and December 8, respectively, 2016, one staff member from Laboratory sent pictures to comment on the inappropriate procedure of finger sticking children for lab work and we should correct it by adopting an evidence-based practice. This staff was granted award during the annual honor awarding ceremony thanks to his persistence in getting it right.

On December 15, 2016, several staff members sent in pictures to complain of the lack of parking space in the basement parking lot for staff because some vehicles had been there for a long time without being used apparently and some vehicles not from staff were parked here during the night. With this complaint, the Security Dept. immediately started out by developing a census of vehicles to remove those not driven in by staff. Later on, the Security Dept. worked together with Discipline Inspection Office and Human Resource Dept. to check vehicles registered under a different name from the owners. Since then, there has been more than enough space for staff to park vehicles in the staff parking lot.

On December 22, 2016, a photo from a family member of patient came in with a comment that there was no signage on the door to MR room that reads "Do not bring in lighter." Then, Radiology Dept. immediately added that signage.

On March 13, 2017, a security petrol staff reported that a bicycle of a staff member was lost. Security cameras were installed in that location immediately.

On March 30, 2017, a staff member sent in picture and described that when the paint came off from a bedside stand in patient rooms, we do not have to buy a new one. Instead, we can just repaint it. That would save cost for the hospital. This suggestion was readily taken.

Since Mr. Bai sent in the first picture and by the time this article was written, 6,371 pictures had been collected via the official account, which involved 2,414 problems. Among these

Table 6.1 Summary of the Percentage of Issues Reported via Official Account that Have Been Resolved

Time Frame	*No. of Photos Received*	*No. of Problems Involved*	*No. of Problems Resolved*	*Percentage*
Aug–Dec 2015	1,025	528	375	71
Jan–Dec 2016	3,588	1,300	1,007	77
Jan–May 2017	1,758	586	543	92.7

problems, 1,925 or 80% were resolved. In 2017, further efforts were made to push the resolution of problems reported. This "Look back on photos" campaign promoted the resolution of pending issues (see Table 6.1).

Within less than 2 years, the "Take picture whenever you see a problem" channel drove the immeasurable changes in PHLP. Heinrich's Law has long been held as a classical philosophy in management. It reveals that for every accident that has caused a major injury, there must have been 29 accidents that cause minor injuries, 300 accidents that cause no injuries and 1,000 signs for the accident. In other words, any accident is triggered by the build-up of a lot of minor safety faults, and any uncontained safety fault may lead to an accident. A miss is as good as a mile.

Among all the problems reported to "Take picture whenever you see a problem," general support and facility issues accounted for 51%, the highest of all. It was followed by problems of clinical care that accounted for 17%, IT issues 10%, signage issue 6%, and fire safety, medical equipment and infection control made up 4%, respectively (see Figure 6.2). At the beginning of the operation, most problems reported were facility problem, when we dubbed it "version 1.0." Later when there were more and more clinical problems, it was upgraded as "version 2.0." Nowadays, some patients upload their experience to the official account, when it enters the phase of "version 3.0." In addition to the typical format of picture, we also see more and more video clips.

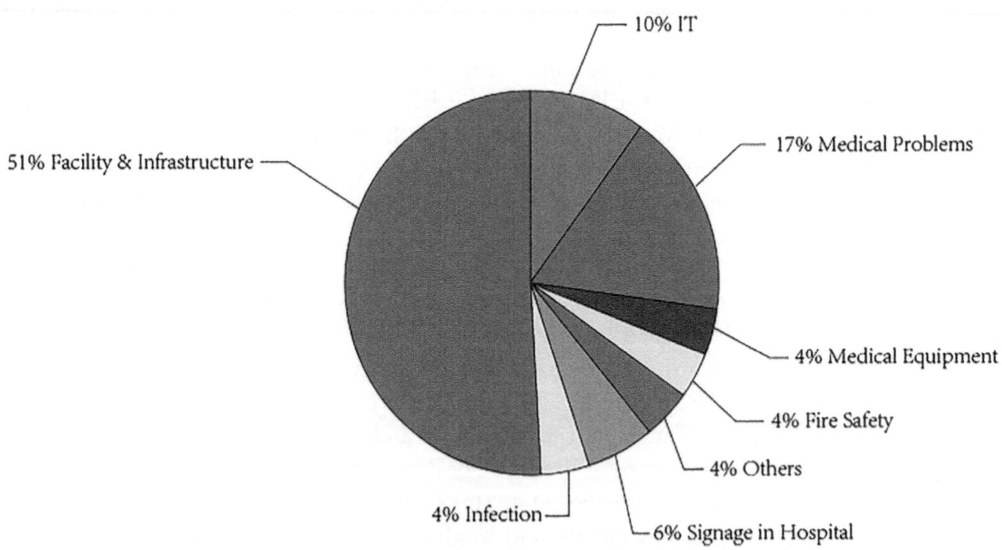

Figure 6.2 Breakdown of problems posed from "Take picture as you want."

The significant role that "Take picture whenever you see a problem" initiative has played in the improvement of our hospital is attributable to the following three aspects:

First and most important is efficiency. In terms of the process of handling, the problems reported to the official account were presented in the morning huddle of leadership members and other administrators, when Mr. Bai presides over the meeting in person. The problems presented received significant attention from relevant administrative departments, which facilitates the immediate action, evidenced by the picture of the outcome. If it is a difficult problem to solve, the leadership members present in the huddle to promote multi-departmental effort for resolution. This form of discussion tears down the barrier among different departments and increases the efficiency of action.

Second, user confidentiality is guaranteed. When one sends a picture to the official account, his or her Wechat user name is displayed, which the user can change anytime at will. So, people do not have concern when reporting problems.

Third, there has been an incentive mechanism. As it encourages staff to point out problems and speak up suggestion whenever they feel like to, the hospital grants award every year to staff who contributed problems that have led to valuable and significant progress in the hospital.

This function has enhanced staff's sense of being "master of the house" and has served as a good channel when staff wants to voice their concern and suggestion. On the other hand, the administrators have become better able to address problems since the operation of this channel by learning to see through the surface to perceive the essence, adopting system thinking and addressing problems with system-based approach, instead of limiting thinking to a specific problem only. They have learned the way to approach problems, analyze causes, develop actions and utilize modern tools of management such as FMEA, RCA, and PDCA.

The "Take picture whenever you see a problem" initiative features a problem-based approach and encourages staff to set long-term targets, start with minor tasks at hand and take action swiftly. In this aspect, it is in line with standard-driven and detail-oriented management of modern hospitals.

"Take Picture Whenever You See a Problem" Has Enabled the All-Round Progress of Quality and Safety

Nowadays, "Take picture whenever you see a problem" has become a part of the life of PHLP staff. Questions like "Have you taken any pictures today?" have even become popular in starting a small talk during break time.

"Take picture whenever you see a problem" does not involve any criteria for subscribers. It is open to hospital staff, staff from contractors, patients, and their families and even the general public. It reflects the inclusiveness of our quality program that values everyone's contribution. The fact that staff, patients and their families are pointing out gaps indicates the risk containment network has covered the entire patient care process from the time when a patient enters the gate to the time when he or she leaves. People can report problems of any process, step, staff or unnoticeable detail any time through "Take picture whenever you see a problem."

Under the holistic view proposed by the inclusive quality program encouraged by JCI, in addition to clinical care, nursing and infection control, quality management should also include facility, equipment, fire safety, emergency response, and hazardous materials. An inclusive quality program looks into not only technical quality but also service quality. This has been reflected from "Take picture whenever you see a problem" because the problems gathered represent all the aspects in a hospital. It even helps us collect staff complaint or concern. Whatever problem posed will be met with resolution.

"Take picture whenever you see a problem" has helped us fix a thousand problems a year, which signifies quality improvement, continuous progress, and PDCA cycle. As a signature management tool of PHLP, it has played a big role in establishing an inclusive outlook on quality.

It was "Take picture whenever you see a problem" that had administrative departments frankly acknowledged problems. At the beginning, it was hard to promote the initiative indeed. From convention, it is difficult to have directors of administrative departments acknowledge problems in face of so many colleagues. But with time, as pictures before and after change had been made were presented, everyone became used to this approach and joined with action. When seeing problems of their own departments from the morning huddles, directors of administrative departments swiftly take action and "cross off the item" by reporting the change that followed. Some administrators even pose problems of their own department, a signal that staff have come to readily acknowledge defects.

At the end of the day, improvement is the purpose of and what we want from "Take picture whenever you see a problem." Since its initiation, more than 2,000 problems have been fixed, and a couple of problems are being solved every day. A problem-based perspective allows us to identify gaps, a target-oriented outlook enables us to solve problem, and outcome-directed attitude brings our attention to change. The culture of continuous improvement has taken shape in the organization.

To us, the culture of safety means a shared value and attitude throughout the organization that prioritize safety. More than merely being a tool or form of management, the "Take picture whenever you see a problem" initiative guides the attention to a safety culture and develops the concept of "safety is a responsibility for all." This program turns the big concept of safety into every small and feasible action so that every one learns to pay attention to safety and participate in safety action. Every staff has come to guarantee safety whenever and wherever.

Case 2: The Regenesis of ER

Introduction

Starting from a single treatment room, the Emergency Room (ER) of PHLP was opened in 1986 and has developed into a service covering 8,610 square feet. In 2015, the new and modern OPD and Surgery Building (building #1, Figure 6.3) was put into service, which covers an area of over 1,000 square feet. However, ER was still in building #9 (see Figure 6.3), a location for clinical services other than the key ones, such as oncology and rehabilitation. Though being in a cramped area with old and broken facilities and equipment, ER had gone through trials and hardships over 30 years and was still accepting a large amount of ER patients.

By the end of 2015, the hospital decided to renovate the ER and the plan had been ready. During JCI baseline survey in February 2016, the consultants recommended to move ER to the new OPD and Surgery Building, which is a common practice around the world. Later on, we had several discussions in the hospital and had the building #1 partly redesigned to accommodate ER. The construction was finished in April 2017. Thanks to the user-friendly layout, processes run well in the new ER. It opens up new prospect for both the ER itself and the hospital as the new ER enjoys easily accessible resources and doubled efficiency, which have significantly improved its capability and patient satisfaction.

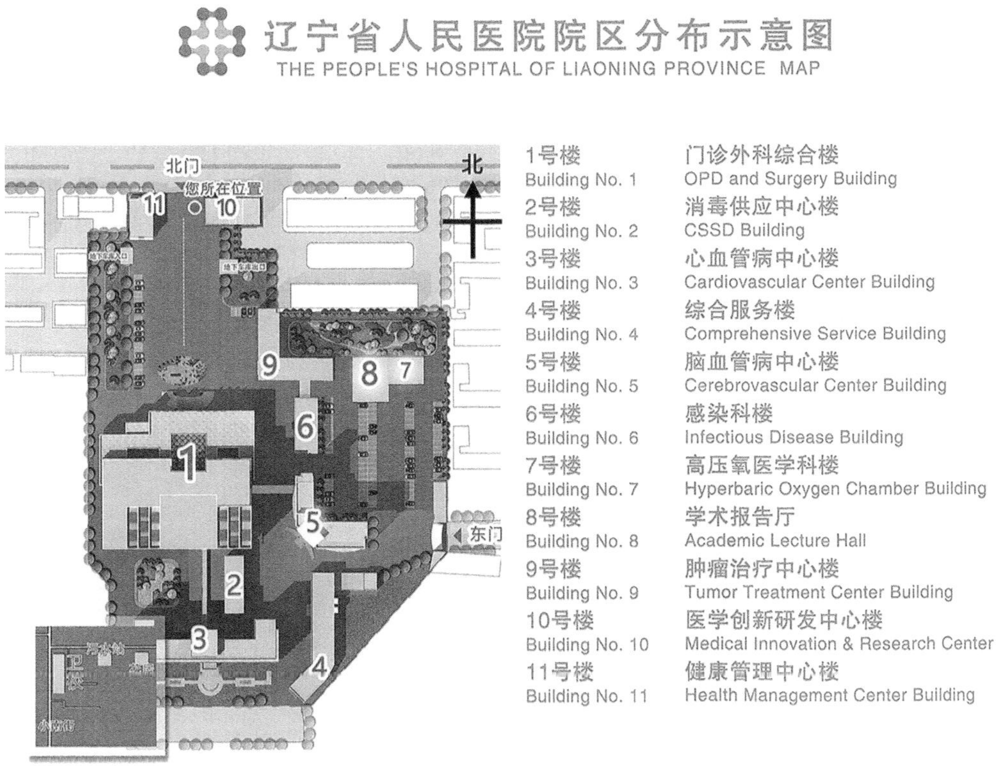

Figure 6.3 The map of the People's Hospital of Liaoning Province.

Baseline Evaluation: Expert Consensus on ER Issue

In December 2015, after "Mr. Bai's longest breakfast ever," Ms. Jilan Liu arrived at PHLP, an organization who had no clue about JCI. On that day, except for the afternoon when she gave lecture, she spent most of the time looking around at the ER (see Figure 6.4a and b). At that time, the ER was still in the old building, and nothing there was unusual to us, since we had been saving countless patients in such an environment day in and day out for years. Nowadays, from the perspective of an initially accredited JCI organization, we find it unbearable to recall what it used to be like there.

Back then, there was no isolation room, observation room, or intensive care room in the old ER. The waiting area was too narrow to allow two stretchers at the same time. When patients were sent in by municipal paramedic service (usually termed "120" in China, which is the hotline number), it was impossible to bring them to the resuscitation room without cutting through the waiting area. Facilities were old and shabby, where stuffing were exposed via damaged surfaces on the exam tables and chairs, and treatment carts were rusty. Medications were prepared in the treatment room by nurses without coverage of air purifier. Fall risks were seen here and there. Cartons of all sizes were piled up at the fire exit of the pharmacy. Temperature was maintained at only 50°F–68°F, and care-providers had to work in cotton-padded overcoat during winter (at the forty-second parallel north, Shenyang witnessed outdoor temperature of only −4°F to 5°F). The list went on and on.

When the need arose to transport a patient from ER to building #1, we had to walk on the road outdoor, and it is imaginable how hard it was during winter. If a patient was transported from ER to cerebrovascular unit in building #5, which are joined by tunnels, we had to go through a ramp of 43 feet, which made it hard for stretcher or gurney. As the cardiovascular unit is located in building #3, it was a 1970-foot walk from ER where people had to exit and enter three buildings. All these were barriers to the saving of lives in danger (Figures 6.5 and 6.6).

ER has been a high-risk and key area for management in every hospital. During our JCI baseline evaluation, 38 problems were identified, ranging from physical layout, facilities, processes, policies to philosophies. For example, ER shared the entrance with inpatient area, long distance between ER and key healthcare locations, emergency triage mechanism not in place,

(a)

(b)

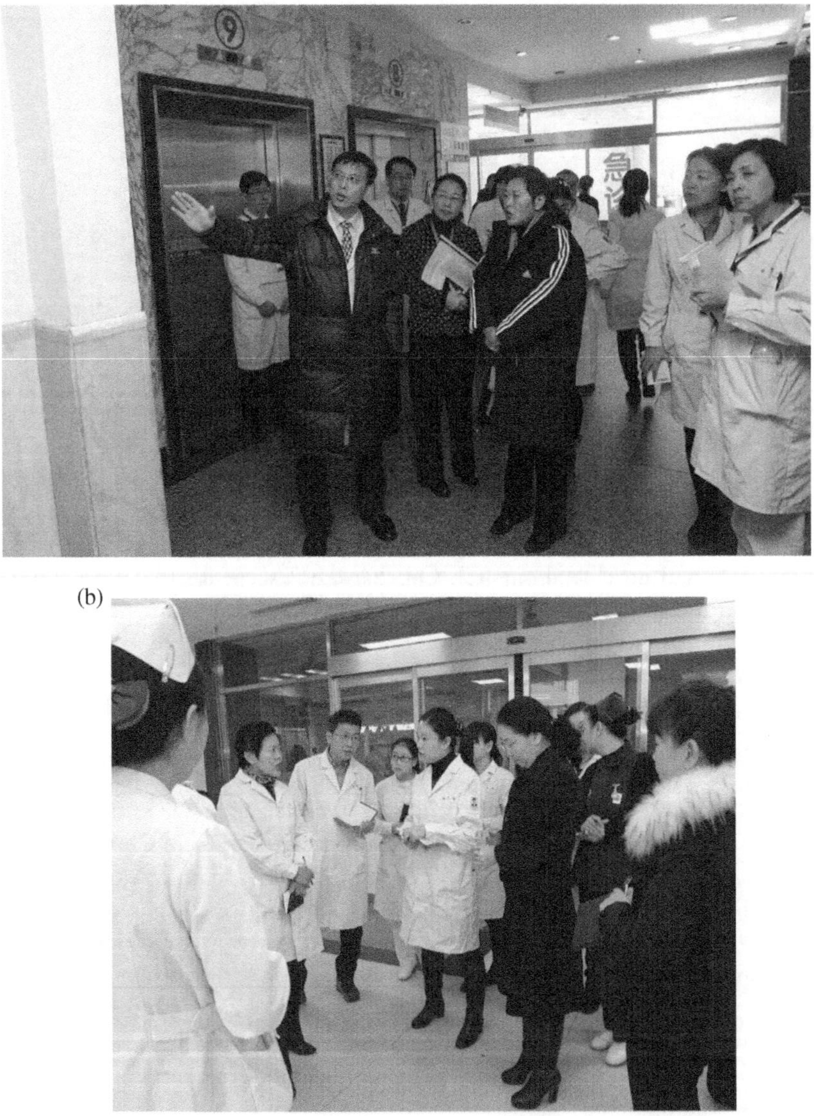

Figure 6.4 Ms. Jilan Liu was touring around the old ER area.

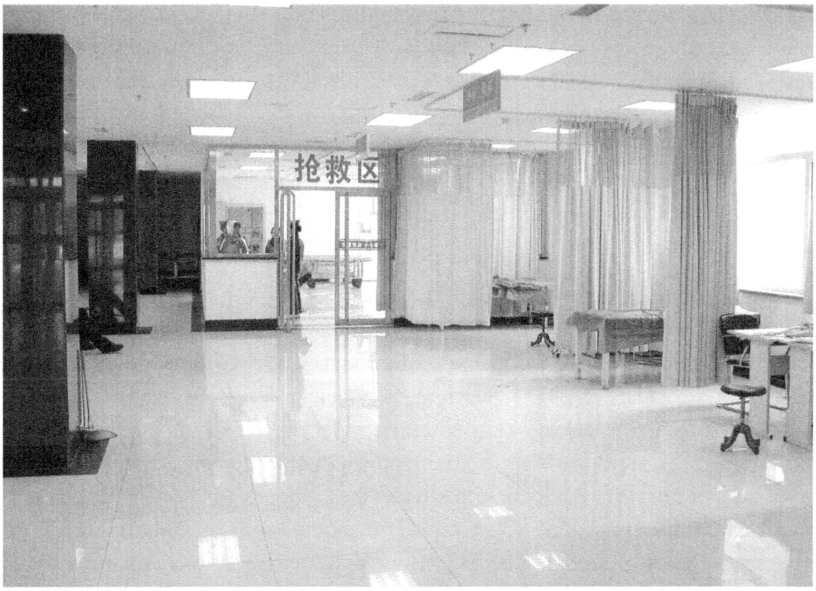

Figure 6.5 **The resuscitation area was far from the ER entrance in the old facility.**

Figure 6.6 **The ramp between ER and other clinical areas, the unavoidable course for patient transport.**

patient privacy unattended to in the ER due to the physical layout, JCI standard compliance issue on the management of emergency medications, isolation room not in place for the observation of patients coming with contagious diseases, areas for resuscitation, and trauma not designated in the resuscitation room in ER and so on.

When we received the JCI baseline evaluation, the plan for ER renovation on its original location had been finished and we had believed that the in-situ renovation might address the issues found in building #9. As baseline evaluation finished, Ms. Liu was wrapped in thought on her way to the airport. Finally, she said:

> I knew you have made up a plan, but I do want to encourage you to rethink about the proper location of ER. It has a bearing on the future of the hospital. ER has been frequently managed and considered as outpatient service in China. However, the trend in the future will feature closer relations between emergency service and inpatient resources. It is more logical to bring emergency service closer to the major care areas for inpatient, in particular for trauma and surgical emergencies, cardiac and cerebral vascular care, respiratory care, diagnostic services, operating room (and DSA, digital subtraction angiography), ICU and CCU. The logic behind this adjacency has been to have better access to shared resources, reduce distance and time of patient transport, and save healthcare professionals from spending time walking a lot. The typical location of ER is an inpatient building. As such, we have suggested you to bring the ER in your new building (#1). This is the most common way to locate an ER in the world. It ensures patient safety and efficiency of care.

We had another discussion within the organization but failed to reach consensus as we agreed that the idea itself did address future needs, but the works needed were too difficult.

One week after the baseline evaluation on February 12, 2016, we received a special email from Ms. Liu, who could not help musing on our ER renovation plan though she was on vacation. Her email reads:

> Though the consultants disagreed with you on the plan of renovation, we did not speak about our contention during the large group exit conference because we wanted to leave it for further discussion. We consultants have concluded that the ER is currently located too far away from the key healthcare services in the hospital. I knew your plan involves establishing operating room, DS, CT and other services in that same building, but that would be too expensive and would not bring the emergency service any closer to other key services. The patient examination area is still to closed to the observation area, which makes it impossible to separate those who wait to be seen. In addition, people have to walk a long distance and go through a ramp before reaching the inpatient ward, ICU or CCU; emergency MRI is not available, and ER has virtually no access to inpatient resonances of healthcare professionals, which creates risk of delay in emergency consultation. These are fundamental barriers that cannot be readily overcome no matter how much resources you invest in. On the other hand, many of the resources in the main building has not been given full use to. If you are to replicate these sets of facilities in another building, that is a waste—you are wasting the house and, more importantly, the equipment, the technologies and the staff.
>
> All in all, ER should be located where access to key healthcare resources is quick and easy. The efficiency of ER is more than efficiency. It is also safety. We believe the provisional ER location indicated in the plan (in the main building #1) is the

Figure 6.7 A designated road exclusive for emergency service.

> best permanent ER location. If you change the plan, finish construction and start emergency services there prior to JCI survey, this new ER would be ready to expand into a strong regional trauma center as your volume grows in the future and serve the hospital's growth strategy. If you do come up with a reconstruction plan for ER in the main building, we would be pleased to review your new plan.

When we discussed the Consultant's suggestion again within the hospital, we did feel it was a formidable challenge to us: at hand were the ready-to-go plans of layout of functions from floor 1 to 4 for the main building (#1) as well as the renovation of ER, with the latter being based on the structure of building #9. If we were to move ER to building #1, we had to redo all the plans and processes. If so, the time when emergency services provided in the new environment would be delayed, even later than the expected day of the actual JCI survey. The layout of outpatient services would be redesigned from the existing plan for building #1. And the resources needed by ER would be rearranged properly. Immediately after we received the email, Mr. Bai summoned the leadership, JCI Office and the design company to discussion a new plan (Figure 6.7).

A Cross-Border Meeting to Decide on the New ER Layout

In February 2016, Mr. Wang Gang was pointed as the Vice President of PHLP in charge of emergency services as he had left the First Hospital of China Medical University. By the end of March, the draft plan for ER in building #1 was completed based on the discussion between the hospital's leadership and the designer company. According to this new plan, emergency registration and cashier, patient reception, resuscitation and emergency pharmacy will be located on the first floor, and isolation zone, end-of-life care, ECG, and emergency laboratory on the second. In April, Ms. Liu and Kathy, another JCI Consultant specialized in facilities and design, provided direction of the new ER plan over video conference and email (Figure 6.8).

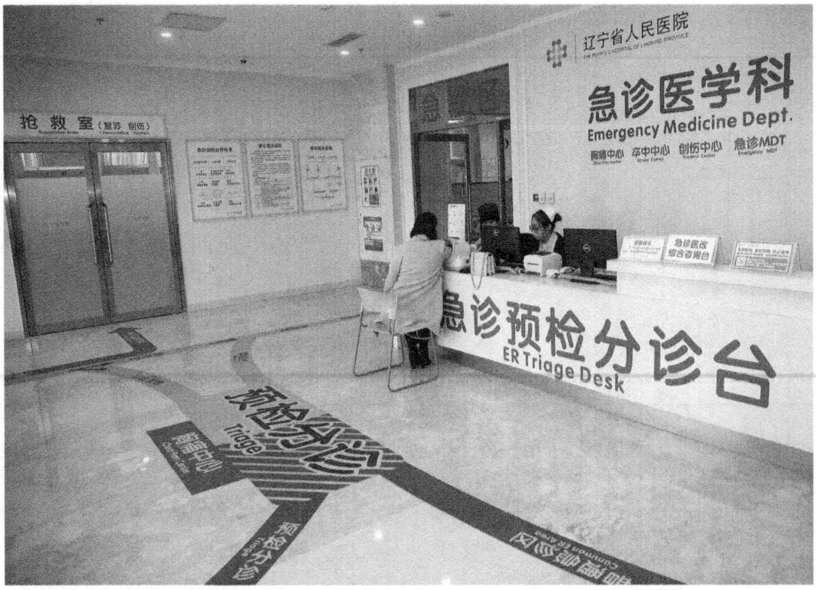

Figure 6.8 The entrance to the new ER location.

The new ER was established. With this new physical layout, ER provides convenience, safety and comfort for patient. It helps save resource, as ER can now use the existing healthcare resources and we no longer had to build CT, operating room and DSA for ER in the old building. Most importantly, it reduces motion and increases operational efficiency for specialist consultation, investigations, and treatment procedures. Demonstrated with the example of chest pain center, the new ER provides for the rapid pull of resources needed for acute myocardial infarction and offers room for redesigning clinical processes. A key measure for a chest pain center is the DTB (door-to-balloon) time, defined as the time interval between the patient's arrival in the hospital and the crossing of catheter guidewire through the culprit vessel. The international recommendation is within 90 min. To reach this bar, we established a clinical pathway and diagnostic process by letting the general resident initiate the process of Catheterization Laboratory and move the care for patients with acute and severe chest pain forward from CCU to the ER. Since then, the time spent before the culprit vessel is accessed in STEMI (ST-Elevated Myocardial Infarction) has been significantly reduced from 150 min on average when the ER was in the old building to 60 min in the new ER. Again, the international standard is within 90 min. Since the operation of the new ER, the compliance to DTB interval increased from 36% in January 2016 to 86.7% (while the national guideline in China sets the bar at 75%) and even 100% for certain months (see Figures 6.9 and 6.10). What's more, we worked with the municipal paramedic service center (120) to bridge the gap between paramedic care before the patient arrives at the hospital and the fast-track mechanism in the hospital. In designated Wechat group chat environment, ECG and other information are sent in while the ambulance is still on its way to the hospital so that we know relevant information before patient arrives. Since the operation of the Chest Pain Center, the mortality for acute myocardial infarction was reduced from 14.29% to 6.67%.

We got to know JCI and JCI Consultants better as we went through the struggle of redesigning and moving the ER. The Consultants have helped us change the conventional mindset on emergency services. Thanks to their profound insight and global experience, we have been able to

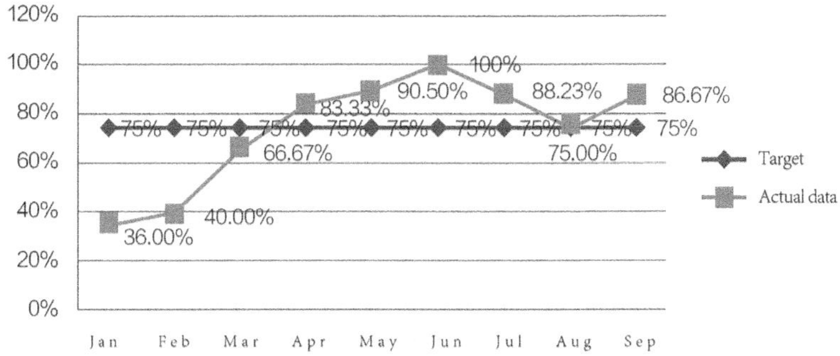

Figure 6.9 The compliance of DTB interval within 90 min during the first 9 months of 2016.

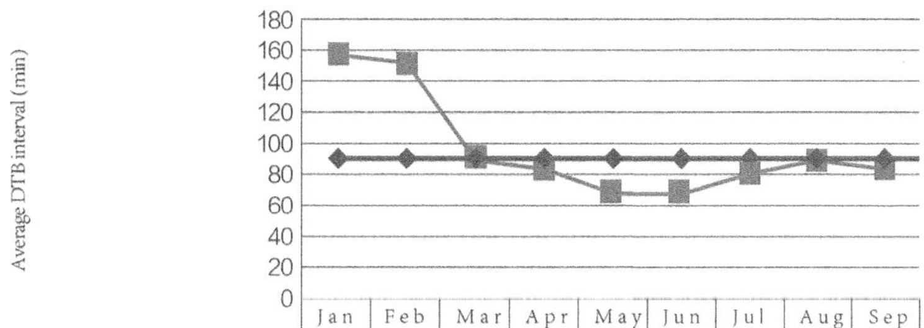

	Jan	Feb	Mar	Apr	May	Jun	Jul	Aug	Sep
Average DTB interval (min)	156.27	151.4	87.67	82.67	67.63	66.64	80.12	87.42	82.93
Target (min)	90	90	90	90	90	90	90	90	90

Figure 6.10 The compliance of DTB interval within 90 min during the first 9 months of 2017.

achieve what we did not think of or what we did not feel confident to do. With the ER process redesigned based on JCI Consultants' recommendation, the hospital has been better accepted among staff and the general public, indicated by the increase in service volume: the ER volume reached a historic high of 35,314 cases from the first 6 months of 2017, a year-on-year increase of 21,177 cases or 66.76%. Moreover, our current location and physical facility have brought us the potential to expand service volume for emergency cases, in particular the severe and critical conditions as well as trauma. Toward the end of June 2017, we received the actual JCI survey, when the ER was in full compliance with JCI standards, being the first ER meeting JCI standards in northeast China.

Chapter 7

Shengjing Hospital of China Medical University

Guo Qiyong, Quan Yu, Mu Rongrong, Li Tao, Gao Xing, Zhang Wei, Zheng Zhi, and Zhao Qi

Shengjing Hospital of China Medical University

Guo Qiyong *is the former President of Shengjing Hospital of China Medical University and the former Vice President of China Medical University.*

He is the Chair of the 3rd Committee of the Radiologists Chapter of the Chinese Medical Doctor Association, Chair of Chinese Society of Radiology, Chair of Medical Imaging Center Management Chapter of the Chinese Hospital Association, Chair of the Liaoning Provincial Society of Radiology, as well as the Chief Editor of Chinese Journal of Radiology.

Quan Yu *is the CIO of Shengjing Hospital of China Medical University. He also serves as a member of the Information Management Chapter and the Information Statistics Chapter of the Chinese Hospital Association, a member of the Information Standardization Chapter of the National Healthcare Standardization Committee, and a member of the Electronic Medical Record and Hospital Informatics Chapter of the Chinese Health Information Association. Quan's contribution has successfully lead the hospital to have achieved HIMSS EMRAM Stage 7, the Adoption Level of Electronic Medical Records Capabilities (Stage 7) and the Maturity of Hospital Information Interoperability (Level 4).*

Hospital Introduction: Shengjing Hospital of China Medical University (SJ Hospital) is a university-affiliated organization with features of comprehensiveness, modern technology, and advanced IT adoption. With 130 years of cultural heritage, SJ Hospital is home to generations of staff who have built and maintained this home-like organization by exploring the unknown and remaining committed to the responsibilities. Throughout these years, based on profound and time-honored history of the SJ Hospital, it has shaped excellent and vigorous culture and become a unique brand of healthcare. Tapping into and innovating its unique culture, the hospital has developed further and demonstrated brilliant vitality.

International Accreditation: HIMSS EMRAM Stage 7 validation in October 2014, and re-validation in September 2017.

Contents

Preface

Overview: Look Up to the Rigorous Doctrine in Healthcare IT

One Should Try to Do Still Better after Having Achieved a Fair Degree of Success

An important reason behind the unrelenting commitment to better healthcare IT adoption in SJ Hospital has been the emphasis attached by the hospital leadership. The hospital has gone through a long process from the initial stage of electronic record to the paperless program and been the leader of healthcare IT in China. When the IT system was initially developed, the hospital was working on improvement by finding and fixing problems. But the progress was still slow.

In 2012, we learned about HIMSS EMRAM and found it extremely relevant to our mindset and direction of hospital development. Therefore, we decided to go through HIMSS EMRAM validation in the hope of expediting overall progress in the paperless program and the infrastructure for big data.

Back then, big data was still a vague concept in China's healthcare sector. As the electronic system had relatively established capability, we started to collect information and data on paper for analysis, in the hope of cost reduction. The efforts paid in HIMSS preparation have resulted in a data pool, while the analysis of the large amount of data has facilitated various kinds of studies. By addressing the large number of requests from the clinicians, IT Dept. became more efficient and such effort had promoted the IT adoption level of the hospital. As we went further in IT adoption, the hospital operated in a more cost-efficient manner. As such, the application of IT should serve not only clinical care but also hospital management.

To facilitate such transformation, SJ Hospital decided to reduce internal barriers of growth, accelerate the IT adoption progress, and bring the hospital to a level closer to international standards by working toward HIMSS EMRAM validation. Flexibility is a key feature of HIMSS EMRAM, as hospitals are evaluated based on the mindset of "patient-centered care" regardless of government policies.

At the end of May 2014, SJ Hospital went straight for a mock survey of HIMSS EMRAM Stage 7 certification without any prior preparation. After the three consultants from HIMSS left, we initiated systematic changes, lasting for 6 months. Finally, we were validated for HIMSS EMRAM Stage 7 in October 2014.

A Tough Fight for Paperless Environment

To work in a paperless manner is one of the requirements of HIMSS EMRAM Stage 7. It was a challenge to our long-held habit. It was far from easy to get it done.

To standardize the way of patient identification features an important step in IT adoption. Hospital visit card or citizen's ID card became the only source to identify a patient. They serve as the unique "key" to the healthcare encounter, which documentation, laboratory and work-up studies as well as printout of results rely on. Initially, the major barrier was physicians who were concerned and resisted the electronic record system. Clinical staff had been writing on white papers for such a long time that they were concerned that they would be in trouble as electronic documentation checked the timeliness of documentation as well.

As a matter of fact, electronic documentation has standardized physician's care to a certain extent by increasing transparency of care data and facilitating hospital management. As the electronic system gradually took shape, we programmed various processes along the journey of care, such as multiple channels for appointment and registration, announcement of queuing information, SMS reminder, and the printout of investigation results from self-service kiosks. In terms of management, we aggregated and analyzed data for timeliness of the first outpatient consultation of the day and incomplete documentation. From the results, we concluded that electronic documentation had saved time and improved efficiency, so that physician could spend more time on patients and get more experience.

The IT Dept. also found themselves improved after working on the paperless initiative. At the beginning of the paperless process, the barriers were still prominent though we had had some foundation. Back then, physicians strongly resisted the paperless process because it meant a fundamental change to the way they work that they had been used to for so long. However, the leadership had remained tough and insistent, and they even used tough means to promote the paperless process, such as removing the printers from the care areas.

But for the IT Dept., our task has been to ensure the normal operation and functionality of the electronic system while fine-tuning user friendliness. For example, we provided the function of templates for physicians to develop their own preferred order templates and record templates. They could develop templates for personal use or share with others in the same or other units. By doing so, physicians became more passionate in helping use improve the electronic system and helped us identify many gaps in the system. Looking back now, it is unanticipated that what people resisted most at the beginning has become the most useful tool in our daily work.

Seeking Harmony Amid Differences

In addition to technical challenge, complicated relationship exists among administrative departments, IT Center, and clinical staff as the hospital built up IT capacity. The better the IT system, the greater changes occurred in the hospital and physicians and nurses came to realize more and more restriction in their work. Therefore, Medical Affairs Dept. and Nursing Dept. collected input from front line staff and submitted the useful ones to the IT Center. On the other hand, Medical Affairs Dept. and Nursing Dept. also bring up requests for the IT Center.

Take the paperless initiative, for example, many clinical staff opposed to the requirement of not printing out patient's records with the conventional mindset that it is impossible for physicians to do their rounds without paper records. At this moment, Medical Affairs Dept. helped collect the opinions of clinical staff, sorted out the good recommendations, and provided them to us. With the comment from front line staff, we developed a wireless program used for rounds, provided computer on wheel, and helped them do rounds without paper. Sometimes we saw administrative departments and clinical staff reach agreement and request for specific features from the IT Center to improve the IT system.

The IT capabilities of the hospital were growing amid these contradictory but harmonious relationships. Though each department has its own roles and responsibilities, when it comes to universal IT adoption, communication was sought among different departments and disciplines. Receiving requests from clinical staff on the electronic features for various processes, IT Dept. provides technical solution, and gradually we formed a culture of interaction between healthcare and IT Dept. as we sought the convergence between the two fields. Meanwhile, as we engaged in more discussion among different departments, we came to learn from each other and thus improved hospital-wide efficiency and team coherence. The effort toward HIMSS EMRAM validation helped every one realize how relevant it was to their own roles and responsibilities. For example, the Medical Director became fluent in starting a discussion from the perspective of IT, and vice versa for the IT Director. Since then, IT Center adopted a role of higher strategic significance.

How the Operating Room (OR) and Anesthesiology Dept. engaged in the paperless process has been impressive? OR has been a vital part in every hospital. In other words, typically, as the door to the surgical suite closes, no supervision is able to get in, whether from administrative departments or patients and their families. However, safety within the OR has always been a top concern of clinical and administrative departments.

Any change to the processes in the OR is a big impact upon the convention and habit. Therefore, the leadership attached high importance and provided full support for the IT Center.

We started with the very basic functions. During the discussions and communication, the clinical staff started to demonstrate a very high level of engagement. When we were bringing the new system alive, staff from the OR pointed out many areas for improvement based on their years of practice and the way that they had used to doing things. In addition to pointing out problems, staff also offered one or several solutions and discussed them with IT staff. One can feel how reciprocal and mutually helpful it was.

Needless to say, the emphasis and commitment from leadership means a lot in the road toward HIMSS EMRAM validation or IT adoption. Taking the opportunity of HIMSS EMRAM validation, the hospital successfully put the OR under supervision in an efficient way. Against all odds, with the strong push from the leadership, we got validated for HIMSS EMRAM Stage 7.

The Advantage of Single Vendor

An important lesson we learned from the IT adoption process was using one single vendor, so that we avoided the challenges of integrating systems from different vendors. However, this does not mean we are free from concern. For example, the OR anesthesia system launched earlier had its own module of ordering and billing different from the main system in the hospital. After discussion, we decided to give up the ordering and billing feature of that electronic system and use the system only for work in the surgical process. The same applied to many other modules that had been added to the main electronic system, we took away repetitive features and kept only those relevant to the processes and procedures. In addition, we have two servers in SJ Hospital for information management. Generally, when there is one single system, one server suffices and does not pose too much pressure on the other server. One more server is required for one more system. Additional complexity and difficulties are introduced with more than one vendor when it comes to system integration, risk, and stress on the servers. IT adoption is not just about spending money on the system, capital, and human resources, but also the coordination of all the three elements.

Thoughts and Reflection

We furthered our understanding of the closed-loop concept as we prepared for HIMSS EMRAM. By now, one can find closed-loop mindset in the system as well as administrative processes for budgeting, tendering, and staffing. To prepare for HIMSS EMRAM validation, instead of adding new software to the environment, we improved the existing ones.

Process improvement is a continuous undertaking involving achieving a paperless environment in transfusion, operation, sterilization service, and outpatient clinic. In 2014, SJ Hospital was the only one in China which managed blood with a paperless process, which we have been proud of. We are more proud of ourselves for the fact that though printers existed during the HIMSS validation, we have taken away the "print" button in many systems while maintaining or even improving the efficiency of the clinical work. Removing the "print" button helps a lot, but it takes enormous courage and IT capabilities from the organization.

We have been pleased to see increased expectation on security of the system, protection, and privacy in the new edition of HIMSS EMRAM requirements. Hopefully, one day we might also see an HIMSS model addressing network structure and the IT servers in the future that helps hospitals improve further. HIMSS EMRAM has been strong in supporting clinical practice and administrative management, but we also realized it does not address performance evaluation of physicians, an important part in healthcare management. We look forward to such a model to be developed by HIMSS in the future.

As we worked toward HIMSS EMRAM validation, we learned new things, overcame difficulties, and enjoyed it a lot. The doubt at the beginning became support and understanding. It is more of a journey toward rigorous doctrine than a test. The most profound inspiration has been that the improvement with IT is not limited to the processes and departments involved but spans to the mindset and professional thinking of staff. If timing, environment, and people determine the fate of an endeavor, as ancient Chinese philosophers believed, then we felt that "people" made the greatest difference in our effort toward HIMSS EMRAM validation.

Chapter 8

Xuanwu Hospital, Capital Medical University

Zhao Guoguang, Li Jia, Wang Lihong, Liang Zhigang, Fei Xiaolu, Wei Lan, Sun Xuemei, Ji Bingxin, Li Xiaoyu, Ying Bo, and Ma Wenhui

Xuanwu Hospital Affiliated to Capital Medical University

Zhao Guoguang, *MD, PhD, is the President of Xuanwu Hospital Affiliated to Capital Medical University, Chief Physician, Professor, and Supervisor of doctoral candidate in neurosurgery. His current roles include Director of National Clinical Institute of Geriatric Diseases, Chairman of Center of Evaluation and Quality Control of Cerebral Injuries of National Health and Family Planning Commission, Vice Chairman of Chinese Congress of Neurological Surgeons, Standing Member of Medical Quality Management Commission of Chinese Hospital Association, Chairman of Beijing Institute of Geriatric Diseases, PI with Epilepsy Institute of Beijing Institute of Major Cerebral Diseases, Co-Chairman of International Minimally Invasive Neurosurgical Society, etc.*

Li Jia, *PhD of Surgery, Chief Physician, Dr. Li is the Vice Secretary of the CPC (Communist Party of China) Committee and Secretary of Discipline Inspection Commission of Xuanwu Hospital who is leading the organization-wide adoption of information technology. His roles include Member of Young Surgeons Committee of Chinese Society of Surgical Oncology; Member of Beijing Surgical Society, its Young Surgeons Committee, and its Colorectal Surgery Chapter; Member of Academic Committee of Chinese Academy of Colorectal Surgery; Chairman of Information Management Committee of Beijing Hospital Association, etc.*

Hospital Introduction: Founded in 1958, Xuanwu Hospital Capital Medical University (hereinafter referred as "Xuanwu Hospital") is now a Level A Tertiary Hospital dedicated to clinical care, medical education, research, disease prevention, health maintenance, and rehabilitation, with neurology and geriatrics as its strong disciplines.

As the clinical facility affiliated to the Capital Medical University, Xuanwu Hospital is one of the cradles for the academic and professional development of neurology in China. It is also the national training base for life science and talent development governed by the Ministry of Education. The hospital offers 20 doctoral programs and 16 master programs and supports the academic activities of Capital Medical University, including the faculties of neurology, general surgery, dermatology and STD as well as geriatrics. The hospital also serves as the national and municipal bases for residency training program, continuous medical education, and examination center.

International Accreditation: September 2015, the first HIMSS EMRAM 6 under the Hospital Administration Bureau of Beijing;

November 2017, HIMSS EMRAM 7.

Contents

Preface

From 6 to 7: Growth Behind the Numbers

In recent years, Xuanwu Hospital Capital Medical University has leveraged the strength of advanced international healthcare quality management standards through learning from the successful experience and approaches adopted in overseas hospitals to better improve the quality management and culture of safety in the hospital. Bold steps have been taken in practice and innovation.

Through taking the international challenges and introducing the concepts of patient safety, care quality, and patient-centricity advocated by HIMSS EMRAM Stage 6 (in 2015), we have been able to better satisfy our patients and forge a better management structure to lead the future development. With improved processes and clinical work flows, the efficiency has been ensured with stronger team cohesion. The international recognition also won the hospital greater local reputation. However, during the process of promoting delicacy management and improving healthcare quality, we increasingly felt that hospital management needed advanced managerial concepts and tools as well as a well-established data-driven culture. Therefore, HIMSS EMRAM Stage 6 is never the end. Only with advanced IT application in healthcare could we realize the goals to promote the development of medical science and the restructuring of healthcare system. That brought us onto the journey toward HIMSS EMRAM Stage 7.

In the new round of medical science development, new service models have emerged based on the technologies related to mobile communication, big data, cloud computing, and cognitive computing. Physicians can obtain more comprehensive, accurate data in real time throughout the life cycle of the patients and population to further discover the pattern of disease occurrence, progression and prognosis and to realize more precise individual care for improved outcomes. Nowadays, we have seen a trend of O2O service model in healthcare, which indicates the necessity to restructure the healthcare and health promotion industry for people to enjoy proper people-centered care with easy access at a reasonable cost. The relationship between patients and healthcare providers would also be reshaped to further upgrade the resources and enhance the service capability.

Xuanwu Hospital was officially validated as an HIMSS EMRAM 7 hospital in November 2017. It is a testimony of our achievements in applying information technology and also a symbol of our excellent service quality supported by information and technology. Xuanwu Hospital will further enhance the sense of gain and build the hospital into a first-class academic teaching hospital and modern medical center renowned in the world to provide satisfying services to our people (Figure 8.1).

Learning: Multidisciplinary Collaboration

During the baseline survey of HIMSS EMRAM Stage 7, the consultants left us with 142 findings for further improvement. After 3 months of intensified improvement actions, we received the mock survey conducted by four consultants in 3 days to assess where we were. Another 100 odd opportunities for improvement were identified. But the progress we had made was commonly recognized. In the following 2 months, the hospital and the vendors fully devoted themselves to the improvement activities and finally brought the systems alive in August 2017.

Figure 8.1 On-site validation of HIMSS EMRAM Stage 7.

The success could not be achieved without the collaboration among all teams through effective communication. Our shared goal was to strengthen the weakness in the hospital to make the process safer and more appropriate. The regular meetings and progress debriefing became an important means of communication to further align the goals and to strengthen the synergy.

Let's take "paperless operation" as an example. Though Xuanwu Hospital had already started our exploration in paperless operation years before the HIMSS validation, we still had many unanswered questions. On February 13, 2017, we invited Jilan Liu to the hospital and introduced the HIMSS EMRAM model and concept to the hospital staff on the launching ceremony of our HIMSS journey. Jilan said that it was the future trend to utilize information technology to support clinical serves and the decision-making process of our physicians. When requests were submitted from the frontline staff, both healthcare and management staff should know the potentials of IT technology. IT staff should communicate more closely with the clinical units to better meet their needs. Inspired by the lecture, we began to view the role of IT from a new perspective and started to expect the Stage 7 validation. Of course, validation was not the ultimate goal. To adopt HIMSS criteria is to ensure patient safety, improve staff efficiency and managerial expertise to facilitate the further development of the hospital as a whole.

HIMSS EMRAM Stage 7 is not an IT project because it requires joint efforts from various units and departments in an organization. We established a complete evaluation system for administrative departments and unit coordinators, which greatly mobilized the participation of the department directors and coordinators.

The VP in charge led the paperless project. The directors of all administrative departments acted as the responsible persons of the supervision groups to review the clinical process. They found 37 occasions where written signature would be required and 106 paper documents that could be digitalized.

The hospital then started the development of the system together with the vendors and the redesign of the processes, including the credible digital signature for physicians during clinical encounters, documentation of surgical notes and other charting process; paperless requests for lab tests, examinations and surgeries; appointment-based check-in for patients.

Growth: A Virtuous Cycle for Managerial Expertise

The purpose of taking the HIMSS challenge is to continuously improve quality with defined goals. During the preparation for HIMSS EMRAM 7, Xuanwu Hospital started from the top-level design to realize the data exchanges and utilization among different business systems through rational planning and the establishment of the integrated platform. This approach helped us to have saved many mistakes as well as cost.

In the past, the IT development had always been the responsibility of the IT Department. But the old process was no longer suitable to achieve Stage 7. The closed-loop management concept, paperless operation, and advanced clinical decision-support system required wider and deeper engagement across the organization. The challenges we faced at the beginning were lack of the personnel who were specialized in medical care, information technology, and hospital management.

In 2016, the IT management in the hospital was restructured and an administration department was established supervised by the original IT Office. The department has three subordinated teams responsible for the hospital business systems, hardware, and integration platform and data analysis and processing, respectively. Then, the hospital reallocated the human resources to organize the task groups responsible for paperless operation, closed-loop management, CDSS, business system upgrade, and development. Each group was participated by the directors of relevant departments and the IT coordinators from the clinical units to review the projects and the launching of new systems (Figures 8.2 and 8.3).

In this process, we also had the opportunities to train the physician champions to participate in the IT development. The improved efficiency and safety brought by the process further encouraged

Figure 8.2 Mock survey of HIMSS EMRAM Stage 7.

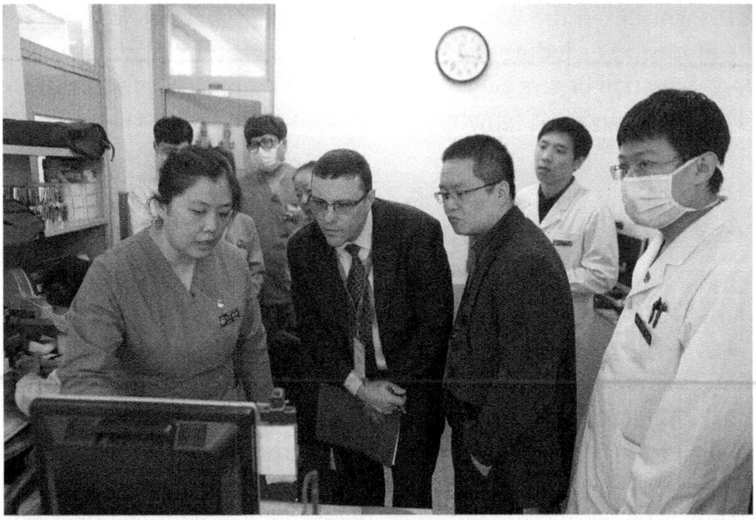

Figure 8.3 On-site validation of HIMSS EMRAM Stage 7.

the participation of our staff. A complete virtuous cycle had been established to engage clinical participation, IT activities, staff training, and hospital management, which further contributed to the quantitative development of the hospital as a whole.

At the final exit meeting of HIMSS EMRAM Stage 7 validation, both Jilan Liu and John Daniels, the surveyor team leader, expressed their congratulations on our achievements. With the guidance of the HIMSS EMRAM criteria, we were able to further improve the effectiveness and usability of our systems to fully meet the needs of the clinical operation and have established a sustainable and manageable platform with stability, efficiency, and safety. A culture to ensure quality, safety, and efficiency through IT development had also been forged under the leadership of the hospital. Prof. Zhao Guoguang, President of the hospital, said that IT development should always be integrated with clinical quality improvement. Through the HIMSS experience, we had initially established a complete IT supporting structure and improved the hospital care quality and managerial expertise. It also laid a solid foundation for our future development.

Case 1: Big Data-Fueled Nursing Quality Monitoring

Progress in Two Indicators

One of the major tasks of our nursing quality team is to evaluate quality with measurable data.

Time Interval of Antibiotics Administration

Usually, medication prescription with a frequency ordered as b.i.d (twice a day) would be given at 8:00 am and 16:00 pm in our hospital. To monitor the process, we collected data through on-site observation and patient interview in all 48 clinical units (including ICUs and regular wards). The background average interval time between the two doses of b.i.d orders was 5.9 h. Later on, the interval was improved to 7.1 h, closer to the ideal 8 h, after continuous monitoring and improvement to ensure sufficient effectiveness of the medication via maintaining expected blood concentration. However, the process was quite challenging because of the missing documentation, manual data collection, limited time for observation, etc. This resulted in a rather small sample size of 100 cases or even less for the quarterly monitoring. Though 100 samples could still reflect the quality of care, it cost too much time and energy and could lead to certain level of statistical bias.

Implementation of Hospital-Acquired Infection Prevention Measures

In 2012, the hospital started to use the data collected by the information system to monitor the nursing quality regarding the prevention of hospital-acquired infection. One indicator we monitored was the implementation of 30° elevation of the bed head for patients on ventilators. The way of data collection was improved compared with that in the previous case. In addition to on-site observation, we also tried to track the performance through the physician orders. The compliance rate was increased from 11.7% to 94.8%, which could be attributed to the active role played by the nursing team. However, the coverage of the system and the indicator was very limited.

In recent years, with the improved information capability in the hospital, the data generated during the nursing activities could assist the nurses to learn more about their performance, reflect the actual quality, and promote scientific management methodologies. With the assistance of the IT systems (HIS, LIS, mobile nursing system, transfusion system, Operation and Anesthesia system, CSSD system, etc.), the trace of the nursing tasks could be documented through the entire process, including prescription administration, nursing procedures, and charting. The discrete data could be stored in the database to be used for further quality analysis and management (see Table 8.1).

Table 8.1 Footprint of Nursing Activities

Nursing Activities	*Data Captured*
Medication administration	Name of the ward, inpatient number, medication prescribed, time of prescription recognition, staff who recognized the prescription, staff who arranged the medication, staff who verified the medication, staff who mixed the medication, staff who initially administered the medication, staff who ended the administration...
Specimen collection	Name of the ward, inpatient number, physician's order, time of order recognition, staff who recognized the prescription, test item, category of test, type of specimen, staff who verified the specimen, start time of collection, end time of collection, staff who collected the specimen, time of handover, time of arrival at the lab, time of verification, time of reporting, time of return...
Vital sign monitoring	Name of ward, inpatient number, planned time of administration, actual time of administration...
Daily care	Name of ward, inpatient number, care item, time of administration, staff who performed the care...
......	......

These data fully support the nursing quality monitoring on timeliness and accuracy during administration, blood transfusion, medication allergy test, specimen collection, patient monitoring, assessment, etc.

Where Do the Data Come From?

At the beginning, the data mining and utilization for nursing quality management relied on a manual process. The administrative department submitted data utilization request in the system. Then, the IT Department would collect and send the data to the applicant if the request was approved to avoid any discrepancy of data from different sources that might impact the analysis results.

With increasing quality data generated from clinical activities, we gradually formed standard analysis approaches for the quality projects, which reduced the process from 5 days in the past to 2 days and provided reliable data analysis models for the later decision-support platform.

Jilan suggested that we fully utilize the power of data integration and data platform to perform clinical decision-making. Soon data analysis models were built into the decision-support platform. Currently, we have realized the real-time analysis of the data involved in the dimensions for nursing quality monitoring with flexible data integration possibilities. Management staff could go to the nursing quality monitoring module and select any items, wards, time period, and other dimensions they want to review. The platform would then generate relevant charts to reduce the time of analysis and the time spent on the process.

Timely Delivery of Blood Gas Specimen (Figure 8.4a and b)

According to the *National Protocol of Clinical Laboratory Test Procedure*, hospitals are required to monitor the delivery time of blood gas specimen. We then started to monitor the delivery time of the specimens on the ward level, unit level, and hospital level to evaluate the timeliness according to the time frame defined.

At the beginning, the results were not satisfactory. We then compared the timely delivery percentage in different time segments within a day and found out that the poor timeliness happened mainly in three segments throughout a day. For example, the volume of specimens usually peaks during 4:00–6:00 am, taking up almost one-third of the daily total. But we had the worst performance in timely delivery. The major contributor to that was one intensive care unit. Cross-department improvement actions were soon taken to tackle the problem. The five major measures included (1) to call the transport worker and take the blood after the worker arrives at the unit, (2) to add designated delivery hotline, (3) to add extra man power during peak hours, (4) to add handover documentation, and (5) to scan the barcode upon the reception of any specimen. The process improved, to some extent, after the measures were implemented for a while. However, due to the manual handover process, the accuracy of the information could not be ensured, which led to the lack of reliable data for further analysis.

We, thus, decided to redesign the information system to allow digital documentation. In the new process, the nurse scans the specimens to be transported, then scans the work badge worn by the worker during the handover. The system would capture the time and a handover record would be generated. In this way, we could make sure that the handover is performed face-to-face and could be documented in real time.

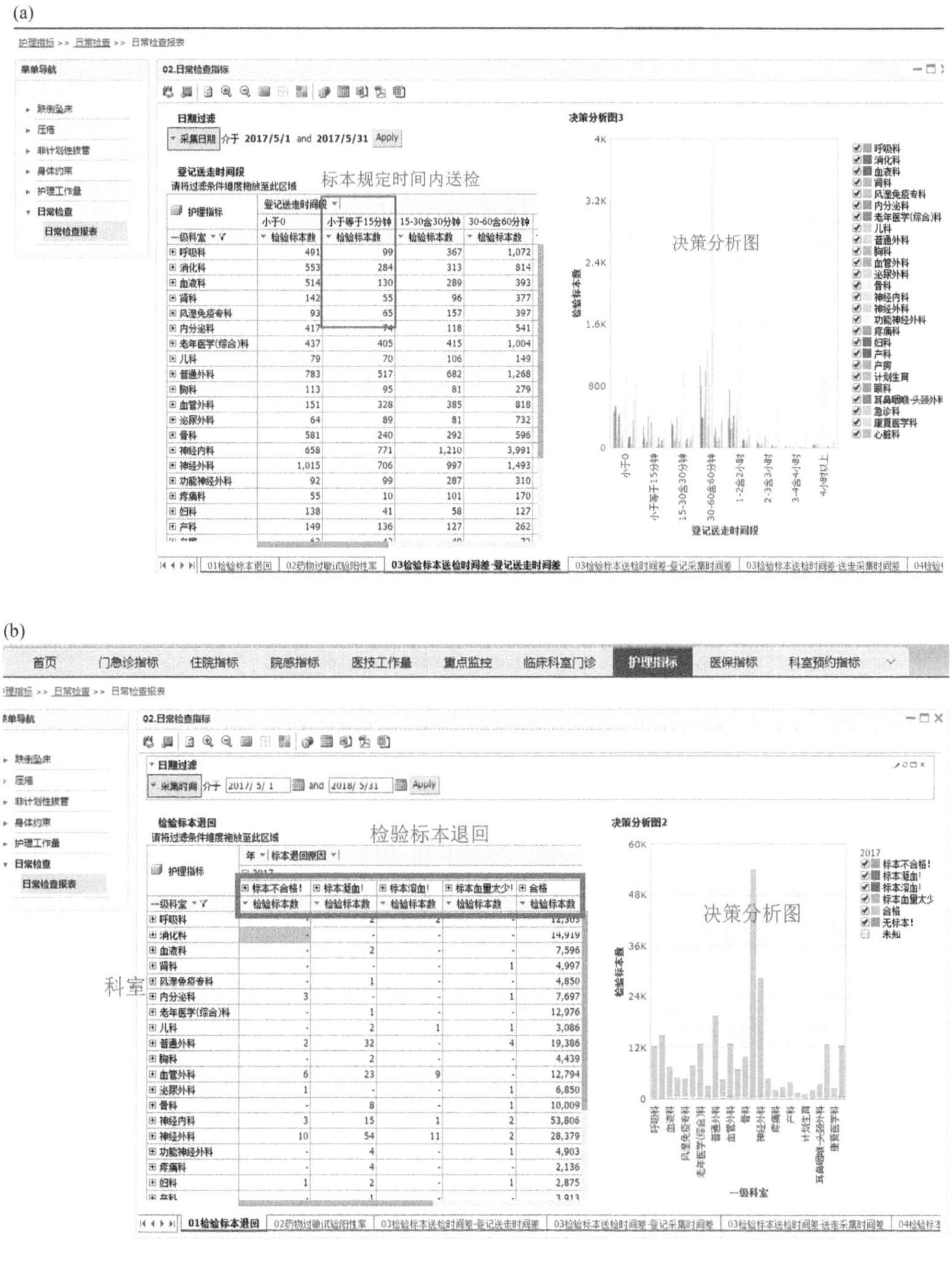

Figure 8.4 Timely delivery of specimens.

In early 2017, the timeliness of blood gas specimen delivery increased to 81.76%. The waiting time before the test was reduced to a mean of 12.22 min. And over 20,000 entries of data had been generated. The improved timeliness (delivery within 15 min) significantly reduced the test result deviation due to the delay.

Anticoagulation Specimen Quality

According to the *Clinical Laboratory Medical Quality Control Indicators (2015)*, the quality of specimens is categorized into clotted specimens, hemolyzed specimens, specimens with substandard volume, and qualified specimen. We reviewed the data regarding the percentage of qualified specimens that need anticoagulant treatment and the percentage of returned specimens on the ward, unit, and hospital levels, respectively, and further probed into the reasons of the specimen rejection. The overlay chart showed the total number and types of specimens that did not meet the quality requirement in a very intuitive way. The aggregation rate reduced from 0.94% to 0.22%. The quality improvement helped to reduce the rejection of the specimens and saved the repetitive collection.

The monitoring on the lab specimens was not limited to that two indicators. Through the data collected regarding the specimen quality and the timeliness of delivery, we could better ensure the quality of tests.

Future Application of Data in Nursing Quality Management

Advantages of Data Application

The data mining and the system optimization for the decision-support platform could push forward the nursing quality improvement through the synergy. The available information breaks through the limits on manual statistical analysis capability by providing whole-sample data to avoid statistical bias that might be resulted from random sampling.

The hospital could retrieve data generated at any time point or period in real time, or capture data generated across certain time span to avoid blind area during quality evaluation. Human factors could also be avoided to ensure that the results are comparable by proper quality standard through a standardized process of data collection, aggregation, and analysis. In addition, continuous data collection could provide constant monitoring on certain quality problem and realize the comparison among different time periods or different units.

With the improved capability of data mining, it could also make our work more efficient, feasible, and cost-effective. On the basis of the secondary utilization of the big data accumulated in the hospital, we will be able to aggregate the value of innovation brought by big data.

The Future of Data Application

The State Council issued the *Action Framework for Promoting Big Data* in 2015 and the *National Strategic Framework for Information Technology Development* in 2016. Data have become a fundamental strategic resource of a country and will exert profound change to our society. Along with the rapid development of information technology and the emergence of digital hospitals, various clinical systems and data generated through the nursing care processes have taken us onto the journey of exploring the utilization of data. But it needs to be emphasized that good application of big data in nursing quality requires a well-developed and well-designed quality control approach. Therefore, the search for proper quality standards should go before data utilization in nursing quality control. Currently, in addition to the nursing sensitivity indicators assigned by the national government, we have implemented over ten indicators related to nursing quality to comprehensively improve patient safety.

The hospital has also adopted scientific management measures (e.g., benchmarking—managing benchmarks—learning from benchmarks) to compare and analyze the quality deviation. The efforts have been made to identify the breakthroughs via case sharing and improved instrument and tools for management. Themed trainings were also organized to ensure the overall upgrade of clinical quality in different units.

The era of information brings changes to our way of thinking. The nursing quality management is marching toward more precise control based on objective data to capture the real clinical process quality in a data-driven off-site manner. We believe that the combination and comprehensive utilization of big data, the optimization of information technology, iteration of quality standards, and various management tools will definitely be the future of nursing quality management.

Case 2: Infection Control: "Zero Underreport"

Hospital-acquired infection is a kind of undesired healthcare quality event resulted from the activities inside a hospital. We established the hospital infection monitoring system through integrating six clinical business systems including physician ordering, lab test, mobile nursing, imaging, operation and anesthesia, and EMR.

The infection control system extracts data for more than 300 indicators from the six systems and makes judgment based on the established diagnosis strategies to flag the cases with certain level of warning and push the information to the monitoring terminals and the physicians' workstations. The diagnosis strategies are a set of complicated assembly developed based on the diagnosis criteria of infectious diseases combined with the qualitative and quantitative indicators captured from the system to make initial judgment on the status of infection.

During the development of the infection monitoring system, quantitative limits were set based on the reference ranges available in LIS. A list of data required to be discrete was developed based on the positive findings (qualitative indicators) of the imaging diagnosis criteria. For example, the imaging diagnosis for "pneumonia" might be indicated as "right lung infection," "lung infection on right lower lobe," "right lower lung inflammation," etc. What we did was to compile a catalog of the data that had to be captured discretely to generate accurate warning to the clinical staff. The diagnosis strategy set is open for adjustment and modification based on the real situation. Currently, the sensitivity and specificity of the warning of the infection monitoring system have reached almost 90%.

The interface of patient infection information contains a large amount of information displayed through a time line in multiple dimensions (see Figure 8.5). When the symptoms or physical signs of a patient indicate infection, or when lab tests/examinations related to infection are prescribed by a physician, the diagnosis strategy embedded in the system would start the judgment process and generate warning to be pushed to the clinical terminals and the infection control monitoring terminals. At the same time, the infection monitoring staff would supervise the response from the physician to make sure he/she responds to the warning in a timely and proper manner so as to diagnose possible infection. The monitoring staff would verify the information reported through the monitoring system and the completion of required documentation (see Figure 8.6).

When a physician wants to review and handle the infection warning, he/she can open the infection information summary displayed in time sequence, including temperature (flagged if $T \geq 38$), high white cell count, positive blood culture, and use of antibiotics. The physician could click the data on the chart to drill down into more detailed information.

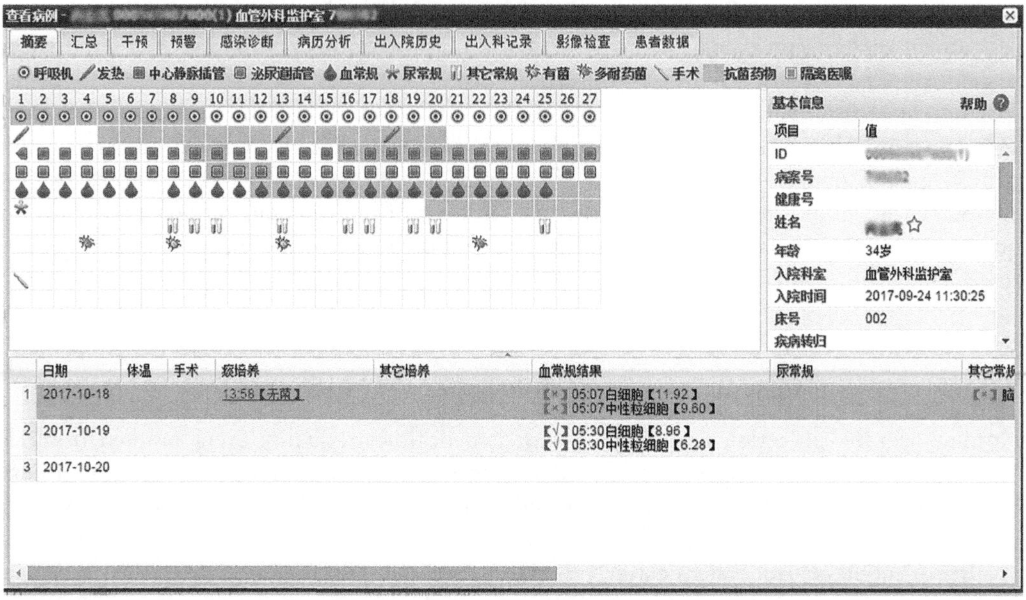

Figure 8.5 Interface of summary information of patient infection.

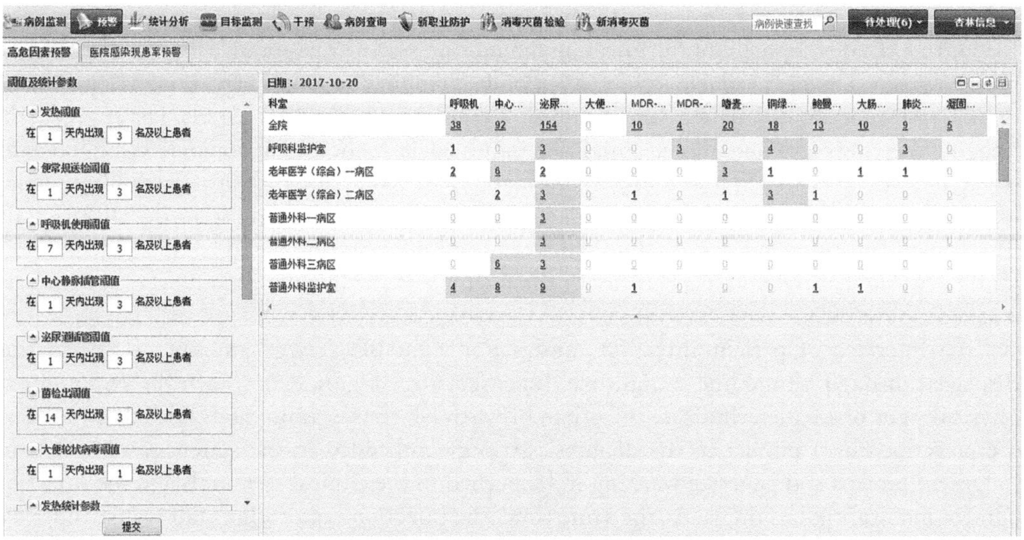

Figure 8.6 Warning on suspected hospital infection outbreak.

Another important function of the infection monitoring system is to send warning on suspected hospital infection outbreak. The interface of the outbreak contains the information of fever patients (three or more) identified in one unit, clustering detection of MDROs and special bacteria, and the number of patients with high-risk factors (e.g., with intravascular catheter, ventilator, urinary catheter) for timely intervention to prevent severe outbreak. The warning on suspected outbreak and sporadic cases are sent simultaneously. That means if there are three or more patients

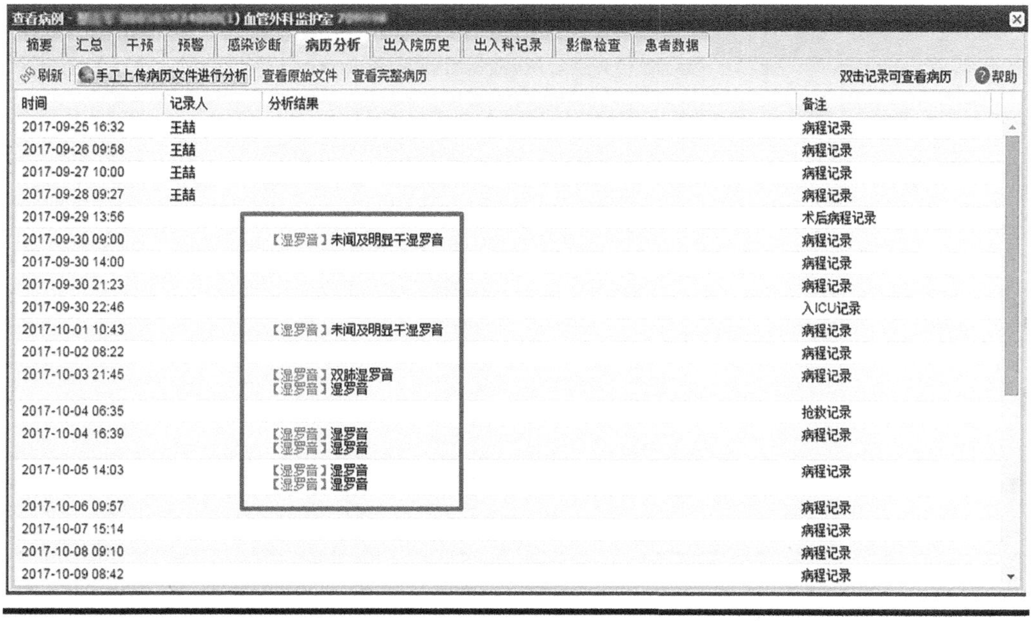

Figure 8.7 Access to EMR by clicking "case analysis—review original document."

identified with fever in one specific unit, warnings would be sent to both the sporadic case and suspected outbreak interfaces to prevent possible delay.

When checking the terminal for infection warnings, the hospital infection monitoring staff could access patient's EMR or go directly to the marked progress notes through the "case analysis—review original document" link (see Figure 8.7). The progress notes are marked with different colors by the system based on the subjective descriptions. The subjective descriptions are categorized into the "positive descriptions" and "negative descriptions" (see Figure 8.8a and b). For example, when staff opens the progress notes through the "review original document" link, he/she could see color-marked descriptions such as "diarrhea," "inflammation suspected" and "skin infection" entered by the physicians for easy and quick scan of key information. The dictionary of the "positive descriptions" and "negative descriptions" is open to the infection control staff for easy maintenance.

Zero Underreport

Though the infection monitoring system had improved the reporting of infection cases and the accuracy rate through pushing warnings, the underreport rate was as high as 15%, far away from our target of "zero." Of course, physician's capability to better identify infection cases needed to be enhanced. Another major cause of underreport was the isolation of the monitoring system from other hospital modules, which meant that the monitoring data were isolated from the EMR system for charting. Most of the underreported cases were caused by inaccurate information communicated. After rounds of communication between the Medical Affairs Department and the IT Department, we decided to solve the problem through modifying the system.

First, the infection monitoring system generates warning information. When physician opens EMR, the warning would pop up on the screen to remind the physician to handle the case in a timely manner.

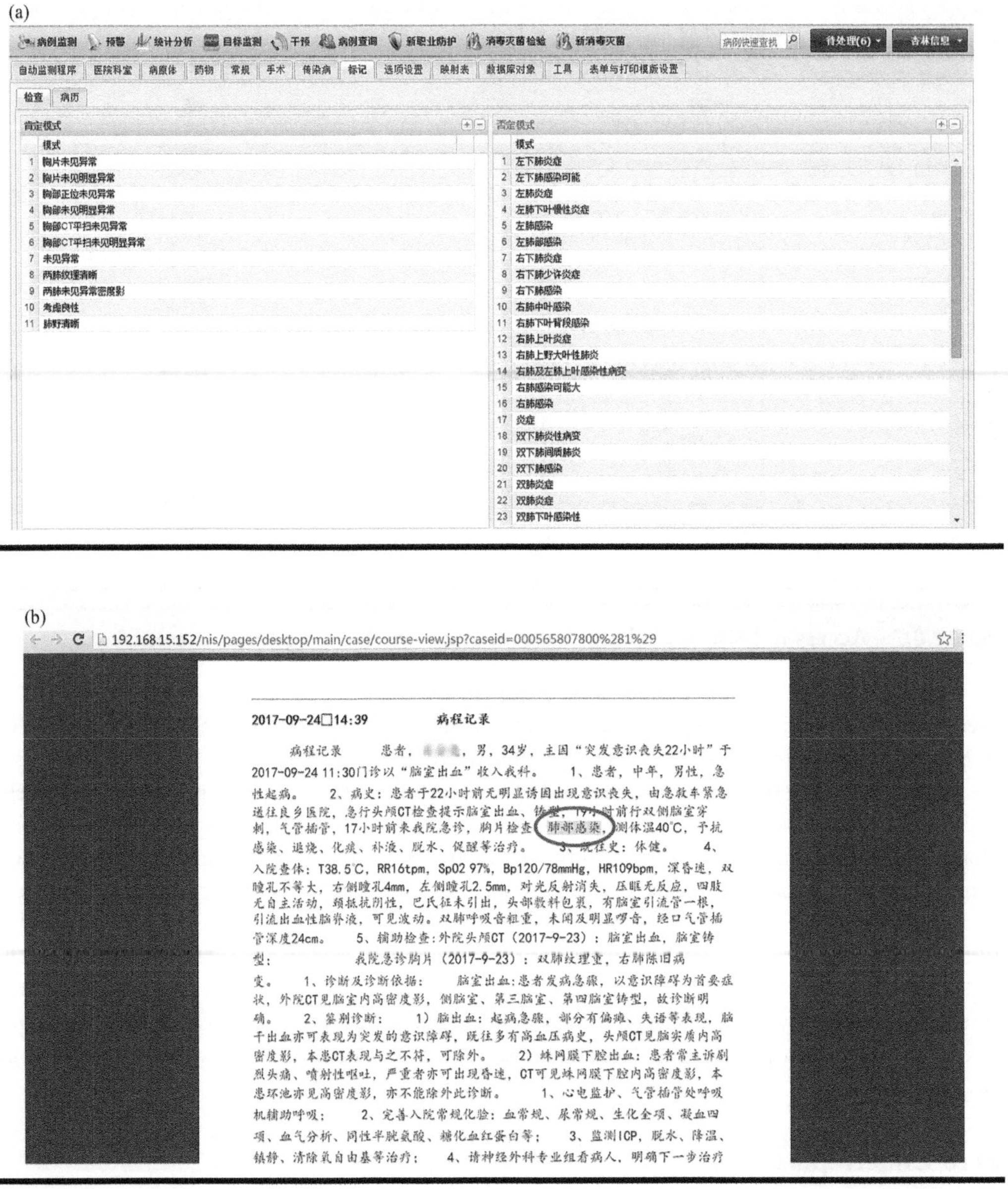

Figure 8.8 Marking on progress notes through "Positive Mode" and "Negative Mode."

Second, during the stay of a patient, the system would require the physician to make a judgment based on the warning. If the case is not hospital-acquired infection but a warning generated due to the lab findings, the physician needs to "rule out" the patient and states reasons. If the physician confirms the infection, he/she has to enter the diagnosis in the ICD-10 library to ensure the accuracy of the entry. The diagnosis would then be marked with "hospital-acquired infection" and automatically updated to the "Admission Note" in the patient's EMR in real time. When the patient is discharged, the cover page of the closed medical record would be generated containing the marked diagnosis.

Third, when a patient is to be discharged, if the infection warning has not yet been responded to, the physician would receive a reminder triggered by the system asking the physician to take actions before discharging the patient. In this way, he information on the cover page of the closed medical record is complete, accurate, and consistent with the data in the infection database could be realized.

With all these in place, we are able to compare the information in the infection monitoring system and the discharge documentation of the patients. The closed loop of infection information processing has been completed (see Figure 8.9).

With the new IT architecture (Figure 8.10), we are able to monitor the entire process from data collection to data utilization.

More importantly, we have achieved our goal of zero underreport with the support of the new system.

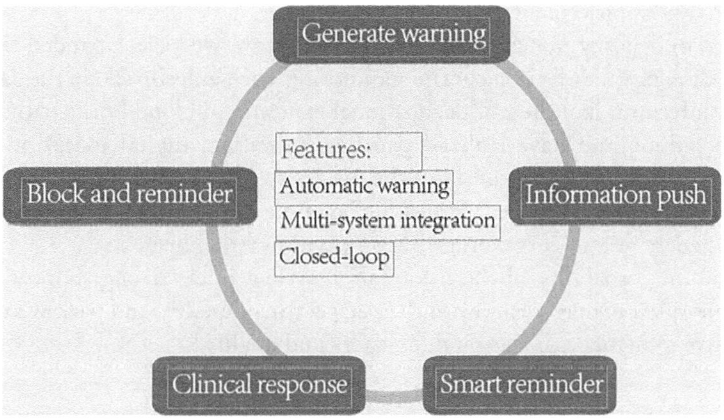

Figure 8.9 Closed loop of hospital infection monitoring.

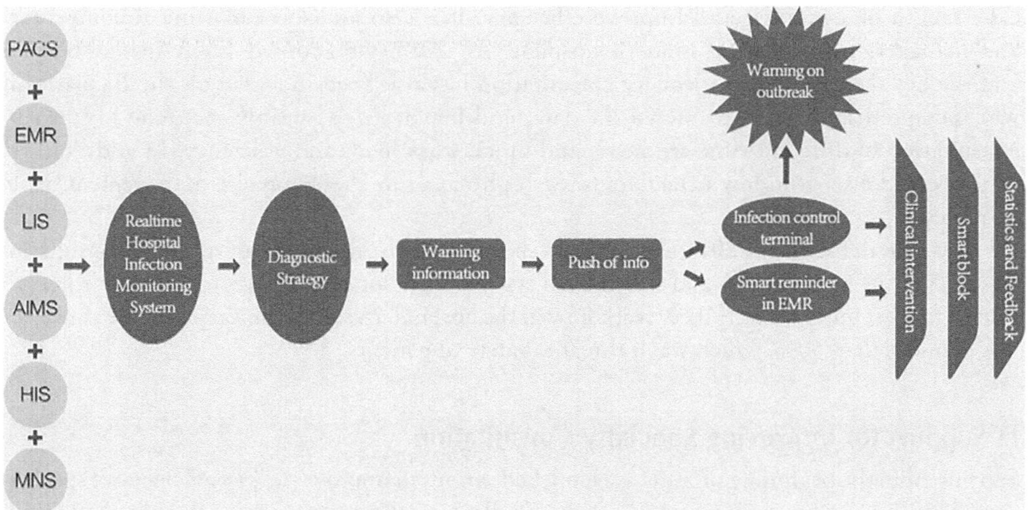

Figure 8.10 Architecture of hospital infection monitoring system.

BI Platform for Decision Support

As a crucial indicator, hospital-acquired infection monitoring data can directly reflect the healthcare quality. Therefore, it should be reported to the decision-making body of the hospital accurately. For this purpose, we completed the closed loop with the support of our BI platform. It can ensure the flexibility and accuracy of data through direct retrieval of the diagnosis on the cover page of closed medical records for analysis.

According to the *Hospital Infection Management Quality Control Indicator* issued by the National Family Planning and Health Commission (now called National Health Commission) in 2015, we selected several monitoring indicators related to hospital-acquired infection on the BI platform to enable real-time display of data. Hospital managers can access the hospital infection monitoring system through the BI platform to review more specific and detail information regarding the infection indicators. More importantly, the comparison and display on the BI platform could support the hospital management, clinical activity management and provide accurate decision evidence for quality improvement.

As the trend of delicacy management continues to grow, we have expanded the utilization of information technology in infection control monitoring, such as feedback on the daily supervision, purchase of disinfectant, handling of occupational exposure to blood borne pathogens, handling of sterilization failure, and have realized paperless operation, digital footprints, and traceable process, which contributed significantly to the efficiency of our daily work. In addition, we also added the "Environmental Hygiene Monitoring" module in the infection monitoring system and realized the paperless full process monitoring on environmental hygiene.

The data mining capability of the information system offers strong support to the decision support of the hospital management from the perspective of quality and patient safety. It offers us a new perspective to manage the hospital for safety and quality.

Case 3: Specialty Consultation: Data-Based Quality and Efficiency

Efficient and high-quality consultation provided by specialists could fully tap the clinical strength of a hospital and improve efficiency. It is also an aspect of clinical competency and managerial expertise of modern hospitals. In 2013, we adopted EMR in our hospital and the key data related to specialty consultation has also been included on the BI platform, which could display and drill down the data on different levels, mainly the trend of specialty consultation of different time segments and units, work load, and efficiency. In addition, the system could also drill down the data to each physician to enable precise management of the activities.

However, in the end of 2015, the statistics showed that the timeliness of specialty consultation was fluctuating around 85% and it had been staying there for almost 2 years. The low efficiency started to exert impact on the daily work flow in the hospital. In some surgical units, the timeliness was even less than 50%, which was a threat to safety of patients.

IT Support for Improving Specialty Consultation

Starting from the beginning of 2016, we launched actions to improve the low efficiency of specialty consultation by utilizing the strength of the IT platform. Other measures taken in the hospital included standard privileging of physicians, circulation of consultation quality monitoring results, inclusion of specialty consultation evaluation into unit KPI management, peer evaluation among physicians, etc.

First of all, we put in place stricter management over the indications to trigger specialty consultation. We divided the cross-disciplinary consultation into three levels. "Emergency Consultation" is limited to emergency and critical patients. The requesting unit calls the physician and the invited physician has to be on site within 10 min. "Scheduled Consultation" is provided to patients who have scheduled surgery in the next 1 or 2 days or who require consultation before discharge. The invited physician should complete the consultation within 24 h. The last type is the "Regular Consultation," which is for the rest of the patients. The consultation is required to be completed within 48 h. Based on the categorization, the inpatient physician initiated the request for specialty consultation in the EMR and selected the level of service requested. The hospital redesigned the process in the information system to require the signature by an attending physician or a higher-level physician before the request could be submitted to ensure the accuracy of the indications and the quality of the consultation service. The privileges of healthcare staff are maintained by the Human Resources Department through the human resources dictionary in the system. A list of consultation items has also been developed to improve efficiency and avoid errors.

The quality of specialty consultation service is guaranteed through stringent control on the privileges of the physicians who could provide specialty consultation. The consulting physician should be an attending or of higher level. The management of the privilege is realized through EMR and maintained by the HR. The units who have chief residents have submitted their staff roster to the Medical Affairs Department for privileging. The privilege would be withdrawn as soon as the chief resident finishes his/her practice in the unit. If the chief resident could not solve the problem, he/she should further refer the case to an attending physician or other physician of higher level for joint consultation.

Peer evaluation has been implemented for further improvement. When the consultation is completed, both the inviting and invited units could evaluate the performance of each other in the EMR system. The scale consists of five levels, namely "Very satisfied," "Satisfied," "Fair," "Not satisfied," and "Poor." Extra comments can be noted on the form as well. The evaluation results and the comments are visible to both sides in the EMR.

The BI platform is utilized to monitor the timeliness of the service provision. Data related to specialty consultation, including all consultation cases, total number of different services (Emergency, Scheduled, and Regular cases) as well as the timeliness are released in the hospital.

The evaluation mechanism has been improved to make the KPI management more comprehensive. The above-mentioned data are released on the information platform of the Medical Affairs Department every month, and further analysis is presented on the quarterly quality meeting on a hospital level. The evaluation on the timeliness of specialty consultation provision has also been included in the KPI management with a threshold of ≥90%.

Precise Management and Quick Respond

After the improvement actions, the timeliness of all three levels of specialty consultation in both June and July 2016 reached over 95%, indicating a significant increase from that in 2015 with statistical significance ($P = 0.000$). The timeliness of the Emergency Consultation increased compared with that in 2015 with statistical significance ($P = 0.043$), but it only stood at 57.89% (see Table 8.2).

Table 8.2 Efficiency of Specialty Consultation (Before and After)

Level of Consultation	*2016.6–7*				*2015.6–7*				*P-Value*
	Total Cases	*Number of Timely Consultation*	*Number of Untimely Consultation*	*Total Timeliness (%)*	*Total Cases*	*Number of Timely Consultation*	*Number of Untimely Consultation*	*Total Timeliness (%)*	
Total	4,383	4,167	216	95.07	4,276	3,313	963	77.48	0.000
Emergency consultation	76	44	32	57.89	125	54	71	43.20	0.043
Special consultation	2,521	2,420	101	95.99	3,442	2,475	697	79.75	0.000
Regular consultation	1,786	1,703	83	95.35	709	514	195	72.50	0.000

As the timeliness further improved, the average length of stay (LOS) and the preoperative LOS had also been reduced. In June and July 2016, the average LOS was 8.21 days, shorter than 8.36 in 2015, and the preoperative LOS was reduced to 3.25 days in 2016 (3.60 in 2015).

At the same time, the satisfaction rate increased as reflected by both the inviting and invited sides. The satisfaction rate toward the inviting units reached 97% and that toward the invited side also hit 95% in June and July 2016.

Our Experience

We summarized our experience with utilizing information system to support the management of specialty consultation:

1. *The qualification and privileges of both the requesting and invited physicians are guaranteed through the restriction designed in the system.*

   Due to insufficient experience or the intention of self-protection, some physicians might initiate a consultation with no indication or select the wrong level of service, which might result in a waste of resources or complains on frequent invitation without proper indications. If the situation is not under control, the physicians would not pay much attention to the specialty consultation, and the quality of the service would be compromised. Besides, if the consulting physician was not competent or held no sufficient qualification, his/her opinions would not be helpful to the care of patients and might lead to misdiagnoses or under-diagnoses. The clinical competency of the physicians is vital to the quality of consultation. So, we established the restrictions in the EMR system according to the privileges of physicians to effectively ensure the quality of consultation and improve the satisfaction rate of the service on both sides. Meanwhile, the flexibility we have left for the involvement of chief residents also provides opportunities for talent development.
2. *EMR system is the carrier and tool for specialty consultation management.*

   We realized the capture of discrete data from the consultation documentation in the EMR after the integration of the two modules, including the time of request, level of consultation, requesting physician, consulting physician, time of the consultation provided, etc. The entire cycle of the specialty consultation from the initiation till the completion is under the supervision by the requesting unit, consulting unit and Quality Control Office for timely intervention should any problem occur. Electronic documentation also prevents problems such as illegibility and left-blank fields, and facilitates the accurate statistics and timely feedback.
3. *Information system-based KPI management is the means to ensure quality and timeliness.*

   Against the background of healthcare reform in the country, the health authorities attach increasing importance to the KPI management in public hospitals to sustain the non-for-profit status of the hospitals and enhance the efficiency to meet the needs from the people. Therefore, one of the indicators to evaluate the operational efficiency of public hospitals adopted by the national authority is the average LOS. Our hospital also hoped to tap our own potential and to enhance their competitiveness through scientific managerial expertise. However, the untimeliness and unsatisfying quality of the consultation commonly existed, which led to repetitive consultation, delayed surgeries, prolonged average LOS, and, eventually lowered hospital efficiency. After we implemented the information platform and monitoring on the timeliness and evaluation, the efficiency was significantly improved and the average LOS was reduced. A closed loop was also formed to ensure quality and safety.

However, we still found that the timeliness of the Emergency Consultation was only around 60%. It might be related to the excessive burden on the patients due to the high volume of patients and consultation requests in large general hospital. At the same time, the segmented expansion of the hospital resulted in undesired building structure, enlarged distance between units, crowded elevators, etc. These added to the difficulties in response within 10 min of the Emergency Consultation. In that case, a more comprehensive management solution was in need.

In the past 1 year of improvement, we already proved that standard physician privileging, publishing of consultation quality monitoring results, inclusion of specialty consultation in the unit KPI management, penalties and incentives for the consulting physicians as well as the peer evaluation could be ways to improve the quality and efficiency. However, with the rapid development of sub-specialties and increasing complicated patients, usually the cases could not be solved by just one or two units. Meanwhile, the patients are more aware of diseases and hold higher expectation of hospital services. The service provided by one unit can no longer satisfy patients' needs. Therefore, the traditional specialty consultation needs to be innovated to provide high-quality multidisciplinary care to patients for improved diagnosis rate, cure rate, and successful resuscitation rate. This must bring new challenges to the delicacy management of hospitals.

Case 4: "Pure" Fast Track

Profile of Mr. He

It was at noon in June 2016 when Mr. He suddenly felt numbness of his left extremities. The body was not listening to his brain and he could not hold up the cup. He needed his wife to help him to walk. And he started to stutter. His wife immediately called 120, the municipal emergency care hot line.

12:13 The ambulance was sent out.

12:23 First aid staff arrived at Mr. He's home, learned about his condition, and decided to bring him onto the ambulance. The ambulance reported to the 120 Control Center that the patient was highly suspected with acute stroke.

12:25 Xuanwu Hospital received the call from 120 who told the hospital that the patient might have acute stroke and requested the Fast Track service. The Triage Desk immediately notified the staff on call for the Thrombolysis Fast Track program.

12:33 The Thrombolysis Team arrived at the ER waiting for Mr. He.

12:38 The ambulance arrived at the hospital. Ambulance staff handed the patient over to the Fast Track physician. While the patient was triaged and registered, the physician started inquiry, physical check-up, and assessment. Orders, lab work, examinations were requested. The ER nurse came to the bedside for phlebotomy. The Fast Track staff assisted the families for payment and accompanied the patient to the CT scan. The care workers immediately delivered the specimens to the lab and performed handover with the lab staff for prioritized test. The Thrombolysis Team decided to perform intravenous thrombolysis ASAP based on the patient condition and CT scan. Then they communicated with the family and started the preparation for the procedure, including borrowing medications from the pharmacy and getting the gurney for thrombolysis (with weighing scale and capability to calculate weight-based dosage and speed of medication administration). The payment would be collected after the patient was treated (but informed consent needed to be obtained first). It took 41 min from the arrival of Mr. He at ER to the initiation of the intravenous thrombolysis treatment (DNT). During the procedure, the changes of patient's condition were under close monitoring. After 1 h, Mr. He's condition was still fluctuating and progressing. The thrombolysis physician notified the physician on the intra-arterial thrombolysis team. The physician arrived at the ER to discuss the treatment plan with the family.

14:56 Family signed the informed consent. Skin preparation was started and the Interventional Procedure Center was notified of the procedure arrangement.

15:05 Patient was sent into the Interventional Procedure Center. After arteriopuncture and administration of contrast, severe stenosis of the right internal carotid was discovered. Stent was inserted. On the second day after the procedure, the muscle strength of the patient's left half of body recovered from Level 0 to Level IV. NIHSS score was improved from 12 to 6. The symptoms were getting better.

Process Redesign Enabled by IT Capability

Generally, 20% of the patients might suffer from disability caused by stroke. It is also a huge social and economic burden. For patients within the 3-h window and 3–4.5-h window after the hit of ischemic stroke, thrombolysis with intravenous rtPA was the only effective treatment if performed with screening on indications and contraindications. Therefore, the continuous improvement of the Fast Track for Stoke could bring more benefit to patients through saving time. In our hospital, we established the patient-centered Fast Track for Stroke in ER to reduce DNT.

Taking the patient in the case just given, there are at least 16 healthcare staff involved in the process, including ambulance staff, 120 Control Center staff, triage nurse, neurologist, staff of the thrombolysis team, second-line physician, phlebotomy nurse, delivery worker, lab staff, radiologist, pharmacy staff, cashier, intra-arterial thrombolysis team staff, interventional procedure physician, anesthesiologist, and nurse of the Interventional Procedure Center. Close and seamless cooperation is the key. Any delay at any point could prolong the time of treatment.

Therefore, quality meetings regarding the Fast Track for Stroke has been convened every week to analyze each step on the process for each patient, find out the causes of delay and discuss the solutions.

At the beginning, hard stops were designed in the IT system to restrict the flow. That means the process only proceed with each step completed in the system. But in emergency cases, staff would bypass the entire IT system. It, of course, did not meet the needs of the patients. We invested a lot of time and man power in the improvement actions to reduce the time to the maximum, and achieved outstanding results. The mean of DNT has reduced from 100 min before 2015 to 41 min today. According to the international requirement, DNT should be controlled under 60 min. As a matter of fact, we already had 90% of our thrombolysis patients treated within 60 min. However, we had to pay extra cost for the process.

In June 2017, Jilan came to our hospital and learned about the Fast Track process. She first recognized the efficiency of the flow, but also pointed out that the information system was not well integrated with other systems in the hospital, and that some of the manual process could be supported by IT through systematic improvement.

She also said that good IT system should be the support of clinical operation to objectively and truly reflect the details of clinical operation, and help to identify the problems through aggregation and analysis for the quality improvement of the hospital as a whole. Patient identification and safety could not be fully ensured without the assistance from IT system. The top-level design required the participation of various departments. The information system for the Fast Track work flow actually involved various aspects to make the clinical work more convenient and bring more benefit to the patients. It would also be helpful in quality control through providing evidences and closed-loop management. Though it might not be easy, but it would worth our efforts.

Jilan's comment enlightened us. Soon we established the IT Improvement Group consisting of IT Department, Medical Affairs Department, Outpatient Department, Nursing Department, ER, Pharmacy, Laboratory, Radiology, and Financial Department. They met on a weekly basis to develop action plans and discuss the feasibility. Process design should always base on the reality of our hospital. The principle we followed was to enhance the communication and reminder functions in the system between physicians, nurses, and ancillary units and provide stronger support and guidance to the clinical operation.

Based on that, we made the following changes to the Fast Track for Stroke flow (see Figure 8.11).

1. Reminder function. When triage nurse enters the patient's chief complaints into the triage system, for example, limb weakness, or alalia, the system would pop up a window reading: Within 3h or Not? Initiate Fast Track or Not? Reminders are important to triage nurses because of their busy duty. In particular, for new staff, it could help them identify high-risk patients to ensure the best treatment opportunities.
2. Physician–nurse communication through system in the past, when nurse identified a high-risk patient, he/she needed to accompany the patient to the consultation room and asked the physician to see the patient first. After the improvement, the process can be realized electronically. The nurse only needs to initiate the Fast Track for a patient. Then an eye-catching icon would appear next to the patient name in the system. When the information is sent to the physician's side, the patient would be prioritized at the top of the patient list on the physician's screen.
3. Enhanced communication between physician and ancillary departments. If a patient does not need Fast Track treatment, staff can choose to end the process. Otherwise, the prescribed

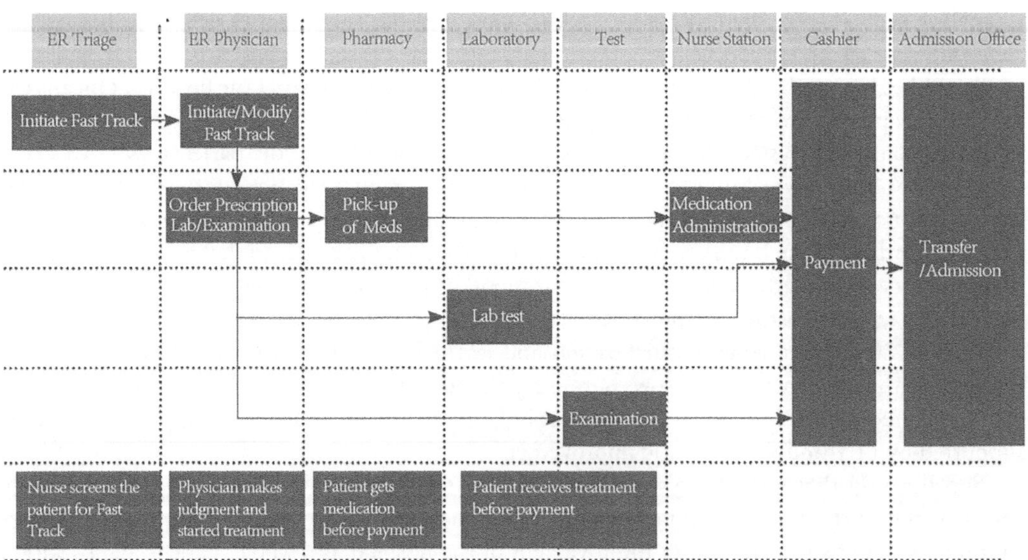

Figure 8.11 Flow chart of Fast Track for Stroke.

orders would be directly sent to the ancillary departments with a prioritization icon next to the patient name to remind the physicians from those units to perform tests or examinations on the patient first. We removed the billing system from this work flow to ensure that patient treatment is before the payment. In the past, the payment could also be settled afterwards. But the physician had to remember to stamp on the paper chart as a symbol for Fast Track service. Now we have the system to help us do all these trivial things.

4. Medication safety. In the past, physician would borrow medications from the ER Pharmacy in advance to save time. In the new process, the system can remind the pharmacists that the prescribed medication is for the patient on Fast Track service. The pharmacy would immediately dispense the medication to ensure medication safety for the patient.
5. Quality control over phlebotomy. The documentation of the phlebotomy was done manually by the nurse and was not included in the electronic system. But now, the nurse can scan the wristband on the patient, which generates the information of blood sampling in the mobile nursing system to ensure the complete footprints of all care measures performed.
6. Real-time update of pre-hospital information. Currently, the 120 Control Center calls the triage nurse at ER, and the nurse would further notify the thrombolysis team staff. During the quality control process, we found that the pre-hospital emergency information was not immediately provided by the 120 Control Center upon the arrival of the patient. We are now working with the 120 Control Center on developing an APP for information transmission to ensure the availability of the pre-hospital information for the physicians when they receive the patient in the hospital to make decisions on the following actions.

According to the requirements of HIMSS EMRAM Stage 7, Xuanwu Hospital has already achieved a paperless environment, closed-loop management for major clinical processes and advanced CDSS and the appropriateness medication use rules defined by our own hospital. The CDSS was built based on Mayo's knowledge base. The BI platform has also enabled us to fully utilize the data and make decisions accordingly.

Guided by the HIMSS EMRAM Stage 7 criteria, Xuanwu Hospital has pushed the IT capability of the hospital to a new height to ensure patient safety, make the work easier for our staff, and support the clinical processes. This has laid a solid foundation for IT-driven hospital administration and our JCI journey in the future.

Chapter 9

Longhua Hospital Shanghai University of Traditional Chinese Medicine

Xiao Zhen, Tang Yijun, Xu Liwen, Xi Yan,
Dong Liang, Chen Xinlin, and Shi Jingyi

Longhua Hospital Shanghai University of Traditional Chinese Medicine

Xiao Zhen, *Chief Physician, Master of Public Management, and Researcher of Healthcare Administration.*

Since the assignment as the President of Longhua Hospital, Dr. Xiao has led the organization through a series of remarkable progress, including the approval as clinical trial center for Traditional Chinese Medicine (TCM) by the State Administration of TCM in 2017 and JCI Accreditation of Academic Medical Center in 2018. Dr. Xiao has roles of Vice Chairman of Shanghai Association of Chinese Medicine, Vice Chairman of Hospital Administration Chapter of China Association of Chinese Medicine, etc.

Chen Xinlin, *MD, Chief Physician, Supervisor of graduate candidate*

Dr. Chen, Vice President of Longhua Hospital Affiliated to Shanghai University of Traditional Chinese Medicine, has devoted herself to clinical care, education, and research for 16 years and built up expertise in integrative care for cardiovascular diseases, hospital administration, and the passage of TCM as a tradition. Dr. Chen is the Vice Chairman of Chinese-Western Integrative Care Chapter of Chinese Society of Gerontology and Geriatrics, among others.

Shi Jingyi, *Chief Physician*

Dr. Shi is the Director of President's Office, the JCI Preparation Office, and Hospital Group Office of Longhua Hospital Affiliated to Shanghai University of Traditional Chinese Medicine.

With familiarity in processes of hospital administration, Dr. Shi has demonstrated skills in coordination. She has participated in decision-making processes for major changes and as program manager for writing hospital development strategies, developing appraisal standards for TCM hospitals in Shanghai and international exchanges and communication. Her research interest lies in performance appraisal of various categories of staff and the impact of process redesign on the staff appraisal. Dr. Shi isMember of Pediatrics Chapter of Chinese Association on Chinese Medicine, among others.

Hospital Introduction: Founded in July 1960, Longhua Hospital Shanghai University of Traditional Chinese Medicine (hereinafter referred to as "Longhua Hospital") was one of the four clinical centers for traditional Chinese medicine (TCM) with the longest history in China. When initially founded, the hospital recruited more than 30 high-profile TCM doctors from the general public and appointed them as the founders of the major disciplines that the hospital was set up with. Before then, they had practiced and studied privately at home. But starting from then, they came to practice and exchange together, propagated the doctrine, and imparted professional knowledge. Their commitment to TCM practice has laid the foundation for the hospital's culture of encouraging diversity, open-mindedness, inclusiveness, and creativity.

Longhua Hospital has become a national TCM research center and one of the role models for TCM hospitals in China with its strong character and expertise of TCM, thanks to its long-lasting pursuance of TCM-focused care through the strategy of "earning reputation for doctors, disciplines, hospitals and practice"; the mission of "putting quality and patient at the first place, inheriting traditional doctrine, breaking new grounds and pursuing excellence"; the strategy of "focusing on TCM and integrating TCM with western medicine" and the vision of "establishing ourselves as a respectable and reputable hospital with a strong TCM profile" over the past five decades.

International Accreditation: In 2012, Longhua Hospital achieved the highest score among all the tertiary TCM hospitals in the level-based national re-accreditation of TCM hospitals, whereas the Ethics Committee received SIDCER (Developing Capacity in Ethical Review) and CAP (Capability Accreditation Program of Ethics Review System for Chinese Medicine Research) certifications.

In October 2016, Longhua Hospital was validated for HIMSS EMRAM Stage 6, becoming the seventeenth hospital of HIMSS EMRAM Stage 6 and the first comprehensive TCM hospital in China.

In July 2017, we received JCI (Joint Commission International) consultants for a JCI mock survey.

Contents

Preface

A Few Thoughts on Synergy of IT Dept. and JCI Office

In line with the shifting focus for modern medicine from single-disciplinary development to global crossover of interdisciplinary resources, the national strategy for TCM in China is to help TCM more readily recognized and accepted in the world. With this strategy in mind, the leadership of Longhua Hospital has regarded healthcare quality and patient safety as the endless pursuit of the organization. As the hospital has been working on both JCI accreditation and HIMSS EMRAM validation, with the effort to enhance compliance to standards, significant progress has been achieved in healthcare quality as well as the management of medication, infection control, equipment, utility, and human resources. The adoption of IT as well as the evidence-based, data-driven management has put our hospital on a new starting point.

When we meet JCI surveyors or HIMSS validators again in the future, the administrators of Longhua Hospital will definitely recall the heated discussions with JCI and HIMSS experts on how the process should flow for patient transport and quality control. Such thinking is also reminiscent of how hard they worked on meeting the JCI and HIMSS requirements altogether, a synergistic couple, to push management and patient safety to the best we could.

At the Directors Meeting, July 30, 2015

At the meeting of directors from all the units, the leadership announced an important plan: the hospital would work toward the JCI accreditation for academic medical center, and a team of experts would be performing a baseline assessment from August 10 to 19.

Among the multiple reasons cited by the leadership, this one was the most relatable to me: "As one of the top TCM hospitals in China who has strong feature of global perspectives, to hold ourselves against higher standards is a necessary step to take." The hospital needed this common goal to inspire staff to strive for better. On the patients' side, a set of international standards of high quality to ensure the safety of care is needed. The hospital already secured the first place in the national re-accreditation for tertiary TCM hospitals in 2012, and a title of "National Civilized Organization" in 2015. Decades of endeavor have earned us great achievements, which has slowly generated complacency among older staff like me. As such, it takes an extraordinary goal to reignite the momentum of the entire staff.

Reflection: to generate change because of the problems that bite us as a hospital operates and develops, it may face such problems as inflexible service process, ineffective means for communication and compromised appropriateness of care. When problem arises, managers may be eager to define its nature but seldom quantifies the magnitude of the problem. Common to any hospital, these phenomena are attributed to a mixture of features, from the inability to adapt from technical and managerial aspects, to the unfavorable contradiction and pattern of the healthcare industry in general. Therefore, every hospital administrator is faced with the urgent task to enhance quality and efficacy, and make the benefits of reform and changes perceivable to the general public without compromising the beneficence nature of hospitals. We wanted to have our practice assessed by accreditation schemes from third-party authorities not because of the piece of certificate that may signify administrative achievement. Rather, it is the advanced philosophies of management that we have been looking for. We have hoped to improve ourselves by working toward accreditation so as to have a better chance of addressing problems that may haunt us in the mid-and-long run, adjusting our goal for development and driving quality as well as efficacy.

The hospital determined its mission to be "putting quality and patient at the first place, inheriting traditional doctrine, breaking new grounds and pursuing excellence." When the leadership made that announcement, none of the comprehensive TCM hospitals in China had been accredited by JCI. In considering the adoption of JCI standards, the leadership had discussions with staff from time to time on questions such as "Is there contradiction between management models from other countries and those in China?" "Is there contradiction between modern management models born out of western medicine and the actual operation of TCM?" "Shall we take a stepwise approach and start with certain units that practice western medicine, or roll out a one-off hospital-wide program?" and "Shall we set a standard goal at international organization or a higher one at international academic medical center?" To seek answers, we worked to get a comprehensive understanding of how we were doing as well as interpret and learn from the standards. In addition to group discussion for justification, the leadership also discussed with Ms. Jilan Liu, former JCI Principal Consultant. Finally, the tissue was brought to the Party and Government

Representatives' Meeting for discussion and solution, where the decision was made to roll out organization-wide preparation for JCI accreditation of academic medical center, the first tertiary TCM hospital in China to set this goal. This decision was listed as a key part in the hospital development plan for the thirteenth Five-Year Period.

In Longhua Hospital, administrators have held the belief that there is no clear boundary between western and Chinese medicine when it comes to hospital administration, and that TCM has advantage in individualized care in greater detail. It is expectable that certain philosophies or routines will be changed, and certain processes may even be overturned when we implement JCI standards. However, at the end of the day, these are for improving the quality of care as well as the level of management, driving change of mindset in service provision, enriching the content of service, and making a stride toward greater global influence of TCM.

Another reason behind the leadership's decision has been our pioneering role in IT and standards adoption, as well as adapting TCM for modern era, signified by our responsibilities of being a national center for TCM clinical research and a large tertiary TCM hospital. Examples of our pioneering role are as follows:

- The title of "National Model Organization for IT Adoption for TCM" was granted to us in 2009.
- Longhua Hospital achieved the highest score among all the tertiary TCM hospitals in the level-based national re-accreditation of TCM hospitals in 2012.
- Ethics Committee received SIDCER (Developing Capacity in Ethical Review) and CAP (Capability Accreditation Program of Ethics Review System for Chinese Medicine Research) certifications.
- The hospital was certified for 5S for its on-site management, and ISO5189 for the clinical laboratory platform.
- It was recognized as "National Civilized Unit" in the fourth routine review, and the phase-I clinical trial office received the certification of ISO17025.

Being an early adopter of evidence-based international standards of healthcare services, the hospital is undertaking supply-side reform while bearing in mind the reason why we started. With this new approach, we want to provide individualized care of high quality in considerate and empathetic ways, where diagnosis and treatment are based on overall analysis of the illness and the patient's condition, an inheritance of TCM. The goal of our JCI accreditation is to improve patient safety and management expertise, and promote sustained development as a TCM hospital.

Exit Conference of the JCI Baseline Assessment and Mock Survey, August 21, 2015

On the last day of this baseline evaluation, an exit conference was held.

Before the baseline evaluation was started, the leadership had not told us, the staff members, to do anything to prepare, probably because they wanted us to realize how standards relate to what we were doing daily. The same was true for consultants as well, who were presented with authentic, though slightly surprising, picture of the hospital. In the conference, the JCI consultants reviewed the result from the baseline evaluation and pointed out the areas that we were going to work on. Specifically, Ms. Jilan Liu, JCI consultant, guided us through a presentation of 127 pages with us and laid out the gaps observed and how we could do better. It just so happened that it was on the seventh day of the seventh month of the Chinese calendar, the Qixi Day (a Chinese festival that celebrates the annual meeting of the Cowherd and the Weaver girl in Chinese mythology, who had been banished to the opposite sides of the Milky Way because their love was not allowed). The review presentation struck me that the distance between us and the JCI standards was similar to the Milky Way that have kept the Cowherd and the Weaver girl apart.

What struck me the most from the 2-week mock survey was the difference between the philosophies behind the JCI standards and those we have used to in hospital administration. In terms of mindset, without doubt, the JCI standards represent the benchmark of safety-oriented care for the patients; in terms of practice, the JCI standards reflect patient flow as a whole; as for inclusiveness, when talking about patient care, the JCI standards address not only the classical areas of clinical units and medical technologies but also general support and logistics, which have been marginalized in the management model that we have used. Realizing these differences, the focus of the works on patient-care process shifted to the upgrading of service process, clinical process in particular, with new mindset, and the overall enhancement operation efficiency.

Shortly after the consultants left, IT Dept. worked in great detail to sort out the JCI standards relevant to IT in the fifth edition JCI standards. Some works needed to be done for each standard in the MOI (Management of Information) chapter itself as well as 22 extra standards from other chapters. This constituted a puzzle for the working group for JCI accreditation, clinical administrative departments, and IT Dept.

Xiao Zhen, CEO of our hospital, reflected further on the review from baseline evaluation, saying

> Don't be scared by the fact that our problems were cited. The purpose of finding problems is to address them. Failing to perceive problem doesn't mean there is no problem. The intent of going for JCI accreditation is to reach the ultimate goal of "greater patient safety and higher healthcare quality". The journey towards JCI accreditation will witness our works to fix, improve and implement policies, as well as our effort to reach a higher aim as one hospital. I have no doubt in achieving this goal with hard work from all of you.

Back to the problem list with over 400 items provided by the JCI consultants, seeing it for the first time, most of us were astonished as we came to realize the processes and practices that we had been so used to turned out to be wrong.

Most strikingly, the terms we had been familiar with were elaborated in greater detail, such as the governance of the hospital, sentinel event, the culture of safety, and ethics. The stark contrast was well presented in the pharmacy when a consultant from another country asked the pharmacist who was dispensing medications to patients. He asked

> I'm bring my kid to see a doctor. I don't have money with me. It's not for any emergency condition. I just want some health boosters for my kid. The physician has given prescription, but I haven't paid because I don't have money with me. So, if I come to you, will you give me the medication? What would you do?

Quite frankly, the pharmacist replied "If you're not emergency patients who are entitled to the Fast Track, then I had to ask the patient to get money and come back later." Hearing this, to our surprise, the consultant pointed out that in addition to sticking to the code of conduct, staff should also help patients find solution, instead of keeping denying their access to care. To address such issue, JCI Accreditation Office held a discussion with colleagues from Party Committee

Office, Medical Affairs Dept., Ethics Office and Science and Technology Dept. and came up with detailed rules of ethics in the organization as well as a revised code of conduct.

JCI Forum Held by CN-healthcare.com, October 26, 2015

The group of chapter managers for the JCI accreditation standards was brought to the JCI Forum held by CN-healthcare.com in Hangzhou (Zhejiang Province, east China), which signified the leadership's determination of transforming the hospital with JCI accreditation. To be honest, I learned a lot from the conference, where colleagues from JCI accredited hospitals shared their experience as well as department-specific comments. With the knowledge gained from the conference, we got better ideas of what to do as chapter managers.

Speakers from different hospitals unanimously emphasized the role of IT Dept. in the preparation of JCI accreditation. Some of them even admitted how IT system hindered the process as it fell short of the demand for JCI accreditation. Listening with rapt attention, I came to realize JCI accreditation is by no means a simple thing that needs input from clinical administrative departments only.

This new awareness was also developed among ourselves when we received evaluation that accreditation, whichever the program is, does not involve any single department alone. Rather, it takes the conjoined effort from all the units and departments throughout the organization. The evaluation is a test to the usability of our IT system and, more importantly, to the operation and management capability of a hospital, the communication and collaboration efficacy of staff and the organizational culture of safety.

Apart from the IT issue alone, the most daunting task in the preparation for JCI accreditation and HIMSS EMRAM validation has been the coordination and communication among all the administrative departments and clinical units. The IT Dept. is responsible for the overall architecture and general performance of the IT system in the hospital while it facilitates and satisfies the demands of clinical units. The wrong approach is to act like a group of blind men trying to size up an elephant, where the men feeling the nose, trunk, and leg mistakenly consider the elephant to be like a rope, a wall, or a pillar. In other words, in such scenario, each man mistakes the part he touches for the whole animal.

Considering the heavy workload for JCI preparations, the JCI Accreditation Office required every administrative department to designate a coordinator for JCI preparation. IT Center did more than that by designating four coordinators. This was a logical arrangement: one addresses the standards related to IT Center from MOI chapter; one handles requests from other departments and units for MOI compliance; one facilitates the demands for IT functions from chapters from IPSG (International Patient Safety Goals), ACC (Access to Care and Continuity of Care), PFR (Patient and Family Rights), AOP (Assessment of Patients), COP (Care of Patients), ASC (Anesthesia and Surgical Care), MMU (Medication Management and Use), PFE (Patient and Family Education), QPS (Quality Improvement and Patient Safety) as well as PCI (Prevention and Control of Infections); and the other manages the IT support needed from the other chapters of the JCI standards. After a hospital-wide thorough discussion, we recognized that the key link in the preparation for JCI accreditation lies in clinical administrative departments, while the key message from the JCI standards has been "patient-centered" standards. Likewise, the IT Center figured that the needs for IT support through IPSG to PCI chapters can be summarized as the need for an upgraded electronic medical record system, which is the most important role of IT Center in the preparation for JCI accreditation. Based on these conclusions, the leadership decided to start with the upgrading of electronic medical record to accelerate the readiness for JCI accreditation.

HIMSS Greater China 2015 Annual Conference, December 13, 2015

I stayed in Tianjin (northern coastal city) for the second HIMSS Greater China Annual Conference. It was a wonderful event and such a learning experience. I was deeply amazed by the extent of synergy between JCI and HIMSS in terms of tasks involved in the preparation. They share similarities in all aspects at all levels.

HIMSS EMRAM has been designed with Stages 0 to 7, with focus on ensuring patient safety and improving healthcare quality. The content addressed on each stage may differ, but the philosophy behind the stages has remained consistent. The consistency of care and the access to patient information are represented on each stage. To prepare for HIMSS EMRAM Stage 6 validation, the first tasks from key processes for a hospital are closed-loop medication administration, clinical decision support, and structured data elements in documentation. The essence behind these three key processes is patient identification and medication management required by JCI standards. Put it another way, for every standard from HIMSS EMRAM Stage 6, you can find how it fits in the clinical practice from JCI standards. For IT Dept., if we are successfully validated for HIMSS EMRAM, we will be confident in the compliance with JCI standards for various patient-care processes. It is safe to say that we should work toward HIMSS EMRAM validation first, during which we get a sense of the process and philosophies of JCI survey and lay a foundation with a practicable and sustainable IT foundation for our final goal of JCI accreditation.

Among the six organizations validated for HIMSS EMRAM Stage 6 or 7 in 2015, five had received JCI accreditation as well. These figures have validated our impression. Ms. Jilan Liu once commented that JCI accreditation helps hospital to manage staff with policies instead of administrative power, while HIMSS EMRAM sustains the policy-driven management with data-driven behavior. Based on her comment, the next logical conclusion would be: the key to convince people in management is no greater than data.

On the one hand, data-based argument is one of the key features of delicacy management in modern hospitals. On the other hand, data provide the foundation for quality and efficacy by ensuring compliance to processes, which increases efficiency. Therefore, the Quality Dept. works with IT Center and other relevant departments to generate the quarterly report on organizational quality and safety from data collected by HIS and the other systems for adverse event reporting, and present the report to the decision-makers. Data have enabled administrators to look at earlier steps in the processes and look into the bottom where the actual work takes place, and to understand the operation from fact-based reasoning instead of intuition. Without data, we were reduced to reactively dealing with the consequence of error, but with data, we could proactively prevent error. Over time, we gradually free ourselves from binary thinking and base decisions more objective facts and science.

The Proposal of Preparing for HIMSS EMRAM Stage 6 Was Approved, February 4, 2016

That day was important as the decision to work toward HIMSS EMRAM Stage 6 was formally approved. By upgrading the IT system, we are confident that we can provide better support to administrative departments, for the preparation toward JCI accreditation as well as to patients, and sustain the new changes made to various processes.

Reflection: the step-wise approach to our goal of JCI accreditation involves "lay the foundation—revise processes—establish mechanism—seek sustainability—serve the develop of the hospital." Specifically, to "lay the foundation" in the first step features the coordination of physical facilities and upgraded mindset, such as the adoption of IT, based on accreditation standards. During this phase, we came to realize that HIMSS EMRAM and JCI requirements lead to the same destination by different routes while each has its emphasis. Bearing in mind the goal of accreditation from both sets of standards and working toward them have helped us identify the hindrance of IT capabilities for JCI accreditation. With consultation and survey, we will have better chance of finding the proper solution and means to address problems, avoiding detours, and saving resources.

HIMSS EMRAM Stage 6 Baseline Survey, February 24, 2016

HIMSS consultants spent 1 day in our organization for a baseline assessment when they pointed out gaps for us to improve in terms of IT adoption. In face of the gaps, interestingly, we no longer felt difficult in getting things into shape, because we were looking at the problems identified during JCI baseline evaluation but reflected from the IT perspective. Again, as HIMSS EMRAM and JCI requirements lead to the same destination, though by different routes, they share the same emphasis on IT adoption. That's how our confidence was built.

Another good solution is an interfacing engine through which CDR and many other tasks will be more readily resolved. Fortunately, it had been installed already for the National HIT Interoperability Maturity Grading. Indeed, it is never wrong to start early!

Both the JCI and HIMSS consultant teams provided ideas and strategies for us to further our management and IT adoption, which would lead us to an overall upgrade. During several rounds of consultation and evaluation, the experts had rigorous and detailed assessment of the organization and talked with staff in terms of IT adoption, quality management and control, medication management, nosocomial infection control and management of staffing, medical education, facility and equipment, human subjects, among others. They found gaps while walking through processes and shared recommendation for improvement, which were exactly what we expected from these activities.

The Meeting to Collect Request for JCI Compliance, June 8, 2016

I participated in the organizational meeting where we talked about the updates of JCI preparation and what supports were still needed. It was the first time that I got a better picture of how to update the IT system for JCI standard compliance. Coming back from the meeting, I made a list of requests of IT features from all the departments. Comparing this list with the list from the previous HIMSS baseline assessment, I found they were highly similar. They were different only in the scope of impact: HIMSS EMRAM Stage 6 requires these functions to be available in several key units, while JCI accreditation requires consistent practice throughout the entire organization. For IT Dept., it would be natural to work toward JCI standard compliance first, and then HIMSS EMRAM Stage 6 requirement. Subsequently, we spread the upgraded processes that have met JCI standards to the rest of the hospital as a step forward toward HIMS EMRAM Stage 7 compliance.

Suddenly, I realized my admiration for experts who have developed the JCI standards and HIMSS standards. I wondered if they were living close to each other or even being neighbors so that they had many chances to discuss. Otherwise, how can these two sets of standards make such a perfect couple?

This meeting helped all of us, from frontline staff to administrators, understand the details about how to upgrade the IT system and reach consensus, as was shared by Xiao Zhen, CEO of the hospital: "To address IT upgrade first is a booster to JCI accreditation. Before we did this, we had the goal but did not have the means. But now, with the incessant means springing from HIMSS EMRAM validation, we have both the goal and the means."

In that meeting, the leadership, directors of administrative departments, chapter managers of JCI standards and staff from JCI Accreditation Office as well as IT Dept. focused on this roadmap, imagined themselves as patients who enter the hospital and complete all the steps, and freely spoke out their experience. The heated discussion and analysis lasted for 4 h, and the participants finally settled on the overall plan of IT upgrading. The way that we reached conclusion was probably an indirect managerial byproduct of the endeavor to work toward the two accreditation schemes.

HIMSS EMRAM Stage 6 On-site Validation, October 28, 2016

We finally got the HIMSS EMRAM Stage 6 on-site validation visit today after a year of hard work. This success did not come easily. It was not possible without the joint effort from all levels of staff from every department. The result itself was expectable, and what I found truly exciting were the comments from validators and the leaders from our hospital.

When extending her congratulations to Longhua Hospital for its certification of HIMSS EMRAM Stage 6, Ms. Jilan Liu, one of the validators, commented that:

> As a large-scale and modern comprehensive hospital with profound tradition and details of TCM, Longhua is outstanding for its electronic medical record and the modern TCM traits in the operating system. Longhua Hospital's experience of IT adoption has a far-reaching influence on the development of TCM in China as it, on one hand, has affirmed and given full play to the concept of individualized care where diagnosis and treatment is based on an overall analysis of the illness and the patient's condition, and on the other hand, has explored means to increase compliance to the standards of TCM practice and hospital administration, consistency of processes and adoption of international trend. Longhua's success in improving patient safety, healthcare quality and operational efficiency has corroborated that IT adoption knows no boundaries of nations or traditions of medicine.

Chen Xinlin, Deputy CEO of the hospital, shared,

> As a large-scale, tertiary-A and comprehensive TCM hospital, we have been making earnest effort in IT adoption and ranked the top among TCM hospitals in this aspect. At this moment when we are preparing for JCI accreditation, we are in urgent need of IT capabilities as support and means for the most prominent quality and safety requirement from the JCI standards. Therefore, the HIMSS EMRAM validation and our effort behind it come at perfect timing. To work on both accreditation schemes simultaneously may apparently delay the progress of JCI accreditation preparation, our initial intent, but as a common belief in China goes, 'sharpening the axe won't slow down the cutting of firewood'. I believe the spin-off of IT advantage from

Figure 9.1 A photo from HIMSS EMRAM Stage 6 validation.

> HIMSS EMRAM validation is conducive to steady and sure JCI standard compliance in sustainable way that reduces waste. In this sense, HIMSS EMRAM validation helps us get several ends at once (Figure 9.1).

In the past, when speaking of IT Dept., some staff might relate it to laying out Internet cable, repairing computers and managing the OA system. However, after going through the preparation of both accreditation schemes, these people may admire IT Dept. as an omnipotent colleague who is always found behind every activity in the hospital.

In the exit report of HIMSS EMRAM Stage 6 on-site validation, the address from the leadership echoed their prior forecast when the proposal of HIMSS EMRAM validation was still going through discussion. The forecast involved three aspects:

First, the work that we have done for HIMSS EMRAM validation have become the basis for JCI preparation with a series of reproducible processes and policies;

Second, the efforts made for HIMSS EMRAM validation is rewarding as it provides tangible support to the hospital's commitment to patient safety and higher quality;

Third, TCM hospital does not differ from hospital of western medicine in terms of the applicability of HIMSS EMRAM requirements, within which TCM hospitals can demonstrate its strength and make breakthroughs in the appropriateness review of TCM prescription, a daunting challenge.

A Hospital-Wide Meeting for Requesting Support for JCI Accreditation Preparation, May 21, 2017

I participated in the hospital-wide meeting where the JCI standard chapter managers gathered to explain their need. It was a heated discussion and exciting meeting where we, IT Dept., gathered much more requests and ideas.

Now, as we have got experienced, we were not scared at all. During the review scheduled twice a week, we always discussed the requests from the departments in charge of particular chapters in the JCI standards. We have a 400-item list of requests, and it was just getting longer. But my colleagues in IT Center still found this job rewarding because we had no problem in thinking of solution for every request, developing a feasible plan and taking action efficiently. To other departments, IT is more than important. It is the solution to problems. That is a commendable progress.

There was an episode in the routine meeting of our department 2 days ago. When we were discussing the templates of physician documentation for Emergency Room, the project manager from the software vendor drew our attention to the consistency of electronic documentation in the EMR system to ensure consistent care for patients in the hospital. His comment surprised us in that JCI philosophies have not only made its way to everyone's mind in the hospital but also blown the mind of professionals from the healthcare IT industry.

From this scenario, we truly felt that everyone had been on the move for JCI accreditation. Apparently, everyone knows the quote "position is offered to competent people."

Actually, the needs for IT support from JCI standard compliance are present throughout most chapters in the standard manual. In particular, many demands spring from the healthcare organization management standards in GLD (Governance, Leadership and Direction), FMS (Facility Management and Safety), SQE (Staff Qualifications and Education), and MOI chapters. It is worthwhile to discuss these demands. It will be of great help for the compliance of these chapters if we can turn all those demands into reality by IT means.

Exit Meeting of JCI Mock Survey, July 21, 2017

We had gone through the JCI mock survey finally, securing the pass to the actual JCI survey.

During the mock survey, divided into administrator, physician and nurse consultants, the experts had rigorous and detailed survey in the organization and talked with staff on a series of topics: quality control and management of medication, nosocomial infection, staffing, medical education, facility, equipment, and human subjects. They found gaps while walking through processes and shared recommendation for improvement.

They commended us on the achievements in the international safety goals, quality management, and administrative management, where expectation had been met. Now that we had known the gaps to fix and the strategy and means of fixing them, we were filled with confidence toward the success of JCI accreditation.

As the mock survey ended, the challenge of the hospital just began. That was particularly true for IT Dept.

Reflection: As all the staff had become more united during the preparation for the mock survey, we received a significantly better report than that from the baseline assessment. More significantly, progress on quality and safety was demonstrated by managerial data from all the aspects, such as clinical care, education, and research. That was a big encouragement for everyone, from administrators to frontline staff. One thing we have learned from this process is that no boundary exists between TCM and western medicine, or between China and the rest of the world when it comes to standard-driven management. As the first TCM hospital in China to work toward both JCI accreditation and HIMSS EMRAM validation, it has been like crossing the river by feeling the stones, and we are on the right tract now. We are confident in the result of the actual survey.

At a group dinner after the mock survey, a clinician, also my good friend and colleague, told me, "After these years of preparation and mock survey, I gradually learned what JCI accreditation is. You've done such good work and overcome various barriers. Over the past two years, I felt new changes every day and our hospital has become safer with higher quality."

I smiled with a knowing look. But it was clear to all of us that there was still a long way to go for the specialized and general (such as JCI Accreditation Office and IT Dept.) administrative departments. Unlike JCI accredited hospitals, we were still halfway toward JCI accreditation. Preparations were still underway until the actual survey scheduled next year.

There is a Chinese expression that says the going is toughest toward the end of a journey. In the advanced stage of reform, Longhua Hospital still faces problems of the policies and mechanisms, and the process improvement will not be made at one go. Fortunately, we decided to improve ourselves against JCI and HIMSS standards. Both of them are powerful instruments for patient safety and quality of care, so that we feel like holding the Heavenly Sword on one hand and Dragon Sabre* on the other.

Case 1: Pharmacy Went Ahead of the Rest and Successfully Adopted IT in Traditional Chinese Medications

Traditional Chinese medications are the key feature of traditional Chinese medical practice. As a hospital focusing on TCM care, we provide medication services of defining characteristics, where 60% of outpatient and inpatient prescriptions have been Chinese herbs, and around 700 inpatients take Chinese medicinal every day.

However, the dosing, administration route and compatibility of Chinese herbs have been based on its unique philosophy, which makes TCM pharmacy management distinct from that of western medicine pharmacy. The priorities of standardization and IT adoption, therefore, became the quality control of Chinese herbs, appropriateness review and accurate, detailed and individualized dosing.

Driven by these problems, the Pharmacy Dept. went ahead of the rest in closing the loop (supply—prescription appropriateness review—administration—monitoring) in Chinese herb management with the principle of "breaking new grounds without leaving the original aim, and inheriting the doctrine but not rigidly adhering to it" and based on international standards of HIMSS EMRAM and JCI. Thanks to the upgraded IT system, we got to overcome the bottleneck in the processes of quality control, appropriateness review and administration (see Figure 9.2). Under the guideline of "adapting ancient wisdom to modern times and foreign ideas to the practice in China," Longhua Hospital has made it to the upfront of the wave of TCM modernization with a towering tree of medication safety hierarchy.

Soil: Quality Management of Supply of Chinese Herbs

Chinese herbs are medicinals readily used in clinical care prepared and processed from raw ingredients. They are both medicinals and special products, which determines that the consistency and reliability of herb quality are suboptimal. What's more, it was hard to ensure proper storage

* These are a formidable pair of weapons from Heavenly Sword and Dragon Sabre, a popular novel of martial heroes in the Chinese culture from Louis CHA Leung-yung.

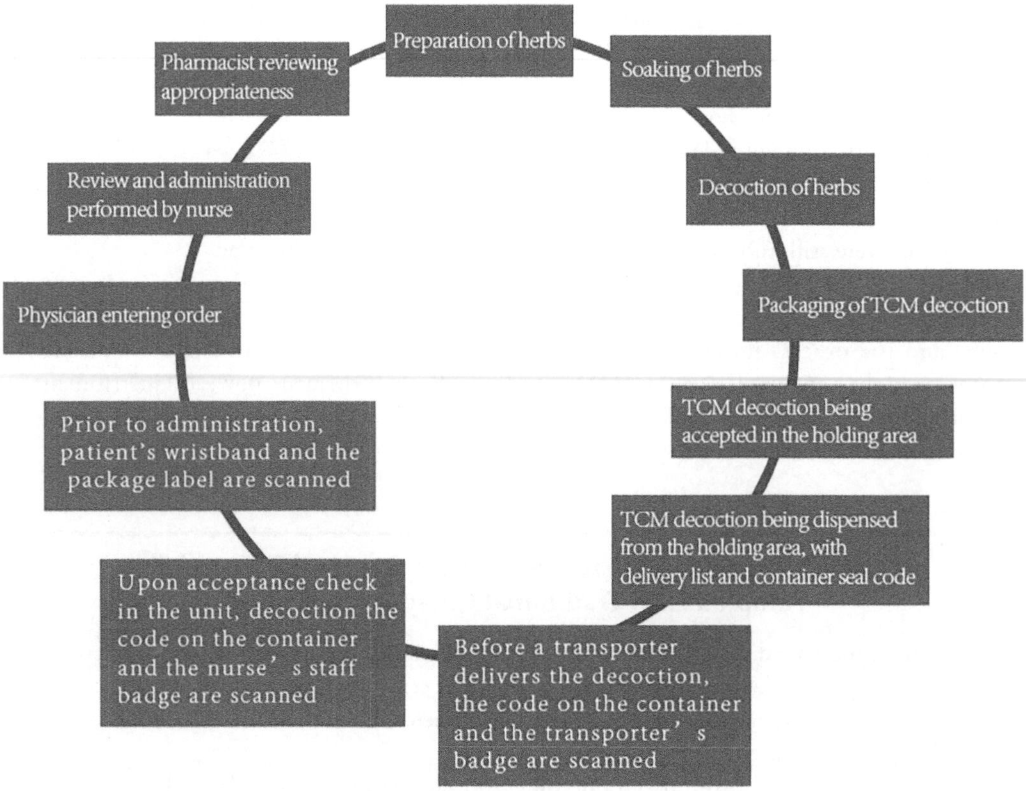

Figure 9.2 The closed-loop management of TCM decoction for inpatients.

condition before the herbs arrive at our warehouse due to the limitation in physical facilities of a third-party supplier such as location and humidity- and temperature-control equipment. That makes the quality assurance before arrival out of our control. That was evidenced by calls coming from patients to TCM Pharmacy, or Outpatient Office or general administrator on duty (during nights, weekends, and holidays), who complained about the herbs they had been given were dusty, mingled with impurities or of wrong specification.

Faced with these challenges, based on the JCI standards on supply-chain management and evidence-based purchasing, the Pharmacy Dept. took a step forward by collaborating with relevant departments to translate innovative management idea into reality. They worked together to modify policies on evidence-based medication purchasing, supply-chain management and warehouse management; monitor steps involved in herbal management, which included management and evaluation of suppliers, herb quality examination during acceptance and storage of herbs. By doing so, we met the standards for modern pharmacy management (for western medication) in terms of quality control, traceability, and ongoing monitoring.

The hospital purchased and installed temperature as well as humidity detectors, and designated two chief pharmacists as quality inspectors in the newly established Quality Inspection Office. They check and document Chinese herbs arriving with different batch number or different packaging dates for their property, impunity status, water content, sulfur dioxide, weight of each small pack and label. As Chinese herbs are not exactly homogeneous in quality, the Quality

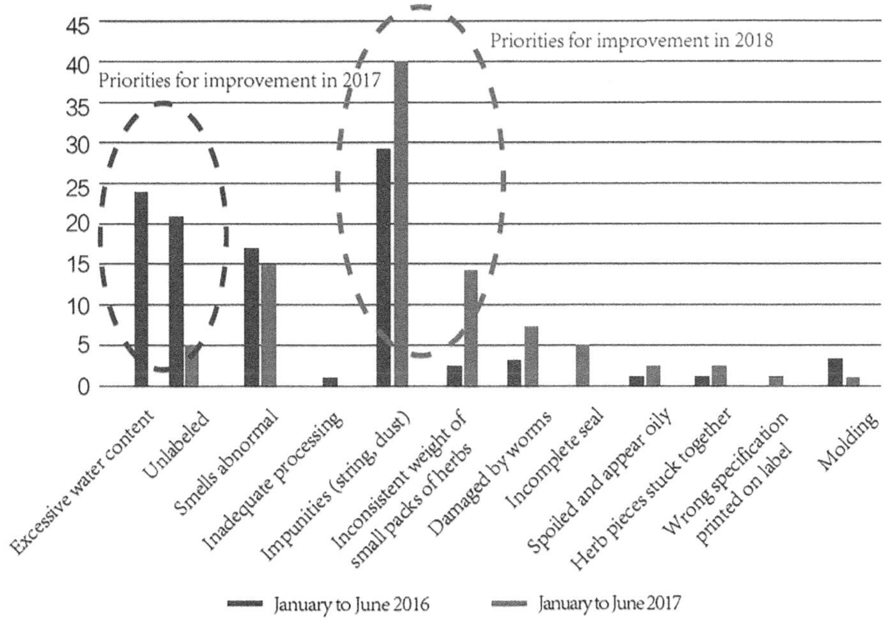

Figure 9.3 Year-on-year analysis of inferiorities identified during internal inspection in Longhua Hospital.

Inspection Office samples a certain proportion of herbs from the warehouse to verify quality. The team also analyzes causes for any inferiority (see Figure 9.3) and develops solution.

Always speak with data. The data gathered from quality inspection are provided to the suppliers, which indicate the areas where evaluation should provide. Based on our observation, the suppliers take corrective efforts and produce reports. For example, excessive water content was found consistently in the herbs checked by the Quality Inspection Office in 2016. After cause analysis, we figured that the water content in the initial product had been acceptable, and the problem arose from the interval between the initial product was ready and the final packaging. When influenced by weather, or when the water content was toward the higher end of the acceptable range of the product, the final products in small packages may become moist. With this cause identified, the hospital required all the suppliers and manufacturers to rectify by maintaining the environment for proper humidity and temperature, reducing water content to the lower end of the acceptable range, and measuring water content again before packaging. With these measures in place, water content for herbs was consistently acceptable in 2017, an important prerequisite for herb quality. Chinese herbs are special in that we usually do not change suppliers. However, when a particular herb is found unacceptable twice in 6 months, the hospital will look for another supplier to ensure herb quality.

The Tree Trunk: To Drive the Management and Appropriateness Review for TCM Prescriptions with IT

It is common that TCM hospitals provide integrative care by combining TCM and western therapies. If used properly, such integrative care will achieve twice the result with only half the effort, if not treating a disease by addressing both its root cause and symptoms, working concordantly to reinforce each other and reducing adverse reactions. Used improperly, though, may result in reduced efficacy, increased toxicity or adverse reactions and even severe consequence.

Another challenge for TCM is that TCM doctors are so used to hand-writing prescriptions, which complicates the management with illegible hand-writing, not using standard language, off-label use, and overdose. Also, administration route and special preparation method are not routinely specified in TCM prescription or medication list, which is a requirement from JCI standards on MMU.

On one hand, incompatibility among different herbs and overdose of toxic herbs are unavoidable risks for TCM, apart from the practice of integrative therapy popular among TCM hospitals. On the other hand, TCM, and integrative therapy in particular, has been underrepresented among the existing software of appropriateness review, which have been tailored to western medicine. Considering the fact that Chinese herbs account for 60% of outpatient prescriptions, a defining feature of our organization, we added functions of TCM prescription in the appropriateness review software that we use. The newly added features include, for example, incompatible combination of western medicine and herbs (or Chinese patient medicine), incompatibility among herbs (summarized as 18 antagonisms and 19 mutual inhibitors) and overdose of toxic herbs.

Pharmacist reviews and fills a TCM herbal prescription based on the specifications for TCM herbs from the Regulation on Prescription, according to Article 29 of the Regulation of TCM Herbs in Hospitals issued by the Chinese national health authority in 2007. In other words, when there is risk for medication safety in the prescription, whether being any of the 18 antagonisms and 19 mutual inhibitors, or contraindication for pregnant women or overdose, the pharmacist does not fill the prescription until the ordering physician confirms this prescription (with another signature) or makes some changes. To meet this requirement as well as guidelines for modern pharmacy management, the Pharmacy, IT Dept. and JCI Accreditation Office worked together and upgraded the appropriateness review software that serves as a proactive review mechanism. Since then, medication safety has been significantly improved.

The mechanism works in this way: physician gives a prescription in the CPOE (computerized physician order entry) while the software to review the prescription. If the software approves the order, it is then sent to the Pharmacy. Otherwise, it is directed to the Appropriateness Review Center for Outpatient Prescriptions, where pharmacists review orders manually. If the prescription fails the pharmacist review again, a message is sent to the ordering physician who may change the order. The review software reduces medication risk by catching near-misses early on.

When pharmacists review orders, they may also view the patients' laboratory results on the system and determine if the order for special patient should be approved. For example, when a patient has poor blood coagulation, a TCM pharmacist looks up the results of recent laboratory tests on the system, such as physiological, biochemistry, and coagulation results. When seeing blood invigorating herbs (such as Honghua, or *Carthamus tinctorius L.*), the pharmacist would alert the physician of the compromised coagulation capability of the patient via the appropriateness review software. For another example, if a physician orders blood invigorating and stasis dissolving herbs or Chinese patent medicine (such as Sanleng, or *Sparganium stoloniferum*; and leech) for a pregnant woman, a contraindication alert will pop up on the screen.

Leaves: Accurate, Detailed, and Individualized Ordering and Administration

"Observing, listening, inquiry and pulse feeling" as diagnostic techniques and "to establish diagnosis and treatment based on a thorough analysis of the illness and the patient's condition" are the unique features of TCM and conceptually consistent with individualized medicine, the essence of modern medicine. It has been based on the rules of "four properties (cold, hot, warm and cool) and five tastes (pungent, sweet, sour, bitter and salty)" and "developing a formula with the principle herb (King), the associate herb (Minister), the adjuvant (Assistant) and the guiding herb (Messenger)." To work properly, Chinese herbs should be grouped in various combinations of dose form, administration route, preparation technique, and optimal timing of administration. In terms of dosage form, doctor can choose from oral decoction (the most typical form), pill, powder, suppository, poultice, alcohol extract, vinegar extract, enema, washing decoction, bathing decoction, fumigant, ear drops, nasal irrigate, nasal insufflation, etc., based on the patient's physique and condition. In terms of preparation techniques, options include to be decocted first, decocted later, melted, reconstituted in boiling water, concentrated, decocted for short time, etc., where the amount of water needed varies. As for the optimal timing of drug administration, it could be taking on an empty stomach, before/during/after meal ingestion and before bedtime, depending on the property of the herbs, diagnosis, patient's physique, and natural season. Special delivery method may also be needed for certain diseases, such as enema and inunction.

The complexity of dose form and administration methods of TCM means ward nurses and pharmacists have to provide very different patient education from western medicine. This requires more effective communication between physicians, nurses, and pharmacists for better medication safety and efficacy. While upgrading the closed-loop medication administration capability, the Nursing Dept., Medical Affairs Dept., Pharmacy Dept., IT Center and JCI Accreditation Office keep seeking solution to individualized medication plan without compromising safety.

Take enema technique for example. To administer TCM decoction via enema or deliver it to the colon in drips has been used on patients with partial bowel obstruction due to gastrointestinal neoplasm who are not able to take decoction orally in the Oncology Unit I. The decoction of the formula Da Cheng Qi Tang (also known as the Decoction for Potent Purgation), among others, is delivered via anus to the rectum or colon and retained there for absorption via colon mucosa. Being absorbed by the body, the decoction cools the heat and detoxicates the bowel, softens the stool and dissipates clumps, purges the interior excess, invigorates blood and dissipates stasis. When giving such order, the physician specifies the timing of administration, temperature for the decoction, drip speed, and route. All the relevant information is sent to the pharmacist who reviews order and communicated to nurses via the labels on medication and the physician's order itself. Before, during and after the administrative procedure, nurses perform overall assessment on patient and inform physicians when needed. So, the entire process involves several sub-processes such as patient identification, assessment, closed-loop medication administration, and medication quality control.

Sixty percent of our inpatients receive TCM therapies, and around 700 inpatients are on Chinese herbal medicine every day, whether oral or topical administration. The Da Cheng Qi Tang decoction administered via enema is just one of them. To ensure efficacy of medicinals, the clinical administrative departments and IT Center worked to ensure they are dispensed in single dose units to ensure they are delivered to patients when needed every day based on the timing for use. When we were working toward JCI accreditation and HIMSS EMRAM Stage 6, the relevant administrative departments upgraded the closed-loop administration process for TCM decoction for inpatients, and provided the timing and route (for ingestion/topical application or anal dripping) of administration on the package of decoction to ensure safe and timely administration.

What's more, realizing our management method had been sketchy and nonspecific, we adopted new measures to ensure medication safety. After being given, an order goes through appropriateness review before being accepted in the pharmacy where staff scans its bar-code. In the preparation step, staff scans each pack of herbs for verification before soaking the herbs in water.

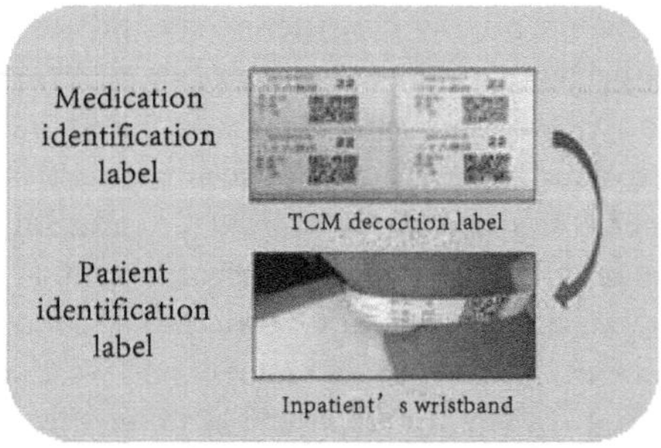

Figure 9.4 Verification between patient identity and medication order.

When herbs are in the decoction machine and ready for boiling, staff scans the machine and the label on the package again before turning on the machine. By the end when the decoction is done, it is collected in pack and labeled. With the IT system, every step in the entire preparation process can be monitored specifically to ensure accuracy of the preparation, traceability of the decoction, standard compliance of the decoction process and medication safety.

According to the requirement on patient identification and medication management from the IPSG of JCI standards, the clinical administrative departments worked with IT Dept. to generate unique QR code labels on the TCM decoction package that contains inpatient information such as ward, admission number, the date when the therapy starts, and volume, and ensure this information is consistent with that from the QR code on patient's wristband. Before giving the decoction to patients, nurses from clinical units scan the codes for verification of patient's identity and medication order to ensure patients receive the right decoction (see Figure 9.4).

If the order involves enema, the nurse learns from the patient's assessment, orders, and therapies to provide proper patient education in a timely fashion, closely monitors patient's vital signs and documents the administration. During a patient's stay in the hospital, the IT system provides information on assessment results from physicians, daily monitoring and administration record from nurses, as well as the appropriateness review and medication instructions from pharmacists to the multidisciplinary team of physicians, nurses, and pharmacists to facilitate update of patient's care plan. This mechanism reinforces the team care concept throughout the hospital so that everyone, from administrators to frontline staff, understands that it is a team effort, instead of individual effort, that treats patient. In addition, this mechanism has boosted effective communication in the hospital.

Outcome Evaluation

When correctly decocted and taken, every ingredient in a TCM prescription gets to demonstrate its expected efficacy. To this end, the hospital upgraded its mechanism of appropriateness review and administration by adding TCM functions to the existing EMR, and launched integrative review mechanism instead of doing it for western versus Chinese medicine individually. Being more inclusive and efficacious, this model has facilitated better communication among staff, provided more specific information on administration method and enhanced medication safety.

With the afore-mentioned process changes, we have achieved higher patient satisfaction and reduced medication error (see Table 9.1).

The adoption of IT has helped with the analysis of near-misses from preparation, which concluded that the wrong specification was picked from the shelf because the medication had been

Table 9.1 Medication Error Due to Wrong Dispensing of TCM

	Reason for Compliant			
Year	*Wrong Specification*	*Wrong Volume*	*Wrong Medicinal*	*Missing Ingredient*
January–June 2016	2	4	1	10
January–June 2017	0	0	0	6

Table 9.2 Preparation Errors of TCM Prescriptions

	Time Frame	
Metric	*January–March 2017*	*April–May 2017*
Wrong specification	0.07%	0
Wrong volume	0.06%	0
Wrong medicinal	0.04%	0

moved to another place but the code provided on the prescription was still the old one. As such, we immediately updated the code of location to reflect the actual storage (see Table 9.2).

The IT system has also improved efficiency of clinical pharmacists, whose daily volume of prescription to be reviewed was increased from 120 per day per person between January and June 2016, to 170 between January and June 2017.

The preparation for the dual accreditation of "JCI+HIMSS" has witnessed the concerted effects from the Pharmacy Dept. and IT Dept., where the Pharmacy Dept. proposed ideas and IT Dept. provided technology to support them. Their synergy has resulted in the transition from traditional to modern management of Chinese herbs, better quality of the management, safer care, and better patient outcome. From the hospital's perspective, this pool of big data gathered with the IT system can be used to demonstrate the science within TCM, how TCM fits into modern medicine and how TCM can be promoted to the global community.

Chapter 10

Children's Hospital of Shanghai

Yu Guangjun, Liu Yongbin, Sun Huajun, Liu Haifeng, Gao Chunhui, Wei Mingyue, Shi Minhua, Ling Qiming, and Chen Min

Children's Hospital of Shanghai

Yu Guangjun, *Master of Pediatrics, Ph.D., and Researcher of Health Management, and Supervisor of doctoral candidates*

Dr. Yu is the President of Children's Hospital of Shanghai (afflicted to Shanghai Jiang Tong University). His academic affiliations include Vice Chairman of Pediatrics Committee of Chinese Research Hospital Association and Shanghai Pediatrician Association, among others. As a lead professional in Shanghai, he has been awarded a Top-10 Young Administrator in Healthcare and Exemplary Individual in Women and Child Care in Shanghai.

His 20 years of career have centered on health policy, hospital management, regional integration of health information, and children's wellbeing. Mr. Yu has received the National Award on Science and Technology Progress and the Science and Technology Innovation Award of Chinese Hospital Association, among others. In addition to over 50 articles published in key Chinese journals and SCI-index journals, Mr. Yu has authored several books, such as The Cloud Technology of Health Care.

Liu Yongbin, *Bachelor of Pharmacology, Master of Public Administration*

Mr. Liu is an Associate Research Investigator of Healthcare Administration and Director of Medical Affairs Department of Children's Hospital of Shanghai with expertise in the operation and quality of medical care, patient safety, redesigning service processes, addressing patient complaints, and IT adoption.

Mr. Liu is a young editor of Journal of China Health Quality Management *and Member of Ambulatory Surgery Chapter of Shanghai Hospital Association, among his various roles. Mr. Liu has led many administrative studies, some of which were awarded in contests. For example, the project* Clinical Pathway Realized through IT System *was awarded the third prize in Science and Technology Innovation Award held by Chinese Hospital Association.*

Sun Huajun, *PhD, Chief Pharmacist*

Dr. Sun is the Director of Pharmacy Department of Children's Hospital of Shanghai. He has specialized in to pharmacology projects of national, municipal, and military levels, published over 60 articles, authored two monographs and contributed to several others. Dr. Sun has received many academic awards in the military medical field.

His roles include Vice Chairman of Prescription Evaluation Chapter of China Medical Education Association and Member of Clinical Pharmaceutical Administration of Shanghai Hospital Association, among others. Dr. Sun is also Editor of Journal of Pediatric Pharmacy, Pharmaceutical Care and Research, *etc.*

Hospital Introduction: Children's Hospital of Shanghai (CHS) was founded by Dr. Fu Wenshou, a renowned pediatrician of the early 20th century in China, and Dr. Su Zufei, the founder of pediatric nutritional studies of the same period in China, when it was initially named as Refugee Children's Hospital of Shanghai. As the first hospital in China specialized in pediatrics, now CHS is a tertiary-A pediatric hospital providing clinical care, health maintenance, education, science and research as well as rehabilitation.

International Accreditation: It was certified as HIMSS EMRAM Stage 6 in October 2016.

Contents

Preface

Overview: HIMSS Empowers Transformation of Healthcare Model

CHS started to use electronic medical record in selected units in 2008. Back then, the electronic system allowed only documentation with limited function. In the year that followed, the electronic system was applied universally in the hospital, enabling ordering and nursing documentation. However, the individual systems of the electronic system were not integrative and the process was not systemically in place.

In 2014, as the new hospital building was going to be constructed, with the principle of "integrative planning, top-level design and simultaneous implementation," we took the opportunity to redesign clinical processes and the way they would be reflected in the electronic system. At the end of 2015, with the aspiration to make greater use of IT system in healthcare, we decided to go for HIMSS certification. It was all about "seeking greater improvement by evaluation and certification." As such, with international mindset of healthcare IT management, we started with clinical need to improve and optimize the IT system. After 1-year's hard work, we received HIMSS EMRAM Stage 6 certification in November 2016.

With those efforts toward HIMSS EMRAM Stage 6, the leadership and staff got the gist of the HIMSS standards and had a better idea about the direction and goal of IT adoption in healthcare. Then in 2016, the leadership listed "going for certification of HIMSS EMRAM Stage 7" as a priority of the annual plan for 2017 for the hospital to score new height. Throughout these years, we have witnessed better logics for IT application in healthcare among staff, improved care processes, higher standards of care, and had the first-hand experience on how HIMSS EMRAM Stage 7 initiate the trend of standardizing care, addressing details and seeking sustainability (Figure 10.1).

Figure 10.1 A photo from HIMSS EMRAM Stage 6 validation.

Base Ourselves on Clinical Need and Let Mindset Direct Action

Conventional notion has it that IT adoption is something for the IT Dept. alone, and the IT adoption level is determined by the technical power of IT Dept. As such, our standard for IT adoption in the hospital mainly involved the physical technology and paid little attention to the value of IT in clinical care.

During the mock evaluation for HIMSS EMRAM Stage 6, consultants emphasized several occasions that at the end of the day, IT adoption in healthcare should facilitate patient safety, sustainable quality improvement, and efficiency of care. Without these goals in the sight, the effort made in IT adoption would deviate from the proper tract for the sound development of the hospital.

With the suggestions from consultants, we held multi-departmental learning sessions to expand our understanding of HIMSS standards. As we went deeper in understanding the standards, we realized greater change was taking shape in our mindset: we stick to the philosophy of "providing patient-centered care and upholding quality and safety"; take measures to ensure patient safety and healthcare quality, improve quality over time, and optimize service processes; keep in mind "standards, models and processes"; and achieve systemic upgrade of philosophy of hospital management.

All the transformations are made for better patient safety and healthcare quality, regardless of using technology means or not. The HIMSS EMRAM validation is intended to facilitate transformation in healthcare via technologies, paying significant attention to whether technology has contributed to higher safety, efficiency, and user-experience in healthcare setting. HIMSS EMRAM validation helps hospitals to upgrade the IT adoption level, provide effective and practical technical tools and means for care providers, help staff reduce error amid busy schedule, and improve efficiency (Figure 10.2).

Figure 10.2 A photo from HIMSS EMRAM Stage 6 validation.

Establish Links between "The Two Mountains"

We assumed that interconnectivity of information means a simple feature of reading data from other systems from the electronic system. However, consultants figured that this simple need required staff to run and log on to another system, or click a tab in the computer during our mock evaluation. This problem of isolated information was especially thorny when staff looked up care related data.

Specifically, information did not flow between nurses and physicians. In other words, physician had no access to nursing note, while nurses did not have access to the physician's progress note, either. For the four vital signs and relevant information (including temperature, heart rate, respiration and blood pressure as well as height and weight for children) in the physician's admission note, they were from the vital sign sheet maintained by nurses. When a physician needed such data, he or she had to look up the vital sign sheet and document the data manually. The IT adoption early on changed only the media of information from paper to electronic system. It did not bring out radical change to healthcare quality, efficiency, and patient safety. If we are to realize interconnectivity of data, single source of data entering, and automatic capturing of data when needed, the old version of electronic system did not work.

Secondly, information did not flow among clinical care, medical technologies, and pharmacy. On the electronic system of their own specialty, imaging study professionals and pharmacists had access to the patient's identity and diagnosis only and were not able to see care related data. When clinical data are not available to radiologist, ultrasonologist, ECG professional, and pathologist, the accuracy of the work-up results are at stake. As for appropriateness review, pharmacist needs to make decision based on information of medication, laboratory results, and patient's condition. But if the patient's clinical information is not available, pharmacist is reduced to looking into the prescription only without a picture of the patient behind the prescription. That is not conducive to medication safety and proper use of medication.

What's more, conventionally, IT Dept. in hospitals boasted how good they were by saying the number of discipline-specific systems we had, but rarely spoke of the number of service processes covered by IT in the hospital. If most of the systems are for a few departments only, the systems only deliver value to a limited number of areas, no matter how many systems are there in the hospital. A metaphor is the fingers of a hand, which work coordinately for a particular gesture (a service process) with optimum efficiency and efficacy when all the fingers are mandated by one neural signal (clinical task).

Healthcare service is multi-departmental by nature. The departments involved include clinical units, Nursing Dept., Pharmacy Dept., investigation departments, Finance Dept., Engineering Dept., etc. The output of one step serves as the input for the next step, when information for the process is generated again and so on. As the task involves several departments, the same goes for information flow. To facilitate continuity of care, patient care information should be the principle line in the information system for integration of data from other departments and systems.

Interconnectivity has been achieved among equipment and devices. According to the HIMSS requirement, we divided IT adoption into five categories: paperless application of IT, closed-loop information provision, data interfacing, information security, and data management. There are 120 detailed tasks generated from these categories, and each task would be addressed by staff from clinical care, medical technologies, nursing, IT Dept. and the software developer. Specifically, physicians, nurses, and staff from investigation departments propose request for IT function based on care processes, quality standards, patient safety, data collection, and application. The IT Dept. turns these clinical requests into IT requests for the software developer to program and upgrade the electronic system.

In clinical care, equipment and devices are meant to receive the right instruction, identify the right patient, perceive abnormal data, and generate correct care data. As such, each medical equipment is a smart dot in the network of health information, instead of an isolated machine. Examples of such equipment include machines for radiological studies, ultrasound studies, laboratory assays, and ECG; cardiac monitor, ventilator, infusion pump, and automatic dispensing machine.

To begin with, IT Dept. performed a census of all the medical equipment in the hospital, listing the name of equipment, model, quantity, location, status of interfacing with IT system, name of the IT system, and manufacturer. From that census, we listed 3,513 pieces of equipment, of which only 196 had been interfaced with the electronic system. Some equipment (such as ventilator and some cardiac monitors) had not been interfaced because the older models did not come with adapter and interface feature, and interfacing would be feasible only until they are replaced by new models.

Reflection

During the process of preparing for HIMSS EMRAM Stage 6, we came to realize that we did not know much about the things that we assumed we had known very well. We had such feeling because the HIMSS standards are more practical and the bar is being raised constantly. HIMSS EMRAM validation represents new mindset, model and standards for management, and the successful certification of HIMSS EMRAM Stage 6 is only a starting line where we strive for standard compliance, delicacy management, and sustainable improvement.

At the end of the day, HIMSS EMRAM validation is for patient safety, healthcare quality, continuous improvement, and process optimization. All the measures are for patient care, and IT adoption serves as the means, instead of goals.

We shoulder heavy responsibilities for furthering the program of smart pediatric hospital. Based on the achievement in IT adoption, we will continue to work hard toward the goal of becoming a leading hospital in China with international reputation, thoughtfulness to details, rich culture, and smart technology.

Case 1: Closed-Loop Management for Medication Tracking

The management mechanism is not effective without closing the loops along clinical processes. Management process without closed loop is like electrical circuit with gaps between elements: it is of no use no matter how many wires are used or how thick the wires are. Closed-loop management composes of steps laid out in the forward sequence as well as feedback mechanism. Therefore, it is also called "feedback-control system." As closed loop is a requirement for HIMSS, we worked on closing the loops in 14 aspects of management: medications, transfusion, surgery, sterilization supply, breast milk, investigation, laboratory assay, consultation, critical value, nutrition, patient tracking, tracking of implant, antibiotics, and infection control.

Take the closed-loop management for medication as an example. The process involves acceptance of product, storage on the shelf in the warehouse, delivery from the warehouse, storage on the shelf of pharmacy, ordering, preparation, delivery to the clinical area, hand-over, and administration. Each step listed here involves a closed loop of its own. In other words, there are small loops within the big loop, and all the loops are connected. Any problem of any loop will result in risk to patients. Therefore, we adopt IT system to facilitate closed-loop medication administration. Real-time control helps us control the process when it happens, instead of after it has happened. It is a fundamental guarantee of medication safety on the patient's side.

Complete Fields and Clear Label

As the traditional belief goes, a handy tool makes a handy man. The first step toward closed-loop medication management is to complete the fields in the drug formulary. Conventionally, drug formulary includes the fields of generic name, chemical name, trade name, manufacturer, expiration date, price, etc. The drug formulary is useful for purchasing and ordering by physician.

We worked on the existing formulary by adding new drug categories and subcategories, limiting route of administration, and defining the dispensing pharmacy. The field of "drug category" is used to:

1. Control privilege to drug use. For example, only with privilege for narcotics can a physician orders narcotics and Schedule-I psychotropics, as the privileging for medications is a fool-proofing practice against error.
2. Data aggregation and analysis of medications, or the summary of volume of all the categories of drugs being used.

On the other hand, the field of "drug sub-category" is used to:

1. Level-based management, such as that for antibiotics (where antibiotics are grouped into different levels and linked to the prescription privilege of physicians), judgment of the selection of diagnostic and therapeutic treatment (such as the library developed for diagnosing infectious diseases and selection of antibiotics);

2. "To limit the routes of administration" is a fool-proofing practice that ensures "correct usage." For example, benzathine benzylpenicillin can be intramuscularly administered only; if administered via intravenous drip, it may cause vascular thrombosis. Intravenous bolus injection of 10% potassium chloride may cause cardiac arrest. And chemo drugs should not be ordered from Emergency Dept., indicating certain limit in the electronic system to "restrict the availability to certain pharmacy" is a fool-proofing mechanism to ensure "no room for mistake."

As the fields of drug formulary were completed, we started to cover every step in the process with barcode for labeling.

- Inpatient wears wristband with barcode. The barcode on the wristband provides patient information of name, sex, date of birth, age, location, bed number, admission/outpatient/ER (Emergency Room) number, which serves as an index for any care data of an inpatient.
- Medications in boxes are accepted into the warehouse with "barcode of the box." This barcode includes name, specification, production source, batch number, and quantity.
- The medication package is printed with "barcode for medication supervision," which includes name, specification, production source, and batch number.
- The medication package is printed with "commercial barcode," which includes name, specification, production source, etc. "Barcode for medication supervision" and "commercial barcode" are referred to as "package barcodes."
- The shelves in the drug warehouse are labeled with "shelf barcode," which serves as the primary index for the location of the shelf and is matched with the code for the section of the shelf. Such shelf barcode is available on the drug refrigerator and safe as well.
- As one shelf may accommodate several types of medications, there is "barcode for the section" on the shelf for each type of medication. This barcode for the section serves as the primary index for the actual location of a drug on the shelf and is matched with the name and information of the medication.
- Whenever a medication order is given, a "code for medication order" is generated for the information of that particular order. It includes patient's identity, medication name, dosage, route of administration, timing of administration, and precaution.
- Single-unit medications of an inpatient can be packed together and put with a label of "package code," which serves as a primary index for several codes for the medication order involving patient identity.
- The "barcode for drug container (cart)" is put on the transport container (cart) for drug. This barcode includes the information of all the drugs in the container of that transport.
- Transporter wear "ID card with barcode" to facilitate the traceability of medication during transport.

Again, alert for medication is reflected as barcode to ensure the right drugs are taken off from the "right section." Therefore, the label for the section on the shelf is also necessary.

1. Labeling of similar medication (see Figure 10.3). Similar medications refer to medications with the similar package, pronunciation of name, and the same name but different strengths. These categories are referred to specifically as "look-alike," "sound-alike" and "multiple-strengths" drugs. Labeling for alert is needed for these medications with higher risk of error in preparation.

2. After being prepared, the medication is properly labeled with the patient's name, admission number, medication name, dose, concentration, preparation time, expiration date, and precaution. Commonly seen precautions for medication involve labeling for high-risk medication, drip speed for intravenous infusion, storage condition, the type of infusion apparatus needed and the need for light-proof strategy. For example, penicillin is labeled with red stickers with words of "penicillin-like medication" (see Figure 10.4).

Figure 10.3 Labeling of similar medication.

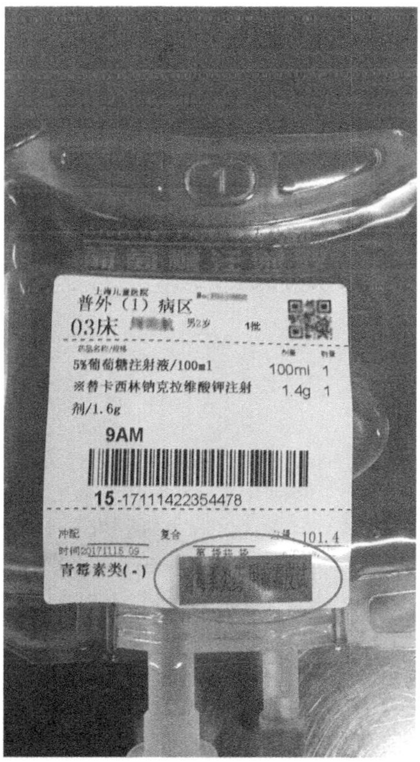

Figure 10.4 Red label for penicillin-type medications.

The Closed-Loop "Journey" of Medication

Following the effort to complete fields for the drug formulary and attach clear labels, we worked to improve the closed-loop process based on barcode and verification. Specifically, it involves closed-loop processes of acceptance and dispensing of medication from the warehouse, drug ordering, preparation, transport, and administration.

The "long journey" of a medication begins as soon as it reaches the doorstep of the hospital (see Figure 10.5):

- Upon acceptance into the warehouse, the barcode on the drug box is scanned by pharmacist as a step for acceptance check. The pharmacist puts a medication on the right shelf as he or she scans the barcode on the box as well as that on the section of the shelf.
- Upon releasing from the warehouse, a staff scans the barcode on the medication box or package barcode.
- Upon acceptance into the pharmacy, a pharmacist always scans the package barcodes and the barcode on the section of the shelf to ensure they are consistent before putting the medication on that section of the shelf.
- A pharmacist from the inpatient pharmacy works on a computer to receive single-dose order for an inpatient and prints out a barcode for medication order.
- Before preparation, a staff scans the package barcode (if it is dispensed as one box as a whole) or the barcode on the section of the shelf (if it is dispensed in individual dose from the original package), and the barcode for medication order.
- This inpatient pharmacist packs single-dose medications of the same patient and put a barcode of package on the sachet.

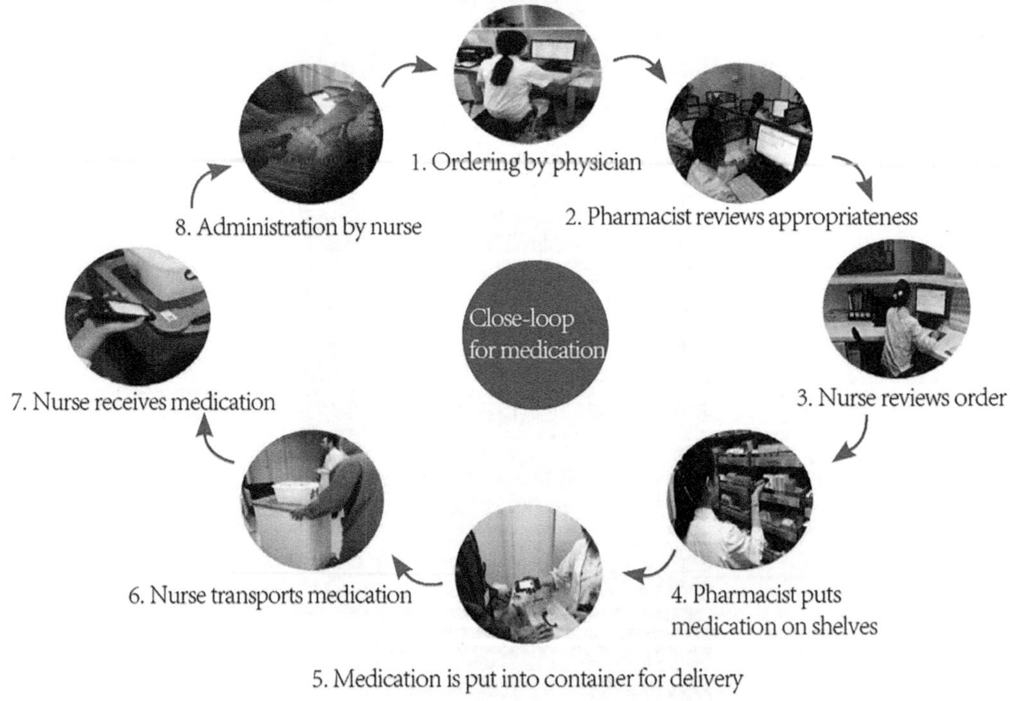

Figure 10.5 Closed-loop process for single-dose oral medication for inpatients.

- A pharmacist puts medications of all the patients of the same clinical unit into a transport container (or cart) and links the medications with the barcode of drug container (cart).
- A transporter scans personal barcode and the barcode on the transport container (or cart) to indicate he or she has received the medication.
- When the transporter has arrived at the clinical unit, a nurse logs onto the Nursing Software or PDA device to document the acceptance of medication container (or cart), opens it and takes out the medications.
- A nurse brings the PDA device to a patient and scans the barcode on the patient's wristband (for the patient's ID number) as well as the barcode for medication order, so that the consistency among the order, patient and medication is verified. If any one of these three pieces of information does not match the others, the PDA gives off alert to the nurse and stops the process of electronic documentation.

To make it easier for physicians to give order and pharmacists to review, and reduce error from wrong calculation from dosing, we added calculation in the system for the number of packs of medication needed for a certain dose determined by the physician. Physicians have been used to ordering medications in milligram (mg) for oral agents and milliliter (ml) for injections, but medications are packed into units of box, sachet, tablet, or bottle. As such, to prepare the prescription, a pharmacist has to do the math manually to come up with the number of packages for a particular order. This model means a lot of work for pharmacist to do the math while not ensuring the dose is the "right" one.

Therefore, we programmed the rules between medication dose and the number of packages into the electronic system, ensuring that the total dose of medication from that number of packages would always be equal to or higher than that prescribed by the physician. When physician enters the dose of the medication, pharmacist pays attention to the number of packages of medication needed and prints out medication label, which indicates the dose and frequency of that administration as well as specifications.

The entire process of drug dispensing has been documented by the electronic system via closed-loop management for tracking. Now we are able to track who does what at which time (when) during which moment (where) and how the result is. This has reduced workload of pharmacist and improved efficiency.

This barcode-based technology has facilitated us by automatically identifying medication, calculating the number of packs of medication and cost; reduced workload in medication dispensing and error of wrong-pick due to human judgment; and enhanced efficiency. As calculating the number of packs for the dose needed is a necessary step in drug dispensing, an electronic solution for calculation definitely results in time-saving benefit for pharmacist, higher confidence of right dosage and less workload.

Feedback control is another feature of this electronic process, where the right patient and right medication are better ensured. To conclude, electronic system has improved consistent compliance to all the policies and regulations for safe medication. The CDS alert, reminder, control, and direction have provided physicians with more support in medication use, and further ensured the correct medication in the right dose is administered through the right route with the proper precautions followed. The fool-proof mechanism, in particular, has controlled orders and guarded against severe adverse event involving medication.

Chapter 11

The First Affiliated Hospital of Nanchang University

Shi Jun, Cao Lei, Gong Jianguo, Zhang Faming, Liu Qiang, Deng Pei, and Lan Chunyu

The First Affiliated Hospital of Nanchang University

Shi Jun, *Former President of The First Affiliated Hospital of Nanchang University Mr. Shi steered the hospital toward "patient-centered care," furtherance of reform, innovation, and ever-improving healthcare quality. After leading a team and surveying the front-line work, he set the goal of becoming "a national-top, research-oriented, and modern hospital" in 2014. Shortly after 8 months, he blueprinted the strategy of becoming "a national medical center for the southern region."*

Mr. Cao Lei *is the Director of IT Department of The First Affiliated Hospital of Nanchang University. He has boosted the IT system and electronic health record of the hospital and established information integration platform and data repository, which have facilitated the interconnectivity of systems, smart analytics, and service integration. Thanks to these efforts, the hospital has been ranked among the top hospitals in China for smart technologies in health informatics.*

Hospital Introduction: Founded in 1939, The First Affiliated Hospital of Nanchang University (hereinafter referred to as FAHNU) has developed into a tertiary-A comprehensive hospital under the direct supervision of the provincial government of Jiangxi Province providing medical care, education, research, and preventive medicine. As a leading hospital of Jiangxi Province, it has been a rising star among various types of hospital rankings in the country: it has been shortlisted in "The Top 100 State-of-the-art Hospitals in

China" by Asclepius Healthcare (Hongkong) for 3 years straight, "List of China's Best Hospitals" released by Hospital Management Institute of Fudan University for 2 years at a stretch, and the 100 hospitals most influential in technology in 2014, 2015, and 2016.

International Accreditation: It was certified as HIMSS EMRAM Stage 6 in November 2016.

Contents

Preface

The Journey to HIMSS EMRAM Stage 6

To Upgrade the IT System—Development Is the Absolute Pursuit

Before starting to work toward HIMSS certification, our IT system had taken shape with functions for clinical care, administration, and management. Over recent years, new and smart ideas of IT have kept emerging thanks to advancement of the industry. To better serve the need from clinical care, patients, and healthcare professionals, the hospital has been constantly upgrading the IT system. However, gaps were widely present in the practical level.

A thorough survey of the existing IT system revealed several issues: (1) Integration was not in place and information existed in an isolated and fragmented pattern, resulting in the unavailability and inaccuracy of information. (2) The IT system did not support healthcare quality control, represented by the inability to monitor infection control, quality control, and medication monitoring; the lack of relevance between patient data and unique identifiers; and missing links along the loop for clinical care. (3) The clinical support system was outpaced by business development and in need of upgrading. (4) The IT system did not enable delicacy management of staff, finance, and resources as loops were not closed in the IT system. And (5) operational data were not coordinated to allow for data retrieval, analysis, and evaluation, let alone decision support for the hospital leadership.

The adoption of IT involves more than the physical layout of resources. More importantly, we need to develop proper mindset for IT adoption. Specifically, professionals in healthcare informatics need to understand IT adoption in the background of development, while healthcare professionals and administrators should think of things around from IT perspective. The furtherance of IT adoption in a hospital is not possible without the input from healthcare professionals and administrators. Only when they realize the role of IT function in their practice can concrete progress be made and momentum sustained in IT adoption.

To keep abreast of the trend in healthcare and become a hospital in line with international standards, we started the assessment of our IT system in September 2015, based on which we developed a mid- to long-term goal for IT adoption and set the target at compliance to HIMSS EMRAM Stage 6 by the end of 2016.

Guided by the principle of "centralized planning, step-wise implementation and priority-based scheduling," we took a step-wise approach to improving our IT capability with the goal of becoming one of the smartest and best hospitals in China.

Integration Platform Facilitating Interconnectivity

The information integration platform was already in place before we set foot on the HIMSS journey, providing important basis for the HIMSS EMRAM Stage 6 certification. On the data exchange level, various business systems have been integrated via search engine. On the data center level, the main data management system has met the need for standardized dictionary, and patient information has been better managed in standardized manner via EMPI (enterprise master patient index). CDR (clinical data repository) has enabled hospital-wide data sharing and data storage in standardized manager. And on the application level, HBI (hospital business intelligence) provides quick and accurate display of spreadsheet for decision making. The data integration platform is depicted in Figure 11.1.

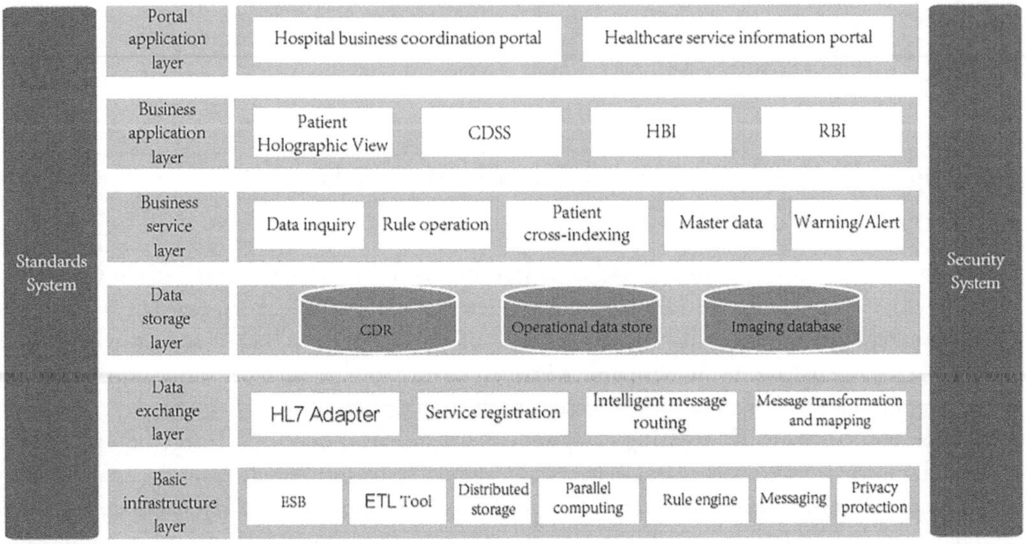

Figure 11.1 The integration platform.

The integration platform is intended to address the isolation of information. It has been achieved by integrating all the business units via ESB (enterprise service bus) and using standardized format for data communication. The smoother data flow and utilization has enabled convenient access of the patients to care and services and higher efficiency of the staff.

To Build Data Repository for Better Data Utilization

CDR enables storage of patient data generated from any care process and accessible through patient's unique index. Data have been collected and converted via IE integration platform as shown in Figure 11.2.

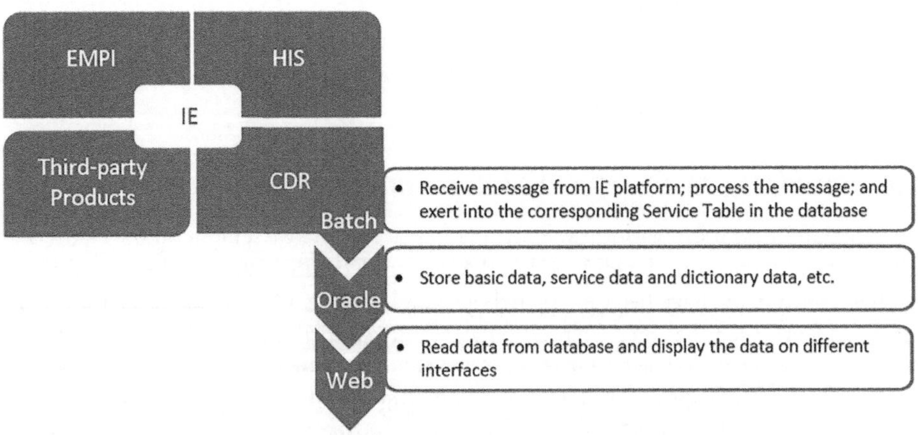

Figure 11.2 The integration platform with IE.

Complete and detailed clinical data from every previous encounter in the hospital are available from the CDR. From the user interface, healthcare professionals can see clinical data from any point of a patient's journey in the hospital. Since they get to see any patient data (such as visit note, allergy to medication, orders, diagnoses, lab results, investigation results, records, and surgical information), they are better able to analyze patient condition comprehensively and objectively. Patient information can be displayed via ordinary, time-based and service-specific (inpatient, for example) dimensions, so that users can find the information in ways they prefer.

As the integration platform has been based on SOA and ESB, data transmission via Web Service and MQ interfaces, and clinical data interfacing via HL7V3 standards, all the clinical processes and data formats have been standardized. The integration engine enables ESB-based system upgrading. The structure of integration platform is shown in Figure 11.3.

With CDR, we are able to ensure (1) access to real-time data, (2) integrity of patient data, and (3) closed-loop management. All the clinical data are managed in CDR with EMPI. As long as clinical data are generated, the all-in-one search engine upgrades the data in the CDR accordingly based on business rules to ensure timeliness and retention of clinical data. As all the clinical data are fed to the CDR, closed-loop management becomes possible. The all-in-one search engine of CDR is shown in Figure 11.4.

For example, the closed-loop management of medication orders centers around the order and tracks as well as manages the entire care process. On an established template of process mapping, the progress of an order is displayed via symbols or on a list of time points. Figure 11.5 features the display of closed-loop management for workup appointment.

As such, the CDR has gathered patient's care data based on EMPI along the time axis with the purpose of closed-loop management, so that users can pull up data specific to outpatient, inpatient, the overall care and medication for clinical decision making. The establishment of CDR has improved the structure and granularity of clinical data, and provided better support for decision making and resources for clinical care and research.

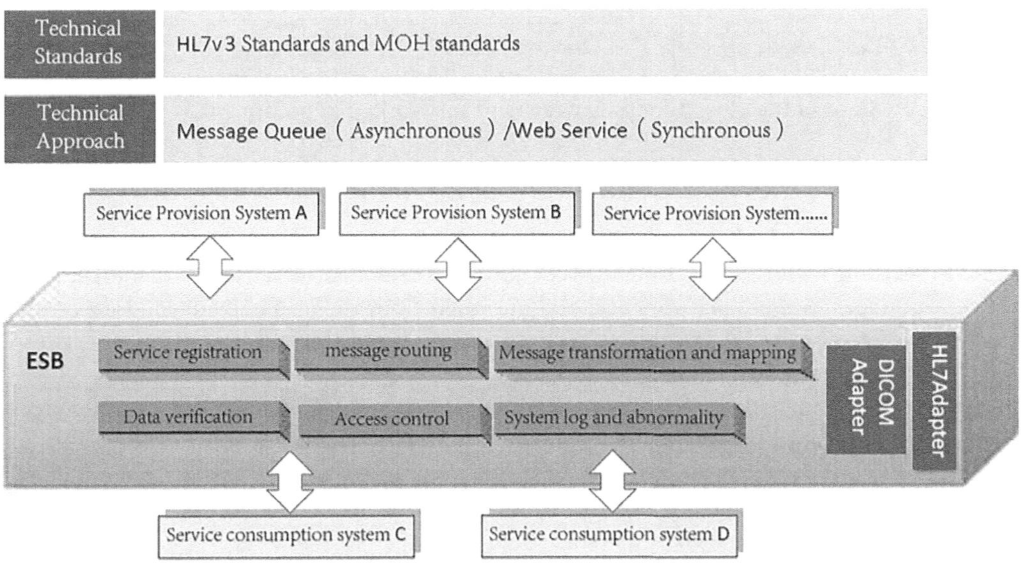

Figure 11.3 Service-oriented integration platform.

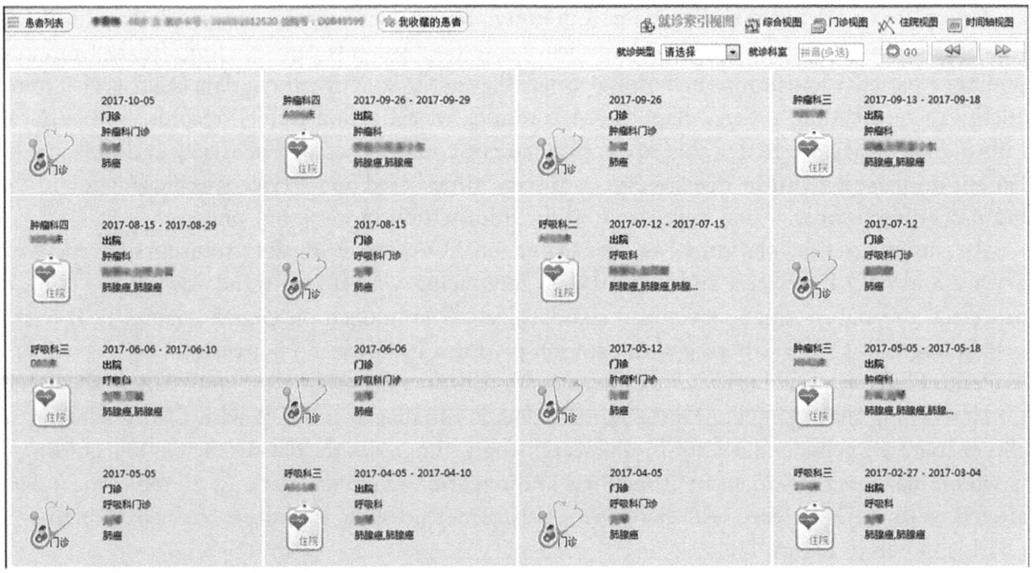

Figure 11.4 Integrative view of CDR.

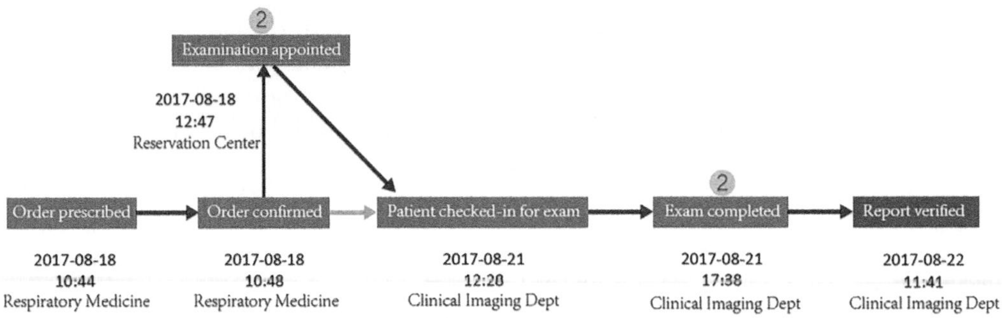

Figure 11.5 Steps in the closed-loop management for workup appointment.

IT Adoption for the Management of Staff, Finance, and Supplies

The philosophy of the ERP has reflected the ideas and processes of hospital management, integrated the existing resources and conducted comprehensive resource management of staff, property, assets, education, research, performance, and operation from the hospital-wide and department levels. It has been conducive to evidence-based management of the hospital with comprehensive data analysis and integrated data service.

During system upgrade and process optimization, we took advantage of IT advancement to establish data exchange pathways among different internal systems and with other health care organizations via data platform. This real-time interconnectivity of data has facilitated multifaceted care services, detailed diagnostic and therapeutic care, science-based operational management, and diversified regional coordination.

What's more, the upgraded system enables us to pull up valuable data through data search engine and turn the result from data analysis into practice. In other words, the alert of business intelligence is triggered by data for decision support for clinical diagnosis, operation management, research, and education. That is when smart healthcare informatics sets in.

The Road to HIMSS EMRAM Stage-6 Certification—Redesigned Processes and Refreshed Mindset

HIMSS EMRAM validation addresses paperless practice, comprehensive coverage of IT function, the value of IT to clinical quality, closed-loop management, CDR utilization, and standardization. The certification indicates the direction of IT system improvement. As such, the purpose of IT adoption is not to satisfy needs only. Instead, it is for the continuous improvement of functionality to provide better and better services for patients, healthcare professionals, and administrators. On the journey of IT adoption, the IT system has been constantly upgraded with the general advancement of society.

Baseline Survey

Quan Yu, Ji Zhou, and Chen Chen, HIMSS experts, made a tour in many units and pharmacies with us to survey the IT adoption as well as processes in the systems in our hospital and gave proper comments. From that baseline survey, gaps in management and processes of medication, emergency care, intensive processes, closed-loop, and PDA were cited.

It was followed by a conference in the hospital with attendants from leadership and administrators. Medical Affairs Dept., Nursing Dept., Pharmacy Dept., Emergency Dept., and Imaging Dept., among others, looked into the problems cited to redesign and optimize processes.

The redesigned processes have improved the safety of all clinical steps and enhanced staff perception on the efficacy of IT adoption, whether they are from clinical units, investigation services, or administrators. As such, staff have been more committed to enhanced IT adoption in the future, and we became more ready for HIMSS EMRAM Stage 6 certification.

Closed-Loop Medication Management via "One Code for Three Codes"

According to requirement of HIMSS EMRAM Stage 6 certification, checking of medication code by IT means should happen in each step along the process of closed-loop medication management, including delivery, storing on, and picking from shelves. However, our IT support for medication management has long been inadequate. To meet standard, we adopted mobile IT system by integrating three codes in only one code for delicacy management of the pharmacy and accuracy in the supply and preparation of medications.

"One code for three codes" means one code is used to represent the validation code, product code, and the drug's code in the HIS. The drug's code in HIS became its unique code for identification. The HIS recognizes three types of code for medication, while picking up according to this sequence: validation code, product code, and HIS code. If the validation code or product code is available from the drug's package, we do not have to put a sticker of HIS code to it. This means a lot for workload: as 80% of the medications in the hospital have validation codes and product codes, staff of the pharmacy only need to work on the HIS code label for the rest 20%.

Putting Medications on the Shelves

According to the HIMSS standards, barcode should be used for checking during dispensing, and barcode should be made available on the shelf for all the medications for pharmacists to verify with PDA device to ensure the right medication is used.

The validation code (or product code) is linked to the HIS code when staff use PDA device to scan the code on the medication shelf and then the validation/product code on the package. As there might be two codes on the package, namely validation code and product code, when the validation code is present, staff scans it; otherwise, staff scans the product code.

Checking is performed when medications are put on the shelf by boxes. Staff scan the codes on the box, shelf and drug package to ensure the consistency among all of them (see Process 1). When inconsistency occurs, the system gives alert (see Figure 11.6). When medications are put on the shelf in single-dose package, staff follow Process 2.

- Process 1: scan the code on medication box → scan the code on shelf → scan the code on single-dose package → save the result
- Process 2: scan the code on shelf → scan the code on single-dose package → save the result

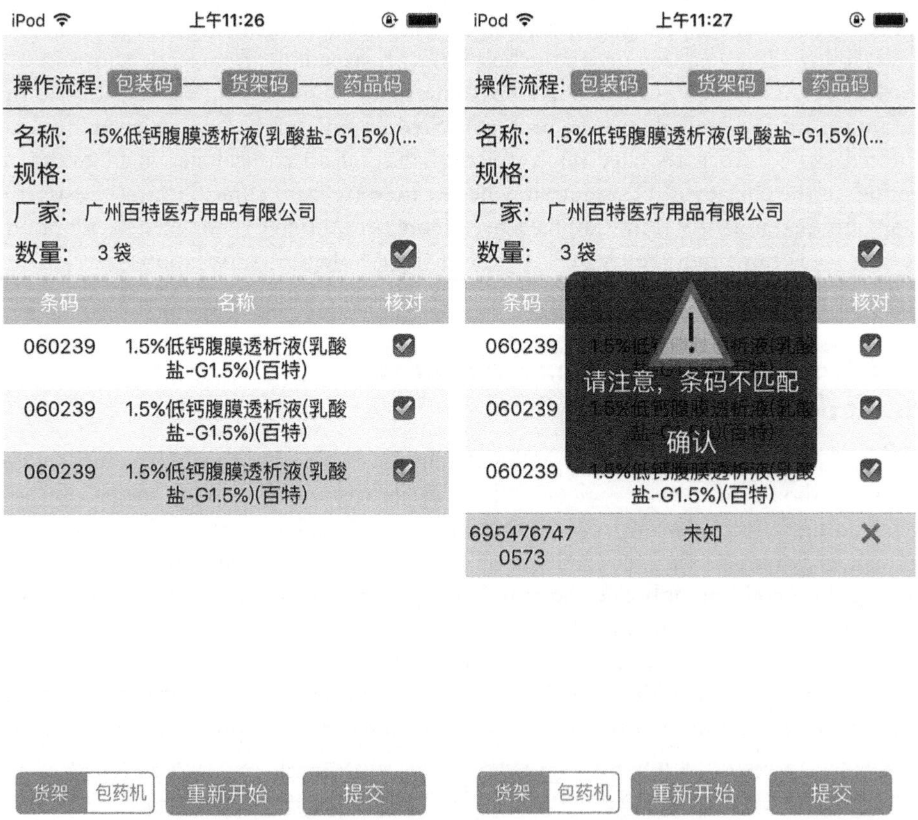

Figure 11.6 Automatic alert from the system.

Appropriateness Review Platform

The validators look for action toward physician's ordering, appropriateness review prior to dispensing in the pharmacy and post hoc prescription evaluation. Thanks to the efforts from Pharmacy Dept., the appropriateness review platform has enabled appropriateness review for medication orders. One can look for all the active orders of a particular patient, the patient's medical record, the communication taken place during review, the conclusion from the review, etc. When reviewing orders, pharmacists have access to the patient's electronic record, CDR, lab, and workup results. The process is mapped out in Figure 11.7.

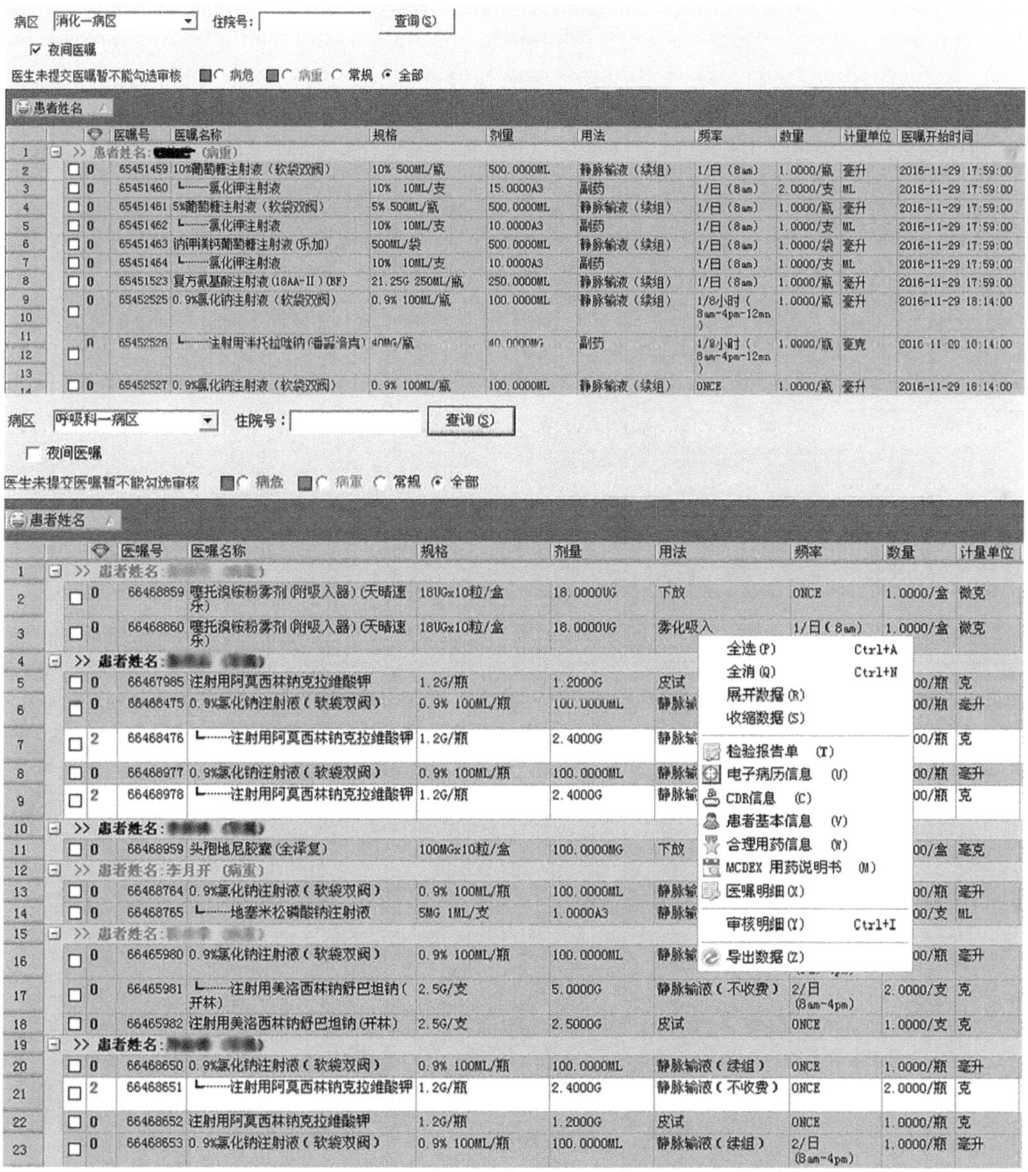

Figure 11.7 Look for patient information via the appropriateness review platform.

Medication Preparation

As the medication dispensing machine has been put into service, oral medications have become available in unit dose to inpatients and managed by barcode throughout the entire process. For certain special medications, the single-dose form is still prepared by staff manually.

Oral medications are checked in multiple steps from being taken out from their original package and packed again for dispensing. It includes feeding the medication into the dispensing machine → scanning the barcode of the dispensing machine → scanning the barcode of the medication container → save the result in the electronic system.

In the PIVAS (Pharmacy Intravenous Admixture Service), one can find the following steps where verification occurs: picking medications from the shelves, sending the medication into preparation room, medication preparation, finishing the preparation, and sending the medication out from the preparation room. The electronic system automatically keeps track of the time, the staff, and the medication involved, which is demonstrated in Figure 11.8.

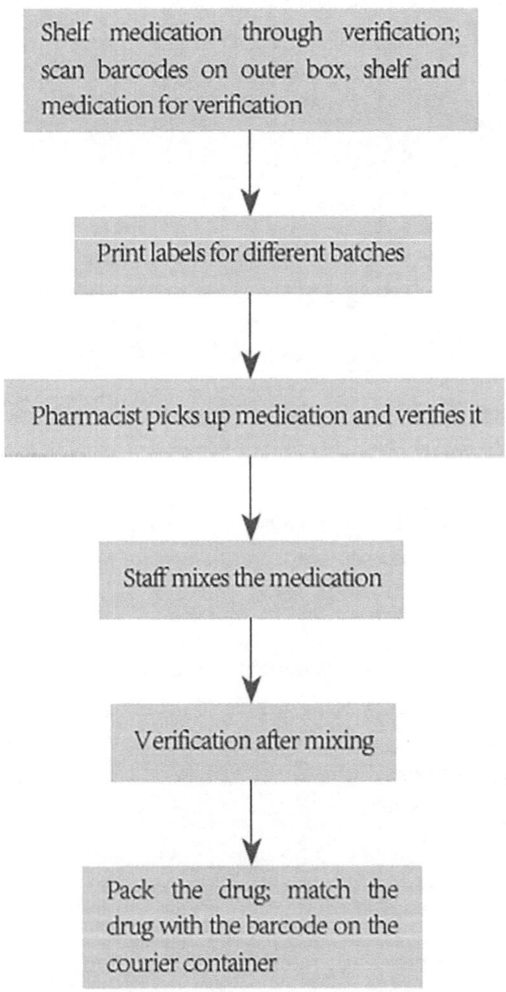

Figure 11.8 Process for medication preparation in PIVAS.

Transport and Handover

The closed-loop management of medication includes transport and handover from the pharmacy to clinical areas. Medications prepared in PIVAS and in Inpatient Pharmacy (oral medication and injection products not prepared yet) before being transported to clinical areas. When it comes to handover involving medication delivery, HIMSS EMRAM Stage 6 requires that:

- Sign-off from pharmacy

  Pharmacy puts the medications of the same unit into a large bag and put a label about the content within on the large bag.

  At signing off, a staff scans the label on the large bag for documentation of staff's name, medications involved, and time.

  At the same time, a staff scans the badge of the carrier to document the carrier's name and time.

  The large bags are put into transport container and locked.
- Reception at the clinical units

  The carrier and a nurse unlock and open the transport container.

  They scan the barcode on the label of the large bag, count the medications within, and document the receiver, medications, and time.

  They scan the badge of the carrier to document the carrier's name and time.
- Medication being picked from the shelf in Pharmacy

  This step is done with a summary list of all the patients:

  A staff scans the barcode (or QR code for PIVAS) on the drug dispensing sheet and the list of medications to be picked from the shelves is displayed on the screen;

  To pick a medication from the shelf, a staff scans the barcode on the drug package and the name of this drug on the list turns red;

  When all the medications have been picked and collected, all the names of the drugs become red and the staff clicks "save" (see Figure 11.9).

Verification with "5R"

To administer medication, a nurse scans patient's barcode/RFID wristband and that on the drug package to trigger the module for "5R" verification, namely the right patient, right medication, right dosage, right route of administration, and right time. If any of the five elements is wrong, an alert pops up on the screen. As the 5R verification is properly done, the electronic system allows medication therapy and updates the drug administration record (see Figure 11.10a–e).

Closed-Loop Transfusion with Safety as Top Priority

In terms of transfusion and its evaluation, we established a three-level system: assessment and evaluation for transfusion, smart pathway for quality management and electronic quality control for continuous improvement. Based on the principles of being science-based, standard-driven, systematic, and safe, this three-level system promotes closed-loop management of the entire transfusion process, real-time quality control of the process, tracking up-stream along the pathway and continuous improvement. The flowchart for transfusion is described in Figure 11.11.

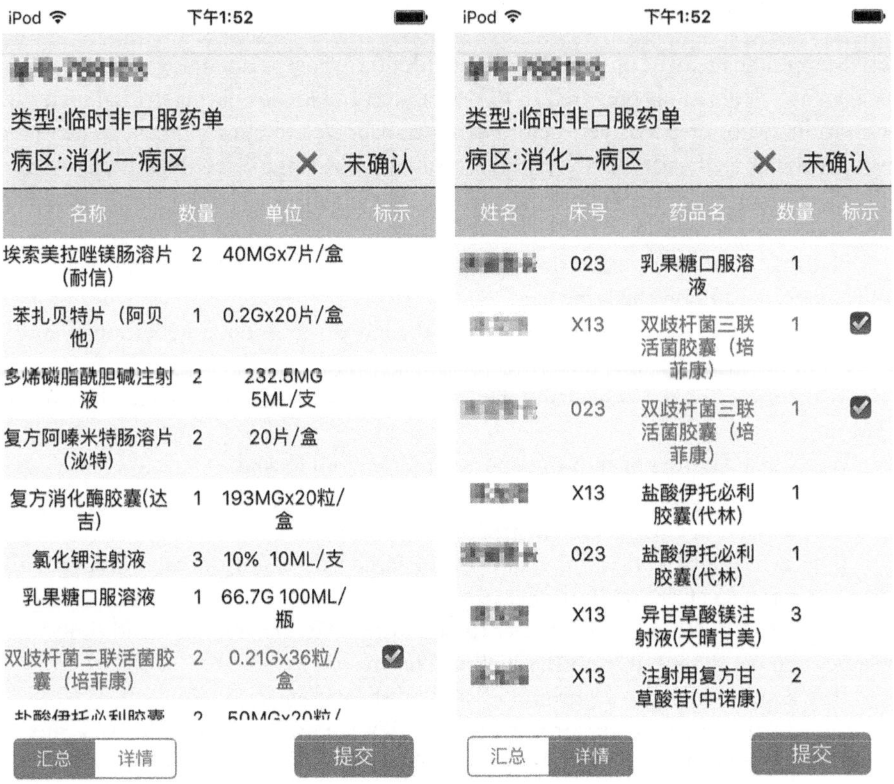

Figure 11.9 When the right medication and the right patient are matched, the entry turns red.

(a)

Figure 11.10 Process of 5R verification.

(Continued)

(b)

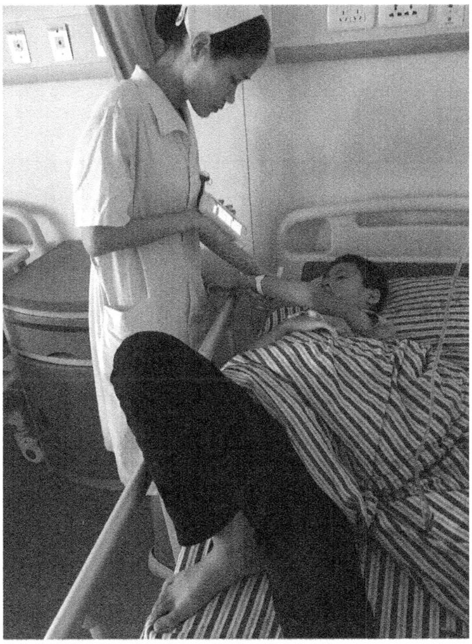

(c)

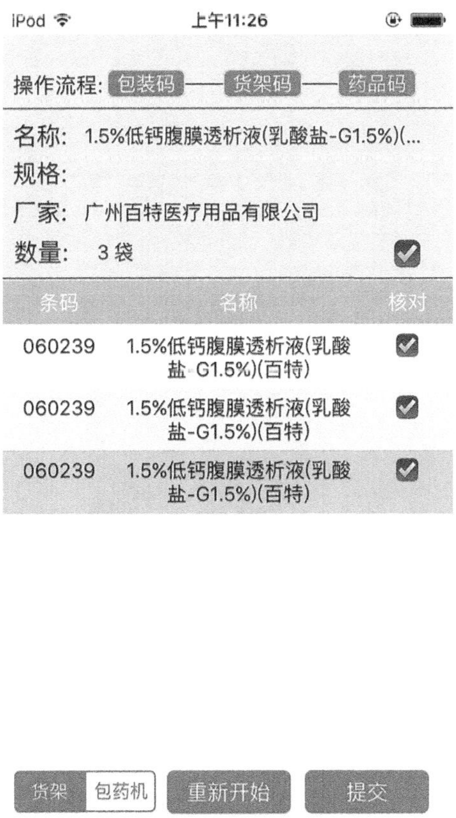

Figure 11.10 (CONTINUED) Process of 5R verification.

(d)

(e)

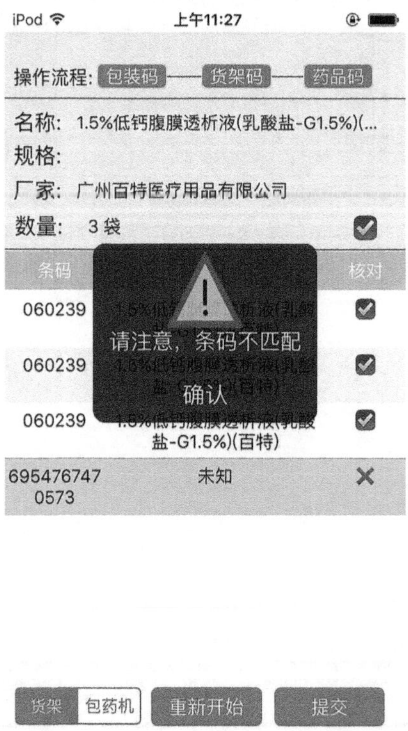

Figure 11.10 (CONTINUED) Process of 5R verification.

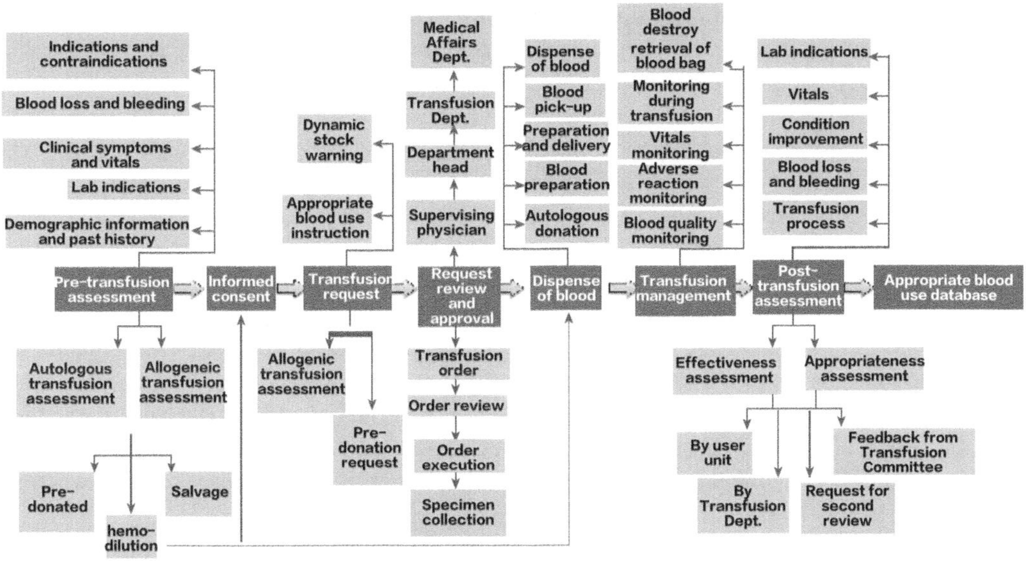

Figure 11.11 Transfusion flowchart.

Closed-loop management of transfusion has been in place along with evaluation for appropriateness and efficacy. A data repository for appropriate transfusion has been established to further the quality of transfusion with PDCA cycles.

Order blood electronically: in the ordering step, all the patient information needed is retrieved from the hospital's system to reduce human error from hand writing. To reduce unnecessary transfusion and preserve blood resources, the electronic system provides reminder for transfusion indication based on the patient's signs and transfusion guideline. Blood can be ordered from the system only when typing and pre-transfusion screening have been done for a patient. And new feature of step-wise approval for large dose transfusion has been added to the electronic system, so that such order is reviewed and approved one by one from senior physician, Director of the unit, Blood Bank, and Medical Affairs Dept., who make the decision based on the dose requested for and acuity.

In reviewing blood orders, Blood Bank should try to prevent blood shortage where no blood can be provided to a physician's order. Therefore, physician of the Blood Bank looks at the signs and indications of patients and prioritizes patients according to the level of need. As such, the valuable but limited resource of blood can be preserved for patients most in need.

Print a form and take blood sample: a nurse goes to a patient to collect blood sample. He or she scans the blood tube and the patient's wristband with PDA to ensure it is the right blood tube for the right patient. The PDA then facilitates the nurse to check ten items of three categories, a process with higher accuracy and lower workload, and documents the time of blood collection and the name of the nurse (blood collector).

Handover of the blood sample: before we upgraded the electronic system, it was impossible to verity electronically the blood sample and the carrier, and there was no way to go back and look for such information from the system. After we upgraded the electronic system, a nurse from the unit scans the samples collected from the unit to be transported, packs them and generates a master barcode. As a carrier arrives at the unit, the nurse scans that master barcode and the carrier's staff information for electronic documentation, and the handover is completed in an efficient way. The receiving end accepts the blood samples in the same way.

Cross-match and verification at dispensing: a nurse verifies the blood and signs for acceptance with PDA scanning to document the time and person involved in that blood reception. The data of blood signed-off from the blood bank and administration time are important elements for quality control.

Verification in the unit: according to the *Policy on Safe Transfusion*, prior to blood administration, two healthcare staff thoroughly go through the blood order, the result of cross-match, and the blood label to verify consistency before the blood is started on the patient. A mandatory process has been programmed into the PDA so that it is not possible for the nurse to skip any step of verification.

Document administration: as the blood is started on the patient, the PDA times and reminds the nurse to assess patients as scheduled.

Collect the empty blood bag: according to *Technical Standards for Transfusion*, every blood bag is collected after the blood is finished, and one should not loss any blood bag. To collect the blood bags: a nurse from the unit scans each bag for documentation and collects the bags in one large bag and seals it off → a support staff scans the code to indicate he or she has taken the bag → the staff from the collection site scans the code to indicate acceptance → the code is scanned when the blood bags are signed off from the organization to disposal facility.

Triage in the Emergency Room (ER)—Assign Triage Level with Only One Click

According to *The Guiding Principles of Triaging ER Patients Based on Condition for Pilot Organizations* (for comments) (document No. 148 of [2011] of Hospital Management Division of Health and Family Planning Commission), Emergency Dept. (ER) of hospitals performs triage and designates three zones for different patients: patients are triaged as one of the four levels and stay in the corresponding zones. Specifically, patients are assessed and categorized as one of four levels: level 1, immediately life-threatening; level 2, imminently life-threatening; level 3, potentially life serious or situational urgency; and level 4, less urgent. ER area is divided into three zones: red, yellow, and green.

In the electronic system for triage, based on signs relevant to level 1 patients, namely respiratory arrest, cardiac arrest, severe dyspnea, shock, or seizure status, when any one sign is positive, with a simple check in that sign from the electronic system, the triage result is immediately available so that life-saving measures can start immediately.

What's more, the electronic system allows fast-track registry as the card readers recognizes several types of cards (such as citizen's ID card and health insurance card), so that patient information is automatically, instead of manually, entered. Alternatively, the system allows staff to generate a file for a John Doe and come back to fill in accurate information later. Based on the zone-assigning rules, the electronic system assigns patient to the appropriate zone, exam room and physician.

Management of Contrast Medium and Allergy

To meet standards for HIMSS EMRAM Stage 6, the PACS should allow electronic ordering, structured report, management of contrast medium and allergy, use of wristband and information communication.

As information is shared and orders are given electronically in the system, investigation departments obtain a patient's history of allergy to contrast medium. During investigation, if contrast medium is indicated, staff administers premedication, and document the result from the skin test in the electronic system, which is then submitted to the CDR. Also, allergy reaction against contrast medium is linked to the system for documentation of adverse events.

During Validation

On November 15, 2016, we finally got to receive the validators lead by Ms. Jilan Liu for HIMSS EMRAM Stage 6 certification. The validators deliberated on our reports, read documents, interviewed staff, and visited various locations to assess how we had been using the electronic system and its functionality. In general, the validation visit was scheduled into morning and afternoon.

In the morning, they went from the Conference Room of Endoscopy Center → Gastrointestinal Unit-1 → Imaging Study → Inpatient Pharmacy → the Conference Room of Endoscopy Center.

In the afternoon, they started from the conference room again and visited Pharmacy for Oral medication → Center for Appropriateness Review → PIVAS for Inpatient → ICU → Admission Office and Medical Record Archive → ER before coming back to the conference room.

The validation started with an introduction of the process and task by John H. Daniel and Ms. Jilan Liu, followed by an overview of the progress in IT adoption of our organization.

During the 1-day survey, the validators visited clinical area, investigation services, pharmacies, ER and ICU, among others. As they arrived at the Gastrointestinal Unit-1, after brief introduction of the team, Gong Yue, the Head Nurse of the unit, started the discussion of how nurses had been using electronic system and PDA. The validators had been impressed by how fluently she described the process and how skillfully she demonstrated the work. After visiting various places, asking many questions, and seeing many demonstrations, the validators had a thorough understanding of our physician's system, nurse's system, PDA, appropriateness review, medication management in the pharmacies, intensive care system, photographing of paper records, single sign-on feature, structured electronic record, clinical pathway, critical value and barcode, and made good comments.

You can feel how delighted we were during the validation (see Figure 11.12).

Figure 11.12 An enjoyable experience of HIMSS validation.

You might wonder: "Are you kidding me?" Indeed, that is a typical snapshot of the validation. We were enjoying the validation itself as well as the good outcomes from process improvement. These outcomes mean concrete help to our organization. Therefore, we have been thankful for Ms. Liu and her colleague validators who have provided a lot of help as we further develop our IT capability. The spin-off from efforts toward HIMSS EMRAM validation include: we have got to learn about the latest trend in IT adoption around the world and expose ourselves to good experiences from international best practice of IT adoption in healthcare. As such, we are better able to plan for the comprehensive development and upgrade of IT adoption in our organization that takes into account local need in China.

Thanks to efforts toward HIMSS EMRAM Stage 6 certification, we have succeeded in applying IT in giving off alert for outlier results, closed-loop management of critical value and guideline- as well as diagnosis-based CDS. As we have the skill and means, when we become more experienced and validated, we expect more application of CDS in the future.

1. Reminder for outlier results

   The IT system provides automatic reminder for outlier results in nursing assessment and provides nursing measures relevant to the scores entered.

   a. In assessment for decubitus, the system automatically generates a score and provides reference for nursing measures (see Figure 11.13).

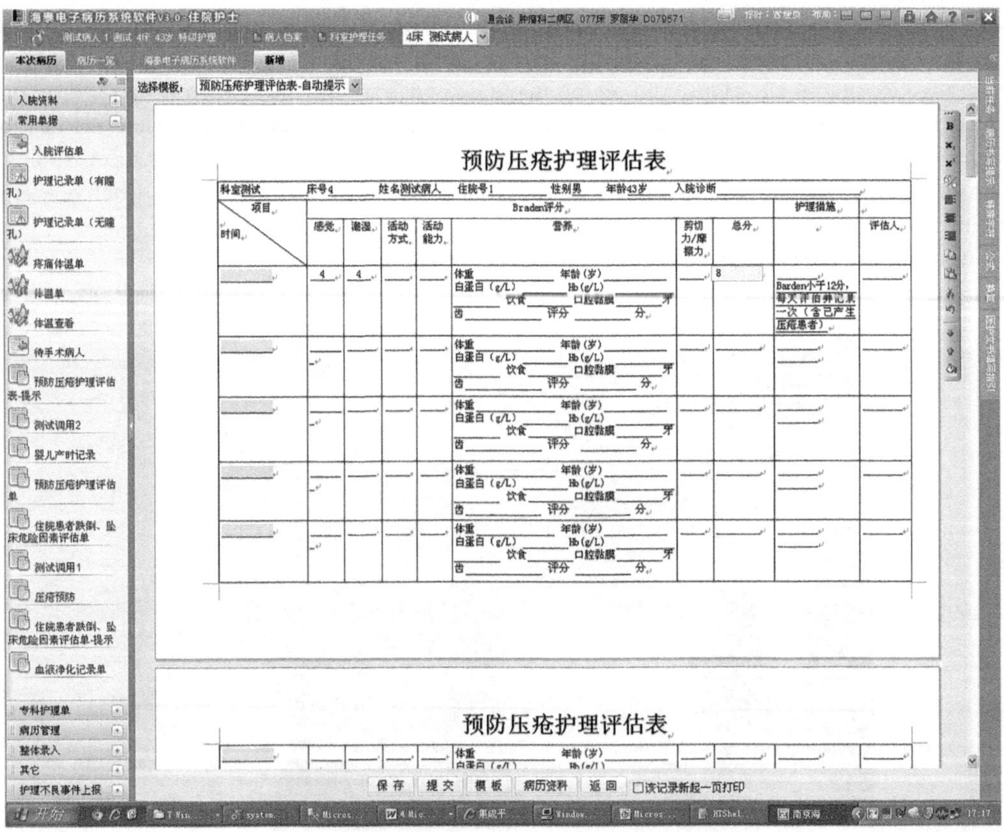

Figure 11.13 Nursing assessment for decubitus prevention.

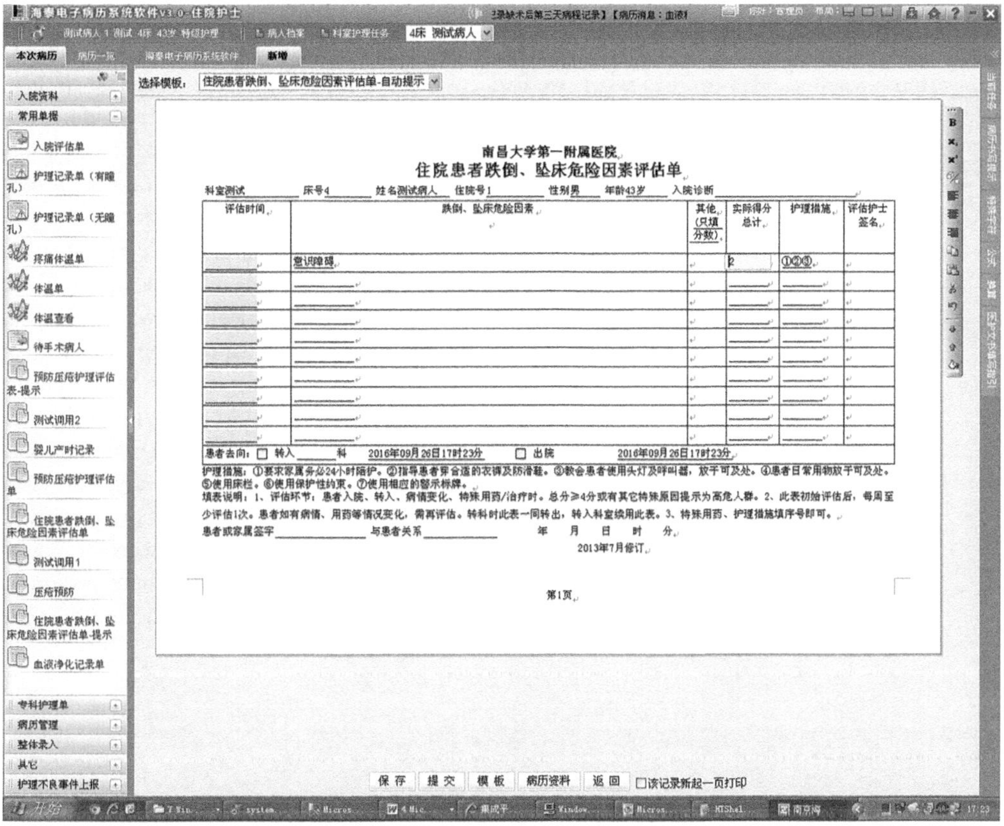

Figure 11.14 Assessment for risk of fall among inpatients.

b. In assessment for fall risk for inpatients, the system automatically generates a score and provides reference for nursing measures (see Figure 11.14).
c. Automatic reminder is available from the Barthel nursing assessment. The electronic system has been programmed with the 15 topics in the Barthel and four options from each one (1: independent; 2: minor help with tool, such as a crutch or proper dinning utensil; 3: minor help from a person; 4: dependent).

2. Closed-loop management of critical values

To meet HIMSS standards, hospitals should be able to achieve the following things in terms of closed-loop management for critical values.

a. The critical result from LIS should be reflected as an immediately recognizable sign on the patient census screen in the nursing station;
b. As staff clicks that sign, he or she is brought to the result of that critical value;
c. The staff can work in the system to announce he or she has received the critical value. Such reply is documented with the staff's name and time.

3. Clinical pathway triggered by the entry of diagnosis

CDS has enabled the initiation of clinical pathway via the entry of diagnosis. As staff enters diagnosis, the electronic system pops up an option of relevant clinical pathway. When the staff clicks the pathway, the system brings up the order set of that pathway.

4. The use of CPOE

CPOE has been universally available in our organization. The penetration of CPOE almost reached 90% in 2015 when we had 2.4 million outpatient visits and 130 thousand admissions a year. CPOE (Computerized Practitioner/Physician Order Entry) refers to the process where healthcare professionals give orders electronically to provide care for patients. All the healthcare professionals with prescription privilege are able to enter orders for medication, workup studies and other care in the electronic system based on national laws and regulations, insurance policy, and practice guideline. The orders given electronically are saved in the medical record. The electronic ordering is also available to physicians of investigation services and anesthesiologist. It is helpful for the use of clinical pathway.

a. Anesthesiologist enters order. The electronic system has enabled the electronic ordering and documentation of anesthetics and other medications used during surgery. When an anesthesiologist enters anesthetics and other medications used during surgery in the *Anesthesia Note*, the electronic system captures that information and generates the orders automatically.
b. Physician of investigation services enters order. When a physician of investigation service orders diagnostic medication, it is documented in the electronic system automatically.
c. Single sign-on feature. For any inpatient, a physician needs to give orders and make notes. These two functions are bridged smartly together in our electronic system (see Figure 11.15). Specifically, in the view of orders, one can pull up the documentation view by just one click on an icon of the patient's entry and *vice versa*.

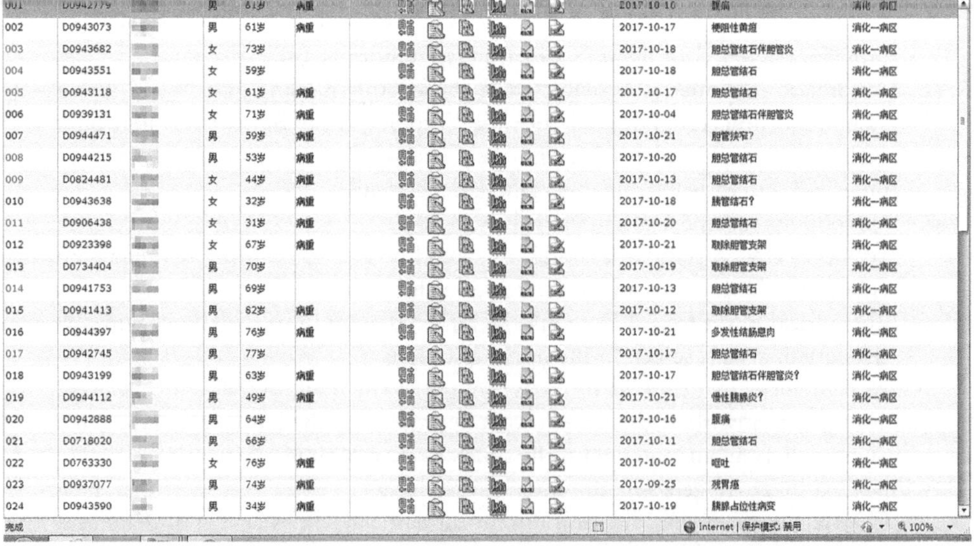

Figure 11.15 The access to the medical record from the ordering module.

5. Structured documentation

   The use of structured electronic documentation is consistent with the trend and clinical need. As such, structural templates and data entry rules are utilized extensively in our electronic system. During documentation, a physician selects the template that he or she prefers to start a structural medical record (see Figure 11.16a–c). Meanwhile, CDR enables staff to look for patient's laboratory and investigation results.

6. Paperless process

   Sounds easy, paperless process is by no means an easy task. It involves several prerequisites: (1) There should be a well-established clinical information system, (2) every piece of medical equipment has the ability of digital interfacing, (3) the hospital gets rid of paper even in signature of informed consents, and (4) paper is not used in any step along the chain of management. To this end, we obsoleted equipment without digital interface, such certain ECG machine and cardiac monitors, and replaced them with those enabling digital data capturing. For necessary papers, such as informed consent with signatures, we scan the completed document and save the electronic file. Outpatient service stopped using paper order sheet and nurses use electronic device every time they perform handover.

(a)

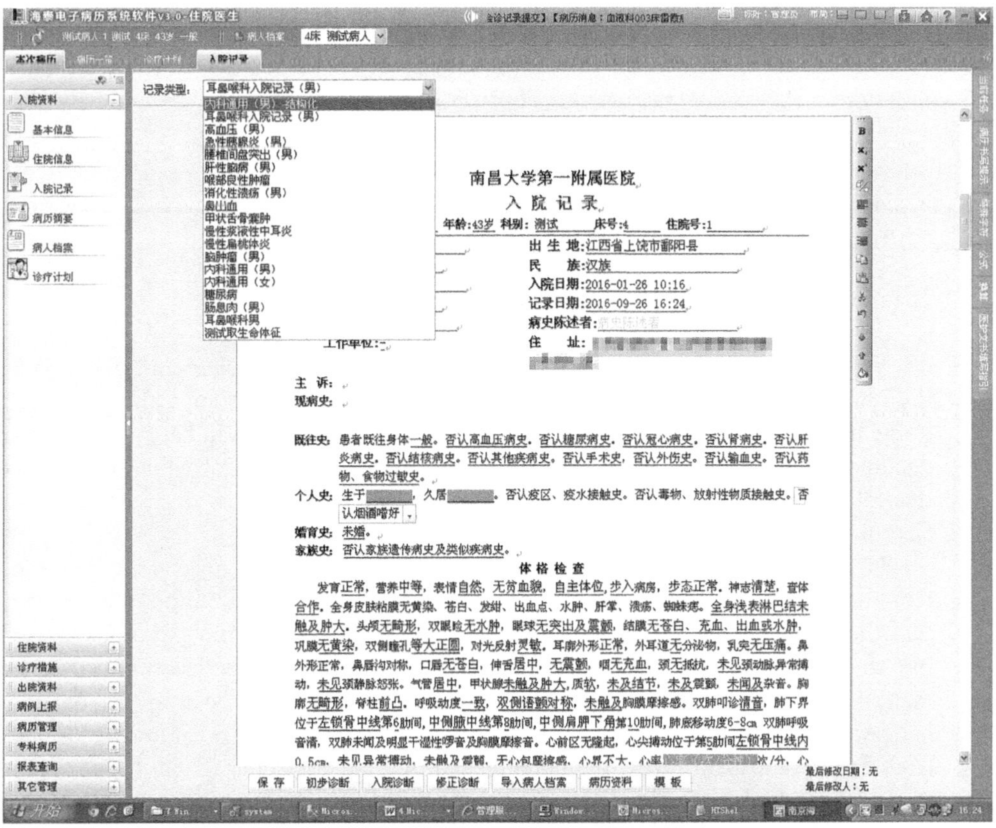

Figure 11.16 Templates for structured record.

(Continued)

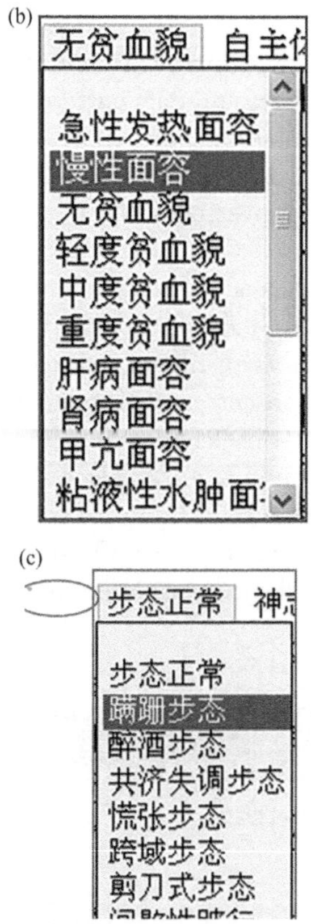

Figure 11.16 (CONTINUED) Templates for structured record.

7. The use of patient barcode

   Upon admission, patient goes through the admission process in the Admission Office, where demographic information is entered into the electronic system and down payment is given. The patient receives a printed wristband from the Admission Office and brings it to the unit where he or she is admitted. A nurse scans the admission barcode with PDA to document the patient's arrival time, as well as the time and staff involved in the clinical care that follows.

8. Scanning of and access to medical record

   For the necessary paper records, consultants recommended us to generate from the system and keep it in the file. As such, all the paper records generated for care are scanned into the electronic system within 24 h. For example, the resuscitation record was scanned into the system, and staff discarded this record as he or she retrospectively entered the information into the electronic system. But consultants also recommended us to keep the original hand-written paper as a scanned file. For another example, hand-written nursing flow sheets from ER and inpatient units are photographed into the electronic system for physicians to read when needed.

   Dr. Lv Huanong, a Vice-CEO of our hospital, gave a good summary of our journey toward HIMSS certification: we went through consultation, mock validation, and actual validation of HIMSS, which have been of great help in the top-level design of IT adoption in the organization and identification of short- and long-term goals as well as implementation strategies. HIMSS emphasizes quality and safety by means of IT adoption, requiring organizations to better define various processes and provide IT means to support patient safety and experience, healthcare quality, standard compliance, management, and capacity building. It encourages hospitals to lay more emphasis on the role of IT application in higher healthcare safety, safer medication practice, automatic retrieval of clinical data, paperless process, centralized, and consistent information provision, continuity, and traceability of data along the processes and the establishment of clinical decision support system. This endeavor will facilitate the realization of a smart comprehensive hospital with smart solutions for documentation, reminder, access to information, control; closed-loop management of medication, infusion, transfusion, laboratory, and investigations; and quality control capability, greater convenience for staff as well as higher efficiency and performance.

Outlook

Based on the actual situation, development strategy, and strengths of ourselves, we learned from others' experience of IT adoption and deploy our efforts in the principles of "top-level design, integration of resources and step-wise approach." We have utilized state-of-the-art IT means as much as possible to enhance capability in clinical care, operational management, coordination with the region, research, and education as well as information integration. We have aimed to establish ourselves as one of the best hospitals in China with smart and excellent care by standardizing care, paying attention to details and using smart technologies.

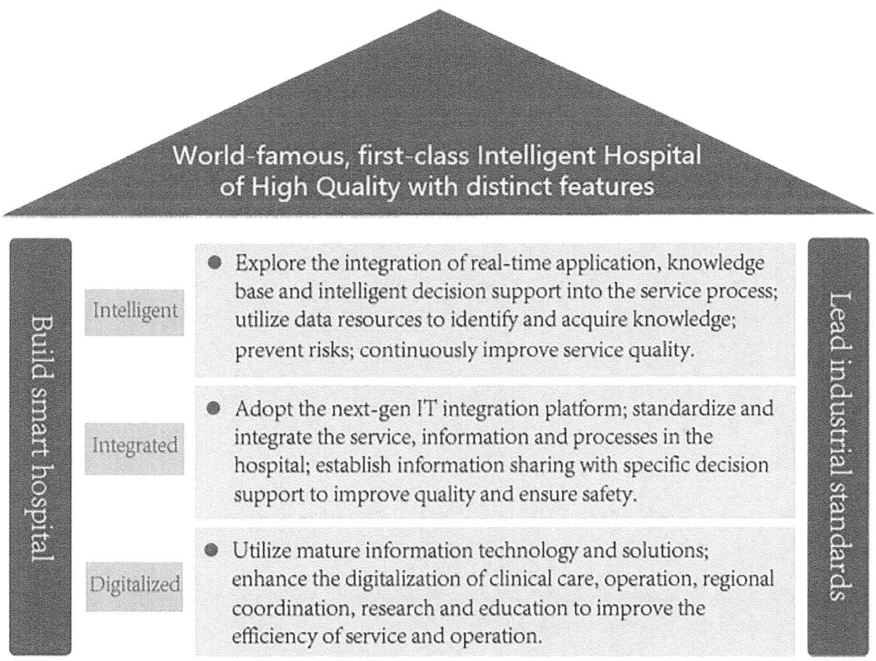

Figure 11.17 The strategic vision of IT adoption of the First Affiliated Hospital of Nanchang University.

In the 2 years to come, we will continue to improve "patient-centered care" with greater IT adoption and further our IT adoption level from being digital-based to integration- and smart-technology-based. To utilize digital technology serves as a prerequisite for strategic planning of the hospital and serve the universal digital practice in clinical care, administration, operation, education, and research. To be centralized and integrative constitutes the essence of the strategic planning of IT adoption in healthcare setting, where IT is utilized to support network-based hospital with centralized and integrative systems (medical, nursing, pharmacy, auxiliary, etc.), all-inclusiveness (clinical care, education, research, process management and smart control), and universal connectivity (among hospitals, communities, insurance companies, finance companies, medical technology services, personal, and family health management). That might be an innovative healthcare model in the age of "Internet+." Smart technologies and features are the long-term strategy of the IT development of our hospital. With this in mind, we will break new grounds in the era of smart business (Figure 11.17).

Chapter 12

People's Shanghai No. 6 People's Hospital

Yin Shankai, Jia Weiping, Fu Yimin,
Chen Ting, and Sun Yu
People's Shanghai No. 6 People's Hospital

Yin Shankai *is a Doctor, Professor, Supervisor of doctoral candidate and Vice President of the Sixth Hospital of Shanghai. He is the Director of Otorhinolaryngology Institute of Shanghai Jiaotong University and Director of Hearing Test Center of Shanghai. He is also the Vice Chairman of Otorhinolaryngology Society of Shanghai Medical Association.*

Jia Weiping *is Medical Doctor, Professor, Supervisor of doctoral candidate and Chief Scientist of "973" key research project in China. Jia Weiping is the Director of Shanghai Clinical Center of Diabetes, Director of Key Diabetes Laboratory of Shanghai and Director of Shanghai Institute of Diabetes; she is also the Chairman of Chinese Diabetes Society and Executive Chairman of IDF-WPR.*

Fu Yimin *assumed her position in IT Center of the Sixth Hospital of Shanghai in 2016 after graduating with Master Degree in business informatics from Monash University (Australia). She is responsible for nursing informatics, nursing electronic system and adoption of glucose platform.*

Sun Yu *shrew himself into Healthcare Informatics 16 years ago with his Master Degree in Engineering from Shanghai Jiaotong University. During his service in the IT Center of the Sixth Hospital of Shanghai during 2012 to 2017, he was responsible for the organization-wide adoption of clinical data depository and clinical support system. In 2018, Mr. Sun became the General Manager of product development in the headquarters of Winning Health Informatics.*

Hospital Introduction: Established in 1904, Shanghai No. 6 People's Hospital and the No. 6 People's Hospital Affiliated to Shanghai Jiao Tong University is a Level-A Tertiary Hospital as well as a large teaching hospital. In 1958, Professor Zhou Yongchang initiated the Ultrasound Medicine together with his colleagues in the hospital, which is later known as the "cradle of China's diagnostic ultrasound medicine." In 1963, Professor Chen Zhongwei, Professor Qian Yunqing, and others successfully performed the first replantation of a severed limb in the medical history in the world, winning the hospital the fame of being the starting point of such technique. Currently, the hospital has 1766 licensed beds and 45 clinical and ancillary units.

International Accreditation: June 2017, HIMSS EMRAM 6.

Contents

Preface

Break Through Bottlenecks, Realize True Information Technology Adoption

Shanghai No. 6 People's Hospital (hereinafter referred as "SH No. 6 Hospital") is an early starter of HIT and now has relevant complete IT infrastructure and architecture. The hospital has a management system centered on HIS as well as the clinical information system based on EMR, covering all aspects from hospital administration to clinical services and logistics support. The information systems have become an important pillar of improving efficiency, processes, and hospital operation management.

From 2006 to 2010 (the "twelfth five-year plan" period), the hospital followed the principle of "overall planning for practical use and gradual implementation for prioritized application" and completed the architecture for data security, redundancy, and backup. We were then accredited as Level 3 in Information Security and Protection by Shanghai Municipality, which further ensures the safety and stability of IT operation in the hospital.

Bottlenecks

Though the IT systems and infrastructure were improving, the number of systems and functional modules had also increased accordingly, which added to the complexity of the management over different processes, and caused weak coupling and interfacing between the systems. The bottleneck gradually took shape.

Back at that time, the data were not standardized and the interfacing was of low efficiency. Diversity of vendors challenged the uniformity of the architectures and standards of different products they offered. The increasing dictionaries related to business data encumbered the efficiency and burdened the maintenance.

The isolated systems and information further added the difficulties in system integrating and data sharing. It was impossible for us to realize centralized storage and sharing of data with products from multiple vendors. The lack of coordinated planning of the overall IT strategy created the situation where systems were isolated from each other. Data could not be shared. Repetitive entries in multiple systems were common. This also led to another problem: inconsistency of data.

To solve those problems, the hospital decided to realize the closed-loop management and clinical decision support system during 2011–2015 (the "thirteenth five-year plan" period). The goal of the hospital for that 5 years was to establish the three major data centers (CDR, management data center, and imaging data center) and the knowledge platform, and to realize the frog leap from being a digital hospital toward an intelligent hospital. Our goals were also in line with the HIMSS EMRAM Stage 6 criteria. Therefore, in November 2016, we launched our HIMSS journey to test the progress we'd made in IT adoption and to evaluate the quality of our performance.

Learn by Practice

After the HIMSS EMRAM 6 baseline survey, the hospital organized a debriefing on the preparation and discussed the findings. The weakness of the hospital existed in the actual implementation in our day-to-day work, as reported by the consultants, mainly lay in the actual utilization of the system. For example, single sign on was not realized; clinical decision support was not effectively utilized; closed loop for medication and blood transfusion was not complete; the system development was not centered on hospital processes.

During the baseline survey, we explained the functions and capabilities in our system, but the consultants said the actual implementation was not evidenced. By that time, we finally understood that IT adoption is a process where the systems are fully utilized by the clinical staff and feedbacks are collected and reviewed for further improvement.

On December 12, 2016, we invited Jilan Liu for a lecture on HIMSS and HIT development. She told us that the purpose of validation is to transform healthcare through information technology to better meet the IT needs of our healthcare staff, improve quality and safety, and enhance the experience of patients. As inspired by the lecture, we began to view the role of IT from a new perspective and started to expect the Stage 6 validation.

We soon established the HIMSS Leading Group, Coordination Groups, Task Groups and Consultant Groups, and selected two pilot units for improved systems and functionalities. The HIMSS Leading Group was chaired by Dr. Jia Weiping, President of the hospital, and

Dr. Fang Binghua, Party Secretary of the hospital. Other important leadership members, including Yin Shankai (VP) and TAO Minfang (VP), also sat on the team together with the heads of key administrative departments (Hospital President Office, CPC Office, Medical Affairs Department, Nursing Department, Medical Equipment Department, IT Center, etc.). They were mainly responsible for coordination of the HIMSS preparation and decision making on major issues. Four task groups were organized for medication, blood transfusion, ICU, and CDSS to be responsible for the process redesign and implementation, feedback and suggestion collection from clinical units, and relevant solutions.

"You have to learn it by practicing it yourself." To meet the HIMSS criteria requires coordinated arrangement from the hospital level and cooperation among multiple departments. We still remember the days when we were fully engaged in the process: Dr. Guo Cheng, Director of Pharmacy, was "obsessed" by medication closed-loop management even in his dreams. Dr. Li Yingchuan, Director of ICU, noted down the key points and asked many questions during the training on "Structured Inpatient Medical Record Documentation." Dr. Shi Haibo, Director of ENT Departments, borrowed the books about HIMSS validation from the IT Center and discussed with them about the preparation. Dr. Zhang Lei, physician of Endocrinology Department, submitted 19 information improvement requests on behalf of his unit. Dr. Zhu Jie, Director of Medical Affairs Department, organized special training on the Policy on Hospital Consultation to be delivered by the IT Center for the chief residents and unit team leaders.

Drops of water finally converged into the river. After more than 6 months of cooperation and mutual support, the hospital finally was validated as a Stage 6 hospital, which would not be possible without the on-site instructions and recommendations from the HIMSS consultants as well as the commitment from the hospital leadership. Dr. Jia Weiping, President of the hospital, moderated many important meetings in the hospital in spite of his tight schedule and formulated the overall organizational structure and principles of actions. Dr. Yin Shankai, VP, emphasized on many occasions that the ultimate purpose of seeking HIMSS validation was to improve the level of IT adoption, enhance the managerial expertise, and tackle the challenges in clinical practices.

All the participation and contribution were paid back with the good news of validation on June 7, 2017. We have every reason to be proud of what we have achieved (Figure 12.1).

Figure 12.1 Shanghai No. 6 People's Hospital HIMSS EMRAM Stage 6.

A New Starting Point

After all the changes put in place, patient safety has been better secured; the cooperation among units and departments has been enhanced; and the efficiency of healthcare staff has also went up. More importantly, the frontline staff started to realize that intelligence could be achieved through their joint efforts with IT Center in tackling problems and designing solutions on a stronger foundation of mutual understanding and trust.

HIMSS EMRAM Stage 6 is not the end point. It empowered us with confidence and strength to pursue our goals in the right way. There is still room in the improvement in CDSS, decision support rules and CDR. We still have a long way to go.

Case 1: Clinical Data Repository (CDR)

Back to Zero

SH No. 6 Hospital first adopted IT solutions as early as in the 1990s. After years of evolution, we had around 110 systems running in the hospital with a total data volume as large as 180 Tb. As the market grew more segmented, more players came into the arena with even more sophisticated solutions, which led to the situation where data could not be shared across systems from different vendors. If the data generated in one system was too large to ensure its efficiency and function, a migration data into several other isolated databases (historical base, annual database, backup database, operation database, etc.) would be a must. But it compromised the effective utilization of data.

In 2015, the hospital started to build the CDR for hosting the data generated from different systems in a centralized way to better utilize and share them. After 2 years of development, we basically finished the architecture of all systems and the CDR, including the design of data flow and the model of the data center.

There had been in total over 6 million entries related to patient demographic information, over 35 million entries regarding patient services, 26 million odd physician orders, nearly 160 million medication prescriptions, more than 15 million lab reports and over 7 million examination reports. Before HIMSS EMRAM validation, we believed that we had realized the integration and sharing of information. With the patient profile view interface (a READ-ONLY module of patient's demographic information, diagnosis, physician's documentation, physician orders, lab reports, examination reports, nursing documentation, surgery and anesthesia, etc.), physicians, and nurses could access all data about one patient anytime anywhere through the system.

However, the HIMSS consultants pointed out that the sharing of patient data was not realized. It was very surprising when we heard that. After the explanation by the consultants, we understood that the "information sharing" defined by ourselves in the past was not on the level of data sharing expected by HIMSS. HIMSS requires CDR serve as the fundamental discrete database to aggregate the discrete data generated from clinical activities and to support the needs of data access by different systems. For example, all information needed by frontline staff should be integrated and displayed on one interface without closing down the current interface and opening the patient profile view. Physicians should be able to quote all types of data from the medical record (diagnosis, demographic information, medication, lab, examinations, etc.) into the chart they are writing. In addition, HIMSS EMRAM model has specific requirements on the closed-loop management of medication and blood transfusion as well as on the CDSS. All these can only be realized through the support of a sufficient CDR.

We knew the tasks would not be easy. First, data cleansing or formatting was not performed in the CDR, which caused chaotic storage. In addition, the primary data in different systems were not consistent, adding to the difficulties in interfacing. Second, the data were not integrated in a patient-centered way. Therefore, the data related to patient care lacked continuity, and no effective data support was available for the CDSS from the CDR. Last but not least, the CDR could not sufficiently support the clinical work because it could not deliver real-time data. In the face of all these setbacks, we decided to redesign the CDR based on the recommendations from the HIMSS consultants.

Always Take One More Step Further

The following steps were adopted to establish our CDR.

First, we defined the general goal of CDR: to organize patient clinical data via EMPI and store all patient clinical information in a complete, standard, and uniform way. Uniform data retrieval service is also provided to the outside to support clinical data sharing as a platform.

Second, we reviewed and analyzed the activities in the hospital and designed 11 clinical business data models according to the clinical service information model standards formulated by the *Health and Family Planning Commission* (see Table 12.1).

Third, EMPI was established to organize all patient clinical data for full integration of heterogeneous data generated by the systems from different vendors in a patient-centered manner. EMPI can automatically match the patient data to merge data for one patient and link patient identity in different systems. Meanwhile, it can remind staff on patient data potentially identified to be linked to one patient to merge the data through automatic search of similar patient. Staff could decide whether to merge the data or not.

Fourth, Master Data Management System (MDM) was established to manage the primary data of high value of re-utilization in different systems to ensure the accuracy, completion, and

Table 12.1 CDR Business Data Model

Patient identifier	Identity registry
Patient service	Appointment, registration
Admission/discharge/transfer	Admission, discharge, transfer between units
Physician order	Prescription, administration
Medical chart	Inpatient medical record
Nursing	Nursing flow sheet, nursing assessment, vital sign monitoring
Laboratory	Lab tests, glucose
Examinations	Radiology, pathology, electrophysiology, other ancillary investigations
Surgery and anesthesia	Surgery and anesthesia
Blood transfusion	Assessment, request, administration, documentation
Health checkup	Health checkup

consistency of data. When data are exchanged among different systems or care providers, the system could eliminate the discrepancy of data in different occasions and realize the standardization of data.

Fifth, the Operational Data Store (ODS) was established. The ODS is the copy of the source system data. It does not eliminate, modify, or integrate data during retrieval. It acquires all historical data from the source systems through data backup restore during the initial loading of data. After that, it captures incremental data through Change Data Capture (CDC) of the clinical data requiring to be available in real time at an interval of every 5 min. For data dictionaries that do not emphasize real-time availability, Extract-Transform-Load (ETL) is adopted to retrieve incremental data from the source systems once every 24 h. In this way, we are able to move the clinical data from the business system database to the ODS.

Sixth, CDR was established. After the ODS was put in place, we then used ETL to retrieve data from ODS to CDR. During the loading, data would be automatically matched via EMPI and standardized through MDM. All data would be cleansed and formatted according to the CDR data models to realize the standardized and modeled storage of clinical data. All historical data were loaded at one time, while incremental data were loaded every 5 min.

Seventh, one external service interface was established. After the CDR had been put in place, all data could be shared with platforms and other business systems through one interface. New system would no longer need special interfacing. All data could be accessed and shared through CDR.

Fruitful Harvest

HIMSS EMRAM Stage 6 changed our perception of CDR and helped us truly understand the meaning of integration and sharing of clinical data.

CDR is an important tool to ensure continuity of patient information from outpatient clinics, ER, inpatient to the follow-up period after discharge. Physicians are able to access all past diagnoses, medical record documentation, lab/examination reports, medication used, and other information in a more intuitive and accurate way. As the infrastructure of CSSD, CDR could assist the analysis of a patient's clinical condition before or during an event.

Besides, CDR plays a significant role in combined medication therapy for infection control among critical patients and surgical patients. Through complicated mathematic algorithm, we are able to monitor the infection risks among patients under combined medication therapy as well as the location of such patients, and send warning automatically for healthcare staff to take effective actions. Thanks to the CDR, it becomes possible to take preventive measures to ensure medical quality.

As the CDR improves, it serves as the most valuable information tool to assist the physicians, nurses, and pharmacists during patient care. Meanwhile, the CDR hosts all clinical data for real-time analysis and statistics to enable identification of problems existing in clinical activities, dashboard for management and operation staff, warning and reminders regarding certain information, which finally leads to the delicacy management practice.

A well-designed CDR requires deep understanding of the practical process in different clinical services and of the needs of the frontline staff and hospital managers. Data availability should be ensured for data loading. During this process, the engineers at the Data Center and business system engineers should work closely with the clinical units and administrative departments. Only in this way, the CDR could truly play the role of data integration and sharing.

Case 2: Give Nurses Back to Patients

Win Over the Hearts

Though SH No. 6 Hospital is a big hospital with complete support with the information system, it still made us worried after we visited other HIMSS EMRAM hospitals before we were validated. The HIMSS EMRAM criteria are comprehensive. It emphasizes the enhanced functionalities and the ubiquitous application of such functionalities. To realize such level of maturity, it requires a high-level managerial expertise regarding information technology development across the hospital. Take nursing as an example, the information system could effectively improve the efficiency and quality of the nursing staff, and bring them the "sense of gain."

Before the validation, we were fully aware that if we wanted to win the battle, we needed to engage each one of our staff and stay practical. In the past, we paid little attention to the engagement of the frontline staff in information development. To quickly complete a task, we sometimes filtered out some of their reasonable requests on purpose. The result was that the system was far from practical and impaired the active participation of the frontline staff, in particular, the nursing staff. The HIMSS consultants often told us that what we planned to do had to enhance the "sense of gain" of the frontline staff to motivate them. Only in this way could we achieve continuous improvement.

To this end, we established the communication mechanism of regular meetings together with the Nursing Department to mainly discuss the problems existing in the nursing practice, possible solutions, and recommendations. The IT Center also decided to go to the units to experience by themselves the daily workload and the work place environment, helping the IT staff think in the shoes of the nurses through more direct communication and a mutual learning process. The hospital also arranged some service training and discussion to improve the understanding of the nursing staff on the system. The enhanced cooperation through learning and understanding has been the guarantee of smooth implementation.

Predicament of "Barcode Scanning"

There was a joke about HIMSS EMRAM criteria among the staff: HIMSS was the assemblages of all kinds of barcode scanning. They believed that "scanning" was a burden on the clinical work flow. But, as pointed out by the consultants, the "scanning" could save much more time than we had thought if we needed to strictly follow the "three checks and seven verifications." If we just verify patient names and the bed numbers, "scanning" would never have a chance to win in terms of speed. But patient names and bed numbers are not sufficient to ensure patient safety.

Actually, before the HIMSS EMRAM validation, we had realized barcode scanning for verification with the mobile nursing system. As requested by the Nursing Department, we developed the bed-side verification, documentation, and inquiry functions in the mobile nursing system which supports printing as well. This saves our nurses from documenting the monitoring on paper and ensures the access to data during quality control. Barcode scanning verification has also been added to the medication handover on the units, refill of the pharmacy shelves and dispensing of discharge medication to patients to complete the closed loop of medication management.

Sleeping data in the system would never bring good experience to the users. Thus, an overview screen was developed for nurses to improve the data accuracy and allow the system to administer the prescription more actively to complete the loop.

Another example is the use of finger pulse oximetry. The small device could often be forgotten on the patients. Then, we put barcode on the device to allow our nurses to collect the patient information regarding the device use in a more convenient way. Such small moves won the applause from the nurses. Closed loop is an urgently needed methodology for clinical practice to ensure the right thing is done in the right way and to simplify the process for our staff.

Paperless Nursing Care

Nursing documentation is part of the nurses' daily work and eats up most of their time. The HIMSS consultants value the digitalization of the nursing documentation and the sharing of information to better support the nurse's work.

We adopted comprehensive structured templates in the nursing system and established the nursing database through which the data could be shared. We also made some improvement to the nursing charts, for example, automatic calculation of the ins/outs, automatic recommendation on nursing tasks for patients at high risks, etc. These functions have reduced the workload of our nurses.

After Stage 6 validation, we received the visit by Ms. Zhu Haihua, CNO of the First Affiliated Hospital of Xiamen University, who shared their experience with us. She mentioned that the adoption of information technology was to give nurses back to the patients, and the system could save the nurses from tedious charting tasks through data collection and sharing. This is not only the aspiration of our nurses, but also the shared goal of IT professionals.

Chapter 13

Sir Run Run Shaw Hospital of Zhejiang University School of Medicine

Cai Xiujun, Pan Hongming, Qiao Kai, Zhuang Yiyu, Cai Bin, Pan Hongying, Wu Dingying, He Jielang, Jiang Zhou, Qian Yin, Wei Li, Huang Chen, Wang Jialing, and Ye Jinming

Sir Run Run Shaw Hospital Affiliated to Zhejiang University School of Medicine

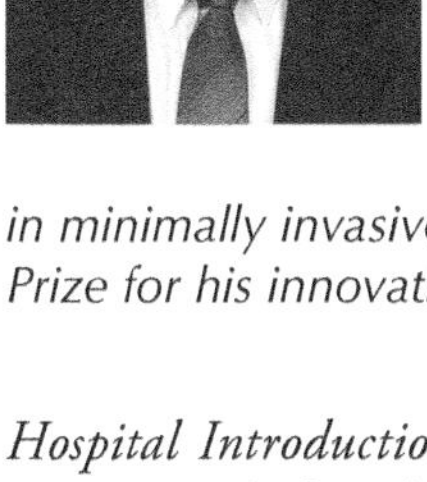

Dr. Cai Xiujun *is the President, Professor, Director of General Surgery Department of Sir Run Run Shaw Hospital Affiliated to Zhejiang University School of Medicine, and director of Key Laboratory for Endoscopy Technique of Zhejiang Province. In addition, he is Vice Director of the Society of Surgery of Chinese Medical Society, Vice Director of the Liver Surgery Group of Society of Surgery of Chinese Medical Society, Vice Director of Pancreatic Cancer Committee of China Anti-cancer Association, the Fellow of American College of Surgery, and the Fellow of Royal College of Surgeons (British). Dr. Cai Xiujun practiced general surgery for 30 years and especially expert in minimally invasive surgery and HPB surgery. He has been awarded the National Prize for his innovation in minimally invasive surgery and HPB surgery.*

Hospital Introduction: Sir Run Run Shaw Hospital of Zhejiang University School of Medicine (referred to as SRRSH hereinafter) is a comprehensive, tertiary-level A, public hospital active in clinical care, medical education, and research, built with the donation from Sir Run Run Shaw, a Hong Kong entertainment mogul and philanthropist, and the resources designated by Zhejiang provincial government in the relevant proportion. Since its foundation in 1994, thanks to the strong leadership support from Zhejiang provincial government, Zhejiang University, and Health and Family Planning Commission of Zhejiang province, SRRSH has been dedicated to the reform of conventional hospital management model and demonstrated the "Shaw's model" that reflects international best practice.

International Accreditation: SRRSH became the first public hospital in the Chinese mainland to be accredited by JCI in 2006 and the first hospital of HIMSS EMRAM Stage 6 in Zhejiang province in November 2015. By August 2017, with the accreditation of HIMSS EMRAM Stage 7, it became the first hospital in the Chinese mainland with both JCI and HIMSS EMRAM Stage 7 accreditation on both campuses concurrently.

Contents

Preface

To Earn the Formidable Combination for the Endless Pursuit of Quality

"SRRSH is the first to make JCI known to people in China. It gets the gist of the JCI accreditation standards and earnestly practices with JCI mentality. JCI started its presence in China with SRRSH, and we are deeply proud to have SRRSH on board! SRRSH is extraordinary to JCI. We are delighted to see you stay on the accreditation track for a decade!" said Dr. Vishal Adma, a JCI surveyor, during the closing ceremony of the fourth JCI survey of SRRSH in October 2016 (see Figure 13.1). We were deeply touched and proud at hearing his words. By then, SRRSH had maintained the record of being the only hospital in the Chinese mainland accredited with flying colors for the fourth time in a row.

The connection between SRRSH and JCI seems to be a part of predestination, implied when it was founded at the beginning. Since it was founded, by taking reference from advanced management models of the U.S. and carrying forward the convention in China, SRRSH formulated a model of hospital management adapted to China's situation in the modern time. With its unique background and international vision, SRRSH has held itself against high standards to achieve excellence and improve its management. Staring with JCI hospital accreditation standards in August 2003, SRRSH got to know about accreditation and became interconnected with JCI as well as HIMSS as it received HIMSS EMRAM Stage 7 status in August 2017. Significant progress has been made on management, quality of care, and patient safety as SRRSH worked to achieve JCI and HIMSS accreditation. The hospital has achieved higher potential for growth, national influence, and recognition as well as compliment with its pioneering models of committee structure, physician credentialing, and privileging, adoption of international patient safety goals, application of IT in healthcare, safety-driven medication use and management, staff education and training programs, job description, performance evaluation, cost management, patient record management, bed allocation, and staff involvement in quality activities.

Figure 13.1 JCI surveyors give SRRSH the thumbs up.

It Is the Culture of Patient Safety That Constitutes the Essence of Healthcare

As a set of widely recognized standards for healthcare organizations around the world, JCI is intended to maximize patient-centered healthcare by encouraging organizations to continuously improve medical quality and safety, and provide safe, quality, and patient-friendly healthcare services by establishing proper healthcare policies and processes as well as standard-driven management. After years of involvement with JCI, SRRSH has gradually brought JCI standards and mindset into its heart and soul thanks to the quality management system it has developed based on JCI standards.

The tracing methodology used during JCI survey features detailed and professional examination on every inch of quality and safety on clinical care, nursing, medical technologies, and general support. The application of risk assessment and quality improvement tools are also covered during the survey, which include Failure Mode Effect Analysis, Hazard Vulnerability Analysis, Infection Control Risk Assessment, and Root Cause Analysis. We have found patient tracer and system tracer methodology very helpful for safety assurance and management of the hospital. Most importantly, as Cai Xiujun, the president of SRRSH, puts it, "We have learned more about the proper culture than methods from JCI!" When you go around SRRSH and ask any staff you chance upon "What is JCI?", he or she will answer "patient safety and continuous improvement of quality" without hesitation.

It is by no means easy to establish the quality and safety culture that centers on patient. SRRSH has followed the philosophy of "serving patient with sincerity, conviction and love" since its foundation, but not until the JCI survey did we realize the delivery of "patient-centered" care requires staff to concertedly increase awareness and act accordingly.

With over two decades' experience in healthcare, Pan Hongying, Vice Director of Nursing Dept. and chief nurse, has contributed to every JCI survey that SRRSH has gone through and thus observed many changes in the hospital. She recognizes that JCI standards emphasize system-based operation and consistency. For patient identification specifically, the bottom line for patient safety is that every staff identifies patient with two identifiers whenever workup, diagnostic and therapeutic procedure, medication administration, and even food delivery takes place. In the tracer activities of JCI survey, the consistency between practice and policies is expected, which allows no error or carelessness. We found it corresponds to the pursuit of our quality culture: do what we have written and write what we are doing.

In the closing ceremony of the fourth JCI survey, Mr. Elijah J. Gilreath, a surveyor, shared a scene that touched him.

> One day, while walking in the corridor of the hospital, I saw a man in a wheelchair, pushed around by his wife. A specimen transporter passed by and noticed they might need some help and came up to help push the wheelchair immediately. At that moment, from that transporter, I truly felt that everyone in the hospital was carrying forward the hospital culture of 'love and support for patients. With this story, I'd like to underline that patient care is not provided by any specific staff. It involves every staff.

Our hospital culture was echoed by the surveyors, with one commenting "We have been impressed with your organization's culture of care, safety, support, and continuing education. We pay tribute to all of your staff. The fact that they provide 'patient-centered' care is commendable."

Every new staff has received orientation specific to JCI standards since 2006, and many staff in SRRSH have experienced more than one JCI survey, most of whom have even gone through four surveys. Every year, the hospital conducts survey of safety culture on staff with patient safety questionnaire from AHRQ (Agency for Healthcare Research & Quality), analyzes and acts on inadvertent events as well as initiates programs of continuous quality improvement (CQI) with tools such as FOCUS-PDCA and six sigma. There were 82 CQI programs in 2016 alone, for example.

If one says JCI accreditation helps hospital establish the quality and safety culture of "patient-centeredness," then HIMSS EMRAM validation is a reinforcer of quality and safety culture. As a pioneer of IT adoption in healthcare in the Chinese mainland, SRRSH has played a leading role in LIS, PACS, medical record, and mobile healthcare. Based on the four-point strategy of "top-level design, stepwise implementation, urgency-based prioritization and ongoing development," SRRSH started to shift from the focus of development from technology intensiveness to clinical decision support capability in 2013. It led to the certification of HIMSS EMRAM Stage 6 in November 2015, after which the organization aimed for HIMSS EMRAM Stage 7 and initiated a series of upgrade projects to increase the extent and sophistication. It was successfully certified in August 2017 thanks to major breakthrough has been realized in closed-loop management, paperless process, clinical decision support, electronic health record, medication management, single sign-on session, subject-specific system, Internet of Things, and interoperability of systems (Figures 13.2 and 13.3).

Being a gold standard of IT adoption in hospitals, HIMSS EMRAM validation promotes compliance to JCI standards on safety, quality, and continuous improvement by standardizing practice with IT approach. During this process, IT was used to close loops in the process, and connect steps in the process. Further delineated in the IT system, policies have been implemented more consistently, which demonstrates how IT adoption serves clinical safety, quality, and patient care. IT has helped close the loops in more than 20 processes, covering medication use, intravenous infusion, transfusion, breast milk, narcotics, drainage assessment, workups, critical values, intervention procedures, surgeries, disinfection and isolation, pain management, premedication, emergency room visits, etc. The highlight of SRRSH lies in the visualization of closed-loop system, where the status of every step is presented in the process map, and any missing step triggers alert to ensure patient safety. Take the closed-loop system of medication as an example, a physician orders medication, a pharmacist reviews the order, and the data are transmitted to dispensing

Figure 13.2 The fourth JCI survey in October 2016.

Figure 13.3 HIMSS EMRAM Stage 7 validation in August 2017.

machine automatically for drug packaging. Before administration, a nurse scans patient's wristband as well as the barcode on the drug package to verify patient's identity, drug name, dose, route, and time. If any piece of information is discordant with that in the system, an alert is given.

We Are by No Means "Mr. Not Bad"

JCI standards represent not only standards to follow but also self-expectation of hospitals. It helps us do a better job by upholding consistency among mindset, standards, attitude, and habits. The significance of triennial survey of JCI accredited organizations is to ensure "high performance by force of habit." It is easy to do well in one day or two, but difficult to do well every day consistently. Therefore, we have carried forward policies and procedures in line with JCI standards to form good habit and reduce risk and error, which include time-out, hand hygiene, and checking for seven pieces of key information during three moments. The standard-driven, complete, and efficacious safety system is initiated as soon as a patient steps into SRRSH. "In terms of patient safety, SRRSH accepts only 'standard compliance' and leaves no room for 'not bad'," said Dr. Cai Xiujun, president of the hospital.

Patient assessment at admission consists of understanding his/her history, getting a complete and accurate idea of the patient's condition and evaluating his/her acceptance of the care and developing individualized and proper plans for the care and discharge. Clinic assessment covers pain, psychology, nutrition, fall, etc. "We provide inpatient at high risk for fall with pajamas with embroidered sign of yellow so that any staff immediately recognizes his/her risk status no matter where the patient goes." "We attach a red label of 'allergy' to the wristband when a patient has allergic history and put similar labels in his/her records and forms for investigation."

Dr. Guo Feng, Vice Director of ICU, and chief physician, has profound experience of how patients benefit from JCI standards. The Center for Severe Pancreatitis, whose establishment took us 3 years to prepare, has decreased mortality from 31.6% to 8.3%. Patients have felt that they are taken care of not by any specific physician, but by the team in SRRSH. We have seen how important it is for the care of the disease.

> The essence of JCI standards lies in having quality and safety assured by all types of rules and regulations by every means. With over 300 standards and over 1000 measurable elements, JCI standards always start with staff, focus on patient, and promote quality and safety. To consistently work according to JCI standards holds the key to providing uniform care and ensuring safety of every patient, no matter if you treat 10 or 2000 patients.

Dr. Cai Bin, Director of Quality Dept., shares that "when working to comply with JCI standards, we became enthusiastic in identifying the gaps unnoticeable in the past and fixing them."

According to HIMSS, standardization is represented with the integration of health information and data, the enhancement with artificial intelligence and the capability of clinical decision support. Take an inpatient with potential cardiac arrest, for example, there are usually observable signs several hours before his or her collapse. Thus, the ability to identify signs and take action as soon as possible is the key to avoiding deterioration. To this end, SRRSH established rapid response team (RRT), the first of its kind in Zhejiang province. Accordingly, specific criteria were developed to define when should one call RRT, which include heart rate above 140 or below 40 beats/min, respiration above 30 or below 8 times/min, and sudden onset of impaired speech. These criteria were embedded into electronic health system, constituting the RRT early warning module. Then, nurse can initiate RRT as soon as any of the criteria is triggered. Upon receiving the call, the RRT should arrive and provide intervention within 5–10 min (Figure 13.4).

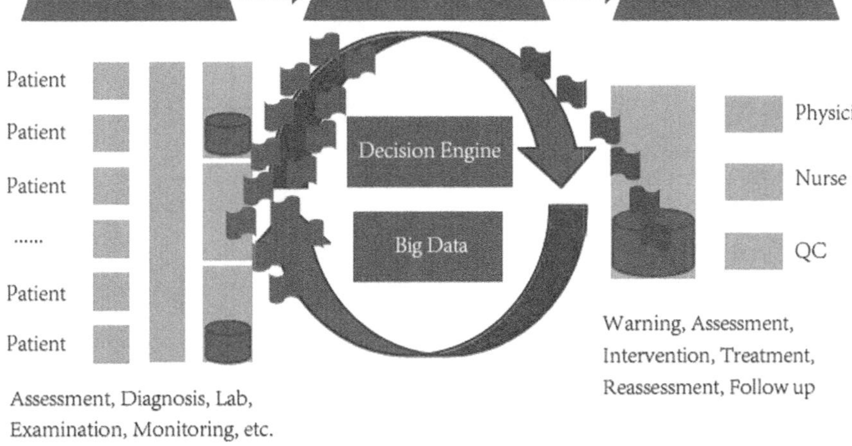

Figure 13.4 Rapid response team (RRT) system.

To Improve Systems and Processes: Do Everything for Patients

Both JCI accreditation and HIMSS EMRAM validation are dedicated for patient safety. As technology advances with time, hospitals become dependent on IT adoption for system and process improvement. In the course of preparation for every JCI survey and HIMSS EMRAM Stage 6 and 7 validations, more importantly, Ms. Jilan Liu, Principle JCR Consultant, Vice President & Executive Director of Greater China at HIMSS, has paid many visits to SRRSH and hailed our effort in the furtherance of patient safety culture, CQI, and the upgrade of IT capability. She shared her expectation over SRRSH that "as the first major comprehensive hospital in China with four JCI accreditation successively, SRRSH has defined the creativity and transformation in the management of public hospital in China and extended its influence among national counterparts. You are among the first in China to start the IT adoption strategy based on your outstanding performance, and have made systematic improvement constantly on patient safety and quality. You have set a good example in furthering clinical care and management with IT capacity and striving toward HIMSS EMRAM Stage 7 certification."

Dr. Liu's comment is well demonstrated in the development of Parenteral Nutrition Software and Resuscitation Management Software used in NICU of SRRSH's Xiasha Campus. During our fourth JCI survey and HIMSS EMRAM Stage 7 validation, surveyors appreciated the uniqueness of our NICU. The fact that NICU, a "neonate member" of the hospital at 2 years old only, was highly regarded during the rigorous surveys was attributable to the care and consideration on many details by the entire NICU team.

A well-known challenge in NICU where neonates are often complicated with weight problem and unique diseases is the individualized dosing for both parenteral and therapeutic agents. The accurate and stable delivery of parenteral nutrient is paramount to the growth and recovery of critically ill neonates, in particular the very low and extremely low birth weight premise. During resuscitation for these critical neonates, efficient and accurate dosing of agents and expedited preparation and administration are favorable for good outcome (Figure 13.5).

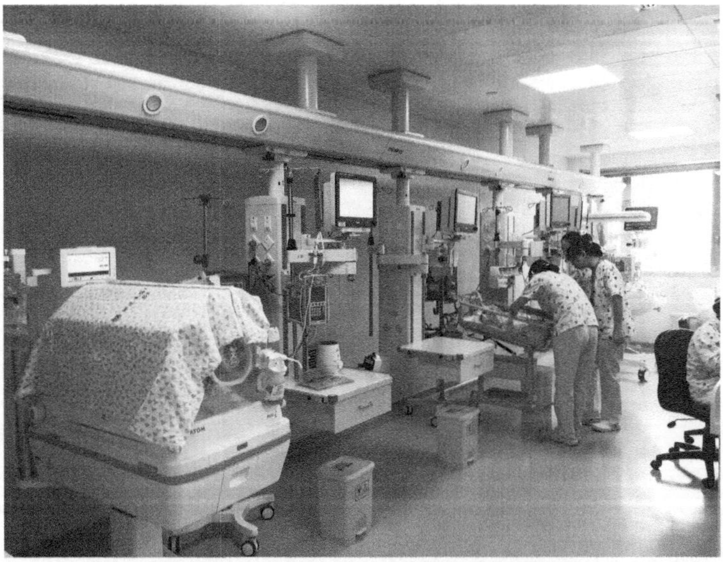

Figure 13.5 NICU in perfect order.

In many hospitals in China, when it comes to parenteral nutrition, the amount of nutritional supplement needed for a neonate and the types and proportion of nutrients are calculated to generate a list of intravenous nutrients. Then, a physician or nurse enters the nutritional order according to that list manually into the electronic system for preparation, either from the intravenous admixture service or from the unit itself, before the infant receives the nutritional agent. In such conventional process, physician has to spend a lot of time and effort just to do the math, while there is inherent risk for safety and imprecision. This process is inadequate for nutritional assurance for critically ill neonates and record tracking for physicians. Under this background, we developed neonatal nutrition software to ensure safety and quality of neonatal care, uniform care, resources available to physicians, less workload, and higher efficiency of physicians. This software has been linked with physician's electronic system and accessible, with user name and password, only to physicians who has been privileged, to ensure only authorized staff are using it.

Once logged in, the physician gets to see the list of key information for inpatients. The information on all the intravenous nutritional preparation is displayed for the physician to consider the need for adjustment in the nutrients mix. As the current weight of the infant is automatically fed by the electronic system, with the tracking record of nutrient intake as well as the easily accessible workup results, all that the physician needs to do to change nutrient constituent is to enter the target for each nutrient. Then the software automatically generates the new combination for intravenous nutritional supplement. In addition to the dosage needed for each nutrient, the volume and drip speed of the intravenous nutritional compound are also provided for the physician. As soon as the physician confirms and saves this information, it becomes intravenous nutritional order in the physician's order list and is sent to nurse and intravenous admixture service. The software has programmed to be so user-friendly that it automatically tunes the dose to the duration of intravenous nutritional support determined (Figures 13.6 and 13.7).

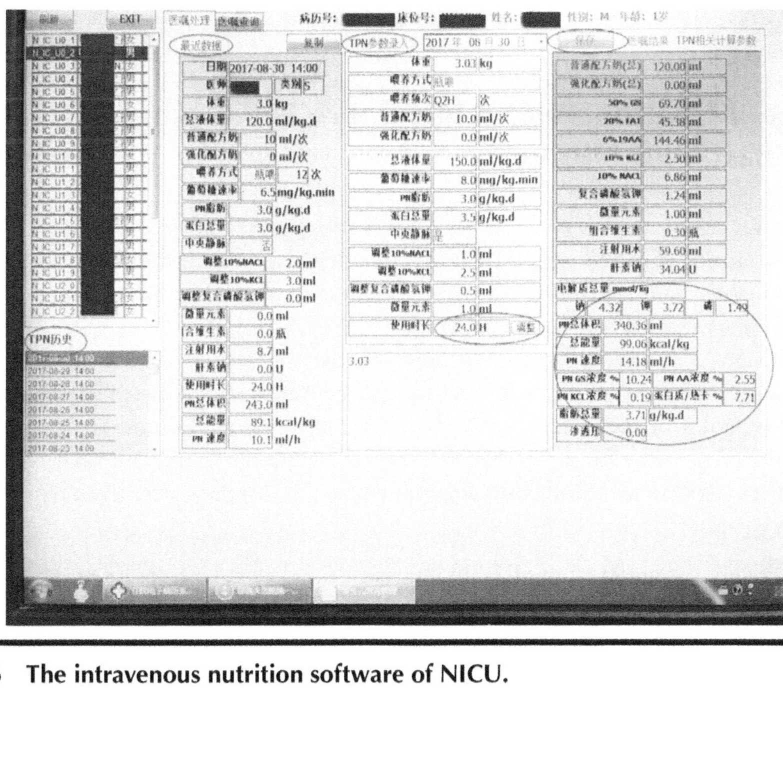

Figure 13.6 The intravenous nutrition software of NICU.

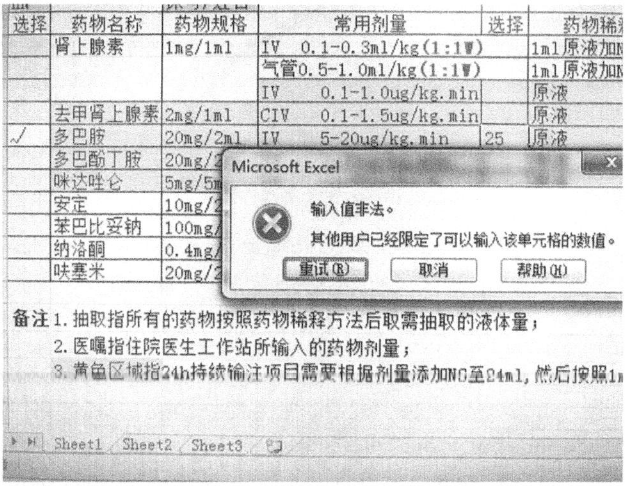

Figure 13.7 The software for resuscitation medication in NICU.

As a safety measure, when overdose or unsafe prescription occurs to the nutrient targets put in by physician, the software turns that information red to remind physicians and makes it impossible to save the information until the physician corrects the figure.

What's more, to ensure the efficiency and accuracy of medication use during resuscitation as well as the timely documentation of ordering, NICU physicians and nurses worked with IT Dept. to develop a simple software of reference information on medication for neonatal resuscitation. During resuscitation, therefore, staff can run the software, enter the neonate's information, select the medication and expected dose and generate medication preparation plan with a hit on "Enter" button. The calculation and the time are maintained in the software for tracking.

In Terms of Healthcare Quality, There Is Nothing Called "Best" but "Better"

JCI survey lasts for one week only, but the quality journey never ends. Every SRRSH staff is learning JCI philosophy by heart, practicing with such mindset and integrate it into his/her habit. By doing so, we will be more science-based in management and clinical practice to better satisfy patients.

HIMSS EMRAM Stage 7 represents the highest standard in healthcare informatics, with this certification marking its commencement instead of destination. Our hospital will break new grounds in the adoption of IT and maintenance of information system. At the end of the day, the state-of-the-art information system supports safer care with higher quality and efficiency as well as attentive care delivered to every patient (Figure 13.8).

As Dr. Cai Xiujun, the president of SRRSH, puts it in the closing ceremonies of the fourth JCI survey and HIMSS EMRAM Stage 7 validation, to get accredited does not constitute our final destination as the journey toward better healthcare quality knows no end. It is an eternal belief and pursuit for SRRSH staff to deliver safe and consistent care of international quality standards (Figure 13.9).

Figure 13.8 The closing ceremony of the fourth JCI survey in October 2016.

Figure 13.9 The closing ceremony of the HIMSS EMRAM Stage 7 validation in August 2017.

Case 1: Put an End to the Uncertainties in Closed-Loop Management for Breast Milk

More and more high-risk neonates survive thanks to the advancement of perinatology and intensive care. Since breast milk provides the best nutrition to neonates in NICU, healthcare organizations document breast milk feeding, required by the National Health and Family Planning Commission in its Announcement of the Review of Baby-Friendly Hospital Accreditation. Babies had been fed with breast milk in NICU before our organization prepared for HIMSS EMRAM Stage 7 certification, with breast-feeding rate at 65% in 2016.

Back then, our electronic system did not provide effective control of or adequate IT support to the administration of breast milk. There were multiple risk points in the transcription, ordering, feeding option, feeding time, documentation, data aggregation, and track capability. There was even a wrong administration of breast milk in NICU in 2016. But now, the electronic supervision of breast feeding based on closed-loop management is in place.

How Breast Feeding Is Managed

Before closed-loop management was in place, breast milk was managed by the following steps.

The family member brought breast milk to the hospital, contained in freezer-safe bags → nurse checked information on the bags written by the family member and visually examined the milk → nurse accepted the milk and documented the total volume received → physician ordered "feeding with breast milk or formula" without having to know if breast milk was available for the baby → the order-handling nurse printed out label and prepared formula according to the physician's order → the patient-care nurse verified the order and baby's information, fed the baby with the milk prepared and documented this in the NICU nursing flow-sheet.

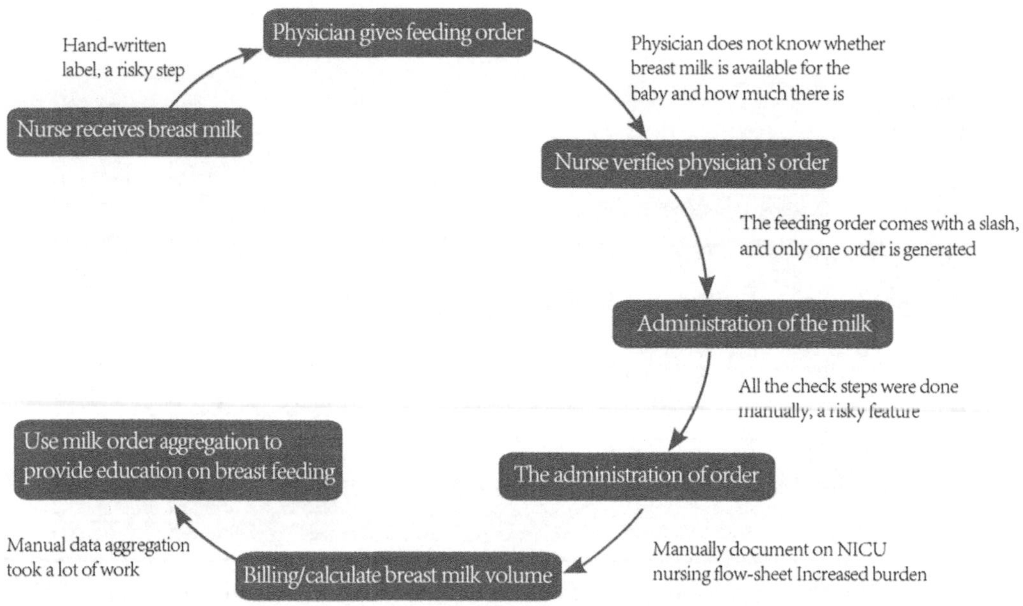

"Feeding with breast milk or formula" meant that if breast milk is available, the baby received breast milk; otherwise, baby was fed on formula. Described in words, this order related to only one instruction.

The problems in this process include:

1. The label might be blurry, or the bed number and medical number might be wrong as the label was written by the family member before s/he handed the breast milk to the nurse for storage in the refrigerator;
2. Not knowing if breast milk was available for the child, the responsible physician was not able to accurately adjust the milk order;

3. It was a risk-prone process as the orders were described in words, there were 12 orders for 1 day and nurse did a lot of work in printing the labels for milks;
4. At that time when PDA (personal digital assistance) was not used yet, nurse manually verified the order and the child's information, which was prone to wrong-baby error;
5. After administering the milk, nurse had to write down the volume of milk given and manually develop the bill, which increased workload;
6. The percentages partial or total breast feeding were all aggregated manually.

The First Step Toward Closed-Loop Management

To overcome the defect in the breast milk management, a task force of closed-loop breast milk management was convened, with the roles and responsibilities listed below:

1. Team leader (the head nurse of NICU): to lead the works of the task group, discuss with group members, identify causes; keep contact with the head nurse in charge of nursing quality, information nurse, and specialty nurse of nursing information; and craft solution based on the causes identified;
2. Educator/coordinator (education nurse of NICU): To detail the steps in the process, communicate changes made to the process to every nurse and evaluate staff;
3. Consultation (the Deputy Director of Nursing Dept./Nursing Quality Management): To manage and direct the entire process;
4. Secretaries (information nurse and nurse of nursing information specialty): To provide facilitation, including the relay of information and the facilitation of program modification;
5. Team members (all the nurses of NICU): To implement changes made to the process and give feedback on the process they are using.

With the conclusion from team discussion, the closed-loop breast milk management process in our hospital has been updated as: nurse receives breast milk → nurse prints out label for the breast milk → nurse stores the breast milk → physician gives individualized breast milk order → nurse confirms the order → nurse prints out the label used for administration and sticks it onto the milk pack → during administration, nurse scans the label and the baby's wrist band with PDA to verify it is the right milk. All the steps constitute a complete train of process (see Figure 13.10).

The nurses constantly provide education on breast feeding to the family members from the beginning of a baby's admission to NICU until discharge. Throughout the process of breast feeding, IT supports of Quick Response (QR) code, wireless network, mobile devices have helped ensure the correct administration of breast milk and data aggregation. Based on data analysis, nurse can give immediate feedback to the family members and increase the percentage of partial and total breast feeding. With these efforts, breast feeding has become safer as well as more process-compliant and facts-driven, contributing to the target of CQI.

During Admission to NICU—Education on Breast Feeding

As soon as a neonate is admitted, a designated staff provides education to the family members and a booklet on this topic. In this 14-page booklet, the background knowledge of breast milk, how it is collected, how to evaluate the quality of each step in breast milk collection at home and how to complete the breast milk quality checklist are described. After studying the booklet, the family

Figure 13.10 Human milk closed-loop management.

member completes a self-evaluation tool from the booklet, which will be reviewed by nurse when they send in milk for the first time. In addition, the family member hands in the quality checklist along with the breast milk each time to ensure the milk has been collected in a way that meets quality expectation of the hospital. Nurse reviews the breast milk quality checklist every day when he/she receives the milk from the family for 21 days (see Table 13.1).

The Quality Control of Breast Milk Starts from Its Source

Breast **milk reception**

When the family brings breast milk in bottles to the nurse station, nurse examines its quality, and work together with the family member in the mobile nursing program. They verify that they have opened the record of the right baby, and enter the volume of each pack of milk in the "milk collected" panel, print out the labels and stick them on each of the milk bottles. Listed on the label are: the name of the baby for the milk, bed number, admission number, date of milk reception, volume of the milk in that bottle and a QR code. All the information is verified by the family member as well. Nurse counts the number of bottles sent in by the family and prints out that number of labels to ensure each bottle has one label. The labels are printed instead of manually completed for error avoidance. As nurse enters the volume of the milk in each bottle, the total volume is automatically generated from the electronic system and brought to physician's milk ordering system (see Figure 13.11).

Breast milk storage

The freezer and refrigerator for breast milk are managed by designated staff from every shift. The staff document the temperature every shift, take out expired milk and clean the storage shelves with disinfectant. Once a month, the freezer and refrigerator are defrosted and cleaned thoroughly.

Table 13.1 Breast Milk Quality Checklist

The following checks are performed everyday
Wash hands step by step according to the six-step guideline in its exact order
Rub hands thoroughly, repeat at least five times on each step and spend at least 30 s to complete all the steps
Clean hands thoroughly under running water
Turn off the tap in a way that avoid recontamination of the hands
Wipe off water with paper/clean towel
Clean the breasts with warm water before attempting to express milk
Let the skin of the breast dry naturally
Fill milk into the bottle till the last 3–4 cm from the cover in case the milk expands in the freezer
Collect milk in sterile, food-grade, and plastic bottle
Put the milk into refrigerator or freezer within 1 h after expression
Store milk in a separate space in the refrigerator or freezer
Put the bottle in straight-up manner in a clean case before putting them into the freezer/refrigerator
Keep breast milk in the refrigerator or freezer and close to the posterior wall
Keep the refrigerator/freezer clean (the corners and gaps in particular), and defrost once every 2–3 months
Maintain food in the fridge in good condition (get rid of spoiled food or food with flavor; do not overfill bottles)
Write mother's information (bed number, name, record number and time of expression) on the label with marker before leaving for the hospital Examine the bottle or pack for any damage or leakage before leaving for the hospital
Keep the thermos table transport kit clean (wash it frequently; avoid floor or dirty surface)
Use thermos table devices for transport
The parts of milk pump were cleaned immediately after use
Disconnect all the parts that are to be cleaned
Use running water in every step
Disinfect any part that has come into contact with milk
Nurse verifies and signs

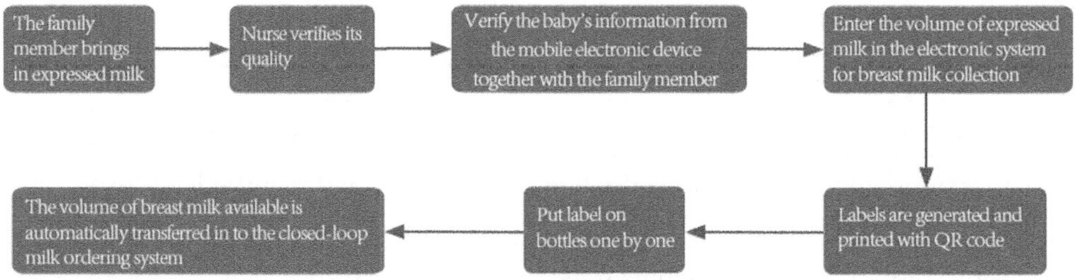

Figure 13.11 The process of receiving expressed milk.

Nurse or secretary lays the labeled bottles with breast milk into cases and one case is for one baby only. Breast milk is stored in medical grade refrigerator (temperature ranged between 2°C and 8°C or 35.6°F and 46.4°F) and freezer (–18°C or –4°F) according to the purpose (see Figure 13.12). Eight hours before milk is needed, the designated staff relocate one from the freezer, in a first-in-first-out manner, to the refrigerator to thaw.

Administration—Interlinking Loops

Ordering breast milk

Physician logs in the ordering system and clicks the baby's file and closed-loop ordering of breast milk (see Figure 13.13). The ordering system automatically provides the total volume of breast

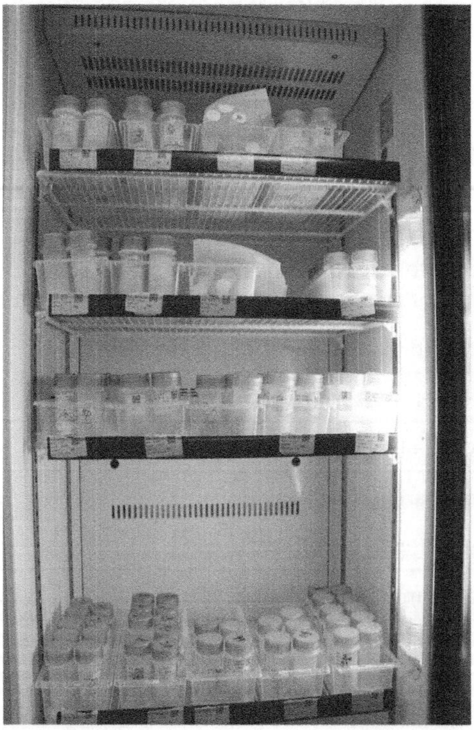

Figure 13.12 Expressed milk stored in refrigerator.

milk available to the baby that day. The physician selects feeding route, frequency, volume of each feed and the type of milk, where breast milk is always the first option. If the milk received at one time is adequate for the entire day, the electronic system generates 12 orders of breast feeding. Otherwise, the electronic system provides as many orders of breast milk as available and other eight suboptimal feeding options are provided to come up with 12 orders in total. Other breast-feeding orders in SRRSH include breast milk, partial-fortified, and total-fortified breast milk.

Nurse verifies order and prints label

Nurse logs in nursing electronic system to verify the order (see Figure 13.14) and has the label printed out from the label printing desk. Provided on the label are patient's name, bed number, record number, the type of milk, volume, feeding route, expected time, and a QR code.

Breast milk (or formula) preparation based on the physician's order

Nurse sticks the label of a particular feed on an empty sterile bottle (or syringe according to the volume needed), scans the QR code on the bottle first and then that on the milk with PDA for the system to match. The PDA indicates "matched" if that is the right milk for the right baby or "the milk does not match, please try again" if the matching fails. Then the nurse does it again.

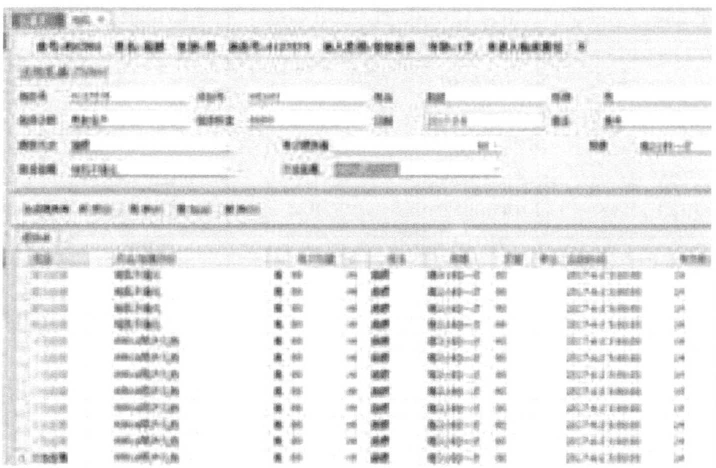

Figure 13.13 Screenshot of closed-loop ordering system for breast feeding.

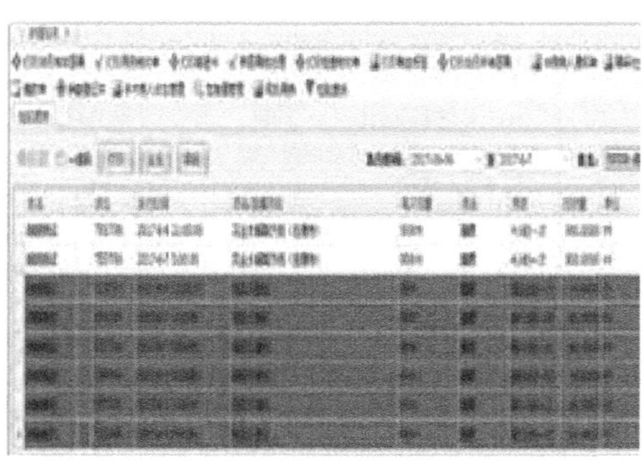

Figure 13.14 Nurse is working with nursing electronic system to verify breast-feeding orders.

Based on the volume specified in the order, with aseptic practice, the nurse pour the breast milk into the sterile empty bottle or draws milk with syringe. Nurse always handles one baby's milk only at a time. After finishing preparing one baby's milk, nurse cleans the table, changes her apron and disinfects her hands before he or she goes on with the next baby's milk. Upon picking up the bottle for administration, nurse gently sways the bottle to blend the milk.

Administering breast milk

Nurse puts the milk in a bed-side milk warmer 15 min prior to administration. When the milk is given to the baby, nurse scans the QR code on the label of the milk bottle, taps the icon of the order to read the milk order, volume, and schedule on his or her PDA. Then the nurse scans the QR code on the baby's wrist band. If they match, the PDA indicates "Success" and the nurse is

Table 13.2 Feeding Order List

Xiasha Campus, Sir Run Run Shaw Hospital of Zhejiang University of School of Medicine							
Feeding order list .... Sep. 29th, 2017; 10:01							
Bed no.	*MR No.*	*Name*	*Type*	*Volume*	*Route*	*Frequency*	*Note*
NICU-01	4380896		Breast milk/81 Kcal preterm formula	0.5 mL	Nasogastric tube	Q4H	
NICU-03	4384050		Nothing by mouth				
NICU-04	4393050		Breast milk/ formula for full-term baby	40 mL	Bottle	Q2H	
NICU-05	4380898		Breast milk/81 Kcal preterm formula	6 mL	Nasogastric tube	Q2H	
NICU-06	4408979		Breast milk/81 Kcal preterm formula	6 mL	Delivered in drips	Q2H	
NICU-07	4407886		Breast milk/81 Kcal preterm formula	25 mL	Bottle	Q2H	
NICU-08	4405109		Breast milk/81Kcal preterm formula	23 mL	Nasogastric tube/ botde	Q2H	
NICU-09	4399106		Breast milk/81 Kcal preterm formula	20 mL	Nasogastric tube/ bottle	Q2H	
NICU-010	4399109		Breast milk/81 Kcal preterm formula	20 mL	Nasogastric tube/ bottle	Q2H	

now ready to administer the milk. If anything fails, the PDA also indicates, for example, "wrong baby, please check again" if they do not match, or "no pending orders" if the order has been stopped or done already.

Based on Data and Continue to Improve

The administration information of order is available. When operating the computer on wheel for nursing information, healthcare professionals can track the administration of "breast feeding" order for its status, category, title, route, frequency, the time of the start and end of the administration as well as that for the order itself.

The electronic system provides enormous support to breast feeding. From the computer, healthcare professionals can print out the feeding orders of all the babies on that day. Nurse prints out feeding order list and sends it to the chat group of parents everyday so that parents know how well they have been compliant to exclusive breast feeding. It is easy for nurse to aggregate total and partial breast-feeding rate for CQI. Meanwhile, a designated nurse reviews the completion of feeding orders to identify babies who are still supplied with formula in addition to breast milk, or whose families have not sent in milk that day. Such review helps push the compliance of the parents to breast feeding.

Closing the loop in the management of breast feeding has helped enhance the quality control over each step in breast feeding and the compliance to process. Specifically, the logical algorithms in the electronic system for ordering breast milk have provided facts of need for physicians to order. The feeding order is prescribed in one step that allows the logical combination of breast milk and formula. This closed-loop management not only ensures safety of breast feeding but also leads to reduced burden among NICU nurses and higher efficiency. Moreover, the organization is able to track the completion of feeding order of any baby as well as the status and whereabouts of a particular serve of milk at any time. With this endeavor, safety, efficiency, traceability, and quality control have been enhanced for breast feeding thanks to IT application. At the end of the day, that is all for the continuous improvement of healthcare quality (Table 13.2).

Case 2: Fall Prevention: Hospital-Wide Coordination with IT Support

An Old Man Who Fell Off at Midnight

One night in 2015 at 11:30 pm, ZOU, a nurse of Hematology Dept., was about to sit down to document her observation from another round in the ward. In general, there were a couple of children with fever, and a couple of children on chemotherapy. Other children were stabilized. She saw most of the children and family members were asleep when she toured around the ward. It was a quiet night compared with other night shifts that she had taken that month.

All of a sudden, a bang from ward No. 8 startled ZOU. She dashed to the ward and found an 87-year-old man, from Bed. 3 of Room. 8, lying at the door to the bathroom with his head in contact with the floor. "Too bad!" ZOU was nervous at the scene though having worked as a nurse for quite a few years. The patients and family members of the same room turned on the lights at hearing the noise. Seeing this scene, the old man's daughter was at a loss.

"Assess him immediately" was the first thing that ZOU thought of. She started to assess the patient: he was responsive but did not give clear answer to questions; pupils were equal in size with unimpaired light reflex; he had elevated blood pressure, rapid heartbeat, and normal oxygen saturation; a hematoma was identified on the occiput with minimal bleeding; and he had mobile upper and lower extremities. With the help from a patient aide, ZOU put the old patient to his bed, called physician, provided cardiac monitoring and oxygen and established an intravenous access. She did all these things coherently without any delay. Again, ZOU asked the old man what happened. He mumbled but ZOU got the general picture: he wanted to use the bathroom but did not want to wake up his daughter, so he got off bed on his own but somehow found himself lay at the door to the bathroom.

Then a physician ordered an emergency CT scan of his head, which identified an epidural hematoma of the left temporal lobe that required close monitoring and hemostatic agent.

This was a severe injury due to fall. Fortunately, ZOU responded immediately and professionally and thus was commended highly by patients and family members of the room, and the family members of the old patient did not blame nurse or the hospital as they regretted as well. However, the managers reflected on the event with horror: what if the nurse did not go to the room immediately; what if nobody found the patient lying at the door of the bathroom; what if the patient was thrown into life-threatening condition or even died from the fall; what if the patient's family members were mad at us…? It was too ghastly to contemplate.

Fall Prevention System with "Structure—Process—Outcome" Logic

Being an unexpected occurrence, fall constitutes the major cause of death and disability from accident for elderly people. Being hard to prevent, fall increases the length of hospital stay, healthcare expenditure, and even the possibility of dispute and conflict. The Centers for Disease Control and Prevention in the U.S. reported 27,483 deaths from fall in 2014. Fall has caused over $2.3 billion every year from the United States Department of Health and Human Service, and around US$71 million extra cost to Hong Kong's healthcare system. In 2014, averagely 0.24 falls occurred to every one thousand patient-days, and 13% of the falls resulted in moderate to severe injury. How to reduce incidence of fall and fall-related injury is a challenge for every hospital. Moreover, reducing risk of injury from fall is one of the safety goals of JCI accreditation standards and China's hospital accreditation standards.

The prevention of fall and fall-induced injury require systemic effort, namely comprehensive and multifaceted preventive actions as well as their adaption to individual fall prevention plan. To make these actions effective, nurses, physicians, physiatrist, and general support staff should work together in multidisciplinary approach. As a four-time JCI accredited organization that just passed the validation of HIMSS EMRAM Stage 7, we set our goal as reduction of fall incidence by means of IT application and multidisciplinary coordination.

With the recommendation from consultants, we finalized a fall prevention management approach of "structure—process—outcome" built upon IT capabilities.

To begin with, the culture of safety and quality was strengthened with policy-driven fall prevention and management practice. The *Policy on Fall Prevention and Management* provides evidence on the definition of fall, the purpose of the policy, the responsibilities of staff involved, the population that needs assessment, moments and tools of assessment, measures to prevent fall, education to patient and family, expected and unexpected outcome, response to a fall event, grading of injury from fall, documentation, and forms. The policy will be updated once every 3 years routinely. In addition, non-punitive process for event reporting was established where staff will receive RMB ten yuan as reward for every inadvertent event they report. Moreover, we adopted the 85:15 ratio in determining the cause of inadvertent event, keeping in mind that 85% of the event was attributed to the system while 15% to the individual involved. Frontline staff have been encouraged to participate in CQI. We raised people's awareness of fall prevention by putting up posters with information on fall prevention along the walls of corridor and handing out fall prevention booklet to every patient with high risk for fall.

Second, a working group of fall prevention and management was established. The group consists of the Deputy Director of Nursing Dept., head nurses, nurses, physicians, general support staff, ancillary healthcare professionals, and IT staff. Every quarter, the group summons to discuss data and cases of fall, analyze causes and craft solution; the fall data and the monitoring on solution execution are discussed in the meetings of Nursing Quality Committee as well as Patient Safety Committee. Staff receive training on fall prevention and management and undertake a case analysis after the training to ensure they understand the details of fall management.

Third, the effective routine practice is maintained and extended to greater detail: keep the bed at the lowest height, bed-rail raised on one side during night time; cup, mobile phone, paper tissue within arm's reach, call button at the side of the pillow and patients attended when they need to go to the toilet. In terms of facility, rooms and corridors are cleared of obstacles and installed with hand rails; "caution wet floor" sign is put up during and after floor is cleaned with water; bathrooms are installed with slippery proof tiles and hand rails; and call bell is provided on both the commode side and shower side, which are check for functionality once a week by the secretary of the nursing unit.

In addition to improve the policies, management and practice, the group maintains fall prevention awareness among caregivers by the means of IT capabilities.

Assessment Tools Augmented by Intelligent Decision-Making System

The fall risk assessment tool that we used listed 11 signs for elevated fall risk. Upon reading it, our consultant commented that it did not reflect the actual fall risk because it did not generate proper score. After literature review, we decided to adopt Morse Fall Scale (MFS) as our hospital-wide fall risk assessment tool (see Figure 13.15). Evidence has it that MFS has high sensitivity, specificity, and positive predictive rate. Therefore, nurses who take care of patients use MFS to assess patient's fall risk everyday.

A nurse enters the result in the electronic nursing system, and the system aggregates the total score. When a patient's MFS score reaches 45 for the first time, the nurse receives a pop-up window of fall risk alert from the electronic system (see Figure 13.16a and b). Then, the nurse provides education to the patient/family member and has them sign the statement on fall risk. Once that statement is saved, the system generates and brings up front nursing diagnosis, goals, and measures to take. After the nurse saves the information, the system brings the nursing diagnosis and goals to the nursing care plan (see Figure 13.17), and the measures to nursing orders as well as nursing task list. The task list directs nurses' work and ensures compliance of fall prevention measures. Thanks to the electronic nursing system, the assessment, diagnosis, plan, and actions are generated efficiently.

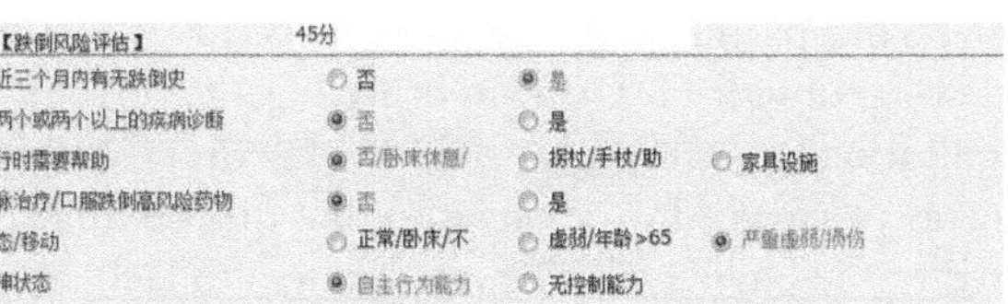

Figure 13.15 The modified fall risk assessment form.

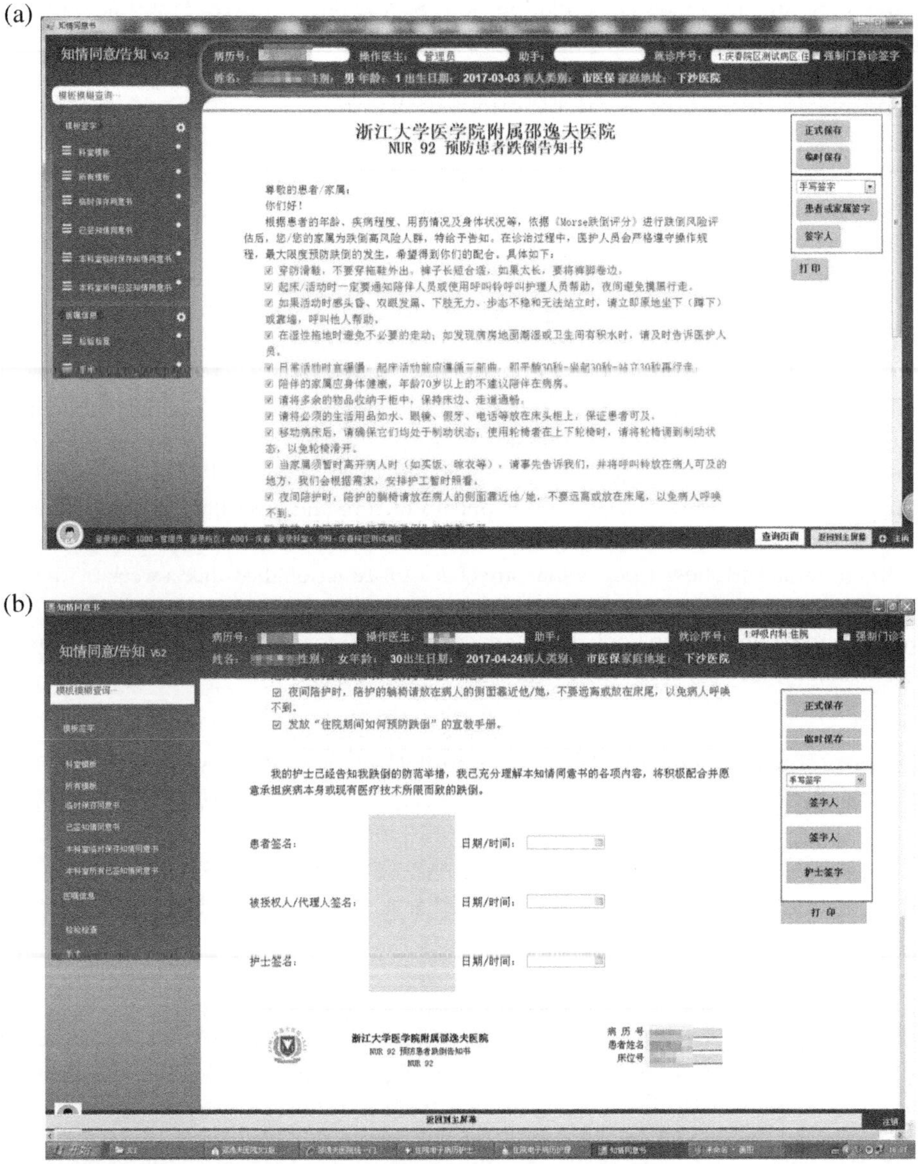

Figure 13.16 The statement of high risk for fall.

Sharing Information for Effective Communication

To ensure all the caregivers of a particular patient have access to all the information of this patient, the Nursing Dept. has worked with IT Dept. to bring together broken pieces of information to foster effective communication by ensuring a patient is effectively identified and known wherever his or her encounter takes place within the organization. For example, the results from fall risk assessment are presented to the physician's electronic system to facilitate their involvement in fall prevention; the alert for high risk is visible in every screen of the nursing electronic system when a nurse logs in the system, verifies and approves order, completes a form of hand-over between shifts

Figure 13.17 Nursing plan.

or between units/campuses. To ensure patients are safe when they leave the unit for investigation, the information of fall risk has been made available to the investigation areas as well. Whenever staff print a form from the electronic system or scan the code, for reservation or report reception, staff of the investigation areas as well as transporters get to see the sign of high risk for fall, and pay special attention to those at high risk for fall during transport.

Apart from electronic communication, physical signs of fall risk are in place to remind caregivers, patients, and families to guard against fall. Fall risk signs in yellow are used throughout the organization (see Figure 13.18a–d). When regarded high risk for fall, an outpatient is given a yellow label for fall risk stuck to his or her clothes, while an inpatient receives the sign on the wrist band, the wall of the bed and the pajama provided by the hospital. At seeing these signs, any staff

(a)

Figure 13.18 The signs for high risk for fall.

(Continued)

(b)

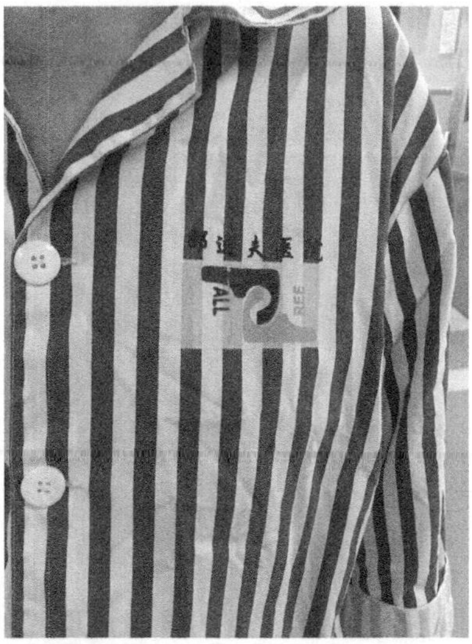

(c)

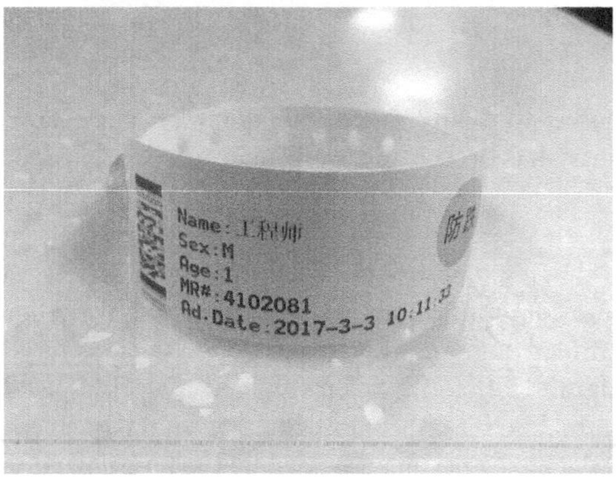

(d)

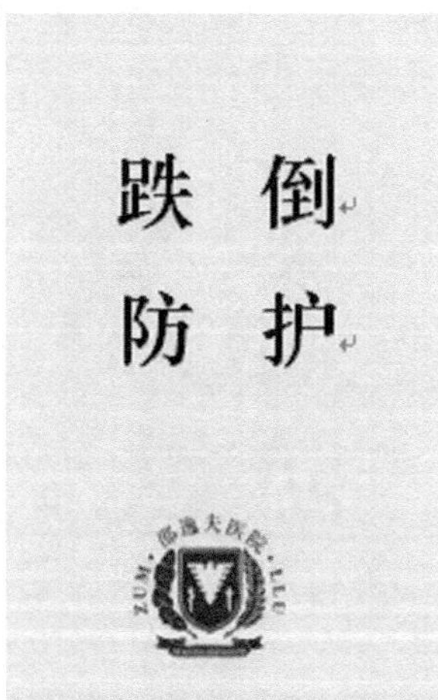

Figure 13.18 (CONTINUED) The signs for high risk for fall.

knows the patient is at high risk for fall. What's more, clinicians provide education to the patients at risk for fall and their family members with Teach-back method.

Quality control is a guarantee to actually implemented measures. Starting from January 2015, SRRSH has reported fall cases to National Database of Nursing Quality Indicator (NDNQI) every month to hold ourselves against international standards and expectations. Fall events are aggregated and analyzed every quarter, which are presented during head nurses' meeting. Fall events requiring special attention is discussed in greater detail. Using a Quality Checklist of Fall Prevention and Management, each nursing unit performs self-evaluation and quality team verifies once a quarter.

Among the 590 teaching hospitals in the NDNQI, our incidence of inpatient fall has been lower than the average since January 2015 (see Figure 13.19). We have been better than the average in terms of incidences of hospital-wide fall injury (Figure 13.20) as well as falls in intensive care units, medical units, surgical units and medical as well as surgical units as a whole (Figure 13.21).

In conclusion, we understood how to develop fall prevention policy thanks to JCI standards and learned to reduce fall incidence and injury with information sharing, multidisciplinary

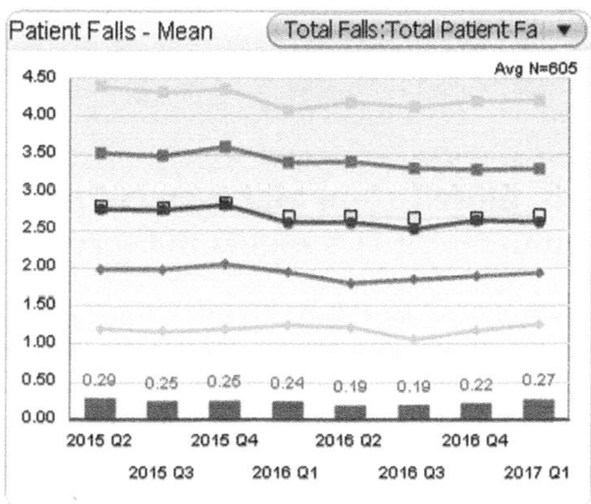

Figure 13.19 Data on incidence of inpatient fall.

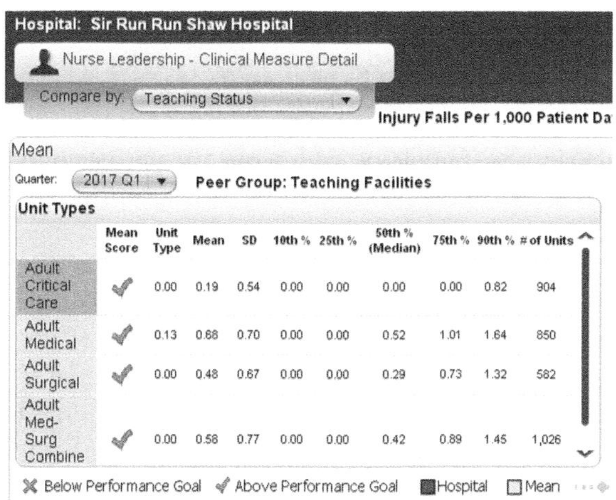

	Mean Score	Unit Type	Mean	SD	10th %	25th %	50th % (Median)	75th %	90th %	# of Units
Adult Critical Care	✓	0.00	0.19	0.54	0.00	0.00	0.00	0.00	0.82	904
Adult Medical	✓	0.13	0.68	0.70	0.00	0.00	0.52	1.01	1.64	850
Adult Surgical	✓	0.00	0.48	0.67	0.00	0.00	0.29	0.73	1.32	582
Adult Med-Surg Combine	✓	0.00	0.58	0.77	0.00	0.00	0.42	0.89	1.45	1,026

Figure 13.20 Breakdown of data on incidence of inpatient fall.

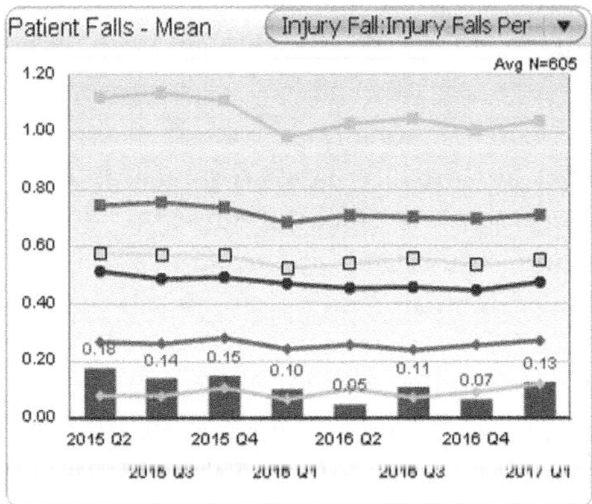

Figure 13.21 Breakdown of data on incidence of inpatient fall based on location.

coordination and joint effort from all the staff by taking advantage of IT capability as we made effort for HIMSS EMRAM Stage 7 certification.

Case 3: Closed-Loop Management of Critical Values with IT Support in Every Step

When started to work for compliance to the second edition of JCI standards in 2006, we were one of the few organizations in China to do so. The standards included many philosophies and processes which were seldom reflected in hospital administration in China. Naturally, our traditional healthcare notions in China were frequently challenged and updated with the modern philosophies as we interpreted standards and reviewed systems and processes. Thanks to our partners from Loma Linda University of the U.S., we came to understand the essence of the JCI standards on critical values. With the reference of the policies and processes of critical values in Loma Linda University Medical Center, we reviewed our laboratory, nursing and medical processes at that time and had multiple discussions on the feasibility of change.

Initial Experience on Critical Value Experience

Our policy on critical values at that time specified that when a critical value was identified, whether from ultrasonography, radiology, endoscopy, or pathology, the investigation physician communicated the critical value via telephone call, according to the defined process. As for Laboratory, they developed and programmed machines to set upper and lower thresholds for laboratory test items; based on this setting, when a value was given as critical, a window popped up on the computer monitor; a laboratory technician then validated the critical value, and communicated the value by talking over the phone. If the critical value belonged to an inpatient, they called the nurse of that floor, who relayed the message to the physician responsible for that patient; if the critical value belonged to an outpatient or ER patient, they made a telephone call to the physician who had ordered the test. The process is mapped out in Figure 13.22.

The policy specified the structure of the information that laboratory technician communicated to the receiver as well as the receiver's read-back over the phone, and required every nursing station

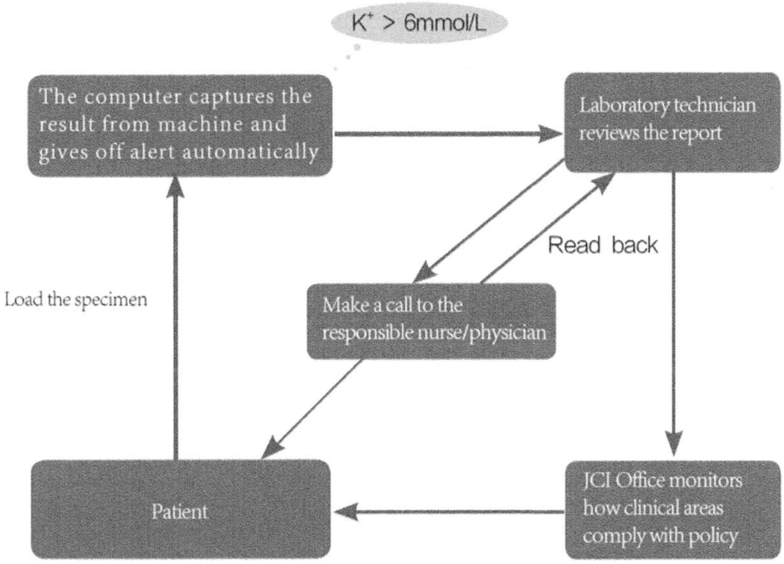

Figure 13.22 The flowchart of the previous process of laboratory critical value reporting.

keep a record of critical value (see Figure 13.23). This record as well as physician's documentation of the critical value was checked regularly by the Quality Dept. (see Figure 13.24).

After the initial JCI survey, the policy and process of critical values maintained unchanged, and the Quality Dept. monitored the compliance regularly, but it was difficult to get everyone work consistently each time. The departments that generated critical values slackened as there were too many steps in the process and real-time monitoring was impossible. Physicians and nurses slackened and complained of the relay and read-back of messages. And the Quality Dept. was not able to expand sample size because a short of human resources…

How can the content and thresholds of critical values be fine-tuned? How can every critical value be reported to the physician accurately, regardless of the lab service, equipment, or clinical unit involved? How can we reduce error from nurses' documentation, read-back and relay of message? How can we ease the burden of nurses and physicians in documentation? How can we effectively reach outpatients or ER patients who have left but with critical value? How can we expand the effective sample size for monitoring of critical value process without increasing staffing?

All these problems had been addressed step by step as the organization went through the ensuing triennial JCI surveys. The critical value process witnessed its qualitative progress with closed-loop electronic system that covers the entire journey of critical value as we worked for the fourth JCI survey in 2016 and, in particular, the HIMSS EMRAM Stage 7 validation.

Rely on Long-Standing Mechanism and Stop "Boy-Who-Cried-Wolf" Scenario

Our long-standing mechanism for critical value management was established as the Quality Dept. led a working group consisting of physician representatives, investigation services and IT Department. They convene once a year to review and analyze performance as well as improve policy and process. They also hold discussion for update of critical value definition as the need arises.

The library of content and thresholds of critical values is constantly maintained and updated. At least once a year, all the investigation services and physicians sit down to review the content

Figure 13.23 The log for critical value maintained in each floor in the past.

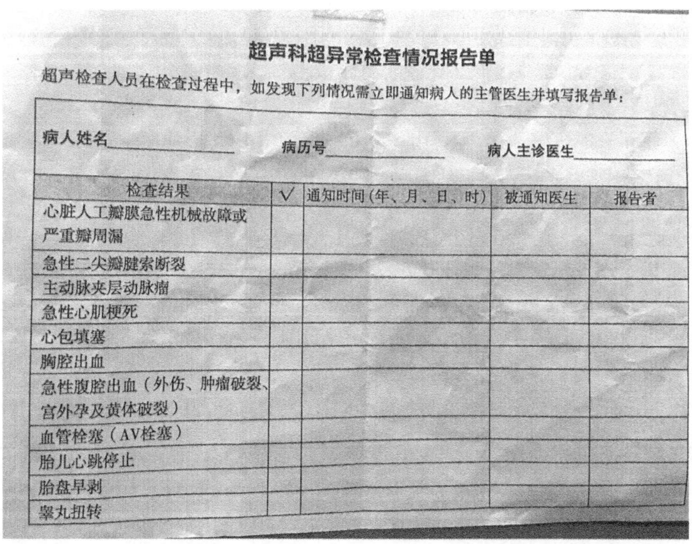

超声科超异常检查情况报告单

超声检查人员在检查过程中，如发现下列情况需立即通知病人的主管医生并填写报告单：

病人姓名________ 病历号________ 病人主诊医生________

检查结果	√	通知时间（年、月、日、时）	被通知医生	报告者
心脏人工瓣膜急性机械故障或严重瓣周漏				
急性二尖瓣腱索断裂				
主动脉夹层动脉瘤				
急性心肌梗死				
心包填塞				
胸腔出血				
急性腹腔出血（外伤、肿瘤破裂、宫外孕及黄体破裂）				
血管栓塞（AV栓塞）				
胎儿心跳停止				
胎盘早剥				
睾丸扭转				

Figure 13.24 Ultrasonography log of critical value observed and some details of the cases.

and thresholds of critical values with the facilitation from the Quality Department. As the critical values are more accurately set, physicians can get rid of alarm fatigue and avoid the risky boy-who-cried-wolf scenario.

Specifically, through monitoring, staff aggregated and analyzed critical values that had been frequently unrepresented in physician's notes, investigated relevant clinical units and concluded three critical value tests most prone to alarm fatigue: the creatinine level of patients with chronic kidney failure who were receiving dialysis, the bilirubin level of patient with chronic obstructive jaundice who had been on standardized therapy, and the hemoglobin of patient with hematological disease who had been on standardized therapy.

After thorough argumentation, policy and process were modify to reflect on the above facts by specifying that when it is reported for the first time during a particular hospitalization, the physician handles it as critical value according to specified process, assesses patient, takes proper action, and documents in the record. The ensuring values of the same test are assessed together with patient's condition, so that if the values do not vary significantly, physician does not need to document the values every time they are reported as long as the values constitute a trend of improvement. Such individualized approach to critical value management avoids alarm fatigue among clinicians because of the "false-positive" results and prevents neglect of critical value that truly need immediate attention.

When we reviewed processes in the way toward the fourth JCI survey, we found critical value process did not cover POCT yet. The working group of critical value decided that the critical value process should apply to the bed-side glucose test performed by nurses.

Efforts were made to improve the critical value process for outpatients. Based on the actual need in clinical care, the critical value policy was improved with better defined process of critical value communication to outpatients and ER patients. First of all, the physician attempts to reach the patient. If fails, the physician informs the Outpatient Office (during open hours) or the general administrator on duty (during the nights, weekends, and holidays), who becomes charged with the responsibility to reach the patient and maintain documentation. Then the Outpatient Office or the general administrator on duty tries to contact the patient. If they fail, they inform the Security Dept. of the hospital to contact the local police station, who then helps to reach the patient or the family member via their public security network.

The Electronic System for Critical Values for Investigation Services Is in Place

The electronic system for critical values for investigation services was put into service (see Figure 13.25a and b), which covers ultrasonography, radiology and imaging, pathology, laboratory, and electrocardiogram. For diagnostic description in words, the system has established rules where specific key words will trigger a critical result, so that any critical result is identified, retrieved, and transmit to the electronic critical value system, no matter which investigation service, equipment, or clinical unit is involved. Data are maintained in this electronic system for tracking and aggregation (see Figures 13.26 and 13.27). Apart from this system, the hospital also put in place an electronic system for messaging, where staff lists are constantly updated to ensure their contact information is current.

(a)

(b)

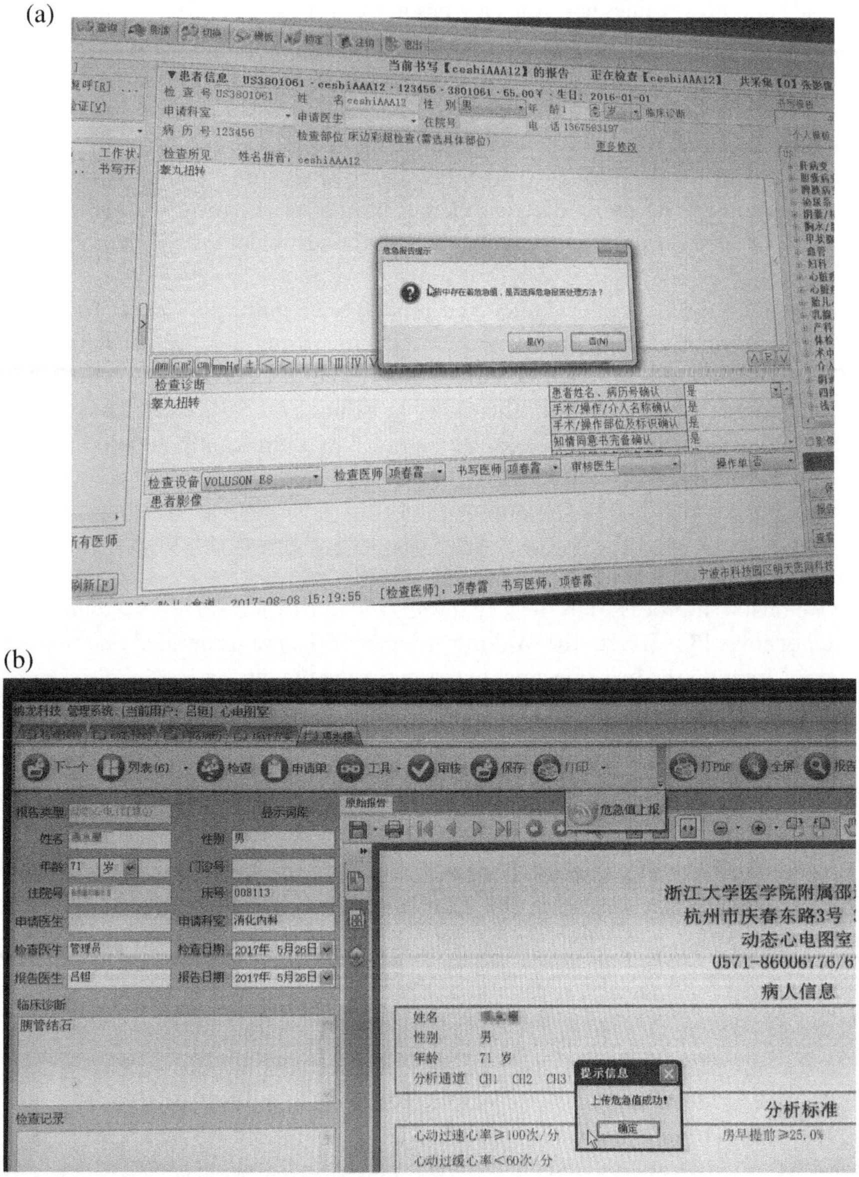

Figure 13.25 The electronic system for critical values for investigation services.

Loops of Reception and Response to Critical Value after Being Triggered by Investigation Services Were Closed

When a critical value is reported, a flashing alarm will appear on the computer monitor of the nursing unit where the patient stays, and the screen freezes and prohibits any operation until the receiver logs in by entering staff number (see Figure 13.28). The electronic system has been programmed in such a way that if the investigation service does not receive the reply from the receiver within 15 min, an alert is seen from its computer monitor. At seeing this, staff of the investigation service should immediately make a call to the nursing station and remind the receiver to see the computer monitor.

Figure 13.26 The screen for critical value aggregation in Radiology and Imaging Service.

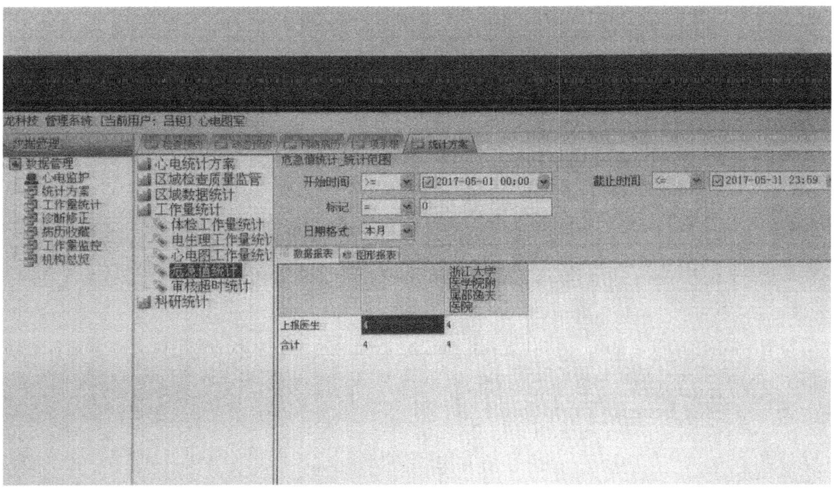

Figure 13.27 The screen for critical value aggregation and search in Electrocardiogram Service.

The electronic system also provides easy access to the response and documentation of the critical value. There are two ways that physicians easily documents the critical value in the electronic medical record: at receiving a critical value, the physician logs on the system, double-clicks "new note" → selects "regular progress note" → and double-clicks "document the response to critical value" (see Figure 13.29). Alternatively, the physician double-clicks the yellow alert for the critical value from the right-lower corner of the monitor, which leads to the documentation panel for critical value response (see Figure 13.30). From the screen of critical value documentation, the physician checks the items involved during that documentation (see Figure 13.31).

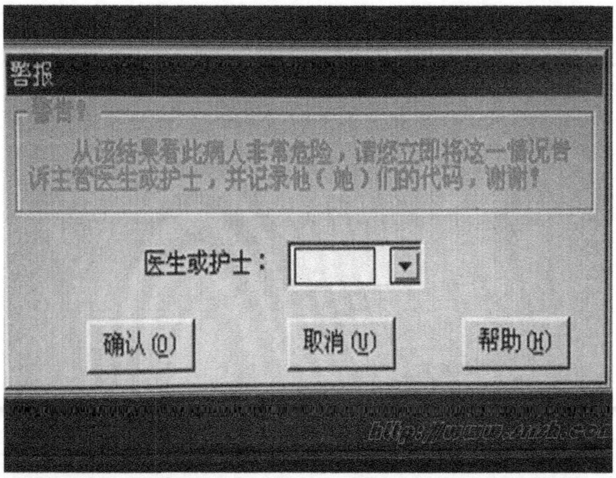

Figure 13.28 An alert window flashing on the computer screen in nursing station where the patient of critical value stays.

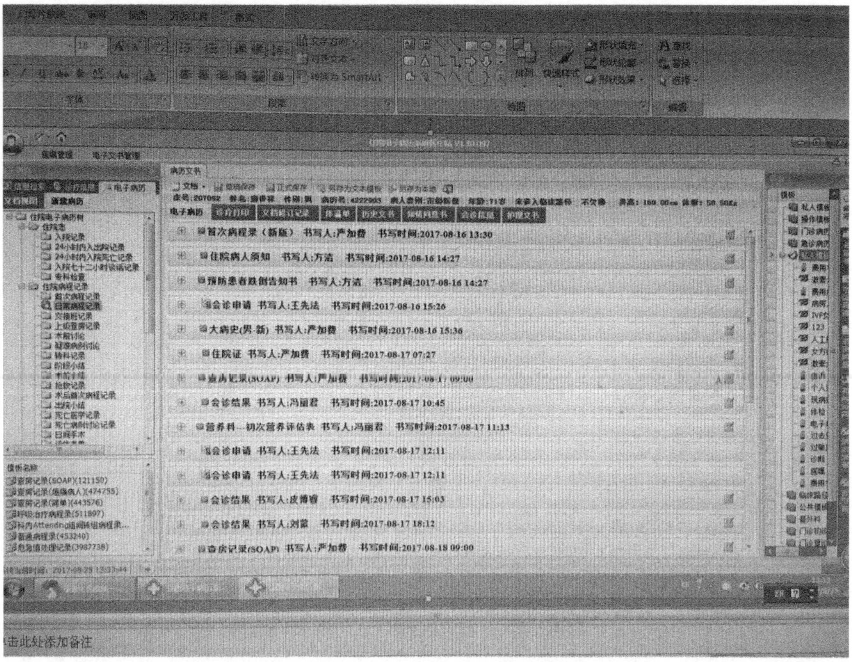

Figure 13.29 One way to document the response to a critical value.

Based on the rules established in the electronic system, the critical value documentation would trigger orders to be given to the patient as a means of clinical decision support to facilitate physician's proper action taken to address the critical value. There is also a library of standard orders for common critical results in the electronic system.

For example, in response to the critical value of insufficient hemoglobin for a patient of gastrointestinal hemorrhage, the physician checks the critical value from the system, and

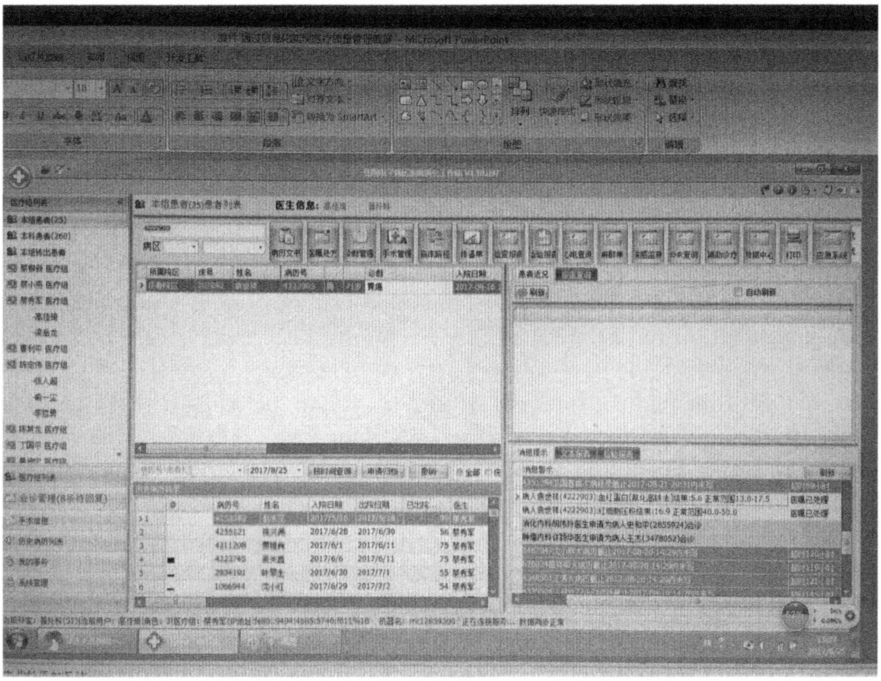

Figure 13.30 An alternative way to document the response to a critical value.

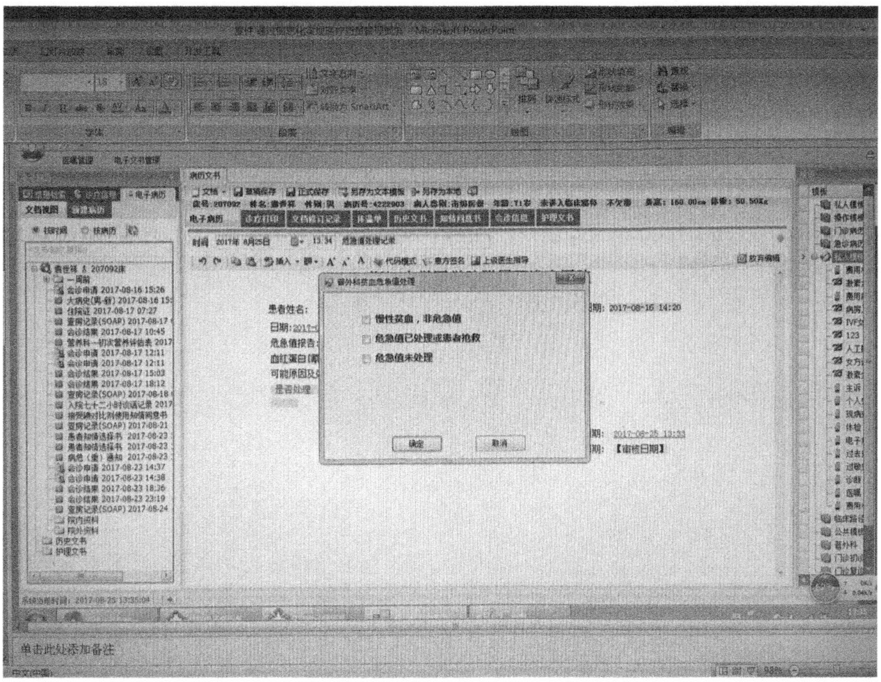

Figure 13.31 The screen of critical value documentation, with the information possibly needed displayed for selection.

the system brings upfront the ordering screen for the physician to pick the proper order, and change the standard order based on patient's specific condition. At the end, the physician saves the order. By now, the documentation of the response to the critical value has been generated automatically, where some pieces of information have been filled in by the system. The physician can edit the words from the editing panel, document his or her action and save that record (see Figures 13.32 and 13.33).

Closed-Loop Management of Critical Values with IT Support in Every Step

At the beginning, the Quality Dept. took a random sample of cases to track the steps in critical value management of "investigation service gives result—the result is delivered via each step needed—physician receives the result and documents the response." But now, all the cases can be monitored in a real-time manner from the electronic system, including how the result is relayed from one step to the next and documented. The closed-loop system of critical value has maximized efficiency as the times, detail and author of critical value generation, sending out, reception, response, and documentation are provided at one screen.

Take Figure 13.34 as example which presents the time when the critical value was sent out from the electronic system, 0 and the blank panel list the cases where the message failed to be sent out for staff of the investigation service to know immediately and call the relevant unit as a remedial measure. This information also enables quality staff to screen out questionable cases quickly and conduct focused analysis.

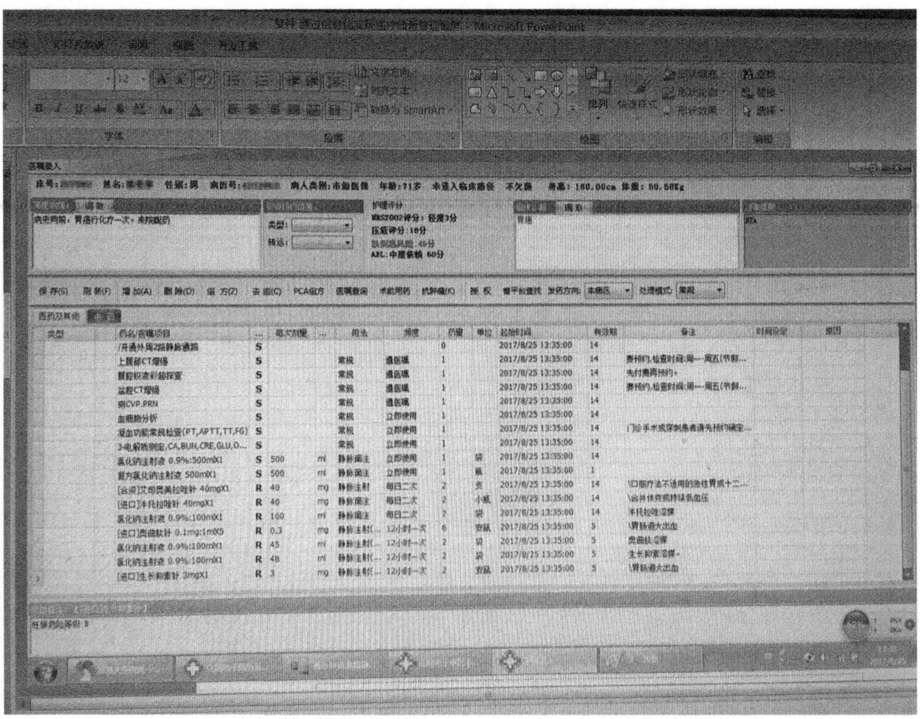

Figure 13.32 The system automatically triggers the orders that physician may need.

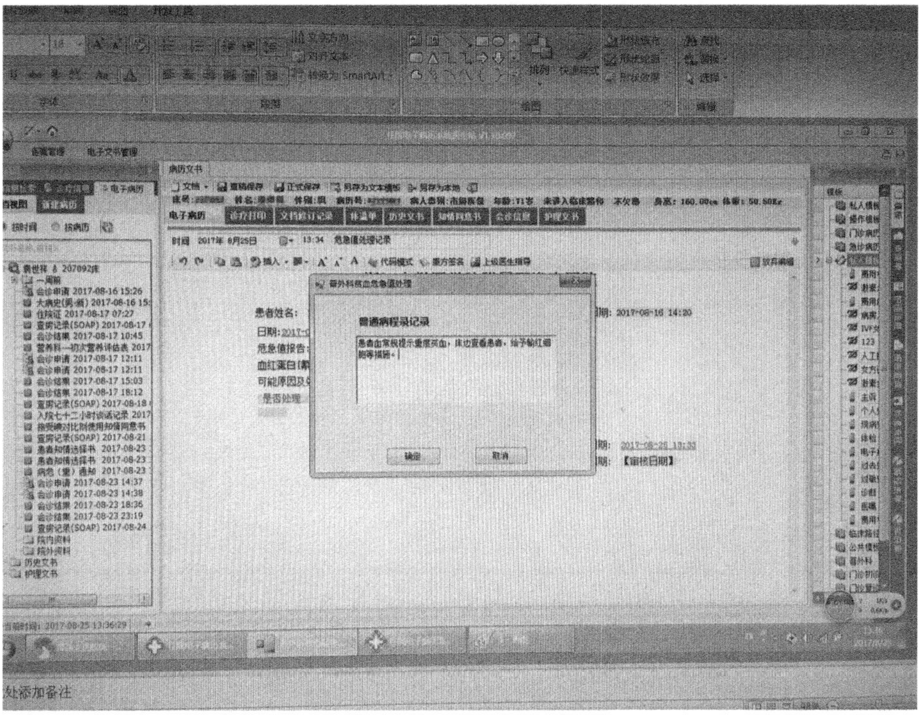

Figure 13.33 The system automatically fills in some of the entries in the documentation of critical value response.

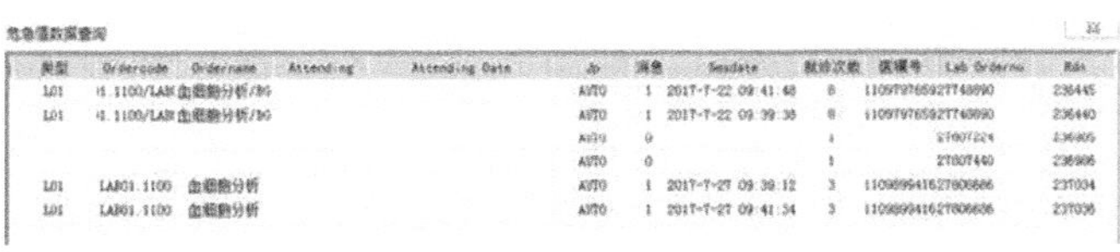

Figure 13.34 Quality monitoring of critical values from the integrated electronic system.

Physicians used to enter critical value as free-form text in their progress note, which was difficult for quality monitoring as the checker should look into every text entry. This became a thing of the past as the updated electronic medical record provides structured documentation of critical values. Also, the loop in quality monitoring has been closed as the electronic system automatically reviews the completion of documentation from each step.

The merit of rule-based operation of the electronic system for critical values has been extended to standardize inpatient glucose monitoring. For example, when a patient's glucose result turns out critical, the electronic system not only triggers a flashing alert to draw the physician's attention but also generates a request for consultation from an endocrinologist ready to be sent out. On the side of the Endocrinology Dept., physicians are able to see glucose critical values throughout the organization to consider if they should provide support of patient education (see Figures 13.35–13.37).

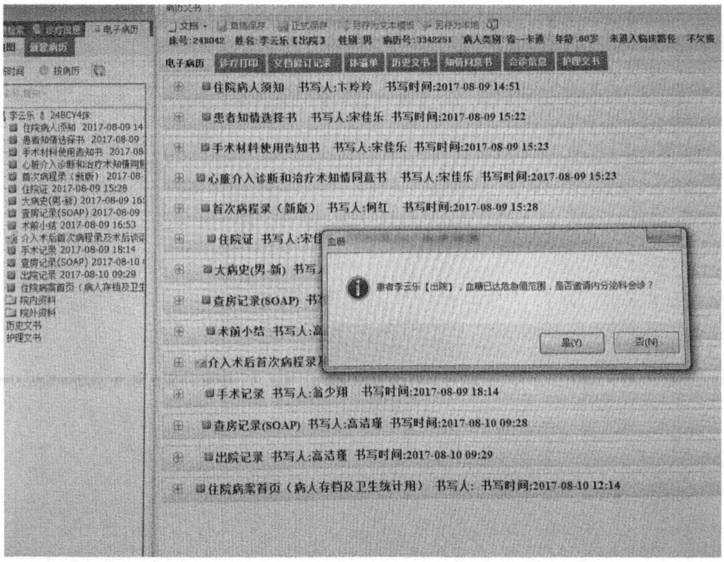

Figure 13.35 A flashing window popped up triggered by a critical value of glucose level and enables physician to order consultation from an endocrinologist.

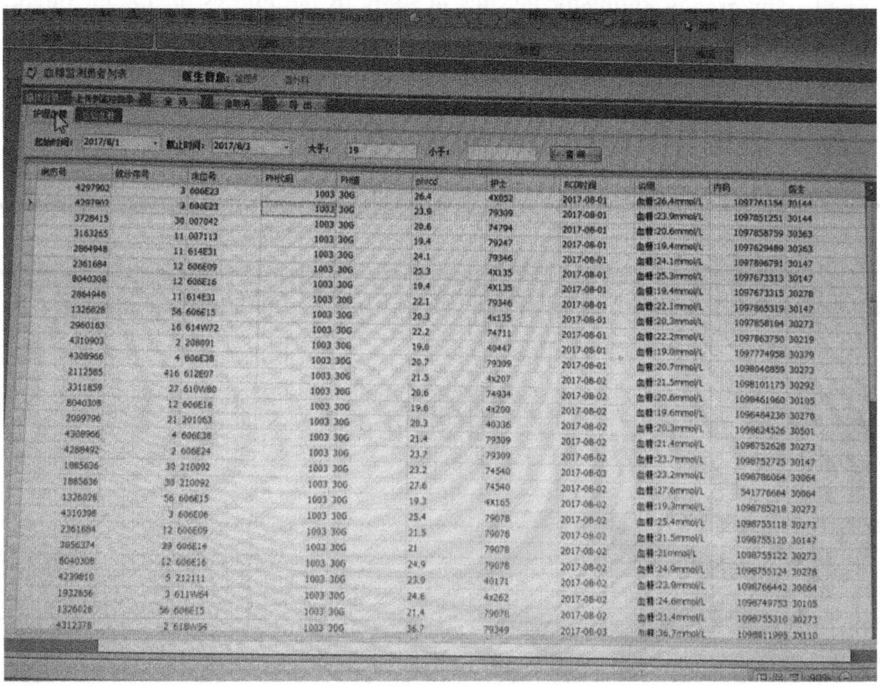

Figure 13.36 Based on the information retrieved from glucose results from the Laboratory, the electronic system allows endocrinologist to get a quick picture of critical values of glucose levels in the organization.

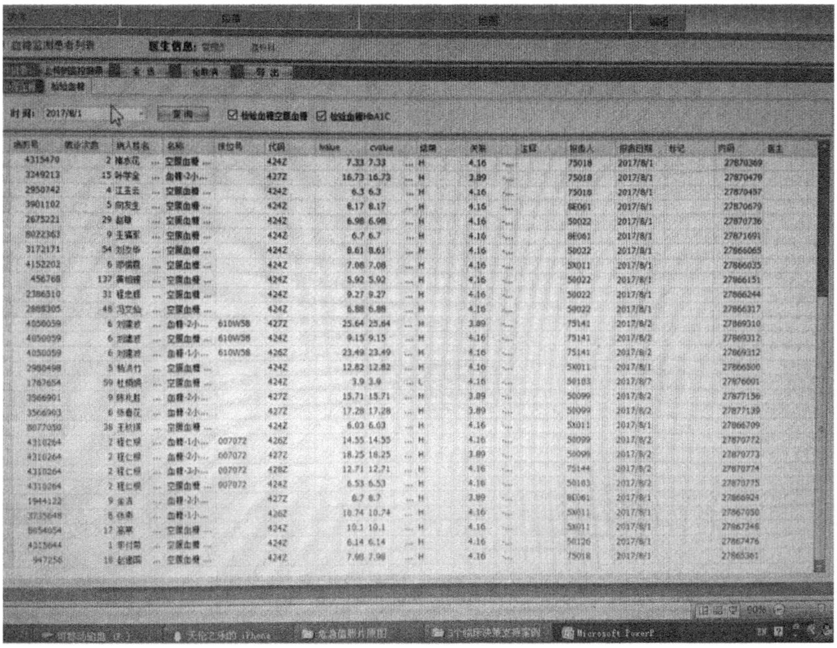

Figure 13.37 The system allows staff to change the upper and lower threshold of critical value or read the POCT glucose results taken by nurse.

Conclusion

Driven by the four JCI surveys, ensured by IT system of HIMSS EMRAM Stage 7 capability and with the strength of multidisciplinary cooperation, SRRSH's efforts in closing loops in critical value management have achieved the expected results of an improved and sophisticated system.

A seasoned nurse with almost 20 years of experience shared that the scariest part of her job was the constantly ringing telephone. At receiving a critical value, she had to rush to the location where the critical value log was kept. It was not uncommon that the log was nowhere to be found because someone else had used it earlier but not returned it to the designated location, and she had to jot down the message on a random piece of paper at hand. Reading from the log, no one felt confident about the integrity of the information of critical values, regardless of the head nurse or quality staff.

A physician exclaimed that "with the definition of critical values, built-in steps in various processes and electronic medical record, the intelligent ordering and documentation system is our wings of safety, efficiency and standardized care."

The frontline staff have tried their best to complete and document each step they have done, only to realize that things may turn out the other way due to excessive workload. But now, as the electronic system keeps track of the time and the author of each step completed in the closed-loop management of critical values, it allows for tracking down to every case. The fact that it recognizes critical values and aggregates data provides resolution to challenges such as how to capture critical values failing to reach the physician, how to ensure the timeliness and accuracy of the result reported and whether clinical action has been taken. In addition, the user-friendly electronic medical record offers controlled facilitation in ordering and documentation as well as efficiency of critical value response by marrying patient safety goals with balanced workload of staff.

Chapter 14

TEDA International Cardiovascular Hospital

Liu Xiaocheng, Dong Jun, Liu Hong, Liu Jianjun, Wu Yunqi, Zhou Yachun, Liu Dongyang, Wang Xin, Han Li, Liu Fei, Yang Chenjing, Xia Chengfeng, Gao Yunfei, Zhang Zan, Zhang Ying, Cui Mei, Wang Yanxia, and Zhang Ye

TEDA International Cardiovascular Hospital

Liu Xiaocheng, *Chief Physician, Professor, and Supervisor of doctoral candidate of cardiovascular surgery*

Dr. Liu is the President of TEDA International Cardiovascular Hospital and fellow of STS and AATS of the US. His honors include "Exemplary Healthcare Professional Returning from Overseas Studies" and "A Top-10 Figure in the News for Healthcare Reform."

After finishing his cardiac surgery fellowship in Prince Charles Hospital of Australia, Dr. Liu returned to China and started the second cardiovascular hospital in China in 1987. There, he performed the first cardiopulmonary transplantation in China. Later, he was appointed the Vice President and CPC Secretary of Union Medical University and established the cardiac surgery service of Peking Union Medical College Hospital. In 2000, he resigned the roles in Beijing and founded TICH in Tianjin Economic and Technology Area, a hospital with brand new managerial structure aligned with the healthcare reform initiative of the State Council. The essence of "patient-centered care" has earned the hospital patient satisfaction and momentum of exponential growth.

Dong Jun, *Chief Physician and Supervisor of graduate candidate*

Dr. Dong is the Executive Vice President of TEDA International Cardiovascular Hospital, Member of Health Quality Committee of Chinese Medical Association and Chinese Nursing Association. She had served as Vice President, Quality Director, and Statistics Expert in the military health system before she came to TICH and led the hospital through a series of international accreditations, which include JCI and its CCPC on specific clinical programs as well as HIMSS Stage 6 and 7. It is the first hospital in China with both JCI and HIMSS certification.

With profound insights in quality, human resources, information system, electronic record, clinical pathway, and performance, she has become productive author of monographs, such as HIMSS, from Zero to One, *and articles and receiver of Scientific Progress Awards at national and military levels.*

Liu Hong, *Vice Chief Nurse*

Ms. Liu is the Director of Quality Control Center of TEDA International Cardiovascular Hospital since 2017 after she had worked 13 years as the Head Nurse of Catheterization Laboratory, when she was involved in the inauguration, administration, technical operation, and nursing care of the unit. Her major role in JCI accreditations from 2009 through 2015 and HIMSS Stage 6 and 7 certification has yielded practical experience in healthcare management. She led a program of work flow and scheduling mechanism in Catheterization Laboratory, which was recognized as a best practice in surveys. On the new position, she devotes herself to quality, risk control, culture of safety and policy improvement.

Contents

Hospital Introduction: Invested by the Tianjin Economic-Technological Development Area (TEDA), TEDA International Cardiovascular Hospital (TICH) was established in 2003 as a Level-A Tertiary Hospital specialized in cardiovascular diseases and the Institute of Cardiovascular Sciences under the management of the Chinese Academy of Medical Sciences & Peking Union Medical College. The hospital is also the Clinical Cardiovascular Science College of Tianjin Medical University, the National Training Base for Interventional Diagnosis and Treatment for Coronary Diseases and Arrhythmia, Base for National Standardized Residency Training, National Practice Base for Hospital Central Sterile Supply Department, and National Demonstration Training Base for Specialized Nursing and Techniques for Cardiovascular Diseases.

The Cardiac Great Vessel Surgery, Cardiovascular Medicine, and Nursing Department are the national Key Clinical Disciplines.

International Accreditation: 2009, 2012, and 2015, JCI accreditation and re-accreditation;

SIDCER: 2012 and 2015, CCPC (by JCI) accreditation and re-accreditation for Heart Failure and Acute Myocardiac Infarction;

2015, HIMSS EMRAM Stage 7;

certification by WHO;

On-site validation by ISO15189 for laboratory for six times;

CAP certification for the Clinical Laboratory for four times.

Preface

Our Story of JCI and HIMSS EMRAM Stage 7

Right after the successful accreditation by JCI in June 2009, the TEDA Hospital management team published the book, *Knowing-how and Doing-so*. How can we make sure that we know how to do things and do it as required? Dr. Liu Xiaocheng, President of TICH, states in the Preface of the book, "Our confidence is consolidated through learning and summarizing, through numerous training, drills, inspections and supervision. It has been the bounce for our staff to make the leap from 'knowing-how' to 'doing-so'." The secret to go from "I don't know" to "I know how to do it" is continuous learning. And the persistence in continuous quality improvement actually comes from repetition of the same tasks.

It is same principle that we followed for our HIMSS validation.

In May 2015, TICH was validated as an HIMSS EMRAM Stage 6 hospital. Later in November the same year, we joined the Stage 7 club. TICH renewed the record of achieving Stage 7 within the shortest time: 6 months. It added to the hospital's Hall of Fame as the third international accreditation after JCI and CCPC. We were also the first hospital in China to be have been accredited by both JCI and HIMSS EMRAM 7.

Through each effort we have made, we learn something new. Even with the strength gained through JCI and CCPC, we still felt that we were a novice when we embarked on the HIMSS journey.

The journey for JCI and HIMSS is a scroll painting that depicted our thinking, ideas, and experience on the landscape, capturing the glory that we have achieved but also our footprints on the wrong tracks. It is the testimony of the culture of safety and team cohesion in the hospital. This is the more valuable legacy left by the international accreditation and validation.

Play on the International Arena: Best Practices from TICH

Dr. Dong Jun, VP of TICH said, "We have been learning from our peers overseas, their concepts and approaches. But today I realized that Chinese hospitals also had very good practices. We should be part of the game on the international arena." During the HIMSS on-site validation, the surveyors were impressed by the smart pharmacy, the white-board screen in the PCI operating area and Business Intelligence (BI) capability that have been implemented in the hospital.

The two automatic dispensers and one smart medication cabinet in the Outpatient Pharmacy are interfaced into the system and realized one integrated medication dispensing flow (see Figure 14.1). The medication is delivered by the system to the pharmacist work station where the pharmacist would further verify the dispensed medication. Then the calling system would call the patients to pick up their medication. Through this way, we could say that we have successfully realized the perfect integration of people, things, and information.

It is not an easy task to achieve. As early as in the designing stage, the vendors of the automatic dispensers did not believe that the interfacing would be possible. But Dr. Liu Xiaocheng, President of the hospital, joined the team and led the design and decision-making process. And the robots were finally interfaced with the hospital systems.

John Daniels, Vice President of HIMSS Analytics, commented, "The level of automation of the Outpatient Pharmacy of the hospital has been the highest so far I have seen during my HIMSS EMRAM Stage 7 visits."

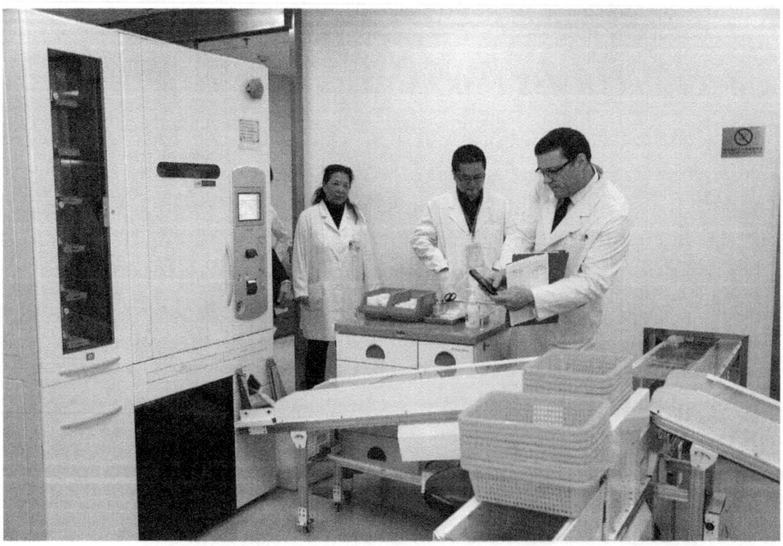

Figure 14.1 Integration of three automatic equipment in outpatient pharmacy.

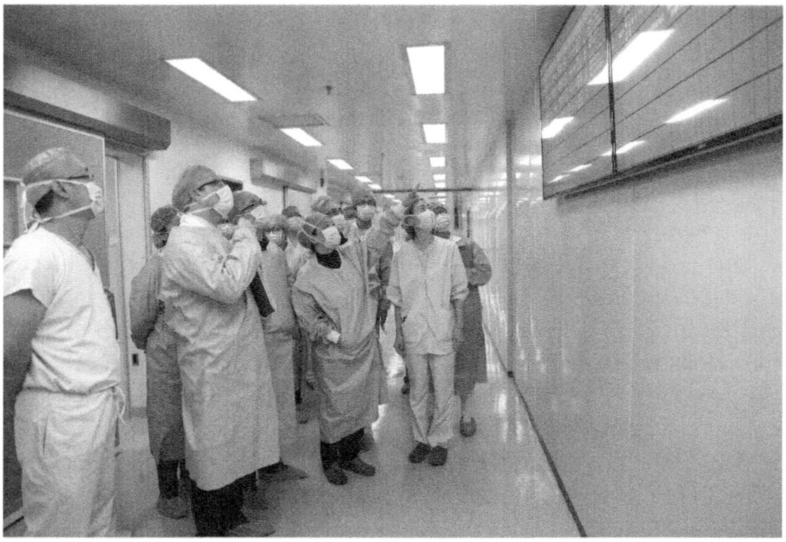

Figure 14.2 Synchronized surgery status screen in PCI operating area and patient waiting area.

The PCI operating room has a white-board screen set up in the waiting area for patients which is synchronized with the operation status screen inside the OR showing the waiting family the progress status of each surgery. Preoperative preparation, surgery going on, and completed surgery are indicated in yellow, green, and red, respectively, to give patient family more specific information about their beloved ones (see Figure 14.2). When communicating with patient families about the patient's conditions, the physician can also retrieve the images from the PACS on the screen to better discuss the conditions and treatment plan with the families.

Michael Pfeffer, CIO of UCLA, commented, "The technology-supported communication in the PCI area allows the family to look at the images. It engages the patient family in the decision-making process. This is the best practices of technology application!"

The screens we put up at the bedside of each ICU patients show both patient's basic information and the risks (e.g., fall, allergy), which greatly support the physician's decision. This idea originally came from our President.

BI is another strength highlighted by the surveyors. The tool of Decision Tree was adopted for our BI platform to deliver a more intuitive view of various data (e.g., length of stay, average cost) for individual diagnoses. As China's healthcare reform went further, the government also released the "zero mark-up" and fixed amount control on healthcare expenditure. In face of the challenges and restrictions on hospitals, the decision support functionality has contributed significantly to the hospital's steady revenue.

Meanwhile, the balanced score card (BSC) has been adopted to be pecked with the evaluation on the unit directors. The BSC shows the fulfillment of the targets as well as the trends at different stages. For example, positive trends are marked in green and negative ones are marked in red.

During the quality improvement case presentation, the critical value management case presented by Dr. Wu Yunqi, director of Medical Affairs Department, and the D2B time for acute myocardial infarction presented by Dr. Song Yu, director of ER were highly recognized by the surveyors. They said that they would share the practices in TICH with more hospitals in the world.

Learning through Repetitive Learning and Practice

Though TICH survived three JCI surveys, it was not until we adopted HIMSS criteria when we understood the essence of JCI standards. You would never know how pear tastes like until you eat one yourself.

Only by practicing and making mistakes could we achieve progress.

1. *Information sharing*. During the HIMSS consultation, the consultants mentioned the lack of information sharing capability in the hospital. We were very surprised because the users could access the data with proper authorization. How come that the data were not shared? We found out that "information" defined by HIMSS was different from ours. What HIMSS requires is the integration of the discrete data not a piece of Office Word file. All the system modules should be integrated onto one interface to allow direct access of the physicians and nurses. Nurses should be able to see all the patient's information without flipping through different modules. In addition, all the medical record documentation should be structured and capture discrete data. Physicians should be able to cite and exert the diagnosis, patient's demographic information and other types of data (e.g., medication, lab, examination) into the record.
2. *CDR*. At the very beginning, we regarded medical record as a matrix-like electronic document listing all the information in time sequence, and designed it according to our own perception of its functionality. However, during the HIMSS EMRAM Stage 6 validation, Jilan Liu was astonished. She said that the CDR was like a water tank that gathers all the data collected and delivers the data as requested. We suddenly realized that what we had was not a CDR. A true CDR is a fundamental database fed with discrete data. It's like the sand or cement that you use to build a tower. When the tower is finished, you no longer see the original raw materials. CDR is the database that supports the operation of the EMR and is required at Stage 2 to include all the patient's laboratory, examination, medication, and imaging information.
3. *Down time contingency plan*. After three rounds of JCI survey, we gradually adopted the manual process to tackle with the downtime with all the examination request sheets, physician order sheets, and patient's information. We thought it was sufficient. But the HIMSS surveyors asked us a question that we could not answer: "Does this standard ask you to turn to a paper process? How would the paper be possible to show you the most important diagnosis and surgeries in the past five days of a patient? How could the physician or a nurse remember all the information of a patient who has been here for 10 days?"

Obviously, the "sufficient contingency plan" was far from sufficient. HIMSS requires a local copy of patient's information that could be accessed during down time so as to support the continuous care of patients. Then we decided to adopt automatic backup download of patient's information generated in the previous 5 days on the local computers and update the backup copy on a regular basis. With this in place, the healthcare staff can access the patient's clinical information during downtime to take care of the patient.

Commitment, Resolution, and Execution

After the HIMSS EMRAM Stage 7 validation, our IT engineers told us that that year was like a 10-year battle for them. Validation is a tool that a hospital could use to drive the continuous improvement of quality.

Improved Organizational Structure

The key of our success in IT adoption is an optimal organizational structure for IT development in the hospital. In the past, the clinical units did not talk with the IT, which further led to underestimated communication. The IT Department received many unreasonable requests that caused unnecessary extra work of the engineers. For this, the hospital restructured the administration of IT development.

Before the restructuring, an IT committee comprising hospital leadership, unit heads, and directors of administrative offices was established. The IT Department was under the management of the committee. After the restructuring, we established the IT Steering Group with IT Department under its management. Three working groups were then organized under the IT Department, namely the Management Working Group, the Medical Working Group, and the Nursing Working Group. They mainly comprised the physicians, nurses and other key users to work together with the engineers in the IT Department (see Figure 14.3).

The new structure played a pivotal role during the HIMSS EMRAM Stage 7 preparation. For example, the engineers once visited the Pediatrics and found out that after the physician had prescribed the medication, the nurse had to manually calculate the dosage based on the child's height and weight and then told the physician. Then the IT Department convened a meeting together with physicians, nurses, and pharmacists to discuss the improvement of the ordering process for pediatric dosing. Now, the Pediatric physicians only need to click a button, "Intelligent Dosing," while ordering medication for the patients, the system would automatically give a dose based on the patient's height and weight. This has saved our nurses from extra work and improved patient safety. Of course, there have been minor fine tunings of the function (e.g., to give dose at the upper limit or the lower limit).

On the one hand, the IT technology realized higher efficiency and safety for the healthcare staff. On the other hand, the healthcare staff have been more actively involved in the process improvement. The enthusiasm from the frontline staff also became the "sweet burden" on the IT Department. Our engineers started to show their valuable contribution to the hospital during this process. But the growing demands from the clinical field have also kept them busy.

Figure 14.3 Process improvement discussion by IT Leading Group.

Self-Training

During the validation, the surveyors were impressed by the staff in the hospital because of their confidence in answering all the questions and demonstrating all the functions in the system. The key is the role of the users, the physicians, and nurses. We adopted many effective measures in the preparation, for example, nurturing the "seeded players" among the physicians and nurses. Each unit selected one "seeded player," who would be responsible for training three colleagues in the unit. And after the three trainees finished their training, they would automatically be promoted as the "trainers" to educate other staff.

"Tests" and "drills" were also our favorite to make sure that everyone could answer the questions or operate the system quickly. Before the system was brought online, the work place of the clinical healthcare staff was their training field. Each step of the care process could become a theme for them to practice every day. When the system was finally alive, they could naturally adapt to the new functions and new flow.

Leadership as the Key

Hospital leadership and management is the key factor of energizing and inspiring the employees. Once the staff are mobilized, they are impeccable. And they can truly benefit from their creativity and efforts via best utilizing the IT technology offered by the hospital.

For TICH, it was not an easy task to achieve Stage 7 in the same year when we was just validated as a Stage 6 hospital. The hospital was very busy with taking care of the patients. After we were validated as a Stage 6 hospital, the explosion in the neighborhood in August added even more clinical burden on the hospital. Dr. Liu Xiaocheng, President of the hospital, was determined to achieve the goal anyway, which was proved that the dedication of the leadership was the most important factor that secured our goal for getting Stage 7.

Starting Point Rather than the End

Data are not necessarily information. Data could be useless if they are not properly used to guide the practice in a hospital. It's like the dashboard on a car. The number of the petroleum volume is just data on the dashboard. But when it indicates that the petroleum volume is low and makes you decide to refill your tank, the data on the dashboard then becomes useful information to trigger your actions.

Information utilization also contains multiple levels regarding its maturity. When the read of the petroleum left in your tank becomes your monthly consumption, the increase or decrease compared with the data from last month becomes a piece of new information that is upgraded through the combination of different data. Data could also spiral and be utilized on a higher level according to the needs of management. But it derives from the very raw data that could generate the primary information, which could further generate the secondary information, contributing to the advancement of management. Information utilization is a step-by-step process, during which, you would find that some data were poor in quality and did not contribute to analysis and decision support. If you need complete, accurate, and reliable data, data governance would be of utmost important to data standardization and collection for generating high quality information.

Dr. Dong Jun, VP of the hospital, once said, "It was HIMSS EMRAM Stage 7 validation that helped us to review the information utilization and allowed me, as the hospital leader, to truly understand the role of information utilization in quality improvement." After the validation, staff in TICH became more aware of the importance of information and keen in mining deeper into the data we have. The needs and requests of information began to surge.

On the exit meeting of HIMSS EMRAM validation, Dr. Liu Xiaocheng said that HIMSS EMRAM model should not ceiling at HIMSS Stage 7. There should be Stages 8, 9, and 10! Only by looking up to higher standards and benchmarks, could we achieve further development in the "post-HIMSS era" of the hospital.

Looking back on the journey we have traversed, Stage 7 was just the beginning of a new voyage of IT adoption. In the language of computer programming, there are only two numbers, "0" and "1." The latter is the maximum one digit could go. If you want to go further, you need to carry yourself into the next digit. That is exactly the process of making progress.

Safety, Quality, Team, and Spirit—The Cultural Legacy from International Standards

Dr. Dong Jun again stood on the podium at the exit meeting of our second triennial JCI survey in July 2015. Instead of delivering a heart-touching speech, she asked three questions: What is JCI? Why did we choose to take the JCI challenge? What has JCI brought to us?

Similar questions were asked when we were validated as an HIMSS EMRAM Stage 7 hospital: What is HIMSS? Why did we choose to take the HIMSS challenge? What has HIMSS brought to us?

"Safety, Quality, Team and Spirit" are the four most suitable words to summarize the cultural asset that we have gained through the process.

Safety

What is safety? Does safety mean quality? This is a pair of confusing concepts. First, safety does not necessarily mean quality, and vice versa. Safety accidents are severe incidents that may result in serious consequences and threats to life, and even lead to collective occurrence. Such kind of accidents can hardly be controlled and cannot be reversed through rectification. Rectification can only be used to mend the harm that have been done. However, safety measures are adopted to prevent any possible harm from happening.

Quality

What is quality? Quality is a kind of criteria that is either met or not met by standards, and has no ceiling for "the best." The quality we expect is to do the right thing in a right way at the first try. In the daily management of a hospital, "no problem" usually is the biggest problem because of the weak awareness of existing problem and potential risks. Quality management is science. The core idea is to make continuous improvement a day-to-day practice.

Team

Both JCI and HIMSS look at the overall practice of a hospital as a whole rather than the competency of one individual staff or one unit. Thus, the role of teamwork can never be over emphasized. The primary principle of the healthcare team of TICH is to put patient first. Physicians, nurses, nursing workers, pharmacists, lab technicians, examination technicians, dieticians, and all other staff work together as a team to provide patient-centered care through a patient-oriented loop.

For example, in addition to physicians and nurses, we have also included dieticians, physiotherapists, and managerial staff on our two CCPC programs. In addition to clinical crossover collaboration, our teams also go patient rounds, administer medications, and conduct rehabilitation together to form a true clinical team for our patients.

Spirit

After several rounds of international accreditation, we gradually formed the spirit of TICH: Hospital, Honor, and Responsibility. We can use three sentences to summarize our experience with JCI and HIMSS. Process is always more important than the results! Patient's satisfaction is always important than awards! Staff's cohesion and pursuit for excellence is always important than the gold seal! As Dr. Liu Xiaocheng said to the media, "TICH is a unique hospital. The JCI accreditation and HIMSS EMRAM validation are new learning experience for us, through which, we have forged the culture for enhanced safety in the hospital. It makes us more determined and confident in pursuing continuous quality improvement."

Conclusion

JCI helps the hospital to do the right thing, and HIMSS ensures that the hospital do the right thing in the right way. HIMSS is not just concepts such as EMR, eMAR, or CDS, but a means to fully implement the measures centering on safety, quality, and continuous improvement from the JCI survey and to consolidate and optimize the policies and procedures.

Case 1: Electronic Coordination System in PCI Operating Room

As a specialized hospital in heart diseases, the Cardiovascular Surgery Department mainly takes surgical patients, while Cardiovascular Medicine Department focuses more on PCI procedures. The Cardiovascular Medicine Department is operated by a huge clinical team covering six independent wards, three levels of nursing care, one Intensive Care Unit, and five PCI Rooms. In 2016 alone, the Cardiovascular Medicine Department completed 13,614 PCI cases. How to ensure the patient safety in face of such a large volume of procedures involving multi-disciplinary collaboration became a huge, complicated challenge. After we were validated as an HIMSS EMRAM Stage 6, more creative ideas popped up among the clinical staff. The head nurse of the PCI Center soon requested a paperless process for patient handover and safety check, the nurses on the ward required to access the patient's condition during surgery, and the physicians wanted the update of the information related to the surgery. All these requests were waiting for the IT Department to take actions.

Real-Time Display of Patient Information

It is always easier to talk about the strategy on paper than to implement them in reality. The IT Department then collected all the requests related to the PCI procedure in June 2015 and convened the first meeting to discuss the "uniform management of PCI patients." The meeting was attended also by Liu Xiaocheng (President) and DONG Jun (VP). Three goals were determined on the meeting: (1) to eliminate all types of paper handover sheets and surgery safety checklists and build the function in the IT system, (2) to remove the communication barriers among different departments/units to improve effective communication, and (3) to engage the patients in the decision-making process regarding the PCI surgery.

The IT Department later on organized numerous meetings, big and small, to specify the requests and translate them into feasible and quantifiable solutions. Through rounds of communication and improvement, a "PCI Operating Room Coordination System" was born. The hospital then set up a process design team based on the final plan chaired by Liu Xiaocheng. The IT Department, Equipment Department, Logistics Department, Surgery Department, PCI Center, ICU, CCU and other clinical units that may be involved in the patient care process were called to join the endeavor. The coordination system was like an airport control tower to coordinate all the aircrafts landing on and taking off from the airport with the capability to display all the information about an individual patient's flow in real time from entering the operating suit, induction of anesthesia, preparation for the surgery, surgery in process and, finally, the departure of the patient from the suit to ICU/CCU/ward.

After a PCI surgery is prescribed, the staff in the PCI Center need to schedule the patient accordingly which would generate a list of all requested surgery displayed on the screens available in the control room, waiting area for patient's families and the nurse station of the ward. When the operating physician requests the patient to be sent to the operating area, the technician in the PCI Center can select the patient on the PDA and click "Send Patient." The screen on the ward would then give a pop-out window with the patient's name, reminding the nurse to send the patient to the PCI Center.

The patient is then handed over from the ward nurse to the PCI nurse at the PCI Center through scanning patient's wristband with patient's ID on it. The patient who is in the waiting area is listed in yellow, indicating that he/she is waiting for the procedure. In the suit, the operating physician and the nurse perform the pre-op safety check by scanning the wristband on the patient again, which would bring up the patient's surgery request and the safety checklist on the PDA. Then the physician and nurse verify all the information as listed on the checklist to confirm that everything has been completed as required. After the nurse saves the checklist on PDA, the patient's entry on the screen would turn into green, indicating that the surgery is in process.

As the handover has been seamlessly integrated with the coordination system, physicians can have a more intuitive overview from the screen about the surgery request list, information about the patients under surgery or in the waiting area, the number of patients on the unit to be sent for surgery, etc. In the office area of the PCI Center, physicians of different disciplines and the director of the center could see the total number of procedures, the occupied suits, and the progression of the procedures (see Figures 14.4 and 14.5).

Patient's family could also learn about the status of their beloved one in the PCI Center on another monitor. After the procedure is over, the OR nurse generates and fills the handover sheet in the electronic system and saves it. Then, the patient's condition would turn into purple which means that the procedure has finished to remind the nurse on the ward and the patient's family that the patient would be sent back.

Correctly Identify Patient with the Support of Technology

In the past, patients were identified manually. But now, we are able to identify patient through scanning their wristbands. In the past, handover was performed on paper charts by the ward nurse and the PCI Center nurse through checking out the items listed. But now, this is completed

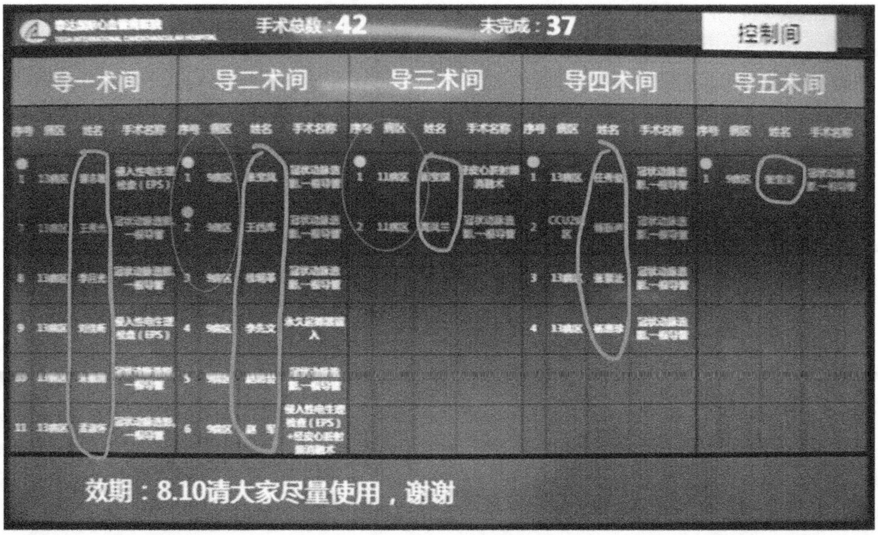

Figure 14.4 Screen in control room of operating suit.

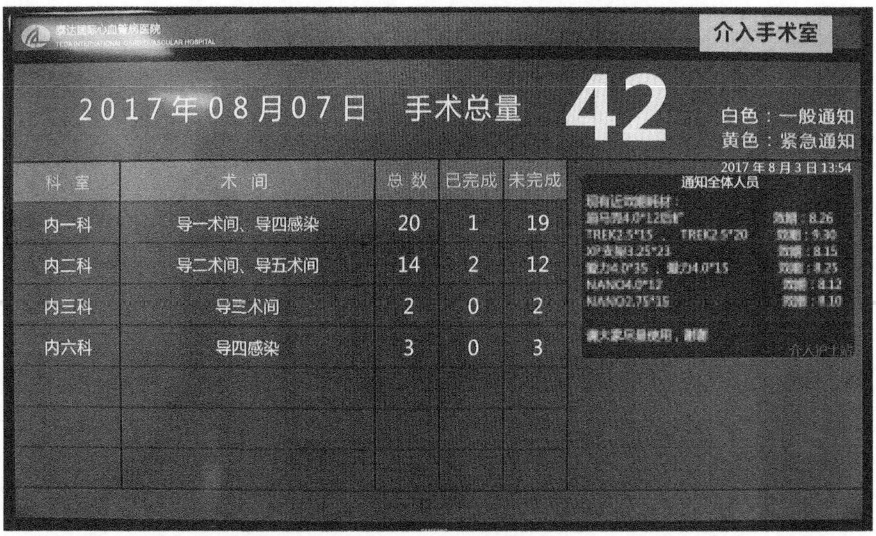

Figure 14.5 Screen in OR office area.

through the coordination system. In this way, we are able to cover the entire loop of the patient's flow (before, during and after the procedure) to minimize risks and errors.

As a compulsory process to be completed for patients transferred between units/departments, hand-written form had been effectively used by clinical staff. But the electronic form is of greater help because it is no longer a fixed form to be completed but rather a type of information generating and feeding data and feed into the database. Each step is strictly controlled in the system to avoid being bypassed by the staff intentionally. It also eliminates the error caused by transcription, improves the efficiency of our nursing staff, and offers potentials in future research.

JCI standard IPSG.2.2 requires the hospital develops and implement a process for handover communication. Breakdowns in communication can occur during any handover of patient care and can result in adverse events. During the JCI triennial survey in 2015, the surveyors traced patients from the ward to OR, OR to ward, ER to OR, and OR to CCU. They observed the accuracy of information communicated during handover, but more importantly, the time footprint of the handover process. With the support of the "PCI Operating Room Coordination System," we are able to integrate the standardized form into HIS. When the patient completes the pre-operation preparation and is sent to the PCI Center (see Figure 14.6), the nurses performing the handover only need to scan the patient's wristband to verify the patient's identity. The system would bring up the patient's pre-op handover sheet, allowing the nurses to verify the medical record, imaging documents, lab results, and other documentation and to match the patient's identity. After both nurses confirm the information, they can finish the handover process by scanning their work badges, respectively.

After the patient is sent into the suit, the operating physician, nurse, and the technician perform the verification again, i.e., Time-Out, where the nurse also scans the patient's wristband with PDA. If the patient's information matches the schedule of the procedure, the system would bring up the surgery information such as patient's medical record number, department/unit, name, age, sex, procedure name, and surgery documentation. While checking the above-mentioned information, the nurse should also look at the patient's allergy and count the supplies required by the physician

泰达国际心血管病医院
TEDA INTERNATIONAL CARDIOVASCULAR HOSPITAL

病案号：[redacted]
姓　名：[redacted]

病区与介入室术前交接

姓名：	[redacted]	**性别：**	{男}	**出生日期：**	[redacted]	**科别：**	{内六科}

介入前查检：
皮肤准备：{已做}；留置针：{有}；活动牙齿：{无}；义齿：{无}；皮试：{不需要}
儿科介入：
禁食水：{单选}；足背动脉标记：{单选}；氧气袋：{单选}；活动牙齿：{单选}；义齿：{单选}；
皮试：{单选}

交接时间：2017/11/22 09:15:11
转入科室：{介入治疗中心}
入院诊断：UAP
术　式：{冠状动脉造影，一根导管}

项目	交接内容
患者一般情况	T:{36 ℃} P:{89 次/分} R:{18 次/分} BP:{134/74 mmHg} 体重：{63 kg}
过敏史	{过敏物质：无}
传染病筛查	传筛：乙肝表面抗原：{阴性}；乙肝表面抗体：{阴性}；乙肝e抗原：{阴性}；乙肝e抗体：{阴性}；丙肝抗体：{阴性}；人类免疫缺陷病毒抗体（1+2）：{阴性}；梅毒螺旋体抗体：{阴性}；梅毒血清反应：{阴性}
其他	活动牙齿{无}　义齿：{无}
备注	
交接人	交班：[redacted]　接班：[redacted]

Figure 14.6 Pre-op handover sheet.

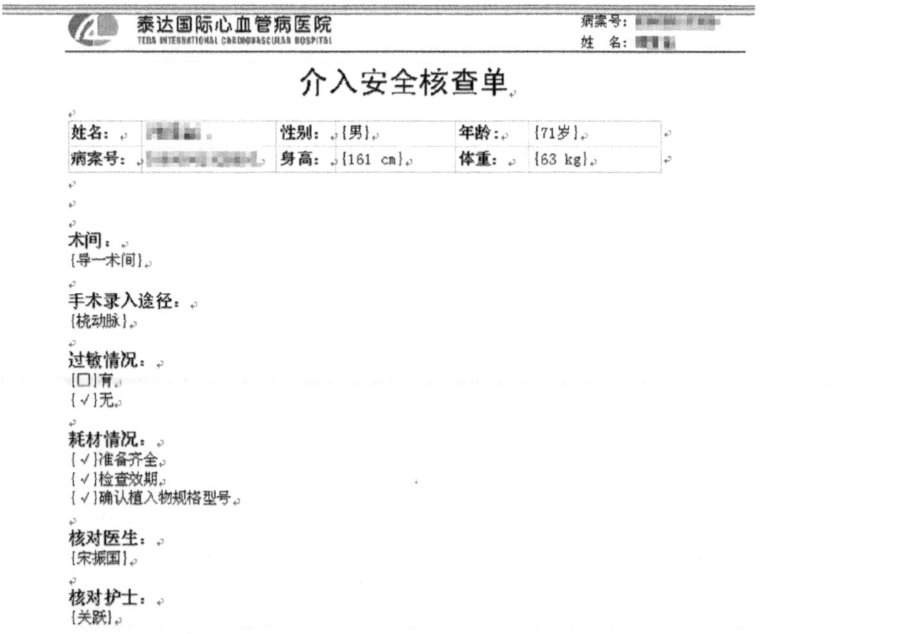

泰达国际心血管病医院
TEDA INTERNATIONAL CARDIOVASCULAR HOSPITAL

病案号: [redacted]
姓　名: [redacted]

介入安全核查单

姓名:	[redacted]	性别:	{男}	年龄:	{71岁}
病案号:	[redacted]	身高:	{161 cm}	体重:	{63 kg}

术间:
{导一术间}

手术录入途径:
{桡动脉}

过敏情况:
{□}有
{√}无

耗材情况:
{√}准备齐全
{√}检查效期
{√}确认植入物规格型号

核对医生:
{宋振国}

核对护士:
{关跃}

Figure 14.7 Safety checklist for PCI.

for the procedure. After the verification, the participating physician and nurse enter their staff passwords, respectively, for completing the Time-Out, and the safety checklist is then saved to the patient's medical record. If the checklist is not confirmed and saved, the staff cannot proceed with the procedure. Before the patient is sent out from the suit, a Sign-Out process is performed. The PCI Safety Checklist (see Figure 14.7) includes the pre-discharge verification initiated by the OR nurse/circulating nurse verbally where the following information needs to be reviewed and checked before the patient leaves the suit: (1) surgery/invasive procedure name; (2) count of instrument, sponges and needles; (3) labeling of specimens; and (4) problems of equipment to be addressed. When Sign-Out is completed, the patient's status would turn green.

The OR nurse submits the Pre-operative Safety Checklist and Surgery Documentation after the procedure is completed. The data would be then fed into the database. Meanwhile, the nurse creates the Post-operative Handover Sheet which could be automatically populated with information already available in the safety checklist and other procedure-related notes. The disposition of patient (i.e., the receiving unit) must be indicated in the handover sheet. The patient's demographic information is populated from the HIS and the name of the procedure is entered by the nurse after it is confirmed by the operating physician. When the handover sheet is verified by the ward nurse, the patient's status would turn purple, indicating that the patient's loop for surgery has been completed.

JCI standard (IPSG. 1) requires that the hospital develop and implement a process to improve accuracy of patient identifications. Wrong-patient errors occur in virtually all aspects of diagnosis and treatment. Patients may be sedated, disoriented, not fully alert, or comatose; may change beds, rooms, or locations within the hospital; may have sensory disabilities; may not remember their identity; or may be subject to other situations that may lead to errors in correct identification. We often forget to identify the patient family as we focus too much on the patient's identity. In China, all surgeries or most of the care/treatment require informed consent from the patient family. Thus, to identify patient family correctly is also important. Based on our practices, we extended the scope of "patient" to include families as well.

Digital and Visualized Physician-Nurse Communication

During the process to adopt the new PCI Operating Room Coordination System, we carried out numerous simulation and test runs. We had thought that correct patient identification and safe patient handover would not be a problem as it is supported by the new process and technology. However, two adverse events warned us of the importance of continuous improvement.

The errors occurred during the physician-patient family conversation regarding two PCI patients in 2015. The root cause was the chaotic environment for conversation: eight units (CCU, Pediatrics, and Internal Medicine Ward 1–6) shared only one conversation room. In most of the cases, one patient would be companied by several family members to communicate the conditions with several physicians in the same room. A solution was needed to solve this situation. The transformation of the conversation room was the priority for the extension of the PCI Operating Room Coordination System. We changed the layout in the area. The previous check-in desk was replaced by four separated conversation rooms (see Figure 14.8).

New screens were installed in the family waiting areas showing the patient's name, unit, sex, and progression of the surgery. When a physician needs to talk to the patient family, he/she calls the patient family to the assigned room through the coordination system and the calling system to make sure that the correct family members were called. During the surgery, if a conversation is required, the technician clicks the button of "call patient family," and the screen would show the patient's name and the assigned conversation room to orient the patient family. Figure 14.9 shows the scene where a physician is talking to the patient family about the condition and investigation findings.

The new setting provides physicians and patient families a relatively quiet, safe, and private environment for conversation assisted with IT system to directly show the image from the suit. This better facilitates the discussion of the surgical plan for the patient between the two sides. This upgrade effectively cut down the incidence of adverse events. The satisfaction rate by the physician increased from 42% to 99%, while the family's satisfaction rate from 39% to 97%.

Figure 14.8 New conversation rooms.

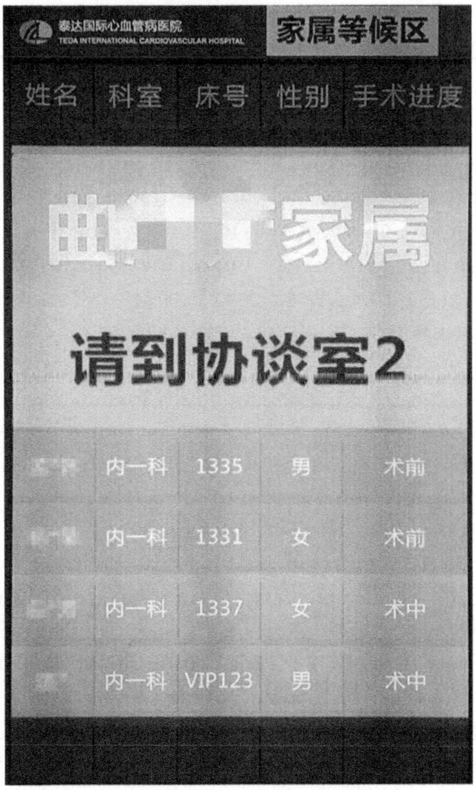

Figure 14.9 Screen in family waiting area.

This was defined as the best practice by the surveyors since such practice, engaging patient family, physician, and nurse, was not commonly found in other hospitals in the world. It is an example of integration of IT system and the Internet of Things to fully combine the flow of people, materials, and information and fully utilize the information system to ensure safety, quality, efficiency and the effectiveness of patient/patient family communication.

Meanwhile, we also realized real-time transmission of the PACS images to the conversation room during the talk. The patient family can also see the image from the angiography on the computer in the conversation room, which was also regarded as a creative measure. This one tiny feature actually required several efforts: first, the collection and retrieval of PACS information; and second, monitoring camera in the conversation room. The purpose of the conversation is to communicate with the patient's family as effectively as possible to make decision for the following treatment. With this new approach, physicians are able to better explain to the patient family with the assistance of the images (Figures 14.9 and 14.10).

Seek Progress through Improvement

On January 21, 2016, one of our physicians found two patients who shared exactly the same name in Chinese: "Dong Xiaojie." Then, who was the family that he should talk to? We later found out that both patients were receiving coronary angiography during the same time slot. But they were admitted to different units (one from Ward 3 and the other Ward 4). How could we better tackle such cases?

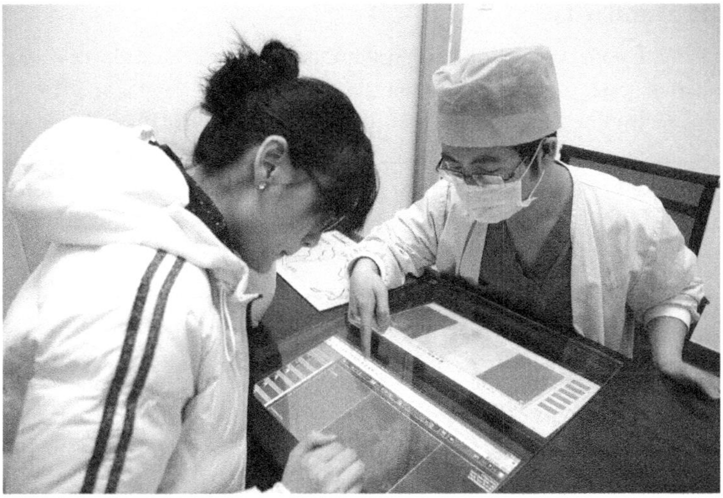

Figure 14.10 Physician informing the patient family about the condition and investigation findings.

Through digging into the causes, it was known that the clinical units had little communication regarding the patient information and they did not know the patients who were scheduled for surgery in other units. Even the PCI staff did not know whether they would have patients with the same name scheduled for procedures. The reason behind this was the high volume of PCI patients. The healthcare staff only communicated the procedure volume and special surgeries during shift handover without checking the names of each patient. Then, a multi-unit meeting was convened on which the directors brainstormed together and identified the major causes: high volume of procedures, insufficient communication about the PCI patients with the same names.

Improvement action was immediately initiated: the PCI Center staff on shift highlight the patients who share the same name on the mobile messaging APP while they are communicating the procedure volume. The clinical units also decided not to schedule the patients with the same names on the same day for PCI procedures. If the PCI Center identified same-name patients from different units before the day of surgery, the staff should inform the clinical unit to schedule them in different time slots. After 8 months of operation, no similar errors ever occurred.

Another problem with patient identification was the patients with no identity certificate. The Medical Affairs Department decided to issue standard identification cards to patients and their families. Pre-op education is provided to patient family members to remind them of bringing their own identification card to the conversation with physicians. A policy regarding the family conversation during PCI procedure was then formulated to clarify the process. Evaluation on the effectiveness was conducted. Staff were trained. In special cases where same-name patients may be scheduled, pictures of the patients would be taken with PDA used by nurses. When verifying the patient's family identity, the physician would show them also the patient's picture for secondary verification in addition to the regular process.

The electronic-based patient handover links the patient's procedure status with the handover documentation, allowing the physicians, nurses, patients, and patient families to view the patient's status anytime anywhere. This process reduces the man-made errors maximally and keeps the objective data about the patient as the evidence for future improvement. The participation of physicians, nurses and patient families in multiple steps in the patient flow loop makes the safety goals much easier to achieve and improved the patient's satisfaction rate.

Go beyond the Standards

The PCI Operating Room Coordination System is the best example of integrating HIMSS EMRAM 7 paperless operation and JCI standards supported by HIS, NIS, LIS, PACS, and Internet of Things technology together, which finally delivers real-time monitoring and feedback on the procedure process. The handover process is no longer an oral or written communication, but a safety action taken by the entire clinical team to better ensure patient safety throughout the patient-centered process.

Case 2: CDSS-Supported Antibiotics Stewardship

It was another busy morning that Dr. Liu, a pediatrician of TICH, became anxious in front of the computer screen, "Why can't I order antibiotics in the system?" "What's wrong? What do you want to prescribe?" asked Dr. Wang, director of Pediatrics. "The child on Bed No. 2. I need ceftriaxone injection for his surgery tomorrow." Dr. Wang sat next to Dr. Liu and started to explain the antibiotics stewardship system on the computer....

The Global Challenge

Drug resistance of bacteria has become one of the major challenges in public health and attracted much attention from governments and societies across the world. It is also a long-known topic to practicing physicians. The overuse and misuse of antibiotics has resulted in the growth of super-bugs that are increasingly resistant to available antibiotics. Health care practitioners are contributing to the development of antimicrobial resistance in several ways. For example, continuing antibiotics when they are no longer necessary, using a broad-spectrum antibiotic when it is not required or continuing the broad-spectrum antibiotic unnecessarily after the sensitivity results are received, using the wrong antibiotic or prescribing the wrong dose, or continuing the prophylactic antibiotic after it is no longer recommended. Therefore, to best control the growth of super-bugs and its spread and to achieve better clinical outcomes, the sixth edition of the JCI standards adds a new requirement on antibiotics stewardship, asking hospital to develop and implement a program for the prudent use of antibiotics based on the principle of antibiotic stewardship.

The Chinese government started a special initiative focusing on the appropriate use of antibiotics as early as in 2011 by releasing a series of policies including the *Guiding Principles of Clinical Antibiotics Use* (2015), *National Guideline on Antibiotics Treatment* and *Management Measures of Clinical Antibiotics Use*, to regulate the clinical practices in hospitals; formulate robust policies and regulations governing clinical antibiotics use; identify the roles of departments and personnel; implement the hierarchical management of antibiotics use, the policy on providing consultation on special antibiotics and the review of physician orders. It requires hospitals to strictly abide by the national policies and regulations regarding the hierarchical management of the drugs as well as the privileges of the physicians supported by an established antibiotics catalog and continuous monitoring.

But how do hospitals realize the goals? TICH again turned to the IT technology.

Don't Wait until It Is Used

TICH responded to the national initiative by launching the antibiotics stewardship program in the hospital several years ago. We established the Antibiotics Stewardship Group comprising the hospital leadership and responsible persons and clinical professionals from the Medical Education Department, Nursing Department, IT Department, Infection Control Department, Pharmacy, and Laboratory.

At the beginning, the clinical pharmacists were responsible for verifying all cases that involve antibiotics use, including the prophylactic antibiotics use for Type I surgical incision and all types of therapeutic antibiotics use. The pharmacists delivered monthly report and feedback to all clinical units and the Quality Control Office together with the comment on appropriateness. The results of monitoring indicators were manually calculated and reported to the hospital leadership. It was no long before the hospital upgraded our IT system and added the statistics of clinical antibiotics use module in the HIS, which helped to analyze the basic information regarding antibiotics use and conduct the monthly indicator analysis for aggregated report and feedback.

However, such statistics after the drug has already been used did not provide much guidance to clinical practice, let alone real-time monitoring on appropriate use of antibiotics. Back at that time, it totally relied on the physician's compliance to the hospital requirements. But the inappropriate use could not be effectively prevented.

Implementation Supported by CDSS

Through our experience with JCI and HIMSS, staff realized that concrete steps and measures were needed to monitor the problems and risks related to clinical practices to prevent incidence from happening. The best tool that we could use was information technology. An integrated decision support function embedded in the clinical pathways following evidence-based guidelines was in urgent need for real-time monitoring and control on the clinical use of antibiotics.

In 2013, TICH was listed as the first pilot hospital in antibiotics stewardship supported by information technology in Tianjin City and started our project to build the module for antibiotics stewardship.

Professional Guidance

The request on antibiotics stewardship was very different from the previous ones as it involved clinical treatment process, medication use, monitoring, and data analysis. When we were lost in such a big maze, the hospital leadership invited the consultants from Taiwan to share with us the experience and practices in Taiwan.

The first step was to give clinical physicians and pharmacists a say in the process. According to the principle of symptom-cluster-based antibiotics use, we built compulsory ordering restrictions on antibiotics in the framework of diagnosis and guidelines to standardize the appropriate use of antibiotics with monitoring indicators adopted for the stewardship. The Antibiotics Stewardship Group then established a team for the Program of Symptom-cluster-based Clinical Use of Common Antibiotics to formulate the program according to the guideline from Taiwan as well as the actual data analysis from the hospital. After repeated discussion, communication, and improvement, the program finally took shape.

At the same time, the IT Department were writing the plan for developing the system module: Once the diagnosis is confirmed, applicable clinical guideline and medication therapy is also determined. Then, the result of lab culture would lead the possibility of changes to the medication therapy, which would further trigger the antibiotics consultation process. The antibiotics consultation request should include the reason and purpose (description of patient's condition), the suggestions, and recommended medication. After the consulting physician gives the information, the treating physician then prescribes the medication and flags it as an order based on consultation. ICD 10 code has been adopted to serve as the evidence for prescription.

By the end of 2013, we brought the Antibiotics Stewardship Module alive.

Physician Privileging Management

In the case we just gave, why could Dr. Liu not prescribe certain medication in the HIS? That was because privilege management had been imposed in the information system to control the prescription of antibiotics. Physicians are only allowed to order certain level of antibiotics according to their privileges. For example, residents can only prescribe non-restricted antibiotics. That is why the physician in the example couldn't prescribe the ceftriaxone injection. In this way, we are able to link the level of antibiotics with the privileges of the physicians. For special antibiotics, only privileged physicians can prescribe such drugs supported by antibiotics use consultation and agreement from professionals with experience in clinical infection. In urgent situation where consultation and agreement could not be obtained in a timely manner or privilege needs to be overwritten for certain medication use, the dosage could not exceed 1 day and documentation is kept in patient's medical record.

Symptom-Cluster-Based Antibiotics Stewardship

The antibiotics are managed based on symptom-clusters in our HIS. We reviewed and identified the infections that could occur in our hospital, including community-acquired pneumonia, ventilator-associated pneumonia and endocarditis and other diagnoses. And antibiotics therapy plans are developed according to the diagnosis-related clinical guidelines, *Guiding Principles of Clinical Antibiotics Use*, *The Sanford Guide to Antimicrobial Therapy*, and *Medication Guideline for Cardiovascular Diseases. The plans are matched with the TICH Formulary* and built into the HIS. For example, if the symptom-cluster indicates a patient has endocarditis, a possible diagnosis is required before antibiotics can be prescribed. The therapeutic medication can only be chosen from a fixed plan: penicillin 1200U IVD q6h; penicillin 1200U IVD q6h+amikacin 500 mg IVD q12h or vancomycin 15 mg/kg IVD q12h. Physicians are not allowed to prescribe other antibiotics in HIS. Such restriction better ensures the appropriate antibiotics use.

Prophylactic and Therapeutic Antibiotics Management

Antibiotics use can be divided into two types: prophylactic antibiotics use and therapeutic antibiotics use. For prophylactic use, the timing, category of antibiotics, and duration of the use shall be managed and monitored. For therapeutic use, the possible diagnosis, treatment plan, and time shall be controlled.

Prophylactic antibiotics use: The system would require a surgery request available before the antibiotic medication can be prescribed and limit the categories of antibiotics with cefazolin sodium injection or cefuroxime sodium injection. A termination time (48 h) of the order would be automatically set for prophylactic use in the system.

Therapeutic antibiotics use: A possible diagnosis is required before the physician could order an antibiotic drug in the system. Physician chooses from the treatment plan and prescribes the drug. The system would recommend dosage and frequency and also set a termination time (regularly 7 days) automatically to ensure the appropriate therapeutic use. When combined use of more than two antibiotic drugs or continuous use over 14 days is prescribed by a physician, the system would automatically trigger the consultation request reminder. The consultation report is then sent back together with recommended antibiotics order after discussion. The prescribing physician would then be able to order the drugs by using the recommended order directly. For example, if the physician believes that one antibiotic drug would not work well on one patient, a combined therapy would require a consultation on antibiotics use. The consultation is also realized through the IT system. After the consultation request is sent, the system would push the request to the specific consultant who then give feedback to the prescribing physician for ordering.

During clinical practice, the automatic termination of the order plays a critical role in ensuring appropriate medication use as well as preventing antibiotics abuse.

Risk Control over Antibiotics

The system compulsorily requires the physician to prescribe the skin test order for any antibiotics requesting a skin test before administration, and negative skin test result is the precondition in the system to allow the ordering of such antibiotics through IV infusion. The control in the system effectively ensures the safety of antibiotics use, and also completes the closed loop of antibiotics stewardship.

Role of CDSS

Back at the time when we did not have the pre-ordering control and technology intervention regarding the antibiotics, we also met our targets of the utilization and DDD of the drug every month. However, the inappropriate time of prophylactic use and therapeutic use without indication remained as problems. With a small module implemented in our IT system, we are now able to consolidate the antibiotics stewardship process, realize real-time monitoring, ensure the implementation of hospital policies and better perform data analysis in an easier way following the principles of appropriate clinical use of antibiotics.

Case 3: No Underreport of Critical Value

For Mr. Wu, the director in charge of medical quality, a new day starts from glancing through the BI dashboard to learn about the performance of critical value reporting of each unit and the hospital average performance. When he sees 98% shown on the screen, he smiles and feels relaxed. That is the way we monitor the critical value reporting in TICH. But before 2015, Mr. Wu's life was not that relaxing.

Critical Values and JCI

JCI defines critical values as results that are significantly outside the normal range may indicate a high-risk or life-threatening condition. The critical values and reporting system of our hospital have been developed based on the discussion involving both the clinical units and the approval by the hospital quality committee. For example, serum potassium (≤3 mol/L or ≥6 mol/L), blood gas pH value (≤7.1 or ≥7.6), and blood urine (≤1 mol/L or ≥25.5 mol/L) are several defined critical values among others for our Laboratory. Therefore, the accuracy of the reporting and the timeliness of recognition of the results play a vital role in responding to the critical value and ensuring the safety of patients through immediate intervention.

Two "Revolutions" of Critical Values

The management of the critical values in TICH went through two "revolutions," and Mr. Wu had experienced both.

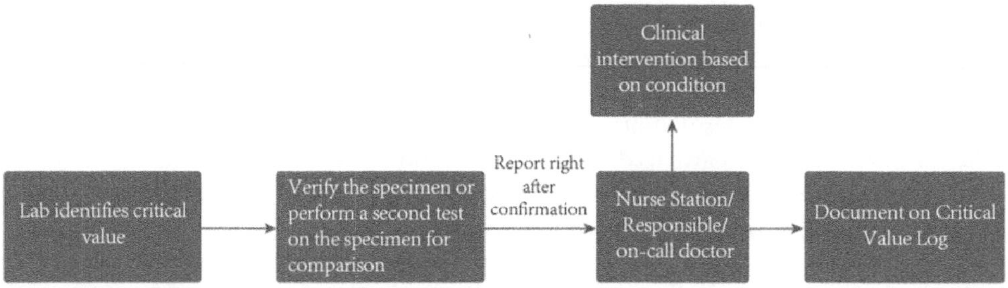

Figure 14.11 Original critical value handling process (before).

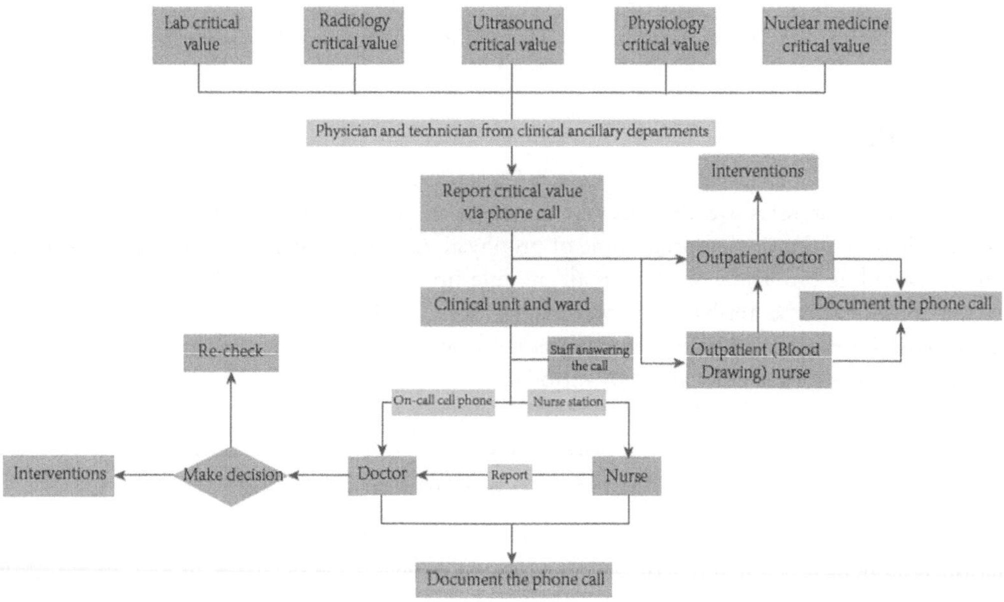

Figure 14.12 Improved critical value handling process (after).

In June 2009, when we were preparing for our first JCI survey, the entire hospital was devoted to the "battle." Critical value communication was one of the six IPSGs, which is also one of the major focuses of the surveyors. Mr. Wu was responsible for the critical value management at that time. The old process of critical value reporting is indicated in Figure 14.11: The Laboratory called the responsible physician, or the physician on-call, or the nurse station. Then the physician documented on the Critical Value Log after intervention had been taken. But during the JCI survey, we identified that the documentation on the units was incomplete and not standardized. At that time, the compliance of staff in handling critical values was only 61.7%.

After the survey, Ms. Dong Jun and Mr. Wu from the Medical Education Department organized all staff for a debriefing on the findings and discussed the improvement on the handling of critical values (see Figure 14.12). The documentation of the phone call communicating the critical values had also been improved to reduce the missing information and errors in the log. It worked. The compliance jumped from 61% in 2009 to 76.6% and then to 83.3% in 2011. Mr. Wu believed that the solution was working.

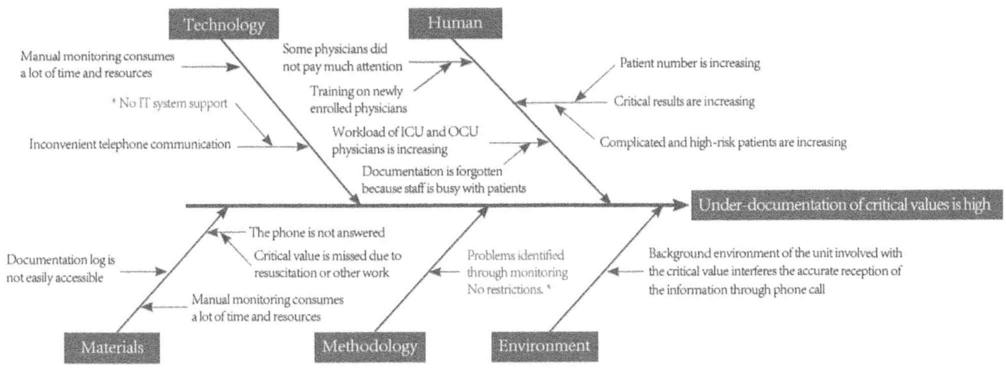

Figure 14.13 Fish bone diagram of high under-documentation rate of critical values.

However, in 2013, the compliance rate stopped improving but dropped to 76.4% at the lowest. Mr. Wu started to receive complains from the frontline staff about all the phone calls and documentation while he was rounding the units. He started to think what went wrong in the new process, and whether there was an easier way to communicate the information in an accurate and timely manner.

Soon, Mr. Wu gathered the staff from the clinical units and Laboratory to further analyze the new process, and used fish bone diagram to find out the causes (see Figure 14.13). It was known that the awareness of the staff was no longer a barrier. However, the lack of IT system support and insufficient control of the process were identified as the major reasons.

As a tool to consolidate the hospital policies and procedures, the information system provides the best control and tracking capability for critical value management. Mr. Wu then reviewed the process again together with the team.

Since 2004 when the hospital was initially established, we integrated the LIS and HIS already, which enables the transmission of the critical values from LIS to HIS. Then how could we notify our physicians in a quick and accurate way? To be quick, it relies on mainly phone calls or text messages, while to be accurate, it requires minimal human interference in the process. We then decided to communicate the critical values through SMS.

The hospital established a close partnership with China Mobile in 2013 to integrate the communications system with the existing LIS and HIS, and equipped our staff on-call with new cell phones to communicate critical values and other urgent information. We then updated the critical value handling process (Figure 14.14) based on the design concept of the closed-loop management (Figure 14.15).

Identification, Communication, Response, and Feedback on Critical Values

The Laboratory performs the tests on the patients' specimens and sets the critical value ranges in LIS that automatically identifies the critical values from all the results. When a critical value is confirmed, the information would then transmit to HIS.

In HIS, what we should do is to enter the phone numbers of the ordering physician, physician on call, unit medical director, director of Medical Education Department and VP in charge. When LIS reports a critical value and HIS receives the information, the system automatically sends a message to the phone of the ordering physician as well as the on-call mobile phone with the patient's medical record number, name, unit, type of outpatient/ER and the critical value, through

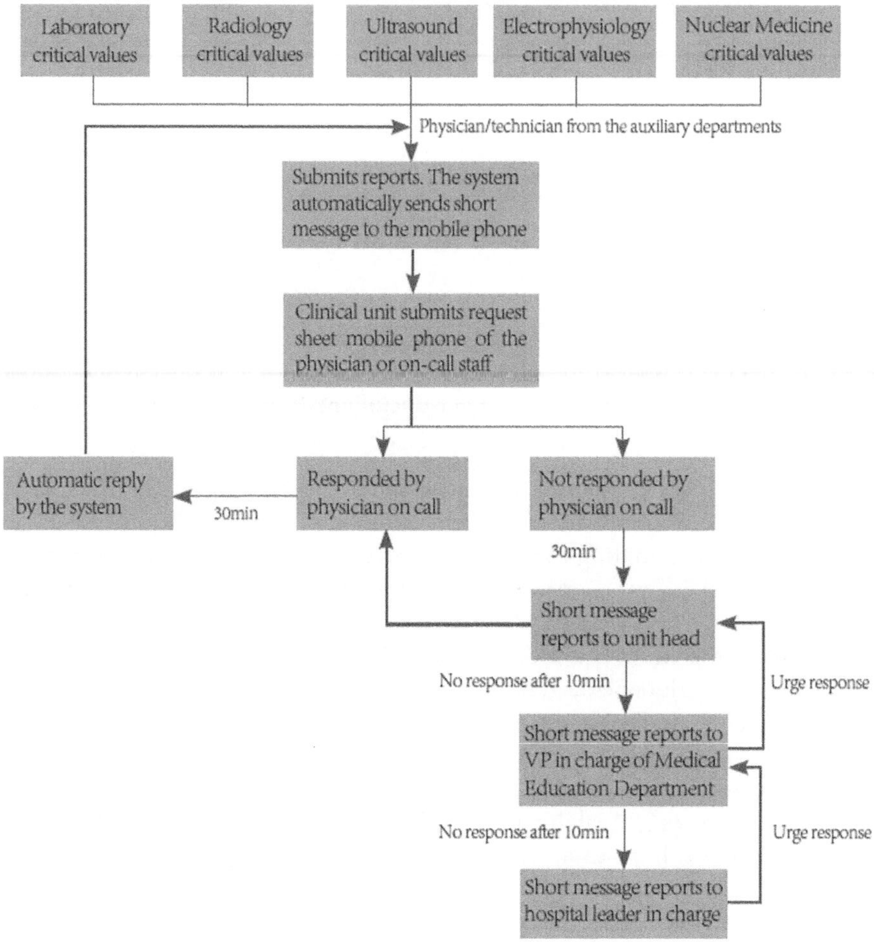

Figure 14.14 Critical value reporting flow chart.

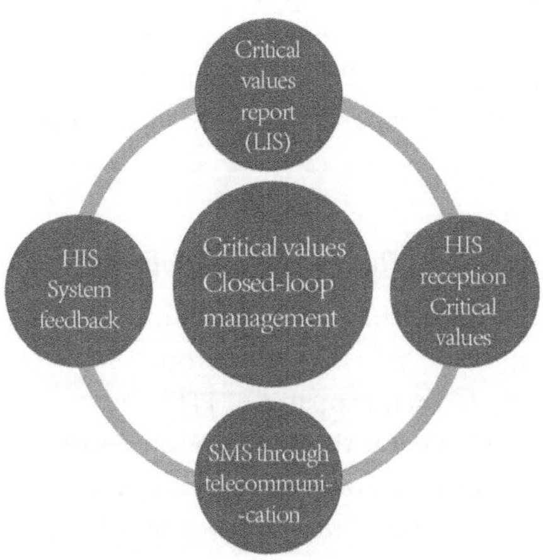

Figure 14.15 Closed loop management of critical value.

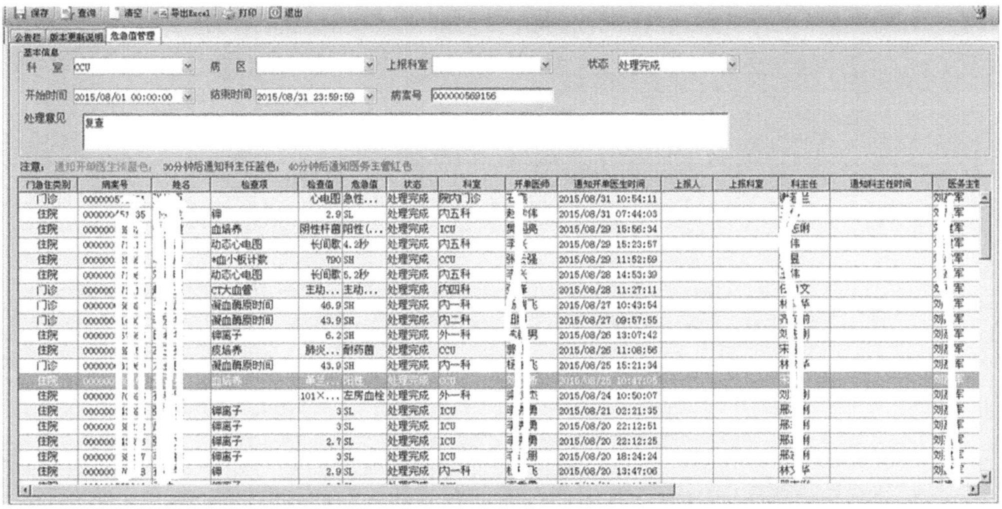

Figure 14.16 Critical value inquiry and handling interface.

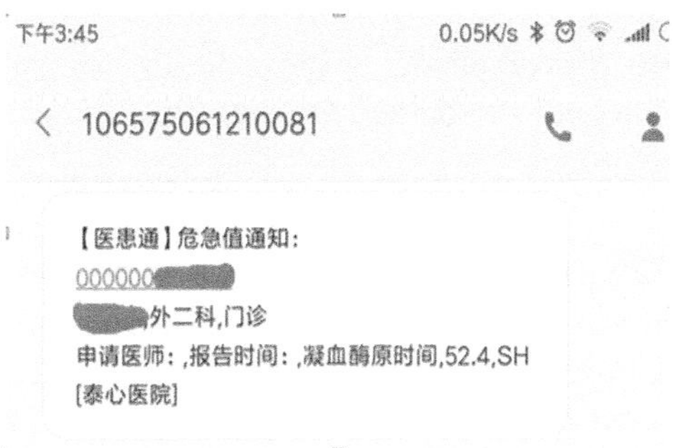

Figure 14.17 Short messaging of critical values.

the communications system. If the physician does not respond within 30 min or confirms in HIS, the system would then send a message to the unit head. The communication would further escalate and notify the director of Medical Education Department at the fortieth minute, and the VP in charge at the fiftieth minute (see Figures 14.16 and 14.17).

Based on that, we fine-tuned the process to ensure faster response to the critical value report on the unit level. We ceilinged the escalation at the level of the director of Medical Education Department to make sure that all the problems are resolved before or at the director level.

We all know that the importance of reporting critical values is to trigger the action taken by the physician to care the patient rather than just communicating this information. Therefore, we require physicians to note down the interventions in HIS as the final step in the closed loop.

After the implementation of the closed loop, the compliance rate increased to above 90% in 2014. The good news is that our physicians can save more time from all the phone calls and critical value documentation. They can go directly in the HIS, take intervention, and chart in the documentation. The Medical Education Department no longer needs to worry about missing information in the report log because each one of the critical values would be documented in HIS. The new system was soon embraced by clinical units and the supervising departments.

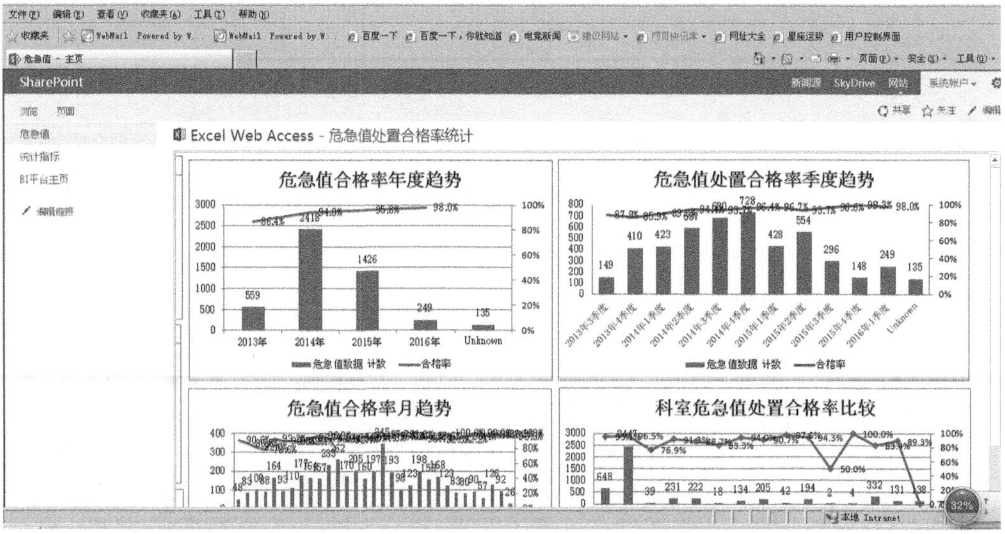

Figure 14.18 BI interface of critical values.

Since the first quarter of 2016, the compliance rate of critical values handling has been maintained above 95%, indicating that the staff's compliance with the hospital procedure as well as the actual practice have been greatly improved.

Critical Value and HIMSS

HIMSS EMRAM Stage 6 requires the hospital utilize the information technology to improve the quality of care. During the validation, we presented the case of our revolution on critical value handling process and achieved positive recognition from the surveyors. After Stage 6, TICH decided to continue the efforts with applying the validation of Stage 7. During the preparation, we established the BI platform and showed to the surveyors all kinds of indicators in the hospital, including the critical value compliance (Figure 14.18). The data were presented from four dimensions (hospital, unit, individual physician, and quarterly data), which covered not only the overall performance but also individual level monitoring. Mr. Wu, as the manager, can access all the information he needs through the HIS interface and BI platform to understand the performance of critical value reporting and handling. This is the best example of utilizing information to support the administrators in the hospital.

The process redesign also reflects the influence brought by JCI and HIMSS, respectively. JCI requires the critical values are communicated in a timely and accurate way to the physicians, but it has no restrictions on the actual solutions. On the other hand, HIMSS encourages hospitals to give a full play of the information technology to realize the purpose, focusing more on the adoption of tools and the concept of closed-loop management. The combination of the two is the best solution for the hospital.

Chapter 15

Guangzhou Women and Children's Medical Center

Xia Huimin, Ding Chunguang, Sun Xin, Wu Weizhe, Cao Xiaojun, Li Lijuan, and Li Minqing
Guangzhou Women and Children's Medical Center

Xia Huimin, *Chief Physician, Professor, and Supervisor of doctoral candidate*

Dr. Xia is the President of Guangzhou Women and Children's Medical Center in his third decade of clinical care and research in pediatric surgery. Over the past 5 years, he has published at least 50 articles in Science Citation-Indexed journals, such as Nature Material, Nature Medicine, *and* Cell, *in addition to more than 10 monographs and textbooks. He has received many awards, such as the Soong Ching Ling Award for Pediatric Medicine from Soong Ching Ling Foundation of China. His innovation in hospital administration and dedication to smart healthcare have yielded HIMSS EMREM Stage 7 for inpatient and outpatient care and many innovative approaches to challenges typically faced by hospitals in China. An example is to initiate trust-based service that allows "seeing doctor before you pay."*

Ding Chunguang, *Senior Economist*

Mr. Ding is the Vice Director of Medical Affairs Department of Guangzhou Women and Children's Medical Center. With degrees in business management, he has worked as an administrator for over 20 years. Mr. Ding has been a champion behind the efforts for accreditation such as JCI, HIMSS, and Tertiary Hospital of China. He is the secretary of Pediatric Quality Control Center of Guangdong Province and Member of Medical Safety and Quality Committee of Guangdong Medical Safety Association. Mr. Ding has published many articles on hospital administration and has co-authored books such as Appraisal Report of Hospitals in China.

Hospital Introduction: Guangzhou Women and Children's Medical Center (hereinafter referred as "GWCMC") was founded in September 2006 based on the merger of the former Guangzhou Children's Hospital and Guangzhou Maternity and Infant Hospital. The hospital covers a land area of 37,425 m^2 with a floor area of nearly 130,000 m^2 to accommodate 1,400 licensed beds.

Currently, there are three National Key Clinical Disciplines approved by the MOH (now called National Health Commission), seven Key Clinical Disciplines and Specialties of Guangdong Province, and two "Twelfth-5 Year Plan" Key Medical Laboratories of Guangdong Province. As a Level-A Tertiary Hospital providing prevention, medical care, health maintenance, research, and education, GWCMC is not only the post-doctoral innovation base of Guangzhou City and Guangdong Province but also serves as the affiliated hospital to Guangzhou Medical University, the teaching hospital affiliated to Sun Yat-sen University, the teaching and practice base of Southern Medical University, and the postgraduate education base of Jinan University. The total outpatient visits of the medical center were 3.76 million in 2016 accompanied with nearly 100,000 discharges and around 60,000 surgeries.

International Accreditation: 2012 and 2015, JCI accreditation and re-accreditation; 2016, HIMSS EMRAM 7.

Contents

Preface

Rebirth from Deep-Rooted Traditions

The story of GWCMC can be dated back to the merge of the two time-honored hospitals.

Guangzhou Children's Hospital was founded on August 1, 1953, formerly known as *Da Paul Hospital*, while Guangzhou Maternity and Infant Hospital was established in 1956. The two hospitals were merged in September, 2006.

However, problems kept emerging after the merger. In particular, after the Zhujiang New Town Campus was open to the public, the issues became even more outstanding: The bumpy outpatient processes, inconsistent policies and treatment criteria, nonuniform care, difficulties in scheduling anesthesiologists, and patient transfers. With the new campus opened in a crowd of high-end offices, the patients would stress more on the quality of care, their own privacy and rights. Underneath the two different ways of operation lies the cultural conflicts between the different facilities. The "three powers" as quoted from LV Hui, Director of HR, were fighting with each other—the staff from the Children's Hospital, the staff from the Women and Neonatology Hospital and the newly enrolled staff for the Zhujiang New Town Campus. Dark clouds were growing up on the leadership.

One day, Dr. Xia Huimin, CEO of GWCMC, noticed that one of their staff was reading a book about international hospital management standards (JCI standards). He thought to himself whether such standards could help to solve our intractable issues. He soon asked the director of the General Affairs Office to search for JCI-related information on the Internet and became the first person in the hospital to learn all those new things. Dr. Xia was convinced that it was something that WE needed after he finished reading through the third edition standards overnight.

At the executive meeting convened in the end of 2009, he proposed to the entire leadership to utilize the JCI accreditation for the delicacy management in the hospital. That idea was applauded on and the hospital officially embarked on the JCI journey. In the next 10 years, GWCMC successfully gained the initial and first triennial accreditation and was validated as HIMSS EMRAM Stage 6 and Stage 7 hospital successively. Ten years on the journey toward international standards is a story full of the wisdom, endeavor, and hard work of all staff of GWCMC and was paid back with well-deserved rewards.

Identify the Gaps and Keep Striving Ahead

Although with thorough preparation, the findings from the first JCI baseline survey made the roller coaster down to the valley: significant gaps were found between GWCMC and the best practices in the world. "Nightmare," "Never," and "Zero" are just a few examples quoted from the consultants' comment on our actual situation back at that time. We were embarrassed by our chaotic environment and messy clinical processes. But that did not prevent us from moving ahead. "Weak foundation is not something we should be afraid of. As long as we could make progress every day, we will be able to catch up!" Dr. Xia made up his mind with no doubt.

"Zero" was the conclusion from the baseline survey in terms of quality improvement. The JCI Office of the hospital invited some quality management experts to education and train the staff on the standards. But most of the trainees fell asleep during the lectures. What was wrong? It turned out that the lecture was too abstract and theoretical for the trainees to understand or to arouse their interest. After rounds of discussion, we decided to try sending champions to be trained under specific topics (e.g., PDCA, QCC, RAC, FMEA) and establishing quality teams to practice in improvement projects. The successful cases were then discussed and shared on the internal training sessions. The training sessions also became more interactive involving dialogs and discussions. Such method achieved positive effects and has been carried on till today.

After the technical challenges had been smoothed out, the next move was to mobilize the staff. We had to leverage the strength from external expertise. The hospital leadership invited a team of experts from Taiwan to assist the improvement. Over 200 projects, small and big, started to gear up the initiative. Ms. Geng Chunhua, CPC Party Secretary of GWCMC, led the supervision team in person to conduct daily checks down to each detail. Ms. Feng Qiong, VP of the hospital, led the logistics team in the hospital with a slogan of "FMS, No Hide-and-Seek!." She toured the hospital every day and talked to the frontline staff. There was once a joke very popular among the hospital staff, saying that "Keep Fire Away, Keep Theft Away and Keep Ms. Jiao (JIAO Yaping, Director of FMS) Away."

From "You Need to" to "I Want to"

A good start did not ensure a smooth journey. We soon reached the bottleneck. Many policies copied from other organizations and advice from the Taiwan team could not be carried through. We were confused by the simple, shallow interpretation of the standards. Was JCI really that unattainable? What a true JCI hospital would look like? Dr. Xia then paid a visit to Jilan Liu, principal JCI consultant, in Seattle when he went there for a conference and toured several hospitals in the U.S. On a weekend, he and Jilan passed by the Seattle Children's Hospital. They decided to take a look but was first refused by the security at the gate. Jilan then showed her JCI consultant badge. And the security guard finally let them go through the door. Dr. Xia was very confused: hospital should be open to everyone; why did they require identification for access? It was his first impression of a JCI hospital that he could never forget afterwards. Later he found out that it was the requirement in the JCI standards: the hospital needs to identify the individuals going in and out of the hospital to ensure a safe and secure environment for the patients, especially in a pediatric hospital. Jilan told Dr. Xia that was what the standards were talking about and the best practice. He brought such concept and practice back to GWCMC. We became the first hospital with security check at the entrance.

"We want practical advices, not empty talk." It became the pet phrase of Dr. Xia. "Practical advice" are the real applicable and proven actions. Till now, "Be Practical" is still part of the culture of the GWCMC.

Jilan Liu then delivered several lectures to explain the JCI standards in our hospital. For example, the JCI standards do not allow bed number to be used as the patient identification. Many staff could not understand the rationale behind this requirement because it was the common practice in Chinese hospitals (even today). Jilan's explanation was that many hospitals made mistakes because of failing to identify patient correctly, and this requirement was to ensure that diagnostic procedure, treatment (medication, surgery, blood transfusion, and others) and other actions were performed on the correct patient. Meanwhile, the standards need to be understood through the perspective of quality and safety. In particular, in the Chinese culture, people would tend to be too rigid to allow flexibility at the frontline, which may harm the progress toward JCI survey.

Jilan and her team, with profound understanding of international standards and rich experience in China's practices, delivered valuable services to the hospital: accurate interpretation, best practices, and zero language barrier. With the guidance from Jilan, the hospital soon formed the consensus on how to pursue further progress. More importantly, the patience of Jilan and her team during the explanation and communication allowed the staff to better understand what should be done and why. We started to realize what would benefit quality and patient safety and what harm would low compliance do to the patients. Jilan told us that JCI standards were reasonable and rational. She said, "If you don't understand the reason behind our recommendation, you just ask us to explain that to you. We will never ask you to do anything that you should not do or cannot do." This actually assured our confidence and willingness to make changes in the hospital with the shared goal among all staff: to ensure patient's safety. Then we started further study of the standards together with Jilan and changed many practices in the hospital through effective communication with the clinical staff. It was surprising that staff began to propose good suggestions instead of keeping JCI away in the past. Since then, we switched from "ordering" to "participating," from "you need to" to "I want to." The pain we had experienced through the journey was finally alleviated. The biggest challenges were in the observation service in ER and the antibiotics stewardship. Dr. Gong Sitang, VP of GWCMC, led the revolution himself and smoothed out the process to reduce excessive observation in ER and antibiotics use in the outpatient setting.

Continuous Improvement with HIMSS

The JCI journey focuses on patient safety and continuous improvement of care. Actually, during the journey, we had a lot of new requests on our IT system but could not realize all of them. The hospital leadership and staff felt that the further development was hindered by the information system. We could not reach our goals with the technology we had in hand at that time. However, the HIT in all hospitals in China was stuck at the bottleneck. We procured all the systems that we could but they were far from satisfying. We were in urgent need of something that we could rely on to break through all these barriers. Then, the news that Peking University People's Hospital and Shengjing Hospital of China Medical University was validated by HIMSS EMRAM Stage 7 traveled across the country and pointed the direction for many hospitals to follow. Maybe that was something that we could rely on to drive the IT development forward.

We started the HIMSS preparation with overtime of the IT staff and barely no clinical participation. Our leaders were worried because of the relaxation of the morale before the true triumph arrived. After the discussion with Jilan, we received the second round of on-site review on behalf of HIMSS Greater China team. The consultant team identified many issues through the on-site review and also provided the interpretation of the standards. Jilan said to us that it was not right to consider HIMSS validation as an IT project. It requires the interoperability within the hospital and across the local community; implementation of closed-loop management concept and decision-making support. To build a digital hospital and smart hospital needs the top-down design from the hospital leadership as well as the bottom-up driving force through advice and suggestions. With the assistant of Jilan and her team, we restructured the organizational structure and management mechanism under which the CEO and CPC Party Secretary were assigned as the major responsible persons and the medical affairs director as the direct coordinator underpinned by extensive clinical participation and IT support. "Closed-loop Groups" were organized to review and redesign the business processes they looked after. They were also responsible for submitting requests and implementing the actions to ensure the clinical and managerial needs were supported by information technology and capability. Each one of the "Closed-loop Groups" consisted of clinical and administrative stakeholders, IT support staff, and representatives and engineers from relevant vendors. Another wave of "mass movement" engulfed GWCMC. We strode forward, convinced, to conquer challenges and gain new progresses.

2016 was important for GWCMC to achieve the HIMSS EMRAM Stage 7. We upgraded, replaced, and optimized many of our systems. Through the close cooperation with the HIMSS consultant team, participation from our frontline staff and the support from our vendors, we worked toward the same goal: to improve our IT capability and clinical adoption maturity and to maximally ensure safety, quality, efficiency as well as the user and patient experience through information technology. It was not easy. But we also had a lot of fun because that was something we were all aiming at and we believed that we were doing what we should do. The cohesion, confidence and resilience of the GWCMC team also blazed our way forward along the HIMSS EMRAM Stage 7 journey. When the HIMSS surveyors announced that we were validated as Stage 7 hospital, the conference hall was filled with excitement.

Knock on Wood! Experience of GWCMC

Ten years of journey following international standards, especially JCI and HIMSS, allows GWCMC to gain a second life after all those efforts and hard work and to sit among the TOP 100 Hospital in China. Day by day, we kept making progress at our pace and finally realized the qualitative change. Such transition would not be possible without the guidance of the international benchmark of hospital management. If you want to be the best, then you need to follow the world-class practices. And GWCMC made it! The secret of our success could be summarized into the following aspects.

Good Understanding of Standards

Survey is based on the accreditation and validation standards. Thus, it's important to start from the standards. Accurate interpretation of the standards is of utmost importance. The core of the standards lies in patient safety and care quality. With HIMSS, it adds efficiency and efficacy, in particular the experience of the system users and patients, on top of quality and safety. The intention, glossary, and even the references of the standards could serve as powerful tools for thorough comprehension. Different cultures and the Chinese translation could lead to misinterpretation of the standards. In such circumstances, opinions and experience from experts could be valuable. This also gives rise to another challenge—how to select the right consultants for your hospital.

A good guidance from the right people could save us a lot of mistakes, and thus time, resources and efforts, and strengthen our confidence. One thing is worthy of remembering: Do not expect each one of your staff to fully understand the standards. It would be much easier to allow chapter champions and coordinators to attend the training first and turn the standards into policies and procedures. The rest of the staff could just be trained on the developed policies and procedures and implement them.

Planning and Task Assignment

This is the basic competence required in managerial expertise. It is also the key during the preparation. A good plan could ensure efficient monitoring on and successful roll-out of the project, and a reasonable goal could serve as the shared and pressing mission that everyone would love to make their due contribution. Clear identification of roles and responsibilities enables transparent and organized project process through well-defined tasks and time frame. Of course, communication exists through the entire project for necessary cooperation and coordination among different stakeholders. GWCMC set up specific cross-department coordination mechanism and designated chapter champions and "closed-loop" responsible persons, which was specifically defined in the policies.

Modification of Policies and Procedures (P&Ps)

This is the foundation for all accreditation and validation as well as the first challenge. During the initial stage, GWCMC made detours because of insufficient understanding of the standards. We copied the P&Ps from other hospitals and applied in our organization directly. It resulted in our initial failure in implementing part of the P&Ps. For example, we adopted the evaluation forms from other hospitals and asked our nurses to use them. They were very reluctant to do that and started to doubt what we were doing. It was OK to refer to the practices in other hospitals, but to fit the reality of your own hospital is the key. Thus, GWCMC developed the "policy of policy" to regular the drafting, reviewing, approving and releasing process of P&Ps. Any P&P needs to be submitted to the hospital executive meeting for review and approval after thorough discussion by relevant clinical units and administrative departments. Only after the approval could the P&P be released followed by regular review and revision.

Training and Drill

It could be a daunting task to train the staff and educate them how to actually put those words in their actions. GWCMC has an average annual OPD visits at 4 million. It is very challenging to ensure the effectiveness of training under such work load. So, we decided to adopt the coordinator mechanism. Each one of the units assigned a senior resident or attending physician as the coordinator who participated the training session on the afternoon of every Wednesday (4:00–6:00 pm). The coordinators would then be responsible for training the staff in his/her own department. Meanwhile, drills were performed to test on some contingency plans. The hospital leaders would trigger the response process without any notice to check the effectiveness of the actions. This has become a routine practice in GWCMC today. To summarize the key points of the policies, we compiled the

"Know-how and Action," a staff education brochure. We also launched the online testing program requiring all the staff to pass the test as the prerequisite for their monthly salary. There was no limit on the number of times one could take the test because learning rather than punishment was the purpose of the tests.

Supervision and Evaluation

It is always easier to say something than to get things done properly. "The compliance of people's action with the hospital P&Ps should be higher than the compliance of hospital's P&Ps with the standards," said one JCI consultant. A supervision team was set up to ensure the execution of the policies and procedures. The team concluded two types of members: the chapter champions and coordinators responsible for supervising the implementation of respective chapters; and special supervising members for simple but hard-to-be-implemented tasks, such as work badge and smoking control. Led by the hospital leaders, the team started weekly checks from which the results were linked to the KPI evaluation of each unit. That was the guarantee of sufficient implementation of our new P&Ps following the JCI standards.

Splendid Rebirth

On our journey in the past 10 years, JCI made us know what we should do, while HIMSS enabled us to do the things in a better way. Patient-centric quality improvement always lies in the heart of a hospital. GWCMC would love to share our experience with our peers to make due contribution to the Healthy China strategy. HIMSS and JCI are like two shining stars in a night sky, leading our path ahead.

Based on our experience in adopting best practices, we have published several books to share our hospital managerial expertise, clinical pathways, and treatment processes of common diseases, such as *Hospital Delicacy Management (Series)*, and *Treatment Process of Common Diseases of Pediatric Internal Medicine, Pediatric Surgery, and Obstetrics/Gynecology*.

According to HIMSS and JCI requirements, we adopted medical record templates; standardized format of data, data sets and files; and clinical data repository (CDR) for data analytics and data mining based on the structured electronic medical record. Leveraging the big data technology, we have developed "Dr. Bear," an intelligent diagnosis and treatment tool, to provide solutions based on the capability of "big data + cognitive computing." We have also set up the disease diagnostic model supported by the EMR and evidence-based medical practice. The model could provide clinical decision support to improve physician's efficiency and diagnostic accuracy through word segmentation and lexical analysis acquired from deep machine learning and training on high-quality EMR. It is called the natural language processing, allowing the system to give suggestions on possible clinical diagnosis of different stage of diseases and provide reference information from other similar cases, tests, and treatment protocols.

We selected 25 diagnoses for cohort studies based on the structured EMR to find the best solutions for treatment and to get closer to the high-level precision medicine techniques and competence. National key laboratories have been erected in our hospital with the power of big data, and the Precision Medicine and Translational Medicine Center as well as the Big Data Center are under construction. Combined with the cohort study, we will be able to transform GWCMC into a research-based hospital.

Case 1: Let's Talk about Medication Management

A New Role Defined: JCI Chapter Coordinator

I knew the hospital was preparing for the JCI survey, but I felt that it was not my business. On morning, when I just finished dispensing the first batch of long-term orders from the pharmacy and was ready to review the new orders from the wards, my cell phone rang. My boss was on the other side, sounding like that he was in good mood, "Weizhe, the hospital is going to take the JCI accreditation. The leaders required each unit to recommend a person who is experienced, knowledgeable, and familiar with the business to be the coordinator. You used to work in the Youth League of the hospital, good at learning, communicating, and organizing. How about signing you in? It's a very good opportunity. You can also have more chances to learn and practice your English. I heard that the hospital also had special subsidies for the coordinators!" "Ok, Boss. Well..." Before I could ask about what a coordinator's job was, my boss hung up the phone. It sounded like a cushy job to me at that time.

"All Those Things Related to Medication Are on You." That was My Assignment

The first thing was to attend the JCI meeting. I entered the room packed with another ten staff. They were all directors and coordinators from other departments, medical affairs, nursing, infection control, logistics, human resources, and IT. As soon as I sat down together with my boss, Dr. Xia and Dr. Zhang, Director of Hospital General Affairs Office, came into the room. "We are going to assign the tasks today. Each one of you will be accountable for different chapters. All those standards containing the word 'medication' and those related to medication are on you," CEO pointed at me and my boss. "Go back and read the standards. Find the gaps and report to the group on the next meeting," my boss whispered to me immediately.

I then went back to my office, started to read the heavy JCI standard manual page by page in both Chinese and English. "It was INDEED a good chance to practice my English!" What a sarcasm!

There are two chapters involving medication. One is the IPSG Chapter (IPSG 1.3 high-alert medication management), and the other is the MMU Chapter. The standards and measurable elements looked cold and dead to me with very limited explanation and no examples. To be honest, it did not talk in human language, at least to me. "Hospital has process to prevent the incidence of medication errors"; "...stored in a way that facilitates safe use"; "...the review on the medication management system." What did all those sentences mean? I went through the entire book and did not find one sentence telling me exactly what to do.

After several training sessions, we still found the standards too vague for us to fully understand. "Are we really going to do this?" I thought to myself. The standards were too unrealistic to be down-to-earth.

MMU = A Big Loop

After rounds of trainings, especially through the interpretation by Jilan and her team, we started to understand the JCI standards. Jilan said that medication management was not only the business of the pharmacy but a process involving all the staff on each step of the drug flow, including healthcare staff, hospital leadership, and even patients' families. The medication management system and procedure support the patients' medication therapies, which require the efforts and coordination among multiple disciplines, established principles and effective processes to improve the selection, storage, prescribing, transcribing, mixing, dispensing, preparation, and monitoring.

The hospital needs to evaluate the safety, effectiveness and cost-efficiency of each type of drugs through monitoring, and the results should further influence the modification to the hospital formulary. This is the big loop of medication management. The entire medication management process is for patients and their safety. That means we need to go hand-in-hand with different departments from the arrival of drugs at the hospital to the bedside administration. It goes beyond merely the chores inside the pharmacy like procurement and dispensing. As required by JCI standards, pharmacists are no longer the keeper of the drugs, but the professionals who provide patient-centric pharmacology services, manage all drugs inside the hospital, and facilitator of quality and services. This is what JCI looks for.

Policies Are Rules

Medication, though, is mainly under the responsibility of the Pharmacy, the P&Ps involving medications cover the entire operation surrounding drugs and many other jobs and roles outside the pharmacy. Therefore, we invited all stakeholders to participate in the P&P drafting. For example, the Nursing Department staff and head nurses were invited to participate in drafting the *Procedure of Medication Use* to make sure that it followed JCI standards and could be implemented in the actual day-to-day work. We also translated the approved polices into concise job-related processes to further define who, when, where, and how. If there was any problem during the trial, relevant chapter coordinator would contact us and then help us to modify the procedure.

Medication Management Is Everybody's Business

Before the baseline, we went to the wards to check their stock medications and found that all of them were filled with the odor of drugs. Unlocked medication room, cabinet packed with base solutions, and different drugs put in the same baskets... These were just a few examples. In one unit, we saw two nurses busy with mixing the STAT medications ordered by the physicians. One nurse picked up one vial of drug from a basket and planned to mix it with the base solution. Right before the needle penetrated into the vial, she suddenly stopped because she found that she picked up the wrong medication. So, she quickly found the correct one in the basket, and then injected the base solution, drew the mixed medication into the syringe and threw the bottle away. At that time, a patient's family came to her and said, "My child is not feeling well." The nurse responded, "I'll be there right away.," while putting the cap back onto the syringe. I was quite confident that nobody would have noticed me if I took the drug away from the treatment cart.

I frowned at the unsafe process with all those chaotically scattered drugs, zero access control, and unlabeled syringes. When the nurse came back from the child, I said to her that drugs needed to be kept safe, and the practice was too dangerous. The nurse said: "I know. But we were too busy. All the meds on the unit could be used up just within a second. We do not have time for tidying up. What about you giving us a pharmacist to manage all the meds for us? We were told that the pharmacy would be on everything related to meds, didn't they?" I was so embarrassed. Where could we find so many pharmacists all those clinical units in three campuses? But we could not give up. We had to let them know that medication management was not the job of pharmacists, and it was the business of every healthcare staff and administrator in the hospital.

"Sending Out" Pharmacists and "Getting Back" the Drugs

The hospital leadership was also aware of the storage issue. But we had a PIVAS for infusion medications in operation. Then why there were so many stock medications on the units? How could we solve the problem? To streamline the process and lower the risks was an urgent task on all of us.

We soon organized a discussion with the staff from medical affairs, pharmacy, nursing, IT, and FMS to analyze the work flow and process. We realized that for the existing long-term inpatient IV orders, they were sent to the PIVAS for verification during the working hours, mixed by the PIVAS and dispensed to the units as "ready to administer." But for newly prescribed long-term orders and STAT orders, they were picked up by the ward nurses from the Inpatient Pharmacy with a master list of physician's medication orders, which would then be prepared and given by the nurses on the unit. This part of orders was not reviewed for appropriateness by a pharmacist before it was used on a patient. Some units adopted the solution of high-volume stock because they worried that the medication could not be picked up from the pharmacy quickly enough to ensure timely administration. Such practice might lead to nonuniform service and even medication loss, error and other issues threatening patient safety.

Thus, we decided to redesign the IV medication flow for inpatients. The PIVAS started to run around the clock to prepare all the long-term and STAT orders for all inpatients to further ensure safe medication use. Due to the complicated process inside PIVAS, the timeliness needs to be compromised. So, the resuscitation and emergency medication orders are not covered by PIVAS. We agreed with the medical affairs and nursing managers that all the medication required be ready within 2 h would be considered as STAT and were allowed to skip the PIVAS. For that part of orders, we set up the minimum stock medication mechanism to meet the clinical needs. The method was then piloted in two units for 1 month and the results were openly published in the hospital. Then we moved on to implement the new mechanism in the other campuses. Feedback were collected and each step of handovers was documented to help us further cut down the delivery time and ensure the quality of medication. The Pharmacy also organized a clinical pharmacist team and a medication quality management team to send out the pharmacists to the wards to learn about the situations and challenges they had faced, educate on the unit staff on appropriate medication use and prescription, assist the management of the minimum stock quantity and the storage, and regularly check on the management and use of drugs on the units.

Through the communication and coordination among different units and departments as well as continuous improvement of the processes, we finally came up with a standardized process across the three facilities and became the first hospital in China to provide 24/7 PIVAS service for three campuses for long-term, STAT and OPD & ED IV orders. Thanks to the PIVAS services, the units now can totally run on the drugs in their crash carts and the minimum stock medications for emergency use. This helped us to reduce 95% of stock medications on the unit and make the medication management process much simpler for the pharmacy.

At the beginning, head nurses refused to return those stock medications to the Pharmacy because they would feel uncomfortable if the medications were not readily available. But my boss demanded, "I need all meds back to my Pharmacy!" The Pharmacy staff wheeled the carts to the units and "took over" the medications "illegally kept" by the staff outside the minimum stock list. But the fact proved that we had released the unnecessary burden on the head nurses. "*The Pharmacy is awesome!* I don't want the medications back to my own unit anymore!" That was the comment from one of our nurses.

The Legendary HIMSS EMRAM Stage 7

The longest journey I've ever decided to take must be the endless accreditation journeys. Isn't that true? Right after GWCMC was successfully accredited by JCI in the triennial survey and the national hospital accreditation program, we did not even have the chance to take a deep breath before we continued with the next goal: HIMSS EMRAM Stage 7, the highest level of the model.

"What is HIMSS EMRAM 7?" "Is it about IT? Electronic Medical Record?" "What does it have to do with our Pharmacy?" "*What is H-I-M-S-S 7? Just don't mess me up.*" "I hope it won't make me lose another 10 kg as JCI did...."

Suddenly, all staff were talking about the new thing when the hospital's decision was made and announced aloud.

Since I was the JCI coordinator, I soon received the materials related to HIMSS EMRAM Stage 7 validation. If JCI was confusing, HIMSS criteria were even worse. All requirements were stated on just a few pages with all the abbreviations meaning nothing to me: EMR, ETL, GPO, UHC, CCR, CCDA, HIT, CPOE, BCE.... The information about pharmacy was just a one-page thing. "Read the documents carefully and see what we should do," ordered my boss, "Just one page? Lucky me!" I said with a smile. Though I did not know what to do, I was convinced that one page would never get worse than JCI with a manual of hundreds of pages.

But the criteria proved me too optimistic.

HIMSS EMRAM Stage 7 stresses on closed-loop management, adoption of information technology, and paperless environment through combining clinical care with artificial intelligence. The requirements on pharmacy are to utilize technology to support the safe medication use process and improve the safety, quality, and efficiency of the hospital services. The data of the entire process need to be documented electronically and be used for clinical decision support through analysis and summarization to serve as the reference for medication management decisions. The one-page statements cover all aspects of medication treatment and care system in the hospital.

What Is Closed-Loop Medication Management?

Safe medication use is one of the key focuses of hospital quality management. It means that right medication is given to the right patient with the right dose at the right time via the right route—the Five-Rights Principle.

After two rounds of JCI surveys, this was not very difficult for us. JCI standards provide the guidance on safe management and use of medication. It concerns the correct types, quantity, and quality of medications throughout the entire process, starting from the supply chain and the storage in the pharmacy to the dispensing process and bedside administration. The analysis of the quality, effectiveness, and adverse reaction of the medications would again influence the decisions on the next procurement. Every step is linked to another seamlessly to from the "closed-loop." In the big loop process, there lie various sub-processes, which we would call them the small loops connected to each other. Standardized dispensing and administration processes supported by information technology could reduce man-made errors to the largest extend. This is what HIMSS wants for the "closed-loop medication management" to ensure safety.

How Many Loops Do We Need?

HIMSS EMRAM Stage 7 requires hospital to fully implement closed-loop medication management supported by barcoding technology starting from the very beginning of physician's ordering. Patient's information is then communicated through the regional HIE capability to complete medication reconciliation including the medication taken by the patient before admission. Physician uses CPOE to order the medication while being supported by clinical decision support system which could provide initial screening of the order to block any order that might cause allergy and overdosing of the patient or that is not allowed to be used on the patient; or remind the physician on proper dosage, route, and drug-drug interaction. Then all the verified orders would reach the pharmacists for further verification. The mixing, administration, and bedside identification are supported by barcode scanning technology. The entire medication use process needs to be documented in the electronic system to trace any possible issue to avoid man-made medication errors. The tracing capability and the documentation and analysis of data realized by IT technology become a strong evidence for treatment and diagnosis. Closed-loop medication management fully supported by technology is one of the key focus areas of HIMSS EMRAM Stage 7 as well as an important symbol of intelligent medication management and a digital hospital.

There are many steps on the loop, but it can be divided into two main parts.

1. Logistics closed-loop to ensure correct types and quantity of drugs

   It could be regarded as an extended supply chain. The logistics supply chain system (procurement, delivery, warehousing, shelving, and dispensing) should be seamlessly integrated to the systems in the pharmacy (automatic dispenser, smart drug cabinet on wards, PIVAS system, etc.) to complete the smart management and dispensing of medication to specific patient or unit. Each step involved is performed with barcode scanning to ensure correct types, quantity, and quality. During the dispensing, the accounting and inventory system of the warehouse needs to be updated to reflect the latest status of the medications. Assisted by IT technology, it should be possible to trace back to the patient for a specific lot of products to identify near misses and patient tracing. This also contributes to improving efficiency and accuracy, saving pharmacists from heavy work load to focus their energy to the appropriateness review.
2. Order closed-loop

   This loop starts from the action of ordering a medication in the system by a physician, goes further through pharmacist review for appropriateness, mixing, dispensing, and ends at the bedside administration. Each step during dispensing, transportation, and actual administration needs to be secured by barcode scanning process. If the barcode does not match the existing information in the system, then the process would be suspended to make sure the correct, transparent, and traceable medication use.

Billing after the Second-Line Verification

In the order closed-loop, the second-line verification (appropriateness review) plays a significant role. The decision support knowledge base is the foundation of verification software that could efficiently screen all the orders and send alerts to pharmacists so as to reduce errors made by the physicians.

In China, most hospitals would purchase the software knowledge base and clinical decision support system directly from a vendor. But as a hospital specialized in women and children's care, no knowledge base product available on the market provides complete functions that we look for. For example, weigh-based dosing or BSA-based dosing calculation is a common practice for pediatric patients, but the existing products did not recommend the individualized proper dosing range for physicians or pharmacists through automatic calculation. They also failed to trigger alerts on inappropriate dosing. Some knowledge base was not built on our hospital's formulary and might cover tens of thousands of drugs, which could cause longer waiting time while doing the checks. What we were looking for were ways to develop a knowledge base covering only the medications on our formulary and supported by allergy checks, pediatric dosing range reminder, special reminders on gestation and lactation status and reminders on kidney and liver function checks to meet the clinical needs and provide rudimentary individualized medication services. Therefore, to develop a second-line verification software specialized for women and children patients was added to our schedule of system integration and closed-loop medication management.

The clinical pharmacists set up the knowledge covering our own formulary based on the HIMSS criteria, manufacturers' instructions and well-recognized guidelines and worked with the software vendor to co-develop the module for our IT system. With the new software, we are able to give a hard stop on medication orders that could never be approved, and reminders on dosing and special population. In addition, we also enabled the real-time communication between the pharmacists and prescribing physicians. If the pharmacist found any order inappropriate, he/she could communicate with the prescribing physician in a timely and precise manner. The new communication capability eliminated the opportunities when patients might need to tell the physicians what was going on with a misinterpreted message.

Currently, the process of dispensing medication in most of Chinese hospitals follows this sequence: prescribing—billing—payment—second-line verification—dispensing—pickup by patient. Many pharmacists would verify the appropriateness of medication orders while dispensing the drug which is highly subject to personal and environmental factors. If a piece of order is rejected, the prescribing physician would need to invalid the order followed by refunding and re-ordering. This complicated process has caused loads of labor and medical disputes.

If we move the second-line verification before the billing and payment, the refund and extra labor could be saved. It can also ensure the full implementation of safety and appropriateness check. As the government released the policy to encourage the independent pharmacies outside hospitals, the patient could be assured that the prescriptions are reviewed by the pharmacist and are safe even if they get the medications from other pharmacies.

GWCMC was the first hospital in South China to fully implement the model of "verification before payment" in the outpatient setting in August 2016. That is exactly the process we want in our hospital for smooth, efficient operation, and for patient safety.

Case 2: One-Stop Service for Obstetrics Clinic

Ms. Zhang was a frequent visitor to the OB clinic of GWCMC from her first pregnancy to her second baby. She told us that compared with the time when she was carrying her first baby, there were more pregnant patients, longer waiting time, and shorter temper even though she was seeing the same doctor in the same place.

As the second-child policy was released to balance the population growth, more families are joining in the "two-children family" club. GWCMC, the first stop of many newborns in this world, is the first place to be hit by the policy. The patient volume increase was "explosive": the outpatient registered an annual pregnancy visits at 161,000, an increase by 13.7% from 2015. Behind the "explosive" scene, the limited space and service processes in the outpatient clinics was significantly challenged by the sudden increase of patients, resulting in much longer waiting time.

How could we improve our efficiency while ensuring quality and safety? Taking the opportunity of HIMSS validation, we set up the Obstetrics Integration Team.

The team reviewed the OB clinic process and brainstormed on possible issues and identified issues through the weekly meetings. Manual calculation and system-assistant calculation, on-site review and interview with pregnant patients… they tried all methods they had to obtain the first-hand data. Soon the team realized the difficulties that the patients were experiencing: the relatively separate steps such as setting up new patient's file, taking vital signs, check-in at nurse station and waiting for visit caused much waiting and queuing time. Repeated queuing and waiting were forced due to lack of an integrated patient flow.

As indicated in Table 15.1, the waiting time before patient check-in at the nurse station took up almost 70% of the total waiting time. Therefore, the team decided to reduce the queuing time for the patients.

HIMSS O-EMRAM Stage 7 focuses on the process improvement and redesign in the outpatient setting to achieve interoperability and optimized processes through technology capability. Thus, the team mapped out a fish-bone chart (see Figure 15.1) to describe the major issues based on their survey and quickly developed the improvement plans to rectify the processes regarding the check-in, human resources, information sharing, location layout of examinations and education (see Table 15.2 for solutions).

Table 15.1 Waiting Time of OB Clinic Patients

No.	*Step*	*Waiting Time (min)*	*Calculation Method*
1	Setting up patient file	25	Manual calculation
2	Examination	10	Manual calculation
3	Nurse station	13	Manual calculation
4	Consultation	21	System calculation

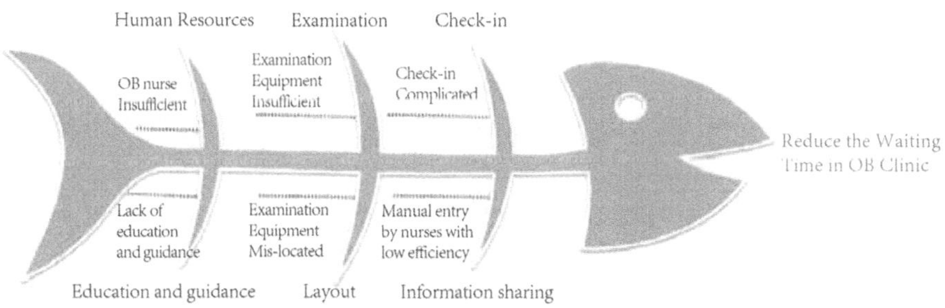

Figure 15.1 Fish-bone chart.

Table 15.2 Current Status and Solutions

No.	*Reality*	*Solution*
1	Complicated check-in process in OB clinic	Use IoT + Internet technology to streamline the check-in process, reduce human resources input and realize interoperability
2	Insufficient OB nurses	
3	Low level of information sharing and manual entry of vital signs	
4	Poor layout of equipment locations	Redesign the locations of different types of equipment
5	Inadequate education and guidance	Enhance education and guidance

Though with the fish-bone chart and improvement plans in place, it was still far from the goal because of all the difficulties during implementation. The most challenging and complained part was the repeated queuing of patients from which the team decided to show the effects of improvement to the frontline staff as well as the patients. They then started to work with the self-service equipment vendor to design and developed the one-stop OB clinic self-service system, combining blood pressure, high and weight and other functions. Linked to the hospital Wechat account, the equipment is able to "read" the patient's identity via barcode or QR code, patient's card or patient's card ID, and then take the patient's vitals. The equipment is put in the self-service area. All patients can use their card or the barcode on the medical record book to get their height, weight and blood pressure documented and transferred, in real time, to the hospital HIS. When the physician sees the patient, he/she could read these data in the EMR.

This high-tech solution integrating the vital-taking and the nurse station check-in together, soon gained its popularity among the mothers. Ms. Zhang also came to the hospital to experience the "high-tech," which, as she described, totally changed the patient experience in the hospital!

Patients could also make appointment through their smart phone. For the initial visit, the IT system would push the personal information registration page to the patient (see Figure 15.2) to allow them finish all the information before they come to the hospital. Upon the actual visit, they only need to verify the information in the registration office. Small as the change might be, it indeed improved the efficiency of nurses to register information with the help of the patients.

Another important criterion of HIMSS O-EMRAM Stage 7 is the paperless environment. The hospital needs to digitalize the care process based on the integration of all silos and information sharing of the complete electronic medical record of patients.

The vital signs measured by the self-service equipment are synchronized to the check-in and scheduling system to save the repeated queuing of patients at the nurse station. The vitals are also shared with other information systems including EMR and Wechat account (see Figure 15.3).

Figure 15.2 Self-service for patient file registration.

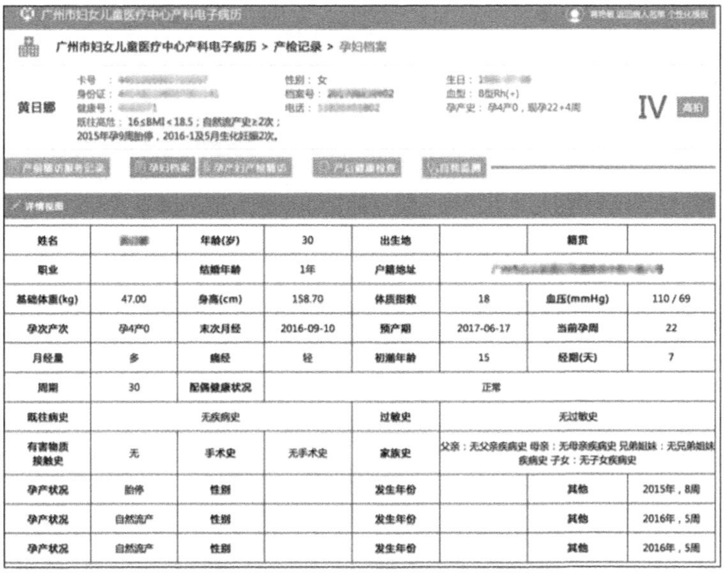

广州市妇女儿童医疗中心产科电子病历 > 产检记录 > 孕妇档案

黄日娜 卡号： 身份证： 健康号：
性别：女 档案号： 电话：
生日： 血型：B型Rh(+) 孕产史：孕4产0，现孕22+4周
IV
既往高危：16≤BMI<18.5；自然流产史≥2次；
2015年孕9周胎停，2016-1及5月生化妊娠2次。

姓名		年龄(岁)	30	出生地		籍贯	
职业		结婚年龄	1年	户籍地址			
基础体重(kg)	47.00	身高(cm)	158.70	体质指数	18	血压(mmHg)	110 / 69
孕次产次	孕4产0	末次月经	2016-09-10	预产期	2017-06-17	当前孕周	22
月经量	多	痛经	轻	初潮年龄	15	经期(天)	7
周期	30	配偶健康状况	正常				
既往病史	无疾病史			过敏史	无过敏史		
有害物质接触史	无	手术史	无手术史	家族史	父亲：无父亲疾病史 母亲：无母亲疾病史 兄弟姐妹：无兄弟姐妹疾病史 子女：无子女疾病史		
孕产状况	胎停	性别		发生年份		其他	2015年，8周
孕产状况	自然流产	性别		发生年份		其他	2016年，5周
孕产状况	自然流产	性别		发生年份		其他	2016年，5周

Figure 15.3 EMR in OB clinic.

In this way, one entry could be used in multiple places to reduce extra entries by physicians and nurses, which is the essence of HIMSS criteria.

We realized paperless operation of the care flow before face-to-face consultation at the beginning of the project. But soon the team found that the follow-up activities still lagged behind since the nurses were documenting the phone calls manually on paper. Another meeting was then arranged to discuss the digitalization of the patient education and follow-up process to close the loop covering activities before, during, and after a clinic visit.

The follow-up system was completed within 1 month with the support from the IT department. Through the system, related education and survey can be sent to the patients based on the follow-up information to realize post-visit management. The healthcare staff can use the education templates in the system to set reminders for patients on regular check-up, follow-up, medication use, discharge education, and activities to realize automatic education. Meanwhile, the system also supports template editing. That means pictures, videos, website links, and other kinds of contents can be added to the system with edited texts and formats.

The online follow-up and education significantly improved staff's efficiency. But the team discovered that few patients and their families would complete all the pushed contents and the follow-up survey. The team then thought of an idea to improve the compliance rate of the patients and families. A pop-up window of a follow-up survey while the user is approaching the key parts of the education material, and it would not disappear and allow continuous reading unless the user finish the forms. It did work as the completion rate of the follow-up survey increased from 30% to 74%.

But the patients were not content with the closed loop: would it be possible to perform measuring and monitoring on the patient's condition at home through utilizing the strength of IoT? It was a really good idea because it actually was an extension of the care of the organization by using terminal devices to monitor the patients, especially to collect data on patients at high risks. They would be able to document their personal health data with the APP set up on the mobile terminals through blue tooth transmission of smart devices or manual entries. After the information is uploaded to the system, healthcare staff then can access the data through PC or APP on the staff terminals inside the hospital. With upper/lower limits set in the system, staff can also receive automatic alerts on abnormal data uploaded by the patients with preset contents, which would automatically kick in the follow-up process of the abnormality in the system. Doctors and nurses could also check on the patient's status and provide monitoring and management of patient's health.

This "para-natal healthcare maintenance" feature extends the loop to include "home care" as the last piece! The team also improved the location layout of all measuring devices and examination equipment in the clinic environment, expanded the room for examinations and added extra equipment (see Figure 15.4). In addition, guidance brochures and *guidance board* of the clinic visit process were made available to provide clear instruction on the newly implemented process for patients.

After 3 months of efforts, the Obstetrics Clinic was reborn with a brand-new look, more efficient staff, and more satisfied patients. With the one-stop self-service platform in place for Obstetrics Clinic, patients can complete their personal profile online before their visits, which cut the waiting time from 20 to 15 min. As the efficiency went up, the hospital now is able to register 70 new patients compared with 50 in the past. On the patient's side, now they spend 28 min less than before (nearly a cut-down of 40%) (see Table 15.3). The hospital receives 161,000 visits for pre-natal check-up every year. That means, in total, we could help patients to save 75,133 h (161,000 × 28/60 = 75,133). Meanwhile, the patient's satisfaction rate increased from 68.7% to 81.3%.

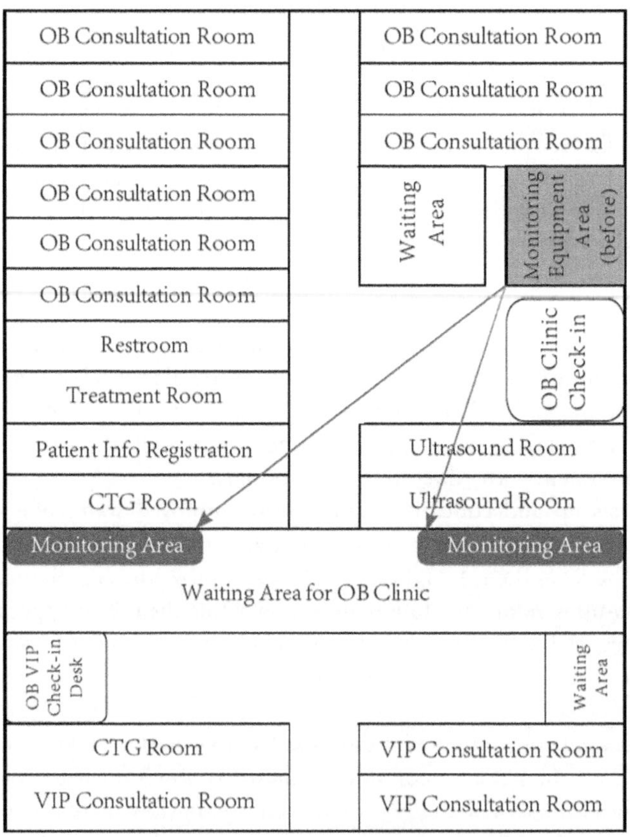

Figure 15.4 Adjustment of monitoring equipment layout.

Table 15.3 Comparison of Waiting Time

Step	*Before (min)*	*After (min)*	*Calculation Method*
Setting up patient file	25	20	Manual calculation
Examination	10	5	Manual calculation
Nurse station	13	0	System calculation
Consultation	21	16	System calculation
Total	69	41	

Case 3: Disease Management: Here Comes Dr. Bear!

One day, a 3-year-old boy started to complain pain in throat with coughing, running nose, sudden fever, and herpes on hands. His teacher immediately sent him to the Infirmary of the kindergarten. The clinician's first impression was normal upper respiratory tract infection. But there were also possibilities of infectious diseases such as hand-food-mouth disease and chicken pox, which might be a threat to the health of other kids. They decided to bring the child to our hospital.

At the triage desk, the nurse entered the symptoms of the child into the system with the support of "Dr. Bear" (an intelligent diagnosis and treatment assistant system for pediatrics): fever, herpes on hands, pain in through, coughing… The suggested diagnosis by "Dr. Bear" was "hand-food-mouth disease," and a visit to the Infectious Disease Clinic was recommended.

It might sound magic. As a matter of fact, "Dr. Bear" is based on the artificial intelligence technology to provide initial diagnosis suggestions to the healthcare staff built on clinical guidance, professional consensus, and medical literature with the support of a huge clinical medical record database. It is designed mainly for the common pediatric diseases such as cold (upper respiratory tract infection), isthmitis, hand-food-mouth disease, and pneumonia. Highly integrated in physician's work flow, "Dr. Bear" could propose follow-up questions on certain entries, suggest possible diagnosis with a sequence, recommend similar medical cases, and continuously enhance its capability with the feedback-and-self-correction mechanism through improving its own algorithm.

Ten years of efforts of GWCMC nurtured and gave birth to the new life—Dr. Bear.

Hospital-Wide Standardized Care Required by JCI

The story started with the standardization of care in the hospital.

Pediatric patients are special population requiring high level of professionalism and rich clinical experience of healthcare staff to give diagnosis and deliver care. However, insufficient experience might result in misdiagnosis, under-diagnosis, incorrect care process and under-standardized practice, bringing unnecessary harm to children physically and psychologically. It is important to standardize all physicians' practice and ensure the same-level of quality, in particular to support the young physicians with less clinical experience. The leadership of GWCMC designated the Medical Affairs Department to organize the clinical care protocols for common diagnosis in different units together with the directors and key staff of each unit.

The first version of our protocols was developed based on the well-accepted clinical protocols and was released in June 2012. These protocols described the basic definitions, clinical symptoms, required examinations, diagnosis, and treatment protocols for common diseases. Frontier information from home and abroad was absorbed; well-established protocols and guidelines were quoted; and experience and research achievements of each units through long time practicing were adopted. But our frontline staff found it not practical because the protocols focused more on theoretical education.

In August 2012, the Medical Affairs Department released an announcement to call for requests from first-line physicians based on which discussion was organized among experts. The following contents were added to the protocols: (1) controlling process on the key steps that might be overlooked during daily work was added to the general clinical care protocol contents, including the standard outpatient/ER/inpatient diagnosis flowchart (describing the care process and major treatment points), triage guidance (clear description of responsible physician level corresponding with acuity), admission criteria, indications for special criticality (clear description of identifying criticality), consultation criteria, discharge criteria and key conversation points; (2) based on the acute onset and atypical symptoms of pediatric patients, the diagnosis and treatment protocols for common symptoms based on the physical signs and common symptoms of pediatrics were included, covering 10 symptoms such as diarrhea, fever, vomiting and jaundice; and (3) we integrated the JCI standards into the diagnosis and treatment and added the critical value reporting and handling process for lab tests, PICU admission, and discharge criteria, ER triage guidance, and nutrition and pain assessment tools.

Patient-Engagement-Based Clinical Pathways for Both Physicians and Nurses

JCI requires that patients and families are engaged in hospital management. Our new operation model is possible to realize this goal. It defines the rights and obligations of both hospital and patients, and gives patients the opportunity to give feedback on the hospital management. The mutually beneficial "collaboration" between the hospital and patients has laid down solid foundation for the good relationship between the hospital and patients as well as for the improved quality of care.

Patients and their families should not be the outsider. Instead, everyone has his/her part to play.

Through the integration of the clinical guidelines and treatment processes in the information system, and following the HIMSS requirement on intelligent closed-loop management for realizing correct, standardized and convenient care flow, GWCMC developed the clinical pathway management system covering medical, nursing and patients' activities. The diagnosis-based clinical pathway system covers both inpatient and outpatient care and is supported by multiple intelligent reminding and controlling functions to ensure the standardized practice on enrolled patients and ensure safe practice.

When a patient comes for clinic visit or admission, the physician could go to the diagnosis entry interface where the system would recommend relevant clinical pathway based on the ICD-10 code of the primary diagnosis entered by the physician. The physician is able to choose not to enroll the patient with reasons clearly stated. If the physician chooses to enroll the patient, the system would progress the patient's care according to the preset pathways and set up the information based on the protocol: (1) task reminder for each visit and daily tasks, including structured medical record, daily therapeutic orders, daily test orders, daily nursing tasks and daily patient education content; (2) reminders for unselected compulsory items; reminders on high-alert medication, expensive supplies, blood product, and discharge medications; (3) important or special control points of certain medical care tasks for admission, pre-operation, post-operation, discharge, critical value, and clinical crisis for information sharing and reminders regarding treatment, nursing, and education among the physicians, nurses and patients; and (4) clinical pathway metrics chart for aggregated information such as enrollment rate, completion rate, variation rate, length of stay, cost of hospitalization, consistency of diagnosis, etc. to monitor the application of clinical pathways and give feedback on the performance (see Figure 15.5).

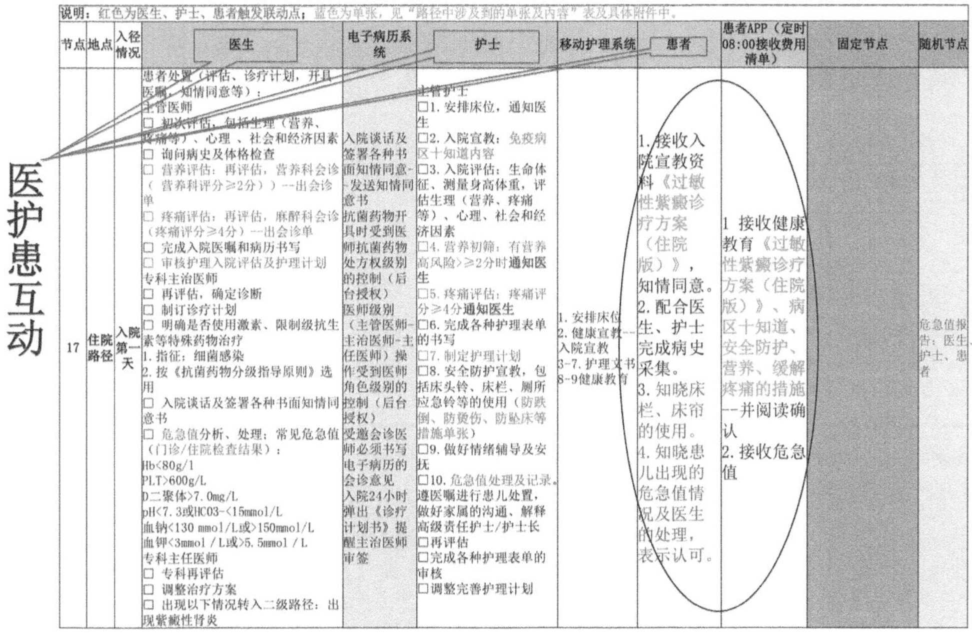

Figure 15.5 Interface of physician-nurse-patient interaction.

Data-Driven Medical Practice

CDSS is used to support diagnosis or clinical care with a wide coverage from diagnosis and onset probability modeling to the effectiveness analysis of alternative care plan. The data could include both individual patient data and data regarding care risks and effective data of feasible care plan stored in the database. While we are paying more attention to patient safety and prevention of medical error, Clinical Decision Support System, and Computerized Physician Order Entry have become the key IT capability in improving patient safety.

Clinical Decision Support System is also one of the key areas required by the HIMSS criteria described in Stages 3, 4, and 6, respectively. The rudimentary level CDS mainly focuses on the checking and reminder on appropriate medication use and duplicated orders during the ordering process by physician. Medium-level CDS includes the trigger of and reminder on clinical pathways, and critical values based on the basic rule engine. Advanced CDS is prediction-based rules and process engine to provide compliance and variation monitoring on clinical pathways and care outcomes.

HIMSS criteria expect all clinical decision support to proactively give reminders based on specific trigger rather than passively through searching by staff. Through the field survey, mapping of care process, and establishment of a multi-dimensional whole-process medical management system, GWCMC developed the care knowledge base, medication knowledge base, auxiliary test/examination knowledge base and linked the diseases to medications and auxiliary tests/examinations through thesaurus mapping. On the basis of structured EMR, we also realized rudimentary and medium-level CDS in our system and partially achieved some advanced CDS capabilities.

Debut of "Dr. Bear"

Not long ago, the Institute of Medical Science of the University of Tokyo diagnosed a 60-year-old women with rare leukemia and offered a care plan for the patient with the assistance of

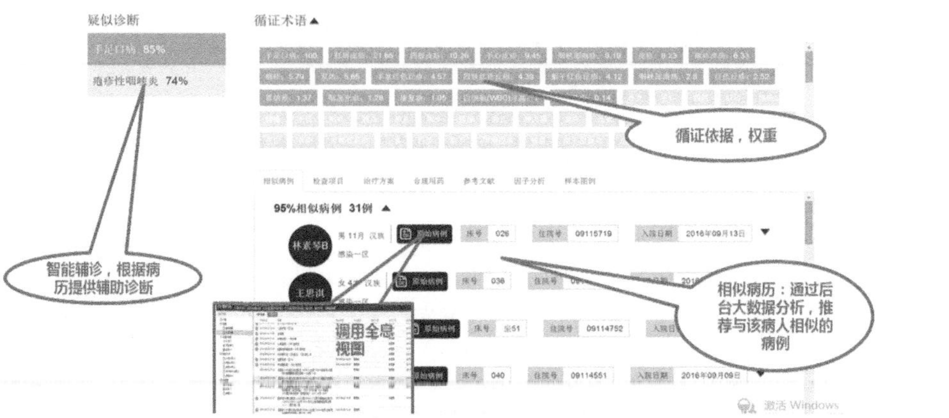

Figure 15.6 Interface of "Dr. Bear."

Figure 15.7 "Dr. Bear" welcoming patients in the OPD hall.

"Watson," the AI system developed by IBM, which ignited the passion of the healthcare sector in applying AI technology.

GWCMC then developed our own pediatric intelligent diagnosis and treatment assistant system, Dr. Bear, according to the lean management requirement by JCI and the technology-enabled healthcare transformation and optimization of care process for better and safer services. HIMSS also expects hospital to realize healthcare information exchange, data integration, and regional sharing of data. Thus, we adopted the structured EMR with chart templates as well as standardized and uniform data element, data set, and documentation that stored in CDR for data analysis and mining. For the medical records generated in the past, we used the semantic analysis technology to realize the structure of the charts and set up the data warehouse for analysis and mining. That is the technical foundation for Dr. Bear (see Figure 15.6).

Dr. Bear (see Figure 15.7) is a clinical solution based on big data and cognitive computing. It is a diagnosis model built upon the knowledge bases with patient EMR as the foundation, which emphasizes the principle of evidence-based medicine. It understands natural language and is trained consistently with high-quality EMR through deep machine learning. In this way, it can give supportive diagnosis on different stages of patient's progress based on the patient's medical record information (admission note, initial progress note, progress/round note, surgical note, lab/examination results). It also provides information to assist decision-making process such as patient case, lab/examination, care plan, references, pictures, appropriate medication use information, etc. Dr. Bear could provide supportive opinions on diagnosis and treatment based on patient-specific situation to significantly improve the efficiency and accuracy of physicians.

Chapter 16

The First Affiliated Hospital of Xiamen University

Jiang Jie, Cai Chengfu, Zhu Haihua, Tong Suijun, Shao Zhiyu, Zhao Min, Ye Feng, Tang Guobao, Yang Yinling, Tang Mingkun, Ma Lei, and Rao Chunmei
The First Affiliated Hospital of Xiamen University

Jiang Jie *is Chief Physician, Professor, and Supervisor of doctoral candidates*

Dr. Jiang is the President of The First Affiliated Hospital of Xiamen University and Vice Dean of School of Medicine of Xiamen University. He is an editor of China Journal of Minimally Invasive Surgery and Hospital Management, *Chairman of Xiamen Society of Cardiothoracic Surgery and Xiamen Medical Doctor Association; and Vice Chairman of the Smart Healthcare Chapter and Hospital Management Chapter of Chinese Medical Doctor Association, among others.*

With profound experience in hospital administration, healthcare models, strategic planning, performance management, and healthcare alliance, he has led the organization through JCI Accreditation of Academic Medical Center and HIMSS Stage 7 certification, the first general hospital in China to have received both certifications.

Cai Chengfu, *Chief Physician, Associate Professor, and Supervisor of graduate candidates.*

Dr. Cai is the Director of Human Resources and HIMSS Office of The First Affiliated Hospital of Xiamen University. Through the preparation of HIMSS certification, Dr. Cai has learned information technology, IT adoption in healthcare as well as digital and smart hospital, and shaped his insights in interconnectivity of IT systems and electronic medical record. He is the Vice General Secretary of Tumor Prevention and Treatment Chapter of Association of Cross-Strait Exchanges in Healthcare, Member of Otorhinolaryngology Chapter of Fujian Society of China-Western Integrative Medicine, etc. Dr. Cai is also an invited editor of Standardized Health Administration *in China.*

Zhu Haihua *is the Director of Nursing Department of The First Affiliated Hospital of Xiamen University. She is Member of Intensive Care Nursing Chapter of Chinese Nursing Association, Chairman of Nursing Committee of Western Medicine Development Center of Association of Cross-Strait Exchanges in Healthcare, and Vice Director of Xiamen Nursing Quality Center. Her expertise includes nursing management, intensive nursing care, JCI, and HIMSS compliance effort, as well as IT adoption.*

Hospital Introduction: The First Affiliated Hospital of Xiamen University was first established in 1937 as the Provincial Hospital of Fujian Province. It is now a large healthcare alliance covering eight campuses, two nursing facilities, and six community healthcare service centers. It is also the first general hospital that has been accredited by both JCI and HIMSS EMRAM Stage 7.

The hospital is the first public organization to realize "full appointment-based visit," "full self-service," and "full patient follow-up" as early as in 2008. In 2014, we became the first "Mobile Hospital" supporting payment through Alipay, a third-party on-line payment platform, in Fujian Province. In 2016, we were recognized as the first Internet+Hospital and won the awards of "Hospital of Innovation," "Top 10 Hospital Innovating Service with IT Support," etc.

International Accreditation: September 2015, JCI accreditation (the tenth academic JCI hospital in China's mainland);

October 2016, HIMSS EMRAM 6;

August 2017, HIMSS EMRAM 7;

On-site validation by ISO15189 for laboratory for several times.

Contents

Preface

JCI + HIMSS: Commitment to Both

JCI or HIMSS, Which One Should Go First? In early 2015, we had the first JCI introduction and experience sharing event. During the discussion, Jilan Liu responded to the question: "JCI or HIMSS, which one should go first?" She said:

> It depended on the hospital's overall situation. If we decided to go for JCI first, it would help us to build our capability while improving patient safety and quality. If we chose HIMSS first, it would add efficiency to safety and quality through providing IT solutions to the JCI requirements. If conditions allowed, the hospital could go for both concurrently.

Back at that time, we had not started the HIMSS preparation. But by looking back into the journey we had made, HIMSS did solve many challenges that we had met in JCI accreditation.

First Encounter with JCI

It was in August 2013, 3 years after our last National Level-A Tertiary Hospital Accreditation conducted by our own government. Through the efforts of several terms of the hospital leadership, we became the No. 1 hospital in Fujian Province in terms of many hospital performance indicators such as outpatient and ED visits. However, in face of the rapid development of medical science and more sophisticated specialty advancement, how to realize delicacy management emerged as the new challenge for our leaders. After rounds of discussion and prudent study, the leadership of the First Affiliated Hospital of Xiamen University with Dr. Jiang Jie as the President decided to follow the JCI standards, the gold standard for hospital across the world, to further improve the hospital management capability. The proposal was greatly supported by Yang Shuyu, then Director of Health and Family Planning Commission of Xiamen Municipality, since when we officially embarked on the JCI journey.

However, JCI was stranger to our staff. To better understand the JCI standards, the hospital organized several rounds of visits to other JCI hospitals for observation and learning participated by the key staff, and invited experts in JCI accreditation to explain the standards supported by case sharing to show the before-and-after differences in their hospitals. In October 2013, we invited a team of experts from Taiwan to perform a baseline study in our hospital and initiated the first round of consultation lasting for 1 year till October 2014.

During that 12 months, the consultants from Taiwan delivered lectures every month and conducted clinical tracers. But the staff felt that "JCI was too high a goal to be achieved in our hospital."

For example, as a hospital with a history over 80 years located in the historical downtown of Xiamen City, the hospital was in extreme needs of extra space. To manage the patients, we actually divided the outpatient area into Zone A and Zone B. Between the two zones was a path where we had both pedestrians and vehicles. The fence on both sides of the path was about 50 cm high. The consultant team pointed out that the fence was too short to prevent possible risks. They also said that JCI standards required the fence to be at least 1 m high to prevent people from crossing over to the vehicle lanes. Otherwise, we would fail the standards.

It was just one of the findings identified by the consultation team. All the "insufficiencies" made us believe that we needed a lot of hardware transformation in order to meet the JCI requirements. Stronger complaints came from the clinical staff: Our hospital would never make it!

The "Ah-Ha" Moment

On October 23, 2014, Jilan brought a team to our hospital for a 6-day Mock Survey (including consultants from South Korea, Lebanon, and US). The team started their day at 8:00 sharp to work with our staff in interviews, document reviews, clinical quality tracer, individual patient tracer, staff qualification interview, medical education review, quality interview, system tracer, closed medical record review, facility tour…

The comprehensive, thorough inspection covered 49 clinical units in four inpatient buildings, two outpatient buildings and the Pharmacology Base. They visited almost every corner of the hospital, including the basement, roof top, portable water supply, kitchen, and sewage treatment to review our practice regarding patient safety, staff health and education and research according to the 1,174 measurable elements in 294 standards of 16 chapters of the manual.

Every morning from 8:00 to 9:00 was the daily debriefing. Our colleagues bombarded the consultants with numerous questions, but Jilan and her team answered all the questions with great patience. At that time, due to the absence of the standard book in Chinese, we did not fulfill the requirement in IPSG.2 to "read back" the critical value. The consultants mentioned this finding repetitively and explained to us the definition and the intent of "read back."

Thus, we started to gradually understand JCI accreditation: As long as we could ensure the patient safety based on our own situation, JCI was not unattainable. The essence of JCI is continuous improvement through constant efforts in adopting effective measures whenever any risk is identified during daily operation. JCI does not require transformation of all hardware in the hospital. The most important thing is to improve patient safety through the collective wisdom of all staff.

The consultant team never gave us the direct solutions but tried their best to inspire and engage the staff in the process. With regard to the fence at the outpatient area, Jilan did not require it to be as high as 1 m. The agreed solution after the discussion among multiple departments was to fix some flags with ropes on the fence and put a sign reading: "DO NOT CROSS." We also arranged security guards to maintain the order during the peak hours in the hospital to ensure the safety of visitors. This method not only cut down the material investment but also protected the visitors.

In just 6 days of Mock Survey, we learned how to perform tracers in our units to track, for instance, a piece of insulin pen, or the meals delivered, or unit-level quality performance.

Implementing JCI Standards: Six Rounds of Supervision

"Document what you do, and do as you document." is the criteria to review the compliance with the JCI standards. The hospital policies need to comply with the national and local laws and regulations. When the laws and regulations set different requirements from JCI standards, then the hospital would be reviewed based on the more stringent requirements.

In April 2015, the hospital officially established the JCI Office and spent 6 months in developing the six rounds of supervision plan (see Table 16.1) to monitor the full implementation of JCI-related policies and procedures. The JCI Office also adopted a triple layered supervision approach to ensure the effectiveness of the monitoring mechanism: (1) Level III: peer check among different units organized by the JCI Office and the regular check by the team headed with the hospital leadership; (2) Level II: focused check by the administrative departments; and (3) Level I: self-check by clinical and ancillary units.

During the first round of supervision, there were only five units who met the requirements. A monitoring report was submitted to the hospital mid-level management meeting in Gantt charts. The hospital leadership's engagement was an important guarantee. For example, Guo Peichai, the then hospital management consultant, organized meetings with the heads of the units who did not perform well, and Qian Yongyue, then VP, led the supervision himself to the units required to take improvement actions.

Hospital knowledge contests and written evaluation on the trainings were conducted to assess the effectiveness of the improvement activities. We reorganized the standards and measurable elements of all chapters into different questions and compiled them into a booklet for all staff, and candidates were selected to participate in the knowledge contests. The candidates were divided into the Unit Head Group, Head Nurse Group, Medical JCI Coordinator Group, and Nursing JCI Coordinator Group. They were tested on their comprehension of the JCI standards and hospital policies.

The purpose was to encourage full implementation of the P&Ps. For that, we organized another two rounds of hospital monitoring.

In the first round, the responsible leaders visited respective units to follow up on their progress and organize the JCI standard learning sessions after the morning hand-off every day. Each one

Table 16.1 Six Rounds of Supervision

Phase	*Objectives*	*Measures*		*Methods*	*Summary*
First round	To identify problems	Cooperation: 95%	Effectiveness: 5%	Self-check and peer evaluation by units	Lack of cooperation and awareness of the importance; action of the management leaders required to ensure implementation
Second round	To identify problems	Cooperation: 95%	Effectiveness: 5%	Self-check and peer evaluation by units	Improved awareness and cooperation in implementing JCI P&Ps
Third round	To improve performance	Cooperation: 40%	Effectiveness: 60%	Focused check by administrative departments; self-check and peer evaluation by units	Failure of clinical units to strictly follow the P&Ps
Fourth round	To continuously improve performance	Cooperation: 20%	Effectiveness: 80%	JCI Office check; self-check and peer evaluation by units	Compliance of clinical units in implementing the P&Ps; revision of policies based on the situation of the units
Fifth round	To continuously improve performance	/	Effectiveness: 100%	Leadership rounds; JCI Office check; self-check by units	Strict implementation of P&Ps in units
Sixth round	To continuously improve performance	/	Effectiveness: 100%	Leadership rounds; JCI Office check; self-check by units	Strict implementation of P&Ps in units

of the hospital leaders was required to complete the visits to all units within his or her scope of responsibilities and was accountable for the effectiveness of the unit-level trainings.

In the second round, we assigned the leaders to each one of the IPSGs and the major challenges encountered in our hospital. Dr. Jiang Jie, President, was responsible for patient identification; Tong Suijun, Party Secretary, for effective communication; Dr. Li Weihua, VP, for equipment safety; Dr. Luo Qi, VP, for surgical safety verification; Dr. Lin Lianfeng, VP, for high-alert medications; Dr. Wang Zhanxiang, VP, for patient fall; Dr. Qian Yongyue, then VP, for radiology appointment; and Mr. Duan Zhiwen, CFO, for fire safety.

We designed questions and answers related to each specific standard. The leaders went to the floors to monitor and test the effectiveness of the training and gave feedback on the results, which further facilitated the mutual learning environment for better implementation of the P&Ps.

Xiamen and International Standards

The first official survey fell on September 21–26, 2015. A team of five surveyors flew in Xiamen and conducted the survey. Different from the Mock Survey, the surveyors were more serious.

The first 2 days was intense but went on well, allowing us to better understand the surveyor team leader: rigorous, thorough, serious, and swift. On the third day, the team leader visited the ER. As a physician specialized in emergency care, the visit was like a tour back home: the crash cart management, the test of defibrillator, the medication management, the documentation of care, the communication between the physicians and nurses. At the physician's work station, the team leader mentioned an obvious defect of the computer system: the nursing documentation could not talk with the physician's module. The only way to access the information was to sign in the other system, which prevented staff from communicating with each other effectively.

Around 9:00 on the morning of the fourth day, the broadcasting system called out for an emergency, "Attention, please. Code 7979 at the Oncology Department. Relevant units be ready for the code." The broadcast repeated for three times. Then, the world set into silence. "Code 7979" is the blue code of the hospital, which requires the code team to arrive at the site within 5 min. The clinician surveyor asked the translator what was going on, and headed for the Oncology Department immediately after he learned that it was the blue code.

It was Mr. Chen, a 75-year-old post-surgery patient receiving chemotherapy because of his lung cancer. He went to the bathroom after his breakfast. And suddenly cardiac and respiration arrest hit him hard. The nurse on call immediately initiated Code 7979. When the surveyor arrived on the unit, the patient was already back thanks to the cooperation between the Oncology Department and the Respiratory Disease Department. He hugged the staff on site and said "Thank You!" to them for saving the patient's life. The applause touched the heart of our colleagues.

On the fifth day, we reviewed the units that had been traced during the week. There were only 3 out of the 85 different areas that had not been visited yet. For the 82 areas, the surveyors had been there at least once, but some had received multiple visits, like the Health Maintenance Department, which had been visited for five times.

After the debriefing on the sixth day, the survey team began their tracers to the last three units. They came back around noon and started their final report and communication with the headquarters. The leadership group meeting was held at 14:30. The hospital leadership, the surveyors, and key managers attended the meeting. The team leader gave a summarized overview on the 6-day of the survey and told us that they would recommend the headquarters accredit us as a JCI hospital.

On October 22, 2016, Dr. Jiang Jie received the gold plaque from Jilan Liu, which marked a special milestone on the history of the healthcare sector of Xiamen. Finally, the 2 years of efforts gained us the JCI gold seal as an academic teaching hospital. The First Affiliated Hospital of Xiamen University became the first accredited JCI hospital in Fujian Province.

Consolidate JCI Standards through HIMSS

JCI accreditation was the first step of the journey pursuing quality and safety. How could we further consolidate what we had achieved and benefit more from lining ourselves with JCI standards? How could we connect the information silos and realize interoperability? How could we improve the efficiency of the staff, enhance their sense of gain and better ensure the patient safety? Three major questions rose above the horizon right after our JCI accreditation. Among all the possible paths, we saw the beacon of HIMSS.

In 2016, Jilan Liu again visited our hospital as the Vice President of HIMSS & Executive President of HIMSS Greater China. She reviewed the IT adoption in the hospital, including single sign on, integration platform, physician-nurse communication platform, decision support, structured EMR, CPOE, closed loop of blood transfusion/medication/human milk, paperless environment, task list, etc. These terms were no longer strangers to us, and the road map for future development started to roll out in front of us.

Tong Suijun, Party Secretary, who was in charge of IT development in the hospital, mentioned that our hospital had a very good foundation in terms of information technology after years of development, and with HIMSS validation, we should not be satisfied with learning from others, but become the experts to line ourselves up to the highest standards, like a BMW 7 series car, the flagship model of BMW.

Dr. Jiang Jie, President of the hospital, stressed that like JCI, HIMSS also called for dedication and courage to take the challenge. The ultimate goal of HIMSS is to encourage better utilization of information and technology to improve quality, safety and efficiency in the hospital for both staff and patients and bring them the sense of gain, and to build our own IT infrastructure and functionalities that are suitable for the hospital. Dr. Jiang also emphasized that the development of information technology and utilization was an endless journey, and, to conquer it, we needed to be down to earth and march forward quickly but steadily.

The hospital then set up an HIMSS Leading Group chaired by Dr. Jiang Jie and executed by the VP in charge of IT. Other hospital VPs served as the deputy team leaders and all heads of the administrative departments participated as members. The HIMSS Leading Group further set up the HIMSS Office consisted of personnel from eight different disciplines (including JCI Office, medical affairs, nursing, pharmacy, management, etc.) to coordinate all activities. We also invited the front-line staff with rich clinical experience and certain level of capabilities in information technology to provide consultation to the clinical IT development, guide the HIMSS progress, and review the outcomes. Each unit set their own HIMSS task group with four designated HIMSS coordinators (two physicians and two nurses) to be responsible for preparing the HIMSS validation and organizing staff training.

Innovative Work Mode

At the beginning of our HIMSS journey, the hospital focused so much on the detailed findings from the consultation of the HIMSS Greater China team that we were not aware of the connections among all those problems. The result was that the solution of one problem incurred another new problem.

We then organized several special meetings and agreed that we need to walk on both of our "legs"—the problem list and the sub-project list. The sub-project list was planned and implemented in a more linear way to review the past, focus on the present, and lead the future; while the problem list was more about the existing problems to be addressed. Based on the consultants' recommendations and the hospital's situation, we drafted a sub-project list including the integration platform, CDR, single sign on, CDSS (medical, nursing and pharmacy services), structured EMR, scanning process, finger-print devices, Wi-Fi deployment, HIE, electronic signature, PDA devices, automatic data collection, paperless environment, patient health management, data analysis, and business intelligence, mobile care (medical and nursing services), and closed-loop management (blood transfusion, human milk, lab/radiology, surgery, pathology). Responsible departments/units were required to report the progress of each sub-project every week.

To ensure the smooth implementation and the coordination among units, administrative departments and vendors, the hospital also experimented on a highly efficient and effective work mode to bring individuals accountable for each one of the tasks to deliver outcomes.

"1+2+N" Mode

The "1+2+N" mode was created to hold personnel accountable for their own tasks and improve efficient, complete communication. "1" was the leading department supervising the progress of a sub-project. "2" referred to the two platforms (the hospital IT Center and the vendor) supporting the project. The leading department directly communicated with the vendors to collect information, and requests and solves any possible problems, while the IT Center reviewed the technical feasibility and application. "N" was all the units/departments involved in one project to cooperate with the leading department in the implementation. The "1+2+N" was designed for small-scale sub-projects. For the projects that involved larger scope and required cross-department coordination, the hospital leadership would then lead a team for the hospital-wide project together with the support from relevant departments and vendors. This new working mode significantly improved our efficiency and better met the needs from our clinical practice to smoothly and rapidly roll out the projects.

Working Meeting Mechanism

The hospital organized weekly working meeting to involve the hospital leadership, responsible persons from all leading departments, project members, and vendors. The leading departments reported the progress of the projects, and the leadership was responsible for solving any possible problems. Designated staff was assigned to take the minutes, develop work plan, and follow-up the implementation. Coordination meetings were convened irregularly to focus on the problems and challenges that needed to be solved.

HIMSS Program Supervision

Each one of the hospital leaders was assigned to specific projects and took the team to track the progress in the clinical units for supervision and feedback on possible challenges and problems.

"One for N" Training Mode

HIMSS EMRAM Stage 7 requires every staff in every unit be familiar with the system he or she uses. Units were encouraged to volunteer in the pilot projects, and some of the units with good foundation and strong willingness were selected to participate in the pilot. Resources investment and incentives were granted to the pilot units.

With regards to staff training, the Medical Affairs Department, Nursing Department, and Pharmacy Department organized the demonstration training every week in the units to train the unit HIMSS coordinators. The unit directors and head nurses were responsible for organizing the training at their own units on the new procedures and system functions provided by the HIMSS coordinators.

Evaluation on the Outcomes

A project assessment team including hospital leadership, leading departments, user units, IT Center and HIMSS Office was established to evaluate the final outcomes of the projects against the HIMSS criteria and the project goals.

Establishment of the Hospital IT Service Center

The Hospital IT Service Center was established to provide consultation and receive feedback on the IT progress for better solving the challenges and difficulties the clinical units had.

Endless Efforts Make Success

On October 26, 2016, the First Affiliated Hospital of Xiamen University became the first hospital in Fujian Province to be validated as an HIMSS EMRAM Stage 6 hospital.

Following in the next year, we received a team of HIMSS Analytics surveyors for the on-site HIMSS EMRAM Stage 7 validation during August 26–28, 2017. On the last day of the survey, the surveyor team agreed that our hospital reached Stage 7.

John Daniels, the team leader, said, "First, I have seen a full-fledged, multi-layered IT governance structure engaging various participants. It is well implemented in your day-to-day work. Second, the hospital is collecting a large volume of discrete data through your system and is utilizing the data to provide clinical and managerial decision support. Third, we have witnessed the reminder function in your system based on proactive prediction. That is one of the best that I have seen so far."

Quan Yu, another validation surveyor, highly recognized our achievements, "The hospital spent 1 year on these progress and optimization, and started to provide food allergy control and food-drug interaction check based on what you already had for Stage 6. This is another step you've taken to guarantee the safety of your patients. The system is capable of recommending nursing measures based on the level of risks of fall, pressure ulcer, pain and other nursing assessment, and generating nursing task list accordingly and reminding the nurses on their due tasks. The complete, useful documentation of the nursing care in the chart can be a good foundation for future data utilization."

HIMSS EMRAM Stage 7 helped us further enhance the strengths we had as well as the overall safety check and emergency response capability. The IT Center is no longer at the margin of the hospital operation. Instead, they have been granted with more responsibilities and tasks as a key department in the hospital. Their support to other units/departments actually initiated a brand-new journey of disciplinary development.

The 3-year cycle of JCI triennial accreditation will fall in 2018. We will continue our journey to better enjoy the fruits from IT development to fulfill our goal of safety, quality, and efficiency! (Figure 16.1)

Figure 16.1 On-site validation of HIMSS EMRAM Stage 7.

Case 1: Big Data-Driven Safe Medication Use

Many hospitals are using the Appropriate Medication Use System to capture the missed errors during the appropriateness review to ensure the safety of medication use. Though many hospitals have established PIVAS (Pharmacy Intravenous Admixture Service), the service could not cover all IV medication required on the clinical floors.

Therefore, in our hospital, we developed the Intelligent Safe Medication Use Decision Support System (hereinafter referred in this case as "the System") and the Intelligent PIVAS Management Platform (hereinafter referred in this case as "the Platform") The System retrieves patient information through the integration platform to realize the full aggregation and sharing of the actual medication data and big data processing through parallel or cross correlation between the medication and patient information. The System could provide big-data-driven clinical decision support for medication safety to solve the practical problems existing in the current medication appropriateness review systems.

The Platform is built based on the digital technology and the IoT solutions to build the automatic monitoring system in the PIVAS management. Information at each step of the IV medication admixture is collected, analyzed, and transmitted for controlling purpose. Staff are trained for their compliance. The new Platform serves the communication and data sharing among physicians, pharmacists, and nurses. It realizes the effective monitoring during the preparation to ensure the quality, mobilize staff's participation. With the Platform in place, staff could work in a more coordinated way with efficient self-monitoring.

The System: An Ideal Mix of Five Modules

The Intelligent Safe Medication Use Decision Support System consists of five modules, including drug allergy, disease/drug contraindications, dose calculation, drug/food interaction and the critical values. The five modules work together, enabling the big data analysis to provide the best therapeutic medication care based on the patient's conditions.

The basis of the drug allergy module is the medication allergy database which is organized according to types of drugs. In addition, we reviewed over 160,000 entries in the database to preclude certain information such as packaging specifications and manufacturers and broke down the compounds into specific ingredients. Medications with the same generic names were then reorganized into the same set according to certain calculation rules. The brand names have also been matched with the corresponding generic ones in the sets as many patients are used to the brand names.

Different from the traditional medication allergy database, the System is capable of performing logic mathematical calculation on the ingredients, the parent nucleus and the adjuvant and has formed data sets related to cross allergies. This is usually missing from the current appropriateness review systems on the market.

The System can automatically capture data in HIS, including the patient's medication allergy history, name of the drug(s) or allergy information, home medication before admission, etc. Then it can fire reminders on the prescribed drug that may related to the allergy history as well as on potential allergy by checking the information against the allergy database to avoid problematic prescriptions.

The drug-disease contraindication module is built based on the standardized disease code database to collect the contraindication listed in the manufacturers' instruction automatically and perform mapping calculation accordingly. When a physician prescribes an order, the System would access the contraindication database, perform calculation based on the available disease, conditions and other information about the patient, and send alert to the physician if it falls in the scope of contraindication.

ICD-10 has been adopted for this module to standardize the description of the diagnoses as many contraindications are linked to one type of diagnosis (as described in the manufacturers' instructions) that may include many sub-diagnoses. In this way, we would be able to avoid any missing contraindication during the review.

The dose calculation module extracts patient data from HIS, maps the data with other discrete data in the rule database for medication use (e.g., diagnosis, special illness, weight, age, height, sex, lab results, medication use history, genetic test results, adverse reaction), and calculates the course of the therapy, dose, and cumulative dose based on the half-life period of the medication. It also performs the pharmacokinetic analysis for antibiotics, chemotherapy medication, cardiovascular, and cerebrovascular medication to avoid duplicated use.

The drug-food interaction module is based on the database comprising the drug-food and disease-food incompatibilities. When a physician prescribes certain medication, the System would provide diet recommendations during the course of medication therapy based on certain rules. This module could effectively prevent the compromised outcomes or adverse events related to drug-food interaction, improve the education and patient compliance, and finally optimize the appropriateness of medication use.

Another innovative solution in the System is the critical value module. A critical value database has been developed for this module together with the critical value dose formula settings. When a critical value is reported on a patient, the System could automatically adjust the dose or give alert based on its logic algorithm.

Coordinated Systems for Process Tracking

The Intelligent PIVAS Management Platform consists of multiple subsystems, including the appropriateness review system by pharmacists, IV admixture tracking and management system,

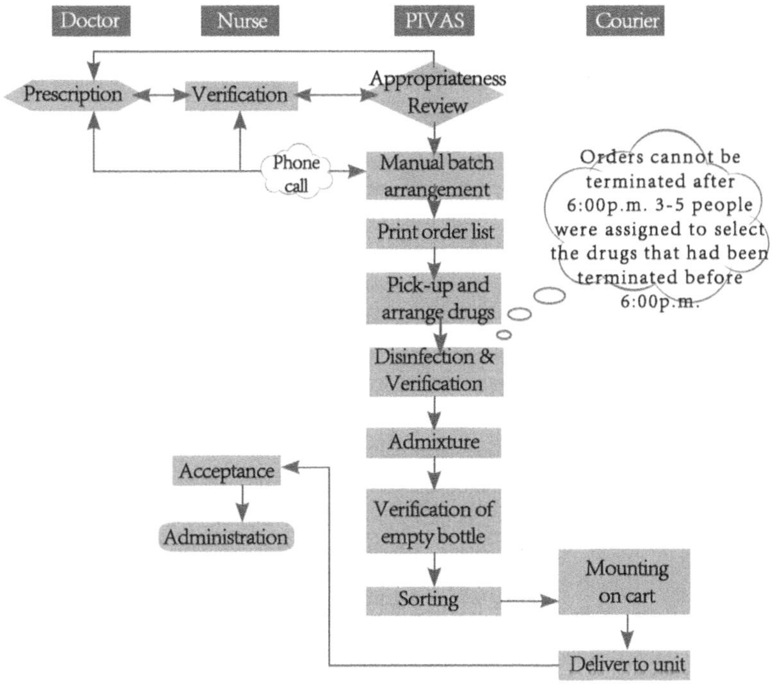

Figure 16.2 Work flow in PIVAS.

automatic batch management system, automatic scheduling system, KPI evaluation system, equipment on-line monitoring system, and expiration management system.

The Platform was first developed to enable reminders and tracking capabilities at each step of the medication flow. A unique barcode is generated by the system for each one of the prescriptions to allow automatic verification from appropriateness review, retrieval of drugs, mixing, empty ampule verification, sorting, dispensing, and administration. Scanning technology is adopted to track the status of the prescription and the staff involved. The real-time digital monitoring has boosted the staff's sense of responsibilities and reduced the errors during the preparation (Figure 16.2).

The Platform also contributes to the resources allocation and management of the prescriptions to further reduce the consumption of medication, supplies as well as the cost of patients. The Platform automatically sorts the prescriptions and categorizes those using half or part of the same ampules/vials into the same slot. With safety as the prerequisite, the syringes, needles and other supplies could be used for the mixing of same medication and base solution to reduce the consumption of supplies. The automatic merger and decision-making of the partial-dose prescriptions by the System significantly reduced the consumption of drugs, the cost of the patients and the hospital, and saved the medical resources. The "Clean Computer," a patented product of the hospital, enables the staff to see through the entire process with the visualized display via providing real-time reminders on high-alert medications and expensive medications to prevent staff from any errors during the admixture.

Due to the change of conditions of patients, physicians might adjust or terminate the orders accordingly. For this, the "Termination with One Click" function has been built in the Platform. As soon as the physician terminates an order, the status would be updated to other modules/systems involved in the following steps. When the staff scans the barcode during review, mixing, and administration, the screen would indicate that the prescription has already been terminated, which cuts down the response time on the chain, saves the waste of medication. It can also play a role in maintaining the good relationships among physicians, nurses, and pharmacists.

The automatic batch management system and the expiration control system support the timely dispensing of the mixed IV medication to the floor according to specific order to ensure the availability and the quality of medication used on the patients.

The System sequences the medications into the most suitable batches according to the actual use and trend of clinical use as well as the patient's individual information. Physicians and nurses can focus their energy and time on the diagnosis and treatment for the patients, while the System takes care of the medication processing from real-time synchronization of termination status, IV speed, safety range for individual patient, arrangement of IV infusion and surgeries and examinations and adjuvant drug control for all long-term and STAT orders, which optimizes the reasonable sequence of the infusion for patients.

A database of medication stability window has been built in the System. Thus, when an IV medication is ready, the System would automatically give an expiration date to the prepared medication for verification on the unit. It can also give reminders on those medication with short stability time after admixture to urge quick dispensing for the safety of medication use.

The flow of IV medication requires team work and sufficient training on PIVAS staff. To that end, staff scheduling and KPI evaluation were also developed to best arrange the shifts, break down tasks, and measure all types of procedures, responsibilities, and standard practice.

In this way, the System guarantees the objectivity, fairness and transparency of the evaluation, and staff's enthusiasm has also been sparkled to achieve better outcome, marking the transition from "governance by people and policies" to "governance by information technology and self-management" (Figure 16.3).

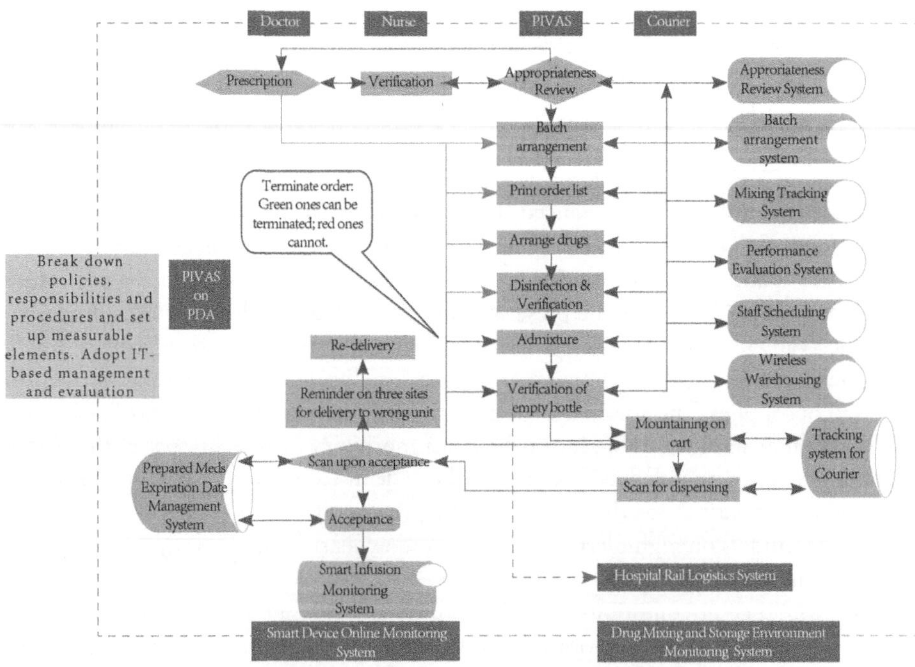

Figure 16.3 Digitalized PIVAS flow.

Effectiveness Evaluation

Supported by the Intelligent Safe Medication Use Decision Support System, the hospital has been able to fully integrate the drug-related data in different systems and realized medication management and data sharing. It gives attention to the factors that may impact the patient's health (allergy, weight, lab/examination results, cumulative dosage, course control, etc.) in the analysis and algorithm and gives decision support based on the conclusion to improve the appropriateness of clinical medication therapy and reduce unnecessary medication use, IV infusion, adjuvant drug use, nutrition treatment, and electrolytes. According to statistics, after the System was brought alive, the IV infusion at the outpatient clinics and ER has been reduced from 35.05% to 0.05%. The infusion among inpatients has been reduced to 6,000 bags per day (2,500 beds). The proportion of medication in the total cost of a patient has been cut down from 35% to 26.7%.

The System also provides valuable information regarding medication use through the eMAR which could be brought up by just one click. It enables the physicians and pharmacists to prescribe and review the orders, and gives recommendations on the order after the calculation of pre-admission medication, medication during hospital stay, allergy, cumulative dosage, individualized dosing and treatment course control. With an emphasis on Internet technology and big data processing, this intelligent system could provide deeper and better information and decision support capability.

The PIVAS of the First Affiliated Hospital of Xiamen University was constructed and put in use in 2005 with a total area of 400 m^2 to process all long-term and STAT IV orders for all 47 inpatient units and those from the outpatient/ER. The daily work load is over 6,000 bags.

The consumption of supplies, cost of medications, and operation expenses have been reduced. Since we introduced the Intelligent PIVAS Management Platform in 2014, we have achieved great benefit in quality, safety, and financial performance. Thanks to the full coverage of the PIVAS service supported by digital tools and fine management process, the hospital has saved more than 1.36 million dollars from medication, supplies, and admixture services fee, equal to the cost of 65 employees for a year.

Based on the statistics, since the implementation of the whole-process KPI evaluation, 750 thousand dollars has been saved from unnecessary medication use, including 4 million from cancer medication and TPN and 1 million from syringes. The area of our PIVAS is only 50% of the national standard. The IT solution helped us to cut the extra space, energy consumption, and optimized staffing.

Staff are mobilized and the team is even stronger. After the Platform was adopted, we have seen reduced mixing time of each staff and errors, higher efficiency in batch scheduling, more timely dispensing of the first batch medication every day, and fewer patient complains. Meanwhile, the data sharing capability has facilitated the communication and cooperation among the physicians, nurses, and pharmacists. The performance evaluation on staff has been improved to adopt the individual-based work load assessment rather than the traditional "collective evaluation." Incentives and punishment have been designed to encourage hard work and contribution from the staff. The time spent on the evaluation has also been reduced. The automatic work load and error calculation helps the managers better evaluate the staff from an objective perspective and reduced the management cost.

Paperless operation: The overall coverage of the PIVAS service supported by technology also contributes to the paperless environment. The System is able to document and save the original admixture data of each piece of the prescriptions in the hospital, which saves the work of our staff in documenting the information, improves efficiency, and ensures the accuracy of data and traceability of the entire process. The paperless operation also reflects our environment-friendly management approach.

In summary, JCI and HIMSS EMRAM Stage 7 have given 19 nurses back to the units to take care of patients and saved much resources in the hospital. With a reduction of the medication proportion in the total care cost to 24.8%, it smoothed out the relationship between the pharmacists. Our effort is paid back through lower investment in man power, finance, and materials; higher output and harmonious development!

Conclusion

The true value of big data in healthcare is the capability of data mining and the analysis of the correlations and rules between data to offer intelligence and automation based on clinical practices. Physicians often rely on their own experience when ordering medications. But due to the different and complex conditions of individual patients, inappropriate medication use is not infrequent.

The Intelligent Safe Medication Use Decision Support System utilizes the big data analysis and calculation capability to aggregate the clinical medication data (e.g., dosing, allergy, critical value, contraindication) to mimic the "human experience" and individualizes the recommendation based on the patient's information and lab/examination results to give intelligent advices.

On the other hand, the Intelligent PIVAS Management Platform effectively solved the problems in staffing and process design and successfully shifted the focus from the "extensive end management" to the "fine process management." The clinical medication use is more appropriate, more timely and safer, and the cooperation among physicians, nurses, and pharmacists is more smoothly.

As a type of healthcare resources, healthcare big data is playing an increasingly pivotal role in today's practices. The research and development in healthcare big data would serve as a powerful support to the development of intelligent healthcare. The healthcare big data is still at its initial stage. But we believe that, with enhanced data analysis capabilities, big-data-driven healthcare would emerge as the future trend.

Case 2: Innovative Life-Cycle Chronic Disease Management

The non-transmissible chronic diseases (hereinafter referred as chronic disease) such as diabetes and hypertension have become the major threat to people's health. On our journey to HIMSS EMRAM Stage 7, we focused on the HIE capability based on the regional health information platform and developed an innovative life-cycle chronic disease care mode.

The Framework

The hospital forged an integrated intelligent management platform involving "hospital—community—home" and covering prevention and care based on the regional health information platform to establish the registry of chronic diseases and implement life-cycle care supported by technology.

Information technology has been adopted to pillar the integrated management platform to include hospitals, communities, disease control and families together and establish the chronic disease registry system.

The innovative mechanism has inspired the motivation of the healthcare professionals, adjusted the scope of basic medication use, guided the patients to go back to the communities and established a prevention and control system of chronic diseases.

Chronic disease care plans have been formulated to tune the rest and work time in the community, and patient clubs for diabetes and hypertension have also been organized to create a caring environment for the patients. The integrated management involving "hospital—community—home" enables life-cycle treatment, health maintenance, and rehabilitation care for the patients.

Implementation

Based on the above-mentioned concept, we redesign the approach of management supported by technology.

First, the integrated management, prevention and treatment platform is installed in the healthcare organizations for providing life-cycle follow-up and care services.

Identification and registry. When a patient is identified and diagnosed with hypertension or diabetes in a tertiary hospital through tests, the system pops up a standardized window of chronic disease profile that is automatically populated with the demographic information (including name, sex, health insurance/citizen ID number, and contact information) of the patient from the hospital system. After recognizing the information, the physician is required to confirm the patient's contact details and give the name of the neighborhood or the community. As soon as the information is saved, it would be updated in the Xiamen Chronic Disease Integrated Prevention and Control System, including the demographic information, neighborhood, diagnosis, prescription, plan of care, diagnosing physician, for the future monitoring, follow-up and preventive intervention (see Figure 16.4).

Community management. The primary level healthcare organizations receive patients with chronic diseases referred by the tertiary hospitals and are responsible for providing standardized health management for the positively diagnosed patients. Patients are followed through clinic visits, phone calls, and home visits. Care services such as treatment, instruction, lifestyle intervention, and occupational rehabilitation are provided. Patients' needs identified during the follow-ups are reported to the specialists in a timely manner (see Figure 16.5).

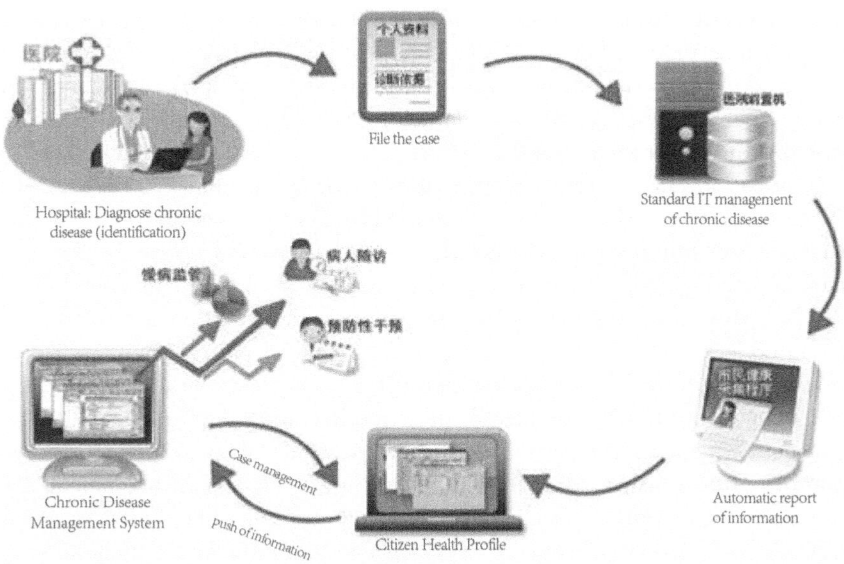

Figure 16.4 Chronic disease diagnosis and registry process in secondary and tertiary hospitals.

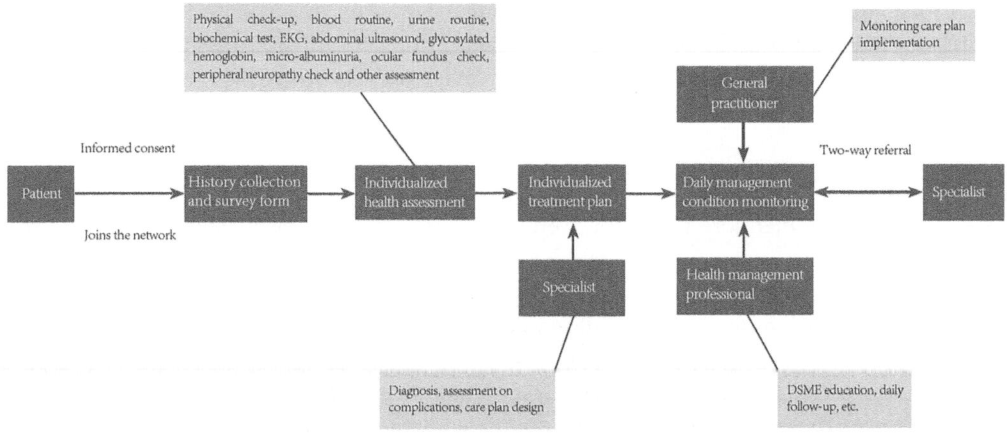

Figure 16.5 Life-cycle management chart of hypertensive/diabetic patients.

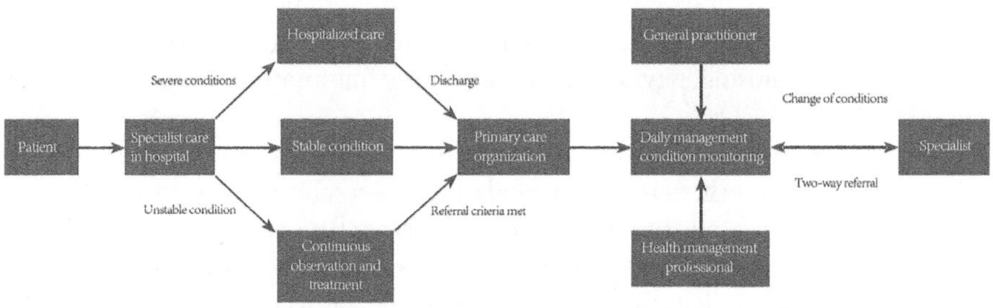

Figure 16.6 "Three-level professional" referral flow.

Upward referral. The community organizations refer patients with hypertension or diabetes to hospitals when necessary. They could appoint specific physicians to see the patients. The physicians then could retrieve the patient's information from the chronic disease management system and set alert to remind the patients about the visit for possible intervention.

Treatment and downward referral. Physicians in the tertiary hospitals could access the patients' information referred by the community organizations and provide treatment accordingly. The outcomes would then report back to the primary level organizations (see Figure 16.6).

Attention from physicians in hospitals. The hospitals could identify new patients with chronic diseases and patients for whom a profile needs to be established on the monitoring platform. They can also review the follow-ups and preventive interventions provided to the patients in the communities.

Intervention from healthcare authorities. The healthcare authorities and CDC could also supervise the situation through the system in both hospitals and communities and get the information regarding new patients, the prevention and interventions taken and the profile management.

Community intervention. The community monitoring platform is implemented to track the management of patients with chronic diseases referred in from hospitals and referred out from the communities as well as the management of patients' profiles. The government also relies on this innovative mechanism to motivate healthcare professionals, adjust the scope of basic medication use, encourage the patients to go back to the communities, and establish a prevention and control system of chronic diseases. Patient clubs for diabetes and hypertension have also been organized to create a caring environment for the patients.

In addition, the comprehensive management system based on the regional information platform has realized the life-cycle care for patients with chronic diseases. To be more specific:

1. The comprehensive health management system enables the synchronization of the patients' visits and disease management, which binds the information from healthcare organizations with that of people's lifestyle and diet. Based on that, health management devices, such as sphygmomanometers and pedometers, have been used by the patients to collect the data about their health status.
2. Patients could upload their health data to the cloud (the Comprehensive Health Management Data Center) to complete the personal HER on the regional health information platform so that the physicians or other healthcare organizations could design better health management plan based on the information.
3. The health data uploaded are analyzed for risk assessment, and feedback is provided to the hospital. Other healthcare organizations or the community service center to serve as the evidence for individualized care plan improvement. With the trend chart and recommendations given by the system, physicians, or health maintenance professionals could better improve the patient's health and the outcomes through regular encounters.
4. The health information or the improved plan of care are synchronized with the communities to allow better understanding of the population health.

The government can then retrieve the data from the platform for big data application through cleansing, aggregation, and analysis. Useful information would then be generated to provide new insights and create new values to the policy making process for the prevention and control of chronic diseases.

The integrated life-cycle management of patients with chronic diseases encompasses the services from both communities and hospitals, both general practitioners and specialists, both self-management and professional interventions covering prevention, treatment and rehabilitation services. It offers a more convenient approach for the patients to enjoy better services and a solution to improving general population health on the local level.

Case 3: Nursing Information: Extraordinary "6+1"

Since the official launching of HIMSS preparation in May 2016, the Nursing Department has prioritized the nursing information on its agenda. The Nursing Department played a cooperative role in optimizing the structured nursing medical record and the nursing PDA functions according to the HIMSS criteria.

Transition of the Role and Effective Communication

The hospital adopted the "1 (leading department) +2 (IT Center and vendor) +N (involved departments)" mode for the implementation of HIMSS EMRAM Stage 6 criteria for effective and rapid development and adoption of new functions and systems in clinical units. As one of the leading departments, the Nursing Department is responsible for changing peoples' mindset and transit the role of nurses from being cooperative to being proactive.

Communication modes were adjusted for more efficient cooperation with the programmers and other IT personnel. Several task groups were organized by the Nursing Department, including Nursing Information Group, Decision Support Group, Human Milk Group, Structured EMR Group, Task List Group, Information Collection Group, and the Blood Transfusion Group. The head nurses of relevant units were assigned to be the group leaders. The Nursing Department decided on the goals and framework of the program. Each group was assigned with defined tasks. The group leader was responsible for proposing requests based on the day-to-day clinical work and communicate directly with the programmers.

The Nursing Department and the programmers identified and confirmed the requests on the routine project meetings. Due to the lack of knowledge about the clinical work flow, the Nursing Department toured the programmers in the units to encourage better understanding of nurses' work and their IT needs. Gradually, a "test—unit pilot—optimization—full implementation" mode was formed for the rollout of new functions and systems for nursing. It took only 2–3 weeks to bring a newly developed function alive based on the request, which greatly cut the R&D cost and time, and improved the efficiency. More importantly, the nursing system has been gradually enhanced.

Stage 6: Continuous Improvement of Nursing System

On July 29, 2016, we had our Mock Survey for HIMSS EMRAM Stage 6, the consultants listed several findings related to nursing, including nursing documentation, nursing clinical decision support, reminder on due/overdue medication administration, and nursing task list. In the following improvement activities, the Nursing Information Group also granted the best support.

CDSS was developed and trialed in pilot units, including the decision support for nursing assessment (pain, pressure ulcer, fall and MEWS) to assist the staff nurses to make the most appropriate decision rapidly and to transform the nursing care to a more evidence-based one with the available information technology.

CDR was installed to collect discrete data from the nursing documentation to realize a higher level of data aggregation, information sharing and process coordination as well as the fine management of nursing care.

The closed-loop management of the human milk and baby formula was embedded in the information system in the Neonatology Department to ensure the safety of breast feeding of the babies who are not roomed-in with their mothers.

The Nursing Department also participated in the redesign of the blood transfusion closed-loop process. A full-process paperless monitoring function was realized in the system to enable the handover and bedside administration to better ensure the safety of blood use.

Imperfect Human Milk Closed-Loop

Human milk closed-loop management was one of the three loops led by the Nursing Department. A closed-loop task team was formed comprising the IT staff, programmers, and physicians and nurses from the Neonatology Department. The task team started from the reality in the clinical unit and reviewed the entire process of the human milk flow, and finished a closed-loop design within 20 days covering the ordering, delivery of human milk to the ward, label printing, storage, thawing, and bedside administration. That was the first loop that we had finished during the preparation.

During the Mock Survey of Stage 7, the consultants pointed out, "The dose of the human milk was not counted in the 24 h intake volume." Again, in the Stage 7 on-site validation, the surveyors identified excessive storage of human milk in the unit, which could cause repetitive thawing and withdrawal, posing infection risk to the little babies.

Proud as we were before the validation, we realized that IT development is an endless journey and should always anchor on the basis of improving patient safety and clinical efficiency.

PDA: Give Nurses Back to Bedside Care

After the first round of JCI survey, the work load resulted from various assessment, documentation and nursing charting increased significantly in addition to the already busy nursing and caring services at the bedside. We heard complaints from physicians and patients that they didn't see nurses much in the patient rooms. On the other hand, the nurses were not happy because of the overtime caused by increasing work they had to handle. To solve this problem, the Nursing Department decided to take the HIMSS opportunity to improve the efficiency of the nurses.

First, PDAs were introduced to the units to replace the PC. This allows our nurses to document at the bed side with all nursing assessment forms then built in the PDA system. Besides, nurses can use PDA to execute physician orders while verifying the medication and food given to the patients and capturing the time of administration in the document.

The patient education, another important part of nurse's work, can also been performed on the PDA: The nurses can input the education content and document in the chart at the same time by clicking on the item they need to perform. Meanwhile, the nurses can also maintain the education content (e.g., admission, medication use, examinations, discharge) on the PC. While providing education to the patient, the nurse only needs to select the template in the PDA and the content would be brought up by the system automatically. This helps to ensure the uniform education across the hospital.

Reminders are also set for new orders, urgent orders, overdue orders/tasks together with the time slot screening function, helping the nurses to be more focused on the urgent/due tasks (see Figures 16.7 and 16.8).

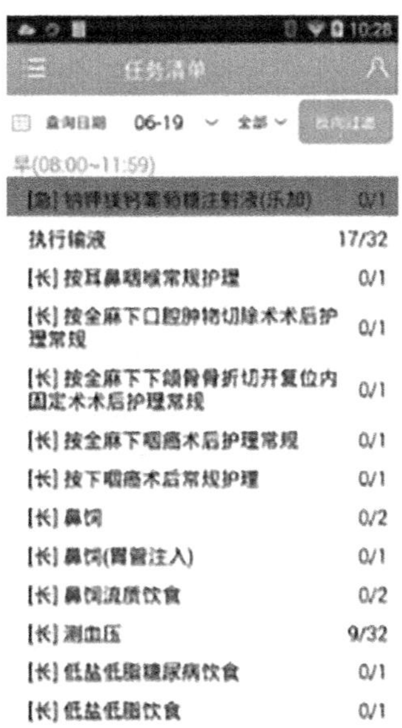

Figure 16.7 Task list (urgent order in red and prioritized).

Figure 16.8 Time slot screening in task list.

Take skin test as an example. Task reminder is built for skin test orders in the PDA. Before the test, the nurse asks open question ("What is your name?") to verify the patient's name and then scans the wristband and the skin test medication. After the order is verified, the nurse injects the medication for penicillin test into the patient. Then the nurse clicks the "administered" button on the PDA screen to confirm the completion of the task, which also triggers the countdown of 15 min in the system. When time is up, the PDA would send a reminder reading "Time is up for skin test on XXX" with vibration and sound alarm. Then the nurse would know that he/she needs to check on the patient's reaction. After checking on the patient, the nurse could directly document the results in the system which would synchronize the information into the Temperature Sheet and STAT Order Sheet in the patient's medical record. If the patient is indicated with negative result, "Penicillin (–)" would show up on the screen. The nurse's signature would also be captured by the system (see Figure 16.9). This improved process makes it an easier and better experience for nurses and further improved the quality and safety of the patients.

We also redesigned the bedside medication administration process in the system. Our nurse uses PDA to scan the patient's wristband and the barcode on the medication for verification. If it is correct, the system requires the nurse to confirm the result of administration again in the system as "administered" or "abnormality." This allows us to capture the exact status and time of medication administration.

The Joy of Being Paperless

With the implementation of digital signature and more forms built in the PDA, like the temperature sheet, glucose sheet, blood pressure documentation, task list, and many others, the EMR adoption became more prevalent in the hospital.

The continuous upgrade of the paperless operation of nursing has reduced the man power and improve the effectiveness of the care on the units. We organized a research team who conducted a survey on the units. The information technology saved each nurse around 55 min during the day shift from printing the charts and signing their names on the paper, and it was a reduction

Figure 16.9 Countdown of skin test and documentation in PDA.

of 30 min during the night shift. Meanwhile, it saved each physician around 35 min from printing the medical record, writing their names and pasting the paper lab results onto the charts. For 1,350 nurses in our hospital, it means that we could save around 1,464 h every day for our nursing staff. According to incomplete statistics, it can also save the hospital around 150 thousand dollars spent on consumables such as paper, ink cartridges, pens, and electricity fees.

The most important thing is that it gives our nurses more time back to the bed side taking care of the patients to observe then, provide patient education, and delivery nursing care. They could spend more time to timely identify the change of conditions of patients and provide instructions on healthy lifestyle, and, finally, facilitate the recovery of the patients. In this way, our patients are safer and content with the hospital. Fewer medical disputes would happen and less social burden would be caused.

Chapter 17

United Family Healthcare

Pan Zhongying, Shi Min, Zhu Yu,
Tian Mu, and Sun Di
United Family Healthcare

Ms. Pan Zhongying/ Sylvia Pan, *Vice President, United Family Healthcare, General Manager/CEO of Beijing Market*

Sylvia has been with United Family Healthcare since 1996. Her career has advanced over the past 20 years due to her hard work, dedication, commitment to excellence, loyalty, and desire to constantly learn and change. Sylvia has held positions as Project Assistant, Government Relations and Accreditation Coordinator, Assistant to General Manager, Assistant General Manager, and Acting General Manager of Shanghai United Family Hospital.

Sylvia holds a Master's degree in Healthcare Business Administration at the University of Colorado, a Master's degree from Peking University's Guanghua Business School and a Bachelor's degree in English literature. Sylvia finished her Ph.D courses of Executive health administration at the University of Alabama at Birmingham and she is currently taking her Ph.D courses at the Johns Hopkins University.

Sylvia became one of the first cohorts of JCI consultant from Mainland China in 2016.

Sylvia is a member of standing committee of Private Hospital Management Branch of Chinese Hospital Association, also the Vice Chairman of Chinese non-government Medical Institutions Association.

Ms. Sun Di/Cindy Sun, *Assistant to the General Manager of Beijing United Family Hospital, Director of Marketing and Sales*

Ms. Cindy Sun joined Beijing United Family Hospital (BJU) in January 2010. During the past 9 years, there were many pioneering marketing breakthroughs. To begin with, the marketing team initiated building Beijing United Hospital's social media network as a strategic project. In 2010, the team first launched the hospital's Weibo matrix and introduced the hospital's general manager and a group of doctors into now well-known Weibo bloggers to the medical blogosphere. In 2013, Ms. Sun was the first to launch WeChat as a channel for hospital promotion and patient education, which was a groundbreaking step in the healthcare industry. In November of 2015, her own lead out sourcing team launched a TMALL flagship shop, making BJU's integrative medical services the first to be made available on this retail online platform. Two years of running the TMALL shop, Ms. Sun and her team has already earned more than 60 million RMB through this platform. She was promoted as Marketing and Sales Director.

Hospital Introduction: Beijing United Family Hospital (BUFH), a subsidiary of United Family Healthcare (UFH), opened in 1997 as a joint venture between Chindex Medical Limited and Beijing Union Technology Development Co. Ltd. UFH has established itself with hospitals and clinics in Beijing, Shanghai, Guangzhou, Wuxi, Tianjin, Qingdao, Bo'ao and Hangzhou as the provider of choice for those seeking premium, personalized healthcare. There are over 400 full-time doctors from 25 different countries and regions working in UFH. Additionally there are over 1000 part-time experts and over 900 nurses on the team.

For two decades, UFH has established an inclusive and all-dimensional service structure that includes prevention, diagnosis, treatment, and rehabilitation and covers the entire life cycle. Over 30 clinical specialties and services can be found in UFH, including cardiac center, oncology center, Da Vinci surgery center, neurosurgery, gynecology and obstetrics, pediatrics, catheterization laboratory, pathology and laboratory, surgery and orthopedics.

International Accreditation: Most of the hospitals and clinics under UFH have been accredited for JCI. Specifically, BUFH is a 5-time JCI-accredited organization, and it was certified with HIMSS EMRAM Stage 6 in November 2017.

Contents

Preface

Resolved to Be an Outstanding Leader

The year 2017 was a remarkable year for BUFH, which marks the twentieth anniversary of its foundation, the fifth-time certification of CAP (College of American Pathologists) in July, the fifth JCI survey in October and the certification of HIMSS EMRAM Stage 6 in November.

UFH has endured great hardships over the past two decades: UFH did not achieve the phenomenal growth that many had expected at the beginning due to the ground-breaking step of foreign investment in healthcare industry in China amid new government policies, the complicated administrative procedures for foreign physicians practicing in China, the unique administrative structure and model distinct from other organizations. The most prominent cause was the type of unprecedented model that UFH has adopted in China. Among one of the first organizations in China to learn about and acknowledge the quality program of JCI, BUFH, and United Family Shunyi Clinic were accredited by JCI in 2005, when they were also the first JCI-accredited organizations in Asia. UFH has played a pioneering role in JCI standard adoption throughout the entire healthcare sector in China. Since then, the other five hospitals and a dozen of clinics under UFH became accredited by JCI in succession, among which were comprehensive hospitals, satellite clinics, rehabilitation facilities, and tumor center. UFH's experience in learning and applying JCI standards to improve its quality program has laid a firm foundation for its rapid progress.

Seeking Common Ground while Reserving Differences

The "international healthcare" feature of UFH has been acclaimed in the healthcare sector, which manifests as international doctors, patients, and insurance (payer). When it was started in 1997 as one of the first joint-venture hospitals in China, BUFH recruited healthcare and administrative professionals from different countries whose experience had represented the diversity of education background and healthcare culture. With direct billing mechanism established with over a hundred international insurance companies and medical transport services, BUFH is serving patients from 183 countries and regions around the world with some 200 full-time staff physicians from over 20 countries and regions.

Such international features have added to the complexity and scale of operational management. With the diversity of staff cultural background, soon after UFH opened in 1998, the leadership realized that the distinction of medical education and training standards from different countries were reflected on the approach of frontline staff. Physicians treated patients of the same sort differently, and adopted different treatment for the same diagnosis, which made it hard to standardize practice. As such, healthcare quality and safety would not happen without a standard-driven and effective system. After several years of discussion and attempts, UFH decided to prepare for JCI accreditation in 2001 by establishing our internal quality standards that would center around JCI standards.

The notability of JCI was a far cry from what it is now since only a scanty few organizations had been accredited throughout Asia. If all that we would achieve would be just a piece of certificate, it was not worth the massive investment of human and material resources. In 2001, with the support from the officials of the Ministry of Health, China Hospital Management Society started to consider international accreditation standards for hospitals. Later on, Peking Union Medical College Press translated and published the JCI standards in 2003, the first of its kind in China. Mr. Cao Ronggui, former Deputy Minister of Health, once said, "The underlying philosophy of the JCI standards is the principle of quality control and continuous quality improvement." This comment can be found in the Preface of this book as well. His comment happened to be in perfect harmony with our initial concern in UFH: "How can we prove we are on the right track and how can we stay on this right track?" Our answer to this concern has been to establish and improve a patient-centered safety and quality standards by going through JCI accreditation. The next question we faced was how to get JCI accreditation and how to adopt JCI standards. There was almost no other hospital in China who we could learn from, and it was costly to request for JCI consultation. It seemed to us that the priorities for investment allocation should be new equipment and facilities and high-level professionals so that we could see the return sooner as a newly established organization (Figure 17.1).

Learning underlies behavior change. Likewise, organizational learning drives changes in organizational behavior to generate new consensus. The hospital leadership believed that internal reform could be sustained by learning JCI standards by ourselves, making trials and experimentation, and summing up experience as well as lessons. Put it another way, an in-depth and thorough understanding of JCI standards can be obtained if we turn knowledge into practice while learning. With this as direction, managers of all levels as well as clinical directors started a drive to study JCI standards, evaluate themselves and correct gaps, and hold ourselves against standards. When staff doctors who had practiced in the U.S. showed us standards and hospital policies for JACHO, taken from their colleagues in the U.S., we came to realize JCI standards were not exactly the same as national standards in the U.S. Instead, JCI standards are more applicable to hospitals outside the U.S. as they have taken into account the diversity of resource availability and the stage of development.

Indeed, this drive furthered our understanding toward JCI standards throughout the entire hospital and built our confidence of a successful JCI accreditation. However, not until 2004 when UFH set up Quality and Safety Dept. and got some first-hand experience with JCI via mock survey did we realize that we had made a lot of detours. For example, administrators had spent a large amount of time on writing policies but they turned out to be irrelevant to the actual work. The reader had difficulty relate the policies to the practice as actual steps and procedures were

Figure 17.1 The general physicians of UFH.

Figure 17.2 UFH nurses and JCI surveyors in 2008.

not described. Also, our initial learning experience included inflexibly reproducing policies used in American hospitals in our own hospital as if it was mere handwork with scissors and paste. Therefore, some descriptions in the policies were fundamentally different from what it was like in real life in Chinese hospitals. Looking back on those days, had we sought professional JCI consultation at the beginning of the preparation for standard interpretation and baseline evaluation, we would have saved some detours and resources, especially time (Figure 17.2).

Since we spent excessive time on self-learning, we did not make it to become the first JCI-accredited hospital in China. But more importantly, our efforts paid off as all the staff had got used to self-learning after the drive to study JCI standards. Also, all the entry-level staff, including house keepers, security guards, and maintenance workers, became aware of their roles in patient safety in addition to their own job responsibilities. Specific training modules had been established as well. As we became more involved in JCI standards, we kept evaluating ourselves and correcting gaps. Finally, in 2005, the hospital and clinic of UFH successfully received the initial accreditation, representing the first health system in Asia being accredited by JCI. Following BUFH, hospitals in Shanghai and Tianjin, the rehabilitation center in Beijing and clinics in Beijing, Shanghai and Guangzhou became JCI accredited in 2008, 2011, and 2014 in succession.

Each survey brings us new insights in the JCI philosophies, and highlights the concept of "seeking harmony but not uniformity, and seeking common ground while reserving differences." These are the basis of reliably high standards of healthcare services driven by concordant and continuous care standards in UFH, a health system with a variety of facilities, including comprehensive hospitals, specialized hospitals, and their subsidiary clinics or independent clinics.

Mutually Supportive for Common Growth

JCI takes care of not only health services but also facility safety, infection control, and administrative management. As an impetus for progression, JCI accreditation has kept clinical and other departments learning and improving to serve the overall growth of the entire organization. UFH will receive the fifth round of JCI survey this year (2017).

Over the past decade or so when UFH has gone through four JCI surveys, its hospitals have grown from ones with main services being general medicine, gynecology and obstetrics and pediatrics to comprehensive hospitals with services expanded to level 2 and 3 care. The growth of Emergency Dept., Surgical Dept., Orthopedics Dept., Neurosurgery Dept., Cardiac Center, and Tumor Center has added to the complexity and challenge of service landscape in UFH as we are handling more and more critical cases and complicated surgeries. In 2016, UFH registered operational revenue of 800 million RMB yuan with 83 beds as healthcare quality has been increasing as a result of JCI standard compliance effort. The level of care has been enhanced as are also performing advanced surgeries with new technologies that require higher level of expertise (represented by minimally invasive surgeries performed by Da Vinci system) in addition to the traditional surgical armamentarium of C-section and general surgeries for children (Figure 17.3).

Over the past 12 years, UFH has come to success along the process of JCI standard adoption. UFH now has mature clinical and administrative teams who provides ever better patient care services. One update that deserves to be mentioned is Ms. Pan Zhongying, CEO of BUFH, has accepted the offer from JCI and been appointed one of the first JCI international consultants from the mainland of China. Ms. Pan has been on the position of CEO since 2008 and involved in three JCI surveys of the hospital in succession. The opportunity came as Mr. Jilan Liu, Principal & JCI Consulting Director, Greater China, encouraged Ms. Pan to join the upcoming JCI consulting team for China toward the end of 2015 to help increase the exposure of JCI standards among a greater number of organizations in China. After receiving training and passing evaluation from central office of JCI at the beginning of 2016, Ms. Pan completed several programs in Japan, Indonesia, and China. Meanwhile, she leads a weekly leadership round in our organization to evaluate clinical areas with JCI standards and provides direction for quality programs. As such,

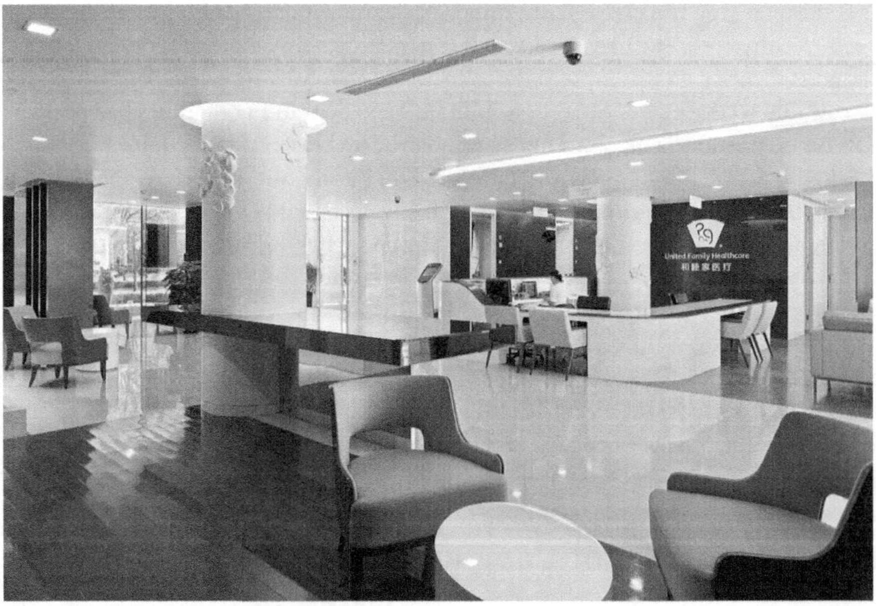

Figure 17.3 United Family New Hope Oncology Center.

she has obtained more direct and first-hand understanding of JCI standards as she has been wearing several hats, ranging from bystander to participator and consultant.

UFH has also witnessed JCI's increasing presence in China over the past decade. Since we received the initial accreditation, delegations from almost a thousand organizations throughout the country have paid visit to us. They have been curious whether JCI standards are more something limited on paper, just like some other hospital accreditation standards do. Here in UFH, they have been able to see how practical and practicable the JCI standards are. We also see an increasing number of JCI hospitals in China, and an ever-growing number of hospitals who take the challenge of accreditation as an opportunity to improve healthcare quality and hospital management.

An Endless Pursuit of Quality

JCI's expectation on quality has never been a mere formality. Therefore, ensuing each JCI survey, we went back to the gaps identified during survey and made correction, and expended this experience to other relevant areas. When conducting survey in the hospital, surveyors not only see the compliance of policies to standards but also look into data aggregated that properly reflect policy compliance. They even verify whether data have been communicated back to staff, so that data are truly driving policy compliance.

In the example of antibiotics, when preparing for the survey in 2008, we delineated the use of preoperative prophylactic antibiotic use in the policy by adapting the latest international guidelines and standards so that the policy would be applicable to China and our organization. Meanwhile, we monitored the compliance of medical staff. Although we made a strict requirement by using standards, we did not aggregate the data we had collected. Therefore, the data had not been used to guide our quality improvement. It was cited as something that we should improve by the surveyors. Such problem of insufficient data aggregation was common among several other metrics identified during UFH's surveys.

To address this issue, the organizations worked to ensure the closed-loop management with data in the years that followed. Data analysis is one thing, but communication of the analysis results is more important. Data are not directing action unless they are communicated to people who generate them. In 2015, the hospital invited international experts to come and provide training on Six-Sigma and Lean management to the key administrators and quality staff regardless of the cost. They walked us through a series of topics, including the design of quality projects as well as data collection, aggregation, analysis, and display. Also, the experts taught us data analysis tools that we got to learn the first time. After the training, 16 participants were awarded with "black-belt." After that training, the entire staff members, from key administrators to frontline clinicians, had more profound understanding of the value of data and the fact that we should use data to justify purpose. Coming back from that training, the quality team was able to provide more professional support to data processing.

Another aspect of the antibiotic case features the never-ending effort to improve quality and patient safety, which represent the core philosophy of ongoing improvement of JCI. In 2017, the Medical Council, whose members are directors of clinical units, unanimously agreed to keep preoperative prophylactic antibiotics as a hospital-wide clinical priority and that it would be included as department-level quality indicator (QI) for Surgical Dept. Having met the benchmark of National Health and Family Planning Commission, UFH still wants to take new challenges and scale new heights.

The JCI mindset is also reflected on the way that data are interpreted. The role of hand hygiene among clinicians in reducing healthcare associated infection has been emphasized in the International Patient Safety Goals. To collect hand hygiene data, most hospitals in China still rely on daily observation by infection control staff. The results are usually above 90% or even 100%, which seems there is little room for improvement. But UFH is not content. We adopted JCI quality improvement tools, among which TST (Targeted Solutions Tool) is intended for issues in healthcare organizations closely related to patient safety but difficult to address by directing organizations to proven solutions. This tool helps with data collection, analysis, and the development of proven and customized solutions. With advice from this toolset, we trained a number of "secret shoppers" who observed how clinicians nearby washed hands by random sampling. The result turned out that hand hygiene compliance was only 50%! International data revealed that the average hand hygiene compliance among clinicians was merely 40%–50% around the world. However, with the concept of continuous improvement in mind, we still regard hand hygiene as a topic that should be the key position for a long time, and we helped improvement by updating hand hygiene posters in the hospital according to WHO hand hygiene guidelines. After 2 months of intensified training, our hand hygiene rate increased significantly to 64%. There have been many examples like this throughout our journey toward quality improvement with JCI adoption. The way we questioned the data we collected on hand hygiene was recognized and encouraged by JCI surveyor. There are many other similar examples where JCI philosophy has helped us improve quality.

To Promote a Fair and Just Culture

The thing that staff in UFH have been proudest of is the use of Edwards Deming's management principle on the basis of the safety culture in line with JCI standards. According to Deming's rule, 85% of the problems in any operation are within the system and are management's responsibility, while only 15% lie with the worker. Whenever an adverse event is reported, the first thing we do is to map out the steps in the event, trying to figure inappropriate or user-unfriendly designs. Based on the defect in the process, we then develop action plan to figure out the root cause of reoccurrence of similar error. Nevertheless, to apply this principle, seeking defect from the system alone is not enough.

When human error is involved, we need to carefully categorize the error based on fair and just culture and properly determine the nature of the behavior, instead of paying no attention at all to the impact of undesirable human behavior. The nature of the behavior ranges from inadvertent error, risky behavior, and indiscreet behavior.

Take driving for example, if one misses the sign of speed limit and drives too fast, that is regarded as inadvertent error. If one sees the sign of speed limit but still over speeds with the impression that everyone else is driving over speed and no measure is in place to track, that is risky behavior. It is similar to drunk driving, a purposeful mistake, and presumptuous crime. When handling adverse event, we always start with identifying system error, but human error is found attributable for around 15% of the time. If dealing with human error, we do not lump them together. Instead, we identify the nature of that error and make reasonable judgment. The key question to ask is: does he or she make this error because of insufficient understanding of policies, or purposeful act? This makes a world of difference and will be handled with different consequences. If the former is the case, the person should be counseled and provided with intensified training. Otherwise, the person's thinking should be corrected.

There is no end to the journey toward quality and safety improvement. We have been always reiterating that, rather than a target, JCI is more of a means that effectively helps and drives us to improve, and encourages us to learn new practices nationally and internationally.

After achieving JCI accreditation, the Laboratory, and Pathology services of BUFH have been accredited by CAP for five times in succession after 2007, which has provided extra guarantee for the safety of Laboratory and Pathology services, a clinically supportive function.

Base Decision on Data

When providing JCI consultation in the same team with Ms. Jilan Liu since 2016, Ms. Pan has noticed something interesting: many HIT operation team members cordially address Ms. Liu as "Teacher Ms. Liu" (to call someone a teacher is the most respectable way to address people in China) and always want to discuss with her how IT can help with JCI standard compliance. The electronic systems of these hospitals that we provided consultation were not from the best brands. Some of them were even inexpensive. But Ms. Liu can always share some practical and efficient solutions for the puzzles that have haunted hospital administrators, where they had difficulty handling the large volume of patients without compromising standard compliance, especially when it involves clinical decision support and the management of clinical pathways. Then Ms. Pan came to realize that hospitals are also going for HIMSS certification, in addition to JCI standards, to redesign their top-level structure of information system and direct clinical practice and application.

In contrast, as an early adopter of EMR, PACS, LIS, and other systems in China, UFH was seeing a lot of complaints from physicians that a large amount of work still required manual operation. By then, Ms. Pan acknowledged that the defects in our information system may become a hindrance of UFH's further development and deserve attention as early as possible. As such, UFH set an important goal of HIMSS EMRAM Stage 6 certification in 2017.

The EMR solution of UFH at that time was highly integrated and conducive to holistic management of health systems, where functions of emergency care, inpatient care, community care, and family care were integrated. The language options included Chinese and English, which was perfect for working environment with cultural diversity. Clinical processes were standardized in the system based on the "fee for service" payment model, and interoperability had met international standards. However, this information system faced the challenge and barrier of insufficient investment from human and material resources, missing pieces along the processes and insufficient detail-based management that was paramount in the trend of paperless work. In terms of data, they were not valid enough, the challenge of quality monitoring over data remained high, and the few methods used for data analysis offered little insight. On top of these, quality monitoring with the use of information system was applied in limited scope, which provided little support for clinical decision making or management.

We have believed that going for HIMSS EMRAM Stage 6 enhances our capability of delicacy management, using data throughout the practice of clinical procedures and pathways and science-based medication management. On the nursing level, the functions we add for HIMSS EMRAM validation will ease nursing workload and reduce error during the administration step taking place at patient's bedside. With all these upcoming benefits, we will have higher transparency and validity throughout in the works. The increased competency of clinical decision making and managerial expertise is demonstrated as better adoption of evidence-based medicine, smarter programming of rules, and the proper balance between consistency among different units and customized need of each unit. Working toward O-EMRAM certification is a challenge to UFH's service model, team-based care, patient education, patient self-management, and the risk-stratified management for chronic disease population. In terms of methodology, HIMSS EMRAM Stage 6 evaluates the functionality of EMR by starting with "a particular point" in the care process to see how the electronic system guides and facilitates care and how interoperable the system is among all the clinical areas. But the bar is higher for HIMSS EMRAM Stage 7 in terms of the scale and complexity involved as the evaluation will involve more aspects and all levels. HIMSS EMRAM validation is a means rather than an end, which drives the application of technology and information throughout the hospital for higher safety, smarter services, and better financial return. By preparing HIMSS EMRAM Stage 6 certification, we expect to empower management with technology, support decision with data, guarantee the improvement of quality and safety, and achieve greater integration between clinical processes and the latest health informatics.

After 20 years of operation and 12 years of experience with JCI accreditation, BUFH's journey has demonstrated that JCI accreditation is only a starting point, and triennial surveys are stations along the journey for us to start again, a process that drives us to challenge and improve ourselves. With all these efforts, we aim to provide patients with safer care of higher quality and centers on patients.

Case 1: Code Purple: Ensuring the Safety in Childbirth Does Not Afford a Single Minute

A benefit from JCI accreditation for healthcare organizations is that they are supported to foresee risk particular to the organization's environment as well as the population they serve, and come up with precaution and response plan. To highlight the importance of risk prevention and the resources support of staffing, material, and finance from leadership level, the FMS (Facility Management and Safety) chapter of the JCI standards has listed disaster as a stand-alone item and required organizations to develop specific plan and test it to ensure proper response when disaster occurs.

For a healthcare organization, the key to guarding against risk is to establish rapid response mechanism based on the risk it faces. At the beginning of preparation for accreditation, UFH established a hospital-wide rapid response system, which involves a standardized rapid response process so that physicians and nurses are better able to concentrate on resuscitation and fewer time is spent on coordination and support seeking communication among units and departments. Based on the well-established code blue process (for cardiac or respiratory arrest) and considering the risk of gynecology and obstetrics, the Gynecology & Obstetrics Dept. innovated a code purple for obstetric patents, which is initiated under any obstetrical emergencies, including premature rupture of placenta, prolapse of umbilical cord, intrapartum, and postpartum hemorrhage, fetal distress, and uterine rupture.

Gynecology and obstetrics have been one of the highest-volume services provided in UFH, though it has been only categorized as a level 2 comprehensive hospital. Pregnant women coming for delivery has been a major population in our organization. With the change of people's preference of child-bearing changes in response to the relaxation of family planning policies in China, more and more couples opt for getting more children than one. This means we will receive pregnant women of higher risks due to higher ages as well as the high prevalence of scarred uterus from cesarean section of the first delivery. By September 2017, over 64.6% puerpera had been giving birth to a second child or more in UFH.

To help pluriparae who have given birth to their first baby via cesarean section try vaginal delivery this time, UFH has provided vaginal birth after cesarean (VBAC) service to encourage natural delivery. This leads to an unneglectable risk of conversion from vaginal delivery to cesarean section and resuscitation as the risk of rupture of the scarred uterus may aggravate as these women attempt to deliver through vagina. The incidence of such conversion is not significantly higher than non-VBAC women, but disastrous consequence may occur on the way to the operating room from the labor room when resuscitation is not effectively provided or actions needed are not taken carefully. Considering its threat to the safety of the mother and the baby, such obstetrics emergency has been prioritized as high risk.

With the collaboration from Quality Control Office and relevant units, a code purple system was established as an emergency mechanism and included in the hospital-wide system of emergency response (see Figure 17.4).

When handling emergency condition, the first-line physician of labor room immediately calls a physician of higher level, who determines if it meets the criteria for code purple. If so, he or she informs a midwife to initiate the code purple process. The General Front Desk of the hospital communicates the code and the location via overhead announcement, and obstetrician, pediatrician, anesthesiologist, ER physician, ICU physician, pediatric nurse, and staff from laboratory, blood bank, ultrasonography, and pharmacy arrive at the site within 3–5 min. The operating room closest to the site of the event immediately gets ready to receive the patient. As soon as the senior

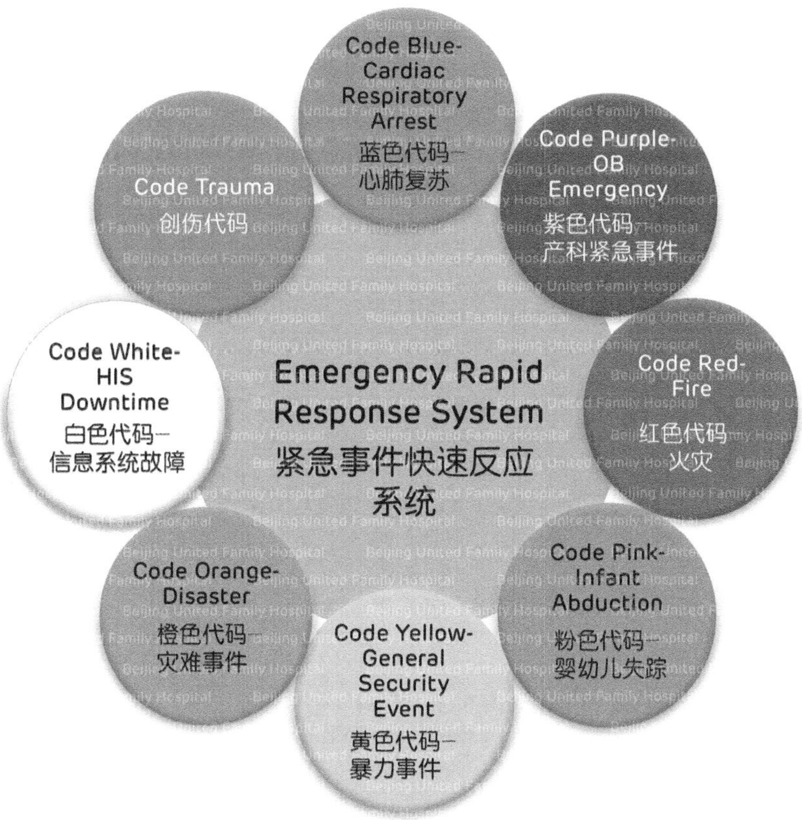

Figure 17.4 Rapid response system of the hospital.

obstetricians arrive at the site of the event, he or she takes over as the general command of the response. As soon as arriving, the midwife establishes the second intravenous access, obstetrician reassesses the women in labor as well as the fetus and staff from Laboratory prepares for transfusion that may be probably needed.

The code purple policy has detailed specification of the steps to take and roles of individuals in the process. It describes, for example, how nurse lets the family know the situation, how the scrub nurse and circulating nurse get ready to start the surgery at any time, and even how security guard is required to come and help with the transport of the patient.

Every time after a code purple event is handled, the obstetric members involved in the case gather to discuss and review the entire event step by step. If they find gaps in the process, they change the process or policy as soon as possible; if they find any member did not provide adequate support, they provide intensified training, so as to improve both the process and the team that handles the event.

Based on JCI requirement on rapid response system of the hospital, we have specified in the policy that if fewer number of event happened than expected in a year, departments in charge of quality and safety organizes drills to ensure every relevant staff is familiar with the process and the steps in resuscitation.

Since the code purple mechanism was established in June 2015, we have had handled 64 purple events, where all the mothers and newborns have been saved. With the 30 min interval between code initiation and delivery of the fetus as our target, we have achieved 13 min on average, with the shortest one being 8 min only. The code of purple has become a code of safety guarantee for the mother and the newborn.

Case 2: Contingency Plan for External Disaster Managed in Great Details

In addition to its own patient care activities, hospital shoulders social responsibility to save life amid public emergencies. Examples can be found in the Boston Marathon bombing in 2013 and Tianjin Binhai (China) Explosion in 2015, when any hospital nearby might be turned into a major rescue provider. Ensuing such public emergency, victims will flood into the closest hospitals nearby in numbers greater than the typical patient volume in the emergency rooms. Such event is categorized as "mass casualty event" among all the emergencies occur in the hospital. "The hospital develops, maintains, and tests an emergency management program to respond to emergencies and natural or other disasters that have the potential of occurring within the community," specified in FMS.6 of the sixth edition of JCI standards. Such emergencies include mass casualty event. Since there is no way to foresee when and where such event will take place, it is impossible to ensure orderly response to an unexpected disaster without an effective contingency plan and the testing of this plan.

For such emergencies, UFH has developed a contingency plan for external disasters based on our own situation and the Hospital Emergency Incident Command System (HEICS), widely used in hospitals in the U.S.

"External disaster" refers to any unforeseeable emergency that occurs outside of the hospital compound and results in medical care needed by multiple patients exceeding the usual capacity of a hospital. It could be airplane crash, collapse of buildings, emergency involving hazardous material (large area of exposure to chemical or radiation), fire, turmoil, collision of multiple vehicles and mass food poisoning outbreak. A basic assumption in the contingency plan for external disaster is the hospital's structure and integrity are not affected. In contrast, "internal disaster"

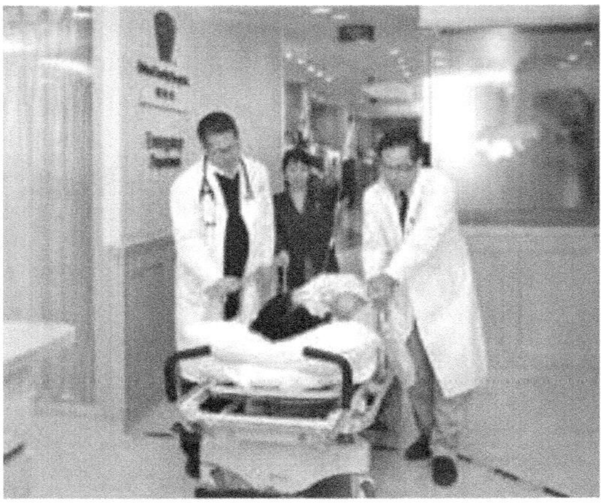

Figure 17.5 The emergency room of UFH.

refers to suspension of services from any cause, which can be power outage of major power outage, earthquake, hospital being destroyed by hurricane and evaluation of patients and staff due to internal fire. Internal disaster is address with a separate contingency plan, so it is not represented in our discussion here.

As a private comprehensive hospital of moderate size (120 beds), BUFH is less competent in trauma and burns than large tertiary-A hospitals in terms of experience, staffing and the number of emergency beds. Therefore, it is particularly relevant for us to develop a contingency plan for external disasters and test the plan regularly to ensure everyone in the hospital is familiar with what to do. The timely activation of the plan and effective resource provision are prerequisites for effective and efficient rescue response (Figure 17.5).

The Contingency Plan for External Disaster for UFH—HEICS

Like a military exercise, there should be principle and trigger criteria for HEICS.

There are two principles involved in our external disaster contingency plan: No. 1, anyone can understand the plan and do what is described in the plan, regardless of whether he or she is a staff or volunteer or anyone else, and whether he or she has been trained in emergency response or not. No. 2, the plan should ensure clinical staff can concentrate on saving patients and victims while other staff provide facilitation and coordination, as staff, clinicians in particular, are valuable resources in disaster response.

If fewer than ten victims come in or when the event is still in the initial phase, physicians alone can response to their need. Only when casualty reaches ten or other need arises shall the entire staff get involved (via code orange). We decided the maximum to be ten because that is our usual maximum volume in the emergency room. If victims keep coming, we need extra resources.

Headquarters for Emergency Response and Emergency Toolkit

In dealing with disaster, who is the general incident command? What should I do? How does communication work? And what shall I start with in face of such complex situation?

Being effective, organized and ready holds the key to disaster response. In UFH, a brief and practical "emergency response toolkit" has been in place in the room for on-call physician in the Emergency Dept. The toolkit includes a meticulously developed contingency plan and all the guidelines, tools and forms that physician, nurse, and administrator may need. Since disasters are rare events, staff are not required to keep every point about disaster in their memory, as long as they have a rough idea about the process and the exact location of this "universal" toolkit (Figure 17.6).

During the Initial Phase of an Event or Dealing with Small Disaster

There are two sets of plans for disasters depending on the severity. The physician of Emergency Dept. and the general administrator on-duty usually opens the toolkit for small disaster first.

The ER physician does the following things:

- Take out the file binder labeled with "Do this first; disaster start here ①" (Figure 17.7a, left), in which "phone tree packet" "ER MD first steps," "command packet" and "security packet" are found;
- Bring the "phone tree packet" to the front desk and have staff there make calls according to the packet. The contingency plan provides a list of persons and their contact information who need to get noticed in the event of disaster. The list makes sure these people receive notice and does not require staff to make judgment;
- Delineate the triage zone and assign a nurse there, and a physician as well if possible, who prioritizes severely injured victim and assigns tasks to physicians coming in to offer help.

The general administrator on-duty does the following things:

Bring more nurses to this area; direct others out of the emergency room to accept victims coming in; assign tasks to staff such as security guards, customer service agents and transporters; and work with ER physician to decide whether to initiate the hospital-wide response by announcing code orange. All the actions and motions possibly needed in such case are clearly and succinctly described in "command packet."

Disaster of Moderate or Large Scale—Code Orange

When the number of victims reaches ten, the announcement of code orange is recommended.

If this decision is made, the ER physician takes out the toolkit labeled with "disaster ②" from "disaster response toolkit" (see Figure 17.7b on the right):

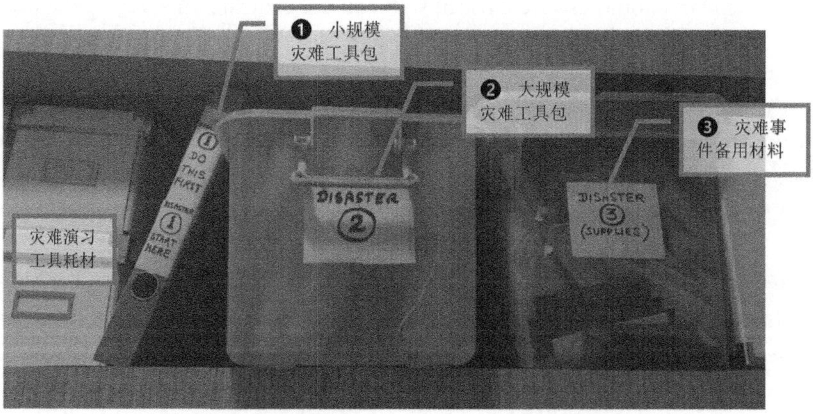

Figure 17.6 Disaster response kits.

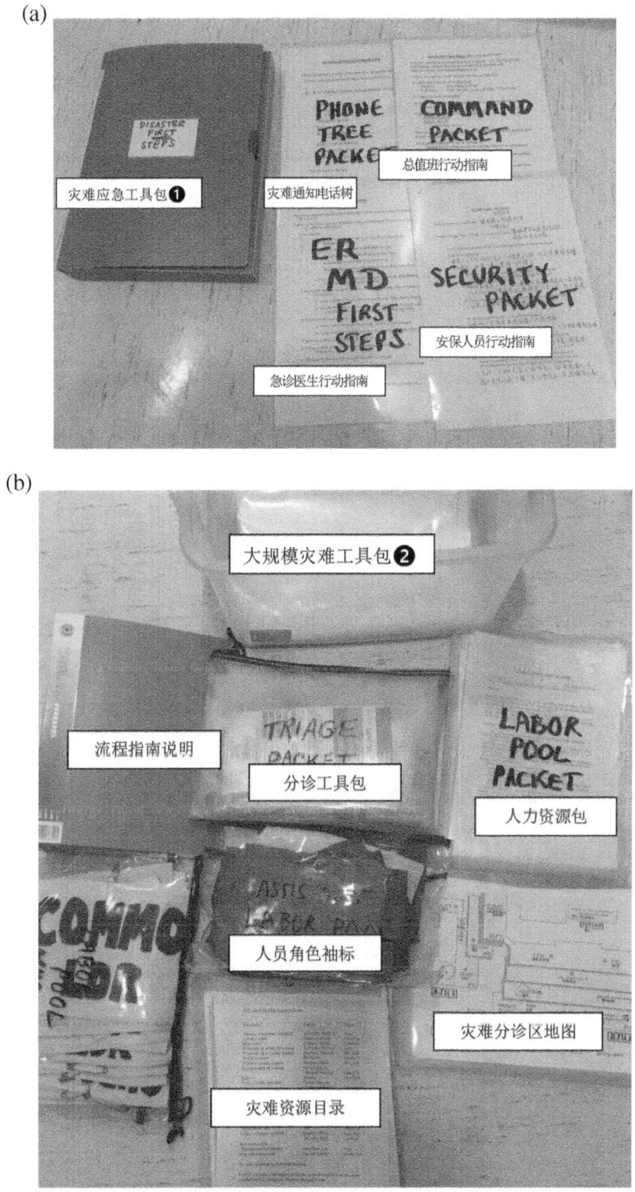

Figure 17.7 Packets in the toolkits.

- Bring the "phone tree packet" from this toolkit ② to the staff of broadcasting service to announce a code orange. The code orange and assembly point are announced via broadcasting to all the occupants in the hospital. Relevant staff and volunteer rush to the assembly point immediately and announce their arrival;
- Establish a patient triage system based on "triage packet";
- Hand "labor pool packet" to the general administrator on duty and return to the physician's own duty.

Patient Triage System

A clear triage system holds the key to efficient medical care to victims as we are using limited healthcare resources for precious lives of patients. All the tools needed for triage system are included in the "triage packet (see Figure 17.8a and b)," which includes the "armband for triage chief," "triage instruction," "triage map," "patient documentation tags," and "patient wristbands." With these tools, any physician can efficiently triage victims coming in and ensure the efficient use of the precious healthcare resources.

The armband for the triage leader is an immediately recognizable indicator of the position of healthcare providers. The triage results determine the sequence of victims to be seen.

(a)

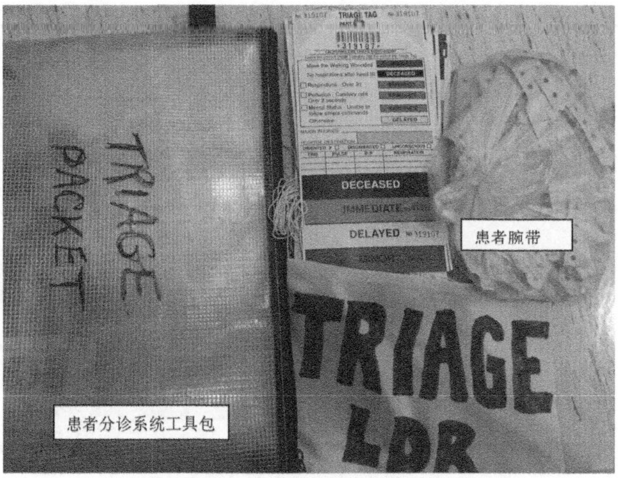

(b)

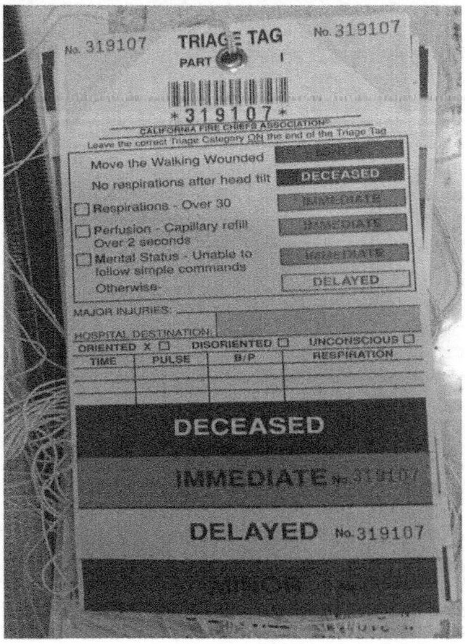

Figure 17.8 Triage packet.

Triage Instruction and Triage Map

In the event of disaster, victims are categorized into four groups, and the criteria for categorization are clearly listed in the instruction. Each group of patients is directed to a specific zone, and the zones are marked in the "triage map." These triage tools are helpful for any physician who does not work here but come to support, so that physicians have uniform criteria for triage. The zones for different level of patients are assigned based on the layout of the hospital under UFH. For example, the most severe patients will be directed to the emergency room.

- Red: immediate, as patient's respiration exceeds 30 breaths/min, capillary refill time is over 2 s or the patient is comatose;
- Green: minimal, as patient can wait for a while as he or she is ambulatory with minor injury;
- Black: deceased; there is no breathing even when the head is tilted to one side;
- Yellow: delayed; conditions not listed above;

Patient Record Tags and Wristbands

The patient tags serve as medical record in the event of disaster, while wristband is a tool for identification. The tag provides key information of patient number, triage category, vital signs, consciousness, other service encounters (if any, such as radiology or ultrasonography) for staff to know immediately at any time. The patient number is consistent between the wristband and tag to avoid misidentification when everything has to move quickly.

The tag and wristband are different from those we routinely used in that the numbers are assigned manually in the event of disaster to avoid any waste of time in entering electronic system or printing. But staff makes sure patient numbers are unique.

The general administrator on-duty does the following things:

- Bring the "disaster ②" toolkit to the assembly point, define zones for each triage category and assign staff. As it is massive disaster, the administrator defines the zones according to the map. The map has been developed with consideration of practicability and convenience according to the triage-based care processes and readily available. Planning beforehand saves time on thinking so that staff can do things required immediately.
- Designate a labor chief, a medical chief, a nursing chief, and an incident command to jointly decide on the scale of the response. For example, based on the role armbands distributed, they determine the size of the HEICS structure involved in this response action, from patient care level to coordination level.

Another advantage of HEICS is it ensures successful cooperation among staff who have been assigned with tasks in this emergency. In other words, when disaster happens, all the people who provide medical care and volunteers can effectively carry out roles defined in the "job action sheet" at hand even without training beforehand. In addition, all the chiefs wear armbands in immediately distinguishable color related to their roles so that staff at the scene can quickly identify them.

For all the roles mentioned above, there are "job action sheet" that explains the title of the role, reporting structure, skills or characters required, and the tasks that they should perform. The tasks are also prioritized into "rank first," "rank second," and "delayed." Based on the scale of disaster, the role assigner decides on role designation of the next phase.

Patient Tracking System

Patient tracking and ongoing monitoring are challenges in disaster response. From our experience on drills for disaster response over these years, we believe necessary documentation and patient tracking are keys to the orderly delivery of care. Therefore, patient tracking mechanism is an indispensable part in the contingency plan so that we can report how we have treated victims to families and authorities and receive the assistance we need in a timely fashion.

The patient tracking plan for external disaster in UFH is laid out as follows:

1. The number from the "patient tag" attached to each patient is used for tracking. As an extra guarantee, patient's wristband also has this number. The staff responsible for patient tracking maintains a list of patients and keeps it current.
2. When a patient is leaving for another care location, the triage physician writes the destination on the yellow form from the top of disaster assessment tag, tears it off and drops it in the box for "floating patients" in the triage area.
3. Every location of the hospital is placed with a "floating patients" box to keep track of every patient leaving that area. For example, when a victim of grade yellow leaves the yellow zone, staff writes his or her name, number, destination and time on the tag and drops it in the floating patient's box. At around 20 min interval, a messenger comes to collect the forms from the boxes and hands them to the patient tracking staff, who updates the information on the whiteboard.
4. An information point can be set up next to the command headquarters where two scribes or messengers stay and document every piece of key information or action throughout the response process.

Miscellaneous

On top of these, the hospital can arrange other activities in the crisis management system, such as press conference and family reception.

Drills for External Disaster

It is important for hospitals to organize disaster drills regularly due to its defining feature of infrequency. The aims of drills are to improve the existing contingency plan and to increase confidence among staff for proper handling as they have the chance to walk it through in real life.

At least two drills on external disaster are required every year in UFH, one as tabletop exercise and the other as a real-life drill. During tabletop exercise, key personnel of the contingency plan participate, including ER director, general physician on-call, general administrator on-call, and staff from quality and safety department, general support section, and other units. They discuss a relevant topic to assess and improve the plan. For example, the topic of tabletop exercise can be "how to respond to disaster more efficiently with IT adoption." A report will be generated from the exercise, and the action proposed will be implemented. Meanwhile, an operation-based drill is necessary to ensure the contingency plan works properly rather than being a mere paper talk.

We may hardly encounter one external disaster in several decades. So the question we ask is how to ensure the drill is realistic so that the plan is properly tested. From UFH's actual works, we found that the crux lies in setting a scenario most relevant to ourselves. For example, scenarios having been simulated in UFH include "influx of international patients with trauma and burns due to airplane landing accident," developed because BUFH is a comprehensive hospital with

演练用于化妆伤者的假血，眼影等

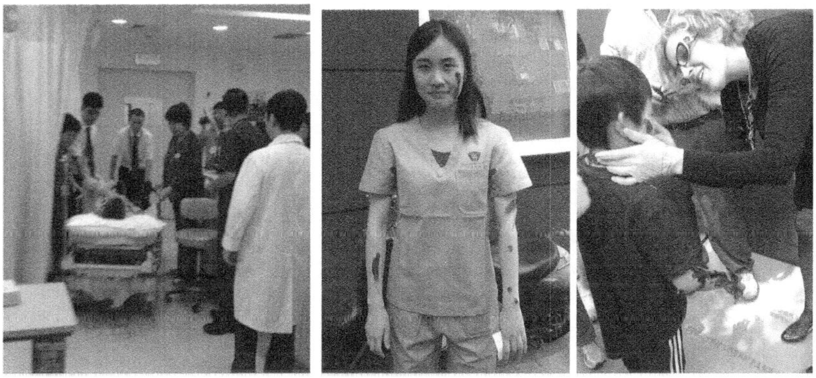

Figure 17.9 Disaster drill in UFH and volunteers.

emergency service who can take care of international patients and is close to the airport; “influx of victims from an explosion in a nearby restaurant” and “group food poisoning event from an international school nearby.” During real-life drills, to make the scenario as real as possible, we invited residents from the community to act as victims (see Figure 17.9)

Thanks to the detailed planning and process delineation from the contingency plans, where the roles of staff in disaster response and the tasks to be done have been clearly specified, as well as the regular tests we take to guard against external disaster, UFH has been able to respond effectively, readily, and orderly when an actual disaster occurs. In 2011, a fire broke out in a hotel nearby from a short circuit of elevator, resulting in the influx of many victims within a short time. ER physician initiated the code orange and staff provided care and referrals needed according to the contingency plan.

The fact that UFH has developed contingency plan for external disasters signals its sense of responsibility to the community. After the sixth edition of JCI standards was released, we modified contingency plans by addressing situations when the personal interests of staff, such as the care for their children as well as senior family members, and their responsibility in disaster response come into conflict. Moreover, psychological consultation will be provided to clinicians and support staff who have been highly involved in caring for the sick and the dying to help them recover from the psychological trauma. Meanwhile, support services are provided to the community as well.

Chapter 18

Shanghai Children's Medical Center Affiliated to Shanghai Jiao Tong University School of Medicine

Jiang Zhongyi, Zhang Min, Shen Nanping,
Xiang Ying, Weng Zihan, He Yi, and Lu Zhaohui
Shanghai Children's Medical Center

Jiang Zhongyi, *Professor and Research Investigator*

Jiang Zhongyi is the President of Shanghai Children's Medical Center affiliated to Shanghai Jiao Tong University School of Medicine, Dean of School of Clinical Medicine of Shanghai Jiao Tong University Children's Medical Center, and Chief of Institute of Pediatric Health Management of China Hospital Development Institute of Shanghai Jiao Tong University.

He has been leading key national and province-level projects of hospital administration and healthcare policies, such as The Analysis of Medical Quality Policies of Chinese Medical Association. *He was awarded "Excellent Hospital President" in 2016 and "Hospital President with Amazing Leadership" in 2018 in China.*

Academic affiliation:

Vice Chairman, Chinese Hospital Management Association

Chairman, Pediatrics Chapter, Biobank Branch, China Medicinal Biotech Association

Vice Chairman, Shanghai Rare Disease Foundation

Vice Chairman, Shanghai Hospital Association

Editor and Appraiser, Chinese Journal of Hospital Administration, etc.

He Yi, *Bachelor of Science*

Mr. He has been working in Shanghai Children's Medical Center for nearly 20 years and became the Director of IT Department in 2012. He has rich experience in hospital information management, architecture design of information system, establishment of medical software systems, computer network technology and system integration.

Lu Zhaohui, *Vice Chief Physician and Supervisor of graduate candidate of Pediatric Thoracic Surgery of Shanghai Children's Medical Center (SCMC)*

Dr. Lu is the Executive Vice President of Women and Children's Hospital of Sanya and the Director of the President's Office and the IT Center of SCMC, Member of Hospital Affairs Committee of Shanghai Association of Hospital Administration, Council Member of Shanghai Volunteer Physician League, and part-time faculty of Medical Education Innovation Program of University of Ottawa. Dr. Lu was awarded "May 4th Youth's Medal" from Shanghai Health and Family Planning Commission in 2016 and nominated for "Top 10 Young Administrators of Healthcare in Shanghai" in 2018.

Hospital Introduction: Shanghai Children's Medical Center (SCMC) Affiliated to Shanghai Jiao Tong University School of Medicine was jointly established by Shanghai Municipal People's Government and US Project HOPE. The center has a capacity of 500 designated beds and 634 available beds, of which ICU beds took up one fifth. It is a state-of-the-art children's medical facility integrating medical care, scientific research, and education.

In 2012, SCMC has obtained the Certificate for Medical Institution Conducting Clinical Trials for Human Used Drug and eight majors are qualified to conduct clinical trials. In addition, SCMC has many outstanding subjects which have significant influence in China and abroad such as cardiovascular and hematologic oncology. In January 2017, approved by the State Council, SCMC became one of the national children's medical centers.

International Accreditation: In 2010, SCMC became the first JCI accredited Grade A Tertiary pediatric hospital in China.

In 2013 and 2016, SCMC passed JCI re-accreditation twice successfully and became the first pediatric hospital accredited by JCI teaching hospital.

In 2015, SCMC won HIMSS-Elsevier Digital Healthcare Award for Outstanding ICT Achievement in HIMSS Asia Pacific Summit.

In 2016, SCMC passed HIMSS EMRAM Stage 6 validation.

Contents

Preface

From Acknowledge to Change, Keep Moving

At the end of 2012, SCMC launched a new round of large-scale information integration platform construction and reconstructed the whole information system. After the implementation (see Figure 18.1), the hospital's business process implementation and healthcare data asset value mining improved a lot and reached a high level.

In November 2016, SCMC successfully passed HIMSS EMRAM Stage 6 (see Figure 18.2) and received compliment from the validation experts. According to John Daniels, Global Vice President of HIMSS, the hospital's information system provided a good interactive interface with all monitoring indicators integrated in the system for frontline clinical employees which proved that SCMC made significant progress in utilizing information technology. Ms. Jilan Liu, HIMSS Vice President, and Chief Executive of HIMSS Greater China, said:

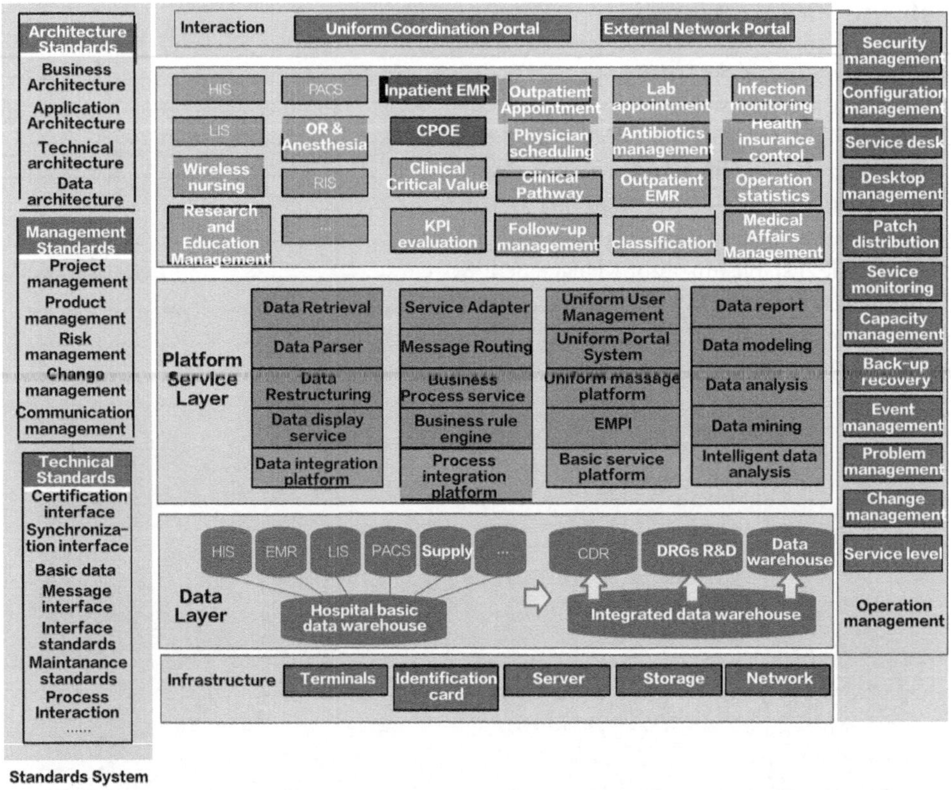

Figure 18.1 Information integration platform construction.

Figure 18.2 A photo from HIMSS EMRAM Stage 6 validation.

During my interaction with SCMC, I realized that having a dynamic management team will help carry out management objectives to process control through implementation which precisely in line with the mission of HIMSS validation that transforming healthcare quality through information and technology will actually benefit clinical employees and patients.

Know Ourselves and Make Changes

Throwback on the past 4 years of implementation, Lu Zhaohui, director of hospital office and CIO of SCMC, was quite emotional.

At the end of 2011, the information management team led by Ji Qingying, vice president of SCMC, and the hospital management level believed that hospital's current implementation was not capable to keep up the development trend at the time. The main problems were as followed: First, SCMC's information system lacked top level design. Thirty subsystems were in tight coupling chaotic state and the system architecture was complicated and inefficient. Second, process management and control was scarce, not to mention the data sharing and standardization in the system. Third, data utilization was incredibly low, from lack of real-time operation and maintenance data, CDR and CSD to accumulation of tremendous healthcare data. Last but possibly the most important, few people regarded information implementation as a key prerequisite for the continuous improvement of hospital quality.

Therefore, in the next year, the information team visited Zhenjiang medical group, Peking University People's Hospital, Shengjing Hospital, and other peer hospital with advanced information implementation, to gain experiences and ideas for the information construction of SCMC.

In November 2012, SCMC decided to partner with Microsoft (China) and launched the reform of the hospital information system (see Figure 18.3), with the cooperation of the leading HIS manufacturers of Wonders Information Company (former Fugao Company).

Comply with the Goals and Achieve the Platform Strategy

The goal of implementation was quite simple actually: make information systems available, usable, and easy to use. However, it was not easy to achieve.

Figure 18.3 Kick-off meeting of data integration platform implementation in 2012.

SCMC named the implementation project as "Data Integration Platform Construction," of which deputy CIO, He Yi, used a vivid metaphor to describe: "The hospital's information systems are the legs of a table. What we are building in the future is a desktop so that we can learn which legs is too long or too short, useful or redundant." At the same time, the hospital was strengthening the exchange and integration of data according to HL7 standards at the platform level.

The First Battle: Reconstruction of Structured EMR

In terms of data sources, EMR, CPOE, and nursing documentation are the three cornerstones of healthcare data. Since handwritten paper medical records have transformed to EMR, tremendous information was accumulated in the system and cannot be efficiently used which must be solved and restructured. Only on this basis can standardization and process control be achieved.

The change of medical records from typing to drop-down options made it hard to copy and paste large segments of texts causing the resistance of clinical doctors. But with stable quality of EMR, less trouble from medical department, and continuous improvement and optimization to allow physicians easily insert any kinds of examination and test results in the records, the objections gradually disappeared.

The information center regarded non-criticism and no objection from the clinical professionals as the biggest compliment. And this is the status quo of the SCMC.

The Second Battle: Nursing Documentation System

At the third World Internet Conference in Wuzhen, Ma Yun said: "Without data, Internet finance is nonsense." So does healthcare information system. The massive, critical, accurate, and real-time clinical data recorded by nurses are a valuable resource for the hospital IT adoption.

Collecting data is an important aspect for electronic nursing documentation. More importantly, our goal is to relive the nurses from their heavy paperwork and give more time with patients. For example, the recognition of "electronic signatures" allows nurses to get rid of printing their care plans every time and finding the right person to sign among frequent shifts.

Until today, the nursing documentation system continues to improve. The nursing department proposed a more comprehensive blueprint for the nursing system structure including nursing assessment, scheduling system, quality control of care, and performance evaluation, etc. Because currently there is no mature nursing system for reference on the market, it is groundbreaking to some extent.

HIMSS validation team spoke highly of the SCMC's nursing system because we have been at the forefront of the industry in terms of interface design, CBI decision support and information sharing among EMR, nutrition assessment and social works, and so on.

This is not only the victory of IT, but the victory of ideas and concepts.

The Third Battle: Release Tightly Coupled System Structure

As mentioned before, in the times when there was no desktop, the hospital systems were complicated and independent. The integration of all systems would require numerous interface design, thus gathering all data on the platform through the new system structure which helped to plug out the makeup ones.

When implementing system platforms, CDR is a necessary component which integrates clinical information systems in the hospital to consolidate and present all patient-centered clinical data to provide decision support. There is a controversy between whether to build CDR or data platform but from our perspective, these two don't really have essential contradiction or conflict. In terms of CDR, it focuses on the integrity and precision of the platform while data platform is an integrated center with data from patients, clinical professionals, and management administrators. Instead of building a data platform aiming at CDR, it would be better to integrate CDR with the goal of building a data platform.

Therefore, the digital integration platform efficiently integrated 38 subsystems of the hospital which realized single sign-on of 1,395 users, established six categories of IT management specifications, teased out 60 main data dictionaries, and defined more than 300 KPIs. Through ESB (Enterprise Service Bus) and master data management, each subsystem could focus on its own professional characteristics and maximize its effectiveness.

Based on the digital integration platform, Patient 360 (or we can call it CDR) has been realized, and the Doctor 360 is a part of the future plan.

The Fourth Battle: Closed-Loop Management and Process Control

The hospital's process management must undertake strictly when it comes to patient safety. For example, the process from doctors issuing prescription, pharmacists checking the prescription, nurses arrange medication, pharmacy dispensing the medication, staff delivering the medication to patients checking and using the medication seems simple but it can be difficult to develop a closed-loop management because too much content related to security management, quality management, and efficiency management involved in the process.

The goal of achieving closed-loop management is simple and clear: to ensure healthcare safety, especially patient safety. Ms. Jilan Liu once mentioned that the operation and maintenance of a hospital was actually composed of countless closed-loop management. From issuing to the final execution of an order required detailed monitoring and recording throughout the entire process. Only in this way can the entire operation and maintenance system be measurable, assessable, and improvable.

System monitoring and quality control are closely connected to each other so we must ensure the smooth progress of process in compliance with regulations. For instance, the system won't reject the signature of an attending doctor to sign a medical history within 24 h of the admission of the patient, or within 48 h, or perhaps longer. But his behavior will be recorded and overtime response will be regarded as an indicator of poor performance in department assessment. Moreover, a surgical record cannot be saved or printed without key parameters such as intraoperative complications and blood loss. In this case, information system is designed to help prevent clinical professionals to make mistakes.

The Fifth Battle: Establishment of Management System

As mentioned before, improving the effectiveness of system's operation and maintenance through management system such as healthcare quality control was merely an example of tightly coupled with clinical services. There were many relatively independent operating systems in other management department of the hospital like comprehensive budget management, three importance and one greatness policy, supply purchasing application, document management, and power operation monitoring, etc. The establishment of these systems contributed to a great benefit when the hospital was standardized, normalized, and efficient.

Take the comprehensive budget management system as an example. It has been operating smoothly from budget preparation, approval to execution and realized the management and control toward the whole process for more than 2 years. The implementation of comprehensive budget management was not only to strictly enforce the financial policy and control the reimbursement process, but also to urge administrators to think clearly about their annual plans and priorities instead of simply solving problems in a chaotic situation. From this perspective, budget management was not about money, but the strategic thinking of the hospital.

The Sixth Battle: Business Intelligence Demonstration

With a large amount of data in the hospital platform, the utilization of these data would test the structure and functions of the system. Data visualization was an effective and intuitive way to present data to the administrators. Through comprehensive assortment, SCMC compiled more than 300 KPIs into a book as the basis for BI data demonstration, and provided real-time business operational indicators as the specific motivation of monthly performance assessment and yearly assessment for department heads to administrators, directors of departments, head nurses, etc.

BI platform allowed the administrators to see data of outpatient visits, average waiting time, number of inpatients and operation, medical income, proportion of consumables and proportion of medicines, etc. (see Figure 18.4), while the directors of departments saw the relative data of responsible department and actually improved service quality, optimized service processes, and reduced medical costs.

Figure 18.4 BI platform interface of SCMC.

Some Accomplishment

System implementation is the way of professional technician and management administrators effectively integrating collected data and processes to be implemented using information and technology. In other words, information system is the IT reflection of the human mindset.

Therefore, when building an information system, the first thing is to think about what you want to do, what is the goal, the process, and the evaluation method without the limitation of information system; then the next thing is to discuss with IT personnel comprehensively and make necessary adjustments or changes; the third step is actual construction and implementation. During operation and maintenance process, it is normal to make some detailed adjustments but there can be no denial of architecture or the process. In many cases, incorrect initial design may lead to the failure of an information system.

During the entire implementation, administrators and implementation team must pay full attention to the needs from the frontline clinical users and apply automatic and intelligent methods of management, monitoring, and guidance into the system to create a spontaneous and silent system environment which is the ultimate goal of information center.

At the same time, it is vital to introduce an internationally recognized standard, HIMSS, as an important benchmark that measures the EHR adoption, integrity, and utilization of the information system. As CEO of SCMC, Jiang Zhongyi said, "If you think your work of implementation is pretty good, then we need some proof to demonstrate our ability such as passing HIMSS validation." Because there is no mature governance system toward implementation in China and less tangible outcome compared to infrastructure construction, hospital administrators are very cautious about investment toward implementation. Answering to decision maker's needs, HIMSS EMRAM provides proof and assessment for turning investment into actual motivation. During HIMSS EMRAM Stage 6 validation preparing process, with help and support from HIMSS team, and with solid foundation of passing two JCI accreditation, we put a lot of effort though still were unprepared for HIMSS EMRAM toward technical approach to achieve the rigorous, systematic, and comprehensive requirements from clinical and management department. After this, we grew up and became more confident.

Keep Moving Forward

Over a decade ago, the implementation of the financial system gradually expanded to the laboratory examination system, EMR system, and CPOE system which brought the hospital information implementation to the front stage under new situation. In the recent years, from passive acceptance to the active development of information implementation, healthcare organizations are facing a new round of revolutions and has become the hot topic and focus in the industry.

In the era of Internet Plus, the goal of SCMC in information implementation is far beyond the *status quo*. Our next step is going to build a high-level information architecture, an intelligent healthcare system, a children's health data platform, a regional dynamic level III tertiary system of diagnosis and treatment, and introduce a commercial insurance system. The information system we built needs to adequately protect and support healthcare services, to show greater value of healthcare big data, and to bring actual benefits to providers, patients, and the entire community.

Case 1: Information Technology for Safety of Medication Administration

Ms. Liu, a newly recruited nurse, was going to give the child in bed 12 intravenous infusion. She used an open question to identify the child's identity, skillfully assessed the venous indwelling needle on its right hand, lightly disinfected and connected the scalp needle, pulled back and confirmed the patency, and then turned around to fetch the intravenous drugs in the nursing disk. Just then, teaching doctor Wang who was supervising Ms. Liu suddenly said, "What needs to be done before giving medicine?" Ms. Liu stopped at a sudden, "Ah! I forget to check with PDA!" Doctor Wang said, "PDA checking is simple, but it is very important for medication safety."

At present, medication errors have become the most prominent problem affecting the safety of inpatient children's medication. Since SCMC passed the JCI accreditation for the first time in 2010, we have been continuously improving and perfecting relevant systems and norms. At the same time, combining with the best practice evidence related to the safety of inpatient children's medication, SCMC has endeavored to seek the most advanced information management method: Form a closed loop of the whole medication process through the application of wireless medical information system, strengthening the elimination of risk factors from the remote link to the close end link, aiming at minimizing the medication errors and ensuring the safety of inpatient children's medication.

Founded in 2004, an Evidence-Based Collaboration Center of the Joanna Briggs Institute and School of Nursing Fudan University was established aiming to generate the best nursing evidence through rigorous and uniform procedures for the practice and decision-making of nursing staff, to guide and drive practice with research. As a benchmark organization in Chinese nursing industry, the center published the *Guidelines for Clinical Nursing Care for Safety of Inpatient Children Medication* and clearly stated that establishing a medication administration system and applying a safe and efficient computer system can reduce the incidence of medication errors. Based on this guideline, we integrated the best evidence and information management process into all safety aspects of inpatient children's medication to avoid medication errors and ensure clinical safety.

Acquiring and Sharing Key Information of Medication

At inpatient admission, inpatient child receives a two-dimensional code wristband containing basic information of the child for system identification from the admission health office. The recorded weight, history of allergies, and medication are saved, updated, and shared at the doctor's and nurse's workstation after admission or transfer.

At the doctor's workstation, the doctor uses personal employee number and password to log in the system, select the child who needs medication, and enter the orders. Based on the child's weight, height, and age, the system automatically provides the recommended dose of the medication. Meanwhile, the system also has safety restrictions and alerts based on weight, height, age, medicine features, and medication status including the maximum dose limit, cumulative amount control, liver, and kidney dysfunction drug alert, penicillin high-risk drug control, potassium chloride, and other high-risk drug control and warning, repeated medication reminders, etc.

On this basis, we provide knowledge bases including prescription manuals and medicine guide as professional references based on PASS system to accomplish automated medication checking which has omitted the process of transcription of doctor's orders. After the doctor submitted the prescribed orders and nurses received them, nurses make arrangements for dispensing after confirming the orders.

All-Along Monitoring from Dispensing to Administration

The pharmacist checks the prescription after receiving the relevant medication application. Then the medicine goes through a series of processes such as taking medicine, entering warehouse, dispensing, leaving warehouses, packing, transferring, and receiving. With individual packages, the medicines will be packed as a whole with two-dimensional code identifications of the basic information of the child, and finally received and signed by the ward.

When a nurse gives medicine to a child, first, she uses open questions to confirm the identity of the child. Second, she uses handhold PDA scans the child's wristband through infrared light. After the scan, PDA's screen will jump directly to the order execution task list of the corresponding child. After scanning the child's medicine bar code, screen will jump to the order execution of the corresponding medicine, which includes all information of the drug, including its name, dose, route, dosage form, time of administration, whether to execute that day, and whether to execute within the regulated period. After confirming all the information, click the allowed, to-be-executed order request (see Figures 18.5 and 18.6).

According to order execution page, the execution of the nursing items can be real-time monitored, including key indicators such as omissions, delays, and planning of care. If the child's identity and medication information are correct, the system will allow to execute; but if the child's identity is incorrect or the medication information is incorrect (if the medication does not match or does not reach the time of administration), the system will not allow the execution.

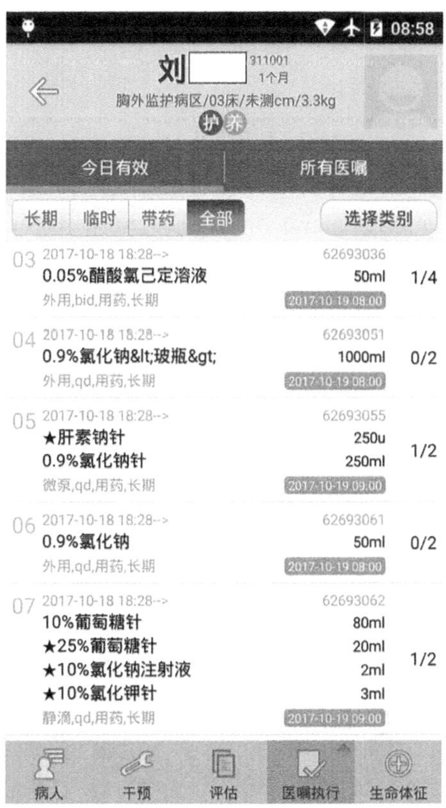

Figure 18.5 Affective medication order of a patient for today.

Figure 18.6 To-be-executed request list of every order within 24 h.

The system automatically records and tracks the actual execution of the orders, including each actual executor and actual execution time of long-term and temporary orders, to assist in the recording and collection of safe medication administration information. After entering the nurse's workstation system, order execution record can be reviewed.

Through the use of information technology, SCMC has built a safe and efficient firewall from standardizing, normalizing, and optimizing complicated operational process to eliminating, controlling, and defending potential or induced working and human errors.

Since implementing information technology based on best practices, nursing-related medication errors have continued to decline from 0.2 per 1,000 patient days to 0.1 per 1,000 patient days which is a significant progress. The exciting news is that high quality process built by well-implemented IT architecture will nurture employee's good work behaviors, habits, and cultures, form a positive human-machine ecosystem, and benefit both clinical professionals and patients.

Case 2: Information Implementation Solved Adverse Events

Adverse events have been the global focus problems for a long time. Since the introduction of JCI accreditation in 2010, SCMC has been working hard to build a set of Adverse Event Management System that meets JCI standards.

From Reporting System to Information Reporting System

According to the *JCI Accreditation Standards for Hospital 4th Edition* and the Chinese Level III rank hospital appraisal standards, and referring to a large number of Chinese and overseas documentations and experience of Chinese hospitals that have passed JCI accreditation, SCMC has classified adverse events into three categories, four levels, and seven types according to the severity of the events (see Table 18.1).

During the preliminary preparation process for the first JCI accreditation, the quality management office of SCMC teased out the adverse event reporting process from following four aspects:

1. Identifying and filling out the reports of adverse events;
2. Analysis and inspect the causes;
3. Revise the description and analysis of the event;
4. Collect and analyze adverse events, and formulate and improve the relevant system of adverse events.

At the same time, encourage medical staff to report adverse events and create a cultural atmosphere without punishment.

Through the process of the adverse event reporting (see Figure 18.7), the quality management office has developed the *Adverse Event Management System* (SCMC-QPS-04), which clearly states several principles:

First, create a culture of no punishment and encourage healthcare professionals to report adverse events. Second, the reporters should state the event in an objective and fair manner, and be responsible for the truthfulness of the content they report. If the reporters do not fully understand the fact, the hospital will not trace accountability of the reporter. Third, except

Table 18.1 Definition of Adverse Event

Level of Adverse Events		
Level	*Category*	*Definition*
Level I	Sentinel events	Unexpected death or permanent loss of extremities, organs or other critical function irrelevant to the diagnosis of a patient during the provision of clinical care; or such event involving a staff working in the hospital
Level II	Event causing adverse consequences	Injury to body or function of a patient or staff that is not caused by the diagnosis but the provision of care or the work in the hospital during the care or work
Level III	Event causing no adverse consequences	Mistake that has been made but did not cause any injury to body/function or just very mild consequence requiring no intervention during the provision of care or work in the hospital
Level IV	Risk	Mistake that has been caught and prevented in time and did not cause or exert potential risk during the provision of care or work in the hospital

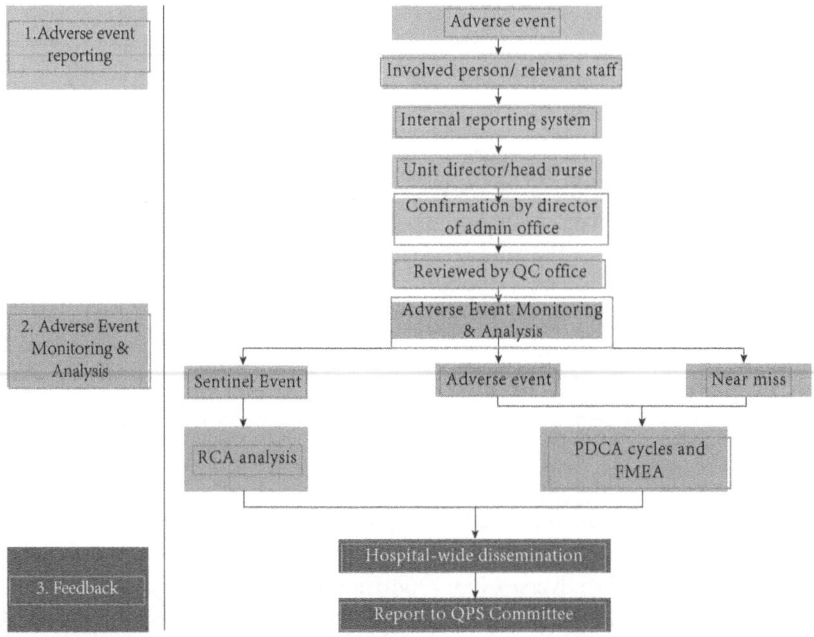

Figure 18.7 Process of the adverse event reporting.

that the hospital has the right to deal with the responsible person of the incident according to the relevant management regulations, the event-occurring department, office, or individual shall not retaliate against the reporter; otherwise, shall be severely punished according to the regulations of the hospital. Fourth, quality management office is responsible for the authority management of the adverse event reporting system in the hospital while information department is responsible for the maintenance of the background data.

At the same time, the clear division of responsibilities for all members included in the adverse events reporting process (see Figure 18.8) facilitated the implementation of the adverse event reporting process. As the hospital-level department for quality and safety improvement, the quality management office was responsible for the acceptance, determination, and documentation of adverse events. The office collected adverse events with high frequency quarterly, and conducted root cause analysis when it's necessary and then reported feedback and put into practice on the hospital's medical quality meeting.

Scientific management must rely on information implementation. How to monitor all four procedures of adverse event report through information became a problem to be resolved at that time.

Normalizing the process and system through information system made adverse event report controllable and easy to trace. The quality management office and the information department formed a team for the adverse event reporting system and cooperated with external companies to open the *in-hospital reporting system* within the hospital's internal OA (see Figure 18.9), and achieved an information reporting of adverse events.

In 2015, the adverse event reporting system performed a comprehensive system upgrade according to the flaws found by hospital employees when using it, and additional functions at

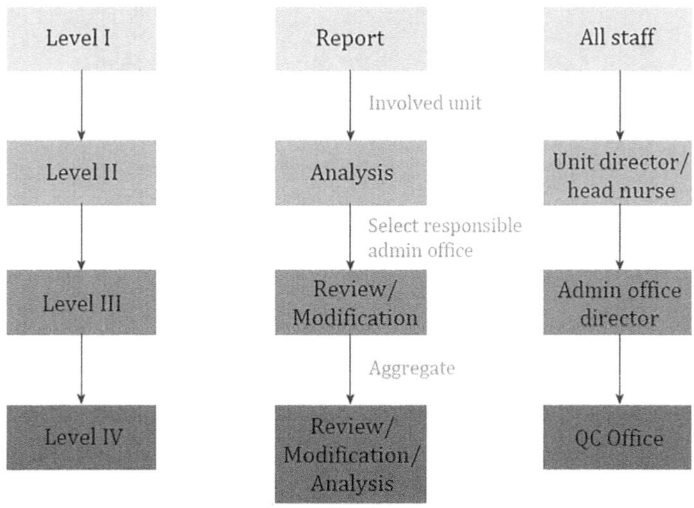

Figure 18.8 Division of responsibility of adverse events reporting.

Figure 18.9 Entry interface of adverse event reporting system.

each reporting level (see Figure 18.10) were added, such as process history, feedback, and report tracking, copying, sending reminders, forwarding, and revoking comment or edit, etc.

The information platform of adverse event reports made it possible for real-time reporting and increased employee's motivation to find and identify problems. All staff in the hospital have the right and obligation to report adverse events, thus creating a quality culture for the hospital.

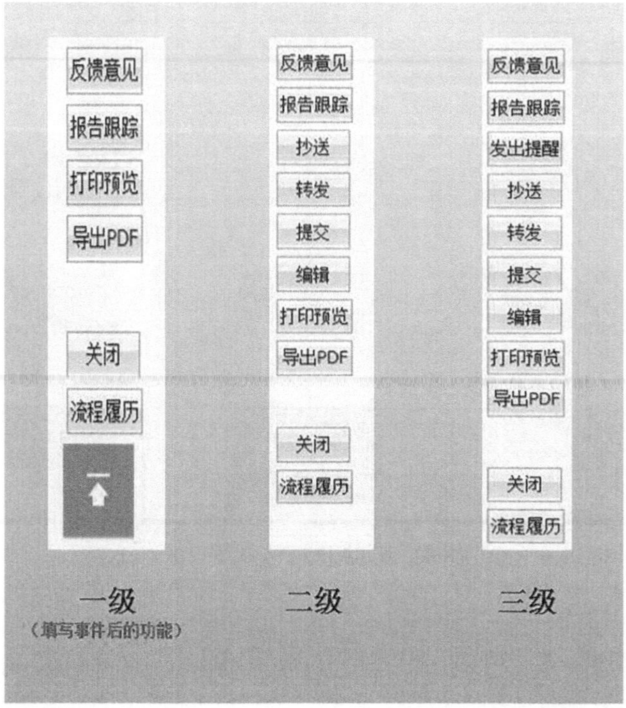

Figure 18.10 Classification of adverse events.

Feedback for Adverse Event Information Process

The reporting of adverse events and data collection were not the ultimate goal of setting up the platform. Instead, the goal was to analyze the type, frequency, departments, and crowds of the events (see Figure 18.11), to combine with risk control assessment, to identify high-risk events and to find the essential reasons using root cause analysis and management tools like PDCA to avoid adverse events. Only by guiding the practice can an information data platform realize its value.

Figure 18.11 Analysis of adverse event.

(Continued)

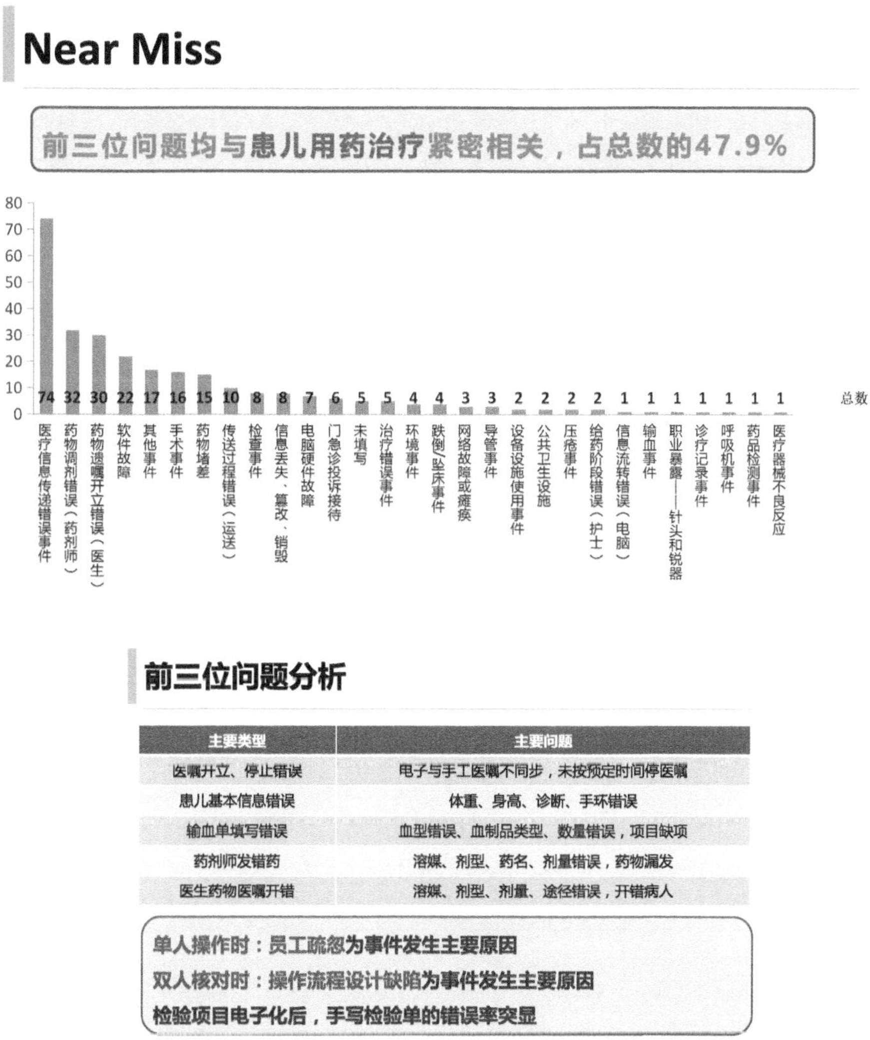

Figure 18.11 (CONTINUED) **Analysis of adverse event.**

Two Interconnected Standards

The core idea of JCI is continuous improvement of patient safety and quality. The arrival of the information age has made it possible to perform process monitoring in an efficient, convenient, and comprehensive way. JCI is focused on whether process, diagnosis, and treatment meet the safety goals while HIMSS provides technical support for meeting JCI standards. Just as the design of the adverse event reporting process, JCI requires effective and timely detection and identification of adverse events, the establishment of an active reporting mechanism, intervention and optimization of medical process by administrative departments, preventive measures to avoid the occurrence of seriwous medical events. All of the management objectives need application of information tools to essentially solve the existing medical risks such as setting up automatic event classification, layer analysis, and timely disposal. These two standards will complement each other and continue to improve healthcare quality to the next level.

Chapter 19

The First Affiliated Hospital of Zhejiang University

Wang Weilin, Zhao Cailian, Zhu Yu,
Jin Jianmin, Lu Xiaoyang, and Qiao Di
The First Affiliated Hospital of Zhejiang University

Prof. Wang Weilin *is the former President of the First Affiliated Hospital, Zhejiang University. He is a Chief Physician and Supervisor of doctoral candidates and has over 30 years of practicing, researching and teaching experience in hepatopancreatobiliary surgery. Prof. Wang is highly skilled in complicated surgeries for liver cancer, pancreatic cancer, liver transplantation and pancreas transplantation.*

Hospital Introduction: The First Affiliated Hospital of Zhejiang University (hereinafter referred to as FAHZU), established in 1947 by Zhu Kezhen (a late former president of Zhejiang University, a prominent scientist, geologist, meteorologist, and educator), is a large tertiary-A hospital with services in clinical care, professional education, and research. It is also the largest provider and instructor of clinical care, education, and research in Zhejiang Province. It covers an area of 1 million square feet and has three campuses: Qingchun Campus, Chengzhan Campus, and Daxuelu Campus.

Over recent years, FAHZU has been a pioneer of reform of public hospitals. By moderating the program "National Key Technologies in Digital Healthcare and the Research of Excellent Regional Application Model," a key science and technology program of the Eleventh Five-Year Period (2006–2010), FAHZU succeeded in establishing a healthcare service network with three level: provincial, county (district) and village and making quality health care services accessible to the grass-roots level.

International Accreditation: JCI accreditation in 2013 and 2017.

Contents

Preface

International Standards Applied in Qingchun Road

What is JCI? When we decided to go for JCI accreditation, few people understood it in China.

In a meeting of intermediate-level administrators, a leadership member described: "In health care around the world, JCI accreditation is like ISO9000 certification for enterprises. It is a high bar. It is a set of quality standards for health care organizations recognized worldwide. It represents the highest standards for health care services and hospital administration. WHO has praised it highly as an accreditation scheme." In common expression, the JCI standards requires hospitals to spare no stone unturned to ensure patient safety and provide the safest care to patient.

Since our preparation started in February 2010, the incoming and outgoing CEOs agreed upon the philosophy in hospital management of "being patient-centered." Both of them regard it as the lofty state of regarding serving patients wholeheartedly as an eternal mission, and seeking "promoting health of mankind with supreme quality in health service."

Dr. Zheng Shusen, the former CEO of FAHZU, Fellow of Chinese Academy of Engineering, commented:

> To improve the service metrics, facilities, equipment and quality according to "international standards" of a hospital as large and comprehensive as an aircraft carrier is the endeavor to spread the philosophy of "being patient-centered" and a systemic

> approach to the problem of expensive and inaccessible health service. The effort we expense is not for a certificate. Rather, it is for the overall guarantee of quality and safety and the convenience for patient.

Similarly, Dr. Wang Weilin, the present CEO of our hospital, said: "JCI accreditation is a new starting point for FAHZU that drives us to pursue the best quality and safety, and stride towards a medical center of international standard by starting with JCI standard compliance on every detail."

When the Old Mindset Clashed with New Ones

During a training for unit-level quality monitors on "How to set up quality program and unit-level monitoring measures," we heard complaint from staff that "Why do you require us to do PDCA as we have been so busy already? Why do we need two measures in each unit? We have to do all these things on our own because we are not supported by the unit director. What's more, we still need to take care of patients and perform other duties." Some also challenged: "What is unit-level policy? What is quality improvement program? What should we talk about in the unit-level quality meeting?"

When Ms. Zhao Cailian, Director of Quality Dept., explained and tried to involve staff in "management and analysis of adverse events," clinicians went into a hubbub of voices, with some questioning "Why should we report adverse event? And at least five reports per month per unit? How can we report if there is no adverse event? Will we get punished from the adverse event reported? Does it have an impact on our annual evaluation and promotion? What types of events are adverse events? Like a broken computer on the floor?"

With these doubts, how could we encourage the clinical units to start quality programs? How could we have them develop monitoring measures? How could we encourage staff to report adverse events voluntarily? Healthcare providers were dealing with excessive pressure from the general public, in addition to the internal stress from the hospital of promotion, position assignment, skill improvement, and healthcare safety. For healthcare safety in particular, clinicians were practicing with the most meticulous care as if treading on thin ice: any error or failure would lead to consequences more severe than accountability and disposition from the organization internally. Against this backdrop, it was not likely that staff would voluntarily report adverse event to avoid any consequence. Rather, they might cover up or try to make the mistake sound less serious. To apply JCI standards at the beginning, we were faced with these challenges in QPS (Quality and Patient Safety) chapter alone, apart from the ignorance toward quality tools like PDCA, RCA, HVA, FMEA, etc.

The attempt to modify the process of correcting an order was met with doubts and questions as well. Before we adopted JCI standards, physicians wrote orders by hand on Standing Order Sheet and Single Dose Order Sheet. Specifically, a physician wrote on the sheet, made a copy, and stated the time of initiation and termination. Then the physician handed the copy to the nurse in charge of general coordination, who then entered the order into the electronic ordering system. Then a nurse in charge of orders compared the order entered against the physician's original writing to ensure the physician had not changed anything. The nurse then submitted the order to the pharmacy. This process sounds complicated, but it was necessary because staff had to ensure the colleague did not enter a wrong order because of illegible writing of the physician, or prevent error when the physician did change the order but forgot to tell nurse.

As we started to apply JCI standards, we got rid of this order transcription process. Instead, we asked physicians to give order directly from the electronic system. Now if a physician changes an order, he or she prints and signs a form that states the change, and gives it to the nurse. The nurse then signs and submits the order.

When this new process was first put into effect, physicians were against it and asking: "Why does it take a physician to enter an order into the electronic system? When a patient needs certain supply or device, physicians do not know how this works in the electronic system." After going through a running-in phase, physicians became accustomed to and compliant with the new process.

Who Moved My Cheese?

"What would you do if you were not afraid?" This sentence comes from the book *Who Moved My Cheese?* Indeed, it is fear that draws us into all kinds of puzzles.

This quote reminds us of the time when we started to prepare for JCI accreditation. The story shared here featured sub-specialty directors of all the laboratories. As the saying goes, "A long-lasting split is always followed by a reunion." With the advancement of time and technology, laboratories of the hospital had gone through many structural changes: everything was done in only one lab at the beginning, but later it grew and was separated into several labs. There were 15 laboratories across the hospital, whether large or small, when we had a JCI mock survey; consultants left us with a definite requirement: all the laboratories should be integrated. That was a real headache! We experienced being overwhelmed for this intimidating task.

The hospital leaders looked at the thick exit report with a heavy heart. Among so many pending tasks, integrating laboratories alone was hard enough. Fifteen of them! It was not easy to maintain fairness at this moment. No director was willing to give up his or her position because the administrative status of the lab itself was an important source of revenue. What's more, the action of integrating the labs alone would open up a can of worms: problems would spring up like domino effect. The CEO and deputy CEO were at a loss what to do. At the end, the decision was made in the CEO and Secretary Meeting that all the labs would be grouped into three labs: central laboratory, surgical laboratory, and laboratory for communicable diseases. It took a long time for all the sub-specialty directors to agree and join together. It was slow and hard. When things became stagnated, we invited Ms. Jilan Liu to reassess our progress. After the visit and interview, Ms. Liu spoke with pleasure: "Small as the sparrow is, it possesses all its internal organs!"

We knew that people had been reluctant and worried about this change, as if their own piece of "cheese" would be taken away. To alleviate our anxiety, Ms. Liu gave a lively administrative training to the leadership and lab directors, when she explained the defects and problems in our laboratory set-up from her international perspective of the current philosophy of healthcare management and JCI standards.

Take the Gastrointestinal Lab and Dermatology Lab as examples, each of them was in a small and shabby room where procedure area and staff area were mixed; only one or two persons were staffed in those labs and it was not uncommon that a report was generated and reviewed by the same person; documents were not aligned into system and policies were not consistently in place; labs were taken charge by directors of clinical units, who did not have the proper qualification as lab manager. All these facts spoke to the ineffective supervision of laboratories. Ms. Liu continued: "If you continue laboratory studies and assays in such setting, accuracy would be at risk, let alone quality and patient safety!"

Wang Weilin, the current CEO and then vice CEO, gave us an analogy:

> You've seen cheese, right? In western countries, cheese is deemed "the best among milk products". Some say "cheese is meat to the poor and banquet to the rich", and "cheese is your happiness". You can imagine how people love cheese. On the decision-making level, we spent a lot of courage and resolution to integrate our labs, because it means we will move the "cheeses" of the directors. The "cheeses" have generated revenue for the labs, but they are detrimental to the benefit of patients and the hospital as a whole for the long run. Think about this: when labs are in many different locations, it takes much labor to deliver specimens; the increase of delivery may result in higher risk of specimen loss and delayed report. At the end of the day, patients would benefit less from our care, the hospital would have difficulty managing things and performance of our laboratories would not be improved. Remember, our goal is to become a best medical center around the world. To this end, we need to set aside the short-term benefits and look into the future.

The professional interpretation from Ms. Liu and the thinking of Dr. Wang in plain language stroke a chord in the heart of the laboratory directors. That discussion was a key driver behind the lab integration process that ensued, an impossible mission without the unanimous understanding among staff and their vision of giving up "personal" interest in exchange for "collective" interest. Being a small piece of history about laboratory only though, it is a vivid example of "The only thing that is constant is change" and a key moment of increased understanding and appreciation toward JCI accreditation.

Changes Reflected in Details

The peak days in a large hospital witness 12,000 outpatients, whose request for admission outnumbers our 3,000 some beds. How can we ensure every patient receives quality care and service? Under the guidance of JCI standards for Accreditation, our hospital has promoted "patient-centered care" by starting from details.

Privacy Protection Reflected in Small Things

In the exam room, Dr. Wang, an orthopedist, is talking to Mr. Li, a patient. In this quiet room, only Dr. Wang's voice is heard. This is a stark contrast to what it used to be before we started to work on JCI compliance: several physicians had to share one exam room. One can imagine how noisy it was in the room, and how patients were examined while being watched by irrelevant people.

The old practice before we were accredited where two to eight physicians shared one exam room was anything but the principle of patient privacy protection featuring "one patient in a room at one time."

If we practiced this principle and divided exam rooms according to the number of physicians they accommodated, then each physician got only a small room without the examining table, let alone high cost. When we were shilly-shally, Ms. Liu recommended us to partition with boards with glass on the top instead, and physicians from the two adjacent cubicles would use the examining table in turn. In this way, physician would work in a comfortable area while "one patient in a room at one time" is achievable. We took Ms. Liu's recommendation and divided into space for exam rooms.

The electronic system of our hospital has adopted new display mechanism when patient names are involved, such as in the outpatient queuing information. The middle name of a patient is replaced by a symbol instead (such as 王× and 张×勤), so that readers do not know the full names.

The line where the queue starts is clearly labeled 1 m from the counters for registration, medication reception and at the phlebotomist, another measure to protect patient privacy. Inspection was performed to all the exam rooms and wards to ensure bedside curtains have been installed wherever needed and patient information has been removed from the bedside card (see Figure 19.1a–f).

(a)
(b)
(c)

Figure 19.1 Measures in place to protect patient privacy.

(Continued)

(d)

(e)

(f)

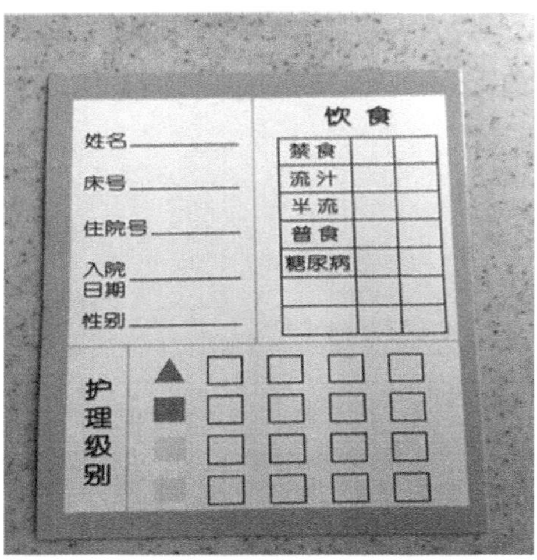

Figure 19.1 (CONTINUED) Measures in place to protect patient privacy.

Thanks to JCI standards, we made every possible effort from policy, facility, mindset, and activity to provide better privacy for patients.

The Same Admission Order in New Format

Before we worked toward JCI standard compliance, when determining a patient needed inpatient care, physician in the outpatient clinic issued admission order on paper or printed that out from the electronic medical record system and gave it to the patient for his/her to go through admission procedure. The admission order included only demographic information, initial diagnosis, and physician's signature, whether written on paper or printed from electronic system.

According to ACC2.1 and ACC2.2 (Access and Continuity of Care), when going through admission process, patient and family receives education on the ward environment, recommended care plan, expected outcome and estimated cost. Initially, we thought it would be fine if we document these pieces of information in the *Note of Discussion with Patients in 72 Hours after Admission.* However, Ms. Liu commented that it would have been earlier than 72 h, and it should be right at admission. A cross-departmental discussion was held among Medical Affairs Dept., Nursing Dept., Admission Service Center, and IT Center where we redesigned the format of admission order and the process of patient admission.

Information added to the admission order included: the purpose of the admission (preventive, therapeutic, palliative, or rehabilitative), reference for decision-making for patient and family (reasons for the admission, care plan, expected outcome and length of stay, priority level of the admission and estimated cost); the telephone number of the unit where the ordering physician works in for patient to seek medical attention during the waiting period; the right to go to other organizations for care and the signature of the patient or family member (see Figure 19.2).

In terms of management, admission orders used to be collected in the Admission Service Center. But now, it becomes the front page of the patient's record closed at discharge (see Figure 19.3).

浙江大学医学院附属第一医院

入院申请单

住院性质:☐ 预防性 ☐ 治疗性 ☐ 姑息性 ☐ 康复性

就诊卡号: 病历号: 姓名:

身份证号: 性别: 年龄: 费用类别:

诊　断:

申请入住科室: 医疗组:

备选入住科室: 病情要求: ☐ 加床 ☐ 普通床 ☐ 特护床

床位类型:☐ 普通 ☐ 100-200/天 ☐ 500/天 ☐ 1000/天

开单医生: 开单时间: 开单科室:

尊敬的患者朋友：您好！感谢您对本院的信任！

为了更好地帮助您了解本次住院相关事宜，医生会告诉您下列信息，有助于您决定是否住院:

*本次住院的原因: ____________________

*计划给您提供的治疗方案: ____________________

*预期治疗结果: ____________________

*大致住院时间: ________ 天; *大致住院费用: ________ *预缴款金额: ________

因医疗资源有限，本院将根据待床患者病情的轻重急缓和登记的先后顺序安排入院；在等待期间，如病情发生变化

请您及时到医院就诊或联系医生，病区联系电话 ________；您也有选择其他医疗疗机构的权利。

患者姓名：(患者/家属签字栏)________ 医生签名:

Figure 19.2 ***Admission Order*** **in new format.**

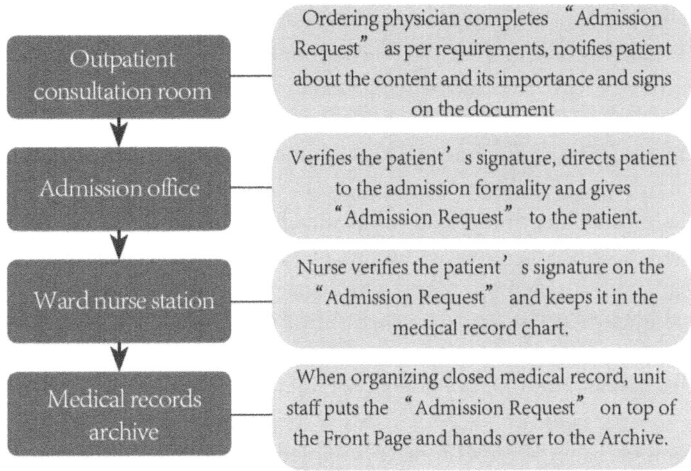

Figure 19.3 Process for *Admission Order.*

Care for Patient's Feeling and Designate Company for Investigation

Yesterday, a physician ordered a MRI exam for Liu, a senior neurological patient admitted 2 days ago. A nurse made reservation via Intranet and informed Liu to arrive at MRI room at 10:00 am today. Specifically, the nurse reassured Liu that he would be accompanied by a designated staff on his way to and from the MRI area.

Happy with the scheduled exam though, Liu was rather dubious of the company described by the nurse. "My wife and children are not with me. Can I make it to the exam alone?" Liu thought to himself. At 9:50 am, the nurse came in Liu's room with Wang, a transporter. At bedside, the nurse instructed Wang of things he needs to pay attention. Then both of them ask Liu's name and verify Liu's record number between his wristband and the order sheet together. Then the nurse and Wang help Liu to get into the wheelchair, and Liu is ready to go to the MRI room in Tower 7. Thirty minutes later, Liu returns to his room under accompany.

JCI lays much emphasis on patient safety. In terms of patient transport alone, hospitals are expected to account for the devices involved in the transport, quality of the service from transporter, disinfection, and isolation and information exchange. Transporters receive standardized training on patient transport service and transport tools are managed in standardized manner. For example, wheelchairs and stretchers receive preventive maintenance regularly.

Case 1: A "Reform" of Patient Identification

One day, the Outpatient Office received another patient who came for complaint. This middle-aged man came in with a report and said: "How can you give me the wrong report? This is so irresponsible. Now I come here to complain!" It turned out that the report he had received was for a lady who happened to share the same first and family names with him.

According to staff of the Outpatient Office, who also suffered unspeakably, they dealt with this type of complaint almost every day. A better policy was needed to prevent such low-level error.

The Trigger of Reform

As the measure that starts the IPSG (International Patient Safety Goals) chapter, patient identification features at least two identifiers, including patient name, medical record number, date of birth, and wristband with bar code. It also specifies that patient room number and other information of their location in the hospital should not be used for identification.

This JCI standard was the trigger for the leadership to launch a "reform" of the way patients would be identified. To this end, the leadership summoned administrators from Quality Dept., Medical Affairs Dept., Nursing Dept., Outpatient Office, Emergency Room, relevant clinical units, Finance Dept., and IT Dept. to have an in-depth discussion. All of us agreed to use name as one of the required identifiers. But for the other uniform identifier, it was hard to reach consensus since different places had different encounters and processes.

Before that discussion, the Quality Dept. conducted a surgery involving 70 diagnostic and therapeutic areas to understand how patients were identified at that time. These areas included Observation Room of Emergency Room, Outpatient Western Pharmacy, TCM (traditional Chinese medicine) Pharmacy, Dentistry, Plastic Surgery, Endoscopy, Outpatient Operating Room, etc. The results revealed that patient identification was not consistently in place. Only one area adopted name and medical record number, which was available on the outpatient registration form. In general, 17 ways of identification were involved among the 70 areas, which were name, sex, age, registration form, card swiping, medical record/history, prescription form, investigation no., guiding form, order no./barcode, citizen's ID card, wristband with hand-written information, ID, radiotherapy no., no. of pacemaker, scanning device and PDA (personal digital assistant) (see Table 19.1). The variety of ways for patient identification was not conducive to overall supervision from the organization level.

After several discussions, summarizing opinions of people involved, the hospital decided to adopt "name + medical record number/date of birth" as the only identifiers for patient identification.

Table 19.1 Ways of Patient Identification Found before We Worked for JCI Compliance

Way of Patient Identification	*Frequency*	*Percentage*
Name	64	91.4
Sex	55	78.5
Medical record/history	28	40
Age	27	38
Card swiping	24	34
Order no./barcode	20	28.5
Scanning device	9	12.8
Registration form	7	10
Guiding form	5	7
Citizen's ID	5	7
Prescription form	3	4
Investigation no.	3	4

This was written into policy and communicated to the entire organization by means varying from weekly routine meeting, Intranet, staff training to staff pamphlet for JCI.

Easier Said than Done, Unexpectedly

To establish medical record number unique to a specific patient, we needed every patient coming in to provide his or her valid citizen's ID issued by the government. To this end, this new requirement was communicated via several means in the outpatient area, including display in the electronic screen at a certain interval, posters on walls, and volunteer providing help in the outpatient lobby. Most patients understood the purpose and supported us. They also talked among themselves, which helped us spread the information. But at the beginning, some patients were confused: "I'm here for doctors, why bother with my ID card?" With patience, volunteers and staff explained to such patients how important it would be to stay with unique medical record numbers, and this was for the safety of care that they receive from our hospital.

It was easier to get patients residing in Hangzhou to understand and support us, but many of those traveling from other cities did not bring their citizen's ID card because they had not heard of the requirement. At hearing this from the Registration Office, the directors figured that this should not be a barrier to care for patients who had traveled from afar. After discussion, we decided that, as long as patient safety is guaranteed, patients who have not provided citizen's ID cards complete the form *Registration for New Patient Coming for the First Time without ID Card in FAHZU* (see Figure 19.4). With this form, patient gets registered for the care as well as in the Outpatient Office. After the patient's visit, Outpatient Office calls back such patients and asks them to send in a copy their valid citizen's ID card to us via fax or photo. In that call, staff also remind the patients to bring their citizen's ID card next time for sure.

After a period of practice with the "name+medical record number/date of birth" as the unique way of identifying patients, we figured another source of confusion: date of birth could be presented as Gregorian calendar or traditional Chinese lunisolar calendar. Therefore, we went back and changed the policy into "name+medical record number" as the unique identifiers for patients.

Figure 19.4 Signs reminding patients coming for the first time but without citizen's ID cards to fill in a form.

Look into Details for Full Compliance

A lot of work has been done by relevant departments to ensure patients are correctly identified.

IT Dept. installed card readers in every registration counter, which automatically obtain patients' names, citizen's ID numbers, and addresses as long as patients put their citizen's ID card on the reader. Once accepted into the electronic system, such information is available in all the registration form, guiding form, investigation form, report, and various electronic systems. When the information is not automatically made available in the HIS (hospital information system) due to the lack of device interfacing, staff write the information by hand on the report while IT Dept. is working on the issue.

In the registration counter, staff put a label with the patient's name, medical record number, and date of birth on the patient's hospital card or health insurance card, whose material has been tested before selection by Finance Dept. To ensure the label would work in the best way for patients, we asked patient's preference as well. Finally, based on patient feedback and our own thinking, we ended up in two ways for how the label should be put: for patients covered by public health insurance, the label of patient information is put on their health record booklets only; for those pay for themselves, the label is put on both the health record booklets and the hospital cards (see Figures 19.5 and 19.6).

When this new policy was implemented, Quality Dept. provided training in succession via simulation exercise and real-time supervision to reduce variation. In this way, people gradually got used to the new way of practice and enhanced policy compliance.

Wristband and PDA Made a Perfect Match

To reduce gaps in the details of patient identification, the hospital allocated PDA devices and wristbands so that wristbands for all inpatients would be scanned with PDA devices, a technology that facilitates nurse in patient identification and takes the advantage of barcoding and wireless network.

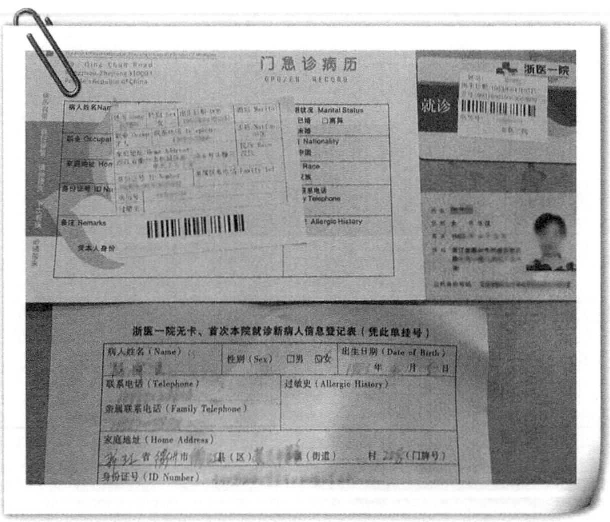

Figure 19.5 The label with patient identity information is attached to both the hospital card and health record booklet for patients paying for themselves.

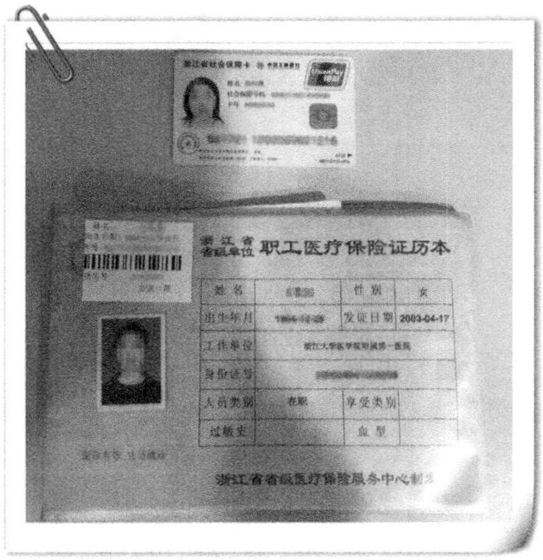

Figure 19.6 The label with patient identity information is attached to both the government insurance card and health record booklet.

To bind medical record number with wristband: Barcoding, a simple, accurate, and reliable technology for graphic identification, has been used widely in logistic management. Therefore, we decided to use this technology to manage our patients. Specifically, inpatient information is encoded in a two-dimensional barcode and printed on patient's wristband, along with name, medical record number, sex and age in routine language. The type of wristband that we specifically selected enables printout from computer, tolerates water and any disinfectants, and are is readable by scanners.

For inpatients, when they have finished admission procedures and go through checkups in the Admission Center, staff there wears the wristband for the patient.

For inpatients who do not need to go through checkups in the Admission Center, they are worn with the wristband by nurse from the floor as they arrive at the unit. The nurse asks patient to speak out his or her own name, verifies the answer with those read from the front page of inpatient record and wristband, and wears it on the patient's wrist once confirms correct (see Figure 19.7). When patient is not able to respond, the family member at the side speaks out patient's name and date of birth.

For patients in the Resuscitation Room of the Emergency Room and Emergency ICU, when sending patients into these areas, nurse verifies their identity with the patients/family members before wearing wristbands for patients.

PDA, a perfect partner of wristband: the hospital promoted the practice of scanning with PDA devices across the organization, a technology that facilitates nurse in patient identification and takes the advantage of barcoding and wireless network. When such technology was not available, nurses had to read and check with their eyes and judgment repeatedly for fear of error, which involved higher workload and stress. However, with technology, nurses no long have to make themselves check again and again, as the device automatically check if the information provided matches with a simply scan on patient's wristband via PDA. If the information does not match, the PDA device gives off alert (see Figure 19.8).

New Model of Patient Identification Based on JCI Standards

To meet JCI standards, we modified our policy on patient identification, which specifies that each patient has a unique medical record number, no matter how many visits that the patient has paid

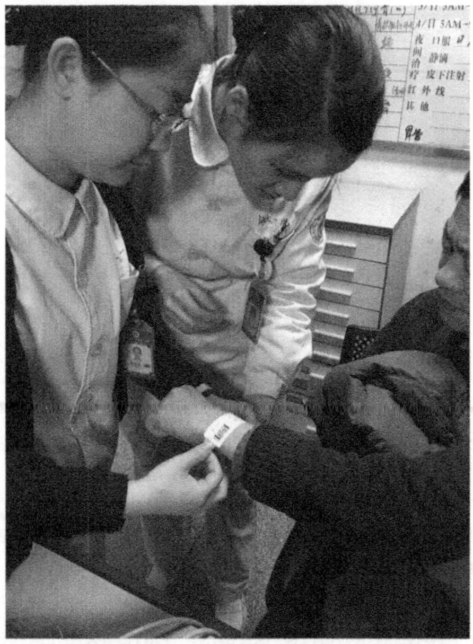

Figure 19.7 Nurses wearing wristband for a patient.

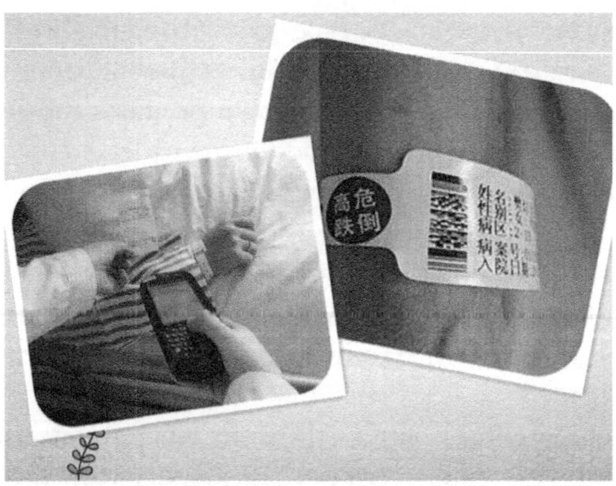

Figure 19.8 Patient identified with PDA device.

to us, and that the unique identifiers for patient are "name+medical record number." Patient's room number or bed number should never be used for identification.

Patient identification should always take place when healthcare professionals give order, perform diagnostic procedure or provide treatment (such as medication, blood or blood product, controlled diet or radiotherapy) or procedures (such as intravenous catheterization and hemodialysis).

The right way of patient identification is:

In the inpatient ward and the Resuscitation Room, Observation Room and Emergency ICU of the Emergency Room, wristbands are used for identification. After patient name is verified, the medical record number is checked with PDA device or manually.

For outpatients and ER patients not admitted to the Resuscitation Room, Observation Room or ICU, identification is performed with medical record booklet, hospital card, investigation order, health insurance card and other materials with patient's name and medical record number.

The key steps are: ask the patient or family member to speak out patient's name, and never identify patients with bed number or room number.

Case 2: PIVAS: The Gatekeeper for Medication Safety

When initially established, the PIVAS (Pharmacy Intravenous Admixture Services) was only able to provide services for the standing orders for selected units, nutritional preparation of 3L and cytotoxic agents. Thanks to the advancement over the past 5 years, it has extended services to more units, single-dose orders, and chemotherapeutic agents as well. It has witness growth in both capacity and volume of services.

Among the variety of medications available from PIVAS, high-alert medications are specifically managed through specific steps in the organization in line with JCI standards.

Mr. Gao Zhe, a pharmacist involved in appropriateness review stationed in the PIVAS, is absorbed in reviewing orders in front of the computer screen while stopping to call physicians from the floor every now and then. In the electronic system for appropriateness review, orders involving high-risk medication are labeled with "危" (the Chinese character for danger) that helps capture the pharmacist's attention. In addition, the module for nutritional preparation comes with "TPN order review" function that displays total energy, carbon/nitrogen ratio, glucose/fat ratio and electrolytes of the preparation for the pharmacist to determine appropriateness. As for chemotherapeutics, a tailored module is in place for the pharmacist to determine their appropriateness as well.

When it comes to storage, high-risk medications are stored in a separated area in the PIVAS, labeled with the alert used consistently across the organization. Meanwhile, specific alerts are in place for look-alike medication, concentrated electrolyte, medications with multiple strengths, and sound-alike medications as reminders to pharmacists. The storage of high-alert medications in the clinical units is inspected when PIVAS staff conduct the monthly tour across the units.

We have been impressed by how the PIVAS improved the management of patient-provided Herceptin.

Herceptin, or trastuzumab for injection, is among the first patient-provided chemotherapeutics prepared in our PIVAS. This expensive medication is good for 28 days only in refrigerator after being opened, but it may take several administrations to finish one bottle of drug because of the course-based dosing schedule. It is a waste if the drug is not used up by its validity after being opened. If Herceptin is managed as a typical patient-provided drug, it is stored in the unit so that staff have to take it back and forth between the unit and PIVAS when it is time for administration. This has created waste of motion, risk of error, and compromised storage condition. As such, PIVAS included Herceptin, a patient-provided medication, into the hospital-wide drug management system where drugs are managed in a centralized manner.

Challenges from Centralized Management

We used to provide herceptin in this way: physician gave the order; patient or the family member purchased it from a pharmacy independent from our hospital, and brought the drug in its original package and receipt to the PIVAS; the PIVAS staff received the drug and established a patient-specific card. Before every administration, a patient had to go to the PIVAS to get registered, and the documentation was also made on a herceptin-specific log at the same time. These documentations were compared for consistency every day.

As the practice became a norm, the number of cards established for herceptin increased to several hundred and was still growing. Staff became anxious about the volume that they foresaw in the near future.

This process was clumsy. For example, one time, a family member of a patient came all the way sweating and arrived at the PIVAS to register with a pharmacist for the patient-provided herceptin. This elderly woman went all the way from the ward to the Dafang Pharmacy outside and to the PIVAS with the medication she had bought, only to find that she did not bring the card. She had to go all the way back to get the card and come again. Other times, a patient or family member might bring in the medication at the wrong time, or break the package themselves, making the acceptance step difficult to handle.

What's more, as the volume kept increasing, the documentation, and daily census become more difficult. For every order of herceptin, the pharmacist had to check if it was the first or repeated exposure of the patient. When the volume expanded to five thick logs with hundreds of patients, staff had to thumb through all the pages and use a calculator to verify again and again for daily census. You can imagine how time-consuming and risk-prone it was. As such, we decided to redesign every step of the process for the patient-provided herceptin.

A "Big Wolf" for the Patient-Provided Medication

In terms of drug delivery, the PIVAS talked to the Dafang Pharmacy, which agreed to deliver the medication to the PIVAS directly, so that the issues of timing and package integrity would be addressed. Mr. Yang Zhihai and Mr. Wu Jun, pharmacists from the PIVAS, developed software for documenting the patient-provided medications. Since the icon of the software is a wolf, it has been nicknamed "the big wolf" by the PIVAS staff. Whenever the medications are delivered from Dafang Pharmacy, the accepting pharmacist runs the software and enters patient information from the medication receipt. As long as an order is given by the physician for a patient, a pharmacist can check if the medication provided by patient has been received from the Dafang Pharmacy. All that patient or family needs to do now is to bring in their chemotherapy card, instead of having to head for several locations with several things in hand. "The big wolf" enables pharmacists to log doses efficiently and provides inventory function. As it keeps track of the volume of medication available to a particular patient, when the staff need to compare the log against the actual count, the log can be displayed in clear and direct way. The software also provides a label of payer of herceptin, whether by the patient or by charity fund (when herceptin was not covered by healthcare insurance, either the patient or charity fund paid for it). Thanks to these measures, herceptin has been better managed with higher efficiency, better accuracy of preparation, and reduced burden from the patient's side.

With the concerted effort of the PIVAS staff, medication, and preparation are managed better with higher compliance to best practice. Every progress made by the PIVAS has not been possible without the prioritized commitment to medication safety, which is well elaborated by the slogan posted at the door to the PIVAS: "The gatekeeper for medication safety."

Chapter 20

The Second Affiliated Hospital of Zhejiang University School of Medicine

Wang Jianan, Zhao Xiaoying, Wang Huafen, Dai Xiaona, Lv Na, Jin Jingfen, Huang Xin, Ye Xiaoyun, Zhang Lili, Ji Nan, Lu Yan, Wang Xin, Jiang Zhixin, and Wei Xingling

The Second Affiliated Hospital of Zhejiang University School of Medicine

Wang Jianan, *MD, PhD, Professor and Supervisor of doctoral candidate*

Dr. Wang is the President of The Second Affiliated Hospital of Zhejiang University School of Medicine. His decade of experience in hospital administration has heavily involved establishment of hospital culture, quality management, cooperation and exchanges. Among his numerous achievements are "The Norman Bethune Medal" and "Hospital President with Amazing Leadership in China."

Zhao Xiaoying, *Chief Physician and Supervisor of doctoral candidates*

Dr. Zhao is a former Vice President of The Second Affiliated Hospital of Zhejiang University School of Medicine and Quality and Safety Consultant. She is the Vice Chairman of Standardized Hospital Management Chapter of the Chinese Hospital Association, with over 20 years of experience in clinical care, education, research, quality, and safety.

Ms. Wang Huafen *is the Director of Quality Department of The Second Affiliated Hospital of Zhejiang University School of Medicine and Chairman of Infection Control Chapter of Zhejiang Nursing Society. She is an expert in hospital quality, nursing performance, infection control, and accreditation preparation.*

Hospital Introduction: The Second Affiliated Hospital of Zhejiang University School of Medicine (hereinafter referred as "SAHZU") is a renowned general hospital engaged in clinical care, education, and research with a complete range of disciplines, strong clinical capabilities, advanced techniques, multidisciplinary collaboration, and excellent managerial expertise.

The hospital was first known as the Universal Benevolence Hospital established by British Church Missionary Society in 1869. During 1885–1925, it served as one of the first hospitals practicing western medicine in China. In early 20th century, the hospital was recognized as the "best hospital in the far east" by peers from both home and abroad and the cradle for many clinical disciplines in Zhejiang Province, including orthopedics, neurology, and neurosurgery.

International Accreditation: 2013, JCI accreditation as a teaching hospital.
2016, JCI triennial accreditation as a teaching hospital.
2017, HIMSS EMRAM 6.

Contents

Preface

Continuous Improvement: The Hospital DNA

SAHZU was accredited as a JCI teaching hospital in January 2013, which injected new vitality to the organization with a history over 140 years. On the debriefing after the JCI survey, Dr. Wang Jian'an, President of the hospital, expressed his gratitude to over 4,000 staff for their perseverance, efforts, understanding, support, and trust. Staff were surprised to see that the eyes of the man who was well known for his toughness and courage filled with tears. But they knew it was the tears of joy for never having given up to pursue the gold standard. With JCI as a guidance, SAHZU has new goals for its future.

A Great Journey Led by International Standards

Things are constantly changing and iterating along with the development of our society. Some wither because they could not catch up with the time, while others prosper by seizing the opportunities. As a hospital with over 100 years of history, SAHZU has also been challenged as we are moving ahead. To grow new buds and blossom in the new era, it is important to forge a new type of culture and requires a good tool for us to leverage.

It was a prudently thought-through decision by the hospital to take the JCI challenge because we believe that JCI will lead us forward. The hospital leadership has been encouraging "going out and introducing in" for continuous quality improvement and lean management. And we noticed that better patient experience and sophisticated improvement were the common pursuit of JCI-accredited hospitals, which also matched the core values of our hospital—"to always put patients and customers first."

We decided to adopt the JCI standards in our facility to inspire our own transformation. When it was first announced to the hospital, many of our staff did buy it because they weighed clinical skills and techniques much more over the JCI survey: "We already have our hands full with all the work we have to do every day. Why bother?" "The Level A Tertiary Hospital accreditation is enough, isn't it?" To break the ice wall and make both our leaders and staff understand the JCI standards better, "training," "Action Plans" and "tracer" became the frequently mentioned words in the hospital through our efforts.

A hospital-wide weekly meeting was fixed on the schedule for the interpretation and learning of JCI standards. Each department and unit organized their own learning sessions and then shared their ideas on the weekly meeting with the mid-level leadership in the hospital. In addition to our communication with the JCI consultants, we also benchmarked ourselves with the standards to identify gaps. And we divided the items into three categories: (1) the ones that we had achieved, (2) the ones that would require some efforts, and (3) the ones that would need the coordination and support at the hospital level or would call for cross-department cooperation.

After rounds of JCI standard learning sessions, we started to revise and develop our hospital policies. We also compiled a JCI training pocket book for our staff. Trainings were organized, for example, the training on culture of safety for our logistics staff to explain what they should do and its importance. For clinical staff, tailored training sessions were scheduled according to their schedules to motivate the participation of the unit heads and the front-line staff. One example was the problem-based learning (PBL) model adopted for the training on QPS, allowing the staff to understand the rationale of the contents.

To better meet the needs of our staff, we had adopted multiple training methods, including specialized training for medical and auxiliary staff, nursing staff, administration and logistics staff; meeting and secondary training; drills; and online training and tests. We also adopted the tracer methodology for onsite inspection and provided one-on-one training on staff who was not familiar with the standards. Screen savers with JCI standards information were designed and put on the computers across the hospital to improve the awareness of our staff and help them better implement the requirements.

With all these efforts, staff started to understand the essence of quality and safety and began to use quality management tools such as PDCA and QCC creatively to solve their day-to-day problems. That was when we realized the capability and potential we had. Maybe SAHZU was born with the pursuit of better quality flowing in our blood.

Quality: The Lifeline of Hospital

Quality Improvement and Patient Safety (QPS) is one of the core focuses covering a wide range of areas in JCI survey. It requires the hospital continuously plan, design, monitor, analyze, and improve the clinical quality and management process. This could never be achieved without excellent planning and leadership.

Therefore, the first thing we did was to establish a triple-level quality management mechanism comprising the Hospital QPS Committee, the Sub-Committees, and the department-level QPS Groups. The hospital president serves as the Chair of the Hospital QPS Committee and department heads the team leaders of the QPS Groups. Their responsibility was to improve and organize regular meetings; as well as identify, discuss, and monitor the issues regarding quality.

Second, hospital-wide priorities were set with monitoring indicators. In 2011, we officially kicked off the preparation for our first survey under the fourth edition which required the hospital to set up at least one monitoring indicator for each one of the 11 clinical areas and nine administrative areas. These indicators basically covered the fundamental scope of service of the hospital. Challenging as they were, the hospital was determined to adopt those indicators under the guidance of the QPS Office. In 2014 when the hospital was preparing for the triennial survey, JCI also made a few significant changes to its new standards. In the new fifth edition, the QPS Chapter became an even greater challenge. For example, the requirements on the unit/service quality became tighter: all departments need to set unit-specific monitoring indicator(s) within the framework of the standards. The indicators should not only reflect the services of the unit, but also be linked to the performance evaluation on physicians and other professionals. In addition, the improvement of resources utilization or treatment outcomes of clinical guidelines also should be evaluated. Compared with the previous edition, the new edition required all staff to be aware of the quality indicators to ensure engagement of all staff. The QPS Office then organized education and mock tracer in each unit supplemented with the quarterly department tracer by the responsible VP in charge of quality. During the triennial survey, the JCI surveyors highly recognized our achievements and said, "Your hospital has put in place a systematic and consistent quality indicator monitoring mechanism to involve all staff. It is the best system I've ever seen."

Third, we also adopted various quality improvement methods in our hospital, including PDCA, QCC, HVA, FMEA, RCA, 6S, etc. These tools encouraged managerial innovation and assisted the improvement of quality.

Last but not the least, a culture of safety was established. Measures such as education and training, nonpunitive reporting of adverse events and hospital quality awards had effectively involved staff to proactively identify issues and to achieve progress together with the hospital. Based on the findings in the culture of safety survey and the risk assessment, we also identified our weaknesses and improvement measures were carried out.

Timely Response for Patient Safety

Hospital is vulnerable to emergencies which require quick response to maximally secure patient safety. It is not an easy task to accomplish.

Before we were JCI accredited, defibrillator was only available in the Cardiac Center, ICU, and OR and just a few units. If a code would occur, nurse had to borrow the defibrillator from those units and might miss the best opportunity of resuscitation of the patient. Thus, we spent nearly 3 million on 100 defibrillators to be allocated across the hospital (see Figure 20.1). We also revised the code policy and procedure and trained all staff to ensure sufficient implementation.

Emergency response system and broadcasting code were set up. For example, 999 refers to the cardiac or pulmonary arrest. Strict zoning was lined out to cover every corner of the hospital facility from the ward, to the garden and basement garage with designated units to be responsible for the response. The code team is required to arrive at the site with a resuscitation kit and start resuscitation within 5 min after 999 is called.

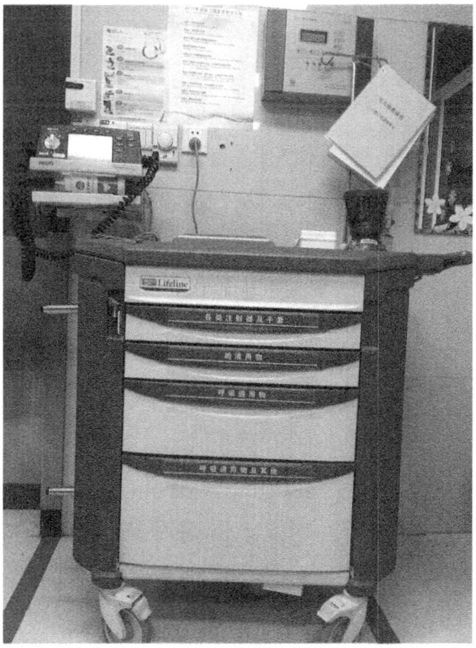

Figure 20.1 Allocation of defibrillators and crash carts on units.

Besides, all other staff except for physicians and nurses, like administrative and logistics staff, security guards, workers, and students, have to receive trainings on the response process and training, and pass the tests.

To better ensure the safety of patients on campus, a Rapid Reaction Team (RRT) responding to the early warning system was organized. The criteria to trigger RRT include respiration rate <8 or >28 bpm, SaO_2 $<90\%$, heart rate >130 or <40 bpm, urine output within 4 h <150 mL, and quick alteration of level of consciousness. When healthcare staff believes that a patient shows such symptom and needs the help from RRT, he/she could call the RRT. The ICU physician responsible for the area should arrive at the bedside within 10 min, start the assessment on the patient, communicate with the responsible physician and assist the following treatment to control the patient's condition and alleviate possible risks. This RRT system is a reassurance to the patients as well as the staff on site.

Culture: The Root of the Fruits

JCI had fundamentally changed the way we think, talk, and act in the hospital. When a problem is identified, both the hospital leader and the staff would say, "We need to do a PDCA." One of our nurses once joked that JCI actually stood for "Joy of Continuous Improvement." A team of excellence was born in SAHZU thanks to the strict standards and our own efforts made through numerous trainings and drills.

On July 5, 2014, a bus was set ablaze and the news shocked the entire country. SAHZU received all 19 adult victims who were severely injured: 1 with a deep burn as bad as 95%, 7 of them 60% burn and 16 of them needing tracheotomy. The call for Code 333 was triggered. Responsible staff soon assembled at the site and started the procedure. Zero death of those burned victims. That was our response to the needs from our society. With the perfectly designed and implemented "Management for life" process, we worked the miracle.

In February 2016, we were successfully re-accredited with excellent performance. Dr. Wang Jian'an believed that it was JCI, the "Golden Name Card," that had laid a good foundation for us to delivery world-class service during the G20 Summit in Hangzhou. JCI makes sure that we protect the patient's privacy, maintain effective communication, and enable a set of complete, robust, and appropriate measures for quality improvement on each step of the care. That is why SAHZU became the only designated hospital to provide medical support during the G20 Summit to the heads of states, including the leaders from the US (Figure 20.2).

Sharing for Staying Excellent

JCI, the Golden Name Card, is more like a name embedded in the culture of safety to serve as the management principles for both leaders and front-line staff. It, indeed, brought along profound perceptional and behavioral changes to SAHZU. We believe that the only way to benefit more patients is to share our successful experience to more hospitals. So, we started to organize the experience sharing events for hospital management professionals from across the country. The mission to share also urges us to stay excellent through learning from domestic and overseas experience, looking up to the highest standards and equipping the hospital with advanced facilities and appropriate policies.

Figure 20.2 Onsite validation of HIMSS EMRAM Stage 6.

HIMSS: Pivotal for Standardization

We know that it could be a long, hard journey to truly realize all the JCI requirements in our daily work, in particular, for a hospital like SAHZU with a history over 100 years. After two rounds of JCI surveys, we realized the maturity model described in the HIMSS EMRAM criteria could be helpful for the consolidation and optimization of the existing policies and procedures in the hospital. It could facilitate our next breakthrough.

With the support from Jilan and the HIMSS Greater China team, we officially launched our HIMSS journey.

HIMSS requires that the information system support the decision-making by the clinical staff based on integrated clinical data; complete, structured, standardized documentation realized through data collection of patient assessment and treatment activities; and strong management with closed loops. All these can help us better implement, monitor and control the medical and nursing care in the hospital, and save more time for healthcare staff to take care of the patients. It is exactly what we wanted!

We will continue our efforts for better quality and self-improvement. As Dr. Wang Jian'an said, "Quality is and will always be the soul of SAHZU!"

Case 1: Inpatient Beds: No Longer in the Pocket of Physicians

Scorched: From Outpatient to Inpatient

Scene 1

10:00 in the morning. Three long queues have formed up in front of the window of Bed Coordination Center and intertwined with the ones for the Admission Office on the opposite side. The elevator lobby is crowded with patients and families. The entire lobby of the Building #6 echoes with noise. Mr. Li, sitting behind the window, takes over the Inpatient Bed Request

Sheet and the Outpatient Card from the patient, reads the card, and asks routine questions with patience. Then, he keys in the information on the Admission Request into the computer, takes out the Bed Appointment Notice, explains the content to the patient and asks for signature.

Then he repeats the same process again for the next patient. Everything seems fine. Suddenly, a man rushes to the window and urges the staff to register him first. The rest of the crowd starts to complain, of course. Mr. Li asks him to queue after other people, but is shouted back, "We went to the Binjiang Campus and queued up for a very long time, and was told to come to the Jiefang Road Campus for admission, appointment and examination. Then we had to queue up again here!"

Scene 2

Ms. Wu, a nurse of the hospital, is busy with her work behind the window standing between her and the crowd. She has to find out the availability of beds from all the paper Admission Requests submitted from different units, match the beds to newly admitted patients and notify them. She has to raise her voice so that she could be heard.

The phone rings again as she just puts it down. "Have you admitted my patient today?" "No more ED patients on my unit!" "Has XXX finished all the pre-admission examinations?" "Why hasn't the patient admitted yet?" "How many patients are waiting for beds? What are their diagnoses?" All these questions pour out from the end of the phone. All she can do is answering the phone while searching through all the admission requests for information. When the day is over, she hears buzz in her brain and her throat is desperately in need of water. She looks through the incoming call record, and it shows 230 calls.

Scene 3

The nurses working at the call center are busy answering phones and making notes.

"Is this SAHZU? I've been waiting for a bed in GI for almost half month. How long will you keep me waiting?"

"I'm so sorry. The GI beds are in shortage right now. There are 15 patients on the waiting list before you."

"What? I'm not going to wait any longer!"

Having put down the phone, the nurse murmurs to herself, "We have open beds in other wards, and also in the GI ward of the Binjiang Campus. But…."

As a hospital with over 100 years of history, many disciplines are recognized as the provincial or even national key disciplines. The hospital welcomes many patients from all over the country who want to seek care here. For some units, the waiting list could be extremely long for a bed. But it is not always the case for some other units. We started to wonder how we could change the situation in which inpatient beds were in the pocket of the physicians and realize a uniform coordination of all beds in the hospital to improve the utilization? We referred to the JCI standards and information technology. New policy was formulated and a IT platform for preadmission process was established to integrate and coordinate the bed resources across the hospital. But it was not an easy task to accomplish.

Bed Coordination Center: Centralized Allocation

In the end of 2011, the hospital set up the Bed Coordination Center. We started with a pilot on several units and then implemented it in both of our campuses. Currently, 90% of our beds are managed by the Bed Coordination Center.

Policy Governing the Bed Resources Was the Foundation of Centralized Management

What we needed to do was to transform the old model where physicians and units arranged their own beds and admission, and to change the tradition of admitting patients to the units designated by their physicians. A hospital-wide coordination meeting was convened by the Hospital Management Committee to discuss the centralized approach together with the Medical Affairs Department, Nursing Department, Bed Coordination Center, IT Center, ED, Quality Office, and heads of clinical units. On the meeting, based on the uniform management required by JCI and the real situation in the hospital, the attendees revised the policies regarding the centralized bed management in both campuses, including *Process of Coordinating and Arranging Inpatient Beds*, *Measures of Admitting Patients from Emergency Department*, *Process of Patient Admission*, etc. After the meeting, the Medical Affairs Department, and the Customer Service Center organized training sessions for all staff on new policies and procedures. Since then, the Bed Coordination Center has been strictly following the principle to "Admit ED First, Prioritize Critical Patients, and Admit Mild Cases as Sequenced." Another principle we have been following is to "Move Physicians for Emergency, Critical and Severe Patients."

Standard Process Is the Remedy to ED Retention

One of the key areas of patient safety and quality by JCI is the effectiveness of a hospital's solution to the boarding patients in the ER.

High volume and insufficient beds in ER are the major causes of the retention. Sometimes, the buck passing among units for complicated and critical cases could also add to the burden on the flow of ER patients.

The Medical Affairs Department organized discussions together with ER, the Bed Coordination Center as well as all clinical unit heads, trying to solve the retention issue. The final conclusion was that no unit or individual could refuse the admission request of an ER patient, the ER physicians' responsibilities and admission process would be revised, and the Bed Coordination Center would follow the principle of "admitting ER patients first." The redesigned process is described below.

The Bed Coordination Center communicates with the specialists at ER at 8:30 am to survey the boarding patients inside the resuscitation room and the consultation rooms, and gives feedback to the ward to ensure timely coordination of beds on the ward for patients according to their criticality. The ER physician makes decision on the unit to admit complicated cases.

Of course, there would be cases where there are too many ED patients for one unit to admit them all, especially for Neurology and Orthopedics with a high proportion of ER admissions. If one unit is full, the Bed Coordination Center should arrange the patients to be admitted to other units after 14:00 according to the principle of "relevant specialties and close location" and "matched specialty for critical patients and cross-disciplinary admission for non-critical patients." Patients would be transferred back to the units where they should be admitted as soon as there is an empty bed. We require the transfer-back to be done within 24–48 h. Noncritical patients can only be admitted to other units after the assessment by the specialist and patient's consent. The responsible physicians of the patients need to follow the patients to wherever they are admitted.

In this way, the Bed Coordination Center is able to coordinate the open beds in different units based on the patients' condition and reallocate the ER patients in a timely manner. This effort saved the patients 5.55 h on average in terms of boarding compared to the figure in 2012.

LEAN Management: Guarantee of Policy Implementation

Based on our own situation, we improved the bed management module in the hospital information system for automatic statistics of diagnosis, waiting time and giving up of the patients.

Based on the real-time monitoring in both campuses, the Medical Affairs Department then could adjust the bed numbers in each unit according to the actual utilization and patient condition. Through communication with all units for surgery schedules of each physician, the Bed Coordination Center could admit surgical patients based on the diagnosis, completion of presurgical tests and examinations and physicians' schedule to avoid prolonged waiting time in the unit and maximize the utilization.

We also give feedback to the heads of units that have longer waiting list to discuss possible solutions; remind all medical teams to follow closely on the inpatients waiting for a bed to adjust the admission plan; and arrange day surgeries for patients who meet the criteria. With all these measures in place, we were able to reduce the patient's waiting time, cut the economic cost for them and alleviate the burden on the units so that patients would not give up waiting.

Efficient Pre-Admission Services Fueled by Information System

In the past, when an outpatient physician confirmed the admission based on the diagnosis, the physician would prescribe a paper admission request and order the preadmission examinations and tests. The patient had to queue up for bed appointment at the Bed Coordination Center, complete the formality and finish all tests and examinations. And the staff responsible for the preadmission tests/examinations had to enter the physician's order while worrying about any possible errors.

But HIMSS pointed out the possible solutions that we could put in place: to enable data sharing for the continuity of care. We then communicated with the IT Department to seek possible improvement in the system. Now, the results of the preadmission tests and examinations from both campuses can be shared through the inpatient EMR.

One-Stop Bed Appointment

In the past, the outpatient system was not linked to the bed management module. Thus, the staff at the Bed Coordination Center had to transcribe the information on the paper admission request as well as the note written by the physician, for example, the medication and surgeries, into the system. This drastically prolonged the waiting time. To reduce the workload caused by repetitive entry and avoid possible errors, the IT Department integrated the OPD system and the bed management system. The physicians were able to enter all information into the computer system, which saves the time of the staff at the Bed Coordination Center and reduced patient's waiting time for appointment. But, patients or families were still required to visit the Bed Coordination Center for appointment, and there were still long queues in front of the windows. This caused much inconvenience to the patients who could not be admitted on the same day. After rounds of brainstorming, we decided to redesign the bed appointment process and adopted the one-stop appointment service.

According to the JCI requirements, a physician should assess patient's condition and needs of prophylactic, palliative, radical and rehabilitative treatment before he/she prescribes the admission request and decide on the type of admission (prioritized or scheduled admission), hospitalization (regular, virtual or day-surgery hospitalization) and the campus for admission. After filling up the estimated cost for the stay, physicians can print out the Bed Appointment Notice to inform the patient and family of the information such as patient condition, initial impression, care plan, special attention, and estimated cost. The patient and family can go home right after they sign the notice.

Then the admission request information is sent to the Bed Coordination Center in both campuses and the one where the patient will be admitting is responsible for arranging and notifying the patient. If the patient wants to know about the progress of bed appointment, he/she can call the hot line printed on the Notice. The bed appointment can be finished at the clinic without wasting patient's time queuing up at the Bed Coordination Center or traveling between the two campuses. The information continuity required by HIMSS makes the life much easier for patients.

We also developed a policy on postponed admission notification. If a prioritized patient could not be admitted within 7 days or a scheduled patient within 60 days, the Bed Coordination Center has to notify the patient.

Order Set for Preadmission Tests/Examinations

The outpatient service in our hospital is very busy. To make sure that physicians order all necessary tests and examinations for patients before admission despite their experience, we set up the 82 order sets based on the diagnosis in different units, as HIMSS also encourages hospitals to adopt order sets in CPOE. The selected order set can be edited according to patient's condition.

For example, in the past, it took our physicians 6.7 min on average to prescribe the presurgery tests and examinations for lung cancer patients, but the time had been reduced to 2.2 min with order sets in place. The ordering time for presurgery tests and examination for thyroid cancer patient had also been reduced to 1.5 min from 3.4 min. While improving the efficiency, diagnosis-based order sets can also ensure uniform service across the organization.

With the joint efforts from the IT and clinical staff, we realized the seamless integration of information generated from different units and ensured the access to both current and history records. Physicians can also trace the progress of the tests/examinations as well as the reports to support their decisions on extra orders and scheduling of surgeries. More importantly, order sets make it more difficult for physicians to miss important tests/examinations.

Cross-Campus Information Sharing

The new campus was open to the public in 2013. But patients were required to finish all the tests and examinations at the campus in which they were going to stay. This caused inconvenience to the patients with virtual admission and day surgery.

To realize the information sharing between the two campuses regarding the tests and examinations, the Bed Coordination Center conducted several rounds of negotiation and system testing with the auxiliary departments. Today, any virtually admitted patient could finish the preadmission tests/examinations at the campus where they see the clinicians and then wait for the bed back at home. They only need to check in with the designated campus when they receive the notification on admission.

For day-surgery patients, after they finish the tests/examinations, the staff will bring them to the day-surgery area for presurgery assessment and check-in at the same campus. The staff are also responsible for the retention and transfer of relevant clinical documents. What patients need to do is to show up on the campus on time for the surgery according to the appointment. For patients who are supposed to be admitted on the same day, they can finish all the admission formality at either campus and then be admitted to the one they are assigned to. For example, if a patient sees an OB clinician at the Jiefanglu Campus, and the physician orders the admission request and preadmission tests and examinations. Then the Bed Coordination Center arranges the patient to be admitted to the Binjiang Campus. However, the patient has not had any food. We allow the patient to complete the admission formality and tests/examinations at the Jiefanglu Campus before going to the Binjiang Campus for admission.

A New Page on the 100-Year History

The centralized and integrated management of bed resources in both campuses and the optimization of the pre-hospitalization processes enable the hospital to fully utilize all the resources and allocate patients in both campuses, which has earned the new campus greater popularity among patients. Three years of efforts gained shorter length of stay, higher bed utilization, and increased number of discharged patients in both campuses.

If we compare the figure from 2016 with that in 2013, we can see that we successfully reduced the preadmission waiting time by 2.46 days for the Jiefanglu Campus and by 0.14 day for the Binjiang Campus. Meanwhile, the bed utilization rate increased by 1.47% for the Jiefanglu Campus and 20.63% for the Binjiang Campus.

The improved outpatient-to-inpatient flow is just one episode of our efforts in improving patient experience and resource utilization. The joint wisdom and efforts of our staff has been the key of the optimized system in place. Today, inpatient beds are no longer the "resources in the pocket of physicians," but a shared resource for patients.

Case 2: Penetration of Standard Care

Scene 1

A 50-year-old female patient complains that she started to have upper epigastric discomfort, pain, loss of appetite, acid regurgitation, and belching. She says that the symptoms have been alleviated obviously after taking anti-acid medication. But she has lost 3 kg in the past 2 months and is diagnosed with gastric cancer after endoscopy. Before admission, nurse A does a full admission assessment on the patient and finds that the patient's BMI is 18.10. The physician does a nutrition screening (NRS) and contacts a nutrition physician for consultation after malnutrition is confirmed. Meanwhile, nurse A documents the information about the patient on the chart, such as light sleep, and hands over the record to the night shift nurse.

Scene 2

A 10-year-old boy with osteosarcoma is waiting for the surgery scheduled on the next day after a cycle of chemotherapy. His responsible physician, B, notices emotional depression of the boy during the presurgery assessment. The physician invites a psychologist to provide support in addition to his own comforting words to the boy.

These are just two examples of our staff's daily work. Our clinical staff are required to perform comprehensive patient assessment, collect relevant information, and provide timely, effective care to the patients. All this started from our JCI journey.

Comprehensive Assessment: Key to Patient Care

Patient assessment is a continuous, dynamic process. Timely, accurate, and patient-specific assessment is also one of the focuses of JCI standards. Healthcare staff should assess the patient's needs within a short period of time and determine the care plan and discharge plan accordingly.

In China, we do not have defined contents for patient assessment. Most of the healthcare staff just follow the common practice and grant special attention to the special populations such as children and the elderly. With a well-developed assessment process in place, it is also required by HIMSS that healthcare staff apply the process in a more efficient way. To that end, the Medical Affairs Department, Nursing Department, Pharmacy, and IT Department revised relevant hospital policies and developed a new patient assessment module in the EMR. Before they brought the new functionality alive hospital wide, a pilot project was carried out in several selected units to test its reliability. They then collected feedback on a regular basis and optimized the process accordingly. After years of efforts, a complete patient assessment and care plan system was born.

Based on the advises from the JCI consultants, including Jilan, we gradually improved our policies on patient assessment to standardize the contents of assessment for outpatients, ED patients, and inpatients; the frequency and time frame of assessment; as well as the requirements on the assessment regarding nutrition, pain, rehabilitation, psychological support, fall/fall from bed, pressure ulcer, catheters, blood transfusion, and restrictions.

With the new policy in place, we started to include more contents for assessment at different frequencies. Therefore, it was in need to improve the EMR system. To this end, the Medical Affairs Department and Nursing Department set up their own EMR groups, respectively, to regularly discuss the action implementation regarding medical and nursing documentation in line with the JCI standards. Multiple meetings had been organized to discuss the sharing of data between physicians and nurses as well as the integration of different modules. The front-line staff also contributed their ideas to continuously improve the systems.

Take blood transfusion as an example.

Before the JCI survey, we adopted the Zhejiang Provincial Quality Nursing Care to assess the patients for blood transfusion before the transfusion, 15 min after it starts and after the transfusion is finished. But the JCI consultants told us that it was not sufficient. Hearing this, the staff were upset because the three-assessment schedule was already keeping the nurses busy. And many patients might have more than one bag of blood/blood products (especially for platelets). They could not imagine how they would be able to handle the intensified monitoring. But the standards should be observed.

After rounds of discussion, we finalized on the scheme: (1) assess the temperature, blood pressure, pulse, and respiration and observe the adverse reaction before and after the transfusion; (2) observe the adverse reaction 15, 30, and 60 min after the transfusion starts as well as after the entire transfusion is finished; and (3) assess the patient every 1 h during transfusion. All the assessment is documented on the Nursing Flow Sheet. Check on temperature, blood pressure, pulse, and respiration is required if adverse reaction is detected by the nurse. And staff are required to document the event.

Facing the increased work load, the only way out was to streamline the process for the nurses. The IT people were then involved in the discussion to develop the template for blood transfusion assessment in the nursing EMR (see Figure 20.3). The nurses can complete the assessment with just clicking and checking on the items.

What HIMSS focuses is not only the convenient entry, but also the recommendation triggered by certain decision support rules. So, as soon as the objective assessment is completed by the nurses, the system would push the assessment information link to the physician's EMR in real time after screening the results, and allow the physician to decide whether it is truly an adverse reaction. For example, a temperature of 38°C is documented by the nurse. But it would be left for the physician to find if it was due to the transfusion, the illness, or the postoperative absorption fever. Physician of the Blood Transfusion Department can be invited if there are any further

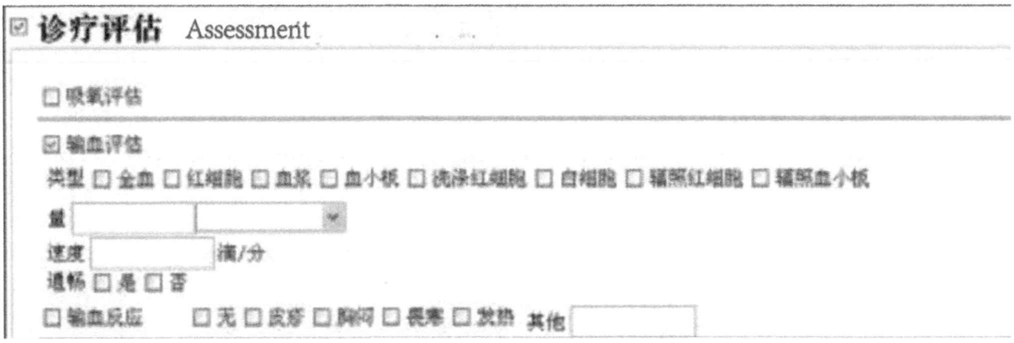

Figure 20.3 Template of blood transfusion nursing sheet.

questions about the patient's condition. The collaboration and interaction between physicians and nurses has greatly improved the accuracy of blood transfusion assessment and ensured the patient safety.

Multidisciplinary Plan for Overall Care

Patient care is a dynamic process involving not only the responsible physician and nurses but also other specialists such as dieticians, rehabilitation therapists, and psychological therapists. The multidisciplinary consultation is the major means of collecting opinions and recommendations from other units. Before we started the JCI journey, the consultation record was kept in the patient's medical record. But as the needs of multidisciplinary consultation increased, it became important for all specialists to understand the history information about the patient, which was a time-consuming task. When the record was not well organized, the missing consultation document might impact the clinical care efficiency.

The JCI standards expect integrated and coordinated care for patients through the cooperation among all departments, units, and services. So we decided to develop a multidisciplinary service protocol based on the existing model and adopted the use of *Multidisciplinary Care Sheet*, which would include patient's demographic information, physician's care plan, nursing problems, and nursing plan, other specialty care plans (nutrition/psychology) and conclusions from other specialty consultation. In such way, both responsible staff and consulting physicians could understand the opinions from other professionals and patient overall conditions in a more straightforward way and more efficiently utilize all kinds of resources for the provision of comprehensive service.

The information on the *Multidisciplinary Care Sheet* is populated automatically from different modules (e.g., care plan from physician's EMR, nursing care from nursing EMR) and updated in real time to save staff from repeated entry.

In the gastric cancer patient case, the care plan, nursing plan, and the dietician's consultation were fully integrated into the *Multidisciplinary Care Sheet.*

The physical checkup upon admission found emaciation, anemia appearance, poor appetite, an intake of 25 g rice at each meal with a major complaint of upper abdominal pain (scored 3). The patient had been cooperative and requested more information about the illness and surgery, and been exited, and had shallow sleep during night time about 4 h. The abdomen was found flat and soft, no pressing pain on epigastrium and no obvious rebound tenderness. The BMI was 18.1. Lab test results: HGB 85 g/L, ALB 30 g/L.

Based on the assessment, the responsible physician developed a care plan that included symptomatic treatment with acid suppression and fluid supply, regular preoperative screening and chest CT to identify the scope of area affected by tumor for developing the next care plan, and dietician's nutrition consultation.

The responsible nurse also developed a nursing care plan related to nursing problems: (1) nutrition disorder (lower than the volume required by the body), (2) chronic pain, and (3) sleep pattern disturbance. Relevant factors, expected goals, time frame, and specific nursing measures were then defined by the nurses.

CDSS for Better Patient Care

As the EMR system improved, we started to think about how to make the system more intelligent. And the CDSS functionality required by HIMSS criteria was exactly what we were looking for. The hospital's IT Center and EMR Team have been working together to push the hospital EMR system toward clinical-oriented intelligence based on JCI requirements since 2011 when we adopted electronic medical record. In July 2017, we received the Mock Survey of HIMSS EMRAM Stage 6 and gained deeper understanding of the CDSS functionality. CDSS is not simply a reminder after assessment. Nor is it a simple aggregation of data. It is a tool to improve care quality and reduce medical errors through providing right information to the right person via the right channel at the right time in a right fashion.

Therefore, we embedded intelligent reminder, decision support, data analysis, and quality management in the CDSS for nursing. Nurses can check the status of the patient right from the patient overview interface to check the safety risks (e.g., fall, pressure ulcer, VTE, isolation) with color coding. Alert would pop out, reading "Please verify the data," when it detects certain gap between the entered data with the regular range or last documented value. Overdue task reminder for assessment, medication administration and care are highly popular among our nurses, in particular junior ones.

Head nurses and the Nursing Department can generate various reports through data mining and analysis, learn about the latest situation on both department and hospital level in real time, for example, imported pressure ulcer/newly developed pressure ulcer, unplanned removal of catheter, making the job much easier for the nursing management.

Patient assessment and care support each other. Timely, accurate assessment is the foundation for the provision of better clinical care. When the cancer patient in the previous case was discharged after surgery, she sent us a banner of appreciation as a token of gratitude. We were also surprised to have received the hand-written festival card from the patient recovered from osteosarcoma. As standardization and processes gradually merge into the DNA of SAHZU, we are able to provide even better care to our patients. If JCI is the guidance to standardize the assessment and care for patients, the CDSS required by HIMSS is the intelligent tool helping us provide complete, accurate clinical care. The combination of the two has laid a solid foundation for us to purse quality and patient safety.

Case 3: College of Training: Carrying Traditions into the Future

We once struggled with the traditional training system. But Dr. Wang Jian'an, President of the hospital, proposed the establishment of the College of Training to integrate the training resources in the hospital and standardize the staff training processes.

The College of Training of SAHZU started its pilot at the end of 2011, headed by the CEO and Party Secretary as the Presidents, and the Executive VP as the Executive President. The faculties are chaired by the directors of relevant administrative departments as well as responsible VPs. The responsible personnel of relevant departments are in charge of the education affairs and the implementation of daily management. The Operation Office is assumed by the Human Resources Department, responsible for the daily management, development, and implementation of strategies, the formulation of training framework and scheduling of courses.

The College of Training provides education and training to all staff in the hospital. The faculties determine the contents of training and the staff who should participate. The college consists of the Faculty of General Training (for all staff), the Faculty of Medical and Technical Training (for physicians and clinical technicians), the Faculty of Nursing Training (for nurses), the Faculty of Administration Training (for all management staff), and the Faculty of Logistics (for all logistic technicians) (see Figure 20.4).

Concepts, knowledge, and skill trainings are provided by specialized faculties based on the level, position, experience of the staff with prioritization mechanism in place to ensure appropriate level and contents of training are delivered to the staff. We also set requirements on continuous education on staff.

The school year starts from January 1st and each semester lasts for 6 months. The college formulates and publicizes the schedule of training before each semester, and completes and releases the statistics of credits as one semester ends. The major training form is on-site lectures supported with live-streamed or online video delivered by internal or external professionals.

The faculties follow the schedule published by the HR every month to organize and implement the training, and are responsible for respective lecturer resources, materials, classrooms, and other affairs. Staff use their badge to check in and out from the classes. The attendance is monitored by the respective faculty and reported to the HR who further releases the information through the intranet. A special section is dedicated to the College of Training on the hospital intranet for notification, online education, evaluation, and credit inquiry. The training information platform ensures the efficiency of communication, diversifies the means of training, and guarantees the smooth roll-out of all activities.

Credit-based evaluation is adopted to assess the quality of learning. Students are required to attend the classes, finish their homework, and obtain certain credits through passing tests. There is a bottom line drawn for the credits of each semester. The credits gained through on-site training

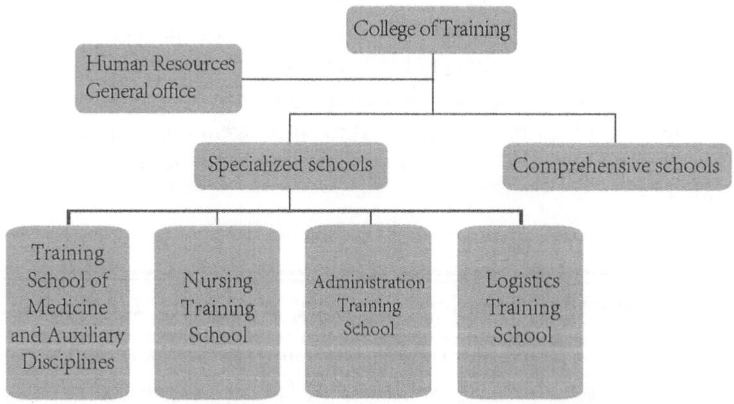

Figure 20.4 Organizational chart of College of Training.

are required to be 40% of the total credits set by respective specialized faculties for specialized training students, and 10% for the Faculty of General Training. The rest credits could be earned through online learning. The unit-based training is required to contribute at least 80% of the credits among all credits earned for specialized courses. The internal professionals who serve as the lecturer could get double credits for the course.

JCI Facilitates the Growth of College of Training

While the College of Training was still piloting its operation model, the hospital launched the JCI accreditation preparation. The college naturally became a platform for JCI-related education, which also drove the rapid growth of the college. "Quality and Patient Safety," the core value of JCI, set a higher bar for the College of Training and stimulated the hospital to pursue practices that embrace such values.

The College of Training started to integrate the courses in different faculties and include the new staff orientation and CPR into the schedule. A more standardized, efficient and effective training mechanism was born to facilitate the SOP education and training for relevant units and departments.

The college also gained progress through the hospital policy and procedure modification. Brainstorming was organized to have involved many more people from different departments and units for possible solutions to potential challenges. For example, the administrative departments worked together to further identified the roles of the management at all levels for the college and formulated the *Management Measures of College of Training, Policy on Orientation for New Staff, Management Measures of Orientation for Non Full-Time Employees, Policy on CPR Training*, and many other policies and procedures. It was to our surprise that the training on policies and procedures enhanced the staff's awareness of the organizational structure and requirements of the college, cleared the obstacles during the pilot, and motivated the staff's participation.

JCI Brings Further IT Adoption to College of Training

At the beginning of 2012, HR hosted a meeting together with the IT Center and major vendors to discuss the IT system for the College of Training, in particular the dedicated column on the hospital intranet and the OA management platform for the college. Three modules were decided to be bring online, namely "Training Plan," "On-line Education," and "Credit Inquiry." The "Training Plan" mainly releases the training schedule for each semester and updates the monthly schedule of all courses. "On-line Education" is built for the training videos and materials with the support of the "On-line Test Platform." "Credit Inquiry" is linked with the "Management System for College of Training," on which students can check their own credits with staff number and log-in password (see Figure 20.5).

Figure 20.5 Information platform of College of Training.

The system was officially launched on March 14, 2012, and soon became the platform for releasing the schedule for the first semester of that year. All types of training materials and online tests modules were made available as well. Due to the complex mix of students, categorized trainings were provided according to students' jobs, titles, and experience. The HR and IT Center then decided to interface the College of Training system with the databases of HR, Nursing Department, and meeting management system. It took us several years to realize the seamless interfacing among different databases. The development of the IT platform is also a continuous process. Through the practices and operation of the college, new functions, such as unit-based statistics, reminder messaging to students who do not meet the credit requirements, internal training record entry, manual entry of credit, and mailbox for college, have been brought online one after another.

Integration of JCI Standards and College of Training

Review the Training Requirements with JCI Standards

During the preparation for JCI survey, we noticed that JCI requires the hospital determine the education needs of staff based on all types of data and information, including quality and safety monitoring. In the old days, staff training followed the traditional way of "working behind closed doors." It means that the training departments developed the courses and lectures based on their own experience rather than any evidence. The JCI standards made us realize that evidence-based training course development is more practical and down-to-earth. The College of Training soon started to work together with the Quality Office to identify the needs for training according to the monitoring indicator data once every 6 months to determine the priorities for training. For example, on August 20, 2012, the data from the Quality Office indicated obvious fluctuation of "surgical site infection" in the hospital. The college then decided to provide special training on the prevention and control of surgical site infection to all staff through the Faculty of General Training. The training course started on September 7 in the same year, and was lectured by Dr. Lu Qun, Deputy Director of the hospital's Infection Control Department. Online course was also made available. There were in total 178 staff who attended the face-to-face training and 2,300 staff who received online training and passed the tests. In the following 6 months, we saw an improvement of the indicator's performance.

We also require all faculties to gather feedback from the students and unit representatives while developing their own training plans. With the great support from the Quality Office (Analysis of Priority Quality Indicators) and all faculties, the colleges were able to better meet the needs and develop more targeted programs, which, in turn, has brought much more benefit to the trainees.

100% Coverage of CPR Training

There is one measurable element in SQE 8.1 by the JCI standards: "Staff members who provide patient care and other staff identified by the hospital to be trained in cardiac life support are identified." We soon realized that the intention is that each member of the staff might encounter a patient suffering from cardiac arrest and immediate resuscitation would be needed. CPR was then included in the curriculum of the College of Training, who organized the training for all staff, including physicians, technicians, nurses, managers, logistics staff as well as outsourced personnel, volunteers, inters, and security guards.

The categorized training system based on different professions, positions, and clinical background was adopted for the CPR training. The HR worked together with the Medical Affairs

Department, Nursing Department, Research and Education Department as well as the College of Training and its specialized faculties to discuss based on the AHA CPR Program and the needs of the daily work, and concluded with a training program in the hospital in May 2012, including the levels of training, trainees, and emergency hot line with 999 as the code for resuscitation. The resuscitation training course comprises three levels, namely CPR, BLS, and ACLS. CPR is provided to all management and logistics staff; BLS for all physicians, clinical technicians and nursing staff; and ACLS for targeted physicians and nurses working in specific units. In 2014 when we set up the Pediatrics Department, PALS was added to the resuscitation training program for the staff working in the Pediatric and other involved units.

The program further defined the scope and attendees of the training and the roles of different administrative departments. HR was coordinating the organization of the resuscitation training and keeping the records. The Nursing Department was responsible for providing the lecturers, deciding on the level-based means and content of the training based and conducting the training and evaluations. The Research and Education Department was assigned with the job to provide facilities and equipment. The Medical Affairs Department was to ensure the trainer resources. All specialized faculties were asked to carry out the training according to the hospital's schedule and requirements. The first round of the resuscitation training was then unveiled its curtain. After the hospital introduced the AHA training program, most of the students graduated from the AHA program became the trainers of the college, and part of them even obtained the AHA trainer qualification. To test the outcome of the training, the HR would lay down the "Little Anne" somewhere in the hospital and call out "HELP" to see the response of the staff.

The quick, effective response to every 999 call has also gradually build the confidence of the staff.

Improved Orientation Based on JCI Standards

The new staff orientation had been something that we had been proud of before we had JCI standards. But the international standards made it even more standardized and comprehensive.

According to SQE 7, "all clinical and nonclinical staff members are oriented to the hospital, the department or unit to which they are assigned, and to their specific job responsibilities at appointment to the staff." Outsourced personnel, volunteers, students, and inters should also be covered in the orientation. The College of Training then developed two different orientation programs for full-time employees and nonemployees, including training preparation, contents, evaluation and attendance, and set clear training program evaluation and feedback mechanism. The orientation can also be divided into general orientation, professional orientation, and department orientation. The general orientation is organized by HR, covering topics like hospital history, culture, and value; hospital policies and procedures; moral and disciplines; basic business knowledge; infection control; emergency response; laws and regulations; behavior; quality management; healthcare insurance, etc. The professional orientation is organized and carried out by the Medical Affairs Department and Nursing Department to provide lecture and demonstration training for physicians, clinical technicians, and nurses regarding relevant protocols and techniques. The professional orientation is organized within the first month after the general one is finished. Department-level orientation is organized by the respective units/departments according to the operation and required knowledge, which could include the goals of services, basic information, structure, service scope, roles and responsibilities, processes, and procedures, occupational safety, hygiene, etc. Credits of the Faculty of General Training would be calculated according to the attendance, in-class performance and evaluation of the general orientation; credits of specialized faculties could be earned through the performance of the professional orientation.

Centralized orientation used to be scheduled in August because of the graduation season falls in July and August every year. But later on, the College of Training set requirements on the orientation for the employees who are recruited throughout the year. Brochure for new staff and orientation materials are distributed upon registration, and collective orientation is organized every 2 months for the staff recruited in the previous 2 months who would also be required to attend the orientation in August.

For the trainings provided to outsourced personnel, volunteers, students, and inters, the responsible departments organize the training and keep relevant documentation. HR is responsible for the College of Training to inspect on the training regularly and provide improvement suggestions on the content and approaches.

Department Training Based on JCI Standards

The education courses provided by the College of Training include general and specialized ones. The former targets at all employees, while the later at specific types of employees. Each department/unit has its own clinical or professional focuses, which causes differences in the needs of training. Thus, it's important to give a full play of the discipline strengths and resources of each unit/department in organizing the trainings.

As SQE 8 requires, "each staff member receives ongoing in-service and other education and training to maintain or to advance his or her skills and knowledge." Department-level training should include the latest theory and technical skills to provide more practical guidance to the staff. At the early years of the College of Training, the department-level training was mainly organized by the department/unit itself according to daily work. The HR would inspect on the execution of the training through reviewing the documents and attendance.

But it was not sufficient to meet the timeliness required by the JCI standards. We, then, decided to promote the department-level training maintenance platform. In September 2015, department-level training was successfully merged with the College of Training under uniform management. The department-level training contributes 0.5 credit per training hour and is calculated to the final credits of a trainee. Designated staff is assigned by each unit to be responsible for the attendance maintenance and upload of training materials. The College of Training serves as a uniform platform for department trainings and saves staff much time from keeping all the documents. Meanwhile, the valid credits become an incentive for the staff to attend the trainings. From the hospital administration perspective, it is also an important means to update the trainings going on the department level.

Blooming with JCI

For the HR Department, the College of Training is like a child of theirs taking a journey full of unknown exploration.

JCI survey brought the team together. All the departments and units granted their greatest support to the development of the College of Training. The training management offices of different faculties, the Quality Office who provides data analysis, the IT Center who develops the platform, the Logistics Department who provides training to the outsourced personnel, the Customer Service Center who delivers training to the volunteers, the Research and Education Department who carries out trainings for the interns, and all units who organize trainings for their own staff, are the ones who are contributing to the growth of the college.

With JCI as a driving force, we have realized that all the personnel working in the hospital, including outsourced staff, volunteers, interns, and security guards are also patient service providers influencing the hospital quality and patient safety. Only through trainings covering all staff can it be possible to practice in line with JCI standards in our day-to-day work and uphold the values of "always putting patients first."

In the tides of quality improvement launched in the hospital, the College of Training has been an extraordinary example of embracing new ideas and transform for better care. Each improvement effort is the rewards from JCI endeavor.

After 5 years of operation, the College of Training has provided numerous high-quality education and training resources online, having laid down a solid foundation for future development.

In addition to the resuscitation training, we also launched the series lectures. The *Washington Manual of Medical Therapeutics and Grand Round* series regarding latest medical development provided by the Faculty of Medical and Technical Training have attracted many staff even though the courses start at 7:00 in the morning. The Faculty of Nursing Trainings targets the students with specific training courses that could meet their sophisticated needs.

The Faculty of Administration Training offers skill trainings for the staff to improve their performance and also develop other hobbies, such as photography, statistics and Photo Shop. The Faculty of Logistics Training carries out training that aligns the staff with the JCI standards. The Faculty of General Training has introduced the core courses such as occupational violence and cross-cultural communication in addition to the infection control, fire safety, and quality management.

As Dr. Wang Jian'an, President of SAZHU, said, "Training is the best welfare for staff." Thus, the College of Training shoulders a noble mission for the development of talents of staff growth. To carry on the professional knowledge and the culture of a hospital is the foundation for the college as well as the driving force of the hospital to strive for a better future. With the guidance of JCI, we are confident that the starry light of the College of Training would lead the way for each one of our staff providing service to our patients to search for better performance.

Chapter 21

Children's Hospital of Fudan University

Huang Guoying, Xu Hong, Qu Xiaowen, Xu Jiahua, Li Zhiping, Wang Chuanqing, Wu Xiaohu, Ge Xiaoling, Ye Chengjie, Liu Gongbao, Gao Xuan, Chen Weiwen, Zheng Feng, and Zhang Yishun
Children's Hospital of Fudan University

Huang Guoying *is the President of the Children's Hospital of Fudan University, Chairman-elect of Chinese Pediatric Society, chief scientist of national key projects, Vice Chief Editor of* Chinese Journal of Pediatrics *and Chief Editor of* Pediatric Medicine.

Dr. Huang's focus of research is non-invasive diagnostics, etiology and early intervention of congenital heart disease, Kawasaki disease with coronary complication and hospital administration. Among the 400 articles that he has published, 110 are found in The Lancet, Pediatrics, Plos Genetics, *etc.*

Hospital Introduction: Founded in 1952, the Children's Hospital of Fudan University is a Level-A Tertiary Hospital accredited by the Health and Family Planning Commission of China (now called National Health Commission). It is also a general children's hospital dedicated to clinical care, medical education, research, and disease prevention. As one of the National Children's Medical Centers in China, the hospital also serves as the education organization for master and doctor programs and postdoctoral research center in pediatrics and has been listed in the "211" project and "985" project with Pediatrics as the national key discipline.

International Accreditation: 2014, the first JCI academic teaching hospital specialized in pediatrics in Asia;

Novembers 2016, HIMSS EMRAM 6.

Contents

Preface

A Journey from "Knowing-How" to "Doing-So"

In recent years, the Children's Hospital of Fudan University (hereinafter referred as "CHFDU") leveraged the strength of advanced international healthcare quality management standards through learning from the successful experience and approaches adopted in overseas hospitals to better improve the quality management and culture of safety in the hospital. And Bold steps have been taken in practice and innovation.

In 2014, the hospital was accredited by JCI as the first academic teaching hospital specialized in pediatrics in Asia in the JCI club. Not long after that, we were validated as an HIMSS

EMRAM Stage 6 hospital in November 2016. Through taking the international challenges and introducing the concepts of patient safety, care quality, and patient-centricity, we have been able to better satisfy our patients and forge a better management structure to lead the future development. With improved processes and clinical work flows, the efficiency has been ensured with stronger team cohesion. The international recognition also won the hospital greater local reputation.

Why JCI?

"We are too busy to care about JCI…" "JCI is all about those details. Why do we have to waste our time on it?" Like many other hospitals in China, the hospital staff did not understand or accept the JCI concept at the beginning.

Then Jilan Liu came to our hospital upon the invitation by Dr. Huang Guoying, President of the hospital, to discuss the value of adopting JCI standards. Jilan simply explained, "JCI standards are patient-centered. The only thing it requires is that the staff do what they should do in the right way. It has nothing more than that." The idea consolidated the leadership's commitment to the JCI journey and became a ring in our mind to always remind us of the reason why we started the journey. Since we decided to take the JCI challenge voluntarily, we were determined to improve the hospital systems, processes, and capability rather than just aiming at the gold seal.

To further align the goals in the hospital, we launched diverse education campaign on different levels, involving the leadership, the management and the frontline staff, for self-learning or centralized training about the JCI standards and other relevant publications introducing JCI experience (such as *From Knowing-how to Doing-so*). On the department level, joint discussions and lectures were organized to interpret the JCI standards. Colleagues from other JCI hospitals were invited to share their experience and strategies. Our own staff had been sent out to other JCI hospital for visits and exchanges.

We also invited consultants from JCI for a comprehensive and systematic baseline survey which lasted for 6 days. Through the thorough evaluation on the hospital's situation, the consultants left us with over 200 findings, including the neglected high-risk processes (e.g., sedation). All management staff agreed with the findings and no one considered them as cavils. All staff participated also benefited from the tracer methodology, through which, we learned that "we were not perfect," and there were many things we could learn from other hospitals in terms of managerial expertise.

The emphasis on patient safety and quality of care had served as the light to help the hospital identify the opportunities of improvement and plan actions based on the reality.

After the baseline, actions were soon put in place through the JCI Leading Group, JCI Office, and the JCI coordinators. As required by the Leading Group, the JCI Office was responsible for reviewing all the policies and procedures; assessing, categorizing and prioritizing the necessary improvement of hardware and redesign of processes based on the recommendations from the baseline; and developing the improvement plans.

Advance through Teamwork

The JCI Office categorized the 200 findings from the baseline survey into three levels and listed all the key issues:

Level I: projects requiring hardware renovation, major policy revision, process redesign, which would cost longer time to gap with the standards (in total 36);

Level II: projects with weak foundation requiring hospital-wide long-term actions through cross-department coordination (in total 28);

Level III: projects with good foundation requiring only simple improvement and achievable within a short period of time (in total 28).

The smooth implementation of those projects could never be possible without the cross-department coordination and effective communication allowing candid and open discussion. The shared goal was to strengthen the weakness in the hospital to make the process safer and more appropriate. To that end, we needed close cooperation of different departments through meetings and discussion to align the targets and give a full play of their respective strengths. For example, the improvement of the outpatient infusion process required the collaboration among the Pharmacy, nurses, physicians, management staff overseeing OPD/ER service, logistics, infrastructure, and IT. Only with the consensus among all these people, would they be able to take an active role in the actions and propose constructive recommendations to ensure smooth implementation.

Challenges were always there during the implementation, in particular for risk management and high-risk processes: conservative thoughts, outdated ideas, old habits… In face of these barriers, the opinions from external experts could be useful. Whenever we argued over certain solutions or captured in certain dilemmas, Jilan would always be there for us to provide the most effective suggestions according to the JCI standards.

At the end of 2013, Jilan suggested that we adopt EMR in the hospital to realize the sharing of patient information and better manage patient clinical data. After rounds of discussion, system development and pilot tests in some of our units, the EMR was finally brought alive. However, many unit directors had spent most of their career using paper medical records. So, it was extremely difficult for them to transit to the EMR in a short time. "It will slow down the visits! I can only see 30 patients compared with 40 in the past!" "The printing is too slow." "It is too noisy." "The paper is always stuck in the machine! I have to fix the printer while fixing my patients"… The complains kept pouring in.

The necessity and feasibility of EMR for outpatient clinics was moved up to the agenda on various meetings organized at the end of that year. On these meetings, Jilan also stressed the importance of information sharing and the EMR adoption, and urged the participation of the staff involved in JCI improvement activities to collect feedback from all stakeholders and further optimize the content and interfaces. After 4 months of arduous efforts, we finally won the support of all physicians on the EMR initiative. The outpatient profiles, the sharing of patient information, access to medical history, use of abbreviation, medical record quality control and other managerial requirements could all be achieved with the new tool, and thus further meet the JCI requirements.

Through this process, we again affirmed the value of cross-department cooperation on the journey toward JCI. To better mobilize the staff from different departments to assist the execution of the leadership's decision and ensure sufficient training for the frontline staff, the JCI Office established an evaluation mechanism on the responsible departments and chapter coordinators, which was called "Gantt Chart+Cooperation Level." "Gantt Chart" showed the progress of each chapter projects, and the "Cooperation Level" was the support level offered to the main responsible department(s). The evaluation results were analyzed and released on a weekly basis and rewards were given every month as the incentives for better outcomes. As they cared about their own performance, the unit directors started to communicate more frequently with the JCI Office.

Jilan was said, "We need to make sure that the teams are racing, but under control. Such incentive measure is worth of sharing."

The final evaluation on our efforts in this "battle" was the mock survey. Three consultants conducted an 8-day mock survey, during which they reviewed the latest progress made and left us with another 200 findings and recommendations. Different from the baseline, the 200 findings from the mock survey were more on the detail level rather than "not met."

Write Down What You Should Do, Do What You Have Written Down, and Document What You Have Done

The initial JCI survey requires a 4-month track record about the hospital performance to demonstrate constant monitoring and data collection. It means that JCI needs to ensure the hospital integrate quality management and monitoring into its daily operation. The focus is the continuous staff training as well as the implementation, monitoring, collection, and aggregation of the data regarding quality improvement.

Staff training was a mammoth project for the hospital. It was not the training itself that posed challenges, but the awareness, understanding, and compliance of each staff in the hospital. The monitoring on individual performance regarding each step and the following analysis, comparison, cause analysis, and improvement were even more critical for the effective improvement. Various methods and formats were adopted for the training: education videos with attendance signature; "Knowing-how and Doing-so" brochure for self-learning and checking; on-site inspection through tracer; knowledge contest with awards granted to outstanding staff; Daily JCI Tips; weekly test with score registry… We had only one goal: to make each one of our staff, workers, and students know how to do things and actually do it in the right way.

As Dr. Huang Guoying, President of the hospital, said, "Write down what you should do; do what you have written down; and document what you have done." The process redesign in the hospital was to improve quality and further ensure the safety of our patients. Therefore, it required that the process be fully implemented, standardized, and integrated into daily practice through policies and be fully complied by each one of our personnel. All the activities need to be documented as the evidence of standard practice or variation. This is also the essence of tracer and JCI requirements.

It requires the hospital to take steps forward to better manage quality improvement activities. All the data collected need to be validated, compared, and analyzed to generate useful information to guide the future actions. The measures and concepts about quality improvement were not familiar to our staff. Thus, how to build the capability in data process and grant sufficient technical support to the clinical departments were the new questions facing the Quality Control Department.

The strategy taken was to organize quality lectures on different departments/units by the staff from the quality office. The topics covered in the lectures included: progress of quality projects; monitoring measures, analysis of fluctuation and recommendations on improvement for hospital-wide and department-level indicators; analysis of the adverse events, sentinel events and relevant improvement actions; clinical pathway management, etc. All the staff were required to attend the lectures, and minutes were kept by designated staff. The monitoring data, causes of fluctuation, and improvement effectiveness were shared with all staff through lectures and posters. The participation of staff in quality activities was also included in the staff evaluation.

During the period to sustain the practice, all projects were on the track steadily, and new systems were operating smoothly. Staff were more aware of the hospital policies, and patient's satisfaction rate and sense of safety were significantly enhanced. A positive culture of safety was growing in the hospital. Staff would remind each other of performing “Time Out” and hand hygiene before procedures. If a child was running in the hospital, staff would stop him/her, or told the parents to attend the child. Smoking would always be dissuaded…

On the leadership interview in our initial survey, David Loose, one of the surveyors, posed a question regarding culture of safety to Dr. Huang Guoying, “Dr. Huang, if a score would be given to the culture of safety in the hospital, how much would you say?” Dr. Huang answered, “Safety has always been a topic in our hospital. However, we did not have the culture of safety in the past. If I have to give a score, I would say 60 at most. But after learning the JCI standards and all the efforts to meet the standards, we have been dedicated to nurturing a culture of safety and it becomes everybody’s responsibility. We are still making progress. So I would say 80 for now. Of course, we will never stop moving ahead for an even safer environment. I can assure you that our goal is 100!”

The accreditation survey started on August 25, 2014 and lasted for 5 days. We were surveyed under the more stringent fifth edition of the standards. The surveyors reviewed our organizational structure, management system, medical service, medication system, infection control, quality indicators, staff qualification, facility safety, research projects and medical education through document review, interviews, system tracers, and individual patient tracers.

Two years of efforts was paid back. Among all 1,171 measurable elements of 294 standards, we only had 24 “partially met” and 1 “not met.” Steward Hamilton said on the exit meeting, “If my granddaughter was sick, I would send her to your hospital for care!” The heart-touching comment was the best rewards to the diligent people of the hospital!

Case 1: Brand New OVA for Outpatient and ER Service

It was an ordinary day of 2013. The queue had already formed in front of the pick-up windows at the Infusion Center. There were still several minutes to 9 o’clock.

An experienced nurse was finding the drugs she was looking for while checking the information on the computer. Her experience kept her efficient and organized.

“Okay… Where is your dexamethasone? The small glass bottle.” She hunted through all the stuff in the bag handed over by the patient’s farther: IV medication, oral medication, drugs for external use, medical record, invoice, lab results… She finally got all the ampules and vials but not the dexamethasone.

The farther looked worried, “Not in the bag?” He grabbed the bag over, trying to find the drug. The patience of the parents standing in the long queue started to vaporize. They began to wave the sheets in their hands, trying to fan away the heat of anxiety.

The farther did not find the drug, either. He took the bag and turned away. The nurse looked at the patient card left behind on the desk and put it into the medication container for the child. It seemed that she was so used to that.

The father rushed to the No. 7 window of the Outpatient Pharmacy and jumped to the first. “Hey, doctor! I just got the medication from you. Did you forget to give me something?”

The young pharmacist asked the farther for the medication list (given to the patient family with medication name, quantity, route, and other information on it). Then the pharmacist responded, “Just a minute. I need to check the video.”

The farther waited anxiously. Suddenly, he got a call from his wife. His wife was with their daughter at the entrance of the Infusion Center. There were too many people in the lobby, and no empty seat was available for her. She had to hold the baby in one arm and carry the belongings in the other hand. She was so worried about her daughter and was sweating even though the air conditioning was working really hard to blowing down the temperature. So, she called her husband to hurry him up. As the father hung up the phone and tried to look into the window, the pharmacist came back. He said, "Please check your pocket. I checked the video and I saw you put the drug into the pocket." The father suddenly recalled that he put the little vial into the pocket because he was afraid of breaking it. But he forgot it because of the long queue.

He thanked the pharmacist, hurried back to the Infusion Center, fished out the dexamethasone, and handed it over to the nurse. The nurse then gave the patient card back to the father together with an infusion sequence number. "Don't lose the number. Otherwise you have to queue up again." she reminded him before he left. He took over the number and thanked the nurse. But he murmured to the nurse, "Don't you think it's a bit dangerous to let the patient's family carry these things around?" The nurse looked at the endless queue and sighed.

It was indeed endless. It was nearly 10 o'clock. The parents waiting for infusion queued up the outpatient lobby, crossed the queue at the pharmacy and ended outside the outpatient building. One parent shared her experience with the "new comer," "If you come here after 9, you have to wait at least 2 hours. So, you'd better have more people come with you. They could queue up here first for you. After you return from the visit with the doctor and pay your bill at Cashier, it would be almost your turn to get the IV." The conversation escaped into the ear of the hospital leaders. It was not the first time they heard about that. They frowned and tried to seek possible solutions.

Meetings had been organized to discuss the IV infusion flow at OPD/ER. Four major issues were identified:

① Medications handed over to parents were at risk of being lost or damaged, or forgotten at home.
② It wasted much time of the staff at the receiving window of the Infusion Center finding and verifying the medication, which was the main cause of the long queue.
③ Drugs requiring refrigeration could not be stored appropriately.
④ Parents had to pick up the medication at the OPD/ER Pharmacy, give the medication to the infusion staff and wait for the infusion, which was of low efficiency because of the queuing.

Meetings had been organized, and staff had been set out to learn from the experience from peer hospitals. However, there was no perfect solution.

It was not until 2012 when the hospital decided to adopt JCI standards and set up the JCI Office that the redesign of the OPD/ER infusion process was moved up as one of the priorities.

With the JCI Office taking the lead, the hospital leadership convened a project meeting joined by the directors from the OPD/ER, Pharmacy, Medical Affairs, Nursing and IT to discuss the initial solution based on the JCI standards and the existing flow and staffing: to designate an area in the Outpatient Pharmacy to IV medication arrangement. After the parents retrieved the oral medications from the Pharmacy, the pharmacist would arrange the medication for IV infusion for the patient and then send to the Infusion Center for mixing according to the schedule. However, most children in our hospital would be prescribed with IV medications. So, we did not implement the idea because we wanted to save man power.

In March 2013, Jilan came to the hospital together with other JCI consultants for the baseline survey. She visited the process in the Infusion Center and reviewed the initial solution we came up with.

According to her, if the IV medications were sent for mixing by batch as scheduled, it might prolong the waiting time of the patients and cause unexpected incidents during the transportation.

She suggested that an infusion admixture pharmacy be established in the Infusion Center like the PIVAS, and that a medication prearrangement system be implemented. After the baseline, the second meeting was convened to review the recommendation from Jilan, and a new plan was born: to establish the IV Pharmacy in the Infusion Center with designated staff to arrange the medication and base solutions for mixing. After the parents picked up the medication and gave to the nurse at the Infusion Center, the nurse would issue an infusion number to the parent. At the same time, the system would transmit the infusion information to the IV Pharmacy for printing the infusion labels, according to which the pharmacist would arrange the medications and base solutions for the patient.

During the mock survey in January 2014, Jilan reviewed the IV infusion process again. She suggested that we establish the OVA (OPD/ER IV Admixture Center) with independent appropriateness review window, dispensing window, and the internal flow as that in the PIVAS. It would be easier for the pharmacists to communicate with the parents and simplify the process by reducing the queuing, crowded patient flow, infection, and security risk. Meanwhile, the concept of adopting information technology to further optimize the work flow was introduced to the hospital. After rounds of discussion with the directors of different departments, the hospital leadership finally decided to overcome the restrictions on staffing and space, and adopt the recommendation from Jilan to establish the best IV infusion process with the resources at our disposal to ensure patient safety.

The task involved a wide range of departments in the hospital. The JCI Office was responsible for coordination and supervision; IT for OVA system development; Pharmacy for pharmacist trainings, reviewing the IV medications, assisting the IT Department in developing the appropriateness review and medication arrangement, assisting the Infrastructure Department in renovating the Infusion Center; Medical Affairs Department for physician training; Nursing Department for nurse training and handover to ensure the proper operation of the work flow during the transition; Promotion Department for posting the new process and notifying the patients and families.

On June 19, 2014, OVA was officially opened to business (see Figure 21.1a and b). The new process significantly improved the experience of our patients and their families. The parents only need to check in at the OVA window with the patient card and prescription. The pharmacist would then review the prescription and generate the infusion number as well as the infusion label. The parent only needs to wait for the nurse to call the number for IV infusion. The pharmacist would arrange the medication according to the infusion label and deliver the medications into the mixing area for final processing.

All the work was paid back with the new process in place: (1) The long queue in front of the Infusion Center window disappeared. There would be only five to six people in the queue at the busiest hours. (2) The families don't need to queue up at the OPD/ER Pharmacy anymore. They are allowed to pick up the oral medications after the infusion. This helps reduce the risks of medication loss during the transportation. (3) The average waiting time has been cut by 2 h. (4) All medications are under the control of pharmacists and reviewed by pharmacists to ensure the effectiveness and safety of the therapy.

We also introduced the concept of HIMSS to the new process by adopting the barcoding system to control the pre-admixture verification, mixing, administration and patrol to verify the information on the infusion label against the infusion number given to the patient. The staff involved in each step and the start/end time of each bag of medication could be tracked in the IV infusion system.

Under the supervision and support from the JCI Office, the pharmacists of OVA continued their efforts in improving the process. Thanks to the project and the satisfying results, the OVA service was awarded as the "Excellent Hospital Service Window" in 2015.

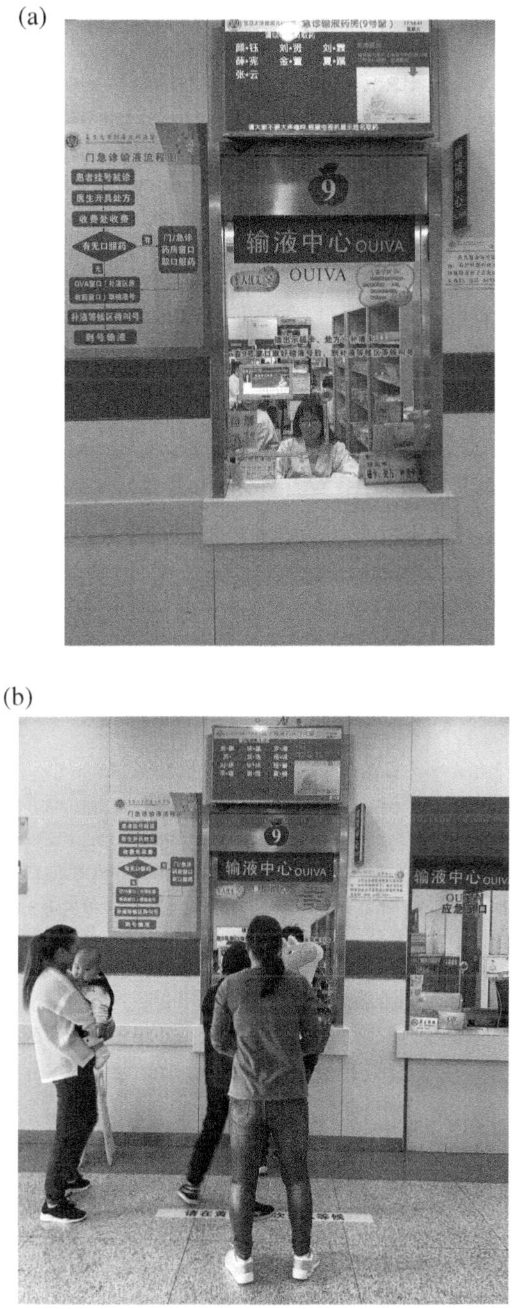

Figure 21.1 OVA (before and after).

After years of continuous improvement, we decided to embark on the HIMSS journey and became an HIMSS EMRAM Stage 6 hospital in 2016. In 2017, to further optimize the information technology, the hospital launched the HIMSS EMRAM Stage 7 campaign. HIMSS EMRAM Stage 7 covers the inpatient and emergency service in the hospital. The OVA operation gained another round of upgrade through the process.

In March 2017, Jilan led a team of HIMSS consultants for the baseline survey to our hospital. During the HIMSS baseline, she offered recommendation on the OVA again to add scanning capability inside the OVA for medication arrangement, and the setting of speed and reminder on dwelling needles in the nurse PDA. In July 2017, we received the mock survey of HIMSS EMRAM Stage 7. By then, we had already realized the barcode scanning process inside the pharmacy.

From 2013 to 2017, the transition of the Infusion Center had saved the time of the families and many more complaints regarding the service flow. Though it took some time for the patient family members to learn about the new process, they were satisfied with it as they just needed one piece of paper and the patient card to receive the infusion service. The hospital leaders don't need to frown at the crowds and chaotic scene at the lobby. And our pharmacists would be reassured when they scan the barcode to verify the medication that the took from the shelves. Our nurses smile more and sigh less while seeing the promising future these changes could bring us.

Case 2: Long-Term Multidisciplinary Collaboration

Though we were very successful in the initial JCI survey, we were left with 24 partially-met findings and 1 not-met finding. The one "not-met" was the multidisciplinary plan of care.

As a Level A Tertiary Hospital specialized in pediatrics, we take all the complicated and critical cases. The special population and the rapid change of conditions pose huge challenges to the daily clinical care in a pediatric hospital. In particular, for the complicated, critical children, they may have dysfunction of multiple organs, which requires the cooperation of different units and disciplines.

Currently, the most common multidisciplinary practice in a Level A Tertiary Hospital is to invite specialty consultation. In our hospital, the annual average number of specialty consultations is over 20,000, including 1,000 emergency cases. We are facing more challenging situation with increasing complicated or critical children admitted to our hospital as the government is promoting the "hierarchical healthcare system." We have seen more patients with three or more systems burdened or suffering from dysfunctions. The JCI surveyors believed that the traditional medical consultation from other specialties could not meet the needs of care of the patients, and such practice could not satisfy the JCI requirements, either. There were mainly two reasons. First, in most of the cases, the physician invited had little time and limited information for them to make sufficient and targeted decision. Second, we did not include nursing, psychology, nutrition, rehabilitation, and other disciplines.

With the support from Jilan and her team, we established a new multidisciplinary cooperation mechanism to develop multidisciplinary plan of care for our patients. The patient assessment was more comprehensive and the consultation process was optimized with the support from the information technology. We also standardized the content of different disciplines to be discussed during the planning of care. A robust quality monitoring and satisfaction rate evaluation system was introduced.

Step 1: Multidisciplinary Collaboration Project Portfolio

The multidisciplinary consultation project portfolio included the top-level projects, improvement projects, and the platform projects. Expert teams were organized for specific projects. The responsible person of each project was required to hold a senior title or be the academic leader. The hospital also developed the time schedule and defined the areas where multidisciplinary consultation service would be provided. When a project was planned, the roles of the team members needed to be defined, and the responsible person was assigned to initiate the discussion and make decisions on the following plan of care.

Step 2: Smooth and Efficient Multidisciplinary Care

For pediatric outpatients, the multidisciplinary consultation project provides primary specialty clinic consultation to the patients. The specialist first receives the child is required to screen and access the patient's condition, completes relevant tests and examinations and documents the medical record. If the child meets the criteria for multidisciplinary consultation, the specialist then makes the consultation appointment for the patient.

For inpatients, when the criteria for multidisciplinary consultation are met, the major responsible specialist makes the appointment for the patient. Designated staff are arranged for multidisciplinary care with special log designed to document the follow-up visits, including the demographic information, opinions of the multidisciplinary discussion, follow-up time, and results.

A more comprehensive assessment and reassessment mechanism was established through all these efforts to cover 13 different sections including nutrition, function, psychology, fall, etc. The effective communication between physicians and nurses, especially regarding high-risk patients, could ensure timely and active interventions from the healthcare staff from different disciplines to be included in the plan of care.

We also utilized the information technology to further improve the consultation process in the system based on the HIS, LIS, PACS, and the information platform we already had. It allows all relevant care providers to access all clinical information about the patient anytime anywhere (e.g., medical record, medications, lab results, pathology findings, images, surgeries, endoscopy image, genetic consultation report), with which, they could generate the partially-structured consultation documentation, the multidisciplinary plan of care and the assessment form based on the patient's diagnosis and other information. At the same time, the hospital management could perform better monitoring on the entire process with defined indicators, for example, the completion rate, the timeliness, and the information provided.

Step 3: Long-Term Multidisciplinary Consultation Mechanism

The responsibility to evaluate the multidisciplinary consultation program falls in the scope of the Medical Affairs Department, who performs the tasks of daily monitoring, evaluation, regular analysis, improvement proposals as well as overall job planning and assignment.

Nurses are designated in each unit to follow up on the outpatients having received multidisciplinary consultation through phone calls every month to collect feedback from the patients and their parents regarding their conditions and experience with the care and further improve the quality of the multidisciplinary care.

The care and service quality has also been included in the medical quality evaluation of the units. The Medical Affairs Department gives feedback to the units on the monthly evaluation. At the organizational level, taking the social benefit and patient satisfaction into consideration, we also implemented favorable policies regarding the staff and units participating in the multidisciplinary service to better motivate the staff and to ensure a sustainable operational model.

For the care plan of patients with two or more burdened or dysfunctional systems, the hospital required cross-department multidisciplinary discussion and identified the standard content that should be covered: current diagnosis, current problem, goal of treatment, solutions, reassessment schedule, and reassessment results. The Medical Affairs Department tracks the discussion by and the cases under the multidisciplinary care and organizes hospital-wide discussion on selected cases on a regular basis.

Further improvement has been implemented in the hospital according to the JCI standards to ensure that the multidisciplinary consultation process is orderly performed through close collaboration to provide safe, continuous care to the patients through a closed loop.

Case 3: From Passive to Active Control on Infection

I officially became a full-time infection control staff on June 1, 2006. What I had to do every day was to search and review medical records in the library. I believe that each one of my colleagues had the same experience back at that time. Our job was to identify the under-reported infection cases that occurred during hospitalization (excluding the cases where patients had latent infection upon admission).

The more cases I caught and documented on my notebook, the more fulfilled I would feel. Of course, those units on my notebook would not be so happy because of the evaluation would become more stringent on them due to the underreporting. The majority of my work hours were spent on the medical records until 2013 when the hospital started its JCI survey preparation. Based on my own experience, I found it increasingly important to adopt information technology in identifying infection risks, adopting timely interventions, and preventing infection outbreak.

In-House Development of Hospital-Acquired Infection Management System

The primary goal was to utilize technology to monitor all the inpatients in the hospital in real time and send warning on possible infection to the management staff.

There was specific infection management software product available on the market. But they could only give warnings based on the lab test results, which was not sufficient because of the pitfall of unidimensional and scattered information in the digital landscape. We then brainstormed with our vendor and decided to develop a special hospital acquired infection management system comprising the following key components: suspicion level monitoring module, outbreak monitoring module, and prevalence monitoring module.

Hospital-Acquired Infection Suspicion Level Monitoring.

There were two major preconditions for this module to work properly: (1) The interfacing of the new system with HIS and LIS should be realized to allow real-time data retrieval; (2) Important data needed to be discrete. The suspicion level monitoring module experienced the following development steps:

Database establishment: The etiology database (Database 1) of pediatric infectious diseases should contain the organism that could cause infection among children such as bacteria, fungus, virus, mycoplasma, spirochete, and chlamydia. Database 2 is the lab result data related to infection diagnosis. Database 3 consists of clinical symptoms and conditions related to different tissue, organ or system infection, including common physical signs and symptoms of all possible infections.

The monitoring module can access information in real-time in HIS and LIS (including symptoms, physical signs, temperature, lab results, other ancillary examination results, risky procedure that may cause infection, and antibiotics therapy, etc.) and calculate the suspicion level according to certain logic algorithm. Warning is then given in prioritized sequence.

The system can automatically rule out the non-hospital-acquired infection cases (colored in gray on the screen). The interface provides an intuitive view over all the cases and leads the confirmed cases into the registry screen.

The data could be extracted from the system and statistics report could be automatically generated. The last check was the reliability and accuracy of the system. It was also a process of continuously improvement.

We spent 2 years finishing the development and the validation of the suspicion level monitoring module and brought it alive in August 2013. With the weapon we have, we don't need to wait for the report from clinical staff, but track all the information from our side. With the overview of all data, we are now able to trace the underreport and remind the physicians of timely registry of the cases (see Figure 21.2).

Suspicion Level Monitoring and Business Intelligence

The new module relieves the work load on the staff and serves to continuously reduce the risks of hospital-acquired infection and improve the patient safety. This requires continuous display of data to demonstrate the trend. HIMSS criteria helped us to have consolidated and optimized the processes we had developed to meet the JCI standards to truly realize quality and safety in the hospital. As required by HIMSS EMRAM Stage 7, Business Intelligence needs to be adopted. It is a powerful tool to assist both clinical and management staff in data analysis and decision-making. Based on the Hospital-acquired Infection Control project, we further realized the real-time display of the data from the suspicion level monitoring module to track the monthly trend of

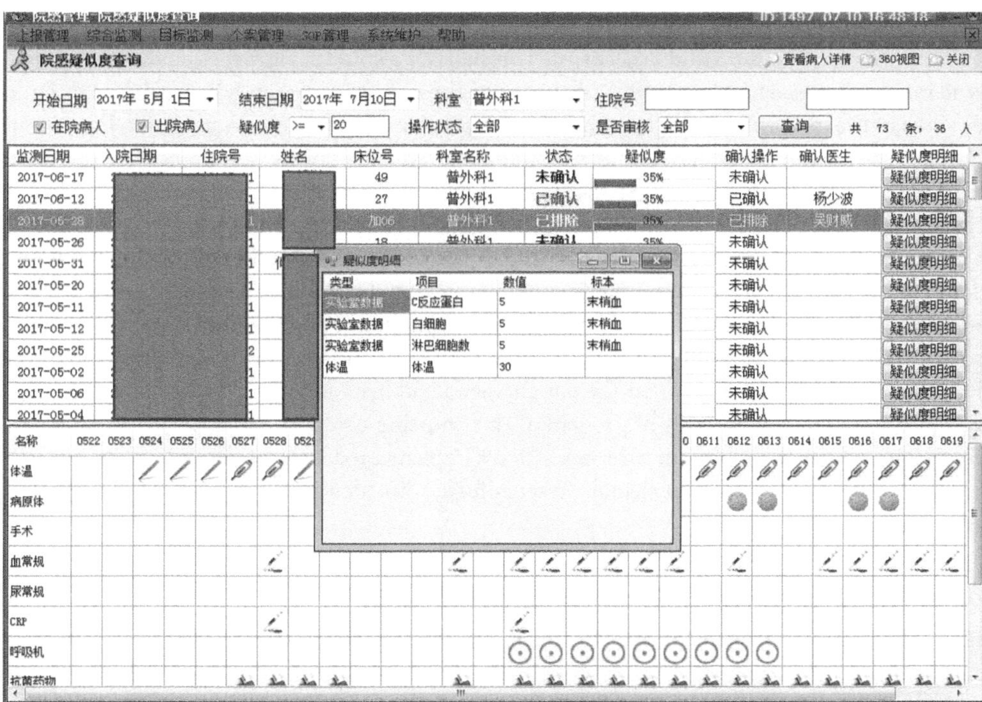

Figure 21.2 Hospital-acquired infection suspicion level monitoring module.

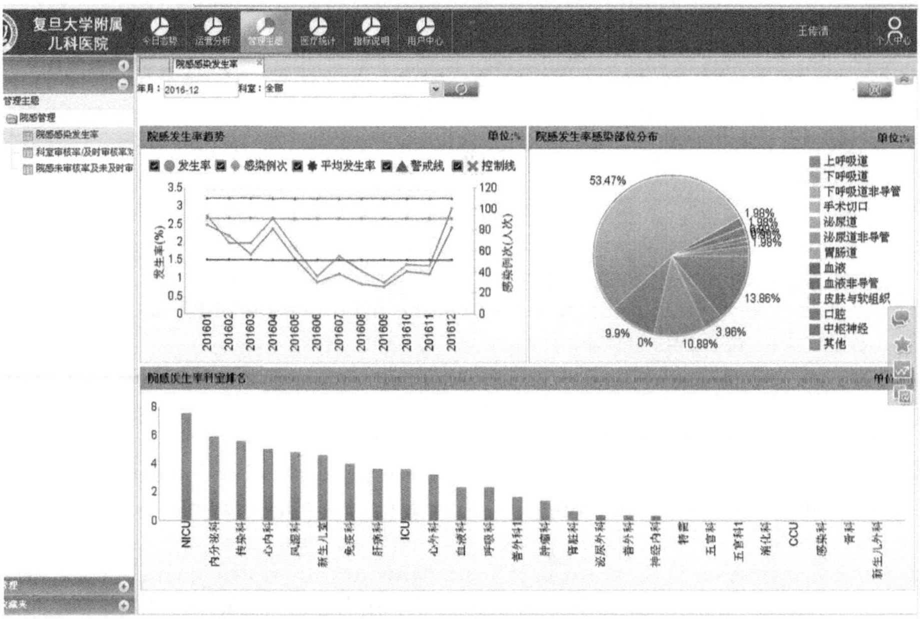

Figure 21.3 BI dashboard of hospital-acquired infection cases.

hospital-acquired infection incidence with charts, and review the trend through the mean line, control lines and threshold line generated from the historical data (see Figure 21.3).

When the trend goes up and exceeds the threshold, we could review the incidence by units or by the infection sites with the support of the multidimensional data analysis model, and dig into the causes of the increasing incidence from the perspective of etiology, locations, etc. For example, in January 2016, the incidence rate of hospital-acquired infection was approaching the control line on the chart. We found out that the unit where we had the most cases was NICU, and that urinary tract infection took up the highest percentage. According to the etiology analysis, the major bacteria were *Klebsiella pneumonia*. Through our analysis, we found that the high-risk populations include low-weight babies, premature babies, and male babies. The source, as we found out through investigation, was the bowel bacteria contamination, and there were quite a number of cases caused by MDROs. Thus, we started the MDRO screening on the patients admitted to the NICU, adopted contact isolation on the patients who had been infected or who carried MDROs, and implemented different levels of urogenital tract nursing care for NICU patients according to their weight. Meanwhile, bundle care was strictly implemented and monitored in the NICU for antibiotics utilization. Soon, the urinary tract infection incidence started to drop in NICU (see Figure 21.4).

Hospital Infection Outbreak Monitoring Module

This module is an extension of the suspicion level monitoring system. When an outbreak is identified (three or more cases caused by the pathogen in one unit within a short period of time), the module would list the information relating to etiology and invasive therapeutic procedures, and give an initial judgment on the suspected outbreak (see Figure 21.5). We would then review the cases listed in the system and initiate the contingency plan if we also suspect an outbreak.

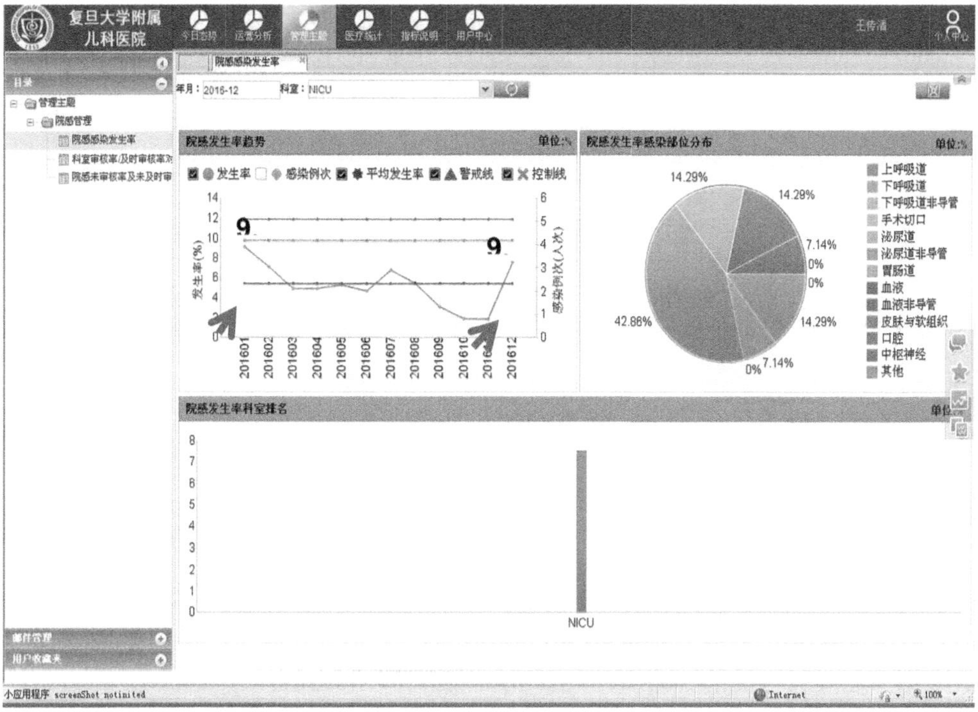

Figure 21.4 NICU incidence rate chart.

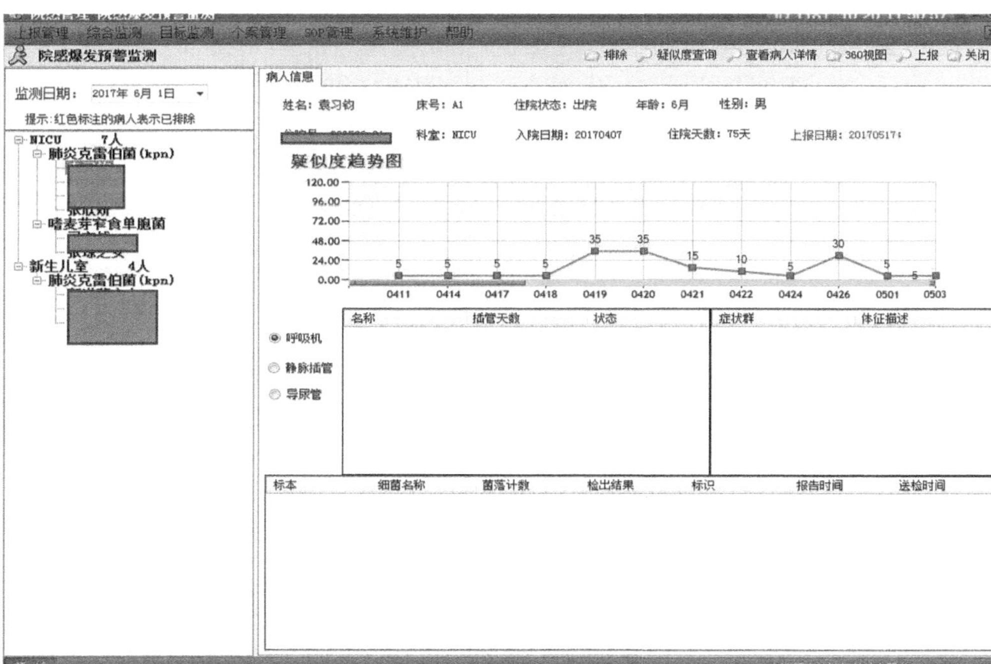

Figure 21.5 Suspected hospital infection outbreak monitoring module.

Hospital-Acquired Infection Prevalence Monitoring Module

This module is another measure we take to supervise the hospital-acquired infection. To calculate the prevalence, we take the total number of hospital-acquired infection cases among inpatients as the numerator (within 24 h) and the total number of patients hospitalized (during the same 24 h) as the denominator. The number includes the discharged patients but excludes the new admissions. The system gets data input from the suspicion level module and automatically generates the prevalence rates for departments as well as for the entire hospital. Such prevalence data could be used as the cross-sectional study in the hospital. The prevalence data could be compared with the data from other organizations to benchmark the performance and find the goals for further improvement.

Statistics Dashboard

The hospital-acquired infection monitoring system could generate various types of statistics reports, for example, the total incidence rate by time, total number of cases by units, prevalence rate by time or units, catheter-associated infection/1,000 catheter days, and verification by physicians over the suspected cases. The reports also provide evidence for hospital-acquired infection risk assessment, and the performance evaluation regarding infection control.

Defects of the Infection Monitoring System

The information system does help us to stay more sensitive about the hospital-acquired infection through the changes and trends displayed to the staff for quicker decision-making. However, the following defects still exist.

Repetitive Warning

If a child was identified with hospital-acquired infection at a certain time point, the system would capture the clinical symptoms, physical signs and lab results that could be related to the infection, and then calculate the suspicion level with color-coded warning. However, as the clinical conditions would continue to exist on the patient, the system would keep giving the warnings regarding the same case even though the case had already been reported. Due to the progression features of different illness, it was quite difficult to avoid repetitive warning. We still need human involvement in the process rather than totally rely on the information system.

Non-Discrete Data

Most of the data captured in the current EMR are discrete, such as the demographic information, major complains, temperature, lab results, examination results, and treatment. But the description of infection in the physician's progress note is still in free text, which could not be accurately captured by the infection monitoring system. For example, if a child had post-operation incision infection but with no fever or abnormal lab results, the system would often miss the case.

Insufficient Key Information

The suspicion level monitoring module is like a robot that gives diagnosis to the patient. If there is no sufficient information, like the temperature and lab/examination results, it may impact the accuracy of the judgment.

System Compatibility

The hospital-acquired infection monitoring system needs to get data input from EMR, LIS, PACS, and other systems, which requires interfaces for data transmission. Any change of the system may influence the smooth data exchanges among different systems and lead to delayed or failed transmission.

The causes of the above-mentioned defects could be multiple, for example, the clinical care behavior, medical record documentation, and level of structured EMR. Therefore, no matter how intelligent the system becomes, it still needs the input from people and relies on us to make the final decisions. We have made a small step forward in adopting information technology to monitor the hospital infection. The next move would be the automatic, comprehensive analysis of the infection risks in the hospital for both staff and admitted patients. We look forward to another leap forward!

Chapter 22

The First Affiliated Hospital of Xinjiang Medical University

Wen Hao, Ma Xuexian, Yang Yuanyuan, Wang Yongxin, Yang Yi, and Fan Ying

The First Affiliated Hospital of Xinjiang Medical University

Wen Hao, *MD, PhD, Professor, Chief Physician and Supervisor of doctoral/graduate candidates*

Dr. Wen is a Former President of The First Affiliated Hospital of Xinjiang Medical University and Director of WHO Collaborating Center for Echinococcosis, who has devoted to the surgical management and transplantation of echinococcosis and other hepatobiliary diseases. Among his more than twenty honors are The Ho Leung Ho Lee Award, Guanghua Engineering Science and Technology Prize and Exemplary Professional Returning from Overseas Studies. He has authored seven monographs, including Echinococcosis, *and almost 150 articles in SCI-indexed journals.*

Hospital Introduction: Founded in 1956, The First Affiliated Hospital of Xinjiang Medical University (hereinafter referred to as FAHXMU) was one of the 156 key projects during the first 5-year period (1953–1957) of China. As a large comprehensive tertiary-A hospital dedicated to clinical care, medical education, research, prevention, and management, FAHXMU is home to seven key clinical programs of national level, six national endoscopic training centers, one national role-model center for standardized residency training (with 26 subjects), national role-model center for laboratory education and national key training center for laboratory.

International Accreditation: Accreditation of Association for Assessment and Accreditation of Laboratory Animal Care (AAALAC) in 2009 and 2014;

Certification of ISO 15189 for medical laboratory in 2009, 2012, and 2015
JCI accreditation in October 2014
HIMSS EMRAM Stage 6 in November 2015

Contents

Preface

Get Rid of Bumptiousness and Shake Off Limitation Like a Butterfly Does to the Cocoon

Returning from Harvard Medical School Full of Experience Learned

Our story started from Harvard Medical School.

Mr. Wen Hao, CEO of the hospital, attended a course for hospital CEOs from China held in Harvard Medical School. During the session on quality evaluation for hospitals in the US,

Mr. Wen was amazed by the JCI accreditation program for hospitals. Excited as he was, he asked the speaker as many questions as he could on JCI accreditation. The first time he was exposed to a systemic introduction of JCI accreditation though, Mr. Wen was fascinated about the JCI standard structure and survey mechanism. Other members of the leadership went to that course other times as well, and all of them became keenly interested in JCI accreditation. Speaking of their experience and thoughts from the course when they were back in the organization, all of them undesignedly yearned for JCI standards. The aspiration resulted from the long course of quality improvement that we had experienced.

In 2005, the Ministry of Health launched a campaign of "the year of hospital administration" featuring "putting patients at the center and focusing on healthcare quality," where results would be evaluated 3 years later. The results from the first evaluation of our hospital were a blow to the confidence of the leadership and staff toward our work. It was the first time that we realized how severe our problems were with quality and safety, and we set out on the tough journey toward quality improvement.

Everything comes to him who waits. The hospital was awarded as an "advanced organization from the national campaign of the year of hospital administration" in 2008. In other quality campaigns held by the Ministry of Health that followed, such as "a long march towards healthcare quality" and "striving for good service, quality and ethics as well as satisfaction from the general public," we achieved good results. In 2012, we passed the national review evaluation for tertiary comprehensive hospitals with flying colors, based on the steady improvement on the capabilities of clinical service and hospital administration. By then, the quality structure had come into being, so as policies and job responsibilities. Processes were more and more compliant with relevant standards and the philosophies of quality and safety had been deeply rooted among staff.

In a time with a mix of opportunities and challenges, the hospital set the strategic goal of "becoming a large educational and research organization strong in clinical care, education, research, prevention and hospital administration, and a leading organization in northwest China with influence spread to Central Asia." We needed an opportunity of quality and managerial expertise to achieve another stride forward in the course of development that features better compliance to relevant norms, standards, and best evidence. To this end, we figured that JCI standards represents the highest standard of healthcare services and management with worldwide recognition. It has been taken as a "boarding pass" to the international market and competition. Our decision to adopt JCI standards conformed to the trend of the times.

To Sound the Clarion Call

Faced with this historic decision, the leadership had been thorough in learning about it and prudent in decision making from the very beginning. As such, in November 2012, Mr. Wen led a team of 18 members to visit and learn in great detail from Huashan Hospital (affiliated to Fudan University, located in Shanghai) and Sir Run Run Shaw Hospital (affiliated to Zhejiang University Medical School, SRRSH, located in Hangzhou, 160 km, or 100 miles, from Shanghai). After visiting the two organizations, the group unanimously agreed that we need JCI accreditation!

A team was designated and sent to SRRSH to learn about JCI standards and practices in a systemic way in December 2012. The team validated how advanced the standards were and how feasible it would be to work toward the accreditation by considering its relevance to national strategies, the development of the hospital and patient services. Summing up the justifications, we finalized the intention to adopt JCI standards.

In January 2013, the *Proposal of Working towards JCI Accreditation* was submitted to the Eighth Staff Congress of the hospital, a mechanism where staff are involved in democratic decision making. During the Congress, Prof. Lin Jianhua, with Huashan Hospital, delivered a speech titled *The Practice of JCI Accreditation for Hospitals and My Thinking* at our invitation. With a heated discussion on all possible aspects, the resolution of "becoming a JCI accredited hospital within two years" was adopted in the congress. It marked a clarion call of our strive toward JCI accreditation.

To Think over the Reasons after Bitter Lessons. There Was No Better Approach than Addressing Problems

We snickered at the same spirit in the structure of standards and the expectations between *JCI Accreditation Standards for Hospitals (the 4th edition)* and the *Accreditation Standards for Tertiary Comprehensive Hospitals in China (2011 edition)*. As we had just received the national accreditation of tertiary comprehensive hospitals, we optimistically believed that "JCI standards are nothing more than this" as we were doing it on the solid foundation demonstrated during the national accreditation. With the guidance from colleagues of Huashan Hospital, we set up JCI Office, designated task groups, interpreted standards, assigned responsibilities as well as developed policies and processes in one breath.

As we went further in the preparation, we came to realize things were not that simple. In July 2013, Ms. Jilan Liu came to provide direction at our invitation. During a hurried tour in patient-care area of just 2 h, when it was like looking at the flowers while passing on horseback, Ms. Liu brought our attention to how JCI and the tracer methodology works and the bunch of safety concerns we had. Only then did we realize the 6-month effort prior to that had not brought us any closer to JCI accreditation. The leadership made a prompt decision to apply for consultation service for JCI accreditation.

In October 2013, we received a 12-day baseline evaluation by a JCI Consultant team lead by Ms. Liu. From this evaluation, we got to have first-hand experience of how JCI accreditation works, what the content of JCI standards would be and what it looks for in real life. As the baseline evaluation finished, the Consulting team left us with a report of 459 problems to resolve. This "unbearable" report dragged us into frustration and disappointment. The leadership did not start by finding out who was to blame. Instead, their comments were full of encouragement. They reminded us that identifying and addressing problem holds the key to improving quality of the hospital.

Mulling over the reasons after bitter lessons, we screwed up courage to analyze problems in great detail, identify the key and challenging tasks that should be addressed upfront, divide responsibilities, and develop plan of action. We then vigorously upgraded physical facilities and IT system; modified policies, processes, and forms; and trained staff.

Time flies when you are very busy. In May 2014, a team of six JCI Consultants arrived again at our invitation for a 6-day mock survey, a check in great detail, even down to the carpet. The Consultants were amazed at our progress based on the assumption that it would be impossible for hospital of this size and scale to achieve progress on the arduous task in such a short period of time.

But the amaze did not stop JCI Consultants from being rigorous as usual toward the actual works in the hospital. Again, the Consultants left us with many problems to work on after the mock survey. Less daunting than the report from the baseline evaluation last time, the report from this mock survey still made us feel despondent. But we nerved up at hearing the encouragement from Ms. Liu, the leader of that Consulting team. Under the guidance from the Consultants, we developed our action plan, which provided clear idea and practice for our improvement.

In the 5 months that followed, the entire staff worked as a formidable force with the united purpose and spared no weekend to work day and night spontaneously. Everywhere of the hospital was lit up as people worked overtime is still a memorable scene to us. As we went deeper in the establishment of policies and various IT functions, optimization of processes, provision of training, and update of signage, we became unprecedentedly passionate in quality improvement. Since the impression of JCI among staff became clearer, "You can actually feel the air of JCI accreditation everywhere around the hospital!", said a nurse.

It is Always Exciting to See the Results

On October 6, 2014, the much-anticipated final exam, JCI accreditation survey, kicked off. Provided by seven surveyors from different parts of the world and lasting for 6 days, the survey strained staff of all levels. It was so tense that you could feel it from the air. On days 1 and 2, the surveyors kept the serious look on their faces. From day 3 on, they became more and more smiley. At seeing this, we also heaved a sigh of relief.

On October 11, the leader of the surveyor team announced to all the staff that FAHXMU passed the JCI accreditation survey. The surveyor team had been impressed by the open-mindedness, confidence, and the passion to learn as well as improve quality among staff of FAHXMU, according to the team leader. At receiving the certificate of JCI accreditation, Mr. Wen described this memorable journey toward JCI accreditation as a time with unparalleled efficiency, selfless dedication, coherence, few grumbles but mutual support, confidence and self-improvement as well as love toward the hospital as one's home. These six unparalleled features not only summed up the effort and gain of the entire staff over the past 622 days but also pay a compliment to the sense of responsibility as masters of the house among staff, who had surmounted difficulties and scrupulously abided by their duties.

Four Aspects of Improvement Thanks to JCI

What did we actually get from JCI accreditation? Mr. Wen's answer to this question was "four benefits."

Benefit 1: More Science-Based Hospital Management

By working toward JCI accreditation, administrative staff unanimously felt that they had been in a course of science-based management of healthcare organizations that provided systemic structure and integrate theory with practice. JCI accreditation drives hospital administration from all aspects, such as leadership and governance, processes and rules, resource allocation, methodology, and culture of safety. After putting heart and soul into these aspects, administrators have gained insight into patient safety and quality of healthcare. What's more, every administrator has learned the steps of continuous improvement in logical sequence: data-based risk assessment for prevention, process monitoring, gap identification, cause analysis, planning, and action. With this new mindset, staff become less prone to managing the hospital based on mere personal experience or volition, and the leadership has enjoyed better communication with clinical departments.

Benefit 2: Higher Quality of Health Service

"Being patient-centered," the philosophy upheld by JCI standards, applies to the entire service process from end to end. We changed our mindset of care from being "disease-centered" to "patient-centered" by starting with a comprehensive assessment involving the current condition and pain; psychological, rehabilitation, and nutritional status; fall risk, finance, culture, religion, and education of a new inpatient, before we develop a comprehensive care and discharge plan. We ensured the continuity and accessibility of patient care from the process level and took comprehensive approach to ensure patient safety and rights, which were directly relevant to care outcome and patient experience.

After learning to be patient-centered, our processes have been better. In the past when administrators developed processes, they thought of whether it would be easy for performers and cost-effective most of the time but paid little attention to how a patient in the process would feel and whether it would be easy for patients. Based on this new approach, we put ourselves into the shoes of patients when we reviewed and modified major processes in the hospital, including way-finding system, infusion process, admission, and discharge process of the resuscitation room of the ER, designing the layout of outpatient area, reservation of service, medication distribution and administration, patient education, and follow-up. This patient-centered thinking has helped us improve patient safety and journey in the hospital.

Another mainstay of quality care is the perfect mastery of skills. According to the SQE (Staff Qualifications and Education) chapter of the JCI standards, we reestablished the evaluation and privileging system of healthcare professionals. To achieve standard compliance, we had to break through the tradition of assuming the performing of a staff member based on his or her positional title, and add metrics related to the volume and quality of service. Under the new model, the competence of medical staff relevant to their positions is evaluated based on a four-part structure, namely the volume of clinical services, the quality of work, performance in the work and ground rules. This new method has helped us ensure that patients receive care up to quality standard from qualified medical staff.

Benefit 3: Further the Lean Management in the Hospital

Hospital administration has been moving toward lean management in accelerated speed. It requires organizations to operate based on a type of quality culture that features clear responsibilities, process consistency, and constant monitoring. We did have mountains of policies, but they existed in name only as they rarely provided direction or supervision to the actual practice. One thing we have learned from JCI standards is to "write what you do, and do what you write" when it comes to policy. This is a prerequisite for bearing the test of "tracing" methodology. With this in mind, we based ourselves on reality to review, integrate, and update policies, processes, and guidelines, after which we provided training and monitoring. We were determined to turn the book of policies into a treasury of knowledge.

An effective evaluation and appraisal mechanism is necessary for the implementation and compliance of policies and processes. The first and foremost task for administrators was how to perform objective and science-based evaluation and monitoring. JCI's prescription is "to justify with data." Accordingly, we set up new monitoring measures, divided measures into organization-wide, department- and unit-level, developed specific monitoring plan for each measure, and validated data collected. Then came the next question: How to obtain the vast amount of data? During a conference discussion, participants placed hope on the Director of IT Center. There was an outbreak of demand for IT support in process redesigning and monitoring. IT function had been in place in the hospital, but it was far from adequate to address the rising need. The IT Adoption Committee swiftly held a meeting to discuss solution, followed shortly by efforts in succession to establish platforms for information integration, mobile nursing system, ICU management, surgery and anesthesia, cardiac monitoring, transfusion, consultation, and adverse effect reporting. As complement, templates for forms, dictionaries, and spreadsheets were completed for review and maintenance. Closed-loop management became available for medication, transfusion, sterilization and supply, inventory, implant, and laboratory after countless discussions between IT staff and clinical staff. As a result, the IT system has been able to retrieve data for over 60% of quality measures. The advances in IT adoption have driven the lean management of the hospital by allowing the consistency, tracking, and monitoring of key processes. The good results by then was a prelude to our pursuance of HIMSS certification.

In general, for the 120 some quality projects undertaken throughout the organization every year that involve the entire staff, science-based management tools have enabled us to conduct deep analysis and systemic improvement on each project, resulting in effective and sustainable resolution of problems. It is a stark contrast to what we did in the past, where we looked into every problem but did not change much on each of them.

Benefit 4: More Diverse Opportunities for Cooperation and Exchange

JCI accreditation has increased our access to higher-level cooperation and exchanges with a wider range of organizations. Under the influence of advanced mindset, staff have been inspired to adopt creative thinking. Some examples of innovative solution in hospital management have been well recognized in the industry. With these good cases, we have been able to share insights and exchange with colleagues in the country and let outsider know us better, an organization in northwest China, a land of unmeasured vastness.

In the course of expanding international healthcare services, JCI accreditation, a business card widely accepted in healthcare around the world, has brought us many opportunities. During an exchange with professionals from Johns Hopkins University School of Medicine, at hearing our status as a JCI accredited organization, the director of orthopedics commented: "You are so terrific that you have been JCI accredited. I feel assured to collaborate and exchange with you in the academic field as we are of the same level of quality, safety and management." Toward the end of the visit to our organization, the professionals from Johns Hopkins University School of Medicine made the decision to establish a two-way exchange program of professional training right away.

Over recent years, we have established exchange and cooperation programs with internationally renowned organizations such as Harvard Medical School, Massachusetts General Hospital and Miami University of the US; Université de Franche-Comté of France and Queensland Institute of Medical Research of Australia; and signed contract of cooperation with several organizations from Central Asia, such as Kazakhastan and Kyrghystan.

From JCI to HIMSS

As JCI standards have been complied and JCI philosophies become deeply rooted among the staff, the momentum of process optimization and quality improvement must be carried forward. On one hand, we were facing increasing number of request from lean management. On the other hand, it was not possible to track and monitor process compliance manually. Against this background, the advantage of IT was ever more prominent. When our delegation attended an annual conference of the Society of Electronic Medical Record for Hospitals in China held in Xi'an (northwest China, about 1,075 km or 668 miles from Beijing), they listened to an introduction of HIMSS provided by Ms. Jilan Liu. The hospital leadership then realized HIMSS would be an opportunity for us to drive IT adoption in the hospital. Therefore, decision was made to work toward HIMSS EMRAM validation so that the intricate and complex needs could be met easier with the technical model of HIMSS.

A sound IT system had been in place, along with systems and platforms. But the interoperability between systems was suboptimal. What's more, closed-loop systems and clinical decision support turned out to be extremely challenging. But the technical difficulties were overcome one by one as the IT Center performed overall planning and deployment and multiple departments joined hands to work together, including medical, nursing, pharmacy, equipment, inventory, clinical, investigation departments as well as our partners.

With these efforts, an integration platform among multiple systems based on data repository was taking shape, with optimized healthcare and managerial processes; ever more powerful dictionaries; increasingly mature closed-loop systems for transfusion, medication, sterilization services, laboratory and expensive supplies; and higher coverage of information provision throughout steps in the patient flow. On November 10, 2015, HIMSS validators worked in our organization and confirmed that our IT application reached the requirement for HIMSS EMRAM Stage 6.

With both JCI accreditation and HIMSS certification, we are convinced that we are better able to go higher and further.

Case 1: The Fast-Track Mechanism for Trauma Care

Belong to a large territory, Xinjiang Uygur Autonomous Region has underdeveloped primary care capability and many areas have limited access to healthcare resources. As public health emergencies such as earthquakes and major traffic accidents happen from time to time, the proper establishment of the model and team of trauma care is essential to responding to emergencies, saving lives, and preventing disability. Such establishment is likened to the fast-track toward life and recovery.

As Pressing as a Fire Singeing One's Eyebrows

The old trauma care model of our hospital had many problems.

First of all, the spectrum of care was narrow and limited to orthopedics and general surgery. In the event of mass casualty or public health emergency, a multidisciplinary approach is needed for triage. As most trauma patients usually come in with multiple injuries, trauma physicians with multidisciplinary knowledge and skills relevant to trauma are needed. But the ER physicians we had were not able to meet such complex need. What's more, the layout of trauma response areas, operating room (OR), and blood bank did not live up to the imminent need of mass casualty.

Second, there were multiple gaps in the processes of trauma care. According to the previous processes, a patient with trauma that involved several disciplines had to be held unnecessarily longer for specialist consultation which took place one after another; there were barriers in the process of moving patients from ER to OR, and it took long time for the OR to be cleared for ER patients during the nights; the life-saving measures needed for trauma patients might be delayed due to the waiting for cross-match results from the blood bank, laboratory results and pre-op preparation; and it was hard to decide on which unit should admit patients with trauma that involved several different disciplines and as such mortality was high.

Starting with these problems, we devoted ourselves to establishing a trauma care team and processes of high performance. It was imperative to develop a mechanism of resuscitation specific to trauma cases, train a team of professionals capable of multidisciplinary care (MTD) and form teams of MTD.

Based on the trauma mortality curve, the primary peak occurs within the first hour after injury when mortality could reach 50%, and the second and the third peaks occur with 1–4 h and 1 week later, respectively. According to Trunkey, who described this pattern, most of the deaths occur during the second peak are preventable. Therefore, the early identification of these patients within the prime time constitutes the key of patient assessment of the early phase in trauma care.

The General Mobilization of the Entire Organization

Step 1 Establish target: We formed the trauma care team that responds to emergencies. It is the best care team that addresses the need of emergency care by providing multidisciplinary integrated care and definite measures as soon as possible to patients with multiple traumas that involve more than one discipline. Moreover, we spread such advanced idea of care to the other parts of the Xinjiang Uygur Autonomous Region in an effort to involve more hospitals to save people as much as possible with the 1 h prime time. Internally, we optimized the process of admission (see Figures 22.1 and 22.2) and the process to bring trauma patients to the OR within 3 h after admission.

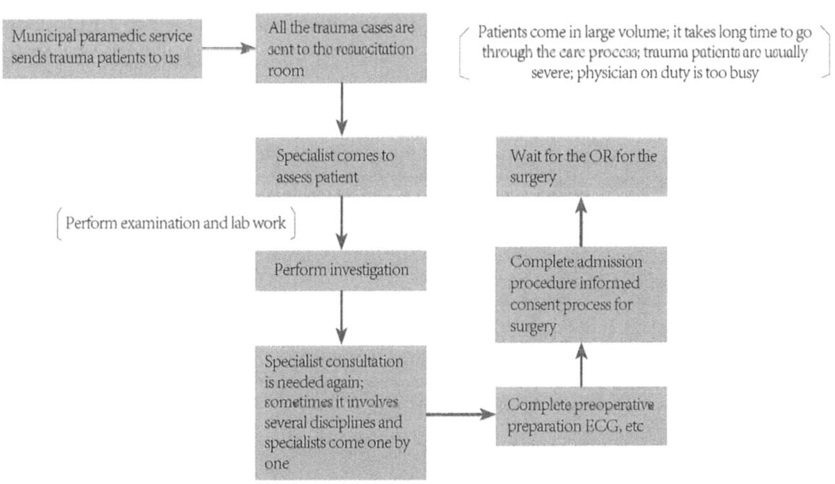

Figure 22.1 The old trauma care process in our ER.

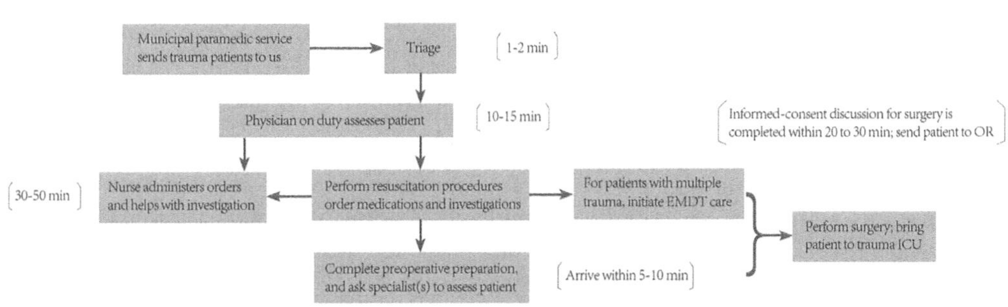

Figure 22.2 The optimized trauma care process and target time frames.

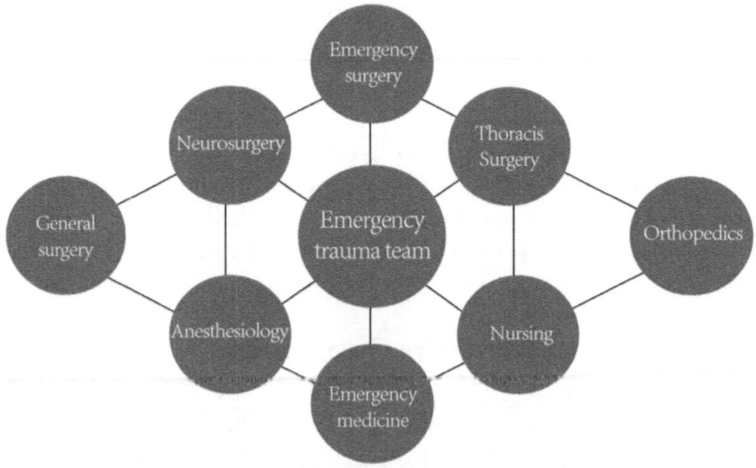

Figure 22.3 The structure of emergency trauma care team.

Step 2 Establish evidence-based structure: Based on the disciplines involved in trauma team of Miami Trauma Center as well as the spectrum of trauma conditions we deal with locally, our trauma team now involves emergency medicine, neurosurgery, thoracic surgery, general surgery, and orthopedics. In terms of operation, three trauma care teams were designated, each of whom includes seven members: a neurosurgeon, a thoracic surgeon, a general surgeon, an orthopedic surgeon, an anesthesiologist, and two nurses (see Figure 22.3).

Step 3 Clear room for a separate resuscitation area: To begin with, based on the existing space in the ER, the EICU was renovated to a separate area that accommodates three trauma cases at the same time. Second, the trauma care shares emergency OR, pharmacy, laboratory, imaging studies (CT and MRI), and cashier with the existing facilities. Third, equipment and supplies specific to trauma care were made available, which include major diagnostic and therapeutic equipment (such as multipurpose patient bed, ventilator, cardiopulmonary monitor, defibrillator, point-of-care X-ray machine, and shadowless lamp), medications, and devices (such as airway reestablishment set, surgical instrument set, puncture sets of various types, catheterization set and devices for external fixation).

Step 4 Make the operation model more rational and effective: Once a member has been assigned into the multidisciplinary team, he or she always participates in the cases assigned to the team, so that team members are familiar with the response to life-threatening trauma and life-saving diagnostic or therapeutic procedures.

One ER surgical and one ER medical physician who have been experienced enough and with the title of senior attending physician or above, as well as two nurses, assume duty everyday. To allow a 3-day interval between two duty days, we designated four resuscitation teams, all are led by the ER surgical physician who would direct the care and facilitate the consultation by anesthesiologist, thoracic surgeon, neurosurgeon, general surgeon, and orthopedic surgeon.

The trauma MDT has been consisted of neurosurgeon, thoracic surgeon, orthopedic surgeon, general surgeon, and anesthesiologist with the title of attending physician or above. When there is major emergency or intractable case, multidisciplinary consultation is needed to direct the patient's care. In that case, physicians designated to the MDT should respond to the call as soon as possible and arrive at the ER within 10 min. The general resident on duty in certain specialties can be assigned as a team member, such as neurosurgery, orthopedics, general surgery, and anesthesiology. If there is no general resident on duty from thoracic surgery, the physician of second-line duty can assume the responsibility. No matter who is designated to the team, he or she should arrive at the ER within 10 min in the case of emergency consultation.

Since the initiation of trauma team care, the ER trauma reanimation room has managed 1,400 some cases in total and 3.2 cases per day. The time spent on emergency trauma care was shortened from 8.7 to 3.1 h. With the new structure of on-duty staffing, unnecessary or repeated consultation has been reduced, reflected by the reduction of the number of consultation assessment received by each trauma patient from 1.8 to 1.3 consultation/case. This has helped shorted the patient's stay in the ER trauma resuscitation room and improved efficiency.

Case 2: Cloud Platform System for Follow-Up: For Discharge Follow-Up at Home

After receiving "haploid allogeneic transplantation of hematopoietic stem cell," Mr. Ma was discharged and required to complete monthly follow-up. Mr. Ma was worried at hearing this follow-up schedule as he lived far away from the hospital and the monthly travel to Urumqi would be difficult. The physician seemed to know his concern and reassured him, saying "Don't worry. The nurse will tell you how this is going to work out in an instant."

Before Mr. Ma went home, a nurse helped him sign in the cloud platform system for follow-up and told him: "After you go home, we will send information about the disease to you every month, and provide follow-up to you all through this cloud platform. All that you need to do is check our messages from time to time." During the recovery phrase, Mr. Ma received regular instruction on health and follow-up specific to the discipline from the cloud platform. He has had easy follow-up thanks to the cloud technology. When Mr. Ma came to the hospital for follow-up visit, he shared:

> I have been receiving information on the rehabilitation of my transplantation procedure from the hospital every month over the past 8 months since I went home. During this time, I experienced itchy skin some time and I turned to the cloud platform on my mobile phone. The rehab instruction there helped me identify this as a sign of post-transplantation rejection. So, I went to visit a local facility right away. I have benefited a lot from this mechanism as I successfully avoid recurrence or aggravation.

Patients experience a long recovery phase after hematopoietic stem cell transplantation, which makes effective follow-up even more important. The cloud system has helped us by sending questionnaire to patients automatically at the first week after discharge, monitoring outcome, recovery, and change in condition after discharge and reminding patients of notification to special medications. The cloud follow-up scheme also provides individualized follow-up based on the required nutritional support, rehab exercise, and prevention of relapse specific to the diagnosis. As all the health information generated from follow-up is electronic, it allows tracking of data and provides evidence for care plan.

What's more, being linked to the electronic medical record and data integration platform of the hospital, this cloud platform for follow-up provides information when being triggered by the smart search engine. As such, an integrated health monitoring model has been in place, which covers every phrase before admission, during hospitalization and after discharge. Moreover, it makes health service accessible at home. With this cloud platform for follow-up, healthcare professionals can provide consultation, screening and instruction on prevention, monitoring, and intervention.

Located in a vast territory with a sparse population, we believe the key of improving service quality lies in how to get our quality healthcare resource through to remote villages. Therefore, it is a knock-out and creative measure specific to the reality here to utilize a cloud platform for follow-up that enables real-time monitoring of patient's health information. It is also an extension of the existing hospital information system, which has been built around electronic medical record. The simplicity and efficiency of the cloud platform for follow-up has resulted in optimized patient-nurse interaction, less burden of nursing work as well as better patient experience and satisfaction.

The benefit of the cloud platform is manifested in other parts of the hospital as well. In Spine Surgery Dept., Ms. Wang, a patient-care nurse, found that communication with patients was difficult sometimes as most patients of Uygur ethnicity do not speak Mandarin, the standard Chinese used across the country. And getting a colleague to help out was not always easy. This difficulty has been readily resolved by the cloud platform. Information of the disease developed in Uygur language is provided by the cloud platform, helping patients to understand what the nurses teach and helping nurses to get education done effectively.

As there is real-time data transmission via wireless network between the cloud platform for follow-up and the nursing module in the Internet-based health education, nurses are now able to enter information while standing at the patient's bedside. The real-time online education for patients reduces repetition of nurses' work and allow nurses to spend more time with patients instead. Consistent and standardized templates of forms have been written into the electronic system with the help from Nursing Dept. These include general education (such as general informed consent for admission, admission education, patient rights and responsibilities and way-finding instruction for investigation areas), and disease-specific education (over 200 diagnoses from 84 clinical units). These contents have been approved by Nursing Dept. and constituted an online library in the cloud platform. Retrieving patients' mobile phone numbers from the health record and triggered by smart rules, the cloud platform regularly sends information as SMS or Wechat message to patient's mobile phone to provide general and disease-specific education, which covers special investigation, special medication, preoperative education, diet instruction, etc. To help patients better understand the diseases they have, information on the causes, pathological change, signs, symptoms, diagnosis, and treatment are described in the platform in simple language and plain diagrams. Patients can read the information of the platform anytime they want to refresh memory.

There is a growing trend of business pattern in health care that intensified rehab instruction and consultation are provided for discharge patients, a vital step in the continuity of care. Internet and mobile devices have helped us follow patients in cost-effective manner with excellent results.

Case 3: Revisiting the Purpose of Assessment by IT Adoption

The proper and evidence-based care plan of a patient should be developed from a thorough assessment of this patient, according to JCI standards. The key assessment items include: general and basic items. General items refer to religious belief, ethnicity, occupation, marital status, time, and way of admission and allergy history, while basic items refer to vital signs, consciousness, vision, hearing, speaking, etc. Other topics of patient assessment include specialty-specific information, ability of daily living, fall risk, decubitus risk, pain, social and psychological condition, nutritional screening, rehabilitation screening, discharge planning, VTE (venous thromboembolism) and unexpected dislodgement of catheter.

To Assess Patient Just because That Motion Should Occur

In the past, the workload of patient assessment was heavy for nurses, who had to collect a large number of data on a wide range of topics. As such, nurses tended to lose alertness while collecting information at admission and copy existing information without much thinking. After gathering data, nurses did not spend much effort in organizing, analyzing or aggregating them. No judgment was generated from the assessment, which made the admission assessment a mere formality as one could not tell immediately from it how sick the patient was and how the patient was doing.

Nurses also found it difficult to remember the contents and frequencies of so many types of assessment, such as various scales for pain and fall assessment, decubitus, and coma assessment. What's worse, the nursing assessment was based more often on subjective feeling. Patients might say certain things at will and the information was biased. This made it even more difficult for nurses to identify hidden facts from the assessment results.

In general, nurses were not in a good position to collect the right data, identify the key issue from the data and use the accurate data for nursing judgment. More often than not, assessment done in such way was reduced to formality and people got indifferent about the purpose of assessment.

Revisiting the Purpose of Assessment

A philosophy of HIMSS has been to enhance the accuracy and efficiency of nursing assessment by reducing the influence of individual judgment and input on assessment results. Therefore, based on the existing IT system in the hospital, while focusing on electronic medical record, we developed a clinical decision support system for nursing assessment by collecting and analyzing demands for nursing assessment, using Oracle 11g as database and developing the program with PL/SQL.

It involves a lot of preparations: We developed the repository for nursing assessment, determined the logics of reasoning, read literature and other information as well as collected demands and suggestions from clinical units toward nursing assessment. Taking advantage of the existing electronic medical record, we developed alert for out of range result of nursing assessment and missing content in the assessment and critical values, along with the repository for nursing interventions needed by high-risk patients and the logical reasoning of nursing plan. After completing these preparations, we had them programmed into the electronic system, and an upgraded nursing system took shape.

The dictionary for data collection for inpatient nursing assessment includes initial nursing assessment, assessments of specific topics (decubitus, fall, ability of daily living, and nutrition), temperature diagram, nursing flow sheet, nursing plan, comprehensive care plan, VTE, and unplanned dislodgement of catheters. The assessment forms were programmed into the electronic system, along with the definition for each option. When the nurse clicks a result for a patient, the system turns that option into red. When a nurse enters a wrong result (such as 45°C for body temperature) or misses any question in the assessment form, the system gives off alert. After a form is finished, the system aggregates the result automatically. When a score is outside of the normal range, indicating the patient is at risk, the system presents the result in blue to draw the attention from the nurse. Meanwhile, the system provides a prompt of the frequency of reassessment and nursing diagnoses. When the nurse clicks on nursing diagnoses, the system then brings up the relevant nursing interventions to remind nurses to take proper actions. On the other hand, the system fills in the comprehensive care plan with the out-of-range results automatically, which has helped the care team better identify a patient's risk level and take proper countermeasures. It ensures every problem of a patient is caught by the care providers, and avoids delay in treatment or inadequate measures due to neglect.

For example, when a patient is identified with high risk for fall, a window pops up that reads "Fall risk result ≥45. Reassess the patient once a day and whenever needed; ask the family member to stay with the patient; raise bed-rail when patient is lying on the bed; keep the floor dry; ask the patient to wear clothes of proper length, etc." When a patient scores ≤9 for decubitus assessment, the pop-up window reads "Reassess the patient every shift and whenever needed; turn over the patient every 2 h; keep the bedding clean and dry; apply cushion, etc." When a medical patient scores ≥4 in VTE, the prompt reads "Assist patient in passive exercise on the bed; encourage patient to get off bed; wear elastic stocking to prevent thromboembolism when needed."

Based on the actual result of each nursing assessment and the risk level behind it, the intelligent electronic medical record presents the relevant instruction to support nurses in decision making. The system also brings the result generated when the nurse goes through the assessment tool to the nursing flow sheet and generates a run chart of that measurement to support the continuity of nursing assessment. With these aggregated data, nurses are able to see how the patient changes dynamically and modify nursing measures when needed.

In the electronic system, various templates of nursing measures are maintained in the library for any possible result from the assessment. Take the assessment of catheter dislodgement for example. A score of 1–3 indicates low risk, and nursing measures include: label all the catheters; secure all the catheters with proper tool and mechanism; evaluate seven key aspects of patients with catheter (patient compliance, fixation, patency, fluid from the drain, dressing, label and pressure); and provide effective patient education. A score of ≥7 indicates high risk of dislodgement and measures include: perform hand-over between shifts at bedside; closely monitor the patient, in particular the catheter; apply proper restraint when patient becomes disoriented, and if so, monitor the skin around the restraints, etc. These options are ready for nurses to choose from, and subject to change the nurse feels needed. It is a major efficiency booster.

The clinical decision support system for nursing assessment as well as the human-computer dialog model has been built on the existing structured electronic medical record system. Thanks to the designs that reflect both JCI and HIMSS standards, our nursing assessment has been more compliant with relevant nursing standards. The IT system in turn supports nurses with intelligence by providing warning, alert, correction needed, and analysis of decisions. By describing how nursing assessment has been in place via IT adoption, we hope that we have demonstrated how JCI and HIMSS are mutually complementary and reinforcing.

Chapter 23

Affiliated Hospital of Jining Medical University

Chen Dongfeng, Chang Li, Qiao Man, Wang Bo, Xu Ran, Wang Guoqian, Liu Zhen, Sun Benzheng, Li Yandong, and Xue Qiang

Affiliated Hospital of Jining Medical University

Chen Dongfeng, *Professor and Supervisor of graduate candidates*

Mr. Chen is the Former President of the Affiliated Hospital of Jining Medical University. Among his leading roles in associations are Member of Chinese Society of Behavioral Medicine, Chairman of Information Management Committee of Shandong Hospital Association, etc.

Receiving training for professional hospital president from Harvard and Peking University programs, Dr. Chen has focused on standardized and lean management in hospital and led an early start on clinical pathway management, diagnosis-related quality and cost control, and humanistic healthcare in China. Under his leadership, the hospital received JCI accreditation in 2015, the first in Shandong province, and HIMSS Stage 6 in 2016.

Dr. Chen has received honors of National and Provincial Exemplary President of Hospital, Excellent Administrator of Patient-trusted Hospital.

Li Yandong, *Vice Chief Physician, Dr. Li is the Director of Standardization Office and Director of Anesthesiology and Member of China International Exchange and Promotion Association for Medical and Healthcare and the Anesthesiology Society of Shandong Province. He has worked intensively for the accreditation of JCI and Tertiary Hospital in China. He has authored and contributed to six monographs and over ten articles, three of which were published in SCI-indexed journals.*

Mr. Xue Qiang *is the Vice Director of IT Center of the Affiliated Hospital of Jining Medical University, who is in charge of software adoption across the hospital. He has worked intensively for the accreditation of JCI, Tertiary Hospital in China, HIMSS Stage 6 and Level-5 as well as Level-6 Usability of Electronic Medical Record in China. He has published more than 20 articles.*

Hospital Introduction: The Affiliated Hospital of Jining Medical University (hereinafter referred to as "AHJMU") is a tertiary-level A comprehensive hospital and a regional medical center in Shandong Province, north China. Built in 1951, it has 2,800 square feet and 3,100 beds. It was ranked the first in terms of composite total score and the composite index of diagnosis complexity in the *Report and Analysis of Inpatient Performance of Tertiary Comprehensive Hospitals in Shandong Province* in 2016 released by the Health and Family Planning Commission of Shandong Province.

International Accreditation: AHJMU was accredited as JCI hospital in July 2015, the first and only academic medical center with JCI accreditation in Shandong Province.

It was certified with HIMSS EMRAM Stage 6 in November 2016.

Contents

Preface

To Achieve Higher Level with the Pair of Accreditations

Sticking to the "patient-centered care and quality driven practice," AHJMU has studied unremittingly and promoted a series of programs in line of public interest, such as price ceiling for each diagnosis and complimentary physician consultations over recent years, which has earned it the reputation of providing "skillful, thoughtful, and affordable" care and provincially and nationally influential brand. As it passed the new version of accreditation of tertiary hospitals in China, the organization witnessed a surge in patient volume.

To satisfy extra patients as the new building was put into use, the hospital has recruited over a thousand new staff over recent years. The strength of administration, functionality, quality, and safety were at risk of attenuation from this large number of freshmen. But the pressure of quality the hospital has been faced with never wane: on one hand, the general public has increasingly higher expectation toward healthcare quality thanks to the ever advancing healthcare technologies; on the other hand, governments from national to local levels have laid unprecedented emphasis on the quality of healthcare services ensuing government policies and regulations such as the *Statement on Furthering the Management of Healthcare Services in Health Care Organizations* and the *Action Plan on Promoting Health Care Quality.*

Amid the dilemma of both quantity and quality, the hospital leadership was faced with challenges of how to sustain the results of standardization gained over the previous years, how to further the transformation for a culture of quality and safety that is unique to our organization, for all-round progress of the hospital and personal growth of staff.

Use JCI as the Key to Resolution

When visiting middle-level staff designated to the Qinghai Red Cross Hospital in 2013, under the Qinghai (Province, on a plateau in southwest China) support program, the leadership of the organization was surprised to see how good quality there was: the priority of patient safety and the awareness of continuous quality improvement (QI) were well reflected from the design and implementation of process and policies from clinical care to general support. After discussing with the administrators in the Qinghai Red Cross Hospital, our leadership came to realize JCI accreditation was behind their excellence. In the same year, we went to the conference on hospital quality management at the invitation of Huashan Hospital of Fudan University, which has been a JCI-accredited organization. At listening to the inclusive presentation from Ms. Jilan Liu, Principle JCR Consultant, our leadership members were exposed to JCI accreditation standards and the philosophy for the first time.

Ms. Liu said:

> The essence of JCI accreditation is "to always focus on patient and continuously improve quality". It provides brand-new perspective on hospital management, and the survey marks just the beginning of the journey. First of all, it constitutes a long-standing mechanism for improvement in face of ever-increasing expectation towards health care from the general public and emerging challenges of healthcare administration with the advancement of healthcare technologies. Secondly, JCI believes that "the problems in hospital administration lie in its system". Therefore, we should dig deeper to find the root cause of the problem from the system and develop systemic solution.

> The way towards JCI accreditation urges hospitals to not only cement the foundation for quality and patient safety but also develop a long-standing mechanism to improve and sustain result based on their own strength. All the hospitals seeking JCI accreditation share a common vision: work hard to truly reach higher patient safety and healthcare quality. Hospital CEOs are always the first to picture this vision. With clear vision and strong sense of mission, they are earnest in leading the hospital towards higher level of quality and patient safety.

Through Ms. Liu's introduction and thorough study, the hospital leadership recognized that JCI accreditation standards are more than just a tool for standardization. More importantly, it represents a research type of mindset that features being evidence-based and that helps us understand the root of the observations or management. The essence of JCI standards of quality and safety fits well into hospital management. The leadership rest on JCI accreditation and took it as a key to the solution we were seeking—we would take the challenge of JCI accreditation as an opportunity to further the standardization process of the organization and establish our own culture of quality and safety.

The preparations for JCI accreditation made progress inch by inch amid various obstacles. Based on JCI accreditation standards and the goals of the hospital, we modified hospital-wide and department-level policies, contingency plans and 633 service guidelines; the admission and discharge criteria of 703 diagnosis of 47 disciplines as well as standardized care process for 337 diseases. With "patient-centered care" as the aim, we established a standard-based management system that covered clinical care, administration, research, and education.

After preparing JCI accreditation for 2 years, both administrators and frontline staff of AHJMU were full of thoughts. Those times were filled with arduous and challenging tasks of establishing new policies and process one after another according to the international standards. For "patient safety goals" and "access and continuity of care," multiple trainings were provided on new policies and processes for staff. The trainings and inspections involved 80,000 attendants, and problems identified during the trials were later addressed with improvement action. We wanted all the staff to get involved, and they did. With their enthusiasm toward better quality, constant communication, and coordination, they joined hands and worked as a great team. This cohesive staff team working toward a common goal maintains the momentum of the hospital.

"You have a stunningly good team. Every staff is working enthusiastically and whole-heartedly to live up to their responsibility of ensuring quality and safe care!" acclaimed Ms. Lim, a JCI surveyor from Singapore.

"I have been to many organizations. As one that has more than 3,000 beds, you have done a really good job and deserve recognition! All of my colleagues and I agree to recommend you as an accredited organization!" during the exit session of the JCI survey, the surveyors' team leader extended his heartfelt congratulations to our hospital.

Isolated Hills of Data

"I got scolded again. What a bad day!" a colleague grumbled at me.

"What happened?" I asked.

> A colleague from another department asked me for a set of data as the leader needed those. I worked so hard to gather them from several electronic systems. But when I

> showed him, he said the data did not make sense because they were different from what actually occurred. So, I was scolded by the leader.

"Poor guy!" I patted on his shoulder but neither of us said anything more.

The next morning, I was seated in the office. I saw joyful people everywhere in the hospital as we became a new member of JCI-accredited hospitals. I might breathe a sigh of relief as I had been nervous for quite a while. Right then, the phone rang. I looked at my phone and became strained right away:

"Hello, boss…"

"Come to my office, now."

> We still need to work on IT adoption. As the national healthcare reform is accelerating, the industry has seen significant changes. We should be vigilant and plan ahead. One time, I wanted a set of data as reference for estimation, but the data provided by the department were inconsistent with facts. I asked, and they said that was because the data had not been interconnected in the electronic system. It turned out that staff had to enter data through different electronic systems and cross-check manually. What the heck? If it takes manual work to interlink information in a JCI accredited organization, then our data are not coherent yet, and certain loops in the information management are not closed yet. Category-based spreadsheet provides only fragmented pieces of information. But without an accurate and holistic picture, how can we use evidence and facts to guide our management and decision making?

From those sincere words, I truly felt his earnest wishes.

> We are an early adopter of health IT, so there are not many role models to learn from. Most of the time, we are crossing the river by feeling the stones. Most of the electronic systems we use now were designed by the users based on their own need without adequate consideration for functions of management and control. Also, some of these systems were developed very long ago while some were newer. What's worse, there was no function for hospital-wide management from the electronic system. All the systems spread out like isolated hills. Put it in "chic, fancy and high-end" metaphor, information flew only on islands or through chimneys. In the way towards JCI accreditation, we painstakingly linked all the electronic systems via the unique identifier numbers of patients. But when it comes to comprehensive integration of all the electronic systems for data mining and business intelligence application, there was still a long way to go. This would be a mission impossible unless the hospital throws itself into an endeavor of IT upgrade.

Taking this unprecedented opportunity, I poured out my grievances from an IT Director's aspect.

"It seems to be a good timing to start the journey towards HIMSS certification." the boss said slowly but affirmatively.

Patient Assessment Done Via Mobile Nursing Electronic System

It takes two prerequisites to be a good hospital: medical safety and service quality. They closely reflect the managerial competence of an organization. Representing the latest international consensus on patient safety philosophies and mindsets, the JCI standards help hospitals to recognize the most urgent safety risks and attain their goals of continual QI. On the other hand, as a non-for-profit global organization built itself from philosophy, HIMSS and its certification promote the IT adoption process of hospitals for optimized care process, higher medical safety, and better patient experience. The emphasis of HIMSS lies in the utilization of IT approaches in reorganizing processes in the hospital.

In terms of patient assessment, our clinicians had tunnel vision about healthcare: physicians cared only about their procedures, diagnosis and alternative diagnosis as well as documentation, and nurses cared only about executing physician's orders, such as injection, infusion, and drug administration. Education was provided to patients but inconsistently. That assessment was far from comprehensive as nutrition, psychology, and social-economic background of the patient was rarely addressed. Attention was directed to the disease instead of the patient. Early recognition of condition and prevention of complication were hardly practiced. Over-treatment, underdiagnosis, and misdiagnosis were present in healthcare as physicians relied too much on experience and care too little about evidence.

In contrast, patient assessment has been grouped into a chapter of its own in the JCI standards to underline the coherence, continuity and dynamics throughout the entire patient journey in seeking care (see Figure 23.1). The JCI standards address patient's condition of all aspects as well as his or her social-economic and psychological needs. To fulfill this end, the hospital needs to define the criteria and frequency for assessment based on evidence. In the practice level, all the care plans and actions shall reflect the results and data from the assessment. In other words, it is the results from assessment that directs the care plan needed in each stage.

Take nursing assessment, for example, to comply with the JCI standards, we established a nursing assessment system with 90 nursing plans, 54 forms, and 17 assessment tools that covered

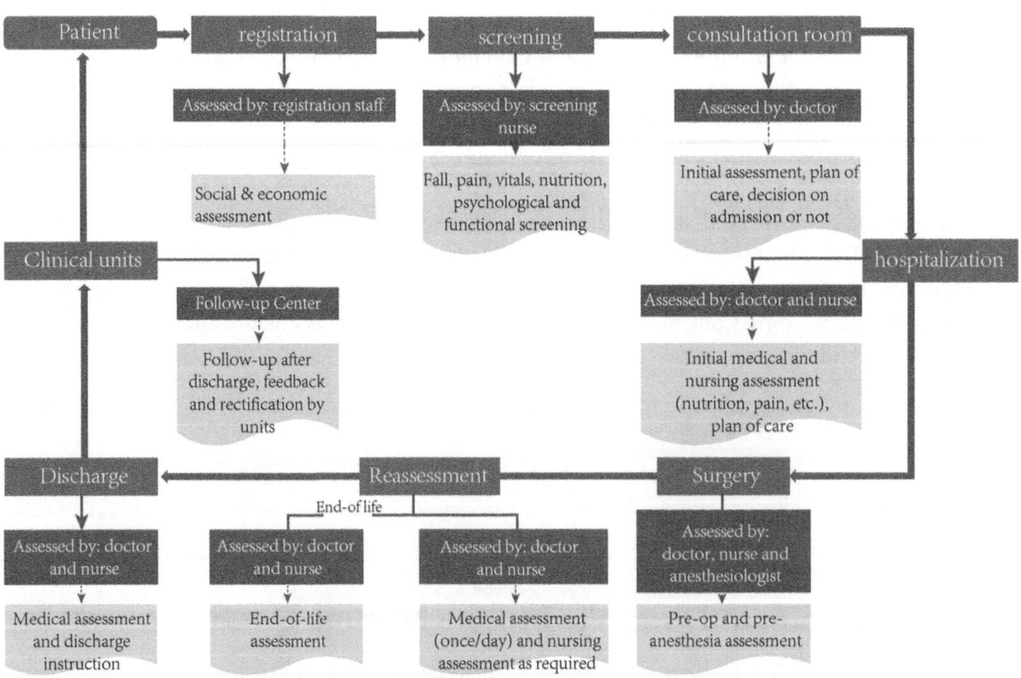

Figure 23.1 Patient assessment that reflects on continuity.

13 topics from six aspects of admission, risk, special population, specialty-specific, discharge, and education need. This system required a lot of skill and workload. Our challenge came how to get them done throughout the organization, how to standardize the assessment and how to ensure uniform care.

The mobile nursing electronic system serves as nurses' assistant and met this challenge. Compared with conventional ways, the mobile nursing electronic system is equally dependent on keeping track of every piece of patents' health information but more efficient and easily accessible. With this, most of the health data have been turned into discrete data. Based on the documentation of data, the mobile nursing electronic system automatically analyzes results and sees if they are out of the normal ranges. If so, it then generates appropriate nursing care plan and the expected outcome for nurses to keep track of the pending nursing tasks. With the temperature, blood pressure, and pulse collected, the mobile nursing electronic system plots graph of vital signs for nurses to visualize how a patient's vital sign changes. What's more, nurses can now use the mobile nursing electronic system to facilitate handover between shifts. When the nurse labels the assessment results to be emphasized during handover by simple tapping on the device, the electronic system will present the selected information for reference during handover. Compared with what nurses had to do in the past, this electronic system has freed up nurses from manual documentation. Functions like this have fundamentally eased the burden off nurses.

The mobile nursing system is also the physicians' eyes by the patient's side. In addition to ward rounds where they get to know the patient's condition and the change of health status, physicians can also keep an eye on patient's progress by reading the data collected and displayed by the mobile nursing system. Nurse enters patients' vital signs (temperature, blood pressure, and pulse) and the status of order administration into the electronic nursing system at the frequency based on nursing level. As the interoperability between the mobile nursing system and the electronic health record has been realized, physicians now can see patients' data from the latter one, which they use more frequently, to make data-driven clinical decisions. Specifically, the mobile nursing system is able to present the assessment results (of pain, nutrition, decubitus, etc.) in the electronic medical record via URL (Uniform Resource Locator), and interface abnormal results (of pain, nutrition, decubitus, etc.) to the electronic medical record as original evidence for physicians to establish diagnosis and care plan. Physicians have felt more supported when they do ward round with the "Physician Round iPad System" module of the mobile nursing system, because they can read nursing data, laboratory and imaging orders and results right at patient's bedside so that they can learn all these things without leaving the patient.

Standing up to the challenges of HIMSS validation, the mobile nursing system has been upgraded with more functions, more completed processes, better usability, higher efficiency, and safer outcomes. It has been connected with electronic laboratory and investigation systems as well as electronic medical record for interoperability, so that data from one system are shared to the others. It has strengthened patient safety by closing the loops in the management of medication and administration, and automatized nursing care plan with its business intelligence.

Quality Guarantee System Empowers Quality Control

Peter Drucker, the founder of modern management, has been quoted as saying, "the purpose of business is to create a customer." This idea applies to hospitals as well, where they ensure quality and safety by adopting new technologies and service models. As a result, patients will receive better care with ensured quality and safety, and staff will be entitled to better outlook for their career as the hospital becomes more inclusive and powerful. In line with this goal, the JCI standards provide a good hint: a managerial structure that supports continuous QI and patient safety (see Figure 23.2) is paramount.

We started to operate according to the JCI philosophy by three means: establishing a patient-centered quality system that involves all the staff, all aspects in the hospital and all steps of processes as well as a code of conduct that emphasizes the paramount principle of patient safety; establishing a problem-based QI mechanism with the adoption of evidence-based management and the logical use of management tools; and creating a non-punitive management culture that features risk management mindset and encourages unexpected event reporting. With such effort, quality control has been extended from clinical areas to other aspects of the hospital, and from administrative departments to every staff member. Thus, the voluntary compliance to the code of conduct and incessant self-improvement among staff constitute the new culture for quality and safety.

The efficacy of quality management structure is not possible without an efficient and user-friendly IT system. To control quality with IT approaches, we have established a clinical quality audit system and a hospital quality supervision system, an integration of multiple IT techniques, as a solution to the routine, long-standing, and sustainable quality engagement.

Evidence-based management is highlighted in the quality metrics monitoring, which has been improved with data-based justification, data operation process and the involvement of all the staff and covered all the aspects in the hospital and all the steps of processes (see Figure 23.3). The works on quality metrics monitoring also serve as the foundation for the hospital quality supervision system, where PDCA cycles in clinical areas can be facilitated with IT competence via the traceable priority metrics of hospital-wide and department levels.

The hospital quality supervision system has standardized the quality works throughout the entire organization, including the levels of unit, administrative departments, and the hospital, by managing their priority metrics, monitoring quality projects, and facilitating management according to hospital accreditation standards of China via a three-level-based platform.

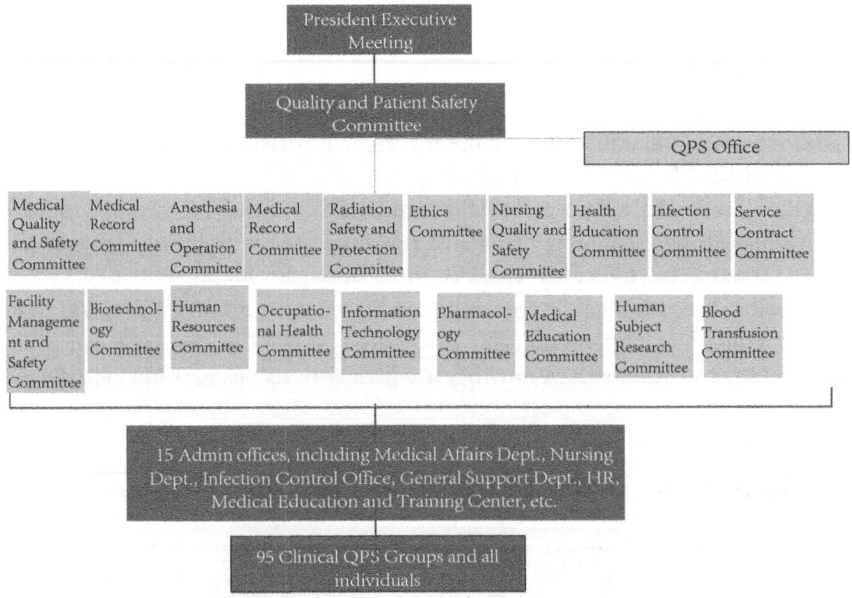

Figure 23.2 The Hospital Quality Committee and its structure.

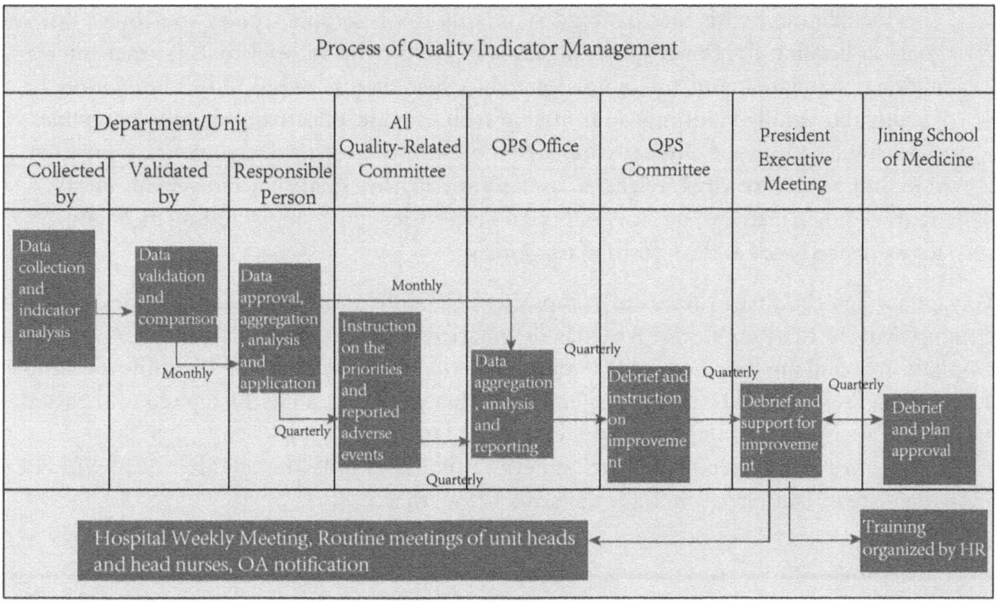

Figure 23.3 The process of quality metrics and projects.

In terms of the utility of the Hospital Quality Supervision System, clinical units have access to the data of the quality metrics relevant to their own. As such, based on the data presented, the units hold a monthly discussion to analyze causes and develop action plan.

For administrative departments, they summarize data from sampling and communicate with relevant units once a month for the hospital-wide metrics, and pick out metrics whose targets are not met yet, generate written report and direct it to the relevant units. In particular, there are key metrics that have significant implication for quality and safety, such as unplanned return to surgery, unplanned readmission within 31 days, return to ICU within 24 h, perioperative mortality, surgical complication, decubitus and fall. Administrative departments take out cases with such adverse outcome and urge the clinical units involved to conduct in-depth discussion and analysis, conclude lessons learned from the cases and take improvement actions.

As for the Quality and Safety Office, which has access to data of all the metrics, both hospital-wide and unit-level ones, it is able to look for metrics whose targets are not reached and communicate this to relevant units, as well as provide reports on unfavorable trends throughout all the units. Specifically, the report describes the target of a particular metric applicable to a particular unit, the result from the same period during last year and the comment on the comparison. If the data have been over the threshold for 3 months at a row or still below the target by the end of the predetermined time-frame, the Quality and Safety Office provides a written report to the unit in charge of that particular metric, who is expected to improve the quality in continuous upward spiral through PDCA cycle. This is an important driver for the hospital-wide communication and exchanges on QI.

To elevate the management of the hospital with the means of IT not only helps us meet JCI standards but also constitutes an important highlight of HIMSS EMRAM Stage 6 certification. From this aspect, we have figured that HIMSS certification, which requires the wide adoption of IT, helps with JCI standard compliance and maintenance. Being interdependent with overlapping features, they reinforce each other.

> The accreditation with international standards is a best opportunity to achieve our goals to become a regional medical center of the provincial level that has met international standards, and to improve patient experience as required by the National Health and Family Planning Commission with our safe, effective and easily accessible care; higher safety of clinical care, infection control, facility, occupational protection and general services; relentless and comprehensive quality improvement efforts; upgraded management, service quality and expertise; and a long-standing mechanism for evidence-based and uniform management.

We were ranked the first in terms of composite total score and the composite index of diagnosis complexity in the Report and Analysis of Inpatient Performance of Tertiary Comprehensive Hospitals in Shandong Province in 2016 released by the Health and Family Planning Commission of Shandong Province, followed by the good news that we were among the top ten in the Ranking of Health Care Quality of Public Hospitals in China in 2016.

Needless to say, it was impossible to achieve "a thousand mile" in and after 2016 without the "individual steps" completed through the years before that.

Case 1: To Turn Policies into Manuals

To Recover Children Safely from Moderate and Deep Sedation

In the Sedation Room on the first floor of the tower where women and children care take place, a baby of only 30 days old was recovering from moderate and deep sedation after a successfully performed MR examination. "Under our close monitoring, this baby will recover soon." said Liu Haiyan, a deputy chief physician of Anesthesiology Dept. who was monitoring the baby. "There are objective criteria to determine if a baby is recovered or not. Anesthesiologist does not let family member to bring the baby home until we see the baby has recovered and reached the required score," she added. Shortly after, the baby woke from sound sleep and was assessed by the anesthesiologist. It reached a safe score from the criteria, and the mother left with the baby in her arms, appearing satisfied. This is a typical scenario in the Sedation Room since the hospital initiated the standardization of moderate and deep sedation (Figures 23.4 and 23.5).

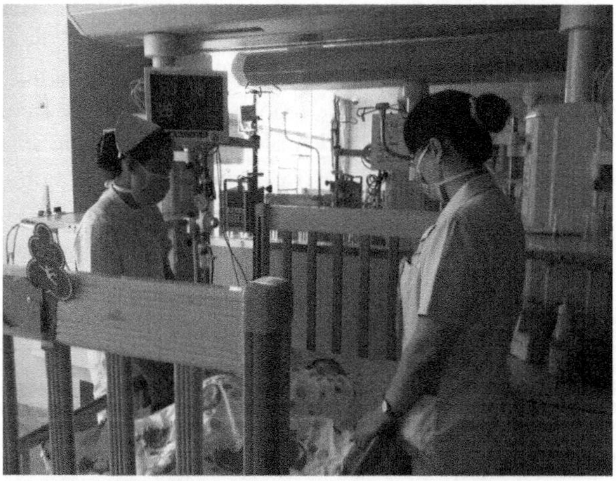

Figure 23.4 A child in recovery phase after moderate and deep sedation.

Figure 23.5 Sedation observation room.

The MR preparation and examination take 20 min or longer, when the patient should stay relatively still. However, as children get annoyed easily by the noise from the machine in operation, it is hard, if not impossible, to keep young children awake and quite for the examination. In many hospitals in China, children are put to moderate and deep sedation before they are received for various work-ups. Moderate and deep sedation differs from general anesthesia, a concept familiar to all of us, in that it puts the patient to sleep with sedative for the purpose of investigation. The patient in moderate and deep sedation is able to maintain voluntary respiration, but vulnerable to respiratory suppression or even asphyxia or death if the dose of sedative is too high, or if the patient is sedated too deeply. Logically, such sedation should be provided by anesthesiologists competent in advanced life support to make judgment and properly use medication based on each patient's constitution, weight, etc.

To put a young child to moderate and deep sedation with chloral hydrate, on one hand, if we have the parent give the child orally, the dose would be inaccurate and staff would have difficulty determining the level of sedation. Sometimes, the parent might have to go back and forth between the physician's exam room and the investigation area, holding the baby in his/her arm, which may not work. This made the investigation difficult. On the other hand, when the investigation was done, the child was taken care of only by the parent, which rendered sedation related complications unnoticed. This was a risk for the child's safety, the parent's discontentment and even medical dispute.

Therefore, to increase the compliance to standard in terms of moderate and deep sedation was an important topic (see Figure 23.6) as the hospital took advantage of the unprecedented opportunity of preparing for JCI accreditation to drive quality, safety, and management up to standards in 2015. A series of measures elevated sedation to a safer and more standard-compliant level throughout the entire organization. As a result, in 2016, moderate and deep sedation was provided to 28,167 cases, of whom 2,976 were infants and young children, with zero severe complication or death.

This significant change started from the modification of one policy.

The Driving Force Spread from Bottom to Top

Sedation is related to many patients and a wide range of departments. Being a risky procedure to patients, sedation involves a series of steps. When every step is performed consistently and up

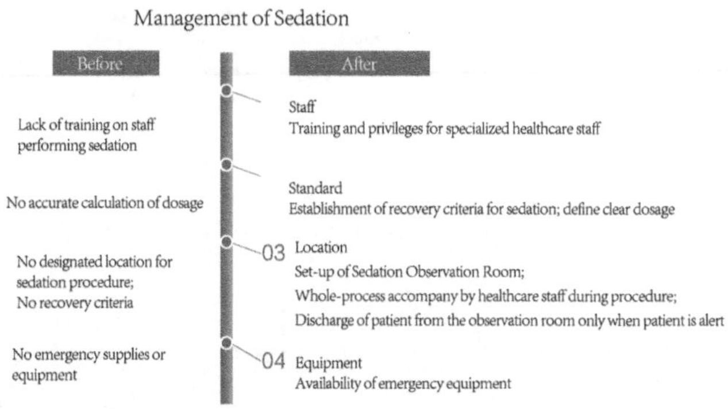

Figure 23.6 Standardized practice in four aspects achieved from the change in policy.

to standards, the likelihood is higher for the appropriate use of moderate and deep sedation and investigation plan, as well as patient safety. To this end, the Anesthesiology Dept. requested a modified mechanism from the Medical Affairs Dept.

The Anesthesiology Dept. started by developing the *Policy on Moderate and Deep Sedation for Diagnostic/Therapeutic Procedure* based on national laws and regulations, the JCI standards as well as the actual situation of the hospital. After reading extensively, including national laws and regulations, standards in healthcare, and guidelines of care, Li Yandong, Director of Anesthesiology Dept., held a multidisciplinary discussion, gathering the entire anesthesia team, physicians, nurses, and administrators of the Medical Affairs Dept., Nursing Dept., and the Office of Standard Compliance. The members of this group heatedly discussed the location where sedation may occur, the necessary qualification of staff involved, and the criteria for recovery assessment, among others. During that brain-storm, everyone voiced his or her opinion, thought out of the box of their individual disciplines to establish every detail of the policy and include more elements from various perspectives. The group established the basis for the *Policy on Moderate and Deep Sedation for Diagnostic/Therapeutic Procedure* after reaching consensus on a range of features, including the necessary qualification of staff providing sedation, pre-sedation assessment, the development and administration of sedation plan, the set-up of Post-Sedation Care Unit, recovery criteria and the readiness of emergency equipment. The development of this policy has reflected the bottom-up approach with thorough discussion, highlighting the involvement of all the relevant disciplines and the collection of inputs from the participants about possible recommendations and strategies.

The Policy Being Fine-Tuned by a Pilot Phase

After being developed, the policy was put into a pilot phase throughout the entire organization, when we expected comments from any part of the organization that reflect the gaps and defects in the policy for us to improve the process. At 1 month into the pilot phase, comments from frontline staff included that the criteria for pre-sedation assessment were not clear enough, how to validate the qualification of staff providing sedation, and the proper human resource allocation for pre-operative patient in severe condition (ASA grade at or above III) who needs sedation.

Based on this feedback, the Anesthesiology Dept. held another round of discussions and modified the policy. During this review, with the purpose of a "succinct, easily practicable, accurate and inclusive" policy, the group drilled down for the gaps in the process and the cause of any barrier. Issues where opinions were strongly divided were brought to the Hospital

Administrator's General Meeting for further discussion in order to reach the best solution and ensure the consistency between the policy and the actual work. During the review that ensued the pilot phase, the standards of the work were further defined in the *Process for Moderate and Deep Sedation, Process for Procedural Sedation for Inconsolable Young Patients, Scoring Criteria for Sedation: Ramsay and RASS Scales* as well as *Discharge Criteria for Sedation*. The qualification of staff providing sedation was also added to relevant policies and processes. The modified policy was presented to the relevant committee for argumentation before being reviewed for concordance and relevance by the Office of Standard Compliance, issued and disseminated to all the units for implementation.

A Policy-Turned User Manual

The policies are developed in five steps in our organization: draft → pilot test → modification → comparison and review → issuance and implementation (see Figure 23.7), where specifics are covered in each step. The purpose has been to develop policies as accessible, readable, and practicable as the manufacturer's user manual for a machine. As the policy is widely accepted among staff, they are more willing to change, make what is described in the policy happen in real life and promote the general compliance to the policy.

Patient is assessed at multiple moments throughout moderate and deep sedation. Patient safety and uniform care are guaranteed as long as healthcare professionals find their roles and places from the policy and follow the steps described for them. Specifically, prior to sedation, a sedation physician assesses the patient's overall condition and documents that; when the patient is under sedation, a nurse continuously monitors and documents the vital signs (such as blood pressure, ECG, oxygen saturation, and respiration frequency); as the sedation ends, the physician assesses the patient's level of recovery, and discharges the patient only when the patient has reached the recovery criteria while educating the family members on the cautions.

With the policy as the evidence for care routine, the hospital set up the Sedation Care Center, led by the Anesthesiology Dept., and supported by the Medical Affairs Dept. and Quality Dept., among others. Based on the layout of outpatient care locations throughout the organization, the Sedation Care Center designated four Post-Sedation Care Rooms as routine sedation locations. These rooms have been equipped (necessary monitoring and resuscitation equipment) and staffed (healthcare professionals) to the same standard. All the staff involved in moderate and deep sedation were trained in lectures, and physicians were allowed to provide sedation only after passing evaluation and receiving privileges. Every quarter, the Sedation Care Center aggregates data related to moderate and deep sedation (including the preventive and remedial actions for complications), analyzes causes, and identifies potential risk to improve the process.

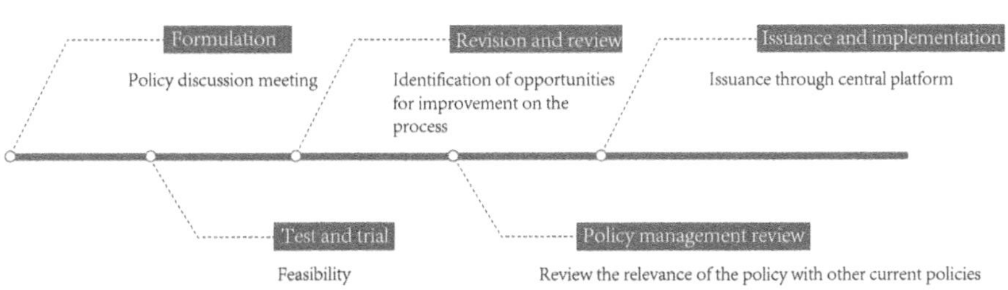

Figure 23.7 The five steps involved in policy development.

By now, moderate and deep sedation has become a strength of our commitment to quality and safety. We did some research and found ourselves the first to define standards for the management of moderate and deep sedation and to designate Diagnostic/Therapeutic Procedure Rooms for Moderate and Deep Sedation.

Our policy structure has been built upon collective wisdom of staff members, and the way that policy is developed and put into practice represents our commitment to continuous QI. Based on the essence of JCI standards, namely quality, safety and service, as well as outstanding mindsets and strategies from local and international organizations, we have involved the entire staff in the policy development process using a bottom-up approach. We have ensured the implementation of policies with the tracing methodology that we have learned from the JCI philosophy as well as a long-standing supervision mechanism of rounds, so as to create a change of mindset among staff: the purpose of policies is to "serve people" instead of "to rule people." With policies, staff got to perform their work accordingly, form new habits, and enhance the competence to serve patients and better ensure patient safety. By then, we can say the practice represents the policy structure.

Case 2: To Increase the Percentage of Correct ST Orders

The Head Nurse Who "Stockpiled Medication"

When returned to the hospital from a refresher program on clinical pharmacy in 2014, I was appointed as the manager for MMU chapter for JCI accreditation thanks to the recommendation of colleagues in the unit. One time, the Pharmacy Dept. summoned pharmacists to inspect and survey how medications were stored in the Treatment Room of clinical wards, with the focus being the volumes and expiration dates. When I got started, I did not have a clue how many there were. Stepping into the Treatment Room, I got dumbfounded: why did people name it Treatment Room while it was technically a stand-alone pharmacy! There were several dozen vials for each of the several dozen medications in the Treatment Room. To make full use of space, the nurse managing the Treatment Room grouped all the boxes of the same medication into the same case, and the cabinet in the Treatment Room was filled with these cases.

"Ms. Head nurse, why do you maintain so many medications? You don't need all of them, right?" I was perplexed about the stockpile strategy of this head nurse.

"My actual concern is whether we have got enough of them! You see, we've got so many patients up here. When emergency occurs, when medications are out of stock, when we do not have enough medication for patients, what shall we do?"

"You do not need to keep so many medications. When emergency occurs, you can easily get it when it is ordered as ST (statim, the Latin for 'immediate')." Without a second thought, I rapped out a solution to the problem.

"Hello pharmacist, don't you know? After an ST order is given, we do not get the medication even after two hours. If the pharmacy can get it to us within 30 minutes, I don't have to do all these things! To maintain this inventory, a nurse may still find herself struggled at the end of the day!" the head nurse spoke with discontent.

"Okay, I got you. I'll talk to my colleagues back in the Pharmacy and come back to you later." I replied with a forced smile.

I checked the expiration date on medications one by one with my head down and found several of them were only good for another 2 months. I glanced at my watch when I finished this check and found that I had spent almost 2 h in this one single Treatment Room!

"Mr. LI, would you please tell me how ST order of medication is filled from inpatient pharmacy?" I asked this young pharmacist happened to be on duty.

"Medication of ST order is delivered along with those of single-dose orders."

"Medication of ST order should arrive at the unit within 30 minutes, right? Why does it take more than two hours?"

"We are overwhelmed by an excessive amount of ST orders from physicians, who may order many other medicines in the name of ST. That is too much for us to handle. See, even this nifedipine of controlled-release form has been ordered as ST." said Mr. Li while showing me the order from the computer screen.

To Retrieve Data and Pinpoint the Key Cause

It takes a survey to justify A comment. Therefore, we did a survey on ST orders with data from November 2014 to January 2015, which showed that only 68% of them were true ST orders. In other words, 25,000 of the 80,000 ST orders had not met the criteria for ST orders. A significant amount of non-emergency medications had been ordered as ST, including nutritional agents, patented Chinese medicine and agents in controlled-released form (see Figure 23.8). They used unnecessarily large amount of manpower and resources and took up delivery resources that should have been reserved for ST orders, and left the medications in urgent need stuck in the way.

Since ST orders were found out of the range of the supervision radar, we decided to initiate a QI program to increase the percentage of correctly given ST orders. This project required multidisciplinary effort as ST order involves physician, pharmacist and IT Departments. The hospital leadership designated Pharmacy Dept. to lead this project and work with a QI team of managers and intermediate level professionals from each of the aforementioned areas. This QI team was assigned to further the progress of the project.

All the members of the QI team summoned to brain-storm the causes for the poor compliance to ST criteria from the aspects of management, facility, people, and environment. They also plotted the causes into a characteristic diagram. Then the QI team evaluated the causes based on the characteristic diagram, assigned score, ranked the causes and highlighted the major ones with circles (see Figure 23.9).

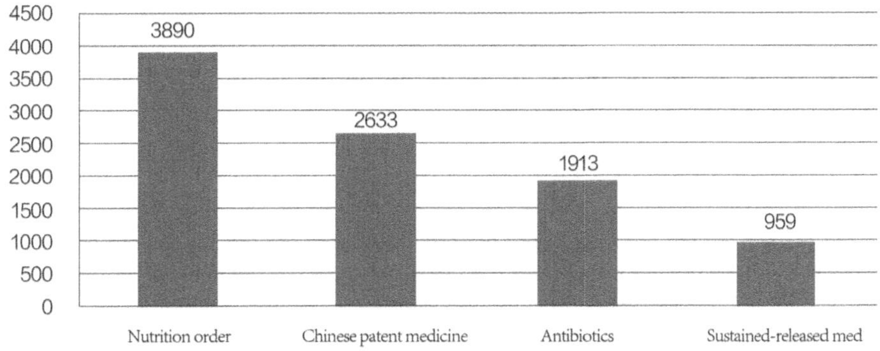

Figure 23.8 The number of incorrect ST orders.

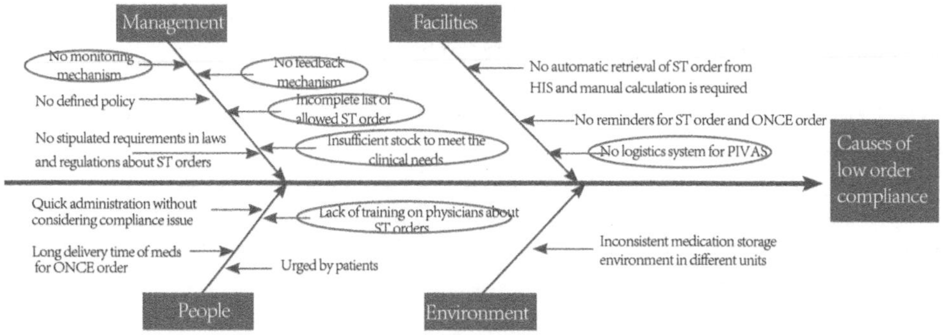

Figure 23.9 Causes for poor compliance of ST orders.

In addition, the QI team analyzed the causes with data on ST orders from November 2014 to January 2015 and converted them into a Pareto Chart, which has been based on the 80:20 rule, and concluded the actual causes: the catalog of ST orders was not clear enough, little training on ST order was provided to physicians, a monitoring and feedback mechanism was not in place, the stock in the clinical units was inadequate and a delivery system was not available to PIVAS (Pharmacy Intravenous Admixture Services).

To Set Goal and Develop Strategies

While data on the compliance of ST order were not available from local and international healthcare standards, we determined ours was 68% from the baseline survey. Based on the actual picture of our quality work, for the purpose of being safe, the QI team set the target as "at least 90% compliance in ST ordering."

The QI team members brain-stormed strategies for each of the true causes and evaluated them based on feasibility, efficacy, and controllability. Based on the 80:20 rule, the QI team selected strategies scored above 40 for implementation and developed action plan with the "4W1H" tool (see Table 23.1).

Table 23.1 Plan Developed Based on "4W1H" Logic

Why	*How*	*When*	*Where*	*Who*
Catalog of ST orders was not up to date	Hospital-wide catalog of ST orders was developed and communicated to staff	January and February 2015	Medical Affairs Dept., Pharmacy Dept., Nursing Dept.	
Physicians had not been trained on ST orders	Clinicians received training on ST orders	February and March 2015	Medical Affairs Dept., Pharmacy Dept.	

(*Continued*)

Table 23.1 (*Continued*) Plan Developed Based on "4W1H" Logic

Why	*How*	*When*	*Where*	*Who*
Communication mechanism was not in place	The Pharmacy Dept. monitors ST orders every month and communicates with clinical units	April–December 2015	Pharmacy Dept.	
The types of stock medication were not adequate	Stock medications based on the catalog of ST orders	April–May 2015	Medical Affairs Dept., Pharmacy Dept.	
PIVAS did not provide delivery service	The delivery system of Infusion Pharmacy covers ST orders	March–April 2015	Pharmacy Dept.	

The Plan was Put into Action Step by Step

- The mechanism of ST order management was established.

  Based on the trend of ST orders observed earlier from surveys, the hospital leadership had a discussion with staff from Medical Affairs Dept., Nursing Dept., Outpatient Dept., Pharmacy Dept., IT Center and clinical units and concluded with a catalog of 108 medications which ST order applies. This catalog was displayed for opinion and feedback on January 27, 2015.

  Then ST order was trained to all the healthcare professionals, who also received evaluation, and highlighted during the weekly meeting on hospital affairs as well as routine meeting for managers of clinical units. The managers, including directors and head nurses, received training and evaluation. Data on ST order were communicated to each unit (see Figure 23.10).

  The Medical Affairs Dept. collected and released the list of physicians who used ST orders incorrectly. The directors of clinical units educated and reminded staff in the unit about the ST order to standardize their utilization of ST order.

  The Pharmacy Dept. provided details of ST orders to the OA account of the unit-level quality controllers or directors to let the units analyze their own data. The Pharmacy Dept. has spent a lot of time and effort in data retrieval, provision and communication with clinical units: it participated in data retrieval and provision for 12 times, involving 125,000 pieces of data; it directed 710 pieces of data to the clinical units; and it engaged in 50 discussions with clinical units about problems in the data (see Figure 23.11a and b).
- To standardize stock medications in the units

  To better manage stock medications in the clinical units, a statement jointly released by the Medical Affairs Dept. and Pharmacy Dept. required clinical units to stock medication based on the *Catalog of Medications Used in Emergency Orders*. Specifically, units shall maintain at most five drugs from the catalog, and units of the same specialty shall maintain the same stock in terms of the types of medications involved (see Table 23.2).

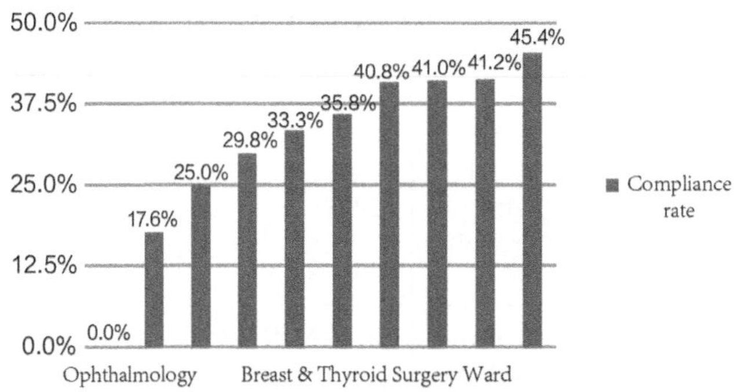

Figure 23.10 The percentage of compliant ST orders throughout all the units.

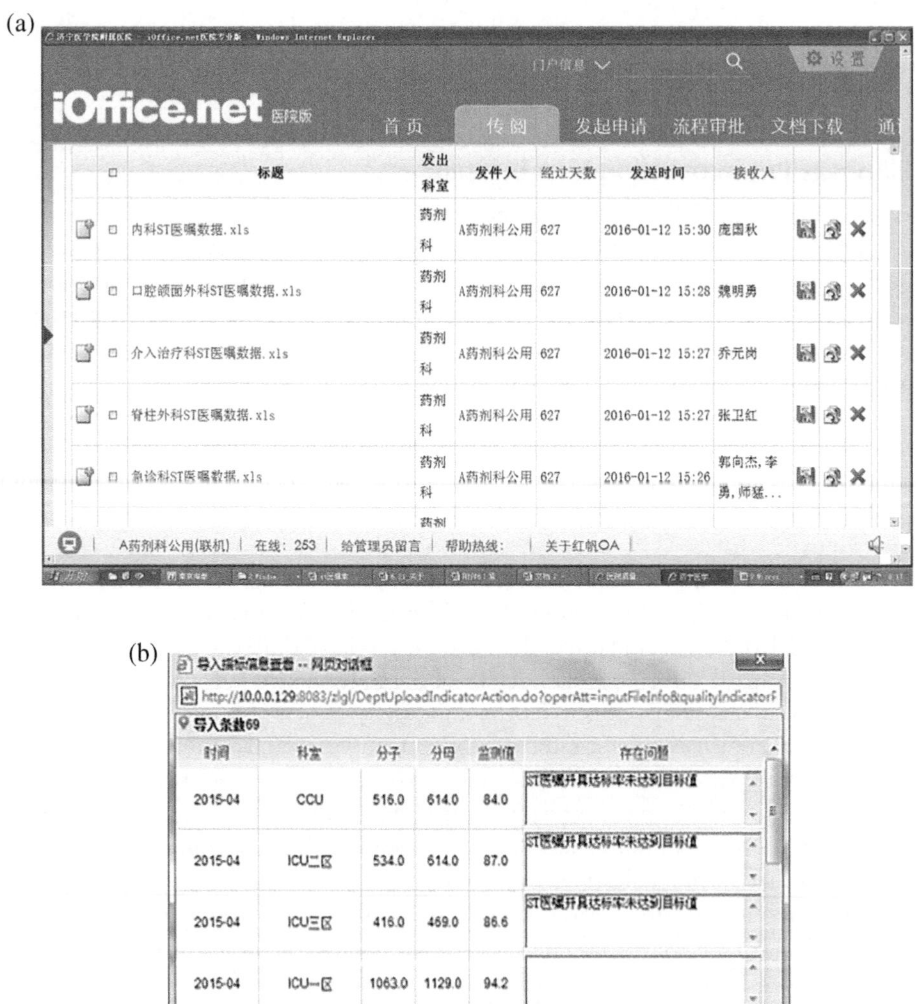

Figure 23.11 ST order being given from the OA system.

Table 23.2 The Master List of Stock Medications in All the Clinical Units (Wards)

Cardiology Dept. (Cardiology I, Cardiology II, Cardiology III, Cardiology IV and Cardiology V)	0.9% sodium chloride injection	500 mL
	0.9% sodium chloride injection	250 mL
	0.9% sodium chloride injection	100 mL
	5% glucose injection	50 mL
	10% glucose injection	500 mL
	Nitroglycerin pills	0.5 mL
	Dopamine hydrochloride injection	2 mL:20 mg
	Deslanoside injection	2 mL:0.4 mg
	Isosorbide dinitrate injection (joint venture)	10 mL:10 mg
	Amiodaronum hydrochloride injection (joint venture)	3 mL:0.15 g
	Diltiazem hydrochloride injection	10 mg
Neurology Dept. (Neurology I, Neurology II, Neurology III and Neurology IV)	Diazepam injection	2 mL:10 mg
	Mannitol injection	250 mL
	0.9% sodium chloride injection	100 mL
	0.9% sodium chloride injection	250 mL
	5% glucose injection	250 mL
	0.9% sodium chloride injection (bottle)	500 mL
	Sterile injectable water	500 mL

- To establish a medication delivery system

  A delivery system was established in the PIVAS (see Figure 23.12) that exclusively handles ST orders based on the fact that the unavailability of delivery system in the PIVAS for ST orders was attributed to the poor efficiency of ST order delivery.

  In the past, the delivery status was not trackable from the electronic system so that clinicians had to make telephone calls to ask the progress or urge a faster delivery. In August 2015, a delivery tracking system (see Figure 23.13) was put into service for staff to easily find the progress of the delivery and expected arrival time. This has helped increase efficiency of ST order delivery.

Outcome Evaluation

From February to December 2015, the system witnessed an increase from 79.5% to 96% for the percentage of correct ST orders, a drop in the number of daily ST orders from 873 to 405, and a decrease of the number of ST orders where the medication has not been listed in the catalog from 8,497 to 640 (see Figures 23.14 and 23.15).

Figure 23.12 The delivery system of Infusion Pharmacy.

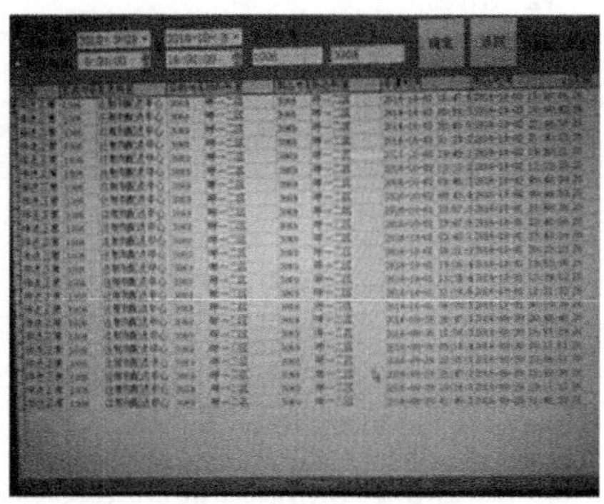

Figure 23.13 The information system of delivery center.

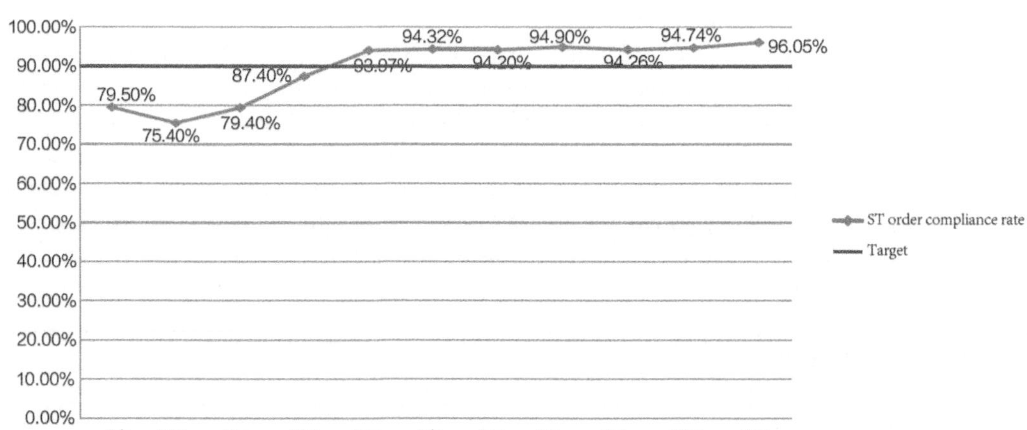

Figure 23.14 Compliance of ST orders.

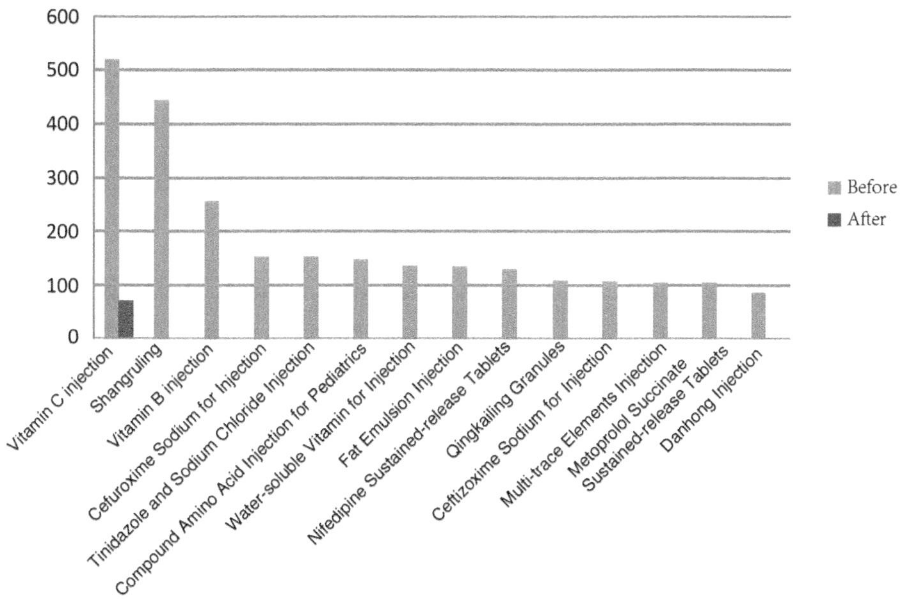

Figure 23.15 ST orders out of the range of the catalog before and after the initiation of this quality project.

Another change generated from this quality program was optimized human resource allocation in that medications of ST orders were delivered by the Infusion Pharmacy instead. By doing so, workload of PIVAS staff was reduced and nurses were freed up from the burden of medication management and able to spend more time with patients. The spin-off was 300,000 yuan of cost saved in a year.

The quality program also ensured medication safety and efficacy in that the risk of degradation had been reduced for unstable agents, such as β-lactam antibiotics and biological products. As the turn-around time of ST orders, from the time when a physician orders it to the time when it arrives at the unit, was shortened from 2 h to 30 min, and delay due to slow delivery became less frequent, medications have a better chance of being administered at the right time.

Review and Areas for Improvement

One year after this quality program was initiated, the percentage of correct ST orders increased to 96% from the baseline of 79.5%. But nine units still did not reach our target by December 2015. From analysis, we identified the following causes:

1. The capacity of prescription review did not live up to the demand. We highlighted the quality of prescription review in the quality program of 2016 with the aim of enhancing pharmacists' capability of reviewing appropriateness of orders, as the year featured "The Year with Emphasis on Pharmacist Prescription Review";
2. The catalog of medications applicable to ST orders was current. Specifically, when certain technology, service, or medication was newly available in the clinical units, the catalog did not reflect such change immediately.

In June 2016, I went to a Treatment Room again during a hospital-wide round for quality and safety, and I found there neat and spacious: there were only five vials of the five stock medications. The head nurse kept telling us how thankful she was for the works we had done. I replied: "Our thanks should go to the JCI philosophy and the hospital leadership for their vision in adopting the JCI accreditation standards. Without them, we would not have been enjoying optimized process, improved efficiency and higher quality and safety in the hospital. At the end of the day, that is for the better quality of care provided to patients."

Case 3: To "Round Up" Hazardous Chemicals with PDCA Cycle

Unlike regular chemicals, hazardous chemicals can be disastrous when leak or explode. A large amount of hazardous chemicals, narcotics, and psychotropics as well as radioactive agents can be found in hospitals for clinical care, research, and experiment. These are also called "hazardous materials" as most of them do harm to human body or environment. If stored or handled inappropriately, they may cause severe adverse event. Many loops in the management of hazardous materials were cited by JCI consultants during the baseline evaluation. For example, the original Program of Hazardous Materials and Waste did not cover all the elements from FMS.5 and FMS.5.1 as the list was not inclusive enough and the storage conditions were not up to standard, among others. Hazardous chemicals were the most important part due to their variety and consequence. Therefore, starting with hazardous chemicals, we adopted PDCA cycle to manage hazardous materials and achieved the expected result, strengthened the management of chemicals as well as other hazardous substances and further guaranteed patient safety.

The Causes for Noncompliant Management of Hazardous Chemicals

In the face of the problems identified for hazardous material management during the first baseline assessment, we sought and analyzed causes from facts gathered on the sites and brain-storm sessions. Four causes were cited (see Figure 23.16):

Figure 23.16 The causes for noncompliant management of hazardous chemicals laid out in fish-bone diagram.

1. The supervising departments and managers did not have enough awareness of safety risks;
2. The policies and processes did not comply with standards, and there was no written policies or plans;
3. Physical facility was insufficient as the storage and protection equipment on the sites were not up to standards;
4. Training was inadequate as the managers and supervisors on the site did not receive training on professional knowledge and were not fully informed of the proper response to emergencies involving hazardous materials.

As such, the immediate priority of the hospital was to standardize the management of hazardous chemicals.

P—The Plan of Continuous Improvement

To standardize the on-site management of chemicals and other hazardous materials, we developed a plan of continuous improvement based on FMS.5 and FMS.5.1 (Facility Management and Safety) of the JCI accreditation standards and have been working to implement tasks from the plan, which governs the inventory, handling, storage, and use of hazardous materials, as well as the containment and disposal of hazardous waste (see Table 23.3).

The Security Dept. took the lead and summoned a working group of QI for hazardous materials to complete relevant tasks in collaboration with Medication Purchasing Office, Material Delivery Center, Laboratory, Pathology, Central Laboratory, Medical Affairs Dept., Nursing Dept., Infection Control Office, Pharmacy Dept., PIVAS, Nuclear Medicine, Radiology Dept., IT Center, General Support Dept., Medical Equipment Dept., House-keeping and General Service Office and the Catering Center.

The goal was to improve and standardize management throughout the organization and to ensure over 95% compliance of hazardous chemical inventory in clinical units, where compliance was defined as the number of units where the number of hazardous materials had been within the maximum level of inventory divided by the number of units that maintains hazardous chemicals.

D—Implement the Plan

Based on the plan of continuous improvement for hazardous materials, tasks were implemented based on the time-line specified in the plan.

Phase 1: To Finalize the Master List of Hazardous Chemicals Throughout the Entire Organization

With a thorough understanding from all the previous purchases, storage, and delivery of hazardous chemicals, we came to divide the 70 hazardous chemicals into eight categories, specifying their type, brand name, specification, quantity, and location, based on *The Categories and Signs for Common Hazardous Chemicals* (code: GB 13690-1992), *The Categories, Brand Names and Codes of Hazardous Products* (code: GB 6944-2005), as well as *The Regulation on Hazardous Chemical Safety*.

Table 23.3 The Plan of Continuous Improvement for Hazardous Materials

Timeline	*Due Date*	*Tasks*	*Responsible persons*
Phase 1	2014 April–July	1. Review the processes of purchasing, storing, delivering, using and obsoleting hazardous chemicals 2. Census the type, volume, and location of all the hazardous chemicals in the hospital 3. Discuss to determine the maximum volume of hazardous chemicals allowed in each unit/department (as their maximum inventory) 4. Develop the master list of all the hazardous chemicals in the hospital, specifying the type, volume, and location	2
Phase 2	2014 July–December	1. Develop written policies and processes for hazardous chemicals based on standards: ① written policies, process and mechanisms of hazardous material management were developed and updated, including the *Program of Hazardous Materials and Waste of 2014* and the *Policy of Hazardous Chemical Safety*; ② *Material Safety Data Sheet (MSDS)* was developed and provided to the units 2. Improve the storage and protection mechanisms on the sites: ① cabinets dedicated for hazardous chemicals of various sizes were provided, whose number totaled 123; ② these cabinets are locked and maintained by designated staff members; ③ the construction plan was developed for the upgrade of hazardous chemical warehouses according to standards; ④ electronic access control system has been consistently installed in Utility Rooms and Waste Rooms in clinical areas; ⑤ radioactive elements were stored in lead shield containers; ⑥ the disposal process and route of hazardous waste have been defined, which is managed by designated individuals with handover documentation; ⑦ the checklist used during inspection for hazardous chemicals has been developed and metric-based monitoring is done every month in the sites. 3. The emergency response mechanism has been defined: ① the spill kits for hazardous materials as well as the emergency response for exposure and spill are in place; ② the management of areas where hazardous chemicals are found and the steps involved in handling a spill are standardized	2

(*Continued*)

Table 23.3 (*Continued*) The Plan of Continuous Improvement for Hazardous Materials

Timeline	*Due Date*	*Tasks*	*Responsible persons*
Phase 3	2015 January–May	1. *The Program of Hazardous Materials and Waste for 2015* was developed to keep current, which specifies the goals of the program and the departments responsible for the hazardous materials and waste 2. Hazardous chemicals are continuously monitored with quality metrics and inspected by Security Dept. every month to ensure expectation had been met, which was at least 95% of compliance of the maximum level of inventory allowed 3. The process for adding new hazardous chemical or increasing inventory level was standardized 4. The electronic system for "supply and operation" was put into use, so that: ① every unit/department reports their inventory of hazardous chemicals in terms of types, volume, and locations; ② the electronic version of MSDS is always accessible 5. The use of signs for hazardous chemicals (which apply to dispensing containers as well) and the practice of inventory log was standardized among units 6. The mechanism of training on hazardous chemicals was standardized to ensure staff who handle and manage materials have received orientation and in-service training 7. The overhead announcement mechanism for spill event of hazardous chemicals has been established and an event is announced as "code orange, location, 7777" for three times 8. The hospital-wide contingency drill program has included spill of hazardous chemicals and this should be done at least once a year	2

Phase 2: To Develop Policies and Processes

Written policies and processes were developed for hazardous materials according to standards. To standardize the management of hazardous materials and waste throughout the entire organization, the *Program of Hazardous Materials for 2014* was developed based on FMS.5 and FMS.5.1 of the JCI accreditation standards to ensure the program had covered every relevant standards and measurable elements. Secondly, modification was made to *Policy of Hazardous Materials*, *Policy of Inspection to Storage Locations of Hazardous Chemicals*, *Policy of Hazardous Chemical Warehouse*, and *Contingency Plan for Events Involving Hazardous Materials*. What's more, *Material Safety Data Sheet (MSDS)* was developed based on the master list of hazardous chemicals throughout the entire organization, which has addressed the safe handling and use of the chemicals. The MSDS was provided to all the areas in the hospital and these locations were required to make it immediately available.

The storage locations have been made more appropriate and protective equipment have been in place. To ensure the proper storage and safe use of hazardous chemicals, the hospital has established comprehensive protective measures to prevent loss or exposure.

In terms of storage: ① based on the master list of hazardous chemicals in the house, the hospital purchased fire resistant, explosion proof and well-vented cabinets designated for hazardous chemicals in four sizes and provided to each unit based on their inventory level. The units were required to put the cabinet in a Treatment Room with access control mechanism; ② all the cabinets are secured with two locks, maintained individually by two staff members from the unit, and an *Inventory Log for Hazardous Chemicals* is maintained and kept current; ③ a construction plan was developed to modify the walls of hazardous chemical warehouses of the Medication Purchasing Office, and Pathology Dept., among others, to address the need for proper temperature, humidity, ventilation, and drainage.

In terms of use: considering the risk of leakage or spill when hazardous chemicals are stored in a cabinet for an extended period of time, units are required to apply for the minimum volume needed each time and minimize their local inventory level.

In terms of inspection: an inspector of hazardous chemicals has been designated to do monthly rounds to audit the storage, use, inventory log and disposal of hazardous chemicals in each unit, and check the emergency supplies and facilities for hazardous chemicals. The inspector documents the monthly rounds. In addition, the local inspector of hazardous chemicals in each unit checks the eye-wash equipment, shower, and other emergency facilities regularly. For the eye-wash equipment specifically, the local inspector keeps the water running for 10–15 min to ensure water quality from the pipe.

An emergency response mechanism was put in place. One part of the emergency response involves proper equipment. The *MSDS* has been uniformly developed based on the types of hazardous chemicals we have maintained in the organization and provided to the chemical locations, where spill kits are available with 33 pieces of items of 15 categories. Apart from these, eye-wash equipment, shower, and other relevant devices have been installed in high-risk areas such as Laboratory, Pathology Dept., Central Laboratory, and Warehouse. The other part involves clearly defined handling process. As different types of chemical require different approach of response during emergency, staff should refer to the *MSDS* for instruction.

Phase 3: Daily Management and Emergency Response

Signs of hazardous chemicals were made clear to staff and put up in consistent ways according to standards. Units keep their own inventory logs according to standards and fill in the replenishment and use every day to keep the record current. The Electronic System for Material, Delivery, and Operation has been developed and used to standardize the management of hazardous chemicals throughout different units. The monthly maximum quantity for each unit has been programmed in the electronic system so that units can never get more than what they are allowed to have. This is an effective means to strictly control the stock level in each unit and reduce risk. To ensure emergency is immediately handled effectively, the hospital organizes annual hospital-wide training on hazardous chemical safety, which covers the storage, use, and emergency response of hazardous chemicals. In addition, at least two drills are performed each year for spill, leakage, and loss of hazardous chemicals to refresh staff's awareness and ability of emergency response.

Table 23.4 Problems in the Use of Common Hazardous Chemicals and Strategies

No.	*Problem*	*Solution*
1	The actual volume has exceeded its permitted maximum	The maximum inventory level is defined and units would fail an application if the volume requested for exceeds the maximum
2	Unsafe storage environment	Designated yellow cabinets that protect chemicals from fire, heat, and collision are used and put up with proper signs
3	Inappropriate storage	Chemicals of different types are laid out in different shelves/separating areas on the same shelf
4	Unclear label	Each type of chemical is attached with immediately recognizable sign according to national regulations
5	Willful utilization	Cabinets are locked and inventory is maintained with the *Inventory hog for Hazardous Chemicals*

C—Check with Quality Metrics

Based on our own experience as well as relevant literature, we found there were 69 chemicals in our hospital. With data on the problems in the use of common hazardous chemicals, we identified causes and strategies as listed in Table 23.4.

A—Act to Sustain Improvement

Actions were taken from April 2014 to May 2015, which included the standardization of the process of "filing request → request being reviewed and approved → storage → use → training." Supervision of the use and management was done through the inventory log of hazardous chemicals via the Electronic System for Material, Delivery, and Operation as well as monthly on-site inspection to ensure the practice is in line with policies and standards (see Figures 23.17–23.19).

The multidisciplinary collaboration driven by the QI group has made a difference in the practice level. The inspection of 119 units throughout the hospital for the management of hazardous chemicals in 2015 revealed that compliance was below 80% for 81 units in January, with a slight increase overall in February; ranged from 80% to 90% in March and reached 95% in April.

Figure 23.17 Storage condition before we started the QI project.

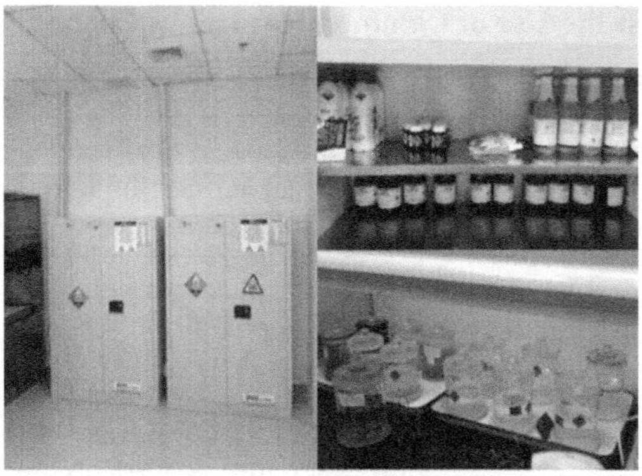

Figure 23.18 Storage condition after we started the QI project.

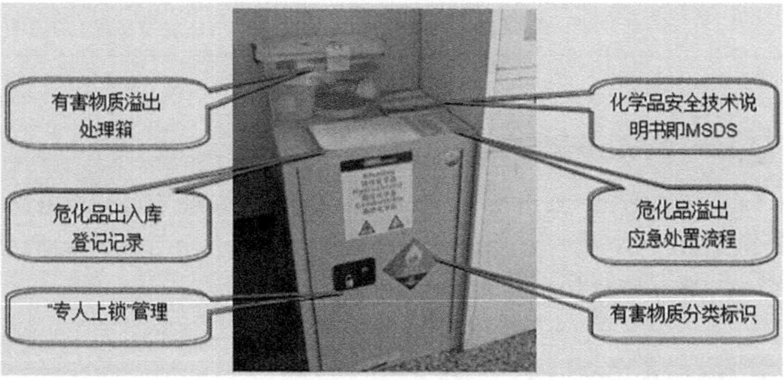

Figure 23.19 Cabinet designated for hazardous chemicals put in place as one of the changes.

The continuous monitoring has revealed that the compliance of hazardous material management has remained stable above 95%. Our experience in managing hazardous chemicals was described in an article, which was published in *Chinese Journal of Medical Management Sciences* and shared in several conferences of hospital management in China. What's more, we filed application for an invention patent for the Quantity-based Monitoring System for Hazardous Chemicals that we had developed. The series of measure that we have taken have improved the compliance of steps in hazardous chemical management to standards, reduced the impact and risk of the hazardous chemicals, ensured facility and environment safety, and snuff out any real danger.

Chapter 24

Ping An Wanjia Healthcare Investment Management Co., Ltd (Ping An Wanjia Healthcare in Short)

Fan Shaofei, Zhou Kang, Wu Jing,
Huang Shujuan, Xie Linling, Huang Yan, Luo Xi,
He Xinzhu, Gu Shibo, and Meng Fanfeng
Ping An Wanjia Healthcare

Fan Shaofei, *Chairman of the Board and CEO of Ping An Wanjia Healthcare, a subsidiary of Ping An Group, joined the healthcare sector 20 years ago and has become expert in the investment and management of large organizations as well as operation in healthcare organizations. His previous roles include Senior Vice President of the China-North Asia Region of Parkway Healthcare, Manager of Healthcare Investment of Fosun Group, and founder of Kangrui Healthcare Investment and Management Co. Ltd. With Master Degree in healthcare administration from University of Berne (Swiss) and EMBA degree from China Europe International Business School (CEIBS), and unique insights in industrial chain of healthcare and innovation of business models in and beyond China, Mr. Fan is an expert in clinic development and healthcare investment as well as operation.*

Zhou Kang (Kevin) *is Associate Partner of Ernst & Young (China) Advisory Limited based in Shanghai China, specializing in strategy and management consulting. Kevin has more than 20 years of experience in strategies, operation and business in healthcare and insurance. Kevin has worked in Ping An and Accenture, and holds master's degree of Health Statistics.*

Wu Jing, *Director of the Healthcare Performance Department, Ping An HealthKonnect, has been engaged in healthcare and the elderly care industry for more than 10 years and has extensive experience in strategy, operation, and project management, especially in primary care and the elderly care and rehabilitation field. She has worked in Ping An Group, Care-ray Healthcare Investment and An Tai Senior Rehabilitation Centre, and has obtained an MBA from Tsinghua University.*

Company Introduction: As the largest insurance company in China, Ping An Insurance (Group) Company of China ranked thirty-ninth on Fortune 500 Companies 2017 and eighth globally among all financial companies. In 2016, the operation revenue of Ping An was 774.488 billion yuan with a profit of 72.368 billion yuan. We have 131 million individual clients with an average number of contracts of 2.21 and an average profit of 311.51 yuan per client. The number of Internet client is 346 million. Ping An launched the "Open Platform + Open Market 3.0" in 2016 to focus on big finance and assets as well as big health and care. Wanjia Healthcare is an important piece of the Ping An big health and care following the principle of patient-centered improved experience.

Wanjia Healthcare aims at becoming the largest healthcare service platform through integrating the primary healthcare organizations across the country and establishing the accreditation standards for healthcare.

Contents

Preface

JCI Standards and Wanjia

Healthcare Strategic Upgrade of Ping An and Wanjia Platform

"A man of honor has things that must be done and things that must not." That is the strategy of Ping An. Therefore, it focuses on the markets of big financial assets and big health which are highly related to the insurance business of the group with the largest market size and the most promising prospects. There is a trend in the financial sector to transit from the sales-driven model to the service-based model. It is expected that the total volume of China's healthcare and services would exceed 1.2 trillion dollars by 2020 and continue to reach 2.4 trillion dollars by 2030.

With healthcare positioned as one of the two core strategies, Ping An Group will invest in business related to patient access, service providers, and payers. An overall strategic layout of the healthcare sector of Ping An will mainly center on healthcare insurance, commercial insurance, health management, and information service with a secondary emphasis on healthcare organizations, distribution and retail of medications and third-party services.

The demands on healthcare and relevant services in China concentrate on the primary level. However, 80% of the resources are centralized in the cities, among which, 80% are in the large and medium size hospitals. Such phenomena drive patients to large hospitals to seek the best care, and further leads to the "overpopulation" in those hospitals. This results in the uncoordinated expansion of large hospitals to meet the patients' needs. On the other hand, the number of primary organizations shrinks with decreasing resources. The reality of China's healthcare is a colossus of weak primary healthcare organizations, strong symphonic effect from large hospitals, restriction on the fluidity of physicians due to the current system, and limited effectiveness of healthcare insurance due to different reimbursement methods.

To follow the national policies to facilitate the development of the hierarchical healthcare system, social investment, multisited licensure for physicians, and cost control on healthcare insurance, Ping An Group decided to integrate government health insurance and commercial products to build a platform of healthcare and services to provide better access to quality service for the people in China.

Ping An Wanjia is dedicated to integrating the quality resources of primary healthcare organizations and establishing the first safety and quality accreditation standards, to meet the needs on fine operation, increased revenue, standard practice, and customer satisfaction through empowering and connecting the primary level organizations.

As Fan Shaofei, Chair and CEO of Ping An Wanjia, states that Ping An Wanjia's goal is to establish platform, connect clinics and set up standards to realize the China's dream of "Healthy Families and Healthy China"!

Wangjia Standard Accreditation and Consultation Service

China has achieved tremendous progress in health promotion, but is still facing multiple challenges. The quality of care remains as an important topic for China's healthcare system.

Many people believe that the quality of care varies among different level of healthcare organizations, which creates the bottleneck in shunting patients to the primary level clinics. It is evidenced that many healthcare staff in the primary clinics are not competent in diagnosing and treating patients. However, personal competence is closely related to their own experience. Distinct gaps among healthcare organizations on different levels and that between urban and rural areas have exerted influenced on the training and experience of physicians. Lack of competent staff has limited the quality of the services on the primary level and prolonged the hospitalization of patients. That is recognized as the indication of poor quality. At the same time, patient experience needs to be further improved. Physicians and nurses are not friendly; there is too little time for the consultation; physicians order unnecessary treatment/medications... These are just a few of the examples of patients complaints that one can hear every day.

People start to realize that quality is a systematic problem rather than the responsibility of only one physician, unit or organization. Policies and institutional framework would be necessary for the improvement of healthcare quality, including clearly defined vision and goals, uniform leadership, standard quality monitoring system, coordinated supervision, framework for quality improvement, transparency, and accountability. Based on that, a comprehensive quality improvement strategy and effective implementation should be achieved.

Ping An Wanjia Healthcare is committed to the establishment of a PPP industrial chain for healthcare to link patients, service provider, and payers through the Wanjia platform. We hope to establish business relationship and achieve in-depth cooperation through four layers, namely online service, accreditation, franchising, and flagship organizations. Meanwhile, we are also going to conduct safety and quality accreditation in these four types of organizations to forge a healthcare network centered on quality and safety.

The evaluation system of Ping An Wanjia centers on safety and quality to help hospitals establish a quality management system and improve operation efficiency. A star-rating accreditation system will be adopted from the perspective of "China's practice of international standards." A combination of primary accreditation and professional accreditation will be implemented to build a complete and standardized accreditation process. Meanwhile, an accreditation team consisting of local surveyors and a resources platform will be established to ensure the fairness of the evaluation.

First Stage: Communication on Business Demands and the Hierarchical System

Before Ping An Wanjia entered the cooperation with JCI, we discussed about the positioning of business demands, program planning, and the specific steps of the first stage of the program. Positioning of goals and analysis of demands, and program planning were the two major tasks.

Discussion of Wanjia Accreditation Standards

In March 2016, when the overall strategy and implementation approach became clear, the leadership of Ping An Wanjia decided to start the discussion on the strategic positioning of the safety-and-quality-based accreditation standards. Mr. Fan Shaofei, Chair and CEO of Ping An Wanjia, Ms. Wu Jing, Director of Accreditation and Consultation Sector, invited Jilan Liu, principal JCI consultant, to discuss the significance of the cooperation between JCI and Wanjia. After the discussion and analysis, the target clients would be the primary level clinics and the outpatient departments of the primary level healthcare organizations. The focus of the evaluation would be the quality control system and the operational management in the clinics. The cooperation between JCI and Wanjia would be based on the Ambulatory Care Standards, which was to be modified according to the local situations and types of clinics.

After 2 months of communication and discussion with JCI Consulting Department, Ping An Wanjia finally signed the cooperation agreement with JCI on May 21, 2016. The signing ceremony was held in the Pin An Building in Shanghai (see Figure 24.1). Paula Wilson, Global Vice President of JCI, and Jilan Liu conducted in-depth discussion with Mr. Fan Shaofei, Chair of Ping An Wanjia, Ms. Xu Zhihong, General Manager, Mr. He Liquan, CTO, Ms. Wu Jing, Director of Accreditation and Consultation Sector and the Wanjia team in the hope of leveraging on the experience and advanced concepts to help Chinese healthcare organizations enhance their awareness of safety and quality, optimize quality management system, diversify the management tools for the benefit of primary level healthcare organizations and the local people in China.

Figure 24.1 Signing ceremony of Ping An Wanjia—JCI cooperation.

Demand Positioning and Design of Wanjia Accreditation System

In early August 2016, Jilan Liu (medical service), Thomas (administration service) and Terence (nursing service) from JCI visited the headquarters of Ping An Wanjia in Shanghai. Ms. Wu Jing attended the meeting. She was responsible for the development, design, and operation of the standards, accreditation process, and consultation business. A Project Team of Wanjia Accreditation Standards Development was formed during the meeting. The project team was responsible for the standard demand positioning, system structure, content of the standards, survey process, and the application effectiveness of the accreditation. The design and planning of the Wanjia Hierarchical Accreditation Standards was officially launched (see Figure 24.2).

Figure 24.2 Launching meeting of JCI—Wanjia Healthcare Standards Development Cooperation.

1. Analysis of the demand positioning and the discussion of the situation in China

   All team members on the accreditation program at the headquarters of Wanjia were devoted to the discussion that lasted for 1 week. In the first 2 days, introduction on the current accreditation activities targeting on the private healthcare organizations and primary ones was provided to the JCI team for sufficient understanding and communication. Wanjia also invited the experts from Chinese Non-government Medical Institutions Association (CNMIA) and Shanghai Association for Non-government Medical Institutions (SHANMI) to contribute their input to the discussion. The former is now piloting on the accreditation on non-government hospitals, and the latter has been conducting accreditation on non-government organizations for 5 years. During the meeting, Hao Deming, Chair of CNMIA, and relevant leaders and experts shared the current situation of the accreditation of three pilot hospitals in China. Yan Dongfang, Chair of SHANMI and his team also shared their experience with the accreditation and evaluation in more than 50 healthcare organizations in Shanghai.

   On the third day of discussion, the experts on the project team and our colleagues reviewed the current accreditation activities piloted locally in China based on the analysis of the demands and strategies of Wanjia. The two sides initiated the first round of discussion on the framework of the Wanjia standards. During the discussion, Jilan told us that TJC also had tried the hierarchical accreditation at the very beginning. Tomas recommended that the principles of the JCI structure be kept in integrity in the basic management system. Terence shared the experience from Turkey as well as the experience of regional primary healthcare safety and quality network in other countries, which had provided sufficient evidence for Wanjia to establish the hierarchical accreditation standards (see Figure 24.3).

   At first, we were worried that the bar was too high for the primary level clinics to meet. But Jilan said that we should not worry about where they started or the number of organizations who could perform well in the accreditation. She also shared with us the experience of HIMSS in developing the hierarchical criteria. In the United States, 70% of the hospitals were at HIMSS EMRAM Stages 0–2 at the early days when the model was first launched. After 10 years of promotion and the upgrade of HIT, today, the United States has nearly 70% hospitals reaching Stages 5–7. Jilan said, "The standards need to encourage the healthcare organizations to make leap forward. Only in this way can the standards facilitate the

Figure 24.3 Discussion among experts from home and abroad.

development of the entire industry." The cases of other international or regional accreditation experience offered were exactly what we could learn from.

Currently, the supervision from the local healthcare authorities on the clinics is rather weak. But the local people have turned to the primary level healthcare organizations due to the limited access to the service provided in large hospitals. However, they also bring their high expectations on safety and quality as well as good patient experience to those organizations. That is the trend that Wanjia wants to catch and land its focus on.

As a set of international standards accommodating healthcare organizations from all over the world, while trying to remove the language restrictions in the standards as much as possible and emphasize on the flexibility by applicable laws and regulations, JCI, to some extent, still keeps the high-level requirements on quality and patient safety from their domestic criteria in the United States. It could take Chinese hospitals very long time to reach the standards through constant preparation and improvement. For the clinics that are small in scale, staffing, and investment, it could be an even harder journey for them. Therefore, Wanjia worked to balance the international benchmark and the reality in China to find an appropriate approach to develop the hierarchical standards based on the JCI standards as well as the local accreditation practice. The project team finally decided to adopt the primary level and the advanced level standards to tailor to the needs of patients' expectation on healthcare.

2. Field visits and training on standards

On the fourth day of our discussion, our colleagues from Wanjia showed to the JCI experts specific cases and toured them to some clinics that had the intention to cooperate with us to familiar them with the four types of clinics that would be included on the Wanjia platform in the future, namely the online clinic, accreditation clinic, franchised clinic and flagship clinic (see Figure 24.4). Based on the summary and findings from the field visits, JCI team started the second round of discussion regarding the positioning analysis. All of the three experts recognized that there were big gaps between the primary healthcare organizations in China (both clinics and outpatient departments of primary level hospitals) and the standards, and that differences indeed existed among the four types of clinics regarding their awareness and current situations. Therefore, it was rational and necessary to establish the hierarchical standards.

Figure 24.4 Field visits by JCI team to targeted clinics.

Figure 24.5 Training on Wanjia accreditation team by JCI team.

On the fifth day, JCI team provided training to all the Wanjia accreditation staff based on the JCI Accreditation Standards for Ambulatory Care through sharing cases and discussions regarding the hospital processes and structures of patient care (see Figure 24.5). The standards interpretation, Q&A, scenario case analysis were the basic foundation for the development of Wanjia's hierarchical standards. The project team finally summarized on the demands positioning and achieved consensus on the development of the standards. The JCI team would review and modify the standards after the draft would be finished. Then based on the feedback on the modification, the standards would be finalized after evaluation.

Development of Hierarchical Standards

The Wanjia Hierarchical Accreditation Standards is the tool for standard practices regarding safety and quality in primary level healthcare organizations in the hope of standardizing the healthcare services and establishing the management system through the process of aligning clinics to the requirements. Evidence-based methodologies and objective environment were adopted to the development of the standards which were written based on rounds of discussions with accreditation experts through (1) demands positioning and design, (2) field survey and training, (3) standards drafting, (4) review by experts, (5) modification based on recommendations, and (6) test on the standards and finalization of the standards.

The actual development of the standards was consisted by the following steps.

Drafting

From August to September 2016, the initial drafting started. The project team experts went through each one of the standards with our colleagues and the standards were modified or edited based on consensus. The drafting was based on the ambulatory care standards developed by JCI which provided the foundation and basic framework of the Wanjia standards. The JCI consultants also offered in-depth insight on the standards as well as detailed and tailored recommendations based on the weakness identified through the field visits. These are all now reflected in the measurable elements of the standards.

Three Rounds of Consultation

From September to November 2016, with the assistance from the experts, we started three rounds of consultation, based on which we summarized the recommendations and modified the first draft. For the first round of consultation, we invited the experts from the JCI hospitals in China: over 20 professionals from the well-known large tertiary and secondary hospitals in Jiangsu Province, Zhejiang Province, and Shanghai. We organized a consultation meeting that lasted for 1 week to further discuss the appropriateness and feasibility of the standards, and made revisions to the draft. Mr. Zhou Kang, General Manager of Strategic Development Department of Ping An Wanjia, participated in the discussion on behalf of the company leadership. Ms. Wu Jing and other team members also joined the discussion on specific chapters (see Figure 24.6). Through the discussion during that round of consultation, detailed design, feasibility analysis, and discussion were conducted in the aspects of patient safety, clinical process and overall management system in China's clinics to ensure the appropriateness and feasibility of the localization of international standards based on Chinese practices.

From 21 to 23 September 2016, the second round of consultation was initiated. Experts from social organizations, accreditation organizations, and higher education institutions, such as China National Health Development Research Center of the National Health and Family Planning Commission, NICE (UK), DNV GL accreditation, Shanghai Jiao Tong University School of Medicine and Shanghai Medical College of Fudan University, were invited. The consultants from different backgrounds contributed their inputs to the revision of the standards from the perspectives of the national policies, current development in China, concepts and trends of international accreditation, best practices of international accreditation and research on operation and management of the domestic healthcare organizations. The invited experts recognized the comprehensiveness and feasibility of the drafted standards. Mr. Zhao Kun, Director of China National Health Development Research Center, officials from the Health and Family Planning Commission of

Figure 24.6 First round of consultation.

Liaoning Province, and experts from NICE shared their research achievements on the standards and their experience in implementing accreditation activities on organizations on the provincial, municipal, and county levels. They recommended that the standards include more layers and be more inclusive to cover more healthcare organizations.

In November 2016, the third round of consultation was conducted. The experts from the healthcare safety and quality administration authorities of over 13 provincial capital cities and local-level cities, industrial associations as well as experts involved in healthcare accreditation activities attended the review and discussion (see Figure 24.7). Based on the recommendations from the previous two rounds of consultation, in-depth interpretation and sufficient discussion were directed to the revised primary level standards as well as the advanced standards (newly added). We discussed the design of the layered framework and improvement on each standard and measurable element together with the experts. It was vital to the comprehensiveness of the hierarchical standard system and the well-organized process of standards development and review.

Translation, Revision, and Review of the Standards

During the process of standards development, accurate translation between English and Chinese was necessary. As the development process involved many rounds of discussion with both domestic and foreign experts, translation became an important task. Jilan, as the chief designer of the standards, took the responsibility to coordinate the JCI consultants, the Wanjia team members and the domestic experts.

We had foreseen the needs of localization of the translation of the standards, and the entire discussion and development was in bilingual (English and Chinese). Thanks to the engagement of Jilan throughout process, we successfully managed the training, drafting, and consultation in both languages. This had cleared away the language barrier and paved the way for the ideal localization and better understanding of the standards.

Figure 24.7 Third round of consultation and launching meeting of Wanjia accreditation.

Test and Finalization of the Standards

Based on the aggregated recommendations from all experts involved, trainings on the standards, consultation on improvement and the test on the survey process were important to establish the understanding of the new standards of the clinics and ensure the sustainability of the accreditation activities. Test surveys were conducted by the Wanjia team on both the primary and advanced standards. The standards were tested out in different specialized organizations in different geographic areas. After multiple tests, Ping An Wanjia proved that the developed standards were effective and appropriate and could benchmark the hospitals with the advanced concepts and practices. On December 3, 2016, the launching ceremony of the Wanjia Clinic Accreditation Standards was staged. Many experts who participated in the process of the standards development attended the event to celebrate the moment together with the colleagues from the primary clinics that had successfully accredited. Mr. Fan Shaofei, together with the representatives from the government authorities, research institutes, international accreditation organizations, and accredited clinics, released the standards (see Figure 24.8). Among the VIPs, we were honored to have Mr. Zhao Kun, Director of China National Health Development Research Center, Jilan Liu, JCI Principal Consultant, Prof. Bao Yong, Shanghai Jiao Tong University School of Medicine, Mr. Bo Huijie, Director of Medical Business and Marketing Director of DNV GL China, and Ms. Zhou Wenwen, Director of Chengdu Dongda Community Healthcare Center. They also expressed their expectations and said that it was an effective way to standardize the practices in the healthcare sector through standards and that there was no end to the journey of standards development because it needed to be continuously updated and improved based on the actual accreditation activities in China. They hoped that Wanjia could establish a routine standards revision mechanism to ensure the feasibility of the standards as well as its leading role in the healthcare industry.

Figure 24.8 Release of Wanjia accreditation standards for clinics.

Introduction to Wanjia Standards

International Patient Safety Goals (IPSG)

JCI accreditation centers on patient safety and the quality of healthcare, which also applies to the healthcare organizations targeted for the Wanjia standards. It will never be of less importance despite of the country, scale, number of disciplines, staffing ratio, and investment. In both international and domestic accreditation, the standards listed in the IPSG chapter are the minimum requirements.

For any healthcare organization, it is of utmost importance to identify patients correctly. Wanjia standards also emphasizes the implementation of the mechanism of patient identification to uniformly identify patients in the healthcare organization. There are risks of mistakenly identify a patient in almost all processes of diagnosis and treatment. The standards require clinics adopt two identifiers to identify a patient and ensure the consistency across the organization.

For large JCI hospitals, the challenging part in IPSG is the standard regarding effective communication. Compared with those hospitals, the primary level clinics are of smaller physical scale, fewer disciplines, and fewer types of services. Therefore, it is less challenging for clinics to achieve that standard. The standards in this chapter stress on the improvement of handover communication during various processes in the hospital to help healthcare staff communicate with each other more effectively, reduce potential risks, and improve patient's experience.

JCI standards also pay special attention to the infection risk mitigation in the organizations. Infection prevention and control is the challenge facing every healthcare organization. It is more so for the primary level clinics due to lack of staff and investment. Nevertheless, for those clinics, it is required that an effective hand hygiene management plan be fully implemented according to commonly recognized protocols such as the ones released by WHO, the American CDC and other international organizations, and adequate hand hygiene facilities be available for staff to enhance the awareness of the staff and reduce the care-associated infection.

Accessibility and Continuity of Care (ACC)

The standards related to accessibility and continuity of care mainly are designed to promote the cooperation and communication among healthcare staff throughout the flow of the patients. The Wanjia standards basically adopted the requirements stated in the JCI standards, but also adapted a bit to fit the Chinese situation.

Starting from the third edition of the JCI Accreditation Standards for Ambulatory Care, it requires an outpatient profile be established for complex patients, i.e., patients who might have chronic diseases with cumulative medical care records, or who might have multiple diagnoses and require multidisciplinary care. The outpatient profile could help physicians comprehensively assess the patient and support the development of the care plan effectively. As we all know, physicians usually have very limited time for one patient. Sometimes, patients might suspect the thoroughness of the physician, and they would worry about misdiagnoses. The profile is a means to solve this tension between healthcare staff and patients. But for clinics that are not operating up to their full capacity, to establish an outpatient profile for complex patients is not the priority of improvement yet. Therefore, it is listed as an alternative for clinics to pursue.

As part of patient's experience, the convenience, comfortableness, and the privacy protection are also considered in the accessibility and continuity of care. In addition to the choice of public transportation, patients can also choose to see the doctor driving by themselves. It has become an objective indicator of quality service to provide sufficient parking facilities to patients. The Wanjia standards include both the convenience and the accessibility of the paths and the facilities of the clinics.

People-centered process design and pain-free experience are of course significant. It is of same importance to ensure enough space in the waiting area and the comfortableness of the chairs. People who seek care in a healthcare organization are weak even if they are not suffering from serious conditions. The unnecessary fatigue caused by a poor waiting environment might accelerate the progression of the illness or emergency situation like faint.

Except for the physical capacity, the space layout of the waiting area, the arrangement of the chairs and the proper direction provided to the patients can also contribute to the privacy protection. So, when designing the waiting area, the clinics need to consider the privacy in the area where people may talk or exchange privacy information. These constitute the new requirements from patients on the healthcare organizations.

Patient and Family Rights (PFR)

The primary level clinics should protect the patient and family rights by laws and regulations (e.g., right to informed consent, privacy protection, equal treatment) and notify them of the liabilities they need to perform (e.g., to provide complete healthcare information, cooperate during tests and examinations, respect the staff and other patients, abide by the infection control and environment management policies and follow the instructions on self-care). There are no specific standards requiring that a formal written notification be given to the patients regarding their rights and liabilities, but there is standard asking the clinic to post such information in public areas in the facility.

The safety of patients is the basic requirement for the clinics. But at the presence of other risks (e.g., abuse, negligence, refusal of staff to provide service), protective measures, and contingency plans are required in the advanced version of the standards. The coordination of the leadership is also included in the advanced version of the standards because of the difficulties in understanding the intent and the tight schedule of the leaders. The standards require the clinics to reduce and overcome the common barriers during the service provision to ensure the accessibility of the care that the patients seek, for example, to communicate with the patients in the language they could understand.

The respect to the patients' religions and values is included in the advanced version of the standards. In China, the majority of the patients in the primary level clinics are Chinese, and according to a sampling survey, there are only 7% people in China's mainland follow religions. Therefore, religious taboos are rare in the clinic settings.

Informed consent must be obtained for high-risk procedures. It is also because we have very strict accountability and punishment on malpractice of healthcare staff in China. In the Criminal Law of People's Republic of China (1997), the legislation authority collected various opinions and defined the crime of medical accident: "Healthcare staff shall be sentenced to a set term of imprisonment under 3 years or detention if death or severe harm to physical health has been caused to the patient due to the fact that the healthcare staff had been seriously irresponsible during the care" (Article 335, Criminal Law of People's Republic of China Revised). Compared with the law enforcement in Germany and Japan, the practice in China is more direct and clearer.

Assessment of Patient (AOP) and Care of Patient (COP)

AOP is the basis of all clinical care. The purpose of assessment is to determine the treatment and services that could meet the needs of patient's health. JCI standards identify the assessment that needs to be performed for developing a plan of care, including pain, fall, nutrition, and function, and defined the population that might need special assessment. The patients with positive findings during the screening would need further reassessment to continuously evaluate the effectiveness of the intervention and to understand the change of conditions. The goal is to ensure accurate provision of services and following care. The awareness of the AOPs is not well established among the primary level clinics in China. But considering its importance, the standards set different requirements on different levels.

In China, the people do not trust the private clinics as much as they do for larger hospitals. So, the clinics usually encounter patients with mild conditions and simple symptoms. They don't spend much time in the clinic. This makes it a very different situation from the overseas practice. In the short run, basic assessment could be required for the primary level clinics (e.g., privately-owned clinic) to include simple screening on pain, fall, nutrition, and function. The requirements on the special population and further assessment are included in the advanced version of the standards. Due to the short visit of patients in the clinics, it is relevantly less feasible or necessary to reassess the patients. And some disciplines like dieticians are not included in the clinic services. Thus, the requirement on the reassessment on fall and nutrition is simplified. On the basis of meeting the basic needs of assessment, we have localized the AOP standards based on the cost-return ratio regarding staffing, time, and equipment.

Anesthesia and Surgical Care (ASC)

There are not many primary level clinics in China that operate an anesthesia and surgery service. The approval of surgical services is very strictly in China, which also limits the possibility to open such services in primary level clinics due to limited resources and competency. Usually, it would be very difficult for those clinics to obtain the qualification or license for anesthesia and surgical care. The only types of procedures they might perform are of basic level with low risks. However, JCI standards set necessary requirements on the assessment, staff qualification, patient monitoring, and informed consent practice for all invasive procedures including those low risk procedures. Thus, the original framework of the JCI standards is kept in this chapter.

Medication Management and Use (MMU)

The Wanjia standards keep almost all requirements regarding MMU in the JCI standards. Though there are differences of the roles of staff in different countries, the principle of adopting an effective medication management process to ensure patient safety is universal. Based on the requirements stated in the national regulations and policies, all healthcare organizations need to prepare resuscitation medications according to their own needs. Thus, MMU chapter is applicable to all clinics.

Patient and Family Engagement (PFE)

JCI standards changed the "E" from education to engagement for this chapter to emphasize the participation of patients and their families during the process of care and to list the patient's experience and satisfaction rate as one of the key indicators. The primary level standards follow the principle of ensuring individualized, effective patient and family education and engagement, and require the clinic staff to pay attention to the willingness, acceptance, and understanding of the education while providing health education. In the advanced version of the standards, it emphasizes the empathy of staff while interacting with the patients to reflect the people-centered services provided by the clinics. It also requires clinics establish a management system over human resources and work load to match the implementation of the standards, and adopt third-party satisfaction survey and social supervision.

Quality Improvement and Patient Safety (QPS)

The participation of all staff is encouraged despite the level of management tool utilization. The basic version standards require that the clinic establish a safety program for patient care; manage the collection, aggregation, and analysis of data; perform root-cause analysis on sentinel events; establish a reporting process for near misses or adverse events; and aggregate, analyze, and design a process to reduce or eliminate risks. It requires clinics to identify the causes of a sentinel event or an adverse event and adopt improvement measures. In the advanced version standards, the clinics should be able to perform root-cause analysis, proactive risk analysis, and implement quality improvement programs.

Chinese primary level clinics are late comers in quality improvement and lack staff skilled in quality improvement. Therefore, we do not set compulsory requirements on that. Meanwhile, the requirements regarding data validation have been removed from the standards due to the following reasons: (1) The types and quantity of data that could be collected by the primary level clinics are limited so that the stability and accuracy cannot be ensured. (2) It is very challenging for primary level clinics to ensure sufficient and qualified human resources or invest enough time in data collection. (3) The staff turnover rate is high in the primary level clinics, which also adds to the difficulties in data collection and validation. (4) There are no requirements regarding data validation in the hospital accreditation program in China, which makes it difficult for the healthcare staff to perform the task. This is a typical example of localization of the JCI standards based on the realities in China.

Prevention and Control of Infections (PCI)

The primary level clinics should follow the local laws, regulations and the administrative requirements to develop the goals of infection prevention and control based on their own features and key programs. The primary level clinics should review and identify the infection control risks and implement actions on a regular basis. The difference between the primary version and the advanced version mainly lies in the requirements on the infection control job and qualifications of infection control staff.

It was not until 1986 that the practice of infection control and management was adopted in China's healthcare organizations. This causes the lack of sufficient infection control professionals. Based on this situation, the primary version standards require that clinics have designated infection control staff who have received infection control training and evaluation and have relevant experience. If the local authority requires infection control staff to be licensed, the regulation is observed.

Governance, Leadership and Direction (GLD)

The GLD chapter sets standards on the operational management of the healthcare organizations from the governing entity and the management levels. Wanjia standards emphasize the responsibilities of the governing body and management staff to standardize the basic management framework in the clinics. To achieve that goal, clear definition of the responsibilities of the management staff on each level is an effective means. This chapter also requires an ethics framework to be established to create a decision-making environment that promotes the practices that meet the ethical standards. Wanjia standards stress that the management staff set the examples for other staff to take the ethical responsibilities in their organizations. A code of conduct to regulate staff's practices is expected to be developed for full implementation of the organization's vision, mission, and values.

It also encourages the primary level clinics to establish a culture of safety. The establishment of the culture of safety is quite challenging for primary level clinics. Currently, there is a trend to blame individual staff for misses and errors, which hampers the promotion of a culture of safety. In certain circumstances, individuals are not the ones who should be blamed. Therefore, we encourage the clinics to establish the culture of safety by adopting an accountability mechanism and improving transparency in work place to truly improve the retention of staff and the weakness in the organizations. It is also an approach to promote culture of safety in these primary level organizations.

JCI also has set requirements related to the clinical environment for care, treatment, and training on other healthcare professionals, as well as the practice of human subject trials. The limited service capacity and the mixed competency of the staff is the reality of the primary level clinics in China. After the field visits conducted by the project team, we finally decided to remove the standards related to these subjects in GLD from the Wanjia standards for primary level clinics.

Facility Management and Safety

In the Wanjia standards, the Facility Management and Safety (FMS) chapter stresses that the physical infrastructure and facilities in the primary level clinics should meet the requirements stated in the applicable laws and regulations for safety. All leaders should be familiar with and observe the requirements in the applicable laws and regulations and take any necessary improvement actions to meet the requirements. In the part related to safety and security, Wanjia standards ask the clinics to develop a systematic management mechanism to ensure the safety of the facilities; conduct regular facility tours, collect and report the data of incidents that have occurred, areas that have potential risks and other events to support the managers and leaders in the decision-making process, mitigate potential risks and ensure a safe environment for staff, patients, and family members.

Fire safety can never be neglected in either JCI standards or Wanjia standards. We lay strong emphasis on a systematic management program regarding fire safety be established in the clinic to ensure that people could be effectively and efficiently evacuated from the facility when any emergency occurs. We also encourage the clinics to intensify the fire safety training on the staff, establish smoking control policy, inspect on and maintain the fire safety facilities regularly, organize fire drills, and help staff to better understand their roles in a fire to maximally ensure the safety of patients as well as the properties of the organizations.

Staff Qualification and Education

Most of the JCI standards related to Staff Qualification and Education (SQE) have been adopted in the Wanjia standards covering the staffing plan, enrollment, job responsibilities, orientation, on-the-job training, and qualification and privileging. For any healthcare organization, qualified staff is the first and foremost foundation for the provision of quality and safe care to patients. A systematic staff management plan could help healthcare organizations to employ qualified talents, provide good work experience, and improve competency of the organization as a whole, which is also important for the staff themselves as well. Only with a systematic human resources management and organizational structure, could it serve as the bridge for smooth communication among different units.

JCI standards focus a lot on the privileging of physicians, which is also the basic requirement for healthcare staff to perform clinical tasks and the prerequisite to provide care to patients. In China, professional title mechanism is the basis for the privileging in large hospitals. And the national government is encouraging multisited licensure for physicians. With the multisited licensed physicians working as the preceptors in the clinics, the skills and competency of the staff could also be significantly improved. However, even in large hospitals where physicians are of similar skill or competency level, it is very challenging to promote the systematic privileging of physicians. Therefore, the SQE chapter of the Wanjia standards emphasizes the standard management over multisited licensed physicians and full-time physicians, as well as the feasibility to promote physician privileging. These measurable elements were developed through thorough discussion.

Management of Information (MOI)

This chapter in JCI standards focuses on the information communication, covering the communication between the hospital and the local community, between staff and patients and families, between the employees and external care providers as well as the management of medical records and hospital documents. In the Wanjia standards, we stress also the internal and external communication and the systematic management of medical records and hospital documents. We also require a standard management of medical records with a prerequisite of compliance with national laws and regulations. The staff of the clinics should document the medical record for patients in a timely manner following a standard format to provide uniform care to all patients.

Development and Application of Wanjia Hierarchical Standards

In May 2016, JCI signed the cooperation agreement with Ping An Wanjia. And in December 2016, Wanjia officially released the Wanjia Hierarchical Standards. The hierarchical standards need to be implemented through accreditation activities for continuous improvement and update to gain sustainability. Therefore, the priority of our work was given to the establishment of the accreditation survey process that matches the standards and reality, the expansion of the surveyor pool, the optimization of the quality management of the accreditation system and the development of a safe and effective IT platform.

In August 2016, Wanjia started the pilot accreditation. In November 2016, Wanjia officially launched the accreditation. In January 2017, the overall promotion of the accreditation by the Wanjia standards was rolled out across the country. By the end of September 2017, there had been in total over 50,000 clinics joined our online network, including 5,300 accredited clinics by the primary version standards. Thirty clinics decided to participate in the advanced accreditation, and one had successfully accredited. Based on the rapid development of the accreditation service, Wanjia soon launched the consultation service to help the clinics achieve continuous improvement.

Standards is the driving force for the healthy development of the primary healthcare sector in China. Therefore, it should seek stability and sustainability. The application of the standards should be integrated with the improvement of survey methodologies, team building, process management, and system tools. Ping An Wanjia hopes to join hands with JCI and HIMSS to contribute to the safety and quality in China and the accreditation activities among the primary level healthcare organizations through learning and exchanges.

Epilogue

"Sometimes to heal, often to help, and always to comfort". This widespread wisdom in the healthcare community is a perfect portrayal of health care. In the history of human civilization, we are now in possession of such advanced technologies never seen before. However, in reality no plausible means exists to cure all diseases. All we can do is to use the resources available to provide patient-centric care with maximum safety and quality and achieve the best clinical processes and outcomes possible. As the old saying goes, cure the curable, ease the needy, and comfort the incurable; in the face of a curable patient, as much resources should be gathered as we can to cure with the safest care of the highest quality; for a disease that heals itself and needs little intervention if any, information and technologies should be harnessed to educate and comfort; as for the incurable cases, technologies and other resources should be employed for relief and comfort, allowing the patient to pass with dignity. Whether international standards or China practices, in the past, this day or the future, the same intent, and principle hold true.

As the wheel of history rolls on, human civilization is undergoing profound transformation, ranging from the underlying productivity technologies to the day-to-day social lives. At such a historic turning point, the world is witnessing a rapid and comprehensive rise of China. Driven by the national achievements and trends, the healthcare industry in China has accelerated its growth as well to lead the HIT development in today's world, turning the "possibilities" into the actual "implementation." Hospital administration is also being standardized and refined as motivated by the healthcare reform.

In this context, the healthcare community in China has leveraged international standards and the power of information technology to foster the "China's standards" with Chinese characteristics through our own practices. We would love to share the history, principles and strategies of China practices, and the future prospect of development with other countries, contributing the wisdom and ideas from China in the era of healthcare transformation to let China's voice be heard and bring us together.

We hope that the experiences and cases shared by the JCI and HIMSS hospitals in China could serve as the beacon for the healthcare community and the industry to move forward. We wish to respond to the challenge of our times with our pursuit of international standards and healthcare information technology and to meet the needs of our people for better health.

One's merit is amplified when shared and harnessed. We hope that with this book, it might shed light on the path we took and the journey leading ahead.

Appendix: HIMSS Greater China Chronicle

2017

December 8th–10th: The 4th SINO-US Summit & 2017 HIMSS Greater China Annual Conference was held in Beijing

December 4th: Henan Provincial People's Hospital validated at HIMSS EMRAM Stage 6

December 2nd: Ningbo Yinzhou No. 2 Hospital validated at HIMSS EMRAM Stage 7

November 29th: The First Affiliated Hospital of Zhejiang University School of Medicine validated at HIMSS EMRAM Stage 6

November 29th: Taizhou Hospital of Zhejiang Province, Taizhou Enze Medical Center validated at HIMSS EMRAM Stage 6

November 28th: Yueyang Hospital of Integrated Traditional Chinese and Western Medicine, Shanghai University of Traditional Chinese Medicine validated at HIMSS EMRAM Stage 6

November 27th: Baotou Central Hospital validated at HIMSS EMRAM Stage 6

November 17th: Shanghai Seventh People's Hospital validated at HIMSS EMRAM Stage 6

November 16th: Beijing United Family Hospital validated at HIMSS EMRAM Stage 6

November 2nd: Xuanwu Hospital Capital Medical University validated at HIMSS EMRAM Stage 7

October 26th: The Second Affiliated Hospital of Zhejiang University School of Medicine validated at HIMSS EMRAM Stage 6

October 25th: Binzhou Medical University Hospital validated at HIMSS EMRAM Stage 6

October 24th: Hebei Provincial People's Hospital validated at HIMSS EMRAM Stage 6

October 18th: Shanghai Tongren Hospital validated at HIMSS EMRAM Stage 6

October 16th: The First People's Hospital of Tianmen in Hubei Province validated at HIMSS EMRAM Stage 6

September 26th: Shengjing Hospital of China Medical University re-validated at HIMSS EMRAM Stage 7

September 23rd: The First People's Hospital of Jiande validated at HIMSS EMRAM Stage 6

September 23rd: Huai'an First People's Hospital validated at HIMSS EMRAM Stage 6

September 20th: The First Affiliated Hospital of Xiamen University validated at HIMSS O-EMRAM Stage 6

September 16th–17th: The 2nd CPHIMS training course of HIMSS Greater China

September 2nd: Henan Children's Hospital validated at HIMSS EMRAM Stage 6

August 28th: The First Affiliated Hospital of Xiamen University and Sir Run Run Shaw Hospital, School of Medicine, Zhejiang University both validated at HIMSS EMRAM Stage 7

July 27th: The Fifth Hospital of Xiamen validated at HIMSS EMRAM Stage 6
July 16th: Wuxi No. 2 People's Hospital validated at HIMSS EMRAM Stage 6
June 8th: Kunming Children's Hospital validated at HIMSS EMRAM Stage 6
June 7th: Shanghai Sixth People's Hospital validated at HIMSS EMRAM Stage 6
April 12th: China Medical University Hospital (Taiwan) validated at HIMSS EMRAM Stage 6
February 21st 2017: HIMSS China Summit was held in HIMSS 17 Conference in Orlando, U.S.

2016

December 16th–18th: The 3rd SINO-US Summit & 2016 HIMSS Greater China Annual Conference was held in Guangzhou

November 22nd: Northwest Women & Children's Hospital validated at HIMSS EMRAM Stage 6

November 21st: Ningbo Yinzhou No. 2 Hospital validated at HIMSS EMRAM Stage 6

November 19th: Affiliated Hospital of Jining Medical University validated at HIMSS EMRAM Stage 6

November 17th: Shanghai Children's Medical Center validated at HIMSS EMRAM Stage 6

November 16th: Children's Hospital of Fudan University validated at HIMSS EMRAM Stage 6

November 15th: The First Affiliated Hospital of Nanchang University validated at HIMSS EMRAM Stage 6

October 29th: Children's Hospital of Shanghai validated at HIMSS EMRAM Stage 6

October 28th: Longhua Hospital Shanghai University of Traditional Chinese Medicine validated at HIMSS EMRAM Stage 6

October 26th: The First Affiliated Hospital of Xiamen University validated at HIMSS EMRAM Stage 6

October 25th: Guangzhou Women and Children's Medical Center validated at HIMSS EMRAM Stage 7

August 5th: Linkou Changgung Memorial Hospital validated at HIMSS EMRAM Stage 6

March 29th: Huangshi Central Hospital validated at HIMSS EMRAM Stage 6

March 28th: Luoyang Orthopedic-Traumatological Hospital, Henan Province, Orthopedic Hospital of Henan Province (Luoyang) validated at HIMSS EMRAM Stage 6

2015

December 12th–13th: The 2nd SINO-US Summit & 2015 HIMSS Greater China Annual Conference was held in Tianjin

November 23rd: Sir Run Run Shaw Hospital, School of Medicine, Zhejiang University validated at HIMSS EMRAM Stage 6

TEDA International Cardiovascular Hospital validated at HIMSS EMRAM Stage 7

November 10th: The First Affiliated Hospital of Xinjiang Medical University validated at HIMSS EMRAM Stage 6

November 9th: Luoyang Orthopedic-Traumatological Hospital, Henan Province, Orthopedic Hospital of Henan Province (Zhengzhou) both validated at HIMSS EMRAM Stage 6

November: CPHIMS first landed in China. HIMSS Greater China conducted the first CPHIMS training course

September 13th: Xuanwu Hospital Capital Medical University validated at HIMSS EMRAM Stage 6

2014

December 6th–8th: The 1st SINO-US Summit & 2014 HIMSS Greater China Annual Conference was held in Beijing

December 3rd: Affiliated Zhongshan Hospital of Fudan University validated at HIMSS EMRAM Stage 6

November 18th: Tianjin Ninghe Hospital validated at HIMSS EMRAM Stage 6

November 17th: Affiliated Zhongshan Hospital of Dalian University validated at HIMSS EMRAM Stage 6

October 25th: Shengjing Hospital of China Medical University validated at HIMSS EMRAM Stage 7

May 23rd: At special news release event in CHIMA, Jilan Liu, the CEO of HIMSS Greater China & Vice President of HIMSS announced Peking University People's Hospital was the first hospital in China validated at HIMSS EMRAM Stage 7

May 13th: Peking University People's Hospital validated at HIMSS EMRAM Stage 7

March HIMSS Greater China was established. Mainly responsible for HIMSS EMRAM validation, conferences, professional development, certification, etc.

Before 2014

Shengjing Hospital of China Medical University, Peking University People's Hospital, Chang An Hospital, Yantai Yuhuangding Hospital, Taipei Medical University Hospital, Taipei Medical University Shuang Ho Hospital, Taipei Medical University Wan Fang Hospital, and Kaohsiung Medical University Chung-Ho Memorial Hospital were validated at HIMSS EMRAM Stage 6

Index

D

E

I

J

Q

R

S

T

U

V

W

X

Z

For Product Safety Concerns and Information please contact our EU representative GPSR@taylorandfrancis.com Taylor & Francis Verlag GmbH, Kaufingerstraße 24, 80331 München, Germany

Batch number: 10731069

Printed by Printforce, the Netherlands